County Borough Elections in England and Wales, 1919–1938: A Comparative Analysis

Volume 1

County Borough Elections in England and Wales, 1919–1938: A Comparative Analysis

Volume 1
Barnsley – Bournemouth

SAM DAVIES and BOB MORLEY

Ashgate

Aldershot • Brookfield USA • Singapore • Sydney

Published by

Ashgate Publishing Limited
Gower House, Croft Road,
Aldershot, Hampshire GU11 3HR
Great Britain

Ashgate Publishing Company
Old Post Road,
Brookfield, Vermont 05036–9704
USA

ISBN 1–84014–246–4

British Library CIP Data
Davies, Sam
County Borough Elections in England and Wales, 1919–1938:
A Comparative Analysis.
Volume 1: Barnsley to Bournemouth.
1. Local Elections – England – History. 2. Local Elections – England –
Statistics. I. Title. II. Morley, Bob.
324.9'42'083

US Library of Congress CIP Data
County Borough Elections in England and Wales, 1919-1938: A Comparative
Analysis / by Sam Davies & Bob Morley.
p.   cm. Includes bibliographical references and index. Volume 1:
Barnsley–Bournemouth.
I. Local Elections – England – Statistics. 2. Local Elections – Wales –
Statistics. 3. Great Britain – Politics and Government – 1910–1936.
I.Davies, Sam (R.S.W.). II.Morley, Bob (R.E.).
JS3215.C68   1999
324.942'083'021 – dc21   99–12017
                                                          CIP

This volume is printed on acid free paper.

Printed and bound in Great Britain by MPG Books Ltd, Bodmin, Cornwall

Contents

List of tables

List of appendices

List of figures

Abbreviations

The following abbreviations for parties or candidates have been used in the tables. Due to limitations of space, some party names have been abbreviated to a greater degree in some tables than in others. Both forms are given here. Other names of organisations abbreviated in the text of the essays have been given in full on the first occasion they occur in each essay.

Al	Allotments (candidate)
Anti-Soc	Anti-socialist (candidate)
A-W	Anti-Waste Party
C	Conservative and Unionist Party
C Ch	Christian Churches
CHKA or Chka	Company House-Keepers Association (Blackpool only)
Chtr	Charter (candidate, or party)
Cit	Citizens (candidate, or party)
Co C	Coalition Conservative
C L	Coalition Liberal
Com	Communist Party of Great Britain
Const	Constitutionalist (candidate, or party)
Const Lab	Constitutional Labour (candidate)
Coop	Co-operative Party
CWMA	Conservative Working Men's Association
H&A	Hotel and Apartments Association (Blackpool only)
IDL	Irish Democratic League

ILP	Independent Labour Party
Ind or I	Independent (candidate, or party)
Ind C	Independent Conservative (candidate)
Ind L	Independent Liberal (candidate)
Ind Lab or I Lab	Independent Labour (candidate)
L	Liberal Party
Lab	Labour Party
MCU	Middle Classes Union
NFDDSS or Nfds	National Federation of Discharged and Demobilised Sailors and Soldiers
NL	National Liberal
NP	National Party
NUWM or Nuwm	National Unemployed Workers Movement
NDP	National Democratic and Labour Party
O	Other (candidate, or party)
PL	People's League
Prog	Progressive (candidate, or party)
Prog C	Progressive Conservative
R	Ratepayers (candidate, or party)
Sydn	Sydney Rating (candidate)
T	Tenants (candidate, or party)
WCA	Women's Citizens Association
Wkrs	Workers (candidate, or party)

Acknowledgements

Our main acknowledgement is to the staff of the various libraries we have visited in the process of collecting the material for this volume. These include the local history sections of the central libraries of Barnsley, Barrow, Bath, Birkenhead, Birmingham, Blackburn, Blackpool, Bolton, Bootle, Bournemouth, Crosby, Liverpool and Manchester. The assistance we received at all these libraries was marvellous, and without the expertise and knowledge of the local librarians we have met we could never have completed this volume. In addition, the British Library newspaper section at Colindale in London provided some material, and the staff of the libraries of Liverpool John Moores University and Liverpool University were extremely efficient and helpful in locating secondary sources.

Various individuals have also helped us. We are indebted to Phil Cubbin of the human geography section of the School of Social Science at Liverpool John Moores University, who converted our hand-drawn maps into computerised form. Dave McEvoy, our former director of school, has given us great support for this project, including financial assistance for our travel. John Herson was involved in the early discussion of the project, and gave us valuable advice on local history and on the computerisation of our data. Jim Ainsworth assisted with some details on Blackburn. Rob Cowan helped with maps of Bootle. John Walton and Jon Lawrence were both kind enough to give us early sight of their latest publications. John Walton and Neville Kirk read drafts of some of the essays, and offered us expert and constructive criticism. Jo Morley provided great help in collecting material for Bath and Brighton, as did Julie Des Forges for Barrow. Our thanks go to all these colleagues and friends.

At the publishing stage, Mike Savage gave strong support for our project. At Ashgate Alec McAulay provided the initial encouragement and enthusiasm that we needed, and Ruth Peters, Kirsten Weissenberg and Elizabeth Wickens have given us excellent advice and support.

Sam Davies received a Research Fellowship from Liverpool John Moores University which helped in the final stages of the preparation of this volume.

Sam Davies and Bob Morley
Liverpool

March 1999

Introduction

> The national historian still tends to have a curiously distorted view of goings-on 'in the provinces'. Provincial events are seen as shadowy incidents or unaccountable spontaneous upheavals on the periphery of the national scene, which the London wire-pullers try to cope with and put into their correct historical pattern.[1]

> there is a lot be said for trying to move comparison from the national towards the regional or the local because it can help one cut away from the constraints posed by national historiography.[2]

> Towns display the economic standing, the social relations, the cultural appreciation, the governmental dynamic, of the people who inhabit them. Towns summarize civilization ... This is why English towns differ from each other.[3]

> no nation state has ever been able to entirely do away with the local political arena.[4]

These volumes of *County Borough Elections in England and Wales* are intended as an initial but nevertheless important contribution to a much greater task: to put a local perspective into the history of twentieth-century British politics and society. As the words of E.P. Thompson indicate, in the first quote above, there has been a peculiar hostility to the importance of the local dimension in British political history, especially in relation to the study of the twentieth century. This is perhaps unsurprising in a country where political power has long been concentrated at the centre. Whatever the economic and social weight British regions or cities may have possessed historically, London was where national politics was conducted. The contrast with, say, Germany makes the point. City-states like Hamburg or *länder* (local states) like Bavaria retained political significance and power to a much greater extent than Birmingham or Lancashire.

The balance within historical study began to be redressed somewhat by the growth of social history in the second half of this century, and of other more specialised fields such as labour history and women's history. From their

---

[1] Thompson, E.P., 'Homage to Tom Maguire', in Briggs, A. and Saville, J., *Essays in Labour History*, (London, 1967), pp. 276–277.
[2] Breuilly, J., *Labour and Liberalism in Nineteenth Century Europe: Essays in Comparative History*, (Manchester, 1992), p. 20.
[3] Waller, P.J., *Town, City and Nation: England 1850–1914*, (Oxford, 1983), p. 318.
[4] Savage, M., 'The rise of the Labour Party in local perspective', *Journal of Regional and Local Studies*, (1990), p. 2.

perspective, the distinctive economic functions and varied social and cultural features of localities were much more obvious and more important. At least to some extent this greater concern with the local has spilled over into political history. To a degree as well, recent political trends have encouraged this development. The results of British elections in the 1980s and 1990s began to contradict long-held beliefs amongst political scientists in the immutable connections between social class and political allegiance, for instance. Thus other factors such as gender, age and locality have begun to assume greater importance in political analysis. The concept of the so-called 'north–south divide', much invoked after the 1983 and 1987 general elections, is the clearest example of how the political significance of locality has become of greater interest.

The great potential, and also the pitfalls, of local studies have by now been much discussed, and there is not the space here to repeat the debate. It is sufficient to say that a degree of consensus exists that local histories should play some part in the wider understanding of British politics and society. Taking the historians quoted above, E.P. Thompson in 1967 applauded the rise of 'a more mature school of local history, employing sociological techniques'. John Breuilly advocated local studies as components of an 'intra-national comparative history'. Michael Savage saw them as a way of understanding the 'dynamics' of 'formal' and 'practical' politics, specifically working-class politics. P.J. Waller asserted the value of studying a particular variant of the local, the town, despite the strength of the 'anti-urban tradition' in British historiography.[5] Whatever the differences in their aims or their approach, they were all agreed on the importance of local history. However, there is one important qualification to the claims of local history that should not be ignored. Thompson still insisted that the 'national and local pictures' should be 'put together', and Breuilly similarly remarked that 'there still will be a "national" level to consider, not merely as an aggregate of local cases but also in its own right'.[6] Local studies taken on their own become a collection of empirical data, and they must still be put into a national or even wider context to have an historical meaning.

These volumes then must be seen as part of a wider historical project. They are focused on local elections, which were an important part of the political system. By 1918 local government had become a significant arena of party politics. The scope and scale of municipal governance had been extended progressively over the previous century to a point where it was no longer of purely local interest, culminating in the absorption of the Poor Law guardians into municipalities in 1929.[7] Concurrently the local government franchise had been extended beyond the ranks of wealthy property-owners to include most local inhabitants,

---

[5]   Thompson, 'Homage to Tom Maguire', p. 277; Breuilly, *Labour and Liberalism*, pp. 20–23; Waller, *Town, City and Nation*, p. 318; Savage, 'The rise of the Labour Party', pp. 10–13.
[6]   Thompson, 'Homage to Tom Maguire', p. 277; Breuilly , *Labour and Liberalism*, p. 22.
[7]   On the development of local government see Keith-Lucas, B. and Richards, P.G., *A History of Local Government in the Twentieth Century*, (London, 1978); Redlich, J. and Hirst, F.W., *Local Government in England*, (abridged version, London, 1958); Waller, *Town, City and Nation*, chs 6 and 7.

culminating in the enfranchisement of women in the legislation of 1918 and 1928.[8] So the control of municipal power mattered politically in this period, and the elections to decide that control were a real test of the popular will. National political parties therefore played a full role in municipal politics. National issues were reflected in council politics, and the results of local elections were of national significance.

The recording and analysis of British municipal election results between the wars was limited, though. There was, and still is, no official centralized system of collecting local election data. Each council was responsible for recording its own results. In most cases these were simply stored within the council's own internal records, and it was only the local press that published them in varying detail. As a result there was little substantive analysis of local elections as they happened. Subsequently the records have remained scattered in local libraries in the pages of the press and obscure council committee minutes. Historians and political scientists have barely touched this data since, aside from a handful of local studies.[9] Least of all has the data been pulled together to analyse aggregate trends, or to carry out comparative studies. Useful attempts at the former task have been made, but they have all been based on a limited range of available evidence.[10] Genuine comparative studies for the inter-war period have not been attempted at all. This is very much in contrast with other European states such as Germany or the Netherlands, where state systems of collection of results were well developed by the 1920s. Extensive analysis of the data collected was possible in these countries, both at the time and in subsequent historical study.

The volumes of this book will fulfil two main purposes. First, they will constitute a comprehensive work of reference for all county borough election results in England and Wales between the wars. Second, they will provide a multi-layered analysis of municipal politics in the same period. This will include the investigation of politics in the individual boroughs concerned, as well as the comparative study of political issues and movements in different boroughs, and also the identification of aggregate patterns of political behaviour across the country as a whole. In doing so, these volumes will fill an important gap in the historical record. They will take in the crucial period of the rise of Labour, the decline of Liberalism, and the consolidation of Toryism. They will span critical

---

[8] Although the municipal franchise between 1919 and 1938 was not as comprehensive as the parliamentary franchise; see notes at the end of this volume, p. 671.

[9] For instance, Bealey, F., Blondel, J. and McCann, W.P., *Constituency Politics: A Study of Newcastle-under-Lyme*, (London, 1965); Savage, M., *The Dynamics of Working-Class Politics: The Labour Movement in Preston, 1880–1940*, (Cambridge, 1987); Marriot, J., *The Culture of Labourism: The East End between the Wars*, (Edinburgh, 1991); Davies, S., *Liverpool Labour: Social and Political Influences on the Development of the Labour Party in Liverpool, 1900–1939*, (Keele, 1996).

[10] For example, Rhodes, E.C., 'Voting at municipal elections', *Political* Quarterly, vol. 9, pt. 2, (1938), pp. 271–280; Cook, C., *The Age of Alignment: Electoral Politics in Britain, 1922–1929*, (London, 1975), ch. 3; Stevenson J. and Cook, C., *The Slump: Society and Politics during the Depression*, (London, 1977), ch. 13; Rowett, J.S., 'The Labour Party and Local Government: Theory and Practice in the Inter-War Years', (D.Phil. thesis, University of Oxford, 1979), pp. 4–28; 368–389.

years of international political turmoil, as well as economic depression and mass unemployment. Being annual, the local elections will give an idea of how political opinion varied between general elections, especially in the longer gaps such as 1924–29 or 1935–45, or in crisis periods such as 1929–31. The volumes will provide new and detailed   evidence for issues such as the role of women in politics, the significance of ethnic and religious differentiation, the connection between occupational and class divisions and party allegiance, the local impact of the decline of staple industries, and the political significance of housing change and movement of population. The volumes will also illuminate the impact of fringe parties such as the Communist Party and the British Union of Fascists, and pressure groups such as the National Unemployed Workers' Movement and the Middle Classes' Union.

The scope of the volumes is limited to the county boroughs of England and Wales. There were a number of different units of local government which had evolved over the previous century. The boroughs of England and Wales in their modern form had originated in the reform of 1835, representing the main urban centres. The larger boroughs were given county status, as opposed to the generally smaller municipal boroughs. There were eighty-three county boroughs by 1931. Other local government units included the predominantly rural county councils, and the later-developed urban district councils and rural district councils. London had its own structure of local government after the 1899 Act, with twenty-eight metropolitan boroughs and the over-arching London county council. Scotland, with its burghs, and Ireland also had their own separate systems. Collating the election results for all these different units of local government would be a massive task, and for logistical reasons alone it would be necessary to narrow the limits to make it feasible. There are a number of other compelling arguments for concentrating on the county boroughs.

First, the elections for the county boroughs took place annually on the same day (normally the first day in November, except when this was a Sunday, in which case they were held a day later). Thus they were directly comparable. By contrast, the annual rural and urban district council elections were held in the spring, while the elections for the London boroughs took place in November, but only in every third year. Second, the parameters of the elections for the county boroughs were clearly defined and unvarying. One-third of the councillors were elected each year, and for every three councillors there was an additional alderman. This pattern was not necessarily applicable to other tiers of local government. In the London boroughs, for instance, all the councillors came up for election every three years, and there was only one alderman for every six councillors. In the urban districts there were no aldermen at all. Third, party politics in local government was developed to the greatest extent in the larger, urban authorities. Only three out of the eighty-three county boroughs had a population below 50,000 by 1931, and in most cases their elections were fought out on party lines by this period. In the smaller municipal boroughs and district councils, and in the more rural county councils, this was much less the case, making their elections much less interesting and significant politically. London was a special case. Party politics was well-defined there, but many of the boroughs were dominated overwhelmingly by one party, and many seats were therefore regularly uncontested. Detailed changes in political support were thus hard to glean from such scattered and spasmodic evidence.

Concentrating solely on the county boroughs, then, these volumes will cumulatively build up the complete tabulated record of local elections between 1919 and 1938 (the first and last years between the wars when a full round of contests was held). Each of the boroughs will be dealt with alphabetically in turn. Included in the coverage are: summary tables of statistical data relating to the population and employment structure of the borough; maps showing ward boundaries (including any changes during the period); summary tables of the municipal election record, showing results by ward and by year, turnout and Labour Party share of the vote by ward and by year, party gains and losses in each year, and the overall party composition of the council in each year (including aldermen); full lists of the results of the elections held each year in November, arranged by ward, including the names and sex of candidates, party labels, the votes cast for each candidate and the total number of votes, the percentages of the vote for each candidate, the total electorate, the turnout, and any party gains or losses. More detailed explanation of the scope of the material, and the conventions and assumptions used in the tabulated data, will be found in the explanatory notes at the end of each volume.

For each of the boroughs there will also be included an essay. These essays will aim to outline the socio-economic context of the locality and its historical development, to examine significant or interesting aspects of its political traditions and culture, and to draw attention to prominent features of the electoral record. They will also provide a guide to further reading. It should be noted that the length and form of these essays will vary, depending on the available secondary historical sources for each borough, and the nature of the particular issues or events that were important in each borough. While each essay will constitute an original and self-contained piece of analysis which can be read on its own, readers at times will be referred to other essays for detailed analysis of particular topics. This is to avoid excessive repetition of points that apply to more than one borough.

In each volume there will also be a concluding chapter giving the aggregate and comparative analysis for all the boroughs contained in the volume. From Volume 2, there will also be a cumulative analysis for all the volumes completed so far, and later in the series some regional and other comparative investigation will also be provided. In this way it is envisaged that a comprehensive picture of voting behaviour and political life in all the county boroughs will be built up. As a further aid to comparison, there will also be a series of appendixes at the end of each volume, in which all eighty-three county boroughs will be ranked in relation to various aspects of their population and employment structure. Unless otherwise indicated in the notes, these tables have been constructed from data contained in the 1931 census.

To conclude this introduction, it is necessary to stress the strengths, and also the limitations, of the material contained in these volumes. For the first time, detailed and comprehensive data on local elections will be available in one single, consolidated source. This will be an important contribution to future historical research, which others will be able to use and develop as they see fit. At the same time, the analysis of the individual boroughs, the comparative studies, and the aggregated data, which will be included in these volumes, will in themselves provide new insights into the politics of inter-war England and Wales. Two cautionary notes need to be sounded though. First, historical evidence on its own does not, in some empiricist fashion, provide the historical answers. Theories and concepts have to be applied to the evidence in order to make sense of it. The authors will strive to achieve this especially in the essays that accompany the results for each borough, and in the aggregate and comparative analysis for each volume. However, given the large scale of the task it has not been possible to do the in-depth historical research that is still needed for most of the boroughs included here. That is a task for other researchers in future years, who will find these volumes of use.

Second, the other caveat is on the nature of electoral data as an historical source. Recent writing has criticised the often unsophisticated interpretation of such data employed by historians, derived mainly from the assumptions of the political sociology of the 1950s and 1960s.[11] It is plain that a more subtle approach is called for, which for instance sees voting itself as a multi-faceted activity determined by a range of factors, and the relationship between party and voter as more complex than has previously been assumed. No simplistic conclusions should be drawn from the data contained in these volumes, as the essays on each borough will show. Instead what is clear is the diversity of political experience revealed in each borough. In demonstrating this, these volumes accurately reflect 'the attention given in recent work to the importance of locality, or the "politics of place" in influencing electoral behaviour well into the twentieth century'.[12]

---

[11] See the important essay, Lawrence, J. and Taylor, M., 'Introduction: electoral sociology and the historians', in *Party, State and Society: Electoral Behaviour in Britain since 1820*, (Aldershot, 1997), pp. 1–26; also, Lawrence, J., *Speaking for the People: Party, Language and Popular Politics in England, 1867–1914*, (Cambridge, 1998), pp. 21–25.
[12] Lawrence and Taylor, 'Introduction', p. 17.

ONE
Barnsley

BARNSLEY

Barnsley was the sixty-first county borough by size in 1931, with a population of just over 70,000. It was situated in the heart of the South Yorkshire coalfield, the Barnsley seam running in a line roughly from north to south through the town. Along this seam lay numerous pits which comprised the central group of collieries in the coalfield. In the area surrounding Barnsley almost ninety pits can be identified between 1840 and 1880, of which at least ten were located within the inter-war boundaries of the borough. Even after merger and reorganisation, there were still thirty-one large pits in the Barnsley area in 1948.[1] Coal dominated the local economy, and this dominance was strengthened in the borough by the boundary extension of 1921 which took in mining areas to the north and east of the town in the Ardsley and Monk Bretton wards. Moreover, the colliery influence on the town's occupational structure was intensified by the fact that many miners were known to live within the borough but travelled every day to work at pits outside the town.[2] Unsurprisingly, coal-mining was by far the largest male occupational group in Barnsley, comprising 44 per cent of the total in 1931. Only Merthyr in South Wales had a higher proportion amongst the county boroughs. There was no other industrial sector that provided significant levels of male employment. Typically of a mining town, opportunities for female employment were also restricted. Just over 20 per cent of the female population was included in the industry tables of the 1931 census, one of the lowest figures amongst the boroughs. The relatively small number of women workers were concentrated mainly in domestic service, shop-work, and the clothing industry.

Barnsley was a predominantly working-class borough, lying sixty-first and seventy-second respectively in the tables relating to domestic service and self-employment. Given the dependence on one of the main heavy industries hit by the inter-war Depression, unemployment was inevitably high in this period. The monthly average of unemployment in 1929 was 16.3 per cent, rising to 44.6 per cent in 1932, and falling back to 24.3 per cent in 1937. Only a handful of county boroughs in the North-East and South Wales coalfields matched these levels of unemployment. Also unsurprisingly, Barnsley experienced a net loss of population in the 1930s, declining by 2.1 per cent between 1931 and 1938.

Nonconformity was traditionally strong in Barnsley, as in the South Yorkshire region as a whole. Before 1914, mining and nonconformity usually meant Liberalism, or Lib-Labism, in politics, and Barnsley was no exception. On the other hand, as David Howell has pointed out, 'the Miners' Federation of Great Britain symbolised the attachment of sections of the industrial working class to

[1]   Shepherd, G., 'The Growth of the Coal Mining Industry in the Barnsley District 1840–1880; With a Special Reference to the growth of the South Yorkshire Miners Association 1858–1880', (B.A. dissertation, University of Liverpool, 1975), pp. 12a–12b; National Coal Board, *Annual Report and Statement of Accounts, for the Year Ended 31st December 1948*, (London, 1949), p. 230; see also Gray, G.D.B., 'The South Yorkshire Coalfield' in Benson, J. and Neville, R.G., (eds.), *Studies in the Yorkshire Coal Industry*, (Manchester, 1976).
[2]   Benson, J., *British Coalminers in the Nineteenth Century: A Social History*, (London, 1989), p. 83; see also below, p. 13.

Labour politics during the inter-war years', although he goes on to add that 'such a role came about only slowly'.[3] The Yorkshire Miners' Association (YMA) was strongly Lib-Lab up to the end of the nineteenth century, as demonstrated in a famous by-election at Barnsley in 1897, when an Independent Labour Party (ILP) candidate was heavily defeated by a Durham coalowner standing in the Liberal cause. Crucial to the victory of the Liberal, Joseph Walton, was the support of the YMA, and especially of its leader, Ben Pickard, 'the iron man of Barnsley'. Walton went on to hold the constituency until 1922.[4]

The Yorkshire region though was one of the earliest to support affiliation of the Miners' Federation of Great Britain (MFGB) to the Labour Party, which was eventually achieved in 1908. A leading proponent of the shift was the Barnsley-based ILP member, Herbert Smith, who became leader of the Yorkshire Miners in 1906, and later president of the MFGB. Under Smith's leadership, Barnsley gradually shifted to Labour. From 1922 the parliamentary seat was only lost once by Labour, and then only very narrowly in 1931. As Howell says, though, Herbert Smith was known for both his 'industrial toughness complemented by hostility to left-wing critics within the MFGB', and his 'moderate Labourism'. This could be seen as a 'salutary indication of the limits of the change from Lib-Labism to Independent Labour'.[5] In the municipal politics of Barnsley, in which Smith was also very prominent, these limits may also be pertinent.

Turning to the municipal record then, the spatial pattern of political support in Barnsley between the wars can be very clearly defined. A line could be drawn through the centre of the borough roughly from north to south, to the east of which lay the main areas of Labour support, and to the west the areas of support for the anti-Labour forces. To the east Ardsley and Monk Bretton wards, added to the borough in 1921 as already noted, and Central and South East were all Labour strongholds, while the East ward was the most marginal in the borough. This was plainly the more working-class side of town. A number of collieries were actually sited within the Ardsley and Monk Bretton wards, and these wards were also the site of most of the 4,000 council houses constructed on the outskirts of the borough between the wars, including the Cundy Cross, Smithies, Burton Grange and Lundwood estates in Monk Bretton, and the Kendray and Ardsley estates in Ardsley. In addition the California Gardens and Worsbrough Common estates were situated in the South East ward. The Central and South East wards contained the poorest and most densely packed city-centre housing, although from 1927 a scheme to demolish sub-standard houses in these wards saw some of their occupants being rehoused on the new out-of-town council estates. The East ward was more mixed, with some inner-city housing to the south of the ward, but also some more pleasant suburban districts further north towards the Dearne valley. By contrast, the South, South West, West and North wards were all strongholds of

[3] Howell, D., *British Workers and the Independent Labour Party, 1888–1906*, (Manchester, 1983), p. 16.
[4] Rubinstein, D., 'The Independent Labour Party and the Yorkshire miners – the Barnsley by-election of 1897', *International Review of Social History*, (1978), pp. 102–134; Howell, *British Workers*, pp. 18–20.
[5] Howell, *British Workers*, pp. 23–24, 51.

the opposition to Labour. These wards consisted mainly of private housing estates in the western suburbs of the town. The Wilthorpe estate in the North ward was the only council-house development on this western side of town.[6] The clear-cut east–west division is also very obviously reflected in the population statistics of the wards. The five eastern wards had the highest persons per room figures (ranging from 0.98 to 1.16), while the four western wards had the lowest (from 0.82 to 0.92).

With the two parties vying for power in Barnsley dominating four wards each, and one other ward being highly marginal, control of the council was always likely to be precarious. On three occasions between the wars the overall position on the council was tied, and control changed five times between 1921 and 1933. Only in the mid 1930s did Labour gain a stable majority, and this was primarily due to manipulation of the aldermanic system, as discussed below. This would nevertheless make Barnsley one of the stronger county boroughs for Labour between the wars. The overall Labour share of the vote between 1919 and 1938 of 49.1 per cent further supports this estimation. Of the ten boroughs covered in this volume, only Barrow had a marginally higher Labour share of the vote, and future volumes will confirm this view.

The pattern over time can be summarised briefly as follows. At the beginning of the inter-war period Barnsley was ruled by a Liberal–Tory alliance which went under the 'apolitical' name of the Independent party (changed in 1935 to the Citizens' party). The Labour opposition had established itself with a handful of seats before 1914, and made important gains in 1919 and 1920 so that the Independents had only a narrow majority. After the borough had been extended to include Ardsley and Monk Bretton and all the other ward boundaries had been redrawn, the 1921 elections put control of the borough on a knife-edge. After new aldermen had been elected, the council was tied at eighteen each, and Labour briefly assumed power on this basis. Subsequent by-election defeats for Labour, and two losses in the 1922 elections, put the Independents back into power. The tide turned back to Labour between 1924 and 1927, and the council was again tied in 1926 before Labour regained full control in 1927. As in most other boroughs, the catastrophic crisis years of the second Labour government marked a shift against Labour in Barnsley, three losses in 1930 giving power back to the Independents. However, it is interesting that Labour made some recovery in 1931 after the low point of the previous year, actually regaining two seats, and in this regard it was commented that 'Barnsley did not follow the county's example generally'.[7] It would appear that the Labour government's policy failures while still in power, especially over unemployment, were more crucial in Barnsley than the 1931 split in the party and collapse of the government.

More in line with the national trend, Labour recovered strongly in 1932, achieving its highest proportion of the poll since 1926. As a result the council was tied again, and further good results in 1933 gave Labour a sound majority. The later 1930s were rather disappointing in electoral terms for Labour though, its

---

[6] On housing estates, see *Centenary Celebrations Booklet, Barnsley County Borough*, (Barnsley, 1969), unpaginated.

[7] *Barnsley Chronicle*, 7 Nov. 1931.

proportion of the poll falling back after 1934, and seats being lost in three successive years from 1935 to 1937. Despite this, Labour control of the council was maintained. This control was strengthened by a further extension of the borough boundaries to take in Carlton ward to the north-east, another mining ward which added three labour councillors at by-elections held in 1938. However, the main reason for Labour's position being consolidated was its manipulation of the aldermanic system, as noted above, and this needs to be considered in some detail.

As noted elsewhere, the aldermanic system, which persisted in English local government until 1974, could be used to bolster artificially the strength of parties.[8] As one Tory defender of the system put it candidly, 'the Aldermen's bench saves our local government system from the twin evils of democracy and equality'.[9] Given the finely-balanced position of Barnsley council between the wars, the control of the aldermanic elections was bound to be crucial. Thus in 1921, Labour in Barnsley had only one of the six existing aldermen, but it had a majority of the councillors. When aldermen were elected for the two new wards that year, by the councillors alone, Labour was able to install its own nominees, and also replace an Independent alderman up for re-election. After by-elections had been held to fill the seats of the elevated councillors, Labour had drawn level and assumed control. When aldermen next came up for re-election in 1924, the Independents had a majority, and proceeded to evict two Labour aldermen. In 1927, when the roles were reversed, Labour replaced two Independents. Again in 1930 and 1931, three Labour aldermen were voted out by the Independent majority.

In 1933, the two parties met to discuss the issue, and an agreement was struck that in future aldermen would be elected according to the proportional strength of the parties on the council. Under the terms of this agreement, after the November elections of that year Labour was entitled to all five aldermanic seats up for re-election. These included three vacancies that had been created by Labour aldermen resigning and fighting council seats, as they had feared that they would have been thrown off the council if the Independents had won a majority. Instead Labour filled the five vacancies and took control of the council.[10] In 1936, when Labour's overall majority was down to three, Labour abrogated the earlier agreement and filled the three vacancies that came up. Labour then held eight of the nine aldermanic seats, although they had a majority of only one amongst the councillors. By 1937 the Citizens in turn had gained a majority of the councillors. There were no aldermen due for re-election until 1939, but the Citizen's leader in the council promised to give Labour 'something of their own medicine' when the time came. The chairman of the Barnsley Citizen's Association was more explicit, promising 'if we hold the power in the near future we shall not hesitate to use it and replace the Socialist Aldermen with Citizen when the time comes'.[11] The following year the three new councillors for Carlton ward restored Labour's

[8]   See Davies, S., *Liverpool Labour: Social and Political Influences on the Development of the Labour Party in Liverpool, 1900–1939*, (Keele, 1996), pp. 110–119.
[9]   *Parliamentary Debates*, vol. 281, col. 770, 14 Nov. 1933.
[10] *Barnsley Chronicle*, 4 Nov. 1933.
[11] B*arnsley Chronicle,* 6 Nov. 1937.

majority, and Labour took the new aldermanic vacancy, as well as replacing the one remaining Citizen alderman for good measure. All ten aldermen in Barnsley were now Labour men. Plainly the Labour Party was not averse to using the system shamelessly to its own advantage when the opportunity arose, just as its opponents have been shown to do so in other cities like Liverpool.[12]

Turning now to the politics of Barnsley council between the wars, the over-riding importance of the coal industry was plain. On the Labour side mining union officials were prominent as candidates. Herbert Smith himself stood in the West ward (1921, 1924), and in the East (1926, 1933), and was mayor in 1932. His sons Harold and Arthur also won seats in the East ward, so that in 1927 there was a curious situation where all three seats in this ward were held by the same family. This was not the only father–son combination on the Labour side, either, W.E. Dodd succeeding his father in Monk Bretton in 1927. Other miners' union officials to stand included Joseph Jones, secretary of the YMA, (North 1925, South 1927, 1930, and Ardsley 1931, 1934) and George Martin (South 1931, East 1934, 1937).[13] Miners and others employed at the pits were also prominent. For example in 1925 of the nine Labour candidates, three were miners, one was a colliery surveyor and one a miners' checkweighman, in addition to two officials. Of the miners, one, Herbert Rhodes, lived in Central ward but worked at Grimethorpe colliery four miles north-east of Barnsley, and another, George Simpson, lived in Monk Bretton but worked several miles north in Staincross, evidence supporting the point made earlier that many miners lived in Barnsley but travelled outside to their work. The colliery interest was also strong on the Independent side. In 1925 a colliery contractor and a manufacturer of miners' lamps were among their candidates, and in 1926 a colliery overman and a colliery secretary stood. Another example was Joseph Richards, the manager of Barnsley Main colliery and a director of Barnsley FC, who held the West ward for the Independents from 1929.[14]

Naturally issues relating to the coal industry were also important. This was never more obvious than in the momentous events around 1926. The 1925 elections took place in the shadow of the impending General Strike, which dominated the campaign in which Labour made three gains. When the 1926 elections were held the miners had already been locked out for six months following the defeat of the General Strike, and they and their families were suffering terrible distress. A major local relief fund had been mounted in which Labour figures were prominent. Alderman Broley was the chairman, and Herbert Smith's son Arthur the treasurer. Labour made this the main issue of their campaign, with significant results. There was a massive turnout of 80 per cent, the highest figure between the wars, and Labour made two gains and recorded its

---

[12] Davies, *Liverpool Labour*, pp. 111–116.

[13] On the strong influence of the miners' union in local politics, see Tanner, D., 'The Labour Party and electoral politics in the coalfields', in Campbell, A., Fishman, N. and Howell, D., (eds), *Miners, Unions and Politics, 1910–47*, (Aldershot, 1996), especially pp. 78–85; and Taylor, A., 'The politics of labourism in the Yorkshire coalfield, 1926–1945', in Campbell, Fishman and Howell, *Miners, Unions and Politics*, especially pp. 237–241.

[14] *Barnsley Independent*, 30 Oct., 7 Nov. 1925, 30 Oct. 1926, 2 Nov. 1929, *Sheffield Daily Independent*, 2 Nov. 1934.

highest percentage of the poll thus far. Herbert Smith gained the marginal East ward, the local press commenting that 'in view of the industrial position he was about the strongest nominee the Labour Party could run'. Even in the Independent strongholds of the North and West wards, the victors conceded that their majorities were lower than they would otherwise have been due to the miners' dispute.[15]

Another key issue in Barnsley municipal politics was housing. In the 1920s the parties vied with each other in promising the extension of council housing, and various estates were developed on the eastern and northern outskirts of the town. One Independent councillor boasted in 1925 that 953 houses had been constructed in the previous three years while his party had been in power, but where he differed with the Labour party was over the use of direct labour. Two other Independent candidates in the same year, though, including an ex-chairman of the Barnsley Chamber of Commerce, argued that 'the town needs men who will keep the rates down'. A further twist to this issue was added the following year when Labour unsuccessfully challenged the nomination of Herbert Snowden in the South West ward on the grounds that his building firm was in receipt of a subsidy for the building of council houses under the 1923 Housing Act. Snowden ran his building firm with his father, who had also stood for the Independents in the South East ward in 1923. Interestingly, twenty years previously his father had been agent in the same ward for an election in which his tactics had been so dubious that he was disfranchised for seven years and the result annulled. The dividing line between the parties became much sharper with the shift in national policy on housing in the 1930s and the atmosphere of national crisis. 'Efficiency and economy' became the main slogan of the Independents, contrasted with Labour's pledge of 'further municipal socialism within the borough'.[16]

In the years of high unemployment in the 1930s, the other main issue which Labour very successfully played upon was the treatment of the unemployed. The Independents were bitter in their complaints that the 'bogey' of the Means Test had resulted in their losing power in the 1932 elections. They claimed that it had been 'thrust upon them', and that they had enforced it with 'the utmost latitude', while at the same time they had 'endeavoured to curtail unnecessary expenditure to relieve the rates which are a burden on the people'. With unemployment in Barnsley at more than 40 per cent at this time, the voters' verdict on these arguments was harsh, and one Independent alderman declared that he was 'disgusted' at the ratepayers' 'ingratitude'. For the rest of the decade the issue dogged Labour's opponents. In the last elections before the war in 1938 the main discussion point was still the administration of public assistance and winter coal allowances, with Labour claiming that its generous provision while in power would be threatened if it was replaced in office.[17]

In a borough so dominated by the mining industry, it is interesting to consider the involvement of women in local politics. As already noted, women were

---

[15]   *Barnsley Independent*, 6 Nov. 1926.
[16]   *Sheffield Daily Independent*, 2 Nov. 1923; *Barnsley Independent*, 30 Oct. 1925, 30 Oct. 1926; *Barnsley Chronicle*, 4 Nov. 1933, 5 Nov. 1938.
[17]   *Barnsley Chronicle*, 5 Nov. 1932; 5 Nov., 1938.

confined to a restricted role in the local labour market, and it would appear that they were equally restricted in the political sphere. It was reported in 1919, in the first municipal elections since the extension of the franchise to women over 30, that 'a good many women exercised their new power'. However, the first woman candidate in Barnsley was not seen until 1921. Mrs Handford stood for the Independents in the South East ward, and appealed to voters to 'Give one vote to the woman' out of the three votes they had that year. The voters plainly did not respond, as she finished at the bottom of the poll behind five others.[18] In total on the Independent side only six women stood over the whole period 1919 to 1938, and of those only two were elected. These two, Mrs Dennis in East ward and Mrs Soper in North ward, were both married to councillors. The Labour party was even more male-dominated. The ILP, after it had seceded from the Labour Party, did put up one woman in 1933. There was no Labour candidate until Mary Durkin stood in 1937 and 1938.

However, the nomination of Labour's first female candidate was a sign of change in more ways than one. Durkin was a bus conductress, she was young, and she was a single woman, and in all these characteristics she did not conform to the pattern of political representation in Barnsley. Moreover, her style of politics was a novelty as well. In 1938 her campaign in the East ward was described as the 'thrill of the election' and a 'remarkable fight' by the president of the Trades Council and Labour Party, while a Citizen spokesman deplored the aggressive and lively style of the candidate and her supporters. For him it was an 'unfortunate exception' to the 'friendly spirit' that usually prevailed in Barnsley municipal contests. The excitement prevailed to the last, with Durkin losing by a single vote after two recounts.[19] She was described as being 'prominent in the inner circles of the local Labour movement', and represented a real change from the rather stolid image of Herbert Smith's 'moderate Labourism'. Another Labour councillor at an earlier election expressed that stolidity well:

> I have held labour views for nearly 40 years, and have done all I could for the workers. I am one of the old brigade with evolutionary ideas, not revolutionary in the attainment of any principle on behalf of the workers.[20]

There was perhaps a generational change beginning here that was a portent of things to come.

In conclusion, there are a number of points to draw from the record of Barnsley's municipal politics between the wars. First, the fact that it was a one-industry town, and one severely hit by the inter-war Depression, was of great significance. Second, the spatial division of the town in political terms was unusually clear-cut, and reinforced by housing change over the period. Third, the precarious balance between the two main parties made the aldermanic system crucial, and both sides were willing to manipulate it to their advantage. Lastly, the limits of the political change represented by Barnsley Labourism, not only in

[18] *Barnsley Independent*, 8 Nov. 1919, 5 Nov. 1921.
[19] *Barnsley Chronicle*, 5 Nov. 1938.
[20] *Barnsley Independent*, 8 Nov. 1924.

terms of policies, but also in terms of achievement, were plain. This was one of the most favourable environments within which the Labour Party would operate in this period, and yet Labour's control of the borough was always tenuous. The echo of an earlier Lib-Labism still survived, but there must also have been an element of working-class Conservatism running through Barnsley's politics to explain Labour's inability to truly dominate the council. Political apathy may also have played a part.[21] If this was so even of Barnsley, how much more must it have applied to other towns. In this lies an important reason for the consolidation of the inter-war Conservative Party, which will be taken up in other parts of these volumes.

---

[21] This conclusion contrasts somewhat with Duncan Tanner's survey of coalfield politics, based primarily on analysis of parliamentary elections, which emphasises Labour's electoral strength in coalfield areas between the wars. See Tanner, 'The Labour Party and electoral politics', pp. 78-85.

A guide to further reading

Newspapers

Barnsley Chronicle
Barnsley Independent
Sheffield Daily Independent

Secondary sources

Benson, J. and Neville, R.G., (eds.), *Studies in the Yorkshire Coal Industry*, (Manchester, 1976).
Benson, J., *British Coalminers in the Nineteenth Century: A Social History*, (London, 1989).
Centenary Celebrations Booklet, Barnsley County Borough, (Barnsley, 1969).
Elliott, B., (ed.), *Aspects of Barnsley: Discovering Local History*, various volumes, (Sheffield, 1993 and following).
Howell, D., *British Workers and the Independent Labour Party 1888–1906*, (Manchester, 1983), ch. 2.
Pollard, S. and Holmes, C., (eds), *Essays in the Economic and Social History of South Yorkshire*, (Sheffield, 1976).
Rubinstein, D., 'The Independent Labour Party and the Yorkshire miners – the Barnsley by-election of 1897', *International Review of Social History*, XXIII, (1978), pp.102–134.
Shepherd, G., 'The Growth of the Coal Mining Industry in the Barnsley District 1840–1880; With a Special Reference to the growth of the South Yorkshire Miners Association 1858–1880', (B.A. dissertation, University of Liverpool, 1975).
Tanner, D., 'The Labour Party and electoral politics in the coalfields', in Campbell, A., Fishman, N. and Howell, D., (eds), *Miners, Unions and Politics, 1910–47*, (Aldershot, 1996).
Taylor, A., 'The politics of labourism in the Yorkshire coalfield, 1926–1945', in Campbell, Fishman and Howell, *Miners, Unions and Politics.*

Barnsley wards 1919–1920

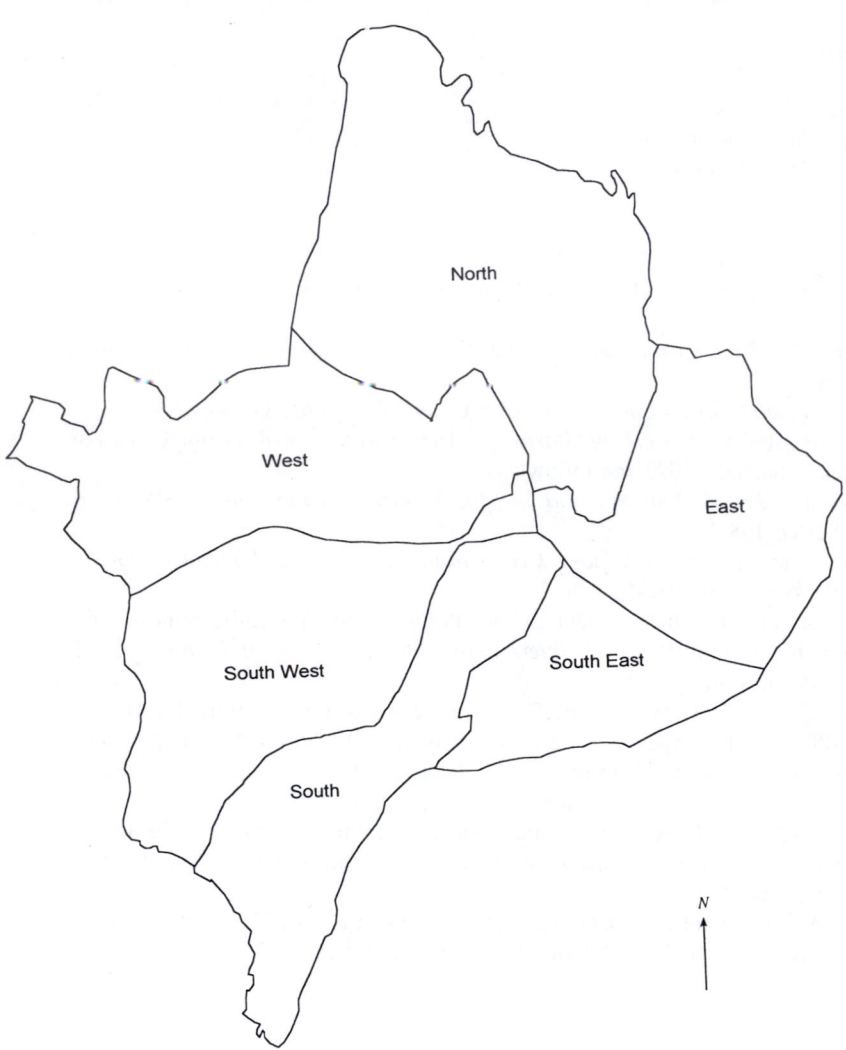

North

West

East

South West

South East

South

N

Barnsley wards 1921–1938

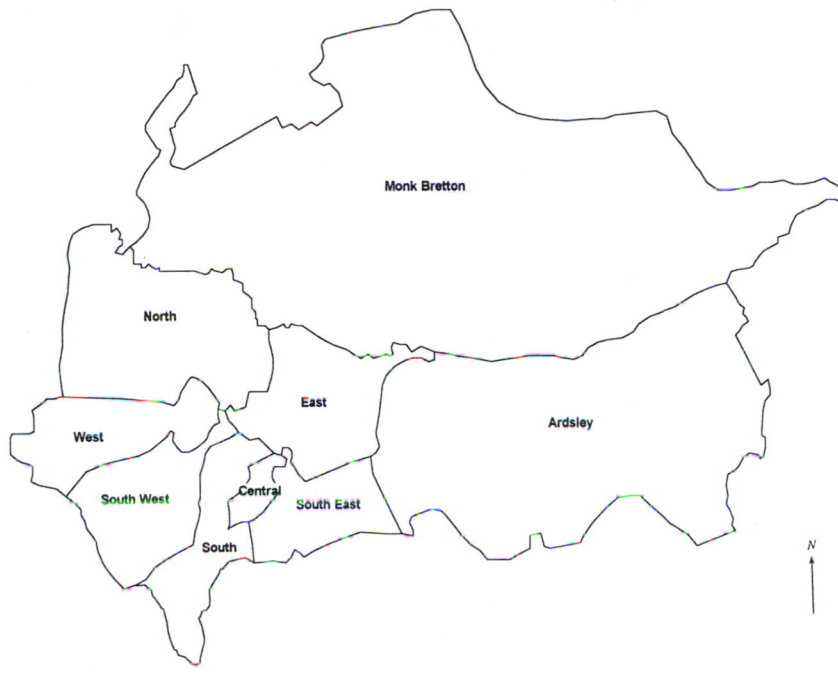

Monk Bretton

North

East

Ardsley

West

South West

Central

South East

South

N

Persons aged fourteen and over classified by industry 1931

	Male	%	Female	%	Total	%
Mining	10,817	44.1	23	0.3	10,840	34.1
Metal and engineering	1,301	5.3	735	10.2	2,036	6.4
Clothing	227	0.9	1,151	15.9	1,378	4.3
Transport	1,510	6.2	186	2.6	1,696	5.3
Commerce and finance	2,927	11.9	1,366	18.9	4,293	13.5
Public admin. and defence	1,878	7.7	500	6.9	2,378	7.5
- Local government	*1,610*	*6.6*	*452*	*6.2*	*2,062*	*6.5*
Personal service	509	2.1	1,910	26.4	2,419	7.6
Other	5,348	21.8	1,366	18.9	6,714	21.1
Total (a)	**24,517**		**7,237**		**31,754**	
Total population (b)	35,863		35,659		71,522	
(a) as % of (b)	68.4		20.3		44.4	
Total out of work (c)	4,785		889		5,674	
(c) as % of (a)	19.5		12.3		17.9	
Managerial and own account	2,003	10.2	494	7.8	2,497	9.6
Operative	17,729	89.8	5,854	92.2	23,583	90.4
Total (excluding out of work)	19,732		6,348		26,080	

Population statistics 1931

Ward	Acres	Population	Persons/acre	Persons/room
Ardsley	1,335	9,419	7.1	0.98
Central	58	6,365	109.7	1.16
East	366	6,987	19.1	1.04
Monk Bretton	2,148	10,520	4.9	1.11
North	636	8,695	13.7	0.82
South	335	6,837	20.4	0.90
South East	287	8,618	30.0	0.98
South West	490	6,852	14.0	0.92
West	381	7,229	19.0	0.86
Total	**6,036**	**71,522**	**11.8**	**0.97**

Overall position on the council 1919–1938

	Position			Gains			Losses		
	Ind[a]	Lab	I Lab	Ind[a]	Lab	I Lab	Ind[a]	Lab	I Lab
1919	14	9	1	0	2	0	2	0	0
1920	13	10	1	0	1	0	1	0	0
1921[b]	18	15	0	-	-	-	-	-	-
1922	22	14	0	3	1	0	1	3	0
1923	23	13	0	1	1	0	1	1	0
1924	22	14	0	1	3	0	2	1	1
1925	20	16	0	0	3	0	3	0	0
1926	18	18	0	0	2	0	2	0	0
1927[c]	16	19	0	1	2	0	2	1	0
1928	16	19	1	1	0	0	0	0	1
1929	16	19	1	0	0	0	0	0	0
1930	20	16	0	3	0	0	0	3	0
1931	19	17	0	0	2	0	2	0	0
1932	18	18	0	0	1	0	1	0	0
1933[d]	15	18	0	0	3	0	3	0	0
1934	14	22	0	0	1	0	1	0	0
1935	15	21	0	1	0	0	0	1	0
1936[e]	16	19	0	2	0	0	0	2	0
1937	15	21	0	2	1	0	1	2	0
1938[f]	14	26	0	0	0	0	0	0	0

Aldermen 1919–38

1919 Ind–5, Lab–1	1929 Ind–4, Lab–5
1920 Ind–5, Lab–1	1930 Ind–4, Lab–5
1921[b] Ind–5, Lab–1	1931 Ind–5, Lab–4
1922 Ind–4, Lab–5	1932 Ind–5, Lab–4
1923 Ind–4, Lab-5	1933[d] Ind–4, Lab–2
1924 Ind–4, Lab–5	1934 Ind–4, Lab–5
1925 Ind–6, Lab–3	1935 Cit–4, Lab–5
1926 Ind–6, Lab–3	1936[e] Cit–3, Lab–5
1927[c] Ind–5, Lab–3	1937 Cit–1, Lab–8
1928 Ind–4, Lab–5	1938[f] Lab–10

[a] From 1935 Ind become Cit.
[b] 1921 - boundary revisions – 3 aldermanic seats vacant.
[c] 1927 - 1 Ind alderman stood down to fight council seat, so 1 seat vacant.
[d] 1933 - 3 Labour aldermen stood down to fight council seats, so 3 seats vacant.
[e] 1936 - 1 Cit alderman stood down to fight council seat, so 1 seat vacant.
[f] 1938 - Carlton ward added, bringing total to 40 seats, and total aldermen to 10.

Municipal elections: winning party 1919–28

Ward	1919	1920	1921	1922	1923	1924	1925	1926	1927	1928
Ardsley (1)	-	-	Ind	Lab	Lab	Lab	Lab	Lab	**Lab**	I Lab
Ardsley (2)	-	-	Ind	-	-	-	-	-	-	-
Ardsley (3)	-	-	Lab	-	-	-	-	-	-	-
Central (1)	-	-	**Lab**	Ind	Lab	Lab	Ind	Lab	Lab	Ind
Central (2)	-	-	**Lab**	-	-	-	-	-	-	-
Central (3)	-	-	**Lab**	-	-	-	-	-	-	-
East	Ind	Lab	Ind	Lab	Ind	**Ind**	Lab	Lab	Lab	Lab
Monk Bretton(1)	-	-	Ind	Ind	Ind	Lab	Lab	Lab	Lab	**Lab**
Monk Bretton(2)	-	-	Ind	-	-	-	-	-	-	-
Monk Bretton(3)	-	-	Ind	-	-	-	-	-	-	-
North	Lab	**Lab**	Ind	Ind	**Ind**	Ind	Ind	Ind	Ind	Ind
South	I Lab	Ind	Lab	Ind	Ind	Ind	Ind	Ind	Lab	Ind
South East (1)	Lab	Lab	Lab	Ind	Lab	**Lab**	Lab	Lab	Lab	Lab
South East (2)	-	-	Lab	-	-	-	-	-	-	
South East (3)	-	-	Lab	-	-	-	-	-	-	
South West	Ind	Ind	Lab	Ind	Ind	Ind	Lab	Ind	Ind	Ind
West	Lab	Ind	Lab	I Lab	Ind	Ind	Ind	Ind	Ind	Ind

Municipal elections: party wins per year 1919–28

	1919	1920	1921	1922	1923	1924	1925	1926	1927	1928
Ind/Cit	2	3	7	6	6	5	4	4	3	5
Lab	3	3	10	2	3	4	5	5	6	3
I Lab	1	0	0	1	0	0	0	0	0	1
Total	6	6	17	9	9	9	9	9	9	9
Turnout %	50.6	52.2	66.0	61.5	63.0	66.8	69.1	80.3	75.7	74.1
Labour %	45.5	48.9	46.2	45.2	45.5	45.1	51.2	52.5	48.2	39.2

Municipal elections: winning party 1929–38

Ward	1929	1930	1931	1932	1933	1934	1935	1936	1937	1938
Ardsley (1)	Lab	Lab	Lab	Lab	Lab	Lab	Lab	Lab	Lab	Lab
Ardsley (2)	-	-	-	-	-	-	-	-	-	-
Ardsley (3)	-	-	-	-	-	-	-	-	-	-
Central (1)	Lab	Ind	Lab	Lab	Lab	Lab	Lab	Lab	Lab	Lab
Central (2)	-	-	-	-	-	-	-	-	-	-
Central (3)	-	-	-	-	-	-	-	-	-	-
East	Ind	Ind	Lab	Lab	Ind	Lab	Cit	Cit	Lab	Cit
Monk Bretton(1)	Lab	Lab	**Lab**	Lab	Lab	Lab	Lab	Lab	Lab	Lab
Monk Bretton(2)	-	-	-	-	-	-	-	-	-	-
Monk Bretton(3)	-	-	-	-	-	-	-	-	-	-
North	Ind	Ind	Ind	Ind	Ind	Ind	Cit	Cit	**Lab**	Cit
South	Ind	Ind	Ind	Ind	Lab	Lab	Cit	Cit	Cit	Cit
South East (1)	Lab	**Lab**	Lab	Lab	Lab	**Lab**	Lab	Lab	Cit	Lab
South East (2)	-	-	-	-	-	-	-	-	-	-
South East (3)	-	-	-	-	-	-	-	-	-	-
South West	Ind	Ind	Ind	Ind	Lab	Ind	Cit	Cit	Cit	Cit
West	Ind	Ind	Ind	Ind	Ind	Ind	Cit	Cit	Cit	Cit

Municipal elections: party wins per year 1929–38

Wins	1929	1930	1931	1932	1933	1934	1935	1936	1937	1938
Ind/Cit	5	6	4	4	3	3	5	5	4	5
Lab	4	3	5	5	6	6	4	4	5	4
I Lab	0	0	0	0	0	0	0	0	0	0
Total	9	9	9	9	9	9	9	9	9	9
Turnout %	60.9	71.1	77.3	75.3	74.9	66.1	75.5	75.4	72.4	68.3
Lab %	45.1	41.9	46.2	53.4	55.6	58.6	48.2	52.4	49.4	52.6

Municipal elections: party wins per ward 1919–38

	I/Cit	Lab	I Lab	Total	Turnout %	Labour % of all votes
Ardsley	2	17	1	20	71.3	60.9
Central	4	16	0	20	76.9	55.3
East	10	10	0	20	75.2	48.4
Monk Bretton	5	15	0	20	59.1	65.3
North	17	3	0	20	72.8	37.6
South	15	4	1	20	68.3	43.1
South East	2	20	0	22	67.2	57.0
South West	17	3	0	20	69.8	44.9
West	17	2	1	20	68.3	35.6
Total	**89**	**90**	**3**	**182**	**69.6**	**49.1**

Seats won by Labour as a percentage of all wins 1919–38   **49.5**

Central ward
(created in the reorganisation of 1921)

Candidate	Party	Votes	%	Electors	Turnout	Gains
1921						
C. Bray	Lab	Unopp.	-		-	-
J.F. Broley	Lab	Unopp.	-		-	-
E. Hinchcliffe	Lab	Unopp.	-		-	-
(3 elected)						
1922						
F. Gommersall	Ind	891	58.3	2,361	64.8	Ind from Lab
G.A. Hunt*	Lab	638	41.7			
Total votes		1,529				
1923						
T. Lang*	Lab	883	60.6	2,348	62.1	-
G.H. Willis	Ind	574	39.4			
Total votes		1,457				
1924						
E.W. Taylor	Lab	812	49.0	*2,473*	67.0	Lab from
J.A. Midgeley	Ind	607	36.6			I Lab
E. Hinchcliffe*	I Lab	239	14.4			
Total votes		1,658				
1925						
F. Gomersall*	Ind	912	52.0	2,597	67.5	-
A. Cassidy	Lab	841	48.0			
Total votes		1,753				
1926						
T. Lang*	Lab	1,286	65.8	*2,534*	77.1	-
H.N. Booker	Ind	667	34.2			
Total votes		1,953				
1927						
E.W. Taylor*	Lab	1,058	59.8	2,471	71.6	-
F. Caffrey	Ind	712	40.2			
Total votes		1,770				
1928						
F. Gommersall*	Ind	1,057	56.6	*2,408*	77.5	-
A. Cassidy	Lab	809	43.4			
Total votes		1,866				

Central ward *(continued)*

Candidate	Party	Votes	%	Electors	Turnout	Gains
1929						
A. Wright*	Lab	932	50.2	2,555	72.6	-
Mrs Gommersall	Ind	923	49.8			
Total votes		1,855				
1930						
J. Raynor	Ind	1,041	51.5	2,546	79.4	Ind from Lab
E.W. Taylor*	Lab	980	48.5			
Total votes		2,021				
1931						
J.F. Broley	Lab	1,149	52.3	2,536	86.6	Lab from Ind
F. Gommersall*	Ind	1,048	47.7			
Total votes		2,197				
1932						
A. Wright*	Lab	1,254	55.2	2,560	88.7	-
F. Gomersall	Ind	1,016	44.8			
Total votes		2,272				
1933						
T. Lang	Lab	1,328	62.2	2,584	82.6	Lab from Ind
J. Raynor*	Ind	771	36.1			
E. Stott	ILP	36	1.7			
Total votes		2,135				
1934						
J.F. Broley*	Lab	1,362	65.9	2,555	80.9	-
J. Raynor	Ind	705	34.1			
Total votes		2,067				
1935						
A. Dunk*	Lab	1,099	57.4	2,313	82.7	-
E. Ashton	Cit	815	42.6			
Total votes		1,914				
1936						
T. Lang*	Lab	1,056	57.2	2,083	88.6	-
E. Ashton	Cit	790	42.8			
Total votes		1,846				

Monk Bretton ward
(added 1921 by extension of the borough)

Candidate	Party	Votes	%	Electors	Turnout	Gains
1921						
J.W. Shaw	Ind	729	23.7	1,701	62.3	-
J.W. Johnson	Ind	693	22.5			
W. Diggle	Ind	646	21.0			
J.C. Dodd	Lab	618	20.1			
E. Cawthrow	Lab	396	12.8			
Total votes		3,082				
Total voters		*1,059*				
(3 elected)						
1922						
W. Diggle*	Ind	648	65.3	1,696	58.5	-
G. Thickett	Lab	345	34.7			
Total votes		993				
1923						
J.W. Johnson*	Ind	920	76.0	1,726	70.1	-
A.G. Sanderson	Lab	290	24.0			
Total votes		1,210				
1924						
J.C. Dodd	Lab	595	50.6	*1,747*	67.3	Lab from Ind
W. Allen	Ind	580	49.4			
Total votes		1,175				
1925						
G.W. Simpson	Lab	709	53.3	1,768	75.3	Lab from Ind
W. Diggle*	Ind	622	46.7			
Total votes		1,331				
1926						
S. Trueman	Lab	1,019	54.0	*2,226*	84.8	Lab from Ind
J.W. Johnson*	Ind	868	46.0			
Total votes		1,887				
1927						
W.E. Dodd	Lab	1,012	54.6	2,684	69.1	-
J. Halmshaw	Ind	842	45.4			
Total votes		1,854				
1928						
T.W. Richardson*	Lab	Unopp.	-		-	-

Monk Bretton ward *(continued)*

Candidate	Party	Votes	%	Electors	Turnout	Gains
1929						
S. Trueman*	Lab	1,254	67.9	3,584	51.6	-
Mrs C.A. White	Ind	594	32.1			
Total votes		1,848				
1930						
E. Sumnall	Lab	1,235	67.5	*3,959*	46.2	-
J.W. Booth	Ind	594	32.5			
Total votes		1,829				
1931						
T.W. Richardson*	Lab	Unopp.	-		-	-
1932						
S. Trueman*	Lab	2,270	82.9	4,710	58.1	-
J.W. Booth	Ind	468	17.1			
Total votes		2,738				
1933						
E. Sumnall*	Lab	2,259	79.9	4,733	59.8	-
G.W. Thompson	Ind	570	20.1			
Total votes		2,829				
1934						
T.W. Richardson*	Lab	1,862	92.5	4,786	42.0	-
T. Degnan	Com	150	7.5			
Total votes		2,012				
1935						
C. Bentley*	Lab	1,895	67.0	4,888	57.9	-
J. Hill	Cit	935	33.0			
Total votes		2,830				
1936						
W. Hunt	Lab	2,165	78.2	4,918	56.3	-
A. Radford	Cit	602	21.8			
Total votes		2,767				
1937						
W. Leach*	Lab	1,765	63.0	4,924	56.9	-
E.M. Burton	Cit	1,035	37.0			
Total votes		2,800				

Monk Bretton ward *(continued)*

Candidate	Party	Votes	%	Electors	Turnout	Gains
1938						
C. Bentley*	Lab	2,117	68.6	4,830	63.9	
E.A. Burton	Cit	967	31.4			
Total votes		3,084				

Overall Labour vote   **65.3%**   **Overall turnout**   **59.1%**

North ward

Candidate	Party	Votes	%	Electors	Turnout	Gains
1919						
C.H. Hesketh	Lab	802	56.1	2,789	51.3	Lab from Ind
T.N. Cretney*	Ind	628	43.9			
Total votes		1,430				
1920						
S.Jones*	Lab	Unopp.	-		-	-
1921						
H.M. Walker*	Ind	1,411	65.3	2,708	79.8	-
C.H. Lee	Lab	749	34.7			
Total votes		2,160				
1922						
H.H. Asquith	Ind	1,304	64.0	3,030	67.2	Ind from Lab
C.H. Hesketh*	Lab	732	36.0			
Total votes		2,036				
1923						
J.S. Rose*	Ind	Unopp.	-		-	-
1924						
H.M. Walker*	Ind	1,371	64.4	*3,193*	66.7	-
T.F. Brown	Lab	758	35.6			
Total votes		2,129				
1925						
R.J. Plummer	Ind	1,481	52.9	3,355	83.4	-
J. Jones	Lab	1,318	47.1			
Total votes		2,799				
1926						
R.J. Soper*	Ind	1,912	65.7	*3,378*	86.2	-
C.G. O'Neill	Lab	999	34.3			
Total votes		2,911				
1927						
H.M. Walker	Ind	1,687	60.2	3,401	82.4	Ind from Lab
E. Sumnall*	Lab	1,116	39.8			
Total votes		2,803				

(Walker became alderman for the ward in 1926, but resigned to fight the council seat)

North ward *(continued)*

Candidate	Party	Votes	%	Electors	Turnout	Gains
1928						
R.J. Plummer*	Ind	1,655	61.7	*3,424*	78.4	-
C. Broadbent	Lab	1,028	38.3			
Total votes		2,683				
1929						
R.J. Soper*	Ind	1,661	65.0	3,931	65.0	-
C. Broadbent	Lab	893	35.0			
Total votes		2,554				
1930						
H.M. Walker*	Ind	2,106	68.4	*3,962*	77.8	-
S. Jones	Lab	975	31.6			
Total votes		3,081				
1931						
R.J. Plummer*	Ind	1,988	67.5	3,993	73.8	-
J. Dickinson	Lab	959	32.5			
Total votes		2,947				
1932						
R.J .Soper MP*	Ind	1,882	62.0	*4,011*	75.7	-
J.C. Place	Lab	1,152	38.0			
Total votes		3,034				
1933						
P.O. Walker*	Ind	1,832	61.0	4,028	74.6	-
J. Dickinson	Lab	1,173	39.0			
Total votes		3,005				
1934						
R.J. Plummer*	Ind	1,602	61.5	4,107	63.5	-
P.A.J. Ruse	Lab	1,004	38.5			
Total votes		2,606				
1935						
Mrs L.J. Soper*	Cit	1,940	66.0	4,227	69.6	-
P.A.J. Ruse	Lab	1,001	34.0			
Total votes		2,941				

North ward *(continued)*

Candidate	Party	Votes	%	Electors	Turnout	Gains
1936						
P.O. Walker*	Cit	2,040	61.1	4,429	75.4	-
W. Leach	Lab	1,298	38.9			
Total votes		3,338				
1937						
P.A.J. Ruse	Lab	Unopp.	-		-	Lab from Cit
(Plummer's nomination invalid)						
1938						
Mrs L.J. Soper*	Cit	1,971	62.3	4,720	67.0	-
W. Heptinstall	Lab	1,192	37.7			
Total votes		3,163				

Overall Labour vote   **37.6%**   **Overall turnout**   **72.8%**

South ward

Candidate	Party	Votes	%	Electors	Turnout	Gains
1919						
A. Chapell*	I Lab	635	58.2	2,868	38.1	-
W. Martin	Lab	457	41.8			
Total votes		1,092				
1920						
H. Foulstone*	Ind	1,314	68.1	3,601	53.6	-
E. Sheerien	Lab	615	31.9			
Total votes		1,929				
1921						
A. Wright*	Lab	918	53.4	2,928	58.7	-
J. Irving	Ind	802	46.6			
Total votes		1,720				
1922						
W. Laughton	Ind	900	60.0	2,898	51.8	-
T. Wilkinson	Lab	601	40.0			
Total votes		1,501				
1923						
H. Foulstone*	Ind	1,109	63.4	2,905	60.2	-
F. Hunter	Lab	639	36.6			
Total votes		1,748				
1924						
C.H. Harris	Ind	1,073	54.4	2,952	66.9	Ind from Lab
A. Wright*	Lab	901	45.6			
Total votes		1,974				
1925						
W. Laughton*	Ind	984	54.6	2,998	60.1	-
J. Roche	Lab	818	45.4			
Total votes		1,802				
1926						
H. Foulstone*	Ind	1,342	57.0	3,004	78.4	-
G. Dobson	Lab	1,013	43.0			
Total votes		2,355				

South ward *(continued)*

Candidate	Party	Votes	%	Electors	Turnout	Gains
1927						
J. Jones	Lab	1,200	51.7	3,010	77.0	Lab from Ind
C. Harris*	Ind	1,119	48.3			
Total votes		2,319				
1928						
T.W. Beevers	Ind	1,343	67.3	*3,016*	66.2	-
H. Godley	Lab	654	32.7			
Total votes		1,997				
1929						
H. Potter	Ind	1,168	62.1	3,025	62.2	-
E. Sumnall	Lab	714	37.9			
Total votes		1,882				
1930						
C. Harris	Ind	1,414	56.5	*3,036*	82.4	Ind from Lab
J. Jones*	Lab	1,089	43.5			
Total votes		2,503				
1931						
T.W. Beevers*	Ind	1,399	59.2	3,047	77.6	-
G. Martin	Lab	965	40.8			
Total votes		2,364				
1932						
H. Potter*	Ind	1,294	54.9	*3,066*	76.8	-
G. Martin	Lab	1,062	45.1			
Total votes		2,356				
1933						
G. Mason	Lab	1,130	50.7	3,085	72.2	Lab from Ind
C. Harris*	Ind	1,098	49.3			
Total votes		2,228				
1934						
W. Durant	Lab	1,174	50.3	3,173	73.6	Lab from Ind
T.W. Beevers*	Ind	1,160	49.7			
Total votes		2,334				

South ward *(continued)*

Candidate	Party	Votes	%	Electors	Turnout	Gains
1935						
H. Potter*	Cit	1,533	61.0	3,167	79.3	-
F. Hunter	Lab	979	39.0			
Total votes		2,512				
1936						
T.W. Beevers	Cit	1,402	54.7	3,199	80.1	Cit from Lab
G. Mason*	Lab	1,159	45.3			
Total votes		2,561				
1937						
A. Hepworth	Cit	1,411	57.8	3,119	78.3	Cit from Lab
W. Durant*	Lab	1,031	42.2			
Total votes		2,442				
1938						
H. Potter*	Cit	1,257	58.8	3,079	69.4	-
A. Lowrey	Lab	879	41.2			
Total votes		2,136				

Overall Labour vote   **43.1%**   **Overall turnout**   **68.3%**

South East ward

Candidate	Party	Votes	%	Electors	Turnout	Gains
1919						
J. Guest	Lab	1,360	52.3	5,890	44.1	-
A.A. Kates	Ind	1,240	47.7			
Total votes		2,600				
1920						
J.F. Broley*	Lab	2,327	59.1	7,691	51.2	-
A. Winter	Ind	1,612	40.9			
Total votes		3,939				
1921						
J. Guest*	Lab	1,424	22.5	3,480	62.5	-
M. Holt	Lab	1,240	19.6			
F. Roebuck	Lab	1,213	19.2			
C.W. Squire	Ind	1,001	15.8			
A. Jenkinson	Ind	844	13.3			
Mrs M.E. Handford	Ind	606	9.6			
Total votes		6,328				
Total voters		*2,175*				
(3 elected)						
1922						
C.W. Squire	Ind	1,222	53.7	3,437	66.2	Ind from Lab
F. Roebuck*	Lab	1,054	46.3			
Total votes		2,276				
1923						
E. Sheerien	Lab	1,247	52.0	3,453	69.5	-
D.R. Snowden	Ind	1,153	48.0			
Total votes		2,400				
1924						
H.M. Cassells*	Lab	Unopp.	-		-	-
1925						
Rev D. Allott	Lab	1,416	57.2	3,516	70.4	Lab from Ind
C.W. Squire*	Ind	1,058	42.8			
Total votes		2,474				
1926						
E. Sheerien*	Lab	1,678	58.2	*3,498*	82.4	-
J. Richards	Ind	1,205	41.8			
Total votes		2,883				

South East ward *(continued)*

Candidate	Party	Votes	%	Electors	Turnout	Gains
1927						
H.M. Cassells*	Lab	1,506	56.4	3,480	76.8	-
H. Potter	Ind	1,165	43.6			
Total votes		2,671				
1928						
Rev D. Allott*	Lab	1,443	67.0	*3,462*	62.2	-
R. Rymer	Ind	667	31.0			
J.F. White	Com	45	2.1			
Total votes		2,155				
1929						
E. Sheerien*	Lab	1,257	51.9	3,665	66.1	-
H. Howe	Ind	1,165	48.1			
Total votes		2,422				
1930						
J. Guest	Lab	Unopp.	-		-	-
1931						
Rev D. Allott*	Lab	1,524	53.2	3,641	78.7	-
H. Howe	Ind	1,341	46.8			
Total votes		2,865				
1932						
E. Sheerien*	Lab	1,625	57.5	*3,632*	77.9	-
J. Earnshaw	Ind	1,203	42.5			
Total votes		2,828				
1933						
J. Guest*	Lab	1,748	67.0	3,623	72.0	-
Mrs G. Bentley	Ind	861	33.0			
Total votes		2,609				
1934						
Rev D. Allott*	Lab	Unopp.	-	3,722	-	-
1935						
H.M. Cassells*	Lab	1,669	59.1	3,745	75.4	-
F.W. Dawson	Cit	1,153	40.9			
Total votes		2,822				

South East ward *(continued)*

Candidate	Party	Votes	%	Electors	Turnout	Gains
1936						
J. Guest*	Lab	1,888	62.0	4,159	73.2	-
H. Jackson	Cit	1,156	38.0			
Total votes		3,044				
1937						
R.H. Raper	Cit	1,284	41.1	4,197	74.4	Cit from Lab
J. Dickinson*	Lab	1,249	40.0			
T. Hunt	I Lab	591	18.9			
Total votes		3,124				
1938						
H.M. Cassells*	Lab	2,071	68.3	4,379	69.2	-
W.H. Greenwood	Cit	961	31.7			
Total votes		3,032				

Overall Labour vote   **57.0%**   **Overall turnout**   **67.2%**

South West ward

Candidate	Party	Votes	%	Electors	Turnout	Gains
1919						
A. Bentley	Ind	619	54.5	2,122	53.5	-
T. Lang	Lab	517	45.5			
Total votes		1,136				
1920						
T. Tipping*	Ind	679	50.5	2,664	50.5	-
T. Lang	Lab	665	49.5			
Total votes		1,344				
1921						
F. Beaumont	Lab	836	52.7	2,599	61.0	Lab from Ind
C.A. White*	Ind	749	47.3			
Total votes		1,585				
1922						
M. Jackson*	Ind	943	53.4	2,649	66.6	-
E. Sheerien	Lab	822	46.6			
Total votes		1,765				
1923						
T Tipping*	Ind	925	55.5	2,650	62.9	-
E.W. Taylor	Lab	741	44.5			
Total votes		1,666				
1924						
C.E. Charlesworth*	Ind	902	53.3	2,679	63.2	-
I. Allen	Lab	791	46.7			
Total votes		1,693				
1925						
H. Rhodes	Lab	916	51.4	2,707	65.8	Lab from Ind
M. Jackson*	Ind	866	48.6			
Total votes		1,782				
1926						
H. Snowden	Ind	1,151	51.7	2,712	82.1	-
J.W. Durnan	Lab	1,075	48.3			
Total votes		2,226				

South West ward *(continued)*

Candidate	Party	Votes	%	Electors	Turnout	Gains
1927						
C.E. Charlesworth*	Ind	1,047	52.1	2,716	74.0	-
H. Jackson	Lab	964	47.9			
Total votes		2,011				
1928						
A. Lightowler	Ind	829	44.5	*2,720*	68.5	Ind from
T.A .Ling	Lab	554	29.7			I Lab
H. Rhodes*	I Lab	481	25.8			
Total votes		1,864				
1929						
H. Snowden*	Ind	1,210	65.0	3,061	60.8	-
W. Heptinstall	Lab	652	35.0			
Total votes		1,862				
1930						
G. Stone	Ind	1,334	65.6	*3,078*	66.0	-
W. Heptinstall	Lab	698	34.4			
Total votes		2,032				
1931						
J.T. Mitchell	Ind	1,311	58.1	3,095	72.9	-
H. Burgin	Lab	945	41.9			
Total votes		2,256				
1932						
H. Snowden*	Ind	1,317	55.2	*3,118*	76.5	-
A. Allen	Lab	1,069	44.8			
Total votes		2,386				
1933						
A. Allen	Lab	1,200	53.0	3,140	72.2	Lab from Ind
G. Stone*	Ind	1,066	47.0			
Total votes		2,266				
1934						
J.T. Mitchell*	Ind	1,237	50.9	3,215	75.6	-
W. Leach	Lab	1,195	49.1			
Total votes		2,432				

South West ward *(continued)*

Candidate	Party	Votes	%	Electors	Turnout	Gains
1935						
H. Snowden	Cit	1,487	58.1	3,249	78.7	-
W. Leach	Lab	1,071	41.9			
Total votes		2,558				
1936						
R.J .Soper	Cit	1,443	53.3	3,323	81.4	Cit from Lab
A. Allen*	Lab	1,263	46.7			
Total votes		2,706				
1937						
W. Arrand	Cit	1,345	52.4	3,356	76.5	-
J. Foster	Lab	1,222	47.6			
Total votes		2,567				
1938						
H. Snowden*	Cit	1,419	57.5	3,339	73.9	-
J. Foster	Lab	1,050	42.5			
Total votes		2,469				

Overall Labour vote   **44.9%**   **Overall turnout**   **69.8%**

West ward

Candidate	Party	Votes	%	Electors	Turnout	Gains
1919						
J. Kellett	Lab	753	40.1	3,318	56.6	Lab from Ind
M. Jackson	Ind	667	35.5			
R.J. Soper	Ind	457				
Total votes		1,877				
1920						
W.G. England*	Ind	1,255	57.3	4,159	52.6	-
E.E. Tilling	Lab	934	42.7			
Total votes		2,189				
1921						
Herbert Smith	Lab	1,043	51.3	3,074	66.1	Lab from Ind
W. Maudsley*	Ind	989	48.7			
Total votes		2,032				
1922						
J. Kellett*	I Lab	794	56.7	2,929	47.8	-
F. Woolerton	Lab	606	43.3			
Total votes		1,400				
1923						
W.G .England*	Ind	1,104	68.1	2,919	55.6	-
J.W. Martin	Lab	518	31.9			
Total votes		1,622				
1924						
B.F. Canter*	Ind	1,551	69.2	2,948	76.0	-
Harold Smith	Lab	689	30.8			
Total votes		2,240				
1925						
J. Kellett*	Ind	1,285	57.2	2,976	75.5	-
Herbert Smith	Lab	961	42.8			
Total votes		2,246				
1926						
B. Harral*	Ind	1,452	62.3	2,931	79.6	-
H. Jackson	Lab	880	37.7			
Total votes		2,332				

West ward *(continued)*

Candidate	Party	Votes	%	Electors	Turnout	Gains
1927						
B.F. Canter*	Ind	1,557	72.9	2,885	74.1	-
F. Hunter	Lab	580	27.1			
Total votes		2,137				
1928						
J.G.E. Rideal	Ind	1,626	74.6	*2,838*	76.8	-
F. Hunter	Lab	554	25.4			
Total votes		2,180				
1929						
J. Richards	Ind	1,317	68.6	3,264	58.9	-
W. Lawton	Lab	604	31.4			
Total votes		1,921				
1930						
B.F. Canter*	Ind	1,678	79.4	*3,253*	65.0	-
W. Beardsley	Lab	435	20.6			
Total votes		2,113				
1931						
J.G.E. Rideal*	Ind	1,752	75.0	3,242	72.1	-
S. Jubb	Lab	585	25.0			
Total votes		2,337				
1932						
J. Richards*	Ind	1,493	62.3	*3,265*	73.4	-
S. Jubb	Lab	904	37.7			
Total votes		2,397				
1933						
W.J. Taylor	Ind	1,216	49.6	3,287	74.6	-
S. Jubb	Lab	970	39.6			
P. Hinchcliffe	Ind	265	10.8			
Miss A. Schofield	ILP	32	1.3			
Total votes		2,451				
1934						
J.G.E. Rideal*	Ind	1,439	59.2	3,302	73.6	-
S. Jubb	Lab	992	40.8			
Total votes		2,431				

West ward *(continued)*

Candidate	Party	Votes	%	Electors	Turnout	Gains
1935						
J. Richards*	Cit	1,607	61.1	3,401	77.3	-
J.H. Foster	Lab	1,021	38.9			
Total votes		2,628				
1936						
W.J. Taylor*	Cit	1,604	60.0	3,387	78.9	-
J.H. Foster	Lab	1,070	40.0			
Total votes		2,674				
1937						
J.G.E. Rideal*	Cit	1,710	70.6	3,426	70.7	-
Miss M. Durkin	Lab	711	29.4			
Total votes		2,421				
1938						
J. Richards*	Cit	1,462	64.9	3,488	64.6	-
H. Tennant	Lab	791	35.1			
Total votes		2,253				

Overall Labour vote   **35.6%**   **Overall turnout**   **68.3%**

TWO
Barrow-in-Furness

BARROW-IN-FURNESS

Barrow-in-Furness was the creation of mid nineteenth-century industrialism and was developed on the bedrock of a longer-established iron trade in the surrounding district of Furness. As late as 1843 there were only twenty-eight houses and 150 people in Barrow village.[1] Located in Lancashire, to the south of the rural Cumbrian Lakeland, this iron-working centre was on the coastal margins and very much separated from the industrial heartlands of the county. The settlement allegedly acquired its name from the small island where the Norseman buried their dead in barrows.[2] The economic development and growth of the town and its subsequent population increase escalated with the building of the Furness Railway from 1846. Rapid development of the iron and steel industry followed the exploitation of the rich local deposits of haematite iron ore. For a few years in the mid-Victorian age, this 'western industrial periphery became a major Bessemer iron and steel centre of Europe and the world.'[3] The Furness Railway was important to Barrow as it took land control and planning decisions which influenced the growth of the iron and steel industry and the Cumberland coalfield.

With the later development of docks, shipbuilding and general engineering the population mushroomed. By the late Victorian age, Barrow was an important industrial centre both regionally and nationally. From a population of 448 in 1851, the town had over 18,000 people in 1871 and almost 58,000 in 1901. With the opening of the first big dock (the Devonshire) in 1867, Gladstone appropriately described the town 'as the youngest child of England's enterprise'.[4] The charter of incorporation, whereby the town attained its borough status, was granted in the same year as the opening of the Devonshire dock. The aristocracy and the gentry provided a landed and semi-feudal impetus to the mid-Victorian industrialisation of Barrow. Thus the rapid transformation from small hamlet to late Victorian heavy industry can be seen as 'an alliance of landowners and capitalists'.[5]

In the late nineteenth century the giant Hodbarrow haematite ore company was the basis of the town's iron and steel processing plants. Hodbarrow also exported the raw ore to the world market. Thus coke brought from the Durham coalfield by the Furness Railway, combined with the local haematite iron ore, underpinned the growth of the local iron and steel plants. H.W. Schneider, Robert Hannay and the Duke of Devonshire were the founders of the Barrow Haematite Steel Company which was to be central to the town's transformation and economic importance. By the early twentieth century, this heavy industrial base provided the materials for the vital defence industries of naval ship construction, heavy armaments and the marine and general engineering of Vickers and Sons.

In the new century, Vickers' was in a unique position in the borough for a number of reasons. From the early twentieth century until the end of the First War

---

[1] *Barrow and District Yearbook*, (1920), p. 81.
[2] Lofthouse, J., *Portrait of Lancashire*, (London, 1977), p. 174.
[3] Marshall, J. D. and Walton, J.K., *The Lake Counties from 1830 to the Mid-twentieth Century*, (Manchester, 1981), p. 29.
[4] *Furness and District Yearbook*, (1939), p. 68.
[5] Walton, J.K., *Lancashire: A Social History* 1558–1939, (Manchester, 1987), p. 216.

naval shipbuilding became Barrow's main industry. The success of Vickers' was based upon its ability to build complete warships with engines, armour and armaments. A merger in 1928 made Vickers Armstrong the UK's largest armaments manufacturing concern. With iron ore processing becoming less important from the Edwardian age due to the gradual exhaustion of reserves, shipbuilding and engineering dominated the industrial structure of inter-war Barrow. Barrow in this era was very much a company town but in two distinct phases. In the nineteenth century the Hodbarrow mine and the Barrow Haematite Steel Company ruled the roost. In the twentieth century it was a town dominated by Vickers'. It was now a company town based on shipbuilding and engineering, both marine and general.

By the end of the First World War then, Barrow had lost or was losing some important industries. There were no large employers of female labour outside of Vickers', as a jute factory that had performed that function had closed down in 1892. Barrow's docks were in decline, never having become of major significance, and the iron industry had virtually run its course. Still firmly in place after 1918 were iron and steel manufacture, shipbuilding, heavy armaments, and marine and general engineering. Also important to the local economy were a railway carriage and wagon works, locomotive construction, an oil refinery, brick and tile manufacture, timber importation and paper making, a wire works and brine-pumping factory. The borough's mid-Victorian characteristics of dynamic economic and population growth were clearly at an end. Its population in 1921 was 74,254, falling to 66,180 in 1931, making it sixty-sixth of our county boroughs ranked in size that year.

Unemployment struck Barrow in the inter-war years, especially during the post-war readjustment of the economy, and during the slump of the early 1930s. Rising unemployment occurred from the early 1920s with the end of the wartime boom in the shipyards. Although the Depression of the early 1930s also hit hard, Walton notes that Barrow shipbuilding 'came off relatively lightly'.[6] Iron and steel performed less strongly because of international competition and the relative expense of Cumberland ores. Walton and Orrell have commented on the weakness, indeed vulnerability, of the borough's economic base in this period.[7] The reliance of Barrow on one strong firm and industry was both its long-term Achilles heel yet short-term salvation. Warship construction at Vickers', including submarines, reached its peak in the First War, fell away in the post-war period and picked up again with rearmament after 1935. Concealed government subsidies kept the vital defence industries going until 1921. The town's economic dependence upon one firm meant that the naval reductions pushed up unemployment by 1922. In that year 60 per cent of those engaged in shipbuilding, nearly half the engineering labour force, and in Barrow as a whole 44 per cent of insured workers, were unemployed.[8] Restructuring and the adaptability of

---

[6] Walton, *Lancashire*, p. 336.
[7] Walton, *Lancashire*, p. 336; Orrell, P.E., 'Barrow-in-Furness: Its Historical and Economic Development 1840–1974', (B.A. dissertation, University of Liverpool, 1975), p. 47.
[8] Orrell, 'Barrow-in-Furness', p. 47.

Vickers' saved Barrow, as the town became from 1921 a major manufacturer of merchant ships. This adaptability, coupled with the strong reputation of the company, saved Barrow from even higher unemployment. The borough fared better in this respect than many similar industrial centres in the same period.

Nevertheless the years 1930–31 saw the closure of a large part of the manufacturing base. A decade earlier the takeover of the Furness Railway by the London, Midland and Scottish Railway had led to the closure of the local railway headquarters. The closure of the carriage and wagon works and locomotive construction followed. Iron and brass foundries, general engineering shops, the brine-pumping works and an oil refinery also disappeared into oblivion. Orrell points out that in the thirty years 1909–39, these industries, including timber firms and the Griffin Iron and Steel Company, had employed 37 per cent of the insured workforce, suggesting that a good deal of the unemployed found alternative employment in local government, municipal undertakings and distributive trades.[9] There is little doubt then that Barrow's economic base narrowed still further in the period of our study. Dock and portside activities were in serious decline, the iron and steel industries languished, while reliance on Vickers' and shipbuilding more than ever put the borough's economic eggs in one basket. The worst years of poverty and unemployment in Barrow were 1922–3, 1931 and 1933. There were 9,000 insured workers unemployed in 1923 and 7,500 in 1931.[10]

The broader parameters of social and economic structure require some comment to help comprehend inter-war municipal politics. In 1931 the metal and engineering category dominated the town with over 62 per cent of a largely male labour force employed in that category. Within this general category too, around 50 per cent of the male labour force, over 12,000 men, were concentrated in shipbuilding and marine engineering. Barrow comes top of the 1931 ranking of county boroughs in its percentage of male workers in shipbuilding (50.9 per cent) and sixteenth in metal and engineering (8.3 per cent). Barrow's working class was very much male and skilled in character, and it was primarily on this working class and its strong trade unions that the Labour party built its strength. There were no large-scale concerns employing female labour, only 18 per cent of females aged fourteen and over being employed insured workers in 1931. The two main sectors of female labour were commerce and finance (23.8 per cent) and personal service (37.5 per cent). With women at just over 19 per cent of the total workforce, Barrow lay eighty-first in that category. Barrow's women were, more than most, confined to home and hearth. Their role in local politics was correspondingly small. Conversely, the absence of a powerful middle class was an important feature. This middle-class 'weakness' can be demonstrated in terms of the relatively low levels of both female domestic service and self-employment in 1931. In that year Barrow, with 3.3 per cent in female domestic service as a percentage of the total population, lay forty-third amongst the county boroughs. In terms of self-employment, Barrow lay sixty-eighth, with just under 10 per cent of the male and female workforce in the 'own account' and 'managers' category. Such a structure helps to explain the strong Labour party in municipal politics and

9   Orrell, 'Barrow-in-Furness', p. 57.
10 Orrell, 'Barrow-in-Furness', p. 76.

the difficulties for the various anti-Labour coalitions that emerged in the inter-war council chamber.

Turning to the early politics of the borough, the paternalism of the aristocracy, especially the Cavendish family, was a significant factor in Barrow in the late nineteenth century. Marshall and Walton note that Barrow's town leadership was disadvantaged by the absence of strongly established middle-class elements and was virtually ruled by 'an industrial junta'.[11] The shipyard and steelworks interests were politically highly influential. The Tory parliamentary candidate in 1885 was a director of the Barrow steelworks, another was a shipowner who placed an order for a ship from Vickers' shortly before the 1895 election.[12] Early twentieth-century local politics was characterised by apathy, uncontested elections and little working-class input. It is worth mentioning however that the first Labour municipal victory was as early as 1892 in Hindpool ward. By 1909, the Labour party, based upon trade union growth, a well-attended trades council, and the Co-operative movement, was making inroads and politicising a council where politics had 'been unknown'.[13] Three important points are made by Marshall and Walton on the pre-war political arena. First, the employers and tradesmen were still in control of the borough. Second, a working-class Liberal vote still existed. Third, the borough had a small Labour group on the council backed by a strong trade-union movement in what was 'a relatively class-conscious town.'[14] Walton refers 'to the confident militancy' of the engineers and shipyard workers in the pre-1914 period.[15]

The post-war Labour party in Barrow was both well-organised and powerful. To reiterate a crucial point made above, the party was based primarily on a skilled and unionised, and predominantly male, working-class movement deriving from the heavy concentration of production and labour in shipbuilding, engineering, armaments manufacture and the iron and steel industries. In terms of municipal politics, Barrow was one of the strongest and most solid Labour county boroughs. Following rapid growth of Labour support in 1919 and 1920, and further significant gains in the mid-1920s, Labour achieved overall control in 1928. The party retained control between 1928 and 1931, and again held power from 1934 to 1938. The fierceness of the inter-party competition in Barrow can be seen by the exceptionally high turnout in municipal elections. With an overall turnout over twenty years of 69 per cent, peaking at 81 per cent in 1925, interest in local elections was vigorously healthy. The fight between Labour and its opponents was a close one, with Labour achieving an average vote of 50 per cent over the period as a whole. There was also an unusually low number of walkovers, only twenty-two out of 160 contests being uncontested. 76 per cent of all contests were straight fights with Labour, and there were only seven contests not involving Labour in the whole twenty-year period.

[11] Marshall and Walton, *The Lake Counties*, p. 125.

[12] Pelling, H., *Social Geography of British Elections, 1885–1910*, (Aldershot, 1994), pp. 274–275.

[13] Quoted in Marshall and Walton, *The Lake Counties*, p. 93.

[14] Marshall and Walton, *The Lake Counties*, p. 137.

[15] Walton, *Lancashire*, p. 274.

Tracing Labour's fortunes in more detail, the newly re-formed party armed with a new constitution did exceptionally well nationally in the municipal elections of 1919. Barrow to a certain extent followed the trend, with Labour securing 52 per cent of the total poll. Labour also did well locally in 1920, substantially increasing its number of councillors to fifteen, and for the first time seriously challenging for control of the council chamber. This was rather out of line with the national picture, with Labour's fortunes generally being in decline in the early 1920s in other county boroughs. Barrow came more into line in 1921 and 1922, when Labour's percentage of the poll dipped to 41 per cent and 44 per cent respectively, an inter-war low point only to be matched by the 1931 debacle. Labour then began to make good progress from 1923 onwards, although 1924 saw a temporary setback, reflecting the national trend and following on closely from the losses in the October 1924 general election.

Unemployment was a local factor that certainly helped Labour in the 1923 election. The local newspaper reported that after the results had been declared, 'the unemployed formed a torch light procession and headed by the drum and fife band marched to the Labour rooms'.[16] The years from 1925 to 1929 saw Labour make great gains in Barrow's council elections. The culmination of this progress took place in 1928, with two gains meaning Labour had fifteen councillors and four aldermen out of the total of thirty-six on the council, and thus overall control for the first time. This very much mirrored the national trend, again repeated in 1929 when Ramsay MacDonald's general election triumph in May was five months later followed by Labour securing 56 per cent of the poll in Barrow, its second-best performance between the wars.

Nationally 1930 was a disaster for Labour, with the MacDonald government's inability to deal with rising unemployment resulting in widespread losses across the country in the November elections. Yet in Barrow, Labour still did reasonably well, holding on to 53 per cent of the vote and sustaining no overall losses. This was a confirmation perhaps of the solidity of the bedrock of support the party enjoyed in the borough, and also perhaps of the relatively minor impact of unemployment in the town at this time. The year 1931 was a different story, with Labour's share of the poll falling dramatically to 43 per cent. Four wards were lost, two of them, Salthouse and Walney, having previously been 'solid' for Labour. The rise in unemployment in 1931, coupled with the political bombshell of MacDonald's 'betrayal', had clearly taken their toll. Recovery was rapid, however, with Labour's share of the vote restored to customary levels in 1932, mirroring the national trend. Nevertheless, Labour lost absolute control of the council with a further two wards lost to the Citizens, a reflection of the fact that the party was defending gains that it had won three years previously at the high point of 1929. The recovery continued in 1933 with one ward being regained, and the party winning its highest inter-war share of the poll at 57 per cent. The following year, the four lost wards of 1931, Central, Ramsden, Salthouse and Walney, were all recovered, and Labour was back in charge and remained so until the Second World War. In the last three years of municipal elections before the war, the general trend of turnout across the nation was down. Barrow only

---

[16] *North Western Daily Mail*, 2 Nov. 1923.

partially reflected this, with turnout falling below the inter-war average for the borough, but still at a relatively healthy low to mid-60s figure. These last pre-war years in Barrow also gave little indication of the Labour upsurge that was to come in 1945. There was not the decline in Labour support that was witnessed in other boroughs, but neither was there any great advance. Labour held its own in a council that was firmly under its control.

Turning to Labour's main opponents, the first observation to be made is that the Conservative party tended to do rather better in parliamentary than in municipal elections in Barrow. Conservatives held the Westminster seat from 1892 until 1906. In that year, with the Liberals allowing Labour to have a straight fight with the Conservatives, the constituency was captured by Charles Duncan for Labour. Pelling attributes this to a heterogeneous body of shipyard and steelworks employees, with Irish Catholics and Scots to the fore, voting 'more or less as a unit for the first time'.[17] Labour held the seat in both 1910 elections, though Pelling still viewed the constituency as marginal. In the inter-war period, Labour held Barrow only in 1924 and in its peak year of 1929. In parliamentary terms, though marginal, Barrow was more a Conservative seat than a Labour one.

By contrast, in municipal elections Tory weakness was reflected in the Conservative party in Barrow restyling itself under the name of the 'Citizens' party in 1928. This reinvention happened in a number of northern towns where party competition with the Labour party was fierce and close. In Barrow municipal elections were genuine contests for control of the council. Middle-class and property-owning groups could not afford the luxury of competition between traditional party organisations. Such contests would have handed Labour control of the borough far sooner than its 1928 triumph. These relatively small groups could thus only achieve their political interests by the fiction of non-partisan politics, and of 'concerned' non-political administration in the interests of all ratepayers. A 1928 membership coupon stated the overt position of the organisation:

> The objects of the Association shall be to provide a medium
> through which Citizens irrespective of Class, Party or Creed, may
> come together for mutual counsel, and to promote efficiency with
> economy in the administration of the affairs of the Borough, to
> the end that trade may be stimulated and employment increased
> therein.[18]

Later in 1933, Captain J. Fisher, chairman of the Barrow Citizens' Association, gave a clue as to the social type his group wanted as councillors. They should be 'the cream of the business element of the town' and 'supporters of big business and employment rather than little businesses and the dole'. The local newspaper stated plainly that 'the majority of the anti-Socialists come under the Citizens banner.'[19] The weakness of the Liberal Party, with only three seats won in the period, pointed in the same direction. Liberals could support the Citizens without

---

[17] Pelling, *Social Geography of British Elections*, p. 275.
[18] *North Western Daily Mail*, 2 Nov., 1928.
[19] *North Western Daily Mail*, 2 Nov. 1933.

the stigma of Toryism. On the other hand, where the Conservatives were on the defensive, they gave themselves a non-political label to rally wider sectors of electoral support.

In any case, all the non-Labour political parties on the council were in their own terms 'anti-socialist'. This had meaning in practical politics in terms of ideology, action and to a degree, organisation. The local *North Western Daily Mail* consistently referred to the political groupings on the council as either 'anti-Socialist' or 'Socialist'. It is apparent that the anti-labour groups acted in unison both in the November elections and in the day-to-day politics of the council chamber. There were only five three-cornered November contests in which anti-socialist candidates fought each other where Labour was standing. When this did happen it was in solidly Conservative–Citizen wards where Labour stood little or no chance of success. Thus in Yarlside (1926 and 1927) and Newbarns (1931) although Conservatives, Citizens or Independents competed against each other, Labour could not secure the ward. Only once in Ramsden ward did a split anti-Labour vote cause embarrassment to Labour's opponents. Here, in 1921, two Independents allowed in a Labour candidate. In 1929 however, it made little difference, as the combined Citizen and Independent poll fell twenty-seven votes short of the Labour candidate. On the rare occasions when Labour did not stand in a ward, Conservatives, Citizens and Independents could compete in straight contests, such as in the rock-solid 'Conservative' ward of Hawcoat where a Citizen versus Independent contest took place in 1934. Usually walkovers were the order of the day, thus confirming the existence of a working anti-Labour arrangement.

Before the advent of the Citizens, the Independents had been one other significant grouping of tradesmen and businessmen of an anti-Labour, though notionally apolitical, orientation. In the early post-war years Independents had controlled the council until 1921. Their true colours were starkly illustrated in 1922 by the local newspaper in announcing the municipal election results. 'It should be pointed out', said the *Mail*, 'that the majority of the Independents are Conservatives'.[20] The Independents were subsequently only a minor group, and the handful remaining on the council clarified their real position somewhat in 1934 when they renamed themselves Independent Conservatives.

Turning now to the spatial geography of political allegiance in Barrow, in 1881 most of the population had been concentrated in the three central wards of Hindpool, Ramsden and Central, which had 30,000 of the 47,000 population. In the 1890s population movement to the outlying wards of Salthouse, Newbarns and Hawcoat began, while Walney increased its population by around 4,000.[21] The Barrow Haematite Steel Company developed in Hindpool, and the original mid-century Scottish-style tenements providing high-density working-class housing still existed there in the inter-war period. This stock of working-class housing was added to by Vickers', which built the company houses of Vickerstown North on Walney Island in the early twentieth century. Before the First World War, Vickerstown North had a population of around 4,000 in 900 company houses,

---

[20] *North Western Daily Mail*, 2 Nov. 1922.
[21] Orrell, 'Barrow-in-Furness', p. 43.

and during the war Vickers' built a further 2,500 houses in Vickerstown South on Walney Island. Walney, with its concentration of engineering and shipyard workers, remained a solid Labour ward like Hindpool. Of the other city-centre wards, Ramsden was a largely Labour ward, with fourteen wins for the party in the twenty years between the wars. Central on the other hand elected as many anti-Labour as Labour councillors, and plural voters concentrated in the retail and business centre would have been influential here. Barrow Island, created in 1929 out of the most working-class section of Walney ward, had the highest number of persons per room in the borough, and unsurprisingly was never lost by Labour.

Inter-war housing construction had little political impact. Between 1921 and 1933 the total number of houses increased from 15,462 to 15,672, an insignificant number reflecting the falling population of the 1920s. But from 1936 to 1939, with the population stabilising, another 3,000 houses were built.[22] 600 municipal houses were built in Devonshire Road and Ainslie Street in the Hawcoat ward, and further council houses were built in Salthouse ward. Salthouse was already a fairly solid Labour ward, whereas Hawcoats was an anti-Labour stronghold, and neither was significantly affected in political terms by these new council estates. There was also some private housing development in the period, with semi-detached housing for the middle classes built on Walney and in Newbarns and Hawcoat.[23] Newbarns, like Hawcoat, was a suburban ward where Labour always had little support, and the private housing developments in Walney were heavily outweighed by the earlier working-class housing.

There was only one major change to the political structure of the borough between the wars. As mentioned above, in 1929 Barrow Island ward was created having previously been part of Walney ward. At the same time Yarlside ward, with its small numbers of voters, was incorporated into Salthouse. These changes took place while Labour was in power, and they both favoured the Labour party, However, they were also defensible on the grounds of equalising electorates across the borough. Walney before 1929 had been rock-solid Labour, and had almost double the number of electors of most of the other wards. The separation of Barrow Island from Walney achieved average electorates for both wards, but the net result was to create an additional Labour ward, as they were both predominantly Labour-supporting after 1929. On the other hand, the incorporation of the small Yarlside ward into Salthouse terminated an anti-Labour seat, the enlarged ward only falling to the Citizens once in 1936. Whether these changes would have been carried through in the same way under Citizen rule is a moot point. On the other hand, there is little evidence in Barrow of the sharp practice in municipal politics that was seen in other county boroughs. There seems to have been little blatant manipulation of the aldermanic elections by any of the political groups. Once Labour achieved near equality in elected councillors in 1920, their aldermanic strength was to reflect a rough parity with the numerical position of their councillors. Subsequently the aldermanic bench largely reflected the party share of councillors in the council chamber, although Labour was over-represented to an extent in the last three years before the war.

[22] Orrell, 'Barrow-in-Furness', p. 77.
[23] Orrell, 'Barrow-in-Furness', p. 77.

One final issue that can be considered is the possible political influence of religious sectarianism, which has been ably examined by Donald MacRaild in his recent study of Victorian Cumbria. Extensive immigration of Scots, Cornish, Staffordshire and above all Irish workers had occurred to provide the labour for the iron and steel industries of mid-Victorian Barrow. The majority of the Irish came from Ulster and included both Catholics and Protestants.[24] There appear to have been some echoes of sectarianism before the First World War. MacRaild notes that late nineteenth-century Barrow had thirteen Orange Lodges.[25] An anti-Catholic base for working-class Conservatism was however not much in evidence in Barrow's municipal politics by the 1920s. In 1921 a degree of sectarianism was seen, when a 'Unionist Labour' candidate wrestled Newbarns ward from Labour, but this was untypical, and took place in a year when Labour's fortunes were at a low ebb. The Unionist Labour victory was 'in large measure due to the party organisation' suggested the *Mail*.[26] The vestiges of sectarianism continued to hold on in the Working Men's Conservative Associations and Conservative clubs, but as a political force it was negligible, and declined through this period. The small Catholic minority of the working class could never be portrayed as a serious threat as far as competition on the job market was concerned, nor was it substantial enough to have a major influence on the local Labour party, as it did in other boroughs such as Bootle (see later in this volume) or Liverpool.[27]

To conclude, Barrow was based economically on heavy industry and in thrall to one large concern – Vickers'. The broad parameters of this simple socio-economic structure provided, as might be expected, the framework for a relatively straightforward set of relationships in municipal politics. The concentration of labour produced a town dominated by a skilled and highly-unionised, and predominantly male, working class. So well organised was this working class locally that the Labour party managed to gain control and eventually hold what was in parliamentary terms a marginal Conservative seat. With high turnouts and few uncontested wards, politics in Barrow were hotly fought. Ranged against Labour were various 'non-partisan', but nevertheless anti-socialist, alliances, organised by the middle class and petty bourgeois tradesmen and shopkeepers to attract the votes of the ratepayers. Working-class Conservatism was not a serious force in Barrow. Conservatives, Citizens, Liberals and Independents were all labels of the anti-Labour *ralliement*. These supposedly apolitical groupings, whatever the label adopted, were the best hope for the middle-class managers, professionals and tradesmen opposed to Labour gaining control of the town. Such was the concentration of working-class numbers in the majority of the wards that Barrow became what in inter-war terms could be regarded as a Labour stronghold. This process was aided by the weakness of the middle class. Crucially, Barrow in the inter-war years retained an important characteristic of its mid-Victorian

[24] MacRaild, D.M., *Culture, Conflict and Migration: The Irish in Victorian Cumbria*, (Liverpool, 1998), p. 27.
[25] MacRaild, *Culture, Conflict and Migration*, p. 145.
[26] *North Western Daily Mail*, 2 Nov. 1921.
[27] See Davies, S., *Liverpool Labour: Social and Political Influences on the Development of the Labour Party in Liverpool, 1900–1939*, (Keele, 1996).

creation. 'The youngest child of England's enterprise' was very much an island of heavy industry and engineering in an agrarian sea. This very much defined the nature of Barrow's inter-war municipal politics and ensured Labour's supremacy.

A guide to further reading

Newspapers

Manchester Guardian
North Western Daily Mail

Secondary sources

Lofthouse, J., *Portrait of Lancashire*, (London, 1977).
MacRaild, D.M., *Culture, Conflict and Migration: The Irish in Victorian Cumbria*, (Liverpool, 1998).
Marshall, J. D. and Walton, J.K., *The Lake Counties from 1830 to the Mid-Twentieth Century*, (Manchester, 1981).
Orrell, P.E., 'Barrow-in-Furness: Its Historical and Economic Development 1840–1974', (B.A. dissertation, University of Liverpool, 1975).
Pelling, H., *Social Geography of British Elections, 1885–1910*, (Aldershot, 1994), pp. 274–275.
Walton, J.K., *Lancashire: A Social History 1558–1939*, (Manchester, 1987).

Barrow-in-Furness wards 1919–1938

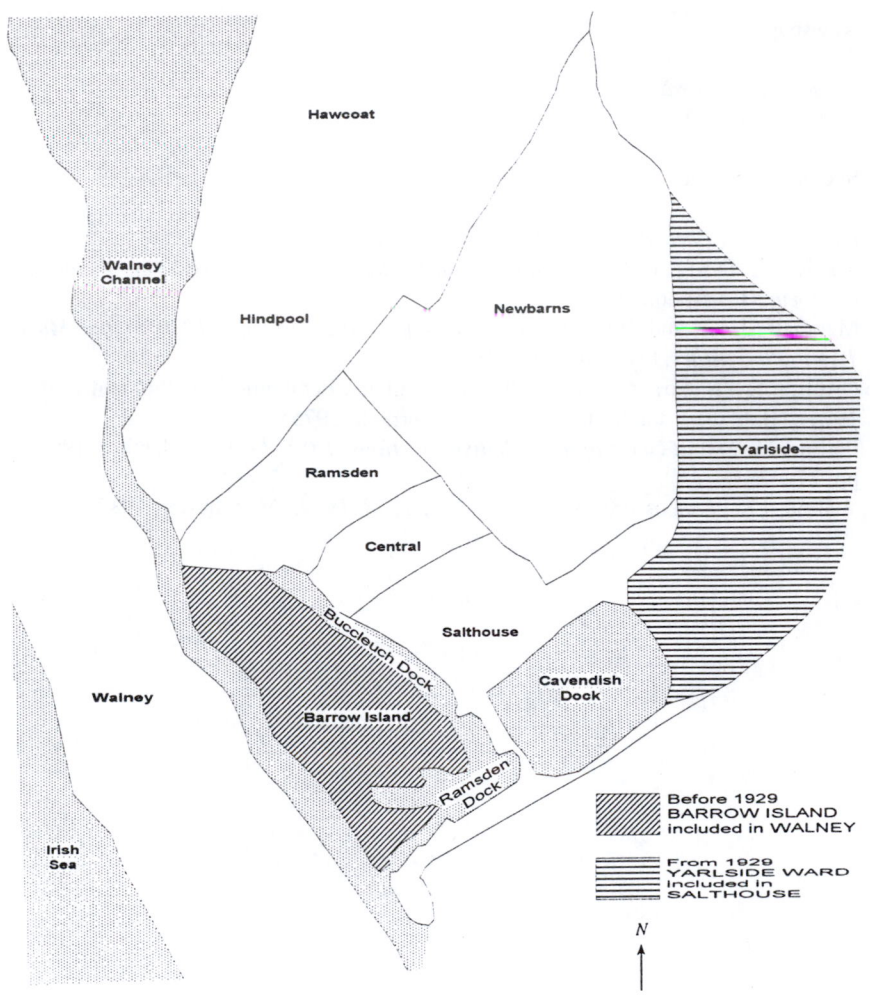

Hawcoat

Walney
Channel

Hindpool

Newbarns

Yarlside

Ramsden

Central

Buccleuch Dock

Salthouse

Walney

Barrow Island

Cavendish
Dock

Ramsden
Dock

Irish
Sea

Before 1929
BARROW ISLAND
included in WALNEY

From 1929
YARLSIDE WARD
included in
SALTHOUSE

N

Persons aged fourteen and over classified by industry 1931

	Male	%	Female	%	Total	%
Metal and engineering	15,029	62.2	376	6.5	15,405	51.4
- Iron and steel	*1,880*	*7.8*	*14*	*0.2*	*1,894*	*6.3*
- Shipbuilding and marine engineering	*12,314*	*50.9*	*339*	*5.8*	*12,653*	*42.2*
Transport	2,141	8.9	40	0.7	2,181	7.3
- Rail	*917*	*3.8*	*17*	*0.3*	*934*	*3.1*
- Water and docks	*858*	*3.5*	*13*	*0.2*	*871*	*2.9*
Commerce and finance	2,359	9.8	1,379	23.8	3,738	12.5
Public admin.and defence	992	4.1	557	9.6	1,549	5.2
- Local government	*751*	*3.1*	*507*	*8.7*	*1,258*	*4.2*
Personal service	447	1.8	2,177	37.5	2,624	8.8
Others	3,206	13.3	1,276	22.0	4,482	15.0
Total (a)	**24,174**		**5,805**		**29,979**	
Total population (b)	34,034		32,168		66,202	
(a) as % of (b)	71.0		18.0		45.3	
Total out of work (c)	4,165		814		4,979	
(c) as % of (a)	17.2		14.0		16.6	
Managerial and own account	1,737	8.7	720	14.4	2,457	9.8
Operative	18,272	91.3	4,271	85.6	22,543	90.2
Total (excluding out of work)	20,009		4,991		25,000	

Population statistics 1931

Ward	Acres	Population	Persons/acre	Persons/room
Barrow Island	640	8,273	12.9	1.15
Central	77	7,609	98.8	0.94
Hawcoat	2,331	8,369	3.6	0.73
Hindpool	335	9,154	27.3	0.97
Newbarns	1,096	8,675	7.9	0.79
Ramsden	137	8,028	58.6	0.94
Salthouse	3,236	8,891	2.7	0.91
Walney	3,150	7,203	2.3	0.86
Total	**11,002**	**66,202**	**6.0**	**0.89**

Overall position on the council 1919–38

	Position				Gains				Losses			
	Ind[a]	C[b]	Lab	L	Ind[a]	C[b]	Lab	L	Ind[a]	C[b]	Lab	L
1919	22	-	10	-	0	-	1	-	1	-	0	-
1920	17	-	15	-	0	-	2	-	2	-	0	-
1921	16	1	15	-	0	1	0	-	0	0	1	-
1922	4	14	14	0	1	1	1	0	0	1	2	0
1923	4	15	13	0	0	1	1	0	1	0	1	0
1924	1	16	13	2	0	3	1	0	2	0	1	1
1925	4	15	13	0	0	0	1	0	1	0	0	0
1926	1	15	15	1	0	0	2	0	2	0	0	0
1927	2	14	16	0	0	0	1	0	0	1	0	0
1928	1	12	19	0	0	0	2	0	0	2	0	0
1929	0	10	22	0	0	0	1	0	0	1	0	0
1930[c]	0	9	22	0	0	1	1	0	0	1	1	0
1931	0	13	19	0	0	4	0	0	0	0	4	0
1932	1	15	16	0	0	2	0	0	0	0	2	0
1933	1	15	16	0	0	0	1	0	0	1	0	0
1934[c]	3	9	19	0	0	0	4	0	0	4	0	0
1935	2	9	21	0	0	0	0	0	0	0	0	0
1936	2	10	20	0	0	3	0	0	0	0	3	0
1937	2	11	19	0	0	1	0	0	0	0	1	0
1938	2	10	20	0	0	0	0	0	0	0	0	0

Aldermen 1919–38

1919 Ind–8	1929 C–2, Lab–6
1920 Ind–7, Lab–1	1930 C–2, Lab–6
1921 Ind–4, Lab–4	1931 C–2, Lab–6
1922 C–4, Lab–4	1932 C–2, Lab–5, Ind–1
1923 C–4, Lab–3, Ind–1	1933 C–4, Lab–3, Ind–1
1924 C–4, Lab–3, Ind–1	1934 C–3, Lab–4, Ind–1
1925 C–4, Lab–3, Ind–1	1935 C–3, Lab–4, Ind–1
1926 C–4, Lab–3, Ind–1	1936 C–2, Lab–6
1927 C–4, Lab–3, Ind–1	1937 C–2, Lab–6
1928 C–3, Lab–4, Ind–1	1938 C–2, Lab–6

[a] Most Independents become Conservatives from 1922;
remaining Independents become Independent Conservatives in 1934.
[b] Conservatives become Citizens from 1928.
[c] One seat vacant in 1930 and 1934.

Municipal elections: winning party 1919–28

Ward	1919	1920	1921	1922	1923	1924	1925	1926	1927	1928
Barrow Island	-	-	-	-	-	-	-	-	-	-
Central	Ind	Ind	Ind	C	Lab	C	C	Lab	Lab	Lab
Hawcoat	Ind	Ind	Ind	Ind	**C**	C	C	C	**C**	**Cit**
Hindpool	Lab	Lab	Lab	C	Lab	Lab	Lab	Lab	Lab	Lab
Newbarns	**Ind**	Lab	C	C	C	C	C	C	C	Cit
Ramsden	Lab	Lab	Lab	Ind	Lab	C	Ind	Lab	Lab	Lab
Salthouse	Lab	**Lab**	Ind	Lab	Lab	Lab	Lab	Lab	Lab	Lab
Walney	Lab	Lab	Lab	Lab	Lab	Lab	Lab	Lab	Lab	Lab
Yarlside	Ind	Ind	Ind	Ind	**C**	C	C	C	C	Cit

Municipal elections: party wins per year 1919–28

	1919	1920	1921	1922	1923	1924	1925	1926	1927	1928
C/Cit	-	-	1	3	3	5	4	3	3	3
Lab	4	5	3	2	5	3	3	5	5	5
Ind	4	3	4	3	0	0	1	0	0	0
Total	8	8	8	8	8	8	8	8	8	8
Turnout %	66.5	75.1	68.0	79.2	73.6	76.2	81.1	68.1	71.7	75.0
Labour %	51.8	52.4	41.0	43.9	54.8	46.0	50.2	49.7	55.9	52.4

Municipal elections: winning party 1929–38

Ward	1929	1930	1931	1932	1933	1934	1935	1936	1937	1938
Barrow Island	Lab	Lab	Lab	Lab	Lab	Lab	**Lab**	Lab	Lab	Lab
Central	Lab	Cit	Cit	Cit	Lab	Lab	Lab	Cit	Lab	Lab
Hawcoat	**Cit**	**Cit**	**Cit**	**Cit**	**Cit**	Cit	**Cit**	**Cit**	**Cit**	Cit
Hindpool	**Lab**	Lab	Lab	Lab	**Lab**	**Lab**	Lab	Lab	Lab	Lab
Newbarns	**Cit**	**Cit**	Cit	**Cit**	**Cit**	Cit	**Cit**	**Cit**	Cit	Cit
Ramsden	Lab	Lab	Cit	Lab	Lab	Lab	Lab	Cit	Cit	Lab
Salthouse	Lab	Lab	Cit	Lab	Lab	Lab	Lab	Cit	Lab	Lab
Walney	Lab	Lab	Cit	Cit	Lab	Lab	Cit	Lab	Lab	Lab
Yarlside	-	-	-	-	-	-	-	-	-	-

Municipal elections: party wins per year 1929–38

	1929	1930	1931	1932	1933	1934	1935	1936	1937	1938
C/Cit	2	3	6	4	2	2	3	5	3	2
Lab	6	5	2	4	6	6	5	3	5	6
Ind	0	0	0	0	0	0	0	0	0	0
Total	8	8	8	8	8	8	8	8	8	8
Turnout %	64.1	61.6	69.1	70.0	70.4	54.4	68.4	63.6	61.9	64.4
Labour %	56.1	52.8	42.7	52.0	57.4	46.1	53.4	53.8	50.9	46.6

Municipal elections: party wins per ward 1919–38

	C/Cit	Lab	Ind	Total	Turnout %	Labour % of all votes
Barrow Island	0	10	0	10	66.1	57.0
Central	7	10	3	20	71.2	48.7
Hawcoat	16	0	4	20	60.3	22.8
Hindpool	1	19	0	20	69.1	58.2
Newbarns	18	1	1	20	69.7	41.1
Ramsden	4	14	2	20	67.1	50.6
Salthouse	2	17	1	20	69.4	52.6
Walney	3	17	0	20	73.2	57.2
Yarlside	6	0	4	10	80.2	27.2
Total	**57**	**88**	**15**	**160**	**69.2**	**49.9**

Seats won by Labour as a percentage of all wins 1919–38   **55.0**

Parliamentary election results

Barrow-in-Furness constituency
(all wards within the borough [1918 boundaries] were included in the constituency)

General election	Winner	Conservative %	Labour %	Liberal %
14 Dec. 1918	C	50.6	49.4	-
15 Nov. 1922	C	53.1	46.9	-
6 Dec. 1923	C	47.5	46.0	6.5
29 Oct. 1924	Lab	48.8	51.2	-
30 May 1929	Lab	44.0	56.0	-
27 Oct. 1931	C	56.8	43.2	-
14 Nov. 1935	C	50.3	49.7	-

Barrow Island ward
(created 1929, previously part of Walney ward)

Candidate	Party	Votes	%	Electors	Turnout	Gains
1929						
P. McKeating	Lab	1,384	58.3	3,555	66.7	Lab from Cit
J. Eddowes	Cit	988	41.7			
Total votes		2,372				
1930						
J.F. Massicks*	Lab	1,222	56.8	3,537	60.8	-
A. Barrie	Cit	929	43.2			
Total votes		2,151				
1931						
Mrs J. Ward	Lab	1,200	50.1	3,567	67.2	-
A. Barrie	Cit	1,196	49.9			
Total votes		2,396				
1932						
P. McKeating*	Lab	1,466	54.1	3,583	75.6	-
J.T. Noble	Cit	1,106	40.8			
Mrs M.E. Robinson	Com	136	5.0			
Total votes		2,708				
1933						
J.F. Massicks*	Lab	1,593	62.1	3,547	72.3	-
J.K. Wardle	Cit	971	37.9			
Total votes		2,564				
1934						
Mrs J.E. Ward*	Lab	1,424	65.4	3,654	59.6	-
Mrs B.A. Burke	Cit	755	34.6			
Total votes		2,179				
1935						
P. McKeating*	Lab	Unopp.	-		-	-
1936						
J.W. Herdman*	Lab	1,353	57.3	3,554	66.4	-
T. Parnham	Cit	1,008	42.7			
Total votes		2,361				

Barrow Island ward *(continued)*

Candidate	Party	Votes	%	Electors	Turnout	Gains
1937						
Mrs J.E. Ward*	Lab	1,270	58.7	3,558	60.8	-
G. Garth	Cit	893	41.3			
Total votes		2,163				
1938						
P. McKeating*	Lab	1,135	50.7	3,441	65.1	-
W. Stevens	Cit	1,104	49.3			
Total votes		2,239				

Overall Labour vote **57.0%** **Overall turnout** **66.1%**

Central ward

Candidate	Party	Votes	%	Electors	Turnout	Gains
1919						
R. Thompson*	Ind	1,301	57.4	3,111	72.8	-
Mrs R .Mills	Lab	964	42.6			
Total votes		2,265				
1920						
O. Smith	Ind	1,323	56.4	3,131	74.9	-
W.H. Mounsey	Lab	1,021	43.6			
Total votes		2,344				
1921						
A. Pass	Ind	1,394	59.1	3,217	73.4	-
J. Holland	Lab	966	40.9			
Total votes		2,360				
1922						
R. Thompson*	C	1,519	58.3	3,209	81.1	-
D. Griffiths	Lab	1,085	41.7			
Total votes		2,604				
1923						
J.V. Holland	Lab	1,178	50.3	3,135	74.7	Lab from Ind
O. Smith*	Ind	1,165	49.7			
Total votes		2,343				
1924						
O. Smith	C	1,395	52.5	3,122	85.2	C from L
S. Lowry	Lab	1,264	47.5			
Total votes		2,659				
1925						
Dr A.F. Rutherford*	C	1,397	52.4	3,209	83.0	-
Mrs R. Mills	Lab	1,267	47.6			
Total votes		2,664				
1926						
J.V. Holland*	Lab	1,289	52.5	3,190	77.0	-
Mrs A. Blackwood	C	1,168	47.5			
Total votes		2,457				

Central ward *(continued)*

Candidate	Party	Votes	%	Electors	Turnout	Gains
1927						
Mrs R. Mills*	Lab	1,218	50.9	3,253	73.6	-
Mrs A. Blackwood	C	1,176	49.1			
Total votes		2,394				
1928						
R. Harper	Lab	1,217	50.5	3,238	74.4	Lab from Cit
T.H. Nicholas	Cit	1,191	49.5			
Total votes		2,408				
1929						
J.V. Holland*	Lab	1,227	54.9	3,485	64.1	-
A. Jones	Cit	1,007	45.1			
Total votes		2,234				
1930						
A. Jones	Cit	1,240	55.9	3,538	62.7	Cit from Lab
A. McConnell	Lab	980	44.1			
Total votes		2,220				
1931						
Mrs A. Blackwood	Cit	1,431	57.2	3,493	71.6	Cit from Lab
R. Harper*	Lab	1,070	42.8			
Total votes		2,501				
1932						
T.T. Hobro	Cit	1,214	51.1	3,513	67.6	Cit from Lab
J.V. Holland*	Lab	1,162	48.9			
Total votes		2,376				
1933						
G. Waite	Lab	1,341	54.9	3,572	68.4	Lab from Cit
A. Jones*	Cit	1,102	45.1			
Total votes		2,443				
1934						
T. Hellen	Lab	1,277	57.8	3,542	62.3	Lab from Cit
A. Barrie	Cit	931	42.2			
Total votes		2,208				

Central ward *(continued)*

Candidate	Party	Votes	%	Electors	Turnout	Gains
1935						
P.J. Bull*	Lab	1,271	52.3	*3,515*	69.1	-
T. Parnham	Cit	1,159	47.7			
Total votes		2,430				
1936						
R. McBurnie	Cit	1,129	50.9	3,488	63.5	Cit from Lab
R. McLauchlan*	Lab	1,087	49.1			
Total votes		2,216				
1937						
G.D. Hastwell*	Lab	1,164	52.2	3,501	63.7	-
T. Parnham	Cit	1,065	47.8			
Total votes		2,229				
1938						
P.J. Bull*	Lab	1,154	51.1	3,388	66.6	-
Mrs S.M. Finlay	Cit	1,104	48.9			
Total votes		2,258				

Overall Labour vote   **48.7%**   **Overall turnout**   **71.2%**

Hawcoat ward

Candidate	Party	Votes	%	Electors	Turnout	Gains
1919						
T. Johnstone*	Ind	1,745	58.1	4,507	66.7	-
T.W. Pickthall	Lab	1,260	41.9			
Total votes		3,005				
1920						
C. Barben*	Ind	2,124	58.7	4,604	78.6	-
C. Mycock	Lab	1,494	41.3			
Total votes		3,618				
1921						
R.T. Dockeray*	Ind	1,620	67.2	4,695	51.3	-
H. Wilson	Ind	790	32.8			
Total votes		2,410				
1922						
W. Bell*	Ind	2,564	73.6	4,916	70.9	-
Mrs S. Robinson	Lab	921	26.4			
Total votes		3,485				
1923						
C. Barben*	C	Unopp.	-		-	-
1924						
R.T. Dockeray*	C	1,931	65.2	4,855	61.0	-
A. McConnell	Ind	1,030	34.8			
Total votes		2,961				
1925						
W. Bell*	C	2,431	66.9	4,951	73.4	-
J. Jones	Lab	1,203	33.1			
Total votes		3,634				
1926						
Mrs M.A. Lee	C	1,185	52.1	4,942	46.0	-
G. Kay	Ind	1,088	47.9			
Total votes		2,273				
1927						
W.J. Ireland*	C	Unopp.	-		-	-
1928						
A.A. Haynes*	Cit	Unopp.	-	4,927	-	-

Hawcoat ward *(continued)*

Candidate	Party	Votes	%	Electors	Turnout	Gains
1929						
Mrs M.A. Lee*	Cit	Unopp.	-		-	-
1930						
W.J. Ireland*	Cit	Unopp.	-	4,325	-	-
1931						
A.A. Haynes*	Cit	Unopp.	-	4,355	-	-
1932						
Mrs M.A. Lee*	Cit	Unopp.	-		-	-
1933						
W. Bell*	Cit	Unopp.	-		-	-
1934						
A.W. Smith*	Cit	1,154	77.0	4,457	33.6	-
A. Abbot	Ind	344	23.0			
Total votes		1,498				
1935						
D. Jackson	Cit	Unopp.	-		-	-
1936						
J.K. Wardle*	Cit	Unopp.	-		-	-
1937						
A.W. Smith*	Cit	Unopp.	-	5,178	-	-
1938						
D.Jackson*	Cit	2,245	67.0	5,589	60.0	-
T.Trewartha	Lab	1,108	33.0			
Total votes		3,353				

Overall Labour vote		**22.8%**		**Overall turnout**		**60.3%**

Hindpool ward

Candidate	Party	Votes	%	Electors	Turnout	Gains
1919						
G. Basterfield*	Lab	1,562	64.0	3,787	64.5	-
F. Butler	Ind	880	36.0			
Total votes		2,442				
1920						
J. Whinnerah*	Lab	1,724	57.5	3,837	78.1	-
F.H. Robinson	Ind	1,273	42.5			
Total votes		2,997				
1921						
J. Doyle	Lab	1,421	50.6	3,972	70.6	-
G.A. Haynes	Ind	1,385	49.4			
Total votes		2,806				
1922						
G.A. Haynes	C	1,619	50.5	3,998	80.2	-
J.V. Holland	Lab	1,588	49.5			
Total votes		3,207				
1923						
D. Griffiths	Lab	1,761	55.6	3,965	79.9	-
W.B. Swann	C	1,406	44.4			
Total votes		3,167				
1924						
J. Doyle*	Lab	1,907	60.4	3,914	80.7	-
C. Whatmore	C	1,252	39.6			
Total votes		3,159				
1925						
W.A. Pickthall	Lab	2,064	64.9	3,952	80.4	Lab from Ind
J.H. Huitson	Ind	1,115	35.1			
Total votes		3,179				
1926						
D. Griffiths*	Lab	1,857	67.9	3,998	68.4	-
J Jamieson	Ind	877	32.1			
Total votes		2,734				

Hindpool ward *(continued)*

Candidate	Party	Votes	%	Electors	Turnout	Gains
1927						
J. Doyle*	Lab	1,732	58.8	3,971	74.2	-
I. Archer	Ind	1,213	41.2			
Total votes		2,945				
1928						
W.A. Pickthall*	Lab	1,724	56.4	3,966	77.1	-
I. Archer	Cit	1,256	41.1			
Mrs M.E. Robinson	Com	77	2.5			
Total votes		3,057				
1929						
D. Griffiths*	Lab	Unopp.	-		-	-
1930						
Mrs M.Jobling	Lab	1,586	59.1	4,286	62.6	-
I. Archer	Ind	1,098	40.9			
Total votes		2,684				
1931						
W.A. Pickthall*	Lab	1,371	49.9	4,291	64.0	-
D. McFarlane	Cit	1,202	43.8			
R.Purcell	Com	172	6.3			
Total votes		2,745				
1932						
R.A. Brunskill*	Lab	1,586	58.7	4,300	62.9	-
D. MacFarlane	Cit	953	35.2			
R.Purcell	Com	165	6.1			
Total votes		2,704				
1933						
Mrs M. Jobling*	Lab	Unopp.	-		-	-
1934						
W.A. Pickthall*	Lab	Unopp.	-		-	-
1935						
R.A. Brunskill*	Lab	1,643	62.2	*4,234*	62.4	-
R.H. Horne	Cit	998	37.8			
Total votes		2,641				

Hindpool ward *(continued)*

Candidate	Party	Votes	%	Electors	Turnout	Gains
1936						
Mrs M. Jobling*	Lab	1,354	62.4	4,210	51.6	-
G. Garth	Cit	817	37.6			
Total votes		2,171				
1937						
J. Miller*	Lab	1,396	60.0	4,164	55.9	-
J.W. Warbrick	Cit	932	40.0			
Total votes		2,328				
1938						
R.A. Brunskill*	Lab	1,433	54.1	4,102	64.6	-
T. Danks	Cit	1,216	45.9			
Total votes		2,649				

Overall Labour vote   **58.2%**   **Overall turnout**   **69.1%**

Newbarns ward

Candidate	Party	Votes	%	Electors	Turnout	Gains
1919						
A. McIntee*	Ind	Unopp.	-	3,317	-	-
1920						
J.W. Postlethwaite	Lab	1,464	53.2	3,536	77.9	Lab from Ind
H.W. Chambers	Ind	1,290	46.8			
Total votes		2,754				
1921						
T. Dickinson	C	1,652	57.2	3,875	74.5	C from Lab
J.E. Ralph*	Lab	1,236	42.8			
Total votes		2,888				
1922						
W. Marsh	C	1,798	58.2	3,881	79.6	C from Lab
P. McKeating*	Lab	1,292	41.8			
Total votes		3,090				
1923						
F. Fisher	C	1,428	51.5	3,736	74.3	C from Lab
J.W. Postlethwaite*	Lab	1,346	48.5			
Total votes		2,774				
1924						
T. Dickinson*	C	1,602	53.3	3,755	80.0	-
W.A. Pickthall	Lab	1,401	46.7			
Total votes		3,003				
1925						
W. Marsh*	C	1,680	54.0	3,848	80.8	-
A.M. McConnell	Lab	1,430	46.0			
Total votes		3,110				
1926						
F. Fisher*	C	1,434	50.6	3,833	73.9	-
S. Sowerbutts	Lab	1,400	49.4			
Total votes		2,834				
1927						
W.F. Clement	C	1,548	53.8	3,828	75.2	-
B. Hartley	Lab	1,332	46.3			
Total votes		2,880				

Newbarns ward *(continued)*

Candidate	Party	Votes	%	Electors	Turnout	Gains
1928						
W. Marsh*	Cit	1,489	53.0	3,740	75.1	-
W.C. Hilton	Lab	1,318	47.0			
Total votes		2,807				
1929						
F. Fisher*	Cit	Unopp.	-		-	-
1930						
W.F. Clement*	Cit	Unopp.	-	4,270	-	-
1931						
Mrs E.A. Ward*	Cit	1,724	61.3	4,274	65.8	-
J. Dickie	Lab	759	27.0			
I.T. Archer	Ind	329	11.7			
Total votes		2,812				
1932						
F. Fisher*	Cit	Unopp.	-		-	-
1933						
W.F. Clement*	Cit	Unopp.	-		-	-
1934						
Mrs E.A. Ward*	Cit	1,265	77.4	4,474	36.5	-
J.A.B. Harvey	Ind	369	22.6			
Total votes		1,634				
1935						
J. Wilson*	Cit	Unopp.	-		-	-
1936						
A. Jones*	Cit	Unopp.	-		-	-
1937						
Mrs E.A. Ward*	Cit	2,229	66.7	5,414	61.7	-
J.G. Waiting	Lab	1,113	33.3			
Total votes		3,342				

Newbarns ward *(continued)*

Candidate	Party	Votes	%	Electors	Turnout	Gains
1938						
T.P. Collinge*	Cit	2,409	62.5	6,050	63.8	-
T.E. Paxton	Lab	1,448	37.5			
Total votes		3,857				

Overall Labour vote   **41.1%**   **Overall turnout**   **69.7%**

Ramsden ward

Candidate	Party	Votes	%	Electors	Turnout	Gains
1919						
R. Bettinson	Lab	1,110	51.1	3,355	64.8	Lab from Ind
W.F.A. Wadham*	Ind	1,064	48.9			
Total votes		2,174				
1920						
I.T. Archer*	Lab	1,307	54.7	3,419	69.9	-
J.H. Huitson	Ind	1,084	45.3			
Total votes		2,391				
1921						
I. Clamp	Lab	989	42.2	3,514	66.6	-
J. Cannon	Ind	804	34.3			
Mrs Ward	Ind	548	23.4			
Total votes		2,341				
1922						
W.E. Roberts	Ind	1,447	53.2	3,433	79.3	Ind from Lab
R. Bettinson*	Lab	1,275	46.8			
Total votes		2,722				
1923						
I.T. Archer*	Lab	1,378	55.1	3,406	73.5	-
Mrs A.S. Livingston	C	1,125	44.9			
Total votes		2,503				
1924						
Mrs A.S. Livingston	C	1,413	51.6	3,389	80.8	C from Lab
I. Clamp*	Lab	1,327	48.4			
Total votes		2,740				
1925						
W.E. Roberts*	Ind	1,390	51.3	3,406	79.6	-
I. Clamp	Lab	1,320	48.7			
Total votes		2,710				
1926						
R. Bettinson	Lab	1,249	54.3	3,419	67.3	Lab from Ind
I.T. Archer*	Ind	1,051	45.7			
Total votes		2,300				

Ramsden ward *(continued)*

Candidate	Party	Votes	%	Electors	Turnout	Gains
1927						
S. Lowry	Lab	1,318	53.6	3,438	71.6	Lab from C
Mrs A.S. Livingston*	C	1,142	46.4			
Total votes		2,460				
1928						
Mrs S. Robinson	Lab	1,220	50.6	3,405	70.8	Lab from Cit
W.E. Roberts*	Cit	1,191	49.4			
Total votes		2,411				
1929						
W.W. Poyntz	Lab	1,127	50.6	3,643	61.1	-
D. Kay	Cit	686	30.8			
I.T. Archer	Ind	414	18.6			
Total votes		2,227				
1930						
C.W. Hilton*	Lab	1,110	51.1	3,652	59.5	-
D. Kay	Cit	1,063	48.9			
Total votes		2,173				
1931						
A.B. McDowell	Cit	1,348	55.1	3,682	66.4	Cit from Lab
Mrs S. Robinson*	Lab	1,098	44.9			
Total votes		2,446				
1932						
W.W. Poyntz*	Lab	1,221	52.3	3,709	63.0	-
T. Taylor	Cit	1,114	47.7			
1933						
C.W. Hilton*	Lab	1,229	54.5	3,690	61.1	-
T. Taylor	Cit	1,025	45.5			
Total votes		2,254				
1934						
Mrs S. Robinson	Lab	1,179	54.8	3,644	59.0	Lab from Cit
T. Taylor	Cit	971	45.2			
Total votes		2,150				

Ramsden ward *(continued)*

Candidate	Party	Votes	%	Electors	Turnout	Gains
1935						
W.W. Poyntz*	Lab	1,245	53.5	*3,611*	64.4	-
A.A. Bennett	Cit	1,080	46.5			
Total votes		2,325				
1936						
R.H. Horne	Cit	1,215	53.6	3,577	63.3	Cit from Lab
C.W. Hilton*	Lab	1,050	46.4			
Total votes		2,265				
1937						
J.T. Harper	Cit	1,078	50.1	3,557	60.5	Cit from Lab
F.J. Longstaffe	Lab	1,075	49.9			
Total votes		2,153				
1938						
W.W. Poyntz*	Lab	1,120	50.3	3,503	63.6	-
W. Roach	Cit	1,108	49.7			
Total votes		2,228				
Overall Labour vote		**50.6%**		**Overall turnout**		**67.1%**

Salthouse ward

(Yarlside ward incorporated in it from 1929)

Candidate	Party	Votes	%	Electors	Turnout	Gains
1919						
J.H. Brown*	Lab	912	59.4	2,206	69.6	-
J. Fisher	Ind	624	40.6			
Total votes		1,536				
1920						
A. Barrie*	Lab	Unopp.	-		-	-
1921						
J. Jamieson	Ind	922	55.3	2,304	72.4	-
D. Griffiths	Lab	745	44.7			
Total votes		1,667				
1922						
W.W. Oldfield	Lab	945	51.8	2,283	80.0	Lab from C
Mrs K. Lee*	C	881	48.2			
Total votes		1,826				
1923						
A. Barrie*	Lab	888	56.4	2,217	71.0	-
E.J. Albion	C	686	43.6			
Total votes		1,574				
1924						
J.F. Massicks	Lab	949	53.1	2,240	79.8	Lab from Ind
J. Jamieson*	Ind	838	46.9			
Total votes		1,787				
1925						
W.H. Rice*	Lab	988	53.6	2,277	80.9	-
R. Crossfield	Ind	855	46.4			
Total votes		1,843				
1926						
I. Clamp	Lab	919	55.6	2,312	71.5	Lab from Ind
A. Barrie*	Ind	734	44.4			
Total votes		1,653				
1927						
J.F. Massicks*	Lab	922	57.3	2,302	69.9	-
Mrs B.A. Pennington	C	687	42.7			
Total votes		1,609				

Salthouse ward *(continued)*

Candidate	Party	Votes	%	Electors	Turnout	Gains
1928						
W.H. Rice*	Lab	1,004	56.6	2,316	76.6	-
D. Kay	Cit	770	43.4			
Total votes		1,774				
1929						
F.W. Milner*	Lab	1,417	58.0	3,910	62.5	-
E.J.E. Warden	Cit	1,027	42.0			
Total votes		2,444				
1930						
J.F. Yeomans	Lab	1,183	51.0	3,873	59.9	Lab from Cit
G.F. Symons	Cit	1,135	49.0			
Total votes		2,318				
1931						
T. Parnham	Cit	1,562	55.6	3,866	72.7	Cit from Lab
G. Waite*	Lab	1,247	44.4			
Total votes		2,809				
1932						
F.W. Milner*	Lab	1,446	50.4	3,928	73.1	-
A.W. Smith	Cit	1,343	46.8			
W.Hart	Com	81	2.8			
Total votes		2,870				
1933						
J.F. Yeomans*	Lab	1,546	54.2	4,074	70.1	-
J.M. Butler	Cit	1,309	45.8			
Total votes		2,855				
1934						
J.T. Gibbon	Lab	1,525	55.3	4,225	65.3	Lab from Cit
T. Parnham*	Cit	1,232	44.7			
Total votes		2,757				
1935						
J.H. Brown	Lab	1,550	52.7	*4,265*	69.0	-
T. Dickinson	Cit	1,393	47.3			
Total votes		2,943				

Salthouse ward *(continued)*

Candidate	Party	Votes	%	Electors	Turnout	Gains
1936						
T. Dickinson	Cit	1,457	51.2	4,306	66.0	Cit from Lab
J.F. Yeomans*	Lab	1,386	48.8			
Total votes		2,843				
1937						
J.T. Gibbon*	Lab	1,499	53.5	4,309	65.0	-
R.F. Bell	Cit	1,304	46.5			
Total votes		2,803				
1938						
J.G. Waiting	Lab	1,443	50.5	4,445	64.3	-
R.F. Bell	Cit	1,413	49.5			
Total votes		2,856				

Overall Labour vote   **52.6%**   **Overall Turnout**   **69.4%**

Walney ward
(Barrow Island ward removed from it after 1928)

Candidate	Party	Votes	%	Electors	Turnout	Gains
1919						
B. Longstaffe	Lab	2,126	56.1	6,073	62.4	-
W. Bell	Ind	1,663	43.9			
Total votes		3,789				
1920						
J. Tyson	Lab	2,809	63.0	6,206	71.8	Lab from Ind
W. Howard	Ind	1,647	37.0			
Total votes		4,456				
1921						
T. Morton*	Lab	2,632	59.1	6,408	69.6	-
A. McConnell	Ind	1,825	40.9			
Total votes		4,457				
1922						
B. Longstaff*	Lab	2,684	50.5	6,416	82.9	-
Dr R. Coffey	C	2,634	49.5			
Total votes		5,318				
1923						
J. Tyson*	Lab	2,590	60.0	6,217	69.5	-
E.R. Flory	C	1,729	40.0			
Total votes		4,319				
1924						
T. Morton*	Lab	3,012	65.7	6,132	74.8	-
F. Burke	C	1,573	34.3			
Total votes		4,585				
1925						
B. Longstaff*	Lab	3,211	58.0	6,327	87.5	-
Dr R. Coffey	C	2,323	42.0			
Total votes		5,534				
1926						
J. Tyson*	Lab	2,833	59.5	6,346	75.0	-
E. Clark	Ind	1,929	40.5			
Total votes		4,762				

Walney ward *(continued)*

Candidate	Party	Votes	%	Electors	Turnout	Gains
1927						
T. Morton*	Lab	2,865	67.2	6,399	66.6	-
D. McFarlane	C	1,397	32.8			
Total votes		4,262				
1928						
H.B. Hartley*	Lab	2,681	55.6	6,401	75.3	-
A.S. Cumming	Cit	2,138	44.4			
Total votes		4,819				
1929						
I. Clamp	Lab	1,323	58.3	3,417	66.5	-
A.S. Cumming	Cit	948	41.7			
Total votes		2,271				
1930						
J.W. Postlethwaite*	Lab	1,184	53.6	3,451	64.0	-
Mrs Lawson	Cit	1,026	46.4			
Total votes		2,210				
1931						
A.S. Cumming	Cit	1,578	58.9	3,446	77.7	Cit from Lab
T. Pinkney	Lab	1,099	41.1			
Total votes		2,677				
1932						
D. Kay	Cit	1,441	52.3	3,464	79.5	Cit from Lab
I. Clamp*	Lab	1,314	47.7			
Total votes		2,755				
1933						
B. Longstaffe	Lab	1,717	60.9	3,496	80.7	-
J. Wilson	Cit	1,104	39.1			
Total votes		2,821				
1934						
J. Brazington	Lab	1,496	59.2	3,470	72.9	Lab from Cit
J.K. Wardle	Cit	1,033	40.8			
Total votes		2,529				

Walney ward *(continued)*

Candidate	Party	Votes	%	Electors	Turnout	Gains
1935						
D. Kay*	Cit	1,505	53.4	*3,603*	78.2	-
J.T. Wardle	Lab	1,312	46.6			
Total votes		2,817				
1936						
J.T. Wardle*	Lab	1,588	59.1	3,737	71.9	-
A.W. Craig	Cit	1,099	40.9			
Total votes		2,687				
1937						
J. Brazington*	Lab	1,428	55.5	3,933	65.4	-
G. Ashworth	Cit	1,144	44.5			
Total votes		2,572				
1938						
A. Morton*	Lab	1,607	53.9	4,307	69.2	-
J. Fisher	Cit	1,372	46.1			
Total votes		2,979				
Overall Labour vote		**57.2%**		**Overall turnout**		**73.2%**

Yarlside ward
(merged into Salthouse ward after 1928)

Candidate	Party	Votes	%	Electors	Turnout	Gains
1919						
T. Pearson*	Ind	331	59.0	686	81.8	-
S. Langford	Lab	230	41.0			
Total votes		561				
1920						
T. Gardiner	Ind	348	64.0	713	76.3	-
F.J. Sharp	Lab	196	36.0			
Total votes		544				
1921						
R.J. Brennan	Ind	298	52.7	701	80.6	-
G.T. Shyvers*	Ind	267	47.3			
Total votes		565				
1922						
T. Pearson*	Ind	364	61.1	720	82.8	-
W.H. Rice	Lab	232	38.9			
Total votes		596				
1923						
T. Gardiner*	C	Unopp.	-		-	-
1924						
J. Mills	C	287	55.2	686	75.8	C from Ind
R.J. Snell	Ind	233	44.8			
Total votes		520				
1925						
E. Waddington*	C	392	68.4	693	82.7	-
J.A. Price	Lab	181	31.6			
Total votes		573				
1926						
W.A. Raby	C	221	40.4	671	81.5	-
A. McConnell	Lab	179	32.7			
Mrs K.A. McNairy	C	147	26.9			
Total votes		547				

Yarlside ward *(continued)*

Candidate	Party	Votes	%	Electors	Turnout	Gains
1927						
J. Jamieson	C	213	38.0	680	82.5	-
G. Kay	Ind	174	31.0			
L.H. Kinrade	Lab	174	31.0			
Total votes		561				
1928						
E. Waddington*	Cit	363	68.8	678	77.9	-
Mrs J.E. Ward	Lab	165	31.3			
Total votes		528				
Overall Labour vote		**27.2%**		**Overall turnout**		**80.2%**

THREE
Bath

BATH

The largest urban centre in Somerset with a population of just under 70,000 in 1921, Bath, the 'Queen of the West', is located thirteen miles south-east of the much larger city of Bristol. Formerly a Roman spa town, the fortunes of Bath had languished for over a millennium, until under the Hanoverian kings its hot springs made it once more a fashionable resort. Although as a spa resort Bath had faded by the 1920s and 1930s, becoming 'a grime-encrusted ... drab place of little charm',[1] tourism remained an important part of the local economy. This was partly reflected in the dominance of small-business interests which aided the Conservative and Liberal control of the fifty-six-seat council throughout the inter-war years.

Nineteenth-century Bath, even after the arrival of the Great Western Railway, did not become an important industrial centre. The Somerset coalfields were close to the boundaries but heavy industry and the concentration of labour barely touched the city. This was partly reflected in local politics, where working-class support for the Labour party was slight outside the two Twerton wards and Widcombe. In its industrial structure Bath remained largely what it was before the twentieth century, a city of small craft industries, with an established service sector in commerce and finance, and some local and national government employment. The new century saw the addition of a metal and light engineering sector, which developed and increased in importance before and after the First World War. Larger enterprises included an iron foundry, lockmaking and clockmaking works. Gas-fitting firms and a railway ironworks provided the staples of more substantial light engineering production. Printing and bookbinding, with a firm of national importance in Pitman's, along with a clothing manufacturer, and flour mills were also firmly established. A large cabinetmaking enterprise at the plant of the wartime aircraft factory was a typical medium-size business.

During the First World War, state intervention saw the growth of eight local factories providing munitions, parts for aircraft and submarines, and even experimental tanks. The munitions industry was unusual in that over a third of the labour force of 3,172 was female, providing a rare opportunity for women to find work outside the service sector. After the war, though, with the rundown of the defence industries, women were forced back into the home and domestic service, especially hotel and catering employment. In 1931, 5,720 women were in personal service accounting for 46.6 per cent of the female labour force.

Despite all these developments, tourism remained the most important sector of the local economy, even though Bath as a tourist resort was in decline during the inter-war years. It was only after 1945 that tourism began to grow again, and in the period considered here the depressed state of this crucial sector was the main cause of unemployment locally. Indeed Bath did not feature in the 1921 census as one of the 148 places inflated by more than 3 per cent of visitors, a key indicator of the state of tourism. Hotels and catering, retailing, and the building industry were all sectors which particularly suffered. The number of people keeping hotels,

---

[1] Davis, G. and Bonsall, P., *Bath: A New History*, (Keele, 1996), p. 145.

lodging houses and public houses in Bath fell between the 1921 and 1931 census returns. Women in this category were especially hard hit, falling by 30 per cent from 536 to 371 in the same decade. The well-being of working-class women who worked in the service sector was also badly affected. Over 300 women in the domestic service category were recorded as out of work in the 1931 census, the second-largest single group after male building workers. This was almost certainly an underestimate of the real figure, given the part-time and casual nature of much hotel and catering work. The underestimation would have been even greater after the Anomalies Act took effect in later 1931. This Act severely restricted part-time workers' entitlement to benefit. Many married women in particular must have disappeared from the statistics to become officially housewives again.[2]

Of course in relative terms inter-war economic depression was much less severe in Bath than in areas of heavy industry, but on the other hand it also missed out on the compensating growth of new industries that other parts of the South and the Midlands experienced. There was no dramatic change in the occupational structure of the city between the wars. Davis and Bonsall point to moderate decline of the primary and secondary manufacturing sectors, with some growth of the service sector and in printing and allied trades.[3] The city remained firmly a residential and tourist centre. Just as the occupational structure changed little, the population increased by a mere 146 in the decade from 1921 to 1931. Nevertheless, Bath rode out the Depression and the unemployment of the 1930s better than more industrial cities. With an unemployment rate of 15 per cent in 1932, Bath was ranked sixty-sixth amongst the eighty-three county boroughs.

While industrial occupations were relatively scarce in Bath, there was conversely a preponderance of middle-class occupations in Bath. The centrality of hotels, lodging houses and public houses was noted above. This was coupled with a large commerce and finance sector. The two indicators of social class employed in these volumes confirm these observations. In terms of domestic service, Bath was ranked seventh amongst the county boroughs, and in terms of management and self-employment it was ranked tenth. This was still a city of high social classification, as Pelling characterised it before 1914.[4] The inter-war municipal franchise could only have magnified the political effects of this, with many in the large business community having more than one vote, while the numerous indoor domestic servants would have had no vote at all.[5]

As far as the religious traditions of Bath were concerned, Anglicanism remained strong amongst the dominant middle class of the city, but this by no means held true for the whole population. There was negligible Irish migration to Bath in the nineteenth century, and no significant recusant minority, so Catholicism was of little consequence. However, there were strong traditions of

---

[2]   For further discussion of the effects of the Anomalies Act, see later in this volume, pp. 349, 417.
[3]   Davis and Bonsall, *Bath*, p. 149.
[4]   Pelling, H., *Social Geography of British Elections 1885-1910*, (Aldershot, 1994), p. 146.
[5]   On the municipal franchise, see the notes at the end of this volume, p. 671.

Nonconformity in the surrounding area, associated especially with the rural weavers of the pre-eighteenth-century woollen industry, and later the Somerset miners. This Nonconformity was reflected in the working class of Bath, and also to some extent amongst small manufacturers.

Given its socio-economic character, it is perhaps unsurprising that Bath was dominated politically by the Conservative and Liberal parties between 1919 and 1938. In parliamentary elections Bath was held by the Conservatives on every occasion except 1923, when the Liberals narrowly won the seat. In municipal elections, Conservatives and Liberals held most of the fourteen wards comfortably. The Labour Party challenge to this dominance was weak. At best Labour held only nine seats on the full council of fifty-six, whereas the Conservatives never fell below twenty-one seats, and the Liberals never below seventeen. Even Independent councillors, who on most issues were closely allied with the Liberal–Tory ruling clique, usually outnumbered Labour on the council.

However, the persistence of Liberalism in Bath politics, despite its precipitate decline nationally in the inter-war period, needs to be noted. In many boroughs in these years, Liberalism was either squeezed out as the third party in a first-past-the-post electoral system, or else Liberals and Tories became effectively merged in an anti-Labour alliance in municipal politics, to the extent that they dropped their distinctive political labels and campaigned as Independents, Citizens or some such apolitical label. In Bath, there appeared to be little to divide Liberals and Tories in terms of municipal policy. One Tory candidate, for instance, stood on a slogan of 'Halt municipal expenditure'. A Liberal, by contrast, denounced the 'wasteful methods' of the council, 'saddling posterity with more than it ought to bear', and deplored the 'enormous sums of money' spent by the Education Committee, adding that they could 'carry education in some directions a great deal too far'.[6] Parsimony over the rates was a shared objective, but nevertheless the Liberal and Conservative parties retained their separate identities, and the Liberals remained the second party in the council.

This in part reflects the fact there was a strong Liberal tradition in Bath, closely associated with Nonconformity. Before 1914 the two Bath parliamentary seats were only marginally Tory, so for instance in 1906 both were lost to the Liberals, and the surrounding constituency of Frome was if anything a Liberal stronghold. After 1918 the predominantly Liberal miners of Frome were converted to Labour to the extent that Labour won the seat in 1923 and 1929. This was replicated in the Twerton area of Bath where the 'artizans and mechanics', who had ensured that the Liberals were 'always sure of a majority' there before 1914, made it Labour territory in municipal elections in the inter-war years. In other parts of Bath, while 'aristocratic' wards like Bathwick and Lansdown were strongly Tory, more socially-mixed wards like Oldfield, St James's and Walcot North and South remained Liberal strongholds, with the main opposition coming

---

[6] *Bath Chronicle and Herald*, 24 Oct. 1931, 5 Nov. 1938.

from Labour. Organised Liberalism did remain unusually strong in Bath's municipal politics.[7]

This was also in part, though, a political sleight of hand. Notwithstanding the survival of Liberalism, the Conservative Party was the strongest political party in Bath. The most remarkable Conservative ward of all was Lansdown. Here Conservatives were returned unopposed for the whole period. With its southern boundary the Roman *Via Julia*, and the imposing Royal Crescent at the city end, and including the golf course, Sion Hill and Summerhill Park, this affluent suburb of large residential housing was the bastion of the Conservatives. Not far behind came Bathwick, St Michael's and Weston wards which were usually retained by the Tories without a contest. With this bedrock of solid support, and strength in other wards as well, the Conservative hold over the council was never in doubt. Given their overall strength, and their minor differences over policy with the Liberals, the Conservatives could afford to ignore some wards altogether and leave them to be fought over by others. Liberal and Tory candidates never opposed each other in municipal elections, and Liberal survival was allowed by the grace-and-favour of Conservatism. This was illustrated starkly in 1938 in the only election between the wars where a Conservative opposed a Liberal. In Walcot North, where there had previously been no Tory intervention, a Conservative gain was recorded at the expense of the Liberals in a three-way contest with Labour.

Turning to the only significant challenge to the two main parties in Bath, it is obvious that Labour was battling against overwhelming odds. Its support was concentrated in a handful of wards, as outlined below, and its weakness on the council was compounded by the use of the aldermanic system, which was controlled by the two main parties. Labour had no aldermen before 1926, and then only a token one until the Second World War. Two or three would have been proportionate to its strength amongst the councillors. There were Labour protests about this, and in 1936 the leader of the Labour Group, Sam Day, declared a 'revolt' against this situation, but to no avail.[8] This was only of marginal significance though in the light of the real weakness of organised labour in the city. This was illustrated in the General Strike of 1926. Nineteen unions combined in Bath to form a Council of Action to organise the strike. The pacific nature of events in Bath was shown by the fact that the Council of Action was afterwards 'complimented and thanked by Mayor and Chief Constable for maintaining perfect order', and on its advice special constables were disbanded after the first day of the strike as 'superfluosities'. A strike bulletin was produced by the Council of Action, but it was reported that only fifty copies were duplicated daily, telling evidence of the extent of labour organisation in Bath.[9]

[7] Pelling, *Social Geography*, pp. 141–157; Craig, F.W.S., *British Parliamentary Election Results 1885–1918,* (2nd edn, Aldershot, 1989), pp. 66, 379; Craig, *British Parliamentary Election Results 1918–1949*, (Glasgow, 1969), pp. 74, 455.

[8] *Bath Chronicle and Herald,* 23 Oct. 1926, 7 Nov. 1936.

[9] Burns, E., *The General Strike May 1926: Trades Councils in Action,* (London, 1975), p. 102.

Labour strength was confined to three main wards, Twerton East and West as noted above, and Widcombe, with some support also in Kingsmead and St James's. The relatively high person per room figures for all these wards indicate the lower social class of these areas of the city. Twerton's working-class Liberalism has already been noted, and it was also the area where the Co-operative movement was established in the city in 1888. Situated to the west of the city, adjoining the River Avon and the Midland and Great Western railway lines, Twerton was where most of the railway workers resided, an occupational group that was reported to be especially supportive of Labour.[10] In addition the council built somewhere in the region of 1,500 new homes between the wars,[11] and the location of these housing projects certainly influenced the Twerton wards. The Southdown housing estate was located on the south-western outskirts of the city within these wards, and the relocation of so many working-class and white-collar residents here certainly helped consolidate Labour's strength.

Widcombe ward, Labour's other main area of support, had dense housing to the east of the central districts. Widcombe was adjacent to the Dolemeads, an Edwardian housing project, where slum renovation and council-house building occurred. Labour also had some support in Kingsmead ward, which contained dense inner-city housing to the north-west of the city, with the main railway station located within its boundaries. It also had workers' flats erected between the wars. Labour's only other foothold was in St James's ward, which was situated in the centre of the city, with some of the oldest and poorest housing. That it was not more strongly Labour was due to the fact that it also contained many of the business voters with retail and commercial premises in the city centre.

Council-housing developments did not guarantee Labour support, of course. The largest housing project was on the southern edge of Bath at Odd Down, where the Fosseway Estate in Lyncombe ward was developed in 1930–31. But Lyncombe was a huge suburban and semi-rural ward with older established settlements of private housing at Lyncombe, Perrymead and Prior Park. In any case, not long after the Fosseway Estate had been started, the National Government in 1933 abolished all central support subsidies with the exception of slum clearance, and Bath's council building experiment was halted. Lyncombe remained a Tory–Independent stronghold. Another new council development at Rudmore Park to the north of the Bristol and Gloucester railway lines was too small to influence the solidly Conservative ward of Weston. To the north-east of the city the Larkhall estate was surrounded by private housing estates in Walcott North ward, which remained Liberal. Finally, the first post-war council estate, built in 1920 at Englishcombe Park south of the inner city, did not produce more than one Labour councillor in the Oldfield ward. Oldfield was again mainly Liberal territory.

[10] *Bath Chronicle and Herald*, 8 Nov. 1919.
[11] Haddon, J., *Bath*, (1973), p. 191, states 2,000 were built; Davis and Bonsall, *Bath*, p. 143, suggest 1,000; the figure of 1,298 given in Appendix 16 of this volume, p. 686, which is for most but not all of the period, suggests a figure somewhere in between.

Surveying the municipal election results in Bath over the period between the wars, variations in political support can be identified. It should be noted though that because of the large number of uncontested seats in most years, the annual percentage figures for Labour support must be treated with some caution. The figures for seats won and net gains are sometimes more reliable indicators of party success in Bath. On that basis, the best years for Labour were 1919, 1926, 1929 and 1932. 1919 was an important year of triumph for Labour in the national context with a breakthrough of many seats gained and well over 2 million votes won. With a new constitution and better organisational structure, the party did well locally in Bath gaining four seats. It was undoubtedly the Bath Labour Party's best year in between the wars, with the *Bath Chronicle* suggesting that Twerton East being 'the most progressive ward ... had shown the way Labour should go'.[12] Walcot South, Westmoreland and Widcombe were the other wards won by Labour. Widcombe and Walcott South were to become Labour strongholds. Westmoreland however, was secured only once more by Labour in 1937.

The cosy apolitical pre-war domination of Bath by the established parties was shattered. Results in the other boroughs in this volume show a picture of low turnout in 1919 across the country coinciding with widespread Labour gains. This might suggest a pattern of middle-class abstention accounting for Labour's success. In Bath, though, Labour secured an overall 40 per cent of the poll on a medium to high turnout of 55 per cent. In the wards where Labour secured victory (Twerton East, Walcot South, Westmorland and Widcombe), there were higher than normal turnouts. Additionally, comparing 1919 to the following year's figures, in most of the wards which were traditionally Liberal or Conservative strongholds there seemed to be little difference in turnout, weakening the argument that the property-owning classes stayed away from the polls in 1919. So in Lyncombe for instance, dominated by Independents and Conservatives, turnout fell by two percentage points to 53.7 per cent in 1920. In Oldfield, dominated by fifteen Liberals in the period, turnout did rise in 1920, but only marginally. Turnout rose substantially in 1920 in only two wards, Walcott North and South, coinciding with a decline in Labour support in both cases. This is the only evidence to support a thesis of middle-class abstention being the reason for Labour's triumph in Bath in 1919, making its success in that year all the more remarkable.

Perhaps what can be said of 1919 and 1920 was that Labour's new independence of Liberalism paid off in Bath. Also in 1919 the anti-Labour forces were fragmented in two wards by a new organisation, the Ratepayers' Guild, putting up two candidates in St James's and Widcombe. In the latter, W.H. Devenish whom the press labelled an Independent, split the middle-class vote and led to a Liberal loss. Altogether 1920 was a mixed year for Labour with at least a consolidation in Twerton West and Widcombe. But also there was some rallying of the propertied classes with two Labour defeats being described as 'heavy' by the *Chronicle*.

---

[12]   *Bath Chronicle*, 8 Nov. 1919.

The first half of the twenties was not so successful for Labour. The party contested only eight seats in 1921, with the *Chronicle* crowing that the Labour 'attacks fail', and Labour's strength on the council remained at nine. There were only four contests in 1922, although Labour held Twerton East. The next year the depths of municipal apathy were plumbed with all wards uncontested. With the 'Red Scare' of the Zinoviev letter fresh in voters' minds, and within weeks of its disastrous general election of 1924, Labour suffered locally in the November elections of that year. This was, on the surface, Labour's worst year in Bath in the inter-war period. No Labour victories were secured, though there were only two contests in Lyncombe and Oldfield. These contests were won by the Conservative and Liberal parties respectively.

The best years for Labour thereafter were 1929, the year of its national success, and 1932, with a good recovery after Ramsay MacDonald's 'betrayal' and the formation of the National Government. In both these peak years Labour secured the election of five councillors. In 1929 four of the five were in uncontested elections in Kingsmead, the Twertons and Widcombe while St James's was held by A.E. Cook by 157 votes in a straight fight with an Independent. Again the same five wards were held in 1932, when Labour secured a clean sweep of walkovers. Here though it is worth noting that Labour were defending the highpoint of 1929. In neither year, however, did Labour make gains against the other parties.

Some analysis is required of the crucial years 1930 and 1931, with the onset of the Depression and the formation of the National Government. These were disastrous years for Labour nationally. In Bath the overall Labour percentage of the poll fell to 29 and then 11 per cent in these two years. Yet Labour incurred no loss of seats in these two years. There were only two contests in 1930, and Labour held Twerton West which was uncontested. Again in 1931 there were only two contests, with Labour securing walkovers in Twerton East and Widcombe. Both years though were bonanza years for the Conservatives and Liberals, these parties securing eight and ten seats respectively, mostly uncontested. One inference to be drawn from so few contests is that Labour did not feel it profitable to put up candidates in traditional areas of Conservative and Liberal strength. In practice this amounted to most wards in Bath. As in many other boroughs as well, the national calls for economy resulted in parties deciding on unofficial electoral agreements, so Labour was spared the worst effects of the decline in its support. Nevertheless, even in wards where the party had previously secured famous victories, Labour was on the retreat in 1930 and 1931. Thus Twerton West was left uncontested by Labour in 1931 and Widcombe was held by W.H. Long for the Liberals with 74.5 per cent of the vote. In the latter ward, Mrs H. Cordiner secured the lowest Labour percentage of the poll (25.5 per cent) for the twenty inter-war years.

Overall, Labour did relatively well in 1932 with five seats secured unopposed. This was, though, a year of complete electoral stasis, when an all-party agreement over seats to avoid any contests was secured, again in a spirit of national economy. Labour, it must be said, seems to have done remarkably well out of this agreement, reflecting perhaps an unusual degree of generosity, or alternatively lack of political astuteness, by their opponents. However, the years 1933 and 1934 were not particularly successful, with most seats now being conceded by Labour, perhaps a quid pro quo for the walkovers it had received earlier. Nationally Labour was expected to do well in the 1935 general election, only to disappoint its followers. By securing one contested victory together with three uncontested wards, it could be suggested that Labour in Bath lived up to an optimism that was to prove false in high politics. In the late 1930s there was little change, and very few contests again in the last two years before the war. In one contest in 1938, Labour's A.C. Butler came last in a rare three-cornered fight in South Walcot, suggesting Labour's support remained weak. Here there was a Conservative gain in a previously Liberal ward, as noted earlier, perhaps a sign of future change. Labour ended the period with eight seats on the council, a position which had hardly altered over the twenty inter-war years.

Finally, it is hard to draw hard-and-fast conclusions from inter-war Bath's municipal politics. First, such was the industrial and occupational structure with its public and service sectors that Bath remained a stronghold of middle-class and petit bourgeois interests. Tourism with its small hotels and lodging houses and small independent businesses, together with the residential nature of Bath, reinforced Conservative, Liberal and Independent strength in the city. With no heavy industry and with artisanal craft production still important, Labour found it difficult to make political inroads. This was reinforced by the lack of an introduction of 'white goods' industries in the 1930s and thus the lack of development of a modern skilled industrial working-class constituency. Second, Liberalism remained untypically active in Bath. The city did not reflect the national pattern of Liberal decline. Third, Labour did indeed establish itself in Bath in the period and had a presence on the council. Interestingly, apart from 1936, Labour remained marginally stronger by at least one council seat than they had in the twenties apart from the peak years in both 1920 and 1921. Then Labour had nine seats on both occasions. Lastly, Bath was unusual when compared with other medium to small southern county boroughs. In place of the non-party anti-Labour alliance of propertied interests, clear party labels were used in the city's politics. No doubt an anti-Labour alliance still operated. This was not however under the usual non-political guise, serving as a cover for established ratepaying and business interests. Such interests usually attempted to run the city's affairs with due economy and restricted welfare expenditure. Perhaps the minimum service Labour performed in Bath was to prevent this fiction.

A guide to further reading

Newspapers

Bath Chronicle and Herald
Western Daily Press

Secondary sources

Davis G. and Bonsall, P., *Bath: A New History*, (Keele, 1996).
Haddon, J., *Bath*, (1973).
Pelling, H., *Social Geography of British Elections 1885–1910*, (Aldershot, 1994), pp. 141–157.

Bath wards 1919–1938

Persons aged fourteen and over classified by industry 1931

	Male	%	Female	%	Total	%
Metal and engineering	2,140	10.6	144	1.2	2,284	7.0
- Engineering	*1,208*	*6.0*	*71*	*0.6*	*1,279*	*3.9*
Clothing	587	2.9	1,163	9.5	1,750	5.4
Building	2,524	12.5	34	0.3	2,558	7.9
Transport	1,764	8.8	53	0.4	1,817	5.6
- Rail	*712*	*3.5*	*18*	*0.1*	*730*	*2.3*
- Road	*961*	*4.8*	*31*	*0.3*	*992*	*3.1*
Commerce and finance	4,268	21.2	2,097	17.1	6,365	19.6
Public admin. and defence	1,816	9.0	534	4.3	2,350	7.3
- Local government	*1,314*	*6.5*	*440*	*3.6*	*1,754*	*5.4*
Professions	884	4.4	1,236	10.1	2,120	6.5
Personal service	1,650	8.2	5,720	46.6	7,370	22.7
Others	4,492	22.3	1,299	10.6	5,791	17.9
Total (a)	**20,125**		**12,280**		**32,405**	
Total population (b)	29,162		39,653		68,815	
(a) as % of (b)	69.0		31.0		47.1	
Total out of work (c)	2,076		545		2,621	
(c) as % of (a)	10.3		4.4		8.1	
Managerial and own account	3,532	19.6	1,464	12.5	4,996	16.8
Operative	14,517	80.4	10,271	87.5	24,788	83.2
Total (excluding out of work)	18,049		11,735		29,784	

Population statistics 1931

Ward	Acres	Population	Persons/acre	Persons/room
Bathwick	596	4,595	7.7	0.55
Kingsmead	176	4,912	27.9	0.79
Lansdown	376	5,361	14.3	0.55
Lyncombe	1,440	6,092	4.2	0.60
Oldfield	301	5,680	18.9	0.64
St James's	80	4,860	60.8	0.95
St Michael's	238	4,244	17.8	0.64
Twerton East	132	4,621	35.0	0.71
Twerton West	713	5,187	7.3	0.87
Walcot North	248	4,406	17.8	0.73
Walcot South	126	4,887	38.8	0.69
Westmoreland	171	4,391	25.7	0.79
Weston	460	5,133	11.2	0.59
Widcombe	95	4,446	46.8	0.84
Total	**5,152**	**68,815**	**13.4**	**0.69**

Overall position on the council 1919–38

	Position				Gains				Losses			
	C	Lab	L	Ind	C	Lab	L	Ind	C	Lab	L	Ind
1919	23	7	20	6	0	4	0	2	2	0	4	0
1920	22	9	18	7	0	2	0	2	1	0	2	1
1921	22	9	18	7	0	0	0	0	0	0	0	0
1922	21	7	18	10	0	0	0	2	1	1	0	0
1923	21	7	18	10	0	0	0	0	0	0	0	0
1924	21	6	19	10	0	0	1	0	0	1	0	0
1925	21	6	19	10	0	0	0	0	0	0	0	0
1926	21	7	18	10	0	0	0	0	0	0	0	0
1927	21	8	18	9	0	1	0	0	0	0	0	1
1928	21	8	18	9	0	0	0	0	0	0	0	0
1929	21	8	17	10	0	0	0	1	0	0	1	0
1930	21	8	17	10	0	0	0	0	0	0	0	0
1931	21	8	17	10	0	0	0	0	0	0	0	0
1932	21	8	17	10	0	0	0	0	0	0	0	0
1933	21	9	17	9	0	1	0	0	0	0	0	1
1934	22	8	18	8	1	0	1	0	0	1	0	1
1935	22	8	18	8	0	0	0	1	0	1	0	0
1936	23	7	18	8	1	0	0	1	0	1	0	1
1937	23	8	18	7	0	1	0	0	0	0	0	1
1938	23	8	17	8	1	0	0	1	1	0	1	0

Aldermen 1919–38

1919 C–7, L–6, Ind–1	1929 C–7, L–5, Lab–1, Ind–1
1920 C–7, L–6, Ind–1	1930 C–7, L–5, Lab–1, Ind–1
1921 C–7, L–6, Ind–1	1931 C–7, L–5, Lab–1, Ind–1
1922 C–7, L–6, Ind–1	1932 C–7, L–5, Lab–1, Ind–1
1923 C–7, L–6, Ind–1	1933 C–7, L–5, Lab–1, Ind–1
1924 C–7, L–6, Ind–1	1934 C–7, L–5, Lab–1, Ind–1
1925 C–7, L–6, Ind–1	1935 C–7, L–5, Lab–1, Ind–1
1926 C–7, L–5, Lab–1, Ind–1	1936 C–7, L–5, Lab–1, Ind–1
1927 C–7, L–5, Lab–1, Ind–1	1937 C–7, L–5, Lab–1, Ind–1
1928 C–7, L–5, Lab–1, Ind–1	1938 C–7, L–5, Lab–1, Ind–1

Municipal elections: winning party 1919–28

Ward	1919	1920	1921	1922	1923	1924	1925	1926	1927	1928
Bathwick	C	C	Ind	C	C	Ind	C	C	Ind	C
Kingsmead	Ind	Lab	C	Ind	Lab	C	Ind	Lab	C	Ind
Lansdown	C	C	C	C	C	C	C	C	C	C
Lyncombe	C	Ind	C	Ind	Ind	C	Ind	Ind	C	Ind
Oldfield	L	L	Lab	L	L	L	L	L	Ind	L
St James's	L	Lab	L	L	Lab	L	L	Lab	L	L
St Michael's	C	C	Ind	C	C	Ind	C	C	Ind	C
Twerton East	Lab	L	Ind	Lab	L	Ind	Lab	L	Ind	Lab
Twerton West	Ind	Lab	Ind	Ind	Lab	Ind	L	Lab	Lab	L
Walcot North	L	L	L	L	L	L	L	L	L	L
Walcot South	Lab	L	L	Ind	L	L	Ind	L	L	L
Westmoreland	Lab	Ind C	C	Ind	C	C	L	C	C	L
Weston	C	C	C	C	C	C	Ind	C	C	Ind
Widcombe	Lab	Lab	L	Lab	Lab	L	Lab	Lab	L	Lab

Municipal elections: party wins per year 1919–28

	1919	1920	1921	1922	1923	1924	1925	1926	1927	1928
C	5	4	5	4	5	5	3	5	5	3
Lab	4	4	1	2	4	0	2	4	1	2
L	3	4	4	3	4	5	5	4	4	6
Ind	2	2	4	5	1	4	4	1	4	3
Total	14	14	14	14	14	14	14	14	14	14
Turnout %	55.3	61.7	64.1	54.7	-	49.5	55.8	54.7	54.1	53.4
Labour %	40.4	27.4	32.4	32.2	-	40.8	51.6	49.4	42.5	16.1

Municipal elections: winning party 1929–38

Ward	1929	1930	1931	1932	1933	1934	1935	1936	1937	1938
Bathwick	C	Ind	C	C	Ind	C	C	C	C	C
Kingsmead	Lab	C	Ind	Lab	C	Ind	Lab	C	Ind	Lab
Lansdown	C	C	C	C	C	C	C	C	C	C
Lyncombe	Ind	C	Ind	Ind	C	Ind	Ind	C	Ind	Ind
Oldfield	L	Ind	L	L	Ind	L	L	Ind	L	L
St James's	Lab	L	L	Lab	L	L	Lab	L	L	Lab
St Michael's	C	Ind	C	C	C	C	C	C	C	C
Twerton East	Lab	Ind	Lab	Lab	Ind	Lab	Lab	Ind	Lab	Lab
Twerton West	Lab	Lab	L	Lab	Lab	L	Lab	Lab	L	Ind
Walcot North	Ind	L	L	Ind	L	L	Ind	L	L	Ind
Walcot South	L	L	L	L	L	L	L	L	L	C
Westmoreland	C	C	L	C	C	L	Ind	Ind	Lab	Ind
Weston	C	C	Ind	C	C	C	C	C	C	Ind
Widcombe	Lab	L	Lab	Lab	L	Lab	Ind	L	Lab	Ind

Municipal elections: party wins per year 1929–38

	1929	1930	1931	1932	1933	1934	1935	1936	1937	1938
C	5	5	3	5	6	4	4	6	4	4
Lab	5	1	2	5	1	2	4	1	3	3
L	2	4	6	2	4	6	2	4	5	1
Ind	2	4	3	2	3	2	4	3	2	6
Total	14	14	14	14	14	14	14	14	14	14
Turnout %	44.8	47.5	54.5	-	58.3	51.6	47.4	45.0	46.5	54.4
Labour %	31.2	29.2	10.7	-	22.9	20.3	36.8	18.7	25.8	8.1

Municipal elections: party wins per ward 1919–38

	C	Lab	L	Ind	Total	Turnout %	Labour % of all votes
Bathwick	15	0	0	5	20	57.9	-
Kingsmead	6	7	0	7	20	52.1	28.5
Lansdown	20	0	0	0	20	-	-
Lyncombe	7	0	0	13	20	45.5	13.2
Oldfield	0	1	15	4	20	56.0	34.5
St James's	0	7	13	0	20	42.7	31.1
St Michael's	16	0	0	4	20	53.7	17.8
Twerton East	0	11	3	6	20	53.3	50.0
Twerton West	0	10	5	5	20	55.1	46.3
Walcot North	0	0	16	4	20	59.4	34.1
Walcot South	1	1	16	2	20	52.5	30.7
Westmoreland	9	2	4	5	20	50.4	29.5
Weston	16	0	0	4	20	60.0	11.4
Widcombe	0	12	6	2	20	59.5	47.5
Total	**65**	**37**	**68**	**50**	**220**	**53.2**	**31.5**

Seats won by Labour as a percentage of all wins 1919–38 **16.8**

Parliamentary election results

Bath constituency
(all wards within the borough [1918 boundaries] were included in the constituency)

General election	Winner	Conservative %	Labour %	Liberal %
14 Dec. 1918	Co C	74.8	25.2	-
15 Nov. 1922	C	50.2	17.8	32.0
6 Dec. 1923	L	48.4	-	51.6
29 Oct. 1924	C	55.8	13.6	30.6
30 May 1929	C	46.9	23.0	30.1
27 Oct. 1931	C	64.0	14.7	21.3
14 Nov. 1935	C	56.6	19.7	23.7

Bathwick ward

Candidate	Party	Votes	%	Electors	Turnout	Gains
1919						
W.A. Shepherd	C	Unopp.	-	1,423	-	-
1920						
A.B. Paget*	C	600	58.8	1,534	66.5	-
H. Chivers	Ind	420	41.2			
Total votes		1,020				
1921						
Mrs Latter-Parsons	Ind	643	61.2	1,597	65.7	-
H. Chivers	Ind	407	38.8			
Total votes		1,050				
1922						
W.A. Sheppard*	C	Unopp.	-	1,710	-	-
1923						
A.B. Paget*	C	Unopp.	-	1,780	-	-
1924						
Mrs Latter-Parsons*	Ind	Unopp.	-	1,821	-	-
1925						
W.A. Sheppard*	C	Unopp.	-	1,887	-	-
1926						
E. Knox*	C	Unopp.	-		-	-
1927						
Mrs Latter-Parsons*	Ind	Unopp.	-	1,993	-	-
1928						
L.K. Bunting	C	Unopp.	-		-	-
1929						
E. Knox*	C	Unopp.	-		-	-
1930						
G. Lipscomb	Ind	Unopp.	-	2,133	-	-
1931						
L.K. Bunting*	C	Unopp.	-		-	-

Bathwick ward *(continued)*

Candidate	Party	Votes	%	Electors	Turnout	Gains
1932						
E. Knox*	C	Unopp.	-		-	-
1933						
G. Lipscomb*	Ind	Unopp.	-	2,217	-	-
1934						
L.K. Bunting*	C	Unopp.	-	2,279	-	-
1935						
J. Plowman*	C	Unopp.	-	2,360	-	-
1936						
G.D. Lock	C	1,048	95.1	2,352	46.9	C from Ind
W.E. Eades	Nuwm	54	4.9			
Total votes		1,102				
1937						
L.K. Bunting*	C	Unopp.	-	2,391	-	-
1938						
J. Plowman*	C	Unopp.	-	2,436	-	-
Overall Labour vote		-		**Overall turnout**		**57.9%**

Kingsmead ward

Candidate	Party	Votes	%	Electors	Turnout	Gains
1919						
J. Evans	Ind	411	41.4	1,921	51.6	Ind from C
F.W. Lee	C	360	36.3			
Mrs H. Cordiner	Lab	221	22.3			
Total votes		992				
1920						
Miss H.A. Hope*	Lab	Unopp.	-	2,047	-	-
1921						
E. White	C	781	56.7	2,148	64.1	-
E.J. Tiley	Lab	596	43.3			
Total votes		1,377				
1922						
J. Evans*	Ind	Unopp.	-	2,201	-	-
1923						
E.J. Tiley*	Lab	Unopp.	-	2,261	-	-
1924						
E. White*	C	Unopp.	-	2,317	-	-
1925						
J. Evans*	Ind	Unopp.	-	2,363	-	-
1926						
E.J. Tiley*	Lab	1,158	78.9	*2,387*	61.5	-
W.H. Devenish	C	309	21.1			
Total votes		1,467				
1927						
E. White*	C	Unopp.	-	2,410	-	-
1928						
J. Evans*	Ind	1,091	83.9	*2,433*	53.4	-
R.E. Hill	Lab	209	16.1			
Total votes		1,300				
1929						
E.J. Tiley*	Lab	Unopp.	-		-	-

Kingsmead ward *(continued)*

Candidate	Party	Votes	%	Electors	Turnout	Gains
1930						
E. White*	C	Unopp.	-	2,480	-	-
1931						
C. Sealy	Ind	912	75.5	*2,541*	47.5	-
W.E. Evans	Lab	296	24.5			
Total votes		1,208				
1932						
E.J. Tiley*	Lab	Unopp.	-		-	-
1933						
E. White*	C	Unopp.	-	2,662	-	-
1934						
C. Sealy*	Ind	817	64.9	2,669	47.1	-
T. Grenfell	Nuwm	441	35.1			
Total votes		1,258				
1935						
E.J. Tiley*	Lab	Unopp.	-	2,647	-	-
1936						
E. White*	C	804	72.6	2,610	42.4	-
T. Grenfell	Nuwm	303	27.4			
Total votes		1,107				
1937						
C. Sealy*	Ind	Unopp.	-	2,580	-	-
1938						
E.J. Tiley*	Lab	Unopp.	-	2,571	-	-

| **Overall Labour vote** | | **28.5%** | | **Overall turnout** | | **52.1%** |

Lansdown ward

Candidate	Party	Votes	%	Electors	Turnout	Gains
1919 J.M.T. Reilly*	C	Unopp.	-	1,720	-	-
1920 T.B. Timmins*	C	Unopp.	-	1,884	-	-
1921 W. Jackman*	C	Unopp.	-	2,025	-	-
1922 J. Van Sommer*	C	Unopp.	-	2,117	-	-
1923 T.B. Timmins*	C	Unopp.	-	2,166	-	-
1924 W. Jackman*	C	Unopp.	-	2,201	-	-
1925 H.S. Davey	C	Unopp.	-	2,247	-	-
1926 T.B. Timmins*	C	Unopp.	-		-	-
1927 A. Bateman*	C	Unopp.	-	2,325	-	-
1928 H.S. Davey*	C	Unopp.	-		-	-
1929 S.H. Rawlings*	C	Unopp.	-		-	-
1930 A. Bateman*	C	Unopp.	-	2,465	-	-
1931 H.S. Davey*	C	Unopp.	-		-	-
1932 S.H. Rawlings*	C	Unopp.	-		-	-

Lansdown ward *(continued)*

Candidate	Party	Votes	%	Electors	Turnout	Gains
1933						
A. Bateman*	C	Unopp.	-	2,505	-	-
1934						
H.S. Davey*	C	Unopp.	-	2,527	-	-
1935						
S.H. Rawlings*	C	Unopp.	-	2,526	-	-
1936						
Mrs H.F.S. Corbett	C	Unopp.	-	2,511	-	-
1937						
B.A.H. Woodd*	C	Unopp.	-	2,569	-	-
1938						
S.H. Rawlings*	C	Unopp.	-	2,627	-	-

Overall Labour vote - **Overall turnout** -

Lyncombe ward

Candidate	Party	Votes	%	Electors	Turnout	Gains
1919						
J.W. Rose*	C	510	55.0	2,213	41.9	-
E.L. Knott	Lab	417	45.0			
Total votes		927				
1920						
S.D. Kennard	Ind	493	53.6	2,261	40.6	Ind from C
F. Mullett*	C	426	46.4			
Total votes		919				
1921						
A.G.F. Spurr*	C	Unopp.	-	2,333	-	-
1922						
F.B. Knight	Ind	640	54.6	2,336	50.2	Ind from C
J.W. Rose*	C	533	45.4			
Total votes		1,173				
1923						
S.D. Kennard*	Ind	Unopp.	-	2,352	-	-
1924						
F.E. Rogers	C	624	71.4	2,378	36.8	-
T. Chamberlain	Lab	250	28.6			
Total votes		874				
1925						
F.B. Knight	Ind	Unopp.	-	2,400	-	-
1926						
S.D. Kennard*	Ind	503	41.4	*2,455*	49.5	-
W.H .Crossman	Ind	503	41.4			
A.F. Marshman	Ind	209	17.2			
Total votes		1,215				

(decided by casting vote of returning officer)

Candidate	Party	Votes	%	Electors	Turnout	Gains
1927						
E. Brake	C	Unopp.	-	2,510	-	-
1928						
Mrs B.L. Devenish	Ind	Unopp.	-		-	-

Lyncombe ward *(continued)*

Candidate	Party	Votes	%	Electors	Turnout	Gains
1929						
S.D. Kennard*	Ind	536	45.9	*2,759*	42.3	-
F.G. Hamilton	C	414	35.4			
Mrs A.J. Cole	Lab	218	18.7			
Total votes		1,168				
1930						
E. Brake*	C	Unopp.	-	2,883	-	-
1931						
Mrs B.L. Devenish*	Ind	Unopp.	-		-	-
1932						
S.D. Kennard*	Ind	Unopp.	-		-	-
1933						
L.G. Adams	C	Unopp.	-	3,766	-	-
1934						
Mrs B.L. Devenish*	Ind	Unopp.	-	3,843	-	-
1935						
F.J. Stayner	Ind	1,146	58.7	3,925	49.8	-
J.W. Andrews	Lab	473	24.2			
E.T. Billett	Ind	334	17.1			
Total votes		1,953				
1936						
L.G. Adams*	C	Unopp.	-	4,133	-	-
1937						
Mrs B.L. Devenish*	Ind	1,416	68.6	4,290	48.1	-
E.L. Knott	Ind	648	31.4			
Total votes		2,064				
1938						
F.J .Stayner*	Ind	Unopp.	-	4,513	-	-

Overall Labour vote		**13.2%**		**Overall turnout**		**45.5%**

Oldfield ward

Candidate	Party	Votes	%	Electors	Turnout	Gains
1919						
C.H. Hacker*	L	722	53.9	2,183	61.4	-
A.E. Cook	Lab	618	46.1			
Total votes		1,340				
1920						
T.T. Stone*	L	793	55.5	2,281	62.6	-
E.H. Cox	Lab	636				
		1,429				
1921						
A.E. Cook	Lab	700	50.4	2,287	60.7	-
W.H. Devenish	C	688	49.6			
Total votes		1,388				
1922						
C.H. Hacker*	L	906	61.4	2,644	55.8	-
E.H. Cox	Lab	570	38.6			
Total votes		1,476				
1923						
T.T. Stone*	L	Unopp.	-	2,678	-	-
1924						
A.H. Stickler	L	723	50.9	2,787	51.0	L from Lab
A.E. Cook*	Lab	698	49.1			
Total votes		1,421				
1925						
C.H. Hacker*	L	Unopp.	-	2,881	-	-
1926						
T.T. Stone*	L	Unopp.	-		-	-
1927						
W.H. Crossman	Ind	1,143	67.8	3,085	54.6	-
R.W. Cornish	Lab	542	32.2			
Total votes		1,685				
1928						
C.H. Hacker*	L	Unopp.	-		-	-

Oldfield ward *(continued)*

Candidate	Party	Votes	%	Electors	Turnout	Gains
1929						
G.J. Long*	L	885	72.3	*3,013*	40.6	-
Mrs H. Cordiner	Lab	339	27.7			
Total votes		1,224				
1930						
W.H. Crossman*	Ind	Unopp.	-	2,977	-	-
1931						
R.G. Cook*	L	Unopp.	-		-	-
1932						
G.J. Long*	L	Unopp.	-		-	-
1933						
A.H. Dawkins*	Ind	1,007	52.5	2,940	65.2	-
F.J. Stayner	Anti-Soc	889	46.4			
S.H. Baker	Ind	22	1.1			
Total votes		1,918				
1934						
R.G. Cook*	L	Unopp.	-	2,982	-	-
1935						
G.J. Long*	L	Unopp.	-	3,003	-	-
1936						
A.H. Dawkins*	Ind	Unopp.	-	3,018	-	-
1937						
E. Taylor*	L	Unopp.	-	3,071	-	-
1938						
G.J. Long*	L	Unopp.	-	3,121	-	-
Overall Labour vote		**34.5%**		**Overall turnout**		**56.0%**

St James's ward

Candidate	Party	Votes	%	Electors	Turnout	Gains
1919						
H.C. Smith	L	655	72.5	1,874	48.2	-
S.D. Kennard	Ind	249	27.5			
Total votes		904				
1920						
C. Cowley*	Lab	Unopp.	-	1,975	-	-
1921						
A. Beasley*	L	Unopp.	-	2,035	-	-
1922						
H.C. Smith*	L	Unopp.	-	2,049	-	-
1923						
C. Cowley*	Lab	Unopp.	-	2,100	-	-
1924						
W. Bray	L	Unopp.	-	2,144	-	-
1925						
H.C. Smith*	L	Unopp.	-	2,176	-	-
1926						
A.E. Cook*	Lab	568	58.0	2,183	44.8	-
E.J. Cocks	Ind	411	42.0			
Total votes		979				
1927						
J.W. Bray*	L	Unopp.	-	2,189	-	-
1928						
H.C. Smith*	L	Unopp.	-		-	-
1929						
A.E. Cook*	Lab	547	58.4	2,140	43.8	-
E.J. Cocks	Ind	390	41.6			
Total votes		937				
1930						
J.W. Bray*	L	Unopp.	-	2,116	-	-

St James's ward *(continued)*

Candidate	Party	Votes	%	Electors	Turnout	Gains
1931						
H.C. Smith*	L	Unopp.	-		-	-
1932						
A.E. Cook*	Lab	Unopp.	-		-	-
1933						
J.W. Bray*	L	Unopp.	-	1,719	-	-
1934						
H.C. Smith*	L	640	78.9	1,667	48.7	-
D. Thompson	Nuwm	171	21.1			
Total votes		811				
1935						
A.E. Cook*	Lab	353	59.3	1,629	36.5	-
W.D. Hughes	Ind	242	40.7			
Total votes		595				
1936						
J.W. Bray*	L	409	84.0	1,552	31.4	-
R. Adams	Nuwm	78	16.0			
Total votes		487				
1937						
C.W. Adams*	L	Unopp.	-	1,534	-	-
1938						
A.E. Cook*	Lab	Unopp.	-	1,494	-	-

Overall Labour vote		**31.1%**		**Overall turnout**		**42.7%**

St Michael's ward

Candidate	Party	Votes	%	Electors	Turnout	Gains
1919						
L.J.E. Bradshaw*	C	Unopp.	-	1,695	-	-
1920						
A.J. Sims*	C	Unopp.	-	1,861	-	-
1921						
T.S. Cotterell	Ind	743	65.9	1,911	59.0	-
H. Morris	Lab	385	34.1			
Total votes		1,128				
1922						
L.J.E. Bradshaw*	C	Unopp.	-	1,980	-	-
1923						
A.J. Sims*	C	Unopp.	-	2,010	-	-
1924						
T.S. Cotterell*	Ind	Unopp.	-	2,042	-	-
1925						
L.J.E. Bradshaw*	C	Unopp.	-	2,079	-	-
1926						
A.J. Sims*	C	Unopp.	-		-	-
1927						
T.S. Cotterell*	Ind	Unopp.	-	2,105	-	-
1928						
J. Percival*	C	Unopp.	-		-	-
1929						
A.J. Sims*	C	Unopp.	-		-	-
1930						
T.S. Cotterell*	Ind	Unopp.	-	2,145	-	-
1931						
J.S. Carpenter	C	Unopp.	-		-	-
1932						
A.J. Sims*	C	Unopp.	-		-	-

St Michael's ward *(continued)*

Candidate	Party	Votes	%	Electors	Turnout	Gains
1933						
A.E. Hopkins*	C	Unopp.	-	2,138	-	-
1934						
J.S. Carpenter*	C	Unopp.	-	2,156	-	-
1935						
W.M. Huntley	C	Unopp.	-	2,147	-	-
1936						
A.E. Hopkins*	C	713	68.8	2,122	48.8	-
C.W. Maxim	Ind	323	31.2			
Total votes		1,036				
1937						
J.S. Carpenter*	C	Unopp.	-	2,156	-	-
1938						
W.M. Huntley*	C	Unopp.	-	2,182	-	-

Overall Labour vote	**17.8%**			**Overall turnout**		**53.7%**

Twerton East ward

Candidate	Party	Votes	%	Electors	Turnout	Gains
1919						
W. Barrett	Lab	888	64.6	2,243	61.3	Lab from L
G.J. Long*	L	486	35.4			
Total votes		1,374				
1920						
F.W. Kitley	L	Unopp.	-	2,248	-	-
1921						
G. Lanning	Ind	712	51.8	2,295	59.9	-
Mrs H. Cordiner	Lab	663	48.2			
Total votes		1,375				
1922						
W. Barrett*	Lab	706	52.8	2,287	58.5	-
A.H. Stickler	L	428	32.0			
M. York	Ind	204				
Total votes		1,338				
1923						
F.W. Kitley*	L	Unopp.	-	2,284	-	-
1924						
G. Lanning*	Ind	733	57.8	2,300	55.2	-
Mrs H. Cordiner	Lab	536	42.2			
Total votes		1,269				
1925						
W. Barrett*	Lab	625	59.6	2,305	45.5	-
E. Tucker	Ind	423	40.4			
Total votes		1,048				
1926						
F.W. Kitley*	L	Unopp.	-			-
1927						
G. Lanning*	Ind	671	54.0	2,358	52.7	-
Mrs F. Hope	Lab	572	46.0			
Total votes		1,243				
1928						
W. Barrett*	Lab	Unopp.	-		-	-

Twerton East ward *(continued)*

Candidate	Party	Votes	%	Electors	Turnout	Gains
1929						
S.J. Amblin*	Lab	Unopp.	-		-	-
1930						
G. Lanning*	Ind	675	66.5	2,455	41.3	-
W.F. Amesbury	Lab	340	33.5			
Total votes		1,015				
1931						
W. Barrett*	Lab	Unopp.	-		-	-
1932						
S.J. Amblin*	Lab	Unopp.	-		-	-
1933						
G. Lanning*	Ind	Unopp.	-	2,508	-	-
1934						
W. Barrett*	Lab	Unopp.	-	2,497	-	-
1935						
S.J. Amblin*	Lab	Unopp.	-	2,511	-	-
1936						
G. Lanning*	Ind	Unopp.	-	2,515	-	-
1937						
W. Barrett*	Lab	Unopp.	-	2,554	-	-
1938						
S.J. Amblin*	Lab	Unopp.	-	2,591	-	-

Overall Labour vote **50.0%** **Overall turnout** **53.3%**

Twerton West ward

Candidate	Party	Votes	%	Electors	Turnout	Gains
1919						
W.G. Reynolds	Ind	596	57.1	1,769	59.0	Ind from L
A.E. Withy*	L	448	42.9			
Total votes		1,044				
1920						
S. Day	Lab	482	41.5	1,895	61.3	Lab from Ind
A.E. Gunning	Ind	315	27.1			
G.J. Long	L	196	16.9			
R. Cox	C	168	14.5			
Total Votes		1,161				
1921						
A.E. Gunning	Ind	652	55.2	1,805	65.4	-
A.E. Bragg	Lab	529	44.8			
Total votes		1,181				
1922						
W.J. Reynolds*	Ind	Unopp.	-	1,847	-	-
1923						
S. Day*	Lab	Unopp.	-	1,851	-	-
1924						
A.E. Gunning*	Ind	657	61.9	1,885	56.3	-
S.J. Amblin	Lab	405	38.1			
Total votes		1,062				
1925						
H .Chivers	L	Unopp.	-	1,898	-	-
1926						
S. Day*	Lab	785	84.7	*1,921*	48.3	-
E. Tucker	Ind	142	15.3			
Total votes		927				
1927						
C.H. Deadman	Lab	586	54.7	1,943	55.1	Lab from Ind
A.E. Gunning*	Ind	485	45.3			
Total votes		1,071				
1928						
H. Chivers*	L	Unopp.	-		-	-

Twerton West ward *(continued)*

Candidate	Party	Votes	%	Electors	Turnout	Gains
1929						
S. Day*	Lab	Unopp.	-		-	-
1930						
C.H. Deadman*	Lab	Unopp.	-	2,528	-	-
1931						
H. Chivers*	L	Unopp.	-		-	-
1932						
S. Day*	Lab	Unopp.	-		-	-
1933						
E.J. Wilding	Lab	728	57.7	2,511	50.2	Lab from Ind
F.F. Batten*	Ind	533	42.3			
Total votes		1,261				
1934						
H. Chivers*	L	Unopp.	-	2,545	-	-
1935						
S. Day*	Lab	Unopp.	-	2,552	-	-
1936						
J.W. Andrews	Lab	703	50.4	2,625	53.1	-
H.W. Carey	Ind	692	49.6			
Total votes		1,395				
1937						
P.E. Bence*	L	790	54.2	2,811	51.9	-
B.E. Vokes	Lab	668	45.8			
Total votes		1,458				
1938						
C.W. Maxim*	Ind	Unopp.	-	2,878	-	-

Overall Labour vote		**46.3%**		**Overall turnout**		**55.1%**

137

Walcot North ward

Candidate	Party	Votes	%	Electors	Turnout	Gains
1919						
E.J. White*	L	576	56.0	1,886	54.5	-
A.E. Stocks	Lab	452	44.0			
Total votes		1,028				
1920						
A.H.W. Taylor	L	947	67.5	1,937	72.4	-
A.E. Stocks	Lab	455	32.5			
Total votes		1,402				
1921						
T. Vezey*	L	Unopp.	-	1,958	-	-
1922						
E.J. White*	L	Unopp.	-	1,979	-	-
1923						
A.H.W. Taylor*	L	Unopp.	-	2,014	-	-
1924						
T. Vezey*	L	Unopp.	-	2,010	-	-
1925						
E.J. White*	L	Unopp.	-	2,033	-	-
1926						
A.H.W. Taylor*	L	Unopp.	-		-	-
1927						
H. Cleaver*	L	Unopp.	-	2,040	-	-
1928						
E.J. White*	L	Unopp.	-		-	-
1929						
G. Burden	Ind	524	40.7	*2,149*	59.8	Ind from L
H.E. Bruton	Lab	416	32.3			
H.J. Lucas	L	346	26.9			
Total votes		1,286				
1930						
H. Cleaver*	L	Unopp.	-	2,204	-	-

Walcot North ward *(continued)*

Candidate	Party	Votes	%	Electors	Turnout	Gains
1931						
E.J. White*	L	Unopp.	-		-	-
1932						
G. Burden*	Ind	Unopp.	-		-	-
1933						
H. Cleaver*	L	Unopp.	-	2,267	-	-
1934						
H.G. Price	L	839	70.4	2,286	52.1	L from Lab
W.A. Eades	Lab	353	29.6			
Total votes		1,192				
1935						
G. Burden*	Ind	Unopp.	-	2,390	-	-
1936						
H. Cleaver*	L	Unopp.	-	2,436	-	-
1937						
H.G. Price*	L	Unopp.	-	2,495	-	-
1938						
G. Burden*	Ind	Unopp.	-	2,559	-	-

Overall Labour vote   **34.1%**   **Overall turnout**   **59.4%**

Walcot South ward

Candidate	Party	Votes	%	Electors	Turnout	Gains
1919						
E. Coleman	Lab	557	50.6	2,014	54.6	Lab from L
J.E. Maber	L	543	49.4			
Total votes		1,100				
1920						
G.T. Cooke*	L	1,016	65.8	2,096	73.7	-
H.H. Morris	Lab	529	34.2			
Total votes		1,545				
1921						
W.J. Baker*	L	Unopp.	-	2,178	-	-
1922						
E. Coleman*	Ind	Unopp.	-	2,205	-	-
1923						
Mrs H. Cooke	L	Unopp.	-	2,265	-	-
1924						
W.J. Baker*	L	Unopp.	-	2,312	-	-
1925						
E. Coleman*	Ind	Unopp.	-	2,321	-	-
1926						
Mrs H. Cooke*	L	Unopp.	-		-	-
1927						
W.J. Baker*	L	Unopp.	-	2,405	-	-
1928						
C.B. Farr*	L	Unopp.	-		-	-
1929						
Mrs H. Cooke*	L	752	73.0	2,485	41.4	-
Mrs H.W. Oldham	Lab	278	27.0			
Total votes		1,030				
1930						
W.J. Baker*	L	Unopp.	-	2,525	-	-

Walcot South ward *(continued)*

Candidate	Party	Votes	%	Electors	Turnout	Gains
1931						
C.B. Farr*	L	Unopp.	-		-	-
1932						
Mrs H. Cooke*	L	Unopp.	-		-	-
1933						
W.J. Baker*	L	Unopp.	-	2,560	-	-
1934						
C.B. Farr*	L	Unopp.	-	2,556	-	-
1935						
Mrs H. Cooke*	L	Unopp.	-	2,558	-	-
1936						
A.H. Smith	L	809	73.3	2,628	42.0	-
H. Male	Lab	295	26.7			
Total votes		1,104				
1937						
C.B. Farr*	L	Unopp.	-	2,610	-	-
1938						
E. Clements	C	695	47.2	2,678	55.0	C from L
G. Williams	L	518	35.1			
A.C. Butler	Lab	261	17.7			
Total votes		1,474				

Overall Labour vote	**30.7%**		**Overall turnout**	**52.5%**

Westmoreland ward

Candidate	Party	Votes	%	Electors	Turnout	Gains
1919						
S.R. Sendell	Lab	607	51.7	1,946	60.4	Lab from C
J.W.C. Southwood*	C	568	48.3			
Total votes		1,175				
1920						
J.W.C. Southwood	Ind C	640	50.8	2,022	62.4	Ind C from L
F.G. Hearse*	L	621	49.2			
Total votes		1,261				
1921						
C. Jenkin*	C	1,173	83.8	2,063	67.8	-
E. Tucker	Ind	226	16.2			
Total votes		1,399				
1922						
A.A. Hunt	Ind	745	66.9	2,064	54.0	Ind from Lab
J.H. Tarrant	Lab	369	33.1			
Total votes		1,114				
1923						
J.W.C. Southwood*	C	Unopp.	-	2,079	-	-
1924						
C. Jenkin*	C	Unopp.	-	2,090	-	-
1925						
A.A. Hunt*	L	Unopp.	-	2,085	-	-
1926						
J.W.C. Southwood*	C	Unopp.	-		-	-
1927						
C. Jenkin*	C	Unopp.	-	2,120	-	-
1928						
A.A. Hunt*	L	Unopp.	-		-	-
1929						
J.W.C. Southwood*	C	692	72.8	*2,185*	43.5	-
Mrs P.S. Padfield	Lab	258	27.2			
Total votes		950				

Westmoreland ward *(continued)*

Candidate	Party	Votes	%	Electors	Turnout	Gains
1930						
C. Jenkin*	C	Unopp.	-	2,218	-	-
1931						
A.A. Hunt*	L	Unopp.	-		-	-
1932						
J.W.C. Southwood*	C	Unopp.	-		-	-
1933						
C. Jenkin*	C	Unopp.	-	2,189	-	-
1934						
A.A. Hunt*	L	542	58.8	2,199	41.9	-
A.C. Stevens	Lab	379	41.2			
Total votes		921				
1935						
J.W.C. Southwood*	Ind	549	57.8	2,170	43.8	-
A.J.J. Mountain	Lab	401	42.2			
Total votes		950				
1936						
B.J. Smith	Ind	562	57.9	2,099	46.3	Ind from Lab
A.J.J. Mountain	Lab	352	36.3			
A.J.Lovell	Ind	57	5.9			
Total votes		971				
1937						
H. Male	Lab	423	59.9	2,001	35.3	Lab from Ind
S.D. Kennard	Ind	283	40.1			
Total votes		706				
1938						
J.W.C. Southwood*	Ind	Unopp.	-	2,000	-	-
Overall Labour vote		**29.5%**		**Overall turnout**		**50.4%**

Weston ward

Candidate	Party	Votes	%	Electors	Turnout	Gains
1919						
A.E. Ommanney	C	Unopp.	-	1,905	-	-
1920						
H.A. Biggs*	C	Unopp.	-	1,948	-	-
1921						
W. Dawe*	C	Unopp.	-	1,955	-	-
1922						
A.E. Ommanney*	C	Unopp.	-	1,966	-	-
1923						
H.A. Biggs*	C	Unopp.	-	2,013	-	-
1924						
W. Dawe*	C	Unopp.	-	2,033	-	-
1925						
G.E. Hughes	Ind	767	61.3	2,043	61.3	-
W.W. Clarke	Lab	485	38.7			
Total votes		1,252				
1926						
H.A. Biggs*	C	682	49.3	2,073	66.8	-
W.W. Clarke	Lab	378	27.3			
A.G. Day	Ind	324	23.4			
Total votes		1,384				
1927						
G.E. Hiskens*	C	Unopp.	-	2,103	-	-
1928						
G.E. Hughes*	Ind	Unopp.	-		-	-
1929						
H.A. Biggs*	C	Unopp.	-		-	-
1930						
G.E. Hiskens*	C	Unopp.	-	2,481	-	-

Weston ward *(continued)*

Candidate	Party	Votes	%	Electors	Turnout	Gains
1931						
C.W. Maxim	Ind	966	62.0	*2,530*	61.5	-
G.E. Hughes*	Ind	591	38.0			
Total votes		1,557				
1932						
H.A. Biggs*	C	Unopp.	-		-	-
1933						
G.E. Hiskens*	C	Unopp.	-	2,629	-	-
1934						
J.R. Torrance	C	836	51.9	2,689	59.9	C from Ind
C.W. Maxim*	Ind	775	48.1			
Total votes		1,611				
1935						
H.A. Biggs*	C	Unopp.	-	2,841	-	-
1936						
G.E. Hiskens*	C	Unopp.	-	2,965	-	-
1937						
J.R. Torrance*	C	Unopp.	-	3,077	-	-
1938						
L.N. Punter	Ind	926	52.7	3,266	53.8	Ind from C
F.E. Barnard*	C	832	47.3			
Total votes		1,758				

(Punter was also described as an Independent Progressive)

Overall Labour vote　　**11.4%**　　　　**Overall turnout**　　**60.0%**

Widcombe ward

Candidate	Party	Votes	%	Electors	Turnout	Gains
1919						
A.W. Hazell	Lab	707	60.6	1,939	60.1	Lab from L
W.H. Devenish	Ind	312	26.8			
G.K. Turvey*	L	147				
Total votes		1,166				
1920						
A.I. Ford	Lab	601	53.2	1,974	57.2	Lab from L
J.W. Crook*	L	529	46.8			
Total votes		1,130				
1921						
W.F. Long	Co.L	968	66.9	2,023	71.5	-
H.W. Webb	Lab	479	33.1			
Total votes		1,447				
1922						
A.W. Hazell*	Lab	Unopp.	-	2,045	-	-
1923						
A.I. Ford*	Lab	Unopp.	-	2,052	-	-
1924						
W.F. Long*	L	Unopp.	-	2,030	-	-
1925						
A.W. Hazell*	Lab	733	57.7	2,052	61.9	-
F.W. Armstrong	Ind	538	42.3			
Total votes		1,271				
1926						
A.I. Ford*	Lab	649	54.6	*2,069*	57.4	-
T. Grenfell	Ind	539	45.4			
Total votes		1,188				
1927						
W.F. Long*	L	Unopp.	-	2,086	-	-
1928						
A.W. Hazell*	Lab	Unopp.	-		-	-
1929						
A.I. Ford*	Lab	Unopp.	-		-	-

Widcombe ward *(continued)*

Candidate	Party	Votes	%	Electors	Turnout	Gains
1930						
W.F. Long*	L	886	74.5	2,186	54.4	-
Mrs H. Cordiner	Lab	304	25.5			
Total votes		1,190				
1931						
W.J. Say	Lab	Unopp.	-		-	-
1932						
M. Moroney*	Lab	Unopp.	-		-	-
1933						
W.F. Long*	L	Unopp.	-	2,114	-	-
1934						
W.J. Say*	Lab	694	55.8	2,115	58.8	-
F.C. Holmes	L	550	44.2			
Total votes		1,244				
1935						
F.C. Holmes	Ind	676	58.0	2,113	55.1	Ind from Lab
Mrs H. Cordiner	Lab	489	42.0			
Total votes		1,165				
1936						
W.F. Long*	L	Unopp.	-	2,110	-	-
1937						
W.J. Say*	Lab	Unopp.	-	2,008	-	-
1938						
F.C. Holmes*	Ind	Unopp.	-	1,976	-	-
Overall Labour vote		**47.5%**		**Overall turnout**		**59.5%**

FOUR
Birkenhead

BIRKENHEAD

The borough of Birkenhead was situated in the Wirral peninsula, on the opposite bank of the River Mersey from Liverpool. Immediately adjoining it to the north was the county borough of Wallasey. The largest town in Cheshire, it was the twenty-fourth largest county borough in 1931 with a population of just under 150,000. It had grown rapidly from the 1840s due to three main developments. First, Laird's (later Cammell Laird's) shipyard was established in 1824, and grew into one of the largest shipbuilders in the country.[1] Second, docks were constructed from the 1840s, and became an important section of the dock system controlled by the Mersey Docks and Harbour Board. Third, as transport links with Liverpool were steadily improved between the 1840s and the 1930s, increasing numbers of the Liverpool middle class began to move to the pleasanter surroundings of the Wirral and commute to work across the river. By the 1930s, 14 per cent of the population of the borough worked in Liverpool.[2]

The occupational structure of the borough reflected these developments very closely. Just over 15 per cent of male workers were in the shipbuilding and repair category, amounting to 7,500 workers in 1931. Another 15 per cent were in the water and dock transport sector, totalling 7,000 workers. In these two categories Birkenhead was ranked eighth and fifth respectively amongst county boroughs. Within these two dominant sections of the local proletariat, the contrast between skilled shipbuilders and unskilled dockers and seafarers was marked. Thus Birkenhead could provide an interesting case-study for analysing the impact on working-class politics of division along skill lines. The trade going through the docks was also specialised in two significant areas which had some impact on the occupational structure of the borough. There was an emphasis on the handling of bulk cargoes, and especially grain imports, in Birkenhead. As a result a large flour-milling sector developed around the West Float section of the docks. The Paul Bros mills (later Homepride) established at the turn of the century, the Ocean Mills of Joseph Rank Ltd erected in 1913, and the mills of Spillers and Bakers Ltd were the most important on the Birkenhead side of the docks. By the 1920s the town claimed to be second only to Minneapolis as a grain-milling centre. Birkenhead also specialised in the import and slaughter of livestock, and around its lairages important meat and meat-product industries were established. These specialisations were reflected in the significant food, drink and tobacco category for Birkenhead in the 1931 census. In the case of milling, though, some of the employment was on the Wallasey side of the docks and would show up there. In proportional terms as well, milling was of greater significance for female as opposed to male employment. The other main sector of male employment was in

---

[1] On this, and other aspects of Birkenhead's industrial development, see Birkenhead Corporation, *The County Borough of Birkenhead: The Official Handbook*, (Cheltenham, no date), pp. 67–141; Lea, M., *Birkenhead, 1877–1974*, (Birkenhead, 1974), pp. 80–91; O'Hara, J., (ed.), *Birkenhead: Guide to Commercial and Industrial Facilities*, (Birkenhead, 1928), pp. 9–16, 23–30, 40, 55, 60–64: Scott, P.A., 'Aspects of the Urban Geography of Birkenhead', (B.A. dissertation, University of Liverpool, 1968), pp. 3–15.
[2] Caradog Jones, G., *Social Survey of Merseyside*, (Liverpool, 1934), vol. 1, p. 57.

commerce and finance with 9,000 workers, a significant number of whom would have been white-collar commuters.

Amongst women there were significant numbers employed in the processing of goods coming in to the docks, over 2,000 working in the paints and chemicals, and aforementioned food, drink and tobacco categories. However, the largest sectors of female employment were commerce and finance with 5,000 workers, and personal service with almost 7,000 workers. These two categories accounted for over 60 per cent of all female employment, and both were an indicator of the substantial middle class of the borough. Thus despite being a major industrial centre with a large working class, Birkenhead was ranked as high as sixteenth amongst county boroughs in terms of female domestic servants per head of population, and twenty-fourth in terms of self-employed and managers as a proportion of the workforce.

Birkenhead was both a proletarian and a bourgeois town then, and its residential pattern at the start of the inter-war period confirmed this. A contemporary description of the borough is evocative:

> [Birkenhead] has unquestionably an industrial character of its own, its industries being mainly associated with the docks and shipbuilding yards ... Except for the shopping area and a few older residential districts most of the town proper is made up of dreary streets of seemingly endless working class houses. Variety is afforded by some patches, especially near the docks, of really bad slums. The social status of the inhabitants improves the further one moves from the river. Rows of villas and new housing estates emerge, together with superior middle-class suburbs, such as Oxton, Bidston and Prenton.[3]

To the north-west, on low land adjacent to the inlet on which the docks were built, a significant proportion of the working-class population of the borough was resident in some of the worst housing. Most of this area was included in Cleveland ward, one of Labour's strongest wards, and many dock-workers lived here. When a prominent member of the National Union of Dock Labourers was mooted as a possible Labour candidate for Cleveland, one of the local newspapers commented that 'he would have been assured of great support'.[4] To the north and east, extending along the Mersey down as far as Laird's shipyard, was further working-class housing of a slightly higher standard. There was a concentration of shipyard workers here, especially in Argyle ward, another Labour stronghold, and parts of Mersey and Clifton wards, which by the mid to late 1920s were predominantly Labour-supporting. The northern section of Grange ward was also predominantly working-class, being sandwiched between the dock and shipyard areas, but it also contained an area of middle-class housing to the south, and it was fairly marginal until Labour captured it in the late 1920s.

Further south along the Mersey from Rock Ferry, and inland on higher ground to the south and west, lay the middle-class suburbs. Here lay Bebington, Egerton,

---

[3] Caradog Jones, *Social Survey of Merseyside*, vol. 1, p. 57.
[4] *Birkenhead and Cheshire Advertiser and Wallasey Guardian*, 25 Oct. 1919.

Oxton and Claughton wards, solid Tory territory, with a degree of Liberal support in Egerton. The persons per room figures for 1931 bore out this residential pattern very well. In the north and east the predominantly working-class wards of Cleveland, Argyle and Mersey had the most crowded residences with more than one person per room on average. At the other extreme to the south and west in the most affluent middle-class wards of Oxton and Prenton (added in 1928), almost two rooms per person was the average. In the wards situated between these two poles, the persons per room figures lay in a middling range.

The development of council housing began to disturb this clear-cut pattern during the inter-war period. Between 1920 and 1938, 3,938 council houses were built by the borough. By 1938 the council owned 11.5 per cent of all the housing stock, and council tenants made up 12 per cent of the total population.[5] Much of this housing was built on the north-western outskirts of the town (initially in Cleveland ward, after the 1934 ward boundary changes in St James's and Gilbrook wards), and on adjoining land outside the borough which was incorporated as Bidston ward in 1928, and then became part of Upton ward in 1934. However, it was to take the much larger developments after 1945, and especially the building of the huge Woodchurch estate to the west of the town in Prenton ward, to transform the social geography of the borough. It should also be noted that almost 4,000 private-sector houses were built between 1920 and 1938, reflecting the continuing attraction of Birkenhead as a commuter centre. The total population of the borough remained virtually stagnant in the 1920s, and fell by something like 5 per cent in the 1930s, a product of the economic problems of the inter-war years.[6] Within that overall pattern, though, population loss was concentrated in the older inner-city areas, while suburban middle-class estates were growing. Argyle, Clifton, Grange and Mersey wards all experienced population loss of over 10 per cent between 1921 and 1931 according to the census data. By contrast, on the southern outskirts, Bebington ward grew by over 60 per cent and Egerton by 10 per cent. To the west, Prenton grew by over 50 per cent and Bidston (later Upton), experienced an almost eight-fold increase in its population.

Turning to the politics of the borough, Birkenhead had an interesting mixture of political traditions. As in other parts of Merseyside, there was a significant Catholic minority here, but not as large proportionally as in Liverpool or Bootle.[7] Much of this minority was concentrated in the Cleveland ward adjacent to the docks, and Catholics made up a sizeable proportion of the dock labour force. The Catholic presence may have been a contributory factor to the strength of Liberalism in pre-1914 Birkenhead. By contrast, Laird's was traditionally an employer of Protestant workers. Even in the post-1945 period, the first question

[5]   Social Science Department, University of Liverpool, *Handbook of Social Statistics Relating to Merseyside*, (Liverpool, 1938), p. 29.
[6]   Fogarty, M.P., *Prospects of the Industrial Areas of Great Britain*, (London, 1945), p. 28.
[7]   As a useful but by no means perfect indicator of this, in the 1861 census, the earliest which can be used for this comparison, the proportion of Irish-born in Birkenhead was 14 per cent, compared with 19 per cent in Liverpool; in 1881 the proportions were 9 and 13 per cent respectively. See also comments on Bootle in this volume, pp. 544–545.

put to shipyard apprentices when they started at Laird's was reputedly, 'Are you a left-footer?' The skilled and predominantly Protestant shipyard workers were concentrated in Argyle ward and to a lesser degree in parts of the Grange, Clifton and Mersey wards.

Despite the influence of sectarianism on the employment patterns of the Birkenhead working class, as a political force in the inter-war years sectarianism seems to have had much less resonance than it did across the Mersey in Liverpool and Bootle. In its earlier history Birkenhead had not been free of sectarian strife. When the Roman Catholic hierarchy and episcopate was established in Britain in 1849, for instance, Protestant objectors held a public meeting in the Town Hall which resulted in a major riot, and other stormy protest meetings were held in the borough that year. Even more serious were the 'Garibaldi riots' of 1862, when Catholics had clashed with Protestant supporters of the Italian patriot.[8] Nevertheless, it was perhaps harder in Birkenhead than across the river for Protestant extremists to portray the proportionally smaller Catholic presence as a 'threat' to Protestant interests. It was also the case that Protestant and Catholic workers were on the whole not competing for the same jobs in Birkenhead, with the well-paid shipyard work being preserved mainly for Protestants. Thus sectarian tensions appeared to become less marked here, at least in overtly political terms anyway. It is significant that the most prominent local populist Orangeman, T. Major Thompson, who claimed to have some support in the working-class areas of the town, was shunned by local Toryism. He won a seat in Grange ward in 1922 when the Conservatives left a seat free for him, but was beaten by a Tory and a Labour candidate in 1925, and by 1926 the Tories were fielding two candidates against him and his share of the vote had fallen to 10 per cent. His later failed attempts to stand in Argyle (1927) and Cleveland (1928) proved that his politics had by now been marginalised in Birkenhead. Certainly the anti-Catholic basis of working-class Conservatism seems to have been much less important in Birkenhead than it was in Liverpool. When Conservative Workingmen met in the borough in the 1919 election campaign, they applauded municipal 'economy', denounced the 'extremism' of trade unionism, and affirmed their belief in the shared interest of employers of workers.[9] Not a hint of religious sectarianism was raised at their public meeting, which would have been impossible across the Mersey.

Rather it was Lib-Labism that held sway amongst the skilled workers of Birkenhead before 1914, another factor in the Liberal tradition here. The influence of the philanthropist W.H. Lever, later Lord Leverhulme, whose Port Sunlight works and model village lay just to the south of the borough, should be noted. He stood as the Liberal candidate for the Birkenhead parliamentary seat (only one before 1918) in the 1892 and 1895 general elections, and at a by-election in 1894, and only narrowly lost to his Conservative opponent on all three occasions. Later, H.H. Vivian, 'a champion of the co-partnership movement', won

---

[8] See Boumphrey, I., *Birkenhead: A Pictorial History*, (Chichester, 1995), unpaginated; Neal, F., 'The Birkenhead Garibaldi Riots of 1862', *Transactions of the Historic Society of Lancashire and Cheshire*, vol. 131, (1981).

[9] *Birkenhead Advertiser*, 29 Oct. 1919.

the seat on a Lib-Lab ticket in 1906, and after losing it in the January election of 1910, regained it in December. However, it should also be noted that the Free Trade question was a potent factor in the constituency. Tariff Reform was denounced by J.M. Laird in 1906, and this no doubt cost the Tories middle-class and working-class votes.[10] Birkenhead was not the Tory stronghold before 1914, then, that it might have been expected to be, given the substantial middle class of the borough and the predominance of Toryism in the Merseyside area. This was also reflected in municipal politics, with Conservative dominance being keenly contested by the Liberals, and in the later Edwardian years, by a growing Labour presence.

In the inter-war period the most striking feature of Birkenhead politics was the apparent divergence between trends at the parliamentary and municipal level. In general elections, Liberalism survived surprisingly well in Birkenhead East, one of the two new seats created in 1918. The prominent local Liberal and stockbroker H.G. White won the seat in 1922, and held it at every subsequent election until the war, with the exception of 1924. By contrast the Labour challenge in this constituency was weak. Even in its peak year of 1929 the Labour candidate only achieved just over 30 per cent of the poll. In Birkenhead West Labour was a more serious contender, winning in 1923 and 1929, but overall the Tories predominated here. So Labour in Birkenhead failed to overthrow the political influence of the two traditional parties in elections to Westminster.

In municipal elections, however, a very different picture emerges. The decline of Liberalism was swift and almost total. In 1918 the Liberals were the second party with fourteen seats on the council, to the Tories' thirty-two and Labour's ten. Labour supplanted them as the second party in 1919, and by 1921 the number of Liberal councillors had been halved. Three Liberal gains in 1923 only represented a temporary revival, and by 1928 there was only one Liberal councillor left, R.P. Fletcher representing Egerton ward. After Fletcher became an alderman following the 1932 elections, no Liberal was elected onto the council for the rest of the period. Over the inter-war years as a whole, Liberals only ever won seats in three adjacent wards in the south-east of the borough, Egerton, Clifton and Claughton. Of these, only Egerton could be said to have a real Liberal presence, with nine Liberal wins overall. Clifton was won only twice, and Claughton once, and neither after 1923.

Labour's rise, on the other hand, was meteoric. After the dramatic breakthrough of five gains in 1919 (reckoned as seven by the local press with the two Co-operative wins), Labour in Birkenhead suffered the same downturn in municipal support in the early 1920s that its sister parties experienced in boroughs up and down the country. Revival came relatively early, though, with five gains in 1923 signalling the turning point locally. By 1926 Labour was the largest single party in terms of councillors, with twenty to the Tories' eighteen, and only the nine Conservative aldermen kept Labour out of power. However, seven aldermen came up for re-election immediately after the November elections, five of whom were Tories. Labour took five of the vacancies, and following a series of by-

---

[10] Pelling, H., *Social Geography of British Elections 1885–1910*, (Aldershot, 1994), p. 251.

elections to replace the elevated councillors, Labour eventually took control of the borough. Further gains consolidated its control over the next three years, before three losses in 1930 reflected a shift seen throughout the country. A catastrophic nine net losses in 1931 completed the reversal of fortune, and the Tories regained control of the borough. Labour made a rapid recovery again from 1932, and with seven gains coinciding with the reorganisation of ward boundaries in 1934, took power again. After this the trend turned against Labour until 1938, and in 1936 Labour lost its overall majority. With twenty-two Labour seats to the Tories' twenty-one and one Liberal alderman, the council was effectively deadlocked. Labour retained control only by virtue of it being the largest single party, with the Tories declining the offer of the Labour leader to take over. Further losses in 1937 gave the Tories a majority again, and they continued in office until the war. Overall, Labour's record of holding power in Birkenhead for eight of the inter-war years, between 1926 and 1931, and between 1934 and 1937, was as good as in any of the boroughs included in this volume.

How can this variation between parliamentary and municipal trends be explained? There is evidence to suppose that it was the voting preferences of shipyard workers that was the key factor here. The suggestion is that many of these workers might have voted Labour in local elections, but Liberal at the national level. Of the wards where they were mainly concentrated, Argyle became a Labour stronghold in municipal elections by 1922, while Mersey and Clifton wards were slower to be won over, but nevertheless were taken by Labour in the late 1920s and after the 1930-31 debacle. Conversely, Liberalism was rapidly eclipsed in these wards. In both Argyle and Mersey, no Liberal candidate after 1918 avoided the ignominy of coming last in the poll. In Clifton there were a couple of Liberal victories in the early 1920s, but by 1923 support for Liberal candidates had all but disappeared here as well. These were three of the five wards that made up the Birkenhead East constituency. Of the other two wards in the constituency, Bebington was a Tory stronghold, again with negligible Liberal support, and only Egerton displayed any significant Liberal sympathies. In sum, Liberalism was virtually non-existent in municipal elections in four of the five wards that constituted the East constituency, yet that same constituency was won by the Liberals five times in six general elections after 1918. On the other hand, significant Labour support in the three wards adjoining Laird's, was not translated into Parliamentary success, Labour rarely getting more than a quarter of the vote in Birkenhead East. The chairman of the Birkenhead Trades and Labour Council stated confidently in 1919 that the municipal election results,

> showed in a marked manner the strength of the Labour influence
> in the eastern division of Birkenhead, which would be an
> important factor at the next Parliamentary election.[11]

In this prediction he was plainly proved wrong.

There are a number of possible reasons why shipyard workers in Birkenhead might have shifted to Labour locally, and yet remained loyal to Liberalism on national issues. There might have been an element of tactical voting here. While

[11]   *Birkenhead News*, 3 Nov. 1919.

Labour could win the three shipyard wards in the constituency, the significant Tory minority in each, combined with the Tory majority in Bebington and solid Liberal–Tory predominance in Egerton, probably meant that Labour was never likely to win the seat in Westminster. Thus some Labour voters, seeing the potential strength of Liberalism in Egerton, might have decided to support the Liberal parliamentary candidate as the lesser of two evils. The strength of the pre-war tradition of Lib-Labism might also have encouraged this possibility. Whether such tactical voting took place in this period is a moot point, as there is no available evidence for it. Even if it did, it was unlikely on its own to explain the exceptional Liberal parliamentary success here. Other local factors must have entered the equation.

While many voters might have been won over to Labour on issues directly related to the council, such as the provision of housing and local services, other issues may have been influential when it came to general elections. As already mentioned, free trade had long been of importance in Birkenhead politics, and it was still relevant in the inter-war years, especially to the shipyard interest. The customary association of free trade with the Liberals may therefore have played a part in their success here. Even more important, defence policy was of great significance to Birkenhead. Laird's built merchant vessels as well, of course, but its naval contracts provided the bedrock of its economic survival in these years. While naval shipbuilding was at a low level generally in the 1920s, Laird's still produced the battleship *Rodney*, the cruiser *Achilles*, and the submarine *Phoenix*, amongst other naval orders. The worst slump years from late 1929 saw the labour force fall to 2,000 by 1931, but gradual recovery was boosted strongly by the order for the aircraft carrier *Ark Royal* in 1935, and later by the battleship *Prince of Wales*.[12] There is no doubt that these contracts sustained employment in Laird's, and without them unemployment in the town would have been more prolonged and more serious. Defence policy was of major significance, then. It is reasonable to suppose that it was a factor in dissuading some shipyard workers, and others as well, from voting Labour at general elections, as Labour in this period was generally not perceived as the party wholeheartedly in favour of defence expenditure.

As stated earlier, Birkenhead provides an interesting case-study for assessing the political impact of the division of the male working class along skill lines. The observations here suggest that slightly different political responses can be identified for the highly-skilled shipyard workers as opposed to the unskilled and predominantly casually-employed dock-workers of Birkenhead. However, these differences are complex, and cannot be reduced to simple generalisations, such as that one or other of the groups gave greater or more consistent support for Labour, as has been suggested elsewhere.[13] Many of the skilled workers of Laird's may not have voted Labour at general elections (for specific and contingent reasons),

---

[12] Lea, *Birkenhead*, pp. 86–91.
[13] See Davies, S., *Liverpool Labour: Social and Political Influences on the Development of the Labour Party in Liverpool, 1900–1939*, (Keele, 1996), pp. 197–231; Adams, T., 'Labour and the First World War: economy, politics and the erosion of local peculiarity', *Journal of Regional and Local Studies*, (1990), pp. 33–40.

but on the other hand their political response at the municipal level seems to be indistinguishable from that of dock-workers, at least as far as the electoral evidence here is concerned. The pattern of support for Labour in Argyle and Cleveland wards, where shipyard workers and dock-workers respectively were most concentrated, was almost identical in terms of strength and variation over time.

Evidence on the occupations of Labour candidates may shed more light on this question.[14] Of seventy-two candidates in Birkenhead between 1919 and 1932 whose occupations have been identified, nineteen (just over a quarter) were trade union officials, fifteen (just over a fifth) were railway workers, another fifteen were clerical or white-collar workers, and seven (a tenth) were insurance agents. The preponderance of officials emphasises the importance of union organisation to the party. Moreover, most of these officials came from one of two unions, the Transport and General Workers (TGWU – from 1922 the main dockers' union) and the Boilermakers (the most important shipyard union). They included some of the most senior figures in the party, including Charles McVey, district secretary of the TGWU, long-serving councillor in Cleveland ward, and Labour mayor in 1937–38 and M.M. Forsythe, local secretary of the Boilermakers and councillor in the Clifton and Mersey wards. Both main male occupational groups seemed to be well-represented amongst Labour's municipal ranks therefore, along with railway workers. The pattern in Argyle and Cleveland wards was also very similar. Of twelve candidates in Argyle, three were officials of the Boilermakers' Union, and another was a rank-and-file boilermaker. In Cleveland, out of twelve candidates five were union officials, three of whom can be identified with the TGWU. In both wards there were also three clerical workers and two insurance agents. Railway workers on the other hand were most strongly represented in Clifton ward, comprising no fewer than eight out of thirteen candidates there. Overall there is nothing to suggest that either dock-workers or shipyard workers were any more or less influential in the local Labour Party, although it would require a much more detailed historical study to flesh out the suggestions offered here.

The other striking feature of Birkenhead's inter-war municipal politics was the blatant chicanery and gerrymandering that was common practice. From 1919 onwards the political battle was resolved into a straightforward fight between Labour and anti-Labour forces, and no holds were barred it seems in this bitter conflict. The 'gentlemanly' agreements to 'play fair' that were seen in other boroughs were rapidly abandoned in Birkenhead. As far as elections to the aldermanic bench were concerned, there was no attempt to maintain party representation on a proportional basis. After 1919 Labour was denied any new aldermen, despite the increase in the number of its councillors, until by 1926 it was grossly under-represented, with only two Labour aldermen to twenty councillors. As pointed out above, once Labour had a majority of the councillors in 1926, the party then seized the opportunity to take power via the aldermanic elections, increasing its share to seven. In 1929 Labour further bolstered its position by taking a further three aldermanic seats, but after the disastrous losses

---

[14] *Birkenhead News*, 26 Oct. 1929; *Birkenhead Advertiser*, 25 Oct. 1919, 27 Oct. 1923, 27 Oct. 1926, 26 Oct. 1927, 26 Oct. 1932.

of 1930 and 1931, half of Labour's total of ten aldermen were replaced by Tories in a tit-for-tat reprisal. When the political pendulum swung the other way again, Labour boosted its share in 1934 and 1935, getting back to nine aldermen, before seeing its aldermanic numbers reduced once more in 1938.

This blatant manipulation of the aldermanic elections for party advantage was not unique to Birkenhead, of course, but the wholesale gerrymandering of ward boundaries that took place in 1934 was less common. There was general agreement at the time that Birkenhead's boundaries badly needed redrawing, there having been no comprehensive changes made to them since the incorporation of the borough in 1877. Proposals had been put forward in 1913 and again in 1921, but on both occasions they had been dropped. Instead piecemeal extensions to the borough had taken place in 1897, 1927 and 1933, so that by 1934 the arrangement of the wards was described by the government commissioner as 'probably unique in the annals of local government'.[15] Originally there had been five larger wards in terms of population (Argyle, Cleveland, Clifton, Egerton and Grange), each represented by six councillors (two elected per year) and two aldermen. Four smaller wards (Bebington, Claughton, Mersey and Oxton) were represented by three councillors and one alderman. After the various extensions, three other wards had been created, one being represented by three councillors (Wirral, 1933), one by two councillors (Prenton, 1928), and one with a single councillor (Bidston, 1928), with an additional two aldermen for the three wards combined. 'Disparities had occurred', concluded the commissioner, and 'equality of representation as between the different wards' was to be the aim of the 1934 overhaul.

However, the instigators of the redistribution were the Tory leaders of the council, only recently in 1931 having regained power after five years of Labour rule, and mindful of Labour's strong recovery in 1932 and 1933. The proposals put forward, and ultimately accepted with only minor amendments, were vehemently condemned as a political fix by Labour. The party leader in the council, W.H. Egan, speaking at the public enquiry, was reported as follows:

> He said he had attended the three meetings of the Parliamentary Committee at which these proposals were discussed, and, in his opinion, insufficient consideration was given to the matter. No more than three hours was [sic] spent in discussing the proposals, and prior to November, 1933, there had been no indication that there was any desire to change the ward boundaries. The areas were not in detail, and he (Mr. Egan) suggested that in two years' time there would be a more suitable time to make the change, in order to give the matter the necessary consideration. The wards were being extended and altered in a way that was neither natural or proper. They had not been put forward for the purpose of expediting [sic], but for the purpose of influencing people in a certain direction.[16]

---

[15] *Birkenhead Advertiser*, 7 Mar. 1934.
[16] *Birkenhead Advertiser*, 7 Mar. 1934.

The original plans for the redistribution had been drawn up by the Conservative agent in Birkenhead, and assurances at the enquiry that 'it does not necessarily follow that a person who is a member of any particular party is going to introduce his politics in a matter of this kind' did not go down very well with the Labour objectors. The Parliamentary Committee of the council, which it was pointed out had a Conservative majority, had approved the plans, it was claimed, after also taking into account alternative Labour proposals, and advice as well from the borough surveyor. Labour remained unconvinced, and continued to protest at the subsequent council meeting where the plans were approved.[17] The new boundaries remained a rancorous issue for the rest of the 1930s, and time and again the Labour leader Egan returned to the theme. In 1934 he said Labour gains were 'despite the redistribution of the wards – a redistribution designed to maintain the Conservative majority'. In 1935 he lamented the 'benefit which the Conservatives have derived from the redistribution'. When Labour lost power in 1937 he complained that 'the redistribution of the wards three years ago was brought about to break our strength, and it has succeeded at last'. In 1938 Egan was still protesting that the redistribution 'was not an equitable one'.[18]

No systematic evidence was presented at the time to back up the Labour objections, but analysis of the data collected here does appear to show that the redistribution worked against Labour's interest. One way to demonstrate this is to calculate the probable Labour representation of wards on the old boundaries, based on the 1932 and 1933 results in each ward (discounting 1931, being a freak year in terms of longer-term trends), and comparing this with the actual representation won between 1934 and 1936, as shown in table 5.1 at the end of this chapter.

As can be seen there, whereas Labour was likely to win a clear majority of the seats available on the old boundaries, the 1934 redistribution tipped the balance against them. This was because many of the changes made to the boundaries, even though they seemed only minor, went to the advantage of the Conservatives. For instance, Grange ward, previously a strong Labour ward returning six councillors, was divided so that the northern section became the Labour stronghold of Cathcart ward with three councillors, while the new Grange ward further south became a Tory stronghold, also with three councillors. The division of the ward was also notably inequitable, with over 6,000 predominantly working-class voters in Cathcart, and 4,500 in the much more middle-class Grange. A more even split would have made Grange a marginal ward at least, or even predominantly Labour. As another example, the three wards of Argyle, Clifton and Mersey, previously all Labour territory returning fifteen councillors between them, were neatly pruned at the edges, leaving three new Labour wards returning only nine councillors. From the more affluent southern end of the old Clifton ward, though, a new three-seat ward was created, Holt, which was at best a Labour marginal (Labour won it twice from 1934 in three-way contests with Liberals and Tories, but then lost it three times in straight fights with Conservatives). In these two examples alone,

---

[17] *Birkenhead Advertiser*, 14 Mar. 1934.
[18] *Liverpool Daily Post*, 2 Nov. 1934, 2 Nov. 1935, 2 Nov. 1937, 2 Nov. 1938.

twenty-one relatively safe Labour seats had been reduced to twelve, and three marginal and three Tory seats had at the same time been created.

Elsewhere, strongly Tory Prenton ward, previously with two councillors, was expanded to take in part of Tory Wirral ward, and was awarded three councillors. The three-councillor Wirral ward was at the same time merged with the one-councillor Labour ward of Bidston to create Upton ward, with three councillors solid for the Tories. The net balance of five Tory councillors to one Labour was transformed into six safe Tory seats. Of the 605 houses in Bidston ward in 1934, 516 had been erected by the council, and representatives of 413 households there signed a petition protesting against the change.[19] They were indignant that their council estate was to be submerged in a huge area consisting otherwise of semi-rural land and middle-class suburbs, particularly as they were physically cut off from the rest of the new Upton ward by the considerable obstacle of Bidston Hill. Further east, the adjacent ward of Cleveland was the only one which was changed to Labour's advantage. Three new wards, St James's, Gilbrook and a much-reduced Cleveland, gave Labour nine seats in total here, replacing the six they had held previously.

Other changes tended to maintain Conservative strength. To the south of the borough the six-seat Egerton, previously Tory with some Liberal strength, was divided in two, the new wards of Devonshire and Egerton both being Tory and between them having six councillors. Bebington and Claughton wards, Conservative strongholds, were both retained with minor changes, and strongly Tory Oxton was unchanged. Significantly as well, Oxton and Claughton survived intact despite the fact that they remained relatively small, with only 2,000 voters in Oxton and less than 3,000 in Claughton. If they had been merged, they would still have been smaller than some Labour wards like Cathcart (over 6,000 voters), Mersey (almost 5,500) and Cleveland (over 5,000). Effectively this meant that Oxton and Claughton received more than double the representation that these Labour wards were given. This highlighted one other notable feature of the 1934 redistribution, that it failed to accomplish its primary aim, which was 'to establish equality of representation as between the different wards'. This can be seen quite clearly by calculating the voter per ward ratio for the pre- and post-1934 boundaries, as shown in table 5.2 at the end of the chapter.

Both before and after the changes, there was a wide variation in the ratio of voters to councillors in different wards. On the old boundaries, at one extreme there were over 2,000 voters per councillor in Cleveland ward and almost 1,900 in Grange, while at the other end of the scale there were around 650 in both Oxton and Prenton. After the changes, Cathcart had over 2,000 voters per councillor, while Prenton had less than 650. Moreover, by characterising wards as either 'Labour' or 'non-Labour' on the basis of the 1932 and 1933 results for the old wards, and the post-1934 results for the new, it becomes obvious that the inequalities tended to favour Labour's opponents. Most of the under-represented wards were 'Labour' wards, and most of the over-represented were 'non-Labour', both before and after 1934. In fact the disadvantage to Labour had if anything increased after the changes. The average voter per councillor ratio increased from

---

[19]   *Birkenhead Advertiser*, 7 Mar. 1934.

1,581 to 1,686 for the 'Labour' wards, while remaining virtually static at 1,194 for the 'non-Labour' wards.

This disparity could to some degree be excused by the fact that one other factor than equality of representation could be taken into account in redrawing boundaries, namely the rateable value of land. Although there was no precise formula for this, wards with high rateable value could be allowed to be smaller than the average, as was made clear at the public inquiry. This revealed the emphasis in the pre-1945 local government system on giving ratepayers an advantaged position in deciding on the composition of the council and the way the rates were spent. The exclusion of certain categories of non-ratepaying citizens from the municipal franchise at this time, and the plural votes allowed to owners of business premises, were both justified on the same grounds.[20] This raises a more general issue of how the municipal electoral system may have been biased against Labour across the country. As far as Birkenhead is concerned, though, it seems clear that the 'rateable value factor' alone could not explain the significant party advantage inherent in the 1934 changes. This gerrymandering must have played some part in the decline in Labour's fortunes in the borough in the second half of the 1930s. However, the general trend away from Labour from 1935 to 1938 revealed in the other boroughs in this volume suggests that it was probably not the only reason.

Birkenhead's inter-war political history cannot be left without some consideration of the impact of the National Unemployed Workers' Movement (NUWM) and the main political force behind the movement, the Communist party.[21] After all, Birkenhead, in September 1932, was where the most significant and best known unemployed riots of the inter-war period took place.[22] What political effect did these sensational and traumatic disturbances have? The 1932 riots have been portrayed by Cook and Stevenson in their important study of the 1930s as rather exceptional phenomena caused by a peculiar and specific sequence of events, and there is much in their argument that the evidence here supports. They correctly point out that unemployment, while in the long term not as bad in Birkenhead as elsewhere, was especially and suddenly severe in 1931

---

[20]   See notes at the end of this volume, p. 671; also, Davies, *Liverpool Labour*, pp. 119–129.

[21]   On the history of the NUWM, and its connections with the Communist Party, see Cook, C. and Stevenson, J., *The Slump: Society and Politics during the Depression*, (London, 1979), pp. 145–194; Croucher, R., *We Refuse to Starve in Silence: A History of the National Unemployed Workers' Movement*, (1987); Merseyside Socialist Research Group, *Genuinely Seeking Work: Mass Unemployment on Merseyside in the 1930s*, (Birkenhead, 1992), ch. 12, pp. 177–200; Davies, S., 'The membership of the National Unemployed Workers' Movement, 1923–1938', *Labour History Review*, vol. 57, pt. 1, (1992), pp. 29–36.

[22]   On the 1932 riots, see Cook and Stevenson, *The Slump*, pp. 170–173, 192–193; Kelly, S.F., *Idle Hands, Clenched Fists: The Depression in a Shipyard Town*, (Nottingham, 1987); Lane, T., 'Some Merseyside militants of the 1930s', in Hikins, H.R., *Building the Union: Studies on the Growth of the Workers' Movement: Merseyside, 1756–1967*, (Liverpool, 1973), pp. 153–177; Shallice, A., *"Remember Birkenhead!"*, (Liverpool, 1982).

and 1932 with the downturn in shipbuilding. This hardship coincided with Labour losing control of the council in November 1931, and 'the tenor of local politics became highly charged in the spring and summer of 1932'. Headlines in the local press such as 'Long Live the Means Test' did nothing to soothe passions. Demonstrations against the Means Test and in favour of increased relief for the unemployed had been initiated by Labour and trade union leaders, and it was only in September that they were outflanked by a more radical set of demands from the NUWM. Cook and Stevenson argue, on very slender evidence, that the legacy of sectarian violence had something to do with the outbreak of the riots, but more convincingly assert that 'customary antagonism towards the police' was an important element behind the rioters' anger. Once rioting took place, Labour leaders were quick to disown the violent turn of events, and the subsequent municipal elections only went to confirm the strength of the support for Labour in the city, and the marginal influence of the NUWM and the Communist Party in electoral terms.

The Communist Party had put up candidates for municipal elections in Birkenhead occasionally before 1932, in Argyle and Clifton wards, with little success. In 1932, though, six Communists stood, including two who had been recently sentenced for their part in the riots, Joe Rawlings, the local leader of the NUWM, and Sid Greenwood. The issue of unemployment and the activities of the NUWM on behalf of the unemployed were, naturally, the centrepieces of their campaign. However, the memory of the events of less than two months previously did not seem to work in their favour. The Communists' most successful candidate in terms of votes cast was Bert Pinguey in Clifton ward, with 254 votes, and four of the other candidates got over 200 votes, but in percentage terms the Communist share of the vote was minimal, the best being the combined share of 7.3 per cent achieved by the two candidates in Argyle. The real feature of the 1932 elections was in fact the big recovery by Labour from its reverses of 1931, with the overall Labour vote going up from 36.5 per cent to 45.4 per cent. Even in what might be regarded as the most propitious of circumstances, then, the impact of the NUWM did little to increase the political appeal of the Communist Party. Birkenhead was no exception to the general picture of electoral failure by the party that has been drawn elsewhere.[23]

One other aspect of the municipal politics of Birkenhead is worth considering briefly now, relating to the question of gender. It is interesting to note that women seemed to play a more significant role here than in most other boroughs, especially as regards the Labour Party. Some of the most prominent Labour leaders in Birkenhead were women, including the first Labour mayor, Mrs M.A. Mercer. Looking at the municipal election candidates in the borough, more than 10 per cent of all candidatures for all parties were won by women (sixty-two out of 596). Labour, with 14.2 per cent of its candidates being women (thirty-three out of 233), had the highest proportion, with the Conservatives and Liberals having 9.0 and 4.5 per cent respectively. The proportion of female Labour candidates was much higher than that for Liverpool (8.7 per cent),[24] for no

---

[23] See Cook and Stevenson, *The Slump*, pp. 127–144.
[24] Davies, *Liverpool Labour*, p. 182.

obvious reasons in the light of the limited evidence available here, especially given the importance in Birkenhead of two male-dominated employment sectors like shipbuilding and the port industry, and the significant part played in the local Labour Party by the unions representing these sectors. The figure is even higher than that for Birmingham (13.1 per cent), as shown later in this volume,[25] even though women played a much greater role in Birmingham's local economy and workforce. What this suggests is that questions of gender and politics cannot be reduced simply to material factors, and that social and cultural influences and traditions need to be considered to fully explain differences in localities. It is to be hoped that future local studies will take up these issues in depth.

In conclusion, Birkenhead was a borough with complex and sometimes contradictory features. Based primarily on shipbuilding and docks, it was also the residence of a substantial middle class. While marked by sectarian division, its politics were not as profoundly affected by this as might be expected. A tradition of Lib-Labism blended in with the rise of the post-1918 Labour Party in municipal politics, but remained distinct at parliamentary elections, at least in part due to considerations of free trade and defence policy. Labour's control of the council for eight of the inter-war years made Birkenhead one of Labour's strongest boroughs, but the politics of the council were perhaps all the more bitter for that. The manipulation of aldermanic elections to party advantage and the gerrymandering of ward boundaries were the result of this bitter political struggle. In 1932, as well, the struggle moved from the council chamber to the streets, and other more radical political forces became significant. But this was only a temporary phenomenon, and did not mark a sea-change in the politics of the borough. Birkenhead was as much a Labour borough in the inter-war years as was possible, in a way that was to become much more common in the main industrial towns and cities of the post-1945 period.

---

[25]   See below, pp. 228–229.

Table 5.1   Predicted effect of 1934 boundary changes on Labour representation on Birkenhead council

Old boundaries 1932–33			New boundaries 1934–36		
Ward	All councillors	Probable Labour councillors	Ward	All councillors	Labour councillors
Argyle	6	6	Argyle	3	3
Bebington	3	0	Bebington	3	0
Bidston	1	1	Cathcart	3	3
Claughton	3	0	Claughton	3	0
Cleveland	6	6	Cleveland	3	3
Clifton	6	6	Clifton	3	3
Egerton	6	0	Devonshire	3	0
Grange	6	6	Egerton	3	0
Mersey	3	3	Gilbrook	3	2
Oxton	3	0	Grange	3	0
Prenton	2	0	Holt	3	2
Wirral	3	0	Mersey	3	3
Total	**48**	**28**	Oxton	3	0
			Prenton	3	0
			St James's	3	3
			Upton	3	1
			Total	**48**	**23**

Table 5.2 Voters per ward in Birkenhead before and after 1934 redistribution

'Labour' wards pre-1934				'Labour' wards post-1934		
Ward	Voters	Coun-cillors	Voters per councillor	Ward	Voters	Coun-cillors	Voters per councillor
Argyle	6,043	6	1,007	Argyle	4,626	3	1,542
Bidston	1,187	1	1,187	Cathcart	6,248	3	2,083
Cleveland	12,253	6	2,042	Cleveland	5,096	3	1,699
Clifton	10,052	6	1,675	Clifton	4,888	3	1,629
Grange	11,334	6	1,889	Gilbrook	4,465	3	1,488
Mersey	3,385	3	1,128	Mersey	5,480	3	1,827
Total	**44,254**	**28**	**1,581**	St James's	4,608	3	1,536
				Total	**35,411**	**21**	**1,686**

'Non-Labour' wards pre-1934				'Non-Labour' wards post-1934		
Ward	Voters	Coun-cillors	Voters per councillor	Ward	Voters	Coun-cillors	Voters per councillor
Bebington	2,597	3	866	Bebington	4,036	3	1,345
Claughton	4,311	3	1,437	Claughton	2,944	3	981
Egerton	11,113	6	1,852	Devonshire	3,967	3	1,322
Oxton	1,926	3	642	Egerton	5,000	3	1,667
Prenton	1,321	2	661	Grange	4,524	3	1,508
Wirral	2,600	3	867	Holt	4,408	3	1,469
Total	**23,868**	**20**	**1,193**	Oxton	2,044	3	681
				Prenton	1,935	3	645
				Upton	3,385	3	1,128
				Total	**32,243**	**27**	**1,194**
All wards pre-1934	**68,122**	**48**	**1,419**	**All wards post-1934**	**67,654**	**48**	**1,409**

A guide to further reading

Newspapers

Birkenhead Advertiser
Birkenhead News
Liverpool Daily Post

Works of reference

Liverpool and Merseyside Official Red Book

Secondary sources

Birkenhead Corporation, *The County Borough of Birkenhead: The Official Handbook*, (Cheltenham, no date).
Boumphrey, I., *Birkenhead: A Pictorial History*, (Chichester, 1995).
Caradog Jones, G., *Social Survey of Merseyside*, (Liverpool , 1924), 3 vols.
Davies, S., *Liverpool Labour: Social and Political Influences on the Development of the Labour Party in Liverpool, 1900–1939*, (Keele, 1996).
Fogarty, M.P., *Prospects of the Industrial Areas of Great Britain*, (London, 1945).
Hikins, H.R., *Building the Union: Studies on the Growth of the Workers' Movement: Merseyside, 1756–1967*, (Liverpool, 1973),
Kelly, S.F., *Idle Hands, Clenched Fists: The Depression in a Shipyard Town*, (Nottingham, 1987).
Lea, M., *Birkenhead, 1877–1974*, (Birkenhead, 1974).
McCulloch, A.L., *The Headland with the Birches: A History of Birkenhead*, (Birkenhead, 1991).
McIntyre, W.R.S., *Birkenhead: Yesterday and Today*, (2nd edn, Liverpool, 1948).
Merseyside Socialist Research Group, *Genuinely Seeking Work: Mass Unemployment on Merseyside in the 1930s*, (Birkenhead, 1992).
Neal, F., 'The Birkenhead Garibaldi Riots of 1862', *Transactions of the Historic Society of Lancashire and Cheshire*, vol. 131, (1981).
O'Hara, J., (ed.), *Birkenhead: Guide to Commercial and Industrial Facilities*, (Birkenhead, 1928).
Pelling, H., *Social Geography of British Elections 1885–1910*, (Aldershot, 1994).
Scott, P.A., 'Aspects of the Urban Geography of Birkenhead', (B.A. dissertation, University of Liverpool, 1968).
Shallice, A., *"Remember Birkenhead!"*, (Liverpool, 1982).
Social Science Department, University of Liverpool, *Handbook of Social Statistics Relating to Merseyside*, (Liverpool, 1938).
Waller, P.J., *Democracy and Sectarianism: A Political and Social History of Liverpool, 1868–1939*, (Liverpool, 1981).

Birkenhead wards 1919–1933

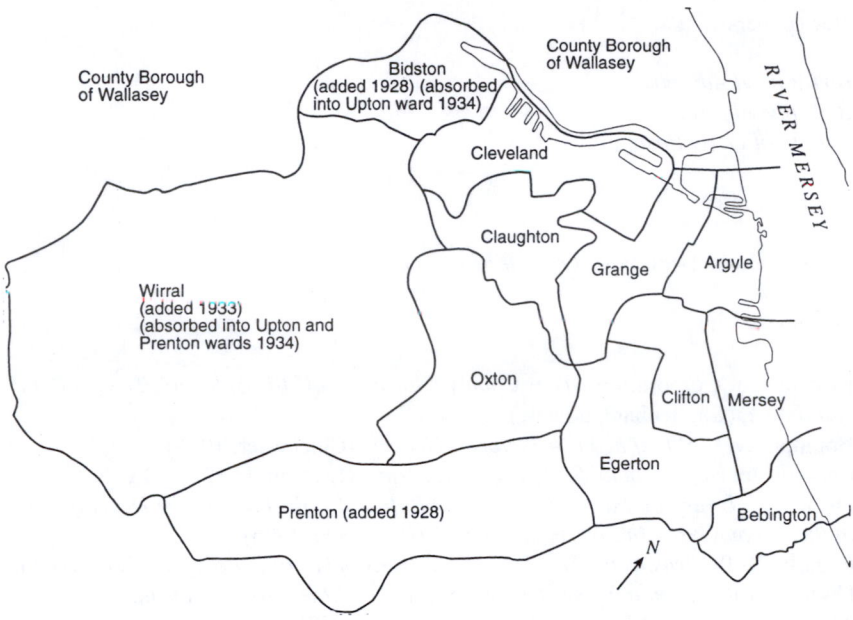

Birkenhead wards 1934–1938

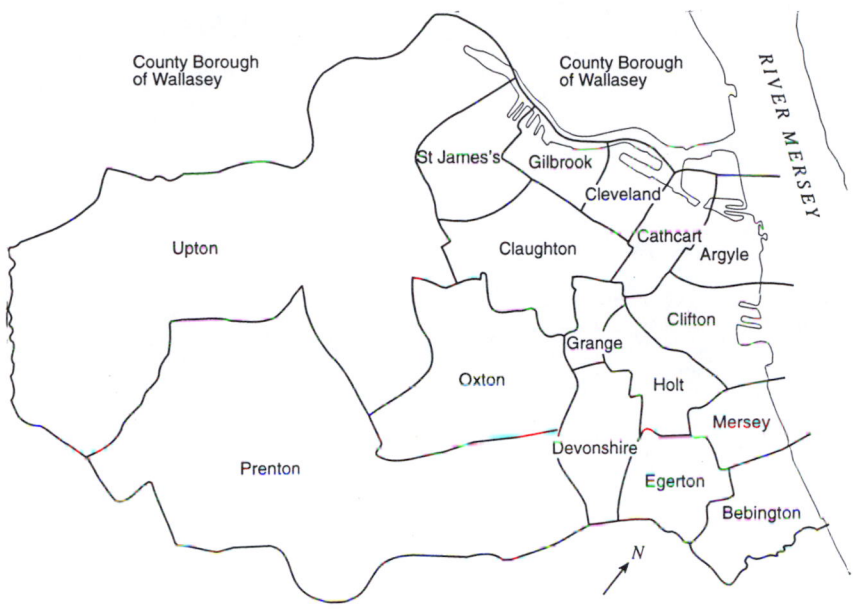

County Borough
of Wallasey

County Borough
of Wallasey

RIVER MERSEY

St James's

Gilbrook

Cleveland

Cathcart

Argyle

Upton

Claughton

Clifton

Grange

Oxton

Holt

Mersey

Prenton

Devonshire

Egerton

Bebington

N

Persons aged fourteen and over classified by industry 1931

	Male	%	Female	%	Total	%
Chemicals, paints, etc.	1,775	3.7	1,171	6.1	2,946	4.4
- Greases, glue, etc.	*1,492*	*3.1*	*1,116*	*5.8*	*2,608*	*3.9*
Metal and engineering	9,548	19.9	273	1.4	9,821	14.6
- Shipbuilding and repair	*7,499*	*15.7*	*74*	*0.4*	*7,573*	*11.3*
Food, drink and tobacco	1,744	3.6	991	5.2	2,735	4.1
Building	3,566	7.5	33	0.2	3,599	5.4
Transport	11,166	23.3	320	1.7	11,486	17.1
- Rail	*2,445*	*5.1*	*58*	*0.3*	*2,503*	*3.7*
- Road	*1,504*	*3.1*	*47*	*0.2*	*1,551*	*2.3*
- Water	*4,175*	*8.7*	*163*	*0.8*	*4,338*	*6.5*
- Docks	*2,902*	*6.1*	*41*	*0.2*	*2,943*	*4.4*
Commerce and finance	9,062	18.9	5,019	26.1	14,081	21.0
Public admin. and defence	3,730	7.8	1,415	7.4	5,145	7.7
- Local government	*3,030*	*6.3*	*1,182*	*6.2*	*4,212*	*6.3*
Professions	981	2.0	1,094	5.7	2,075	3.1
Personal service	1,611	3.4	6,976	36.3	8,587	12.8
Other	4,682	9.8	1,920	10.0	6,602	9.8
Total (a)	**47,865**		**19,212**		**67,077**	
Total population (b)	70,855		76,948		147,803	
(a) as % of (b)	67.6		25.0		45.4	
Total out of work (c)	12,043		2,124		14,167	
(c) as % of (a)	25.2		11.1		21.1	
Managerial and own account	4,855		1,847		6,702	12.7
Operative	30,967	86.4	15,241	89.2	46,208	87.3
Total (excluding out of work)	35,822		17,088		52,910	

Population statistics 1931

Ward	Acres	Population	Persons/acre	Persons/room
Argyle	294	14,520	49.4	1.18
Bebington	247	6,274	25.4	0.85
Bidston	443	3,265	7.4	1.37
Claughton	435	8,725	20.1	0.73
Cleveland	668	29,722	44.5	1.06
Clifton	294	21,530	73.2	0.85
Egerton	627	22,688	36.2	0.74
Grange	332	25,782	77.7	0.96
Mersey	206	8,044	39.0	1.04
Oxton	806	4,503	5.6	0.57
Prenton	1,643	2,750	1.7	0.54
Total	**5,995**	**147,803**	**24.7**	**0.89**

Overall position on the council 1919–38

	Position					Gains					Losses				
	C	Lab	L	Ind	Coop	C	Lab	L	Ind	Coop	C	Lab	L	Ind	Coop
1919	28	15	11	0	2	0	5	0	0	2	4	0	3	0	0
1920	29	15	10	0	2	2	0	0	0	0	0	1	1	0	0
1921	35	12	7	1	1	6	0	0	1	0	0	4	2	0	1
1922	40	6	7	3	0	5	0	0	2	0	0	6	0	0	1
1923	33	11	9	3	0	0	5	3	0	0	7	0	1	0	0
1924[a]	27	17	8	3	0	0	6	0	0	0	5	0	1	0	0
1925	26	20	8	2	0	0	3	0	0	0	2	0	0	1	0
1926	27	22	4	3	0	3	2	0	0	0	2	0	3	0	0
1927	24	29	2	1	0	0	1	0	0	0	0	0	0	1	0
1928	23	34	1	2	0	0	4	0	0	0	4	0	0	0	0
1929[a]	23	33	1	2	0	0	0	0	0	0	0	0	0	0	0
1930	24	33	1	2	0	3	0	0	0	0	0	3	0	0	0
1931	35	22	1	2	0	10	1	0	0	0	1	10	0	0	0
1932[b]	32	20	1	2	0	0	3	0	0	0	3	0	0	0	0
1933[a]	36	25	1	1	0	0	4	0	0	0	4	0	0	0	0
1934	31	32	1	0	0	0	7	0	0	0	6	0	0	1	0
1935	30	33	1	0	0	1	0	0	0	0	0	1	0	0	0
1936	31	32	1	0	0	3	1	0	0	0	1	3	0	0	0
1937[a]	34	28	1	0	0	3	0	0	0	0	0	3	0	0	0
1938[c]	35	26	1	0	0	1	0	0	0	0	0	1	0	0	0

Aldermen 1919–38

1919 C–9, Lab–2, L–3
1920 C–9, Lab–2, L–3
1921 C–9, Lab–2, L–3
1922 C–9, Lab–2, L–3
1923 C–9, Lab–2, L–3
1924 C–9, Lab–2, L–3
1925 C–9, Lab–2, L–3
1926 C–9, Lab–2, L–2, Ind–1
1927 C–6, Lab–7, L–1, Ind–1
1928 C–6, Lab–7, Ind–2

1929 C–6, Lab–7, Ind–2
1930 C–3, Lab–10, Ind–2
1931 C–3, Lab–10, Ind–2
1932[b] C–3, Lab–5, Ind–2
1933 C–9, Lab–5, L–1, Ind–1
1934 C–10, Lab–5, L–1
1935 C–8, Lab–7, L–1
1936 C–6, Lab–9, L–1
1937 C–6, Lab–9, L–1
1938[c] C–6, Lab–7, L–1

[a] 1924, 1929, 1933, 1937 - 1 seat vacant.
[b] 1932 - 5 aldermanic seats vacant.
[c] 1938 - 2 aldermanic seats vacant.

Municipal elections: winning party 1919–28

Ward	1919	1920	1921	1922	1923	1924	1925	1926	1927	1928
Argyle (1)	Lab	C	C	Lab	Lab	Lab	Lab	Lab	Lab	Lab
Argyle (2)	Lab	C	C	C	Lab	Lab	Lab	Lab	Lab	Lab
Bebington	C	C	C	**C**	**C**	**C**	C	C	C	Lab
Bidston	-	-	-	-	-	-	-	-	-	-
Cathcart	-	-	-	-	-	-	-	-	-	-
Claughton	Lab	C	C	C	L	C	C	C	C	C
Cleveland (1)	Lab	**Lab**	Lab	C	Lab	Lab	Lab	Lab	Lab	Lab
Cleveland (2)	Lab	**Lab**	C	Ind	Lab	Lab	Ind	Lab	Lab	Lab
Clifton (1)	Coop	C	L	C	Lab	C	Lab	Lab	Lab	Lab
Clifton (2)	Coop	L	C	C	C	Lab	C	Lab	Lab	Lab
Devonshire	-	-	-	-	-	-	-	-	-	-
Egerton (1)	L	C	**C**	**C**	L	C	C	C	L	C
Egerton (2)	C	C	**L**	**L**	L	L	L	C	C	C
Gilbrook	-	-	-	-	-	-	-	-	-	-
Grange (1)	Lab	C	Ind	Ind	Lab	Lab	C	Lab	Lab	Lab
Grange (2)	Lab	C	C	C	Lab	Ind	Lab	Lab	Lab	Lab
Holt	-	-	-	-	-	-	-	-	-	-
Mersey	C	C	C	C	C	C	C	Lab	C	Lab
Oxton (1)	C	**C**	**C**	**C**	**C**	**C**	**C**	**C**	**C**	**C**
Oxton (2)	-	-	-	-	-	-	-	-	-	-
Prenton (1)	-	-	-	-	-	-	-	-	-	-
Prenton (2)	-	-	-	-	-	-	-	-	-	-
St James's	-	-	-	-	-	-	-	-	-	-
Upton	-	-	-	-	-	-	-	-	-	-

Municipal elections: party wins per year 1919–28

	1919	1920	1921	1922	1923	1924	1925	1926	1927	1928
Summary										
C	4	11	10	10	4	6	7	5	5	4
Lab	7	2	1	1	7	6	5	9	8	10
L	1	1	2	1	3	1	1	0	1	0
Other	2	0	1	2	0	1	1	0	0	0
Total	14	14	14	14	14	14	14	14	14	14
Turnout %	**45.3**	**54.2**	**49.0**	**54.0**	**53.7**	**53.8**	**57.5**	**54.5**	**49.5**	**52.7**
Labour %	**37.0**	**35.6**	**30.3**	**39.1**	**38.4**	**34.9**	**28.2**	**46.7**	**46.7**	**48.9**

Municipal elections: winning party 1929–38

Ward	1929	1930	1931	1932	1933	1934	1935	1936	1937	1938
Argyle (1)	Lab	Lab	C	Lab	Lab	Lab	**Lab**	Lab	Lab	Lab
Argyle (2)	Lab	Lab	C	Lab	Lab	-	-	-	-	-
Bebington	C	C	C	C	C	C	C	C	C	C
Bidston	-	-	Lab	-	-	-	-	-	-	-
Cathcart	-	-	-	-	-	**Lab**	**Lab**	**Lab**	Lab	**Lab**
Claughton	C	C	C	C	C	**C**	C	C	C	C
Cleveland (1)	Lab	Lab	C	Lab	Lab	**Lab**	Lab	Lab	**Lab**	**Lab**
Cleveland (2)	Lab	Lab	C	Lab	Lab	-	-	-	-	-
Clifton (1)	Lab	C	C	Lab	Lab	Lab	Lab	Lab	Lab	Lab
Clifton (2)	Lab	C	C	Lab	Lab	-	-	Lab	-	-
Devonshire	-	-	-	-	-	C	C	C	C	C
Egerton (1)	C	L	C	C	C	C	C	C	C	C
Egerton (2)	C	C	C	C	C	-	-	-	-	-
Gilbrook	-	-	-	-	-	Lab	Lab	C	Void	Lab
Grange (1)	Lab	C	C	Lab	Lab	C	C	C	C	C
Grange (2)	Lab	Lab	C	Lab	Lab	-	-	-	-	-
Holt	-	-	-	-	-	Lab	Lab	C	C	C
Mersey	Lab	C	C	Lab	Lab	Lab	**Lab**	**Lab**	Lab	Lab
Oxton (1)	**C**	**C**	**C**	C	**C**	**C**	**C**	**C**	**C**	**C**
Oxton (2)	-	-	-	-	-	-	-	**C**	-	-
Prenton (1)	-	**C**	**C**	-	**C**	C	**C**	**C**	**C**	**C**
Prenton (2)	-	-	-	-	-	C	-	-	-	-
St James's	-	-	-	-	-	Lab	Lab	Lab	C	Lab
Upton	-	-	-	-	-	Lab	C	C	C	C

Municipal elections: party wins per year 1929–38

	1929	1930	1931	1932	1933	1934	1935	1936	1937	1938
C	5	9	15	5	6	8	8	11	10	9
Lab	9	5	1	9	9	9	8	7	5	7
L	0	1	0	0	0	0	0	0	0	0
Others	0	0	0	0	0	0	0	0	0	0
Total	14	15	16	14	15	17	16	18	15	16
Turnout %	40.3	45.8	59.6	52.8	47.9	42.9	50.4	47.8	48.8	46.3
Labour %	54.9	40.9	36.5	45.4	53.8	49.6	41.2	38.9	40.4	41.1

Municipal elections: party wins per ward 1919–38

	C	Lab	L	Other	Total	Turnout %	Labour % of all votes
Argyle	7	28	0	0	35	48.4	55.0
Bebington	19	1	0	0	20	51.5	34.1
Bidston	0	1	0	0	1	79.7	58.7
Cathcart	0	5	0	0	5	44.4	64.3
Claughton	18	1	1	0	20	56.8	22.6
Cleveland	4	29	0	2	35	49.3	62.6
Clifton	11	21	2	2	36	48.2	39.3
Devonshire	5	0	0	0	5	47.7	7.9
Egerton	26	0	9	0	35	50.7	20.5
Gilbrook	1	3	0	0	4	50.2	52.1
Grange	13	19	0	3	35	51.0	44.4
Holt	3	2	0	0	5	45.2	46.6
Mersey	10	10	0	0	20	47.5	48.8
Oxton	21	0	0	0	21	57.9	5.7
Prenton	9	0	0	0	9	47.6	-
St James's	1	4	0	0	5	53.7	52.8
Upton	4	1	0	0	5	59.6	35.0
Total	**152**	**125**	**12**	**7**	**296**	**50.3**	**41.6**

Seats won by Labour as a percentage of all wins 1919–38   **42.2**

Parliamentary election results

Birkenhead East constituency
(the following wards [1918 boundaries] were included in East: Argyle, Bebington, Clifton, Egerton, Mersey)

General election	Winner	Conservative %	Labour %	Liberal %
14 Dec. 1918	Co C	64.5	26.7	8.8
15 Nov. 1922	L	42.2	-	57.8
6 Dec. 1923	L	36.5	-	63.5
29 Oct. 1924	C	40.3	26.7	33.0
30 May 1929	L	32.3	31.8	35.9
27 Oct. 1931	L	-	26.8	73.2
14 Nov. 1935	L	28.6	23.3	48.1

Birkenhead West constituency
(the following wards [1918 boundaries] were included in West: Claughton, Cleveland, Grange, Oxton)

General election	Winner	Conservative %	Labour %	Liberal %
14 Dec. 1918	Co C	59.4	31.0	9.6
15 Nov. 1922	C	54	46.0	-
6 Dec. 1923	Lab	44.2	55.8	-
29 Oct. 1924	C	50.7	49.3	-
30 May 1929	Lab	39.5	45.9	14.6
27 Oct. 1931	C	63.8	36.2	-
14 Nov. 1935	C	55.9	44.1	-

Argyle ward
(two elected each year until 1934; thereafter one)

Candidate	Party	Votes	%	Electors	Turnout	Gains
1919						
F. Godsell	Lab	1,260	32.2	4,692	46.7	Lab from C
Mrs M.A. Mercer	Lab	987	25.2			Lab from C
W.M. Furnival*	C	706	18.0			
E. Youds	C	695	17.8			
A. McLellan	L	264	6.7			
Total votes		3,912				
Total voters		2,191				
1920						
J. Merritt*	C	1,435	27.9	4,741	56.0	C from L
W.M. Furnival	C	1,310	25.4			
H. Cushing	Lab	1,220	23.7			
J.A. Wood	Lab	1,184	23.0			
Total votes		5,149				
Total voters		2,656				
1921						
W.A. Kidd	C	1,341	28.0	4,648	56.0	C from Lab
J. Johnson	C	1,216	25.3			C from Lab
E.W. Mercer	Lab	856	17.8			
A. Fyles	Lab	804	16.8			
M.C. Ellis	L	580	12.1			
Total votes		4,797				
Total voters		2,602				
1922						
Mrs M.A. Mercer*	Lab	1,383	31.6	5,096	45.8	
E.A. Roberts	C	1,346	30.7			C from Lab
T. McLellan	Lab	1,281	29.2			
A. Constantine	L	373	8.5			
Total votes		4,383				
Total voters		2,335				
1923						
F. Tweedle	Lab	1,433	26.6	5,380	51.4	Lab from C
T. McLellan	Lab	1,429	26.5			Lab from C
J. Merritt*	C	1,314	24.4			
J.A.S. Hassal*	C	1,211	22.5			
Total votes		5,387				
Total voters		2,763				

Argyle ward *(continued)*

Candidate	Party	Votes	%	Electors	Turnout	Gains
1924						
A.E. Farlow	Lab	1,365	25.9	5,614	48.1	Lab from C
H. Booth	Lab	1,362	25.9			Lab from C
J. Johnson*	C	1,309	24.8			
Mrs I.M. Alty	C	1,232	23.4			
Total votes		5,268				
Total voters		2,702				
1925						
Mrs M.A. Mercer*	Lab	2,009	32.1	5,769	56.1	Lab from C
E.A. Newman	Lab	1,737	27.7			
E.A. Roberts*	C	1,284	20.5			
W.R. Dalzell	C	1,237	19.7			
Total votes		6,267				
Total voters		3,239				
1926						
T. McLellan*	Lab	1,953	28.7	5,855	59.2	-
E. Tweedle*	Lab	1,932	28.3			
J. Johnson	C	1,921	28.2			
S.E. Dutton	C	1,009	14.8			
Total votes		6,815				
Total voters		3,467				
1927						
A.E. Farlow*	Lab	1,422	26.1	5,943	49.5	-
S. Parker	Lab	1,326	24.4			
E.V. Couche	C	978	18.0			
E.A. Roberts	C	931	17.1			
T.M. Thompson	Ind	784	14.4			
Total votes		5,441				
Total voters		2,941				
1928						
Mrs A.M. Allen*	Lab	1,665	32.3	5,665	54.2	-
E.A. Newman*	Lab	1,631	31.6			
E.B. Caldwell	C	1,130	21.9			
D. Walsh	L	397	7.7			
A.E. Delf	L	331	6.4			
Total votes		5,154				
Total voters		3,071				

Argyle ward *(continued)*

Candidate	Party	Votes	%	Electors	Turnout	Gains
1929						
T. McLellan*	Lab	1,517	41.0	6,538	36.0	–
P. Allery*	Lab	1,295	35.0			
E.B. Caldwell	C	884	23.9			
Total votes		3,696				
Total voters		2,356				
1930						
J.P. Noon*	Lab	1,127	27.9	6,141	42.3	–
A.E. Farlow*	Lab	1,104	27.3			
E.B. Caldwell	C	1,074	26.6			
Mrs E.C. Harvey	C	627	15.5			
W.H. Bishop	Com	108	2.7			
Total votes		4,040				
Total voters		2,599				
1931						
E.B. Caldwell	C	1,832	28.0	6,063	56.0	C from Lab
W.M. Furnival	C	1,808	27.6			C from Lab
Mrs A.M. Allen*	Lab	1,273	19.4			
E.A. Newman*	Lab	1,232	18.8			
J. Rawlings	Com	212	3.2			
Mrs H. Barriskell	Com	197	3.0			
Total votes		6,554				
Total voters		3,393				
1932						
Mrs A.M. Mercer	Lab	1,639	27.7	5,982	52.1	–
P. Allery*	Lab	1,506	25.4			
A.V. Crutchley	C	1,252	21.1			
W.M. Shennan	C	1,093	18.5			
J. Rawlings	Com	227	3.8			
W.E. Morris	Com	207	3.5			
Total votes		5,924				
Total voters		*3,118*				

Argyle ward *(continued)*

Candidate	Party	Votes	%	Electors	Turnout	Gains
1933						
E.A. Newman	Lab	1,650	29.7	6,043	47.5	-
R. Shaw	Lab	1,648	29.6			
W.J. Parry	C	947	17.0			
C.E. Vines	C	930	16.7			
S.R. Greenwood	Com	196	3.5			
J. Rawlings	Com	192	3.5			
Total votes		5,563				
Total voters		2,870				
1934						
H. Dawson	Lab	1,234	66.8	4,626	39.9	Lab from C
R. Snape	C	613	33.2			
Total votes		1,847				
1935						
P.A. Allery*	Lab	Unopp.	-	4,368	-	-
1936						
E.A. Newman*	Lab	926	57.4	4,293	37.6	-
P.A. Wilson	R	688	42.6			
Total votes		1,614				
1937						
H. Dawson*	Lab	976	57.1	4,064	42.1	-
W. Woollett	C	733	42.9			
Total votes		1,709				
1938						
P.A. Allery*	Lab	845	58.4	3,865	37.4	-
E.R. Caldwell	C	601	41.6			
Total votes		1,446				

Overall Labour vote   **55.0%**   **Overall turnout**   **48.4%**

Bebington ward

Candidate	Party	Votes	%	Electors	Turnout	Gains
1919						
W.H. Bishop	C	398	56.3	1,229	57.5	-
J.A. Wood	Lab	160	22.6			
A.C.G. Wallace	L	149	21.1			
Total votes		707				
1920						
E.H. Hoblyn	C	640	79.8	1,241	64.6	-
A. Dodworth	Lab	162	20.2			
Total votes		802				
1921						
W.D. Woodin	C	569	69.3	1,276	64.3	C from L
G.J. Jackson*	L	252	30.7			
Total votes		821				
1922						
W.H. Bishop*	C	Unopp.	-	1,293	-	-
1923						
E.H. Hoblyn*	C	Unopp.	-		-	-
1924						
W.D. Woodin*	C	Unopp.	-	1,425	-	-
1925						
G.P. Dennis	C	560	54.8	1,578	64.7	-
M.W. Roberts	L	461	45.2			
Total votes		1,021				
1926						
W.H. Bishop	C	541	48.2	1,988	56.4	-
P. Allery	Lab	405	36.1			
T. Cuthbert	L	176	15.7			
Total votes		1,122				
1927						
H. Halsall*	C	691	68.4	2,107	47.9	-
Mrs M. Buckley	Lab	319	31.6			
Total votes		1,010				

Bebington ward *(continued)*

Candidate	Party	Votes	%	Electors	Turnout	Gains
1928						
Mrs M.E. Elliott	Lab	420	27.4	2,280	67.3	Lab from
H. Lees	C	399	26.0			Ind C
S.H. Price	L	397	25.9			
G.P. Dennis*	Ind C	319	20.8			
Total votes		1,535				
1929						
D. Ravenscroft	C	663	56.9	2,555	45.6	-
J. Miller	Lab	503	43.1			
Total votes		1,166				
1930						
H. Halsall*	C	728	67.0	2,494	43.5	-
W.J. Hughes	Lab	358	33.0			
Total votes		1,086				
1931						
C.R.E. Nottingham	C	1,069	70.8	2,518	59.9	C from Lab
Mrs M.E. Elliott*	Lab	440	29.2			
Total votes		1,509				
1932						
D. Ravenscroft*	C	787	53.8	2,592	56.4	-
J. Miller	Lab	643	44.0			
Mrs D. Anderson	Com	32	2.2			
Total votes		1,462				
1933						
W.M. Shennan*	C	714	54.0	2,597	50.9	-
Mrs E. Ward	Lab	609	46.0			
Total votes		1,323				
1934						
J. Baxter*	C	980	54.4	4,036	44.7	-
N.G.L. Percival	Lab	779	43.2			
W.E. Morris	Com	44	2.4			
Total votes		1,803				
1935						
G. Williams	C	1,209	56.7	4,109	51.9	-
N.G.L. Percival	Lab	922	43.3			
Total votes		2,131				

Bebington ward *(continued)*

Candidate	Party	Votes	%	Electors	Turnout	Gains
1936						
T.W.A. Baty	C	1,162	65.2	4,120	43.2	-
Mrs E. Ward	Lab	619	34.8			
Total votes		1,781				
1937						
M. Raney-Smith	C	1,179	56.4	4,081	51.2	-
W. Richardson	Lab	910	43.6			
Total votes		2,089				
1938						
G. Williams*	C	1,157	63.6	4,186	43.4	-
W. Richardson	Lab	661	36.4			
Total votes		1,818				

Overall Labour vote		**34.1%**			**Overall turnout**	**51.5%**

Bidston ward
*(added in 1928, but absorbed into Upton ward in the 1934 reorganisation;
no November election held until 1931)*

Candidate	Party	Votes	%	Electors	Turnout	Gains
1928						
(no election)						
1929						
(no election)						
1930						
(no election)						
1931						
M.M. Forsythe	Lab	561	58.7	1,198	79.7	Lab from C
H. Deverill*	C	394	41.3			
Total votes		955				
1932						
(no election)				1,187		
1933						
(no election)						

Overall Labour vote **58.7%** **Overall turnout** **79.7%**

Cathcart ward
(created in 1934 reorganisation, previously part of Grange ward)

Candidate	Party	Votes	%	Electors	Turnout	Gains
1934						
H.D. Shakeshaft	Lab	Unopp.	-	6,248	-	-
1935						
T.E. Anderson	Lab	Unopp.	-	6,061	-	-
1936						
W.E. Power	Lab	Unopp.	-	5,842	-	-
1937						
H.D. Shakeshaft*	Lab	1,589	64.3	5,573	44.4	-
J.T. Higgins	C	883	35.7			
Total votes		2,472				
1938						
W.H. Egan	Lab	Unopp.	-		-	-
Overall Labour vote		**64.3%**			**Overall turnout**	**44.4%**

Claughton ward

Candidate	Party	Votes	%	Electors	Turnout	Gains
1919						
W.H. Boston	Lab	884	43.7	3,201	63.3	Lab from L
S. Woodward	C	740	36.5			
H. Bickersteth*	L	401	19.8			
Total votes		2,025				
1920						
W.H.B. Yeo*	C	1,089	63.2	3,308	52.1	-
Mrs W.A. Moore	Lab	633	36.8			
Total votes		1,722				
1921						
W.H. Major*	C	1,142	68.2	3,411	49.1	-
E.J. Davis	Lab	532	31.8			
Total votes		1,674				
1922						
J.H. Clegg	C	1,018	52.8	3,406	56.6	C from Lab
D.P. Garner	Lab	491	25.5			
Mrs M.A. Davis	Ind	418	21.7			
Total votes		1,927				
1923						
D. Evans	L	1,007	46.2	3,475	62.7	L from C
W.H.B. Yeo*	C	755	34.6			
A. Fyles	Lab	417	19.1			
Total votes		2,179				
1924						
H. van Gruisen	C	963	39.9	3,524	68.5	-
A.G.W. Owen	L	899	37.3			
H. Collard	Lab	551	22.8			
Total votes		2,413				
1925						
J.H. Clegg*	C	1,037	41.9	3,689	67.1	-
A.G.W. Owen	L	966	39.0			
Mrs A. Jones-Davies	Lab	474	19.1			
Total votes		2,477				

Claughton ward *(continued)*

Candidate	Party	Votes	%	Electors	Turnout	Gains
1926						
R.B. Toosey	C	1,170	51.4	3,745	60.8	C from L
D. Evans*	L	1,107	48.6			
Total votes		2,277				
1927						
H. van Gruisen*	C	1,250	54.8	3,783	60.3	-
W. Davies	Lab	647	28.4			
A.E. Delf	L	383	16.8			
Total votes		2,280				
1928						
J.H. Clegg*	C	1,569	68.9	3,842	59.2	-
W. Davies	Lab	707	31.1			
Total votes		2,276				
1929						
R.B. Toosey*	C	1,351	67.9	4,249	46.9	-
W. Davies	Lab	640	32.1			
Total votes		1,991				
1930						
H. van Gruisen*	C	1,460	62.7	4,166	55.9	-
M.G. Wilkinson	Lab	486	20.9			
J.E. Roberts	L	384	16.5			
Total votes		2,330				
1931						
D.P. Moseley*	C	2,174	79.5	4,227	64.7	-
Mrs M.J. Wilkinson	Lab	560	20.5			
Total votes		2,734				
1932						
F.D.E. Smith	C	1,541	67.2	4,225	54.2	-
E.A. Newman	Lab	711	31.0			
J. Gaskell	Ind	40	1.7			
Total votes		2,292				
1933						
F.H. Macdonald*	C	1,438	69.2	4,311	48.2	-
T.E. Anderson	Lab	640	30.8			
Total votes		2,078				

Claughton ward *(continued)*

Candidate	Party	Votes	%	Electors	Turnout	Gains
1934						
C.E. Vines	C	Unopp.	-	2,944	-	-
1935						
L.G. Davies	C	1,417	85.1	3,169	52.6	-
Mrs M.J. Wilkinson	Lab	249	14.9			
Total votes		1,666				
1936						
F.H. Macdonald*	C	1,279	68.0	3,173	59.3	-
F.A. Robinson	L	327	17.4			
H.L. Cottle	Lab	276	14.7			
Total votes		1,882				
1937						
C.E. Vines*	C	1,165	68.5	3,243	52.5	-
F.A. Robinson	L	536	31.5			
Total votes		1,701				
1938						
L.G. Davies*	C	1,090	73.2	3,251	45.8	-
H. Rhys	L	400	26.8			
Total votes		1,490				

Overall Labour vote   **22.6%**   **Overall turnout**   **56.8%**

Cleveland ward
(two elected each year until 1934; thereafter one)

Candidate	Party	Votes	%	Electors	Turnout	Gains
1919						
W.H. Adams*	Lab	2,306	39.0	8,408	38.9	-
F. Tweedle*	Lab	2,168	36.7			
J. Gouldson	C	633	10.7			
W. Weston	C	518	8.8			
A. Constantine	L	286	4.8			
Total votes		5,911				
Total voters		3,270				
1920						
W.H. Egan	Lab	Unopp.	-		-	-
C. McVey	Lab	Unopp.	-			
1921						
Miss M. Hickey*	Lab	1,928	33.9	8,737	44.1	
H.H. Crutchley	C	1,899	33.4			C from Lab
A. Cargill	Lab	1,859	32.7			
Total votes		5,686				
Total voters		3,852				
1922						
A.Smith	C	2,212	30.8	8,965	56.2	C from Lab
M. Halligan	Ind	1,891	26.4			Ind from Lab
W.H. Adams*	Lab	1,596	22.2			
F. Tweedle*	Lab	1,477	20.6			
Total votes		7,176				
Total voters		5,042				
1923						
W.H. Egan*	Lab	2,986	37.4	9,497	54.3	-
C. McVey*	Lab	2,830	35.5			
J. Smith	C	2,163	27.1			
Total votes		7,979				
Total voters		5,155				
1924						
A. Cargill	Lab	3,286	31.5	9,816	55.7	Lab from C
T.H. Herron	Lab	3,226	30.9			Lab from C
H.H. Crutchley*	C	2,129	20.4			
Miss M. Hickey*	C	1,800	17.2			
Total votes		10,441				
Total voters		5,466				

Cleveland ward *(continued)*

Candidate	Party	Votes	%	Electors	Turnout	Gains
1925						
T.H. Ward	Lab	3,016	38.7	10,363	54.8	Lab from C
M. Halligan*	Ind	2,709	34.7			
Mrs I.M. Alty	C	2,076	26.6			
Total votes		7,801				
Total voters		5,681				
1926						
W.H. Egan*	Lab	3,809	40.0	10,554	55.2	-
C. McVey*	Lab	3,662	38.5			
D.T. Raikes	C	2,045	21.5			
Total votes		9,516				
Total voters		5,828				
1927						
A. Cargill*	Lab	3,095	38.0	10,740	47.6	-
T.H. Herron*	Lab	3,050	37.4			
W.R. Brownell	C	2,004	24.6			
Total votes		8,149				
Total voters		5,117				
1928						
F. Garstang*	Lab	2,851	40.4	10,765	38.8	-
T.H. Ward*	Lab	2,833	40.2			
T.M. Thompson	Ind	1,368	19.4			
Total votes		7,052		3,526		
Total voters		4,177				
1929						
J.B. Birkett*	Lab	2,753	38.3	12,120	36.6	-
E.J. Davies*	Lab	2,750	38.3			
J.S. Allen	C	1,677	23.4			
Total votes		7,180				
Total voters		4,430				
1930						
A. Cargill*	Lab	2,565	25.4	12,450	42.2	-
W. Davies*	Lab	2,528	25.0			
F.H. MacDonald	C	2,521	25.0			
A.D. Toosey	C	2,480	24.6			
Total votes		10,094				
Total voters		5,255				

Cleveland ward *(continued)*

Candidate	Party	Votes	%	Electors	Turnout	Gains
1931						
H. Bullock	C	3,984	26.6	12,345	62.0	C from Lab
J. Baxter	C	3,972	26.5			C from Lab
F. Garstang*	Lab	3,518	23.5			
T.H. Ward*	Lab	3,506	23.4			
Total votes		14,980				
Total voters		7,656				
1932						
W.H. Egan	Lab	3,982	29.7	12,331	57.2	Lab from C
C. McVey	Lab	3,886	29.0			
F.H. Macdonald*	C	2,643	19.7			
G. Wharton	C	2,431	18.1			
S.R. Greenwood	Com	241	1.8			
W. Favager	Com	225	1.7			
Total votes		13,408				
Total voters		*7,057*				
1933						
A. Cargill*	Lab	4,007	32.9	12,253	51.1	-
W. Davies*	Lab	3,934	32.3			
A.E. Farlow	C	2,052	16.8			
J. Furness	C	1,997	16.4			
J. Gaskell	Com	192	1.6			
Total votes		12,182				
Total voters		6,261				
1934						
M. Halligan	Lab	Unopp.	-	5,096	-	Lab from C
1935						
T.H. Herron	Lab	1,565	67.9	4,854	47.5	-
G. Hayes	C	740	32.1			
Total votes		2,305				
1936						
A. Cargill*	Lab	1,285	69.4	4,753	38.9	-
J.T. Higgins	R	566	30.6			
Total votes		1,851				
1937						
M. Halligan*	Lab	Unopp.	-		-	-

Cleveland ward *(continued)*

Candidate	Party	Votes	%	Electors	Turnout	Gains
1938						
C. McVey	Lab	Unopp.	-		-	-

Overall Labour vote   **62.6%**   **Overall turnout**   **49.3%**

Clifton ward
(two elected each year until 1934; thereafter one)

Candidate	Party	Votes	%	Electors	Turnout	Gains
1919						
H. Triplett	Coop	1,559	29.0	8,461	41.5	Coop from C
J. Maddocks	Coop	1,482	27.6			Coop from L
W.N. Dickie*	C	1,251	23.3			
R. Frame*	L	1,080	20.1			
Total votes		5,372				
Total voters		3,513				
1920						
C.G.R. Stephens*	C	2,791	38.1	8,555	54.6	-
R.P. Fletcher*	L	1,817	24.8			
T.H. Salmon	Lab	1,451	19.8			
Mrs M.J. Herron	Lab	1,275	17.4			
Total votes		7,334				
Total voters		4,673				
1921						
W. Jackson*	L	2,400	39.7	8,622	45.9	
W. Blair	C	1,719	28.5			C from Coop
W. Green	Coop	1,029	17.0			
G.A. Price	Coop	890	14.7			
Total votes		6,038				
Total voters		3,961				
1922						
W.L. Milne	C	2,061	24.7	8,765	53.6	C from Coop
G.E. Falcon	C	1,800	21.6			
Mrs W.A. Moore	Lab	1,532	18.4			
T.N. Philip	L	1,496	18.0			
T.H. Ward	Lab	1,443	17.3			
Total votes		8,332				
Total voters		4,696				
1923						
J. Coulthard	Lab	1,989	21.1	9,081	57.6	Lab from L
J.R. Hurrell	C	1,901	20.1			
R.P. Fletcher*	L	1,846	19.5			
W. Richardson	C	1,784	18.9			
R. Frame	L	1,460	15.5			
A. King	Com	466	4.9			
Total votes		9,446				
Total voters		5,230				

Clifton ward *(continued)*

Candidate	Party	Votes	%	Electors	Turnout	Gains
1924						
W. Richardson	C	1,931	37.2	9,230	48.8	
C. Nathan	Lab	1,644	31.7			Lab from L
W. Jackson*	L	1,612	31.1			
Total votes		5,187				
Total voters		4,503				
1925						
Mrs W.A. Moore*	Lab	2,150	27.6	9,310	53.5	-
W.L. Milne*	C	2,053	26.4			
R. Harrop	C	1,959	25.2			
Mrs E.L. Foster	L	1,619	20.8			
Total votes		7,781				
Total voters		4,978				
1926						
J. Coulthard*	Lab	2,137	25.2	9,297	49.9	
H. Triplett	Lab	2,128	25.1			Lab from C
J.R. Hurrell*	C	1,685	19.9			
R. Harrop	C	1,635	19.3			
Mrs E.L. Foster	L	903	10.6			
Total votes		8,488				
Total voters		4,640				
1927						
W. Richardson*	Lab	2,068	24.5	9,212	50.0	-
C. Nathan*	Lab	1,996	23.6			
D. Redfern	C	1,843	21.8			
J.R. Hurrell	C	1,698	20.1			
C. Weaver	L	846	10.0			
Total votes		8,451				
Total voters		4,608				
1928						
Mrs W.A. Moore*	Lab	2,327	24.5	9,076	56.3	
J. Maddocks	Lab	2,275	23.9			Lab from C
W.L. Milne*	C	2,063	21.7			
Mrs R. Grant	C	2,021	21.3			
W.T.C. Hunt	L	712	7.5			
R.E. Heughan	Ind	104	1.1			
Total votes		9,502				
Total voters		5,111				

Clifton ward *(continued)*

Candidate	Party	Votes	%	Electors	Turnout	Gains
1929						
J. Coulthard*	Lab	2,090	33.3	10,098	33.0	-
H. Triplett*	Lab	2,078	33.2			
Mrs R. Grant	C	1,980	31.6			
J. Rawlings	Com	119	1.9			
Total votes		6,267				
Total voters		3,336				
1930						
C.G.R. Stephens	C	2,120	25.2	10,031	45.7	C from Lab
W.L. Milne	C	2,092	24.9			C from Lab
W. Richardson*	Lab	1,714	20.4			
M.M. Forsythe*	Lab	1,649	19.6			
W. Tudor	L	718	8.5			
J. Rawlings	Com	119	1.4			
Total votes		8,412				
Total voters		4,588				
1931						
J.H. Hogkinson	C	3,594	32.5	10,114	56.2	C from Lab
L.G. Davies	C	3,509	31.7			C from Lab
Mrs W.A. Moore*	Lab	1,991	18.0			
J. Maddocks*	Lab	1,971	17.8			
Total votes		11,065				
Total voters		5,689				
1932						
J. Coulthard	Lab	2,462	27.5	9,969	49.9	Lab from C
F. Tweedle	Lab	2,410	26.9			Lab from C
A.J. Milne	C	1,914	21.4			
Mrs R. Grant*	C	1,911	21.3			
J.H. Pinguey	Com	254	2.8			
Total votes		8,951				
Total voters		*4,973*				
1933						
R.W. Melville	Lab	2,417	27.2	10,052	45.7	Lab from C
J. Bennett	Lab	2,384	26.8			Lab from C
S.A. Jones	C	1,942	21.9			
W.L. Milne*	C	1,930	21.7			
J.H. Pinguey	Com	206	2.3			
Total votes		8,879				
Total voters		4,591				

Clifton ward *(continued)*

Candidate	Party	Votes	%	Electors	Turnout	Gains
1934						
T.H. Ward	Lab	1,142	65.0	4,888	35.9	Lab from C
E.B. Caldwell*	C	614	35.0			
Total votes		1,756				
1935						
F. Tweedle*	Lab	1,150	52.8	4,812	45.3	-
E.A. Cropper	C	1,028	47.2			
Total votes		2,178				
1936						
C.A.J. Forrester*	Lab	1,048	26.2	4,834	45.9	
A.S. Knight	Lab	983	24.6			Lab from C
C.D. Gracey	C	764	19.1			
F.H. Neal	C	695	17.4			
D. Wolfe	L	503	12.6			
Total votes		3,993				
Total voters		*2,218*				
(2 elected)						
1937						
T.H. Ward*	Lab	1,024	53.2	4,774	40.3	-
G. Bibby	C	902	46.8			
Total votes		1,926				
1938						
N.G.L. Percival	Lab	927	53.2	4,608	37.8	-
G. Bibby	C	814	46.8			
Total votes		1,741				

Overall Labour vote   **39.3%**   **Overall turnout**   **48.2%**

Devonshire ward
(created in 1934 reorganisation, previously part of Egerton ward)

Candidate	Party	Votes	%	Electors	Turnout	Gains
1934						
J.H. Hodgkinson*	C	929	54.9	3,967	42.7	-
E.E. Emmerson	L	418	24.7			
Mrs L.O. McLellan	Lab	346	20.4			
Total votes		1,693				
1935						
G.S. Prentice*	C	1,494	78.5	3,960	48.1	-
Mrs E. Hill	Lab	410	21.5			
Total votes		1,904				
1936						
H. Bullock	C	1,147	58.9	3,948	49.3	-
R. Baker	L	801	41.1			
Total votes		1,948				
1937						
J.H. Hodgkinson*	C	1,259	63.8	4,085	48.3	-
H. Rhys	L	713	36.2			
Total votes		1,972				
1938						
G.S. Prentice*	C	1,163	57.0	4,089	49.9	-
R.P. Fletcher	L	879	43.0			
Total votes		2,042				

Overall Labour vote   **7.9%**   **Overall turnout**   **47.7%**

Egerton ward
(two elected each year until 1934; thereafter one)

Candidate	Party	Votes	%	Electors	Turnout	Gains
1919
H.G. White	L	1,547	31.0	7,422	45.1	-
E.J. Hughes	C	1,291	25.9
W.E. Williams	C	1,132	22.7
G.A. Price	Lab	1,018	20.4
Total votes		4,988
Total voters		3,348
1920
H. Halsall*	C	2,412	30.8	7,389	58.6	-
W.H. Stott	C	2,401	30.7
M. Hunter	L	1,272	16.2
J.W. Longworth	Lab	883	11.3
W.R. Atkinson	Lab	863	11.0
Total votes		7,831
Total voters		4,332
1921
D.J. Clark	C	Unopp.	-		-	-
J.W. Collin	L	Unopp.	-
1922
E.J. Hughes	C	Unopp.	-	7,715	-	-
H.G. White MP	L	Unopp.	-
1923
G. Dimmer	L	2,251	26.9	7,916	54.3	L from C
E.E. Emmerson	L	2,113	25.3			L from C
G.H. Wright*	C	2,030	24.3
R.M. Evans*	C	1,973	23.6
Total votes		8,367
Total voters		4,295
1924
D.J. Clark*	C	2,339	48.8	8,055	51.9	-
R.P. Fletcher	L	1,684	35.1
J.W. Longworth	Lab	768	16.0
Total votes		4,791
Total voters		4,180

Egerton ward *(continued)*

Candidate	Party	Votes	%	Electors	Turnout	Gains
1925						
E.J. Hughes*	C	2,735	26.0	8,260	65.4	-
R. Moelwyn-Hughes	L	2,675	25.5			
A. Robinson	L	2,557	24.3			
G.S. Prentice	C	2,535	24.1			
Total votes		10,502				
Total voters		5,398				
1926						
G.S. Prentice	C	2,243	28.2	8,427	54.3	C from L
A. Boyd	C	2,229	28.0			C from L
G. Dimmer*	L	1,221	15.4			
E.E. Emmerson*	L	1,154	14.5			
F. Garstang	Lab	1,106	13.9			
Total votes		7,953				
Total voters		4,572				
1927						
R.P. Fletcher*	L	2,341	42.4	8,619	49.8	-
D. McWilliam	C	2,246	40.7			
W.H. Auld	Lab	929	16.8			
Total votes		5,516				
Total voters		4,295				
1928						
E.J. Hughes*	C	2,800	30.8	8,837	58.7	C from L
J. Merritt*	C	2,800	30.8			
H. Allsop	Lab	1,235	13.6			
F. Walton	L	1,199	13.2			
A. Smith	Lab	1,056	11.6			
Total votes		9,090				
Total voters		5,187				
1929						
A. Boyd*	C	2,380	30.1	9,749	45.1	-
G.S. Prentice*	C	2,319	29.3			
W.K. Tunna	L	1,147	14.5			
T.E. Green	Lab	1,038	13.1			
H. Platt	Lab	1,033	13.0			
Total votes		7,917				
Total voters		4,400				

Egerton ward *(continued)*

Candidate	Party	Votes	%	Electors	Turnout	Gains
1930						
R.P. Fletcher*	L	2,554	29.5	9,988	52.0	-
D. McWilliam*	C	2,297	26.5			
H.T. Dunn	C	2,206	25.5			
Mrs S. Grierson	Lab	816	9.4			
R. Melville	Lab	786	9.1			
Total votes		8,659				
Total voters		5,190				
1931						
J. Merritt*	C	4,790	40.7	10,365	58.7	-
E.J. Hughes*	C	4,664	39.6			
R. Melville	Lab	1,235	10.5			
Mrs S. Grierson	Lab	1,080	9.2			
Total votes		11,769				
Total voters		6,089				
1932						
A. Boyd*	C	3,250	40.2	10,928	45.7	-
G.S. Prentice*	C	3,235	40.0			
R. Melville	Lab	1,604	19.8			
Total votes		8,089				
Total voters		*4,993*				
1933						
D. MacWilliam*	C	3,064	33.8	11,113	42.1	-
W.E.R. Short*	C	2,930	32.4			
A.S. Knight	Lab	1,533	16.9			
Mrs A.M. Allen	Lab	1,526	16.9			
Total votes		9,053				
Total voters		4,680				
1934						
J. Furness	C	915	48.4	5,000	37.8	-
G.A. Price	Lab	682	36.1			
W.H. Tunna	L	294	15.5			
Total votes		1,891				
1935						
A. Boyd*	C	1,505	64.7	5,087	45.7	-
Mrs L.O. McLellan	Lab	821	35.3			
Total votes		2,326				

Egerton ward *(continued)*

Candidate	Party	Votes	%	Electors	Turnout	Gains
1936						
W.E.R. Short*	C	1,559	72.3	5,097	42.3	-
Mrs M.J. Herron	Lab	596	27.7			
Total votes		2,155				
1937						
J. Furness*	C	1,603	65.3	5,052	48.6	-
R.N. Melville	Lab	851	34.7			
Total votes		2,454				
1938						
A. Boyd*	C	1,476	59.3	5,130	48.5	-
S. Coulthard	Lab	1,014	40.7			
Total votes		2,490				

Overall Labour vote	**20.5%**		**Overall turnout**	**50.7%**

Gilbrook ward
(created in 1934 reorganisation, previously part of Cleveland ward)

Candidate	Party	Votes	%	Electors	Turnout	Gains
1934						
F. Garstang	Lab	1,247	62.8	4,465	44.5	Lab from C
J. Raney-Smith jun.	C	740	37.2			
Total votes		1,987				
1935						
C.H. Russell	Lab	1,092	47.7	4,288	53.4	-
C.S. Hancox	C	982	42.9			
F.A. Robinson	L	215	9.4			
Total votes		2,289				
1936						
C.S. Hancox	C	1,190	52.4	4,328	52.5	C from Lab
W. Davies*	Lab	1,083	47.6			
Total votes		2,273				
1937						
(election void – fire in ballot box)						
1938						
C.H. Russell*	Lab	1,145	51.6	4,397	50.5	-
B.M. Jager	C	1,075	48.4			
Total votes		2,220				

Overall Labour vote		**52.1%**		**Overall turnout**		**50.2%**

Grange ward
(two elected each year until 1934; thereafter one)

Candidate	Party	Votes	%	Electors	Turnout	Gains
1919						
James Platt	Lab	1,568	21.9	9,022	43.5	Lab from C
J. Coulthard	Lab	1,546	21.6			Lab from L
W. Jackson*	L	945	13.2			
A. Austin	C	898	12.5			
J.R. Saronie*	C	826	11.5			
R. Harrop	Ind	707	9.9			
J. Duff	L	674	9.4			
Total votes		7,164				
Total voters		3,928				
1920						
Dr H.G.F. Dawson*	C	2,470	30.4	9,121	46.1	C from Lab
A. Austin	C	2,245	27.6			
John Platt*	Lab	1,776	21.9			
A. Cargill	Lab	1,634	20.1			
Total votes		8,125				
Total voters		4,204				
1921						
D. Walsh	Ind	1,736	21.6	9,358	51.9	Ind from Lab
R.H. Gossage	C	1,669	20.8			C from L
J.A.S. Hassal	C	1,515	18.9			
John Platt	Lab	1,121	14.0			
C. Nathan*	Lab	1,027	12.8			
Mrs M. Hugh-Jones*	L	957	19.7			
Total votes		8,025				
Total voters		4,857				
1922						
T.M. Thompson	Ind	2,332	28.9	9,532	56.2	Ind from Lab
G.P. Dennis	C	1,962	24.3			C from Lab
James Platt*	Lab	1,409	17.5			
J. Coulthard*	Lab	1,273	15.8			
R.G. Morton	L	1,083	13.4			
Total votes		8,059				
Total voters		5,357				

Grange ward *(continued)*

Candidate	Party	Votes	%	Electors	Turnout	Gains
1923						
W.H. Adams	Lab	2,545	27.5	10,023	47.9	Lab from C
W.E. Power	Lab	2,488	26.8			Lab from C
Dr H.G.F. Dawson*	C	2,149	23.2			
Dr W.R. Dalzell*	C	2,087	22.5			
Total votes		9,269				
Total voters		4,799				
1924						
John Platt	Lab	2,422	24.0	10,232	57.5	Lab from C
D. Walsh*	Ind	2,188	21.7			
R.H. Gossage*	C	2,171	21.5			
W.H.B. Yeo	C	2,020	20.0			
R.M. Hughes	L	1,289	12.8			
Total votes		10,090				
Total voters		5,886				
1925						
E. Marquis	C	2,575	37.4	10,437	55.6	Lab from Ind
S.C. Hills	Lab	2,228	32.4			
T.M. Thompson*	Ind	2,075	30.2			
Total votes		6,878				
Total voters		5,798				
1926						
James Platt*	Lab	2,551	25.1	10,445	52.1	-
W.E. Power*	Lab	2,521	24.8			
R.H. Gossage	C	2,000	19.7			
H. Deverill	C	1,987	19.6			
T.M. Thompson	Ind	1,088	10.7			
Total votes		10,147				
Total voters		5,443				
1927						
M. Poland*	Lab	2,529	25.8	10,490	48.3	
A. Fyles	Lab	2,466	25.1			Lab from Ind
H. Deverill	C	2,434	24.8			
W.T. Dodd	C	2,379	24.3			
Total votes		9,808				
Total voters		5,070				

Grange ward *(continued)*

Candidate	Party	Votes	%	Electors	Turnout	Gains
1928						
S.C. Hills*	Lab	2,836	26.1	10,170	53.0	
T.E. Anderson	Lab	2,766	25.5			Lab from C
E. Marquis*	C	2,654	24.4			
H.D. Smith	C	2,607	24.0			
Total votes		10,863				
Total voters		5,394				
1929						
James Platt*	Lab	2,670	27.3	11,642	43.4	-
W.E. Power*	Lab	2,656	27.1			
E. Marquis	C	2,296	23.4			
H.D. Smith	C	2,174	22.2			
Total votes		9,796				
Total voters		5,047				
1930						
E. Marquis	C	3,062	42.4	11,484	45.1	C from Lab
M. Poland*	Lab	2,106	29.2			
A. Fyles*	Lab	2,047	28.4			
Total votes		7,215				
Total voters		5,181				
1931						
T.E. Jones	C	3,790	28.5	11,378	60.2	C from Lab
W.H. Ward	C	3,763	28.3			C from Lab
S.C. Hills*	Lab	2,929	22.0			
T.E. Anderson*	Lab	2,814	21.2			
Total votes		13,296				
Total voters		6,846				
1932						
W.E. Power*	Lab	2,998	26.0	11,339	56.4	-
James Platt*	Lab	2,887	25.1			
M.C. Ellis	C	2,427	21.1			
W.E.R. Short	C	2,416	21.0			
M. Halligan	Ind	791	6.9			
Total votes		11,519				
Total voters		*6,399*				

Grange ward *(continued)*

Candidate	Party	Votes	%	Electors	Turnout	Gains
1933						
S.C. Hills	Lab	3,513	31.5	11,334	51.0	Lab from C
M. Poland*	Lab	3,502	31.4			
Mrs C.A. Greggains	C	2,105	18.9			
Mrs E.C. Gossage*	C	2,033	18.2			
Total votes		11,153				
Total voters		5,780				
1934						
T.E. Jones*	C	898	41.7	4,524	47.6	-
C.H. Russell	Lab	893	41.5			
J. Jones	L	361	16.8			
Total votes		2,152				
1935						
J.F.J. Wood	C	1,400	77.3	4,496	40.3	C from Lab
W.E. Power*	Lab	410	22.7			
Total votes		1,810				
1936						
J.W. Hislop	C	1,491	65.5	4,410	51.7	C from Lab
H.H. Green	Lab	787	34.5			
Total votes		2,278				
1937						
T.E. Jones*	C	1,356	58.4	4,413	52.6	-
H.L. Cottle	Lab	967	41.6			
Total votes		2,323				
1938						
A.S. Hooper*	C	1,160	50.4	4,205	54.7	-
H.L. Cottle	Lab	1,140	49.6			
Total votes		2,300				

Overall Labour vote		**44.4%**		**Overall turnout**		**51.0%**

Holt ward
(created in 1934 reorganisation, previously part of Clifton and Egerton wards)

Candidate	Party	Votes	%	Electors	Turnout	Gains
1934						
Mrs A.L. Cochrane	Lab	920	49.3	4,408	42.4	Lab from C
L.G. Davies*	C	638	34.2			
F. Cooper	L	309	16.6			
Total votes		1,867				
1935						
J. Coulthard*	Lab	976	45.5	4,405	48.6	-
R. Harrop	C	715	33.4			
R. Baker	L	452	21.1			
Total votes		2,143				
1936						
J. Harris	C	1,051	55.0	4,402	43.4	C from Lab
R.N. Melville*	Lab	861	45.0			
Total votes		1,912				
1937						
J. King	C	1,128	56.5	4,330	46.1	C from Lab
Mrs A.L. Cochrane*	Lab	869	43.5			
Total votes		1,997				
1938						
W.S.B. Carrodus	C	968	50.3	4,257	45.2	C from Lab
J. Coulthard*	Lab	958	49.7			
Total votes		1,926				

Overall Labour vote   **46.6%**   **Overall turnout**   **45.2%**

Mersey ward

Candidate	Party	Votes	%	Electors	Turnout	Gains
1919						
J.C. Paterson	C	631	47.7	2,668	49.6	-
T. McLellan	Lab	603	45.5			
J. Poslewhite	L	90	6.8			
Total votes		1,324				
1920						
L. Lees*	C	1,028	61.3	2,659	63.0	-
T. McLellan	Lab	648	38.7			
Total votes		1,676				
1921						
H. Speed*	C	769	62.9	2,709	45.1	-
T.H. Ward	Lab	454	37.1			
Total votes		1,223				
1922						
W. Courtney	C	835	57.9	2,747	52.5	-
W.E. Power	Lab	607	42.1			
Total votes		1,442				
1923						
L. Lees*	C	895	59.6	2,873	52.3	-
James Platt	Lab	607	40.4			
Total votes		1,502				
1924						
Dr H.G.F. Dawson	C	775	53.0	2,973	49.2	-
J. Miller	Lab	424	29.0			
J.R. Radcliffe	Ind	263	18.0			
Total votes		1,462				
1925						
W. Courtney*	C	922	59.4	3,018	51.5	-
S. McLachlan	Lab	631	40.6			
Total votes		1,553				
1926						
W.M. Ramsay	Lab	917	53.9	3,009	56.6	Lab from C
L. Lees*	C	679	39.9			
Dr F. Walton	L	106	6.2			
Total votes		1,702				

Mersey ward *(continued)*

Candidate	Party	Votes	%	Electors	Turnout	Gains
1927						
Mrs J.C. Forsyth	C	733	53.3	3,001	45.9	-
M.M. Forsythe	Lab	643	46.7			
Total votes		1,376				
1928						
S.C. Eckley	Lab	821	53.4	3,009	51.1	Lab from C
J.R. Hurrell	C	716	46.6			
Total votes		1,537				
1929						
W.M. Ramsay*	Lab	896	57.9	3,354	46.2	-
R. Harrop	C	508	32.8			
E.G. Cooke	L	144	9.3			
Total votes		1,548				
1930						
Mrs J.C. Forsyth*	C	759	57.6	3,419	38.5	-
S. Rowe	Lab	558	42.4			
Total votes		1,317				
1931						
J.R. Hurrell	C	1,111	59.7	3,392	54.8	C from Lab
S.C. Eckley*	Lab	749	40.3			
Total votes		1,860				
1932						
S.C. Eckley	Lab	858	53.0	3,348	48.4	-
T. Shaw	C	702	43.3			
D.H. Evans	I Lab	60	3.7			
Total votes		1,620				
1933						
C.A.J. Forrester	Lab	1,023	59.9	3,385	50.4	Lab from C
Mrs J.C. Forsyth*	C	684	40.1			
Total votes		1,707				
1934						
J. Miller	Lab	1,442	71.4	5,480	36.9	Lab from C
Mrs Molyneux	C	434	21.5			
E.G. Cooke	L	144	7.1			
Total votes		2,020				

Mersey ward *(continued)*

Candidate	Party	Votes	%	Electors	Turnout	Gains
1935						
S.C. Eckley*	Lab	Unopp.	-	5,331	-	-
1936						
M. Poland	Lab	Unopp.	-	5,182	-	-
1937						
W.M. Ramsay*	Lab	1,269	56.3	5,086	44.3	-
P.A. Wilson	C	984	43.7			
Total votes		2,253				
1938						
S.C. Eckley*	Lab	1,036	53.6	5,021	38.5	-
P.A. Wilson	C	896	46.4			
Total votes		1,932				

Overall Labour vote   **48.8%**   **Overall turnout**   **47.5%**

Oxton ward

Candidate	Party	Votes	%	Electors	Turnout	Gains
1919						
A.H. Chalmers*	C	781	92.8	1,558	54.0	-
A. Dodsworth	Lab	61	7.2			
Total votes		842				
1920						
Miss A.A. Laird	C	Unopp.	-		-	-
1921						
S. Woodward	C	Unopp.	-	1,628	-	-
1922						
A.H. Chalmers*	C	Unopp.	-	1,674	-	-
1923						
Miss K.M. Worrall	C	Unopp.	-		-	-
1924						
S. Woodward*	C	Unopp.	-	1,749	-	-
1925						
J.A.S. Hassal*	C	Unopp.	-	1,757	-	-
1926						
Miss K.M. Worrall*	C	Unopp.	-	1,795	-	-
1927						
S. Woodward*	C	Unopp.	-	1,827	-	-
1928						
R.H. Gossage	C	Unopp.	-	1,808	-	-
1929						
Miss K.M. Worrall*	C	Unopp.	-	1,836	-	-
1930						
Dr H.G.F. Dawson	C	Unopp.	-	1,845	-	-
1931						
R.H. Gossage*	C	Unopp.	-	1,890	-	-

Oxton ward *(continued)*

Candidate	Party	Votes	%	Electors	Turnout	Gains
1932						
Miss K.M. Worrall*	C	1,108	95.4	1,905	61.0	-
T.H. Ward	Lab	54	4.6			
Total votes		1,162				
1933						
Mrs R. Grant*	C	Unopp.	-	1,926	-	-
1934						
H. Deverill*	C	Unopp.	-	2,044	-	-
1935						
Miss K.M. Worrall*	C	Unopp.	-	2,921	-	-
1936						
Mrs R. Grant*	C	Unopp.	-	2,893	-	-
T.Q. Howard	C	Unopp.	-			
(2 elected)						
1937						
H. Deverill*	C	Unopp.	-		-	-
1938						
Mrs R. Grant*	C	Unopp.	-		-	-
Overall Labour vote		**5.7%**		**Overall turnout**		**57.9%**

Prenton ward
(added in 1928, but no November election held until 1930)

Candidate	Party	Votes	%	Electors	Turnout	Gains
1928						
(no election)						
1929						
(no election)						
1930						
A.S. Gaskell*	C	Unopp.	-		-	-
1931						
A.W. Baker*	C	Unopp.	-	1,228	-	-
1932						
(no election)				1,312		
1933						
A.S. Gaskell*	C	Unopp.	-	1,321	-	-
1934						
A.W. Baker*	C	801	47.1	1,935	47.6	-
J.R. Hurrell*	C	653	38.4			
F.A. Robinson	L	247	14.5			
Total votes		1,701				
Total voters		922				
(2 elected)						
1935						
J.R. Hurrell*	C	Unopp.	-	2,234	-	-
1936						
A.S. Gaskell*	C	Unopp.	-	2,357	-	-
1937						
A.W. Baker*	C	Unopp.	-		-	-
1938						
Mrs R.N. Copeland*	C	Unopp.			-	-

Overall Labour vote		-		**Overall turnout**		**47.6%**

St James's ward
(created in 1934 reorganisation, formerly part of Cleveland and Claughton wards)

Candidate	Party	Votes	%	Electors	Turnout	Gains
1934						
H. Platt	Lab	1,397	57.2	4,608	53.0	Lab from C
H. Bullock*	C	1,046	42.8			
Total votes		2,443				
1935						
Mrs M.A. Mercer*	Lab	1,577	52.8	5,185	57.6	-
E. Greaves	C	1,411	47.2			
Total votes		2,988				
1936						
R. Shaw*	Lab	1,392	50.2	5,306	52.2	-
T.F. Muir	C	1,380	49.8			
Total votes		2,772				
1937						
J. Molyneaux	C	1,484	51.7	5,264	54.5	C from Lab
H. Platt*	Lab	1,384	48.3			
Total votes		2,868				
1938						
Mrs M.A. Mercer*	Lab	1,526	56.1	5,301	51.3	-
W.H. Pontin	C	1,193	43.9			
Total votes		2,719				

Overall Labour vote   **52.8%**   **Overall turnout**   **53.7%**

Upton ward

(added as Wirral ward in 1933, but no election held in November 1933, and absorbed along with Bidston ward into Upton ward, and part into Prenton ward, in 1934 reorganisation)

Candidate	Party	Votes	%	Electors	Turnout	Gains
1934						
A. Summers	Lab	829	51.0	3,385	48.0	Lab from Ind
I.W. Fletcher*	Ind	797	49.0			
Total votes		1,626				
1935						
S. Higson	C	1,598	68.0	3,457	68.0	-
Mrs E.H. Tomlinson	Lab	752	32.0			
Total votes		2,350				
1936						
C.J. Yates	C	1,500	67.1	3,508	63.7	-
J.R. Mewton	Lab	735	32.9			
Total votes		2,235				
1937						
W.H. Harford Jones	C	1,706	68.9	3,752	66.0	C from Lab
A. Summers*	Lab	770	31.1			
Total votes		2,476				
1938						
S. Higson*	C	1,417	66.9	4,036	52.5	-
A. Summers	Lab	700	33.1			
Total votes		2,117				

Overall Labour vote   **35.0%**   **Overall turnout**   **59.6%**

FIVE
Birmingham

BIRMINGHAM

Birmingham was the second city to London and the largest county borough by some way, with a population of just over one million in 1931. It was still a growing city in the inter-war period, unlike other large industrial cities to the north which had experienced most of their growth before 1914. In the decade between 1911 and 1921 Birmingham's population increased by 11.5 per cent, in the following decade to 1931 by another 7 per cent, and between 1931 and 1938 by almost 4 per cent. Its nineteenth-century status as 'the workshop of the world' was augmented by major new industrial developments during the First World War and again in the 1930s, making it the most dynamic of the larger boroughs.

Birmingham and the adjoining Black Country formed a regional economy which was based mainly on metal manufacture. Birmingham itself specialised in the production of finished metal goods, 'frequently of a kind requiring a high degree of craftsmanship or complicated assembly work'. There was a particular emphasis on non-ferrous metals, and the city had 'probably a wider variety of industries than any other town in Great Britain'.[1] Much of this industry prior to 1860 was carried on in 'small workshops, low roofed and imperfectly lighted ... for the most part situated in back courts', and there were a 'large number of small masters employing a few workmen'. While the scale of industry increased later, small-workshop production around the city centre employing mainly skilled labour remained important down to the inter-war period.[2]

Later industrial development, mostly including diversification into larger-scale production, took place away from the city centre. To the north-west along the Birmingham canal beyond Ladywood a metal-working district developed. To the south-west Cadbury's shifted from its Bridge Street works near the city centre to its new factory at Bournville in 1879, which was supplemented by more metal working in the Stirchley and Selly Oak districts. In the south-east the Birmingham Small Arms Company works at Small Heath was the hub of a new mixed industrial area. Most important of all, to the east and north, railway wagon and motor factories and gas works in the Nechells and Saltley areas, and the General Electric Company's factory at Witton in the Aston area, formed the basis of an extensive industrial district.[3] Conversion to war production between 1914 and 1918 stimulated further development. The Austin motor works at Longbridge in the south-west corner of the city employed 2,800 workers in 1914, and 20,000 by 1918, for instance, and Dunlop's rubber works at Bromford to the east also grew rapidly, becoming 'Fort Dunlop' in 1915.[4]

[1]   Fogarty, M.P., *Prospects of the Industrial Areas of Great Britain*, (London, 1945), pp. 339–340.
[2]   Wise, M.J. and Thorpe, P.O., 'The growth of Birmingham 1800–1950', in British Association, *Birmingham and its Regional Setting; A Scientific Survey*, (Birmingham, 1950), pp. 216, 222.
[3]   Wise and Thorpe, 'The growth of Birmingham', pp. 222–224.
[4]   Briggs, A., *History of Birmingham, vol. II: Borough and City 1865–1938*, (London, 1952), p. 218; Cherry, G.E., *Birmingham: A Study in Geography, History and Planning*, (Chichester, 1994), p. 128.

While there was a brief period of rising unemployment during the transition from war production between 1918 and 1922, 'the long-run process of readaption to the needs of a post-war economy was tackled more successfully in Birmingham than in many other parts of the country'.[5] Based on its traditions of metal working and skilled labour, the city avoided the worst problems of the inter-war Depression through the expansion of the 'new' industries producing automobiles, auto components, electrical equipment, new metal alloys, plastic and other synthetic goods, together with other consumer products. Much of this growth occurred on the outskirts of the city, at Longbridge and Fort Dunlop, and in a broad swathe of factories along the Tame valley from Perry Bar in the north, through Gravelly Hill and Bromford, to Stechford and Castle Bromwich in the East. In the 1930s especially, Birmingham recovered while many other industrial boroughs suffered prolonged depression and unemployment. With 15 per cent out of work in 1932, it was sixty-ninth out of the eighty-three county boroughs. By 1937 Birmingham's unemployment rate had fallen to 4.3 per cent. Only Derby, and the nearby boroughs of Smethwick and Coventry, had marginally lower unemployment figures.

The occupational structure of Birmingham reflected its industrial history. There was a preponderance of skilled workers in the city, especially in the older workshop trades, but also in the newer industries. In 1931 almost 40 per cent of the entire workforce recorded in the industrial tables of the census was in the metals and engineering sector, a higher proportion than any other borough. In proportional terms for specific trades within that sector, though, Birmingham was exceeded by Coventry and Oxford in vehicle construction, by Salford in electrical goods, by Sheffield, Middlesbrough and a number of others in metals, and by various boroughs in general engineering. This was only due to the fact that Birmingham had a much broader base across all these sectors than other more specialised towns. In absolute terms Birmingham occupied a dominant position. Over 55,000 worked in vehicles, compared with 27,000 in Coventry and just over 5,000 in Oxford. Almost 19,000 worked in electrical goods, compared to Manchester's 9,700 and Salford's 6,000. In the metal industries there were over 100,000 in Birmingham, compared to just under 90,000 in Sheffield and 18,500 in Middlesbrough. Only in general engineering was Birmingham overshadowed by a larger centre, Manchester having almost 19,500 in this category as compared with Birmingham's 16,000. It should be added that Birmingham's continued industrial growth of the 1930s could only have strengthened its dominance in these industries, although we have no census figures from 1941 to show this. As far as male workers were concerned, outside these core industries there were also significant numbers employed in food, building, transport, commerce and public administration, emphasising even more the broad base of Birmingham's economy.

The role of women in the employment pattern of Birmingham was distinctive. Outside the textile districts, there were very few boroughs where women worked in significant numbers in manufacturing, as opposed to service, industries. Female employment in the core metal and engineering trades of Birmingham, though, amounted to almost 60,000, 30 per cent of the total. In the long-established

---

[5]   Cherry, *Birmingham*, p. 281.

jewellery trade, women made up 40 per cent of the total workforce in 1931. Women had traditionally always played an important role in Birmingham's workshops, and this tradition was carried over into the industries that developed later. Of the workforce in the rubber industry dominated by Dunlop's in Birmingham, 38 per cent was female. In the food industry dominated by Cadbury's, women comprised 46 per cent of the total. Women were employed in the new industries of the city to a greater extent than when those same industries developed elsewhere. In vehicle construction, women made up a quarter of the labour force in Birmingham, but only 13 per cent in Coventry and 8 per cent in Oxford. In electrical goods, 32 per cent of the Birmingham workforce was female, but the corresponding figure for Salford was 27 per cent, and for Manchester 15 per cent. What this demonstrates is the fact, long known by feminist historians, that the gender disposition of occupational and skill categories is determined not by economic factors alone, but also by socio-cultural expectations. The implications of the heightened importance of women at work for working-class politics in Birmingham will be considered later.[6]

There was also an extensive middle class in Birmingham. The numerous small masters of the earlier workshop trades produced an independent middle-class ethos that was distinctive to Birmingham, often contrasted at the time with the loftier ambitions of northern textile industrialists. The emphasis was on small-scale specialised production, self-sufficiency, domestic markets. If Manchester's middle class was associated with Free Trade, then Birmingham's was linked with Tariff Reform and Protection later. The larger scale of the later industrial developments brought changes in the middle class, especially with the growth of a huge army of managerial and clerical staff. However, the economic well-being of Birmingham's middle class was still in the 1930s dependent primarily on domestic consumption. The other feature of the middle class that needs to be stressed is its strong association with Nonconformity, and especially with 'old Dissent' such as Unitarianism and Quakerism. Nonconformists were also numerous in the working class, mainly in the form of Wesleyan Methodists, Baptists and Congregationalists. By the 1892 religious census Nonconformists outnumbered Anglicans in Birmingham.[7] Nonconformity's overall importance to Birmingham's social and political life has often been noted, but it was particularly influential in municipal politics as will be shown below. One other aspect of Birmingham's population that is noteworthy was the lack of a significant Catholic tradition. There was no great recusant minority, and Irish migration in the nineteenth century was negligible. Of the large cities Birmingham had the least Irish influence, and this also had political implications which will be examined below.[8]

---

[6] On gender and skill, see Phillips, A. and Taylor, B., 'Sex and skill: notes towards a feminist economics', *Feminist Review*, no. 6, (1980); on political implications, Savage, M., *The Dynamics of Working-Class Politics: The Labour Movement in Preston, 1880–1940*, (Cambridge, 1987).

[7] Rose, R.B., 'Protestant Nonconformity', in Stephens, W.B., (ed.), *A History of the County of Warwick: Vol. VII The City of Birmingham*, (1964), pp. 418–428

[8] Reynolds, S., 'Roman Catholicism' in Stephens, *The City of Birmingham*, pp. 397–402.

Turning then to the politics of Birmingham, there were a number of important historical factors that affected the pattern of political support in the city. First, it has been argued that relations between the classes in the workshop-based trades tended to be close and relatively non-antagonistic, leading to a tradition of class collaboration rather than conflict. A shared attachment to Nonconformism may also have helped to cement class alliances. In this account, the significant middle-class influence on Birmingham Chartism was succeeded by the reformism of skilled 'new model unionism' and Lib-Labism, providing barren ground for later attempts at independent labour representation. This did represent a barrier to the early development of the Labour Party in Birmingham, but it must not be overstated. As one recent important study has shown, even in the 1830s and 1840s changes in the scale and nature of the workshop trades were undermining customary relationships and sparking conflict.[9] Change continued later in the century, and by 1914 workers in large-scale factories were supplanting skilled artisans in small workshops as the main force in the Birmingham working class, a change that was to be even more strongly manifested in the inter-war period. Yet the persistent thread of class collaboration can still be traced in the Birmingham labour movement down to the inter-war period. In 1917 a body calling itself the Trade Union Industrial Trades Council broke away from the official Trades Council.[10] It was committed to maintaining the wartime political and industrial truce, and claimed to represent 'patriotic labour'. One of the leaders of the breakaway, Eldred Hallas, won the Duddeston constituency in the 1918 general election for the National Democratic and Labour Party (NDP), a party nationally representing 'patriotic labour' and allied with the Conservative Party. Hallas was one of only ten such MPs elected in 1918, suggesting the unusual strength of support for this explicitly class-collaborationist movement in Birmingham. Hallas subsequently rejoined the Labour Party, and in 1923 he contested the Handsworth ward still espousing his 'patriotic labour' views.[11] But other factors need to be brought in to explain the singular weakness of the Labour Party in Birmingham down to 1939.

It is hard to overestimate the significance of Joseph Chamberlain and the development of Liberal Unionism to Birmingham's political development. The Unitarian Chamberlain made his early fortune in the Birmingham screw-making industry. Independent, fiercely proud of his local base, ambitious and tough-minded, he made his name as a radical in Birmingham municipal politics in the late 1860s and 1870s. He was the only national political leader of his day that had served his apprenticeship in local government. The 'civic gospel' of the closely-knit Nonconformist leadership of the city, emphasising civic duty and the importance of municipal government, was combined with Chamberlain's political skills to produce the Liberal 'caucus'. As Asa Briggs put it, 'Birmingham stood for the most powerful political machine in the kingdom, and the most active and

---

[9] Behagg, C., *Politics and Production in the Early Nineteenth Century,* (London, 1990), chs 4 and 5.
[10] Corbett, J., *The Birmingham Trades Council 1866–1966,* (London, 1966), pp. 110–116.
[11] *Birmingham Post,* 2 Nov. 1923.

adventurous brand of English radical Liberalism'.[12] 'Radical Joe' gained support beyond the ranks of the Birmingham middle class alone, for 'trade unionism was linked with, and dominated by, the ideas of Joseph Chamberlain'.[13] It would not be an exaggeration to say that the Birmingham caucus was the origin of party political organisation in local government in Britain, as well as the model for the modern Liberal Party. In response, Birmingham Toryism was forced also to develop a local political organisation that was ahead of its time. As Briggs points out,

> With a Conservative organization conscious of the need for appealing to working men, and a powerful Liberal organization monopolizing local political power, there was little space left for the growth of independent Labour organizations.[14]

Chamberlain moved on to the national stage in the 1880s, and much of his radicalism was later abandoned, but his influence on Birmingham remained immense. When he split the Liberal Party over Irish Home Rule in 1886, most of Birmingham's Liberals went with him to create the most powerful Liberal Unionist organisation in the country. This transition was made easier by the absence of the Irish interest in Birmingham, unlike other cities where Irish support for Liberalism was electorally significant. In succeeding decades Unionism and Conservatism grew steadily closer together in Birmingham, while Chamberlain still exercised a powerful spell over the city. His Tariff Reform campaign from 1903 was a disastrous political failure nationally, but the domestic-orientated middle class (and at least some of the working class) of Birmingham was far more amenable to the imperialist and protectionist rhetoric of his later years.[15]

Liberal Unionism was already the most powerful political force in Birmingham before 1914, and when in 1918 it was finally merged locally with Toryism its power could be described as almost hegemonic. Candidates for the Conservative and Unionist Party (to give it its full and rarely-used name) have been designated as Conservatives in the election results for Birmingham listed below to be consistent with coverage of other boroughs in these volumes. In the Birmingham press, though, these candidates were never described as anything other than Unionists. In its inter-war guise, Birmingham Unionism was an extraordinary amalgam of political traditions and ideas. Some of the original radicalism of the 1860s was retained, the 'civic gospel' being transmuted into municipal enterprise that elsewhere might have been described as 'Municipal Socialism'. There was also an echo of the era of Lib-Lab politics in the way in which working-class candidates were selected by the Unionist Party for working-class wards. Thus in 1920, for instance, two candidates described as 'Unionist working-men' ousted Labour councillors in the 'entirely or largely industrial'

---

[12] Briggs, *History of Birmingham*, p. 175.

[13] Corbett, *The Birmingham Trades Council*, p. 41.

[14] Briggs, *History of Birmingham*, p. 192.

[15] On Chamberlain's career see Jay, R., *Joseph Chamberlain: A Political Study*, (Oxford, 1981).

wards of Rotton Park and St Paul's.[16] Combined with these features was an emphasis of Empire and protection, and through amalgamation with the local Tory party, another tradition of 'Tory Democracy'. There is no doubt that this Unionism attracted widespread support amongst middle-class and white-collar voters, and also significant numbers of working-class voters. Faced with such a well-organised political machine allied to a popular political ideology, Labour's weakness in Birmingham becomes more understandable. Finally, the relatively buoyant state of Birmingham's inter-war economy perhaps further reinforced support for Unionist policies.

The municipal election results for Birmingham bear out this general picture. Unionist control of the council was never seriously under threat between the wars, and in fact grew more secure over time. Labour made substantial gains in 1919 on an extremely low turnout to bring its total of seats up to twenty-eight. Combined with the remnants of Liberalism from the 1886 split, and various other factions of those who could not accept the 1918 Conservative–Unionist merger, there was a potential opposition of fifty-six seats to the Unionists sixty-six. This was an unstable position though that could not last. As the local press commented on the years 1919 to 1922, 'a strict political classification of the members of the Council is a matter of some difficulty owing to a certain number of the candidates modifying their political designations when at the hustings or after election'.[17] Many of those unattached to the three main parties eventually drifted into the Liberal or Unionist ranks, and by the mid-1920s the Liberals themselves had gone into a permanent decline that mirrored their national fortunes. Labour meanwhile had lost many of its initial gains on a much higher turnout in 1920, and though it recovered some ground in 1921, it fell back again in the mid-1920s. The 1924 elections only a few days after the general election dominated by the Zinoviev letter were especially bad for Labour. Although Labour in Birmingham followed the national trend in 1926 and made big gains, and further gains in the next two years, 1929 represented its inter-war peak. Yet at this stage it held only thirty-six seats to the Unionists seventy-two, and as the Liberals and others had declined so drastically, the Unionist majority was overwhelming.

The collapse of Labour support in 1930 and 1931 was probably as great in Birmingham as anywhere else in the country, with the 1931 elections after the collapse of the second Labour government being particularly disastrous. Again following national trends, there was a Labour recovery between 1932 and 1934, and Labour achieved its highest number of seats on the council. However, the thirty-seven seats it held in 1934 were in a much expanded council, so in proportional terms the Unionist control was greater than in 1929. Following this came four years of substantial Unionist gains from Labour between 1935 and 1938. After the last elections before the second world war, there were 108 Unionists on Birmingham council, an inter-war peak. By contrast, Labour with twenty-two councillors had fewer seats than they had held in 1919. There was plainly no forewarning of the Labour landslide of 1945 in the late-1930s electoral trend in Birmingham.

[16] *Birmingham Post*, 2 Nov. 1920.
[17] *Birmingham Mail*, 2 Nov. 1921.

Looking at the spatial distribution of political support, in the first decade of the period Labour's main strength can be clearly identified in two areas. First, Labour was strong in parts of the old industrial centre of the city, such as the St Bartholomew's, St Martin's and Deritend and Ladywood wards. On the other hand, the city centre wards of St Mary's, St Paul's and Market Hall, which contained most of the central shopping streets, were predominantly Unionist. While the Labour wards here were the site of some of the worst slum housing of the city, the Unionist wards at least in parts contained more salubrious residential quarters such as the New Hall district. Market Hall also contained the highest proportion of plural voters in the city, and St Paul's the second highest, and these business voters no doubt tipped the balance in these wards. Second, Labour support also extended outwards from the centre to the northern (Duddeston and Nechells and Aston wards), eastern (Washwood Heath, Saltley and to a lesser extent Small Heath), and western (All Saints) industrial belts.

Beyond this in the outer suburbs Labour strength in the 1920s was confined solely to the Selly Oak ward which contained most of the Bournville estate and part of the Selly Oak–Stirchley metal-working district. It is noticeable that in Northfield ward where the Longbridge plant was sited, Labour had little support at this stage. This is perhaps not as surprising as it might seem, as very few of the Austin workers lived in the immediate vicinity of the factory and most travelled to work from further afield. Northfield ward itself was still a predominantly suburban middle-class ward, and in 1921 with a population of just over 11,000 was the smallest in the city. It formed part of a ring of suburban wards where Labour had very little support stretching through Harborne, Edgbaston, Soho and Sandwell wards to the west, Handsworth and Erdington to the north, and Yardley, Acock's Green, Sparkhill, Moseley and King's Heath, and King's Norton to the east and south. The only wards where Liberals won seats consistently were King's Norton. and Lozells. Part of the Bournville estate lay in the north of King's Norton, and a Cadbury took the seat unopposed for the Liberals in 1921. In 1924 though the Liberal candidate, the then secretary of the Birmingham Liberal Association, was heavily defeated. In a three-cornered contest the Liberal came bottom of the poll with only 14.5 per cent of the vote, and received almost 2,000 votes fewer than the Unionist victor. When a Liberal and a Unionist next confronted each other two years later, the Liberal this time had a majority of almost 2,000 votes. After this the two parties entered into an agreement so that a Liberal was given a clear run every three years, and the Unionists were given a free run in the intervening elections. A similar agreement allowed a Liberal a clear run in Lozells from 1928, tacitly recognised in 1931 when it was stated that the Liberal 'received unofficial Unionist support'.[18]

The electoral geography of Birmingham changed in the 1930s as the city changed. The new industries developing primarily on the northern and eastern outskirts profoundly altered this side of the borough. Perry Bar to the north was added to the borough in the late 1920s, and eventually became a ward of strong Labour support. Further additions to the borough in the east in 1934 were accompanied by electorally significant ward boundary revisions. The more

[18] *Birmingham Post*, 3 Nov. 1931.

industrial northern end of Yardley ward was combined with added land to create Stechford ward, another mainly Labour ward, leaving Yardley as a Unionist stronghold. The industrial east end of the two Erdington wards was also combined with added land to form Bromford, another Labour ward. The rest of the old Erdington wards became the new Gravelly Hill and Erdington wards, solidly Unionist. Hall Green was created from the southern ends of Sparkhill and Acock's Green, leaving three Unionist strongholds where previously there had been two. There were also minor additions to the Labour wards of Washwood Heath and Saltley which left them politically unchanged, and the transfer of a portion of Moseley and King's Heath to King's Norton which was also politically neutral in its effects.

At the same time there was extensive housing development which also helped to change the political map of Birmingham. Housing was probably the major issue at municipal elections in Birmingham. Immediately after the First World War the Labour Party vociferously advocated a policy of slum clearance in the city centre and more extensive council-house construction. Its major gains in 1919 were attributed mainly to this campaign. However, the electors were described as being 'not nicely discriminating' in this regard, as there was unanimity amongst the parties over the issue, and Birmingham was already 'in the van of authorities to submit detailed schemes' for council housing. The extension of public housing, as well as being politically expedient, could easily be countenanced by the remnants of the old radical tradition in the Unionist party. The Unionist council subsequently embarked on a massive programme of council-house building, and thereby stole a march on Labour. By 1922 the tables had been turned, and the Unionist gains in that year were put down mainly to their housing policy.[19] Over 50,000 council houses were constructed between the wars, more than any other borough in the country. 80 per cent of them were built by 1933. There were also considerable, if still inadequate, slum clearance programmes instituted. Over 50,000 privately-owned houses were also built, mostly in the later 1930s.

Huge council estates were built in the wards of Perry Bar (Kingstanding and Kettle House, 6,302 houses), Northfield (Weoley Castle and Allen's Cross, 4,879), Stechford (Lea Hall and Batchelor's Farm, 4,846), and Bromford (Pype Hays, 1,344). These formed a new bloc of predominantly Labour-supporting wards on the outskirts of the city. The political impact on Northfield was dramatic. Its electorate doubled from 5,000 to 10,000 between 1929 and 1931, and doubled again to over 20,000 by 1938. Labour gained the ward for the first time in 1932, and in the last two elections before the war won it even though elsewhere in the city the party was losing seats. In other cases private housing estates counterbalanced council-house development, as in Hall Green (Fox Hollies, Gospel Farm and Billesley Farm, 6,204 council houses), Erdington (Witton Lodge, 1,374), Yardley (Marlborough House and Fast Pits, 2,171), and Acock's Green (Tylesley Farm and Spring Road, 1,350).[20]

---

[19] *Birmingham Post*, 3 Nov. 1919, 2 Nov. 1922.
[20] Cherry, *Birmingham*, pp. 112–120; see also Fogarty, M.P., *Town and Country Planning*, (London, 1948), ch. 3, pp. 30–48.

It would be wrong, anyway, to assume that council-house dwellers were automatically Labour supporters, especially in a city like Birmingham. Council-house rents were higher than inner-city private rents, and living in suburban estates imposed extra travelling costs. It was mainly the better-paid sections of the working class, and some white-collar workers, who moved to the new estates. Council policy on tenants deliberately encouraged this, prioritising high-wage earners.[21] There was no industry based in the Kingstanding estate in Perry Bar. In a 1938 survey it was found that a high proportion of the population there travelled some distance to work. In the city as a whole, a quarter of all wage-earners travelled at least three miles each way to work.[22] At least some council tenants, if they were not already supporters of Birmingham Unionism, would surely have looked favourably on the party that had provided them with their new houses. Even in Perry Bar where council housing predominated overwhelmingly, Labour did not establish complete control. The Unionist vote only once fell below 40 per cent there, and in 1938 a Unionist gain from Labour was achieved, once again making the point that working-class Unionism was a powerful force in Birmingham politics.

It was also the case that while Labour was establishing some new bridgeheads in the suburbs, it was beginning to lose its older redoubts in the inner city as rehousing took place. After the changes in national policy in 1934–35 brought a greater emphasis on slum clearance and new subsidies to finance it, the effect became clear. While many slum-dwellers were rehoused within the inner city, as many as 30 per cent were decanted to outer estates.[23] In All Saints' ward where Labour had been comparatively strong in the 1920s, the electorate began to fall gradually from 1929, and precipitately from 1934. By 1935 all three seats in the ward were held by the Unionists. In St Bartholomew's a similar depopulation resulted in Labour's share of the vote gradually declining, so that by the late 1930s Unionist candidates were only narrowly losing where previously they had been getting less than 30 per cent of the vote. In St Martin's and Deritend the trend was most obvious, with all three Labour seats in the ward falling to the Unionists in successive years between 1936 and 1938.

Unionist domination of Birmingham's municipal politics remained unthreatened down to 1938, then. This domination was a reflection of real political support, and Birmingham Unionism had no pressing need to manipulate the municipal electoral system in order to bolster its position, as parties tended to do in other boroughs where political control was more tenuous. Thus Labour was sometimes under-represented proportionally on the aldermen's bench in Birmingham, but not outrageously so. The Labour total increased from two to four aldermen between 1919 and 1922, still not proportionally equivalent to the twenty-four Labour councillors. Then as Labour lost seats in the next few years it moved into a position of near parity of aldermanic representation by 1925. By 1928 Labour was again under-represented, with five aldermen to thirty councillors, and it remained so to varying degrees until 1935. The Labour

---

[21]   Fogarty, *Town and Country Planning*, p. 36.
[22]   Fogarty, *Town and Country Planning*, p. 37.
[23]   Cherry, *Birmingham*, pp. 121–124.

aldermen had increased to seven by that year, and to eight by 1938, while Labour was losing council seats in the same period. In 1938, therefore, Labour was actually over-represented, with eight aldermen to only fourteen councillors. If the aldermanic system was misused, then it was more significant in artificially sustaining the Liberal position. From 1929 there were only two Liberal councillors, representing the King's Norton and Lozells wards, and from 1937 only one, but the Liberal position on the council was still boosted by three aldermen until 1933, and two up to 1938.

Nor was there blatant gerrymandering of the ward boundaries by the Unionists. Taking Labour's ten strongest wards between 1919 and 1928 (measured by its overall share of the vote over those ten years), in 1919 there were 4,571 electors for each councillor in those wards. In Labour's ten weakest, there were 3,682 electors per councillor. This reflected Unionist strength in suburban wards, which at this stage tended to be smaller in population terms, and was a slight electoral disadvantage for Labour. By 1933 prior to ward reorganisation when the population of the suburban wards had expanded considerably, the respective figures were 5,231 per councillor for Labour's ten strongest, and 5,344 for their weakest, suggesting no advantage either way. After reorganisation, taking Labour's top and bottom ten wards for the period 1934 to 1938, the respective figures in 1934 were 4,617 for Labour's strongest, and 3,852 for its weakest. The slight electoral balance in favour of Labour's opponents had been restored, but it ought to be stressed that this was a very marginal advantage. Comparable analysis of Liverpool in the same period, for instance, has revealed much greater disparities in ward size severely disadvantaging Labour, as well as far more cynical manipulation of the aldermanic system in that city.[24] Similar evidence can be found in the cases of Barnsley, Blackburn and Bootle in this volume.

Another important question relating to municipal politics in Birmingham that needs to be addressed is the role of women. It was noted above that women occupied an unusually significant position in the workforce of the city, and it is possible that this was reflected in a corresponding prominence in the political sphere. The evidence here is interesting, if not entirely conclusive. Out of a total of 1,191 candidates for all parties in municipal contests between the wars, 107 were women. The comparable figures for a city like Liverpool, where women's role in the local labour market was much more restricted, were 127 women out of 1,717 candidates.[25] In percentage terms women made up 9 per cent of the total in Birmingham, and 7.4 per cent in Liverpool, hardly a striking disparity. However, if these figures are broken down by party, then more noticeable differences emerge. While women candidates varied proportionally very little between Birmingham and Liverpool as far as the Conservative–Unionist and Liberal parties were concerned (5.2 per cent as opposed to 4.4 per cent, 5.1 per cent as opposed to 6.3 per cent respectively), women were significantly better represented in the Labour Party in Birmingham (13.1 per cent as opposed to 8.7 per cent). By

---

[24]   On ward boundary disparities see Davies, S., *Liverpool Labour: Social and Political Influences on the Development of the Labour Party in Liverpool, 1900–1939*, (Keele, 1996), pp. 97–109; on aldermen, pp. 110–119.

[25]   Davies, *Liverpool Labour*, p. 182.

contrast, though, women's role in Birmingham trades-unionism remained marginal, a long-standing 'weakness of the trade unions in the City'.[26]

A tentative conclusion might be that the important position women held in the main manufacturing industries of Birmingham was reflected in involvement in the local Labour Party in a period when women's enfranchisement endowed them with greater political power. Michael Savage's important study of Preston working-class politics has shown how a similar pattern there of increased women's participation was crucial in transforming Labour into a more neighbourhood-based and less economistic party in the later 1920s. He also shows how high unemployment in the 1930s increased competition between male and female workers and shifted the balance back again, with women's influence on the party being reduced as their position in the labour market was eroded, and policy consequently moving back to more traditional economistic lines.[27] It would be interesting to apply this analysis further to the very different circumstances of Birmingham, where increased employment opportunities in the 1930s meant that women played an even greater role in many of the new industries.

As far as women as newly-enfranchised voters are concerned, it would appear that their impact was significant in its effects on the parties. In 1919, it was reported that Labour 'succeeded in prevailing upon the women to go to the poll to a much greater degree than any of the other parties'. In some wards in particular 'the number of women voters was very small indeed'. This factor was much emphasised in explaining Labour's unexpectedly good results on a very low poll in that year.[28] By contrast, there was a much higher turnout in 1920, and Labour was far less successful. Interestingly, a similar pattern was evident when the enfranchisement of women under the age of thirty took effect. Labour did well on a low poll in 1929, but fell back on a much higher poll in 1930. This pattern was repeated in many other boroughs as well, as the results in the rest of this volume confirm. A possible explanation can be surmised that middle-class women were initially put off from voting, perhaps due to general middle-class attitudes to women's role in the public sphere, perhaps even due to disapproval by male partners. Labour's comparative success as a result prompted a rapid shift of middle-class opinion on women voting, leading to the reversal of the following year. However, detailed research is needed to establish whether this hypothesis is acceptable.

This also prompts speculation on one other striking feature of Birmingham's electoral record in the inter-war period. This is the extremely low turnout that prevailed in municipal elections. Birmingham had by far the lowest overall turnout of all the ten boroughs included in this volume. Preliminary work on other towns for future volumes suggests that it had one of the lowest turnout figures of all eighty-three boroughs. In parliamentary elections as well, turnout in Birmingham tended to be below the national average. Taking all Birmingham seats together, the turnout in the 1918 general election was 48 per cent, compared to 56 per cent for England as a whole, in 1923 63 per cent compared to 71 per

---

[26] Corbett, *The Birmingham Trades Council*, pp. 171–173.
[27] Savage, *The Dynamics of Working-Class Politics*, pp. 162–187.
[28] *Birmingham Post*, 3 Nov. 1919.

cent, in 1924 71 per cent compared to 77 per cent, and in 1935 63 per cent compared to 71 per cent. Only in 1922, 1929 and 1931 did the Birmingham turnout come close to the national average. Why should this be so, in reputedly the 'best-governed city in the world'? The overwhelming dominance of Unionism in municipal politics might have accounted for a degree of apathy on the part of voters, but on the other hand boroughs with similar one-party control such as Bath or Blackpool did not experience such high levels of abstention. Turnout was exceptionally low in 1919, with city-centre wards in particular such as Market Hall, St Martin's and St Bartholomew's standing out. Over the whole period, the city-centre wards and also the new council-estate wards such as Perry Bar tended to have the lowest turnout, suggesting that working-class abstention was most marked. The trend over time was also downward generally from the early 1930s as employment and prosperity was rising locally. Perhaps there was a degree of working-class indifference to the claims of the Labour Party peculiar to Birmingham. Perhaps also this indifference grew even more as material standards improved under a Unionist council. Again, only much more detailed analysis could substantiate these tentative suggestions.

In conclusion, Birmingham can be summarised as a dynamic, growing and changing industrial city in the inter-war period. The increasing strength of Unionism and concomitant weakness of Labour were the main characteristics of the municipal politics of the borough. The socio-economic structure of class relationships in the city, the economic growth of the inter-war period, and the political agency of Chamberlain and the Unionist and Conservative leaders that succeeded him, all played a part in consolidating this position. In the second half of the nineteenth century it was commonly said that Birmingham was as Liberal as the sea was salt. Now it was as Unionist. Briggs recounts the following story from 1868:

> Birmingham Liberals were circulating ... a black-edged card announcing that the mortal remains of 'OLD TORYISM' would be consigned to their last resting-place on Tuesday, 17 November. 'A Man that is born a Tory hath but a short time to live, and is full of Humbug: he springeth up like a fungus, and withereth like a cauliflower; and is seen no more; in the midst of life and hope he meets his death.' At the foot of the card, in block capitals, were printed the words NO RESURRECTION.[29]

Birmingham Unionists seventy years later could have reprinted the cards substituting 'socialist' for 'Tory', such was their confident grip on the city. Yet they would have been as wrong in their forecast of no resurrection for their opponents as their Liberal predecessors had been. In the 1945 general election Labour won ten of the thirteen Birmingham seats. In 1946 the Labour Party won control of Birmingham City Council. 'In Birmingham an ice cap has melted and the waters flow', it was commented.[30] No better example could be found of the cataclysmic social change that total war can bring.

---

[29]   Briggs, *History of Birmingham*, p. 167.
[30]   Briggs, A., 'Political History from 1832', in Stephens, *The City of Birmingham*, p. 317.

A guide to further reading

Newspapers

Birmingham Mail
Birmingham Post

Secondary sources

Barnsby, G.J., *Birmingham Working People: A History of the Labour Movement in Birmingham*, 1650–1914, (Wolverhampton, 1989).

Behagg, C., *Politics and Production in the Early Nineteenth Century*, (London, 1990).

Briggs, A., *History of Birmingham, vol. II: Borough and City 1865–1938*, (London, 1952).

British Association, *Birmingham and its Regional Setting; A Scientific Survey*, (Birmingham, 1950).

Cherry, G.E., *Birmingham: A Study in Geography, History and Planning*, (Chichester, 1994).

Corbett, J., *The Birmingham Trades Council 1866–1966*, (London, 1966).

Fogarty, M.P., *Town and Country Planning*, (London, 1948), ch. III, pp. 30–48.

Hastings, R.P., 'The Birmingham labour movement, 1918–1945', *Midland History*, vol. V, (1979–80).

Hopkins, E., 'Working class life in Birmingham between the wars, 1918–1939', *Midland History*, vol. XV, (1990).

Jay, R., *Joseph Chamberlain: A Political Study*, (Oxford, 1981).

Municipal Journal and Public Works Engineer, 'Municipal Birmingham', vol. 40, (12 Jun. 1931), pp. 879–80; 'Birmingham developments', vol. 43, (23 Feb. 1934), p. 266; 'In Birmingham today', vol. 43, (27 Apr. 1934), pp. 567–572.

Smith, M., *Conflict and Compromise: Class Formation in English Society 1830–1914: A Comparative Study of Birmingham and Sheffield*, (London, 1982).

Stephens, W.B., (ed.), *A History of the County of Warwick: Vol. VII The City of Birmingham*, (1964).

Wright, A. and Shackleton, R.M.Y., (eds), *Worlds of Labour: Essays in Birmingham Labour History*, (Birmingham, 1981).

Zuckerman, J. and Eley, G., *Birmingham Heritage*, (London, 1979).

Birmingham wards 1919–1933

Birmingham wards 1934–1938

Persons aged fourteen and over classified by industry 1931

	Male	%	Female	%	Total	%
Metal and engineering	139,602	41.9	58,823	33.9	198,425	39.1
- Metal-working	*25,755*	*7.7*	*6,532*	*3.8*	*32,287*	*6.4*
- Vehicle construction	*42,038*	*12.6*	*13,638*	*7.9*	*55,676*	*11.0*
- Other metal industries	*31,813*	*9.5*	*21,129*	*12.2*	*52,942*	*10.4*
Clothing	3,911	1.2	10,026	5.8	13,937	2.7
Food, drink and tobacco	11,909	3.6	8,678	5.0	20,587	4.1
Building	25,219	7.6	356	0.2	25,575	5.0
Transport	22,654	6.8	935	0.5	23,589	4.7
- Rail	*10,542*	*3.2*	*295*	*0.2*	*10,837*	*2.1*
- Road	*11,222*	*3.4*	*473*	*0.3*	*11,695*	*2.3*
Commerce and finance	47,718	14.3	25,124	14.5	72,842	14.4
Public admin. and defence	20,917	6.3	8,940	5.2	29,857	5.9
- Local government	*14,469*	*4.3*	*6,933*	*4.0*	*21,402*	*4.2*
Personal service	9,867	3.0	28,752	16.6	38,619	7.6
Other	51,673	15.5	31,877	18.4	83,550	16.5
Total (a)	**333,470**		**173,511**		**506,981**	
Total population (b)	476,072		526,531		1,002,603	
(a) as % of (b)	70		33		51	
Total out of work (c)	44,811		17,189		62,000	
(c) as % of (a)	13		10		12	
Managerial and own account	36,104	12.5	12,276	7.9	48,380	10.9
Operative	252,555	87.5	144,046	92.1	396,601	89.1
Total (excluding out of work)	288,659		156,322		444,981	

Population statistics 1931

Ward	Acres	Population	Persons/acre	Persons/room
Acock's Green	2,269	58,516	25.8	0.79
All Saints'	514	38,593	75.1	0.95
Aston	538	35,612	66.2	0.92
Balsall Heath	448	34,805	77.7	0.80
Duddeston and Nechells	570	38,592	67.7	1.09
Edgbaston	2,657	35,539	13.4	0.64
Erdington North	2,706	41,091	15.2	0.81
Erdington South	2,551	29,671	11.6	0.73
Handsworth	1,405	26,980	19.2	0.65
Harborne	2,388	21,769	9.1	0.69
King's Norton	2,825	22,811	8.1	0.73
Ladywood	302	26,275	87.0	1.08
Lozells	364	30,343	83.4	0.79
Market Hall	342	15,712	45.9	1.08
Moseley and King's Heath	3,009	39,728	13.2	0.65
Northfield	5,751	22,753	4.0	0.82
Perry Bar	3,085	20,214	6.6	0.88
Rotton Park	683	39,999	58.6	0.91
St Bartholomew's	517	35,018	67.7	1.12
St Martin's and Deritend	410	39,309	95.9	1.13
St Mary's	353	30,657	86.8	1.19
St Paul's	388	27,532	71.0	1.19
Saltley	1,585	39,930	25.2	0.85
Sandwell	1,538	20,228	13.2	0.67
Selly Oak	1,710	28,558	16.7	0.76
Small Heath	687	32,127	46.8	0.75
Soho	724	25,407	35.1	0.72
Sparkbrook	618	31,741	51.4	0.79
Sparkhill	2,644	42,703	16.2	0.71
Washwood Heath	1,990	38,923	19.6	0.82
Yardley	5,576	31,467	5.6	0.80
Total	**51,147**	**1,002,603**	**19.6**	**0.83**

Overall position on the council 1919–38

	Position				Gains				Losses			
	C	Lab	L	Other	C	Lab	L	Other	C	Lab	L	Other
1919[a]	66	24	17	12	2	6	0	9	12	3	1	1
1920	70	22	14	14	6	1	0	2	2	6	1	0
1921	67	29	18	6	0	6	0	1	4	0	3	0
1922[a]	69	28	12	10	5	2	0	0	1	5	1	0
1923	69	25	12	13	1	1	0	1	1	2	0	0
1924	77	20	10	13	7	0	0	0	0	5	2	0
1925	82	17	7	13	4	0	0	0	0	2	1	1
1926	73	29	7	11	2	8	0	0	7	0	0	3
1927	72	33	5	10	0	3	0	0	2	0	1	0
1928	72	36	4	9	1	4	0	0	4	1	0	0
1929	72	36	5	8	1	1	0	1	0	2	0	1
1930	79	31	5	6	6	0	0	0	0	5	0	1
1931	89	21	5	6	9	0	0	0	0	9	0	0
1932	88	22	5	6	0	4	0	0	4	0	0	0
1933	87	26	5	5	0	1	0	0	1	0	0	0
1934	87	37	4	5	0	7	0	0	7	0	0	0
1935	96	32	4	4	7	0	0	0	0	7	0	0
1936	98	30	4	4	2	0	0	0	0	2	0	0
1937	103	27	3	3	6	1	0	0	1	4	1	1
1938	108	22	3	3	5	0	0	0	0	5	0	0

Aldermen 1919–38

1919[a] C–21, Lab–2, L–6
1920 C–21, Lab–3, L–6
1921 C–21, Lab–4, L–4, Ind–1
1922[a] C–19, Lab–5, L–4, Ind–1
1923 C–20, Lab–5, L–4, Ind–1
1924 C–20, Lab–5, L–4, Ind–1
1925 C–20, Lab–5, L–4, Ind–1
1926 C–21, Lab–5, L–3, Ind–1
1927 C–21, Lab–5, L–3, Ind–1
1928 C–21, Lab–4, L–3, Ind–2

1929 C–21, Lab–4, L–3, Ind–2
1930 C–20, Lab–5, L–3, Ind–2
1931 C–20, Lab–5, L–3, Ind–2
1932 C–20, Lab–4, L–3, Ind–3
1933 C–21, Lab–4, L–3, Ind–2
1934 C–23, Lab–4, L–2, Ind–2
1935 C–23, Lab–7, L–2, Ind–2
1936 C–23, Lab–7, L–2, Ind–2
1937 C–23, Lab–7, L–2, Ind–2
1938 C–22, Lab–8, L–2, Ind–2

[a] 1 aldermanic vacancy 1919 and 1922.

Municipal elections: winning party 1919–28

Ward	1919	1920	1921	1922	1923	1924	1925	1926	1927	1928
Acock's Green	Ind	Ind	C	**R**	**Ind**	C	**Ind**	C	C	Ind
All Saints'	Lab	C	Lab	Lab	Lab	C	C	Lab	C	Lab
Aston	Lab	Lab	C	Lab	C	C	Lab	Lab	Lab	Lab
Balsall Heath	Coop	C	C	C	C	C	C	C	C	C
Bromford (1)	-	-	-	-	-	-	-	-	-	-
Bromford (2)	-	-	-	-	-	-	-	-	-	-
Bromford (3)	-	-	-	-	-	-	-	-	-	-
Duddeston etc.	T	C	Lab	**T**	C	Lab	Lab	Lab	Lab	**Lab**
Edgbaston	**C**	C	**C**	**C**	**C**	C	C	**C**	**C**	**C**
Erdington	-	-	-	-	-	-	-	-	-	-
Erdington North	**C**	C	C	**C**	**C**	C	**C**	C	C	C
Erdington South	C	C	C	C	**C**	C	C	C	C	C
Gravelly Hill	-	-	-	-	-	-	-	-	-	-
Hall Green (1)	-	-	-	-	-	-	-	-	-	-
Hall Green (2)	-	-	-	-	-	-	-	-	-	-
Hall Green (3)	-	-	-	-	-	-	-	-	-	-
Handsworth	Ind	Ind C	**C**	Prog	C	**C**	C	C	C	C
Harborne	C	C	C	C	C	C	C	C	C	**C**
King's Norton	Coop	L	**L**	Lab	**L**	C	C	L	C	C
Ladywood	Lab	C	Lab	C	**C**	C	C	Lab	Lab	Lab
Lozells	L	Ind	C	L	T	C	C	C	C	L
Market Hall	C	**C**	C	C	C	C	C	C	C	C
Moseley etc.	Ind	**C**	**C**	**C**	**C**	**C**	**C**	**C**	C	**C**
Northfield	Ind	C	C	**L**	**C**	C	**L**	C	C	Ind
Perry Bar (1)	-	-	-	-	-	-	-	-	-	-
Perry Bar (2)	-	-	-	-	-	-	-	-	-	-
Rotton Park	C	C	Lab	C	C	C	C	Lab	C	C
St Bartholomew's	L	C	L	Lab	C	L	C	Lab	Lab	Lab
St Martin's etc.	C	**C**	Lab	Lab	C	Lab	Lab	Lab	Lab	Lab
St Mary's	Ind	C	Ind	Ind	C	Ind	**Ind**	Lab	Lab	Ind
St Paul's	C	C	**C**	C	C	C	C	Lab	C	C
Saltley	Lab	Lab	Lab	Lab	Ind	**Lab**	**Lab**	Ind	Lab	Lab
Sandwell	Ind	Ind	Ind C	Ind	Ind	C	**Ind**	Ind	C	Ind
Selly Oak (1)	Coop	C	Lab	**Lab**	Lab	**Lab**	Lab	Lab	Lab	Lab
Selly Oak (2)	-	-	-	-	-	-	-	-	-	-
Small Heath	Lab	L	Lab	C	**L**	C	C	Lab	C	Lab
Soho	Lab	C	C	C	**C**	C	C	C	C	C
Sparkbrook	Lab	C	Lab	C	C	C	C	C	C	C
Sparkhill	C	C	**L**	C	C	C	C	**C**	C	**C**
Stechford (1)	-	-	-	-	-	-	-	-	-	-
Stechford (2)	-	-	-	-	-	-	-	-	-	-
Stechford (3)	-	-	-	-	-	-	-	-	-	-
Washwood Heath	Lab	L	Lab	**Lab**	L	**Lab**	**Lab**	Lab	Lab	**Lab**
Yardley	Lab	Ind	C	Ind	Ind	Ind	**Ind**	Ind	Ind	C

Municipal elections: winning party 1929–38

Ward	1929	1930	1931	1932	1933	1934	1935	1936	1937	1938
Acock's Green	C	C	C	C	C	C	C	C	C	C
All Saints'	Lab	C	C	Lab	C	C	C	C	C	C
Aston	Lab	C	C	Lab	C	C	Lab	C	C	C
Balsall Heath	C	C	C	C	C	C	C	C	C	C
Bromford (1)	-	-	-	-	-	Lab	C	C	C	C
Bromford (2)	-	-	-	-	-	Lab	C	-	-	-
Bromford (3)	-	-	-	-	-	Lab	-	-	-	-
Duddeston etc.	Lab	Lab	C	Lab	Lab	Lab	Lab	Lab	Lab	Lab
Edgbaston	C	C	C	C	C	C	C	C	C	C
Erdington	-	-	-	-	-	C	C	C	C	C
Erdington North	C	C	C	C	C	-	-	-	-	-
Erdington South	C	C	C	C	C	-	-	-	-	-
Gravelly Hill	-	-	-	-	-	C	C	C	C	C
Hall Green (1)	-	-	-	-	-	C	C	C	C	C
Hall Green (2)	-	-	-	-	-	C	-	-	-	-
Hall Green (3)	-	-	-	-	-	C	-	-	-	-
Handsworth	C	C	C	C	C	C	C	C	C	C
Harborne	C	C	C	C	C	C	C	C	C	C
King's Norton	L	C	C	L	C	C	L	C	C	L
Ladywood	C	C	C	C	C	C	C	C	C	C
Lozells	C	C	L	C	C	L	C	C	C	C
Market Hall	C	C	C	C	C	C	C	C	C	C
Moseley etc.	C	C	C	C	C	C	C	C	C	C
Northfield	C	C	C	Lab	C	C	Lab	C	Lab	Lab
Perry Bar (1)	-	-	C	-	Lab	Lab	Lab	Lab	Lab	C
Perry Bar (2)	-	-	-	-	Lab	-	-	-	-	-
Rotton Park	Ind	C	C	C	C	C	C	C	C	C
St Bartholomew's	Lab	Lab	C	Lab	Lab	Lab	Lab	Lab	Lab	Lab
St Martin's etc.	Lab	Lab	C	Lab	Lab	Lab	Lab	C	C	C
St Mary's	Lab	C	Ind	Lab	C	Ind	C	C	C	C
St Paul's	Lab	C	C	Lab	C	C	C	C	C	C
Saltley	Lab	Lab	C	Lab	Lab	Lab	Lab	Lab	Lab	C
Sandwell	Ind	C	Ind	Ind	C	Ind	Ind	C	C	Ind
Selly Oak (1)	Lab	C	C	Lab	Lab	Lab	Lab	Lab	C	C
Selly Oak (2)	-	-	-	-	-	-	-	Lab	-	-
Small Heath	Lab	C	C	Lab	C	Lab	C	C	C	C
Soho	C	C	C	C	C	C	C	C	C	C
Sparkbrook	C	C	C	Lab	C	C	C	C	C	C
Sparkhill	C	C	C	C	C	C	C	C	C	C
Stechford (1)	-	-	-	-	-	C	C	C	C	C
Stechford (2)	-	-	-	-	-	C	-	-	-	-
Stechford (3)	-	-	-	-	-	Lab	-	-	-	-
Washwood Heath	Lab	Lab	C	Lab	Lab	Lab	Lab	C	Lab	Lab
Yardley	C	C	C	C	C	C	C	C	C	C

Municipal elections: party wins per year 1919–28

	1919	1920	1921	1922	1923	1924	1925	1926	1927	1928
C	9	20	15	14	20	22	19	14	20	15
Lab	9	2	10	8	2	5	6	12	9	10
L	2	3	3	2	3	1	1	1	0	1
Other	10	5	2	6	5	2	4	3	1	4
Total	30	30	30	30	30	30	30	30	30	30
Turnout %	29.2	39.0	42.3	46.8	40.4	49.1	43.3	42.3	42.1	40.7
Labour %	30.5	28.9	42.6	38.1	37.8	38.0	40.3	45.5	44.3	45.5

Municipal elections: party wins per year 1929–38

	1929	1930	1931	1932	1933	1934	1935	1936	1937	1938
C	16	25	28	15	24	25	24	29	28	28
Lab	11	5	0	13	8	12	9	6	6	4
L	1	0	1	1	0	1	1	0	0	1
Other	2	0	2	1	0	2	1	0	0	1
Total	30	30	31	30	32	40	35	35	34	34
Turnout %	31.2	37.8	40.5	36.3	36.1	33.0	36.2	31.9	32.6	36.2
Labour %	49.0	39.8	30.9	50.1	46.3	43.0	41.5	39.3	42.1	38.9

Municipal elections: party wins per ward 1919–38

Ward	C	Lab	L	Other	Total	Turnout %	Labour % of all votes
Acock's Green	14	0	0	6	20	30.6	32.9
All Saints'	12	8	0	0	20	38.2	47.7
Aston	10	10	0	0	20	38.7	51.0
Balsall Heath	19	0	0	1	20	35.9	35.6
Bromford	5	3	0	0	8	35.1	47.0
Duddeston etc.	3	15	0	2	20	32.8	58.4
Edgbaston	20	0	0	0	20	40.3	13.0
Erdington	5	0	0	0	5	34.5	38.2
Erdington North	15	0	0	0	15	40.0	37.6
Erdington South	15	0	0	0	15	38.1	29.6
Gravelly Hill	5	0	0	0	5	33.1	30.1
Hall Green	7	0	0	0	7	30.3	35.5
Handsworth	17	0	0	3	20	44.1	17.1
Harborne	20	0	0	0	20	43.1	13.9
King's Norton	10	1	8	1	20	48.0	34.0
Ladywood	15	5	0	0	20	40.7	43.6
Lozells	13	0	5	2	20	37.6	27.0
Market Hall	20	0	0	0	20	32.5	31.3
Moseley etc.	19	0	0	1	20	35.0	19.3
Northfield	12	4	2	2	20	46.9	44.3
Perry Bar	2	6	0	0	8	29.7	52.7
Rotton Park	17	2	0	1	20	44.1	40.6
St Bartholomew's	4	13	3	0	20	30.9	51.7
St Martin's etc.	7	13	0	0	20	37.9	56.2
St Mary's	8	4	0	8	20	28.2	31.1
St Paul's	17	3	0	0	20	33.2	37.0
Saltley	2	16	0	2	20	42.9	56.1
Sandwell	6	0	0	14	20	45.1	18.3
Selly Oak	5	15	0	1	21	50.6	52.7
Small Heath	11	7	2	0	20	42.4	47.2
Soho	19	1	0	0	20	41.1	41.0
Sparkbrook	17	3	0	0	20	35.2	43.4
Sparkhill	19	0	1	0	20	33.8	28.3
Stechford	6	1	0	0	7	36.8	47.7
Washwood Heath	2	16	2	0	20	37.8	53.3
Yardley	12	1	0	7	20	36.5	35.0
Total	410	147	23	51	631	**37.9**	**40.8**

Seats won by Labour as a percentage of all wins 1919–38   **23.3**

Parliamentary election results

Aston constituency
(the following wards [1918 boundaries] were included in Aston:
All Saints' [part], Aston [part], Lozells [part], St Mary's [part])

General election	Winner	Conservative %	Labour %	Liberal %
14 Dec. 1918	Co C	62.4	27.8	-
15 Nov. 1922	C	60.8	39.2	-
6 Dec. 1923	C	56.2	31.8	12.0
29 Oct. 1924	C	54.6	45.4	-
30 May 1929	Lab	47.8	52.2	-
27 Oct. 1931	C	70.8	19.2	-
14 Nov. 1935	C	68.8	31.2	-

Deritend constituency
(the following wards [1918 boundaries] were included in Deritend:
St Bartholomew's, St Martin's and Deritend)

General election	Winner	Conservative %	Labour %	Liberal %
14 Dec. 1918	Co C	82.7	-	17.3
15 Nov. 1922	C	48.9	28.8	22.3
6 Dec. 1923	C	56.1	43.9	-
29 Oct. 1924	C	51.5	48.5	-
30 May 1929	Lab/Coop	42.5	50.7	6.8
27 Oct. 1931	C	66.0	34.0	-
14 Nov. 1935	C	59.5	40.5	-

Duddeston constituency
(the following wards [1918 boundaries] were included in Duddeston:
Duddeston and Nechells, Aston [part], St Mary's [part])

General election	Winner	Conservative %	Labour %	Liberal %
14 Dec. 1918	Co NDP	-	-	20.6
15 Nov. 1922	C	61.1	38.9	-
6 Dec. 1923	C	59.6	37.2	-
29 Oct. 1924	C	51.2	48.8	-
30 May 1929	Lab	39.0	61.0	-
27 Oct. 1931	C	61.1	36.6	-
14 Nov. 1935	C	57.8	42.2	-

Parliamentary election results *(continued)*

Edgbaston constituency
(the following wards [1918 boundaries] were included in Edgbaston:
Edgbaston, Harborne, Market Hall)

General election	Winner	Conservative %	Labour %	Liberal %
14 Dec. 1918	Co C	76.4	-	23.6
15 Nov. 1922	C	-	-	-
6 Dec. 1923	C	72.2	-	27.8
29 Oct. 1924	C	76.6	23.4	-
30 May 1929	C	63.7	23.4	12.9
27 Oct. 1931	C	86.5	13.5	-
14 Nov. 1935	C	81.6	18.4	-

Erdington constituency
(the following wards [1918 boundaries] were included in Erdington:
Erdington North and South, Washwood Heath, Aston [part])

General election	Winner	Conservative %	Labour %	Liberal %
14 Dec. 1918	Co C	66.0	-	6.9
15 Nov. 1922	C	-	-	-
6 Dec. 1923	C	66.0	34.0	-
29 Oct. 1924	C	59.5	40.5	-
30 May 1929	Lab	43.1	43.5	13.4
27 Oct. 1931	C	68.1	31.9	-
14 Nov. 1935	C	58.3	37.4	-

Handsworth constituency
(the following wards [1918 boundaries] were included in Handsworth:
Handsworth, Sandwell, Soho)

General election	Winner	Conservative %	Labour %	Liberal %
14 Dec. 1918	Co C	56.4	-	-
15 Nov. 1922	C	59.6	-	-
6 Dec. 1923	C	-	-	-
29 Oct. 1924	C	65.6	34.4	-
30 May 1929	C	53.9	29.3	16.8
27 Oct. 1931	C	78.4	21.6	-
14 Nov. 1935	C	73.0	27.0	-

Parliamentary election results *(continued)*

King's Norton constituency
(the following wards [1918 boundaries] were included in King's Norton:
Northfield, Selly Oak, King's Norton [part])

General election	Winner	Conservative %	Labour %	Liberal %
14 Dec. 1918	Co C	54.5	-	15.1
15 Nov. 1922	C	41.6	32.8	25.6
6 Dec. 1923	C	43.4	30.7	25.9
29 Oct. 1924	Lab	42.8	43.3	13.9
30 May 1929	C	42.0	40.6	17.4
27 Oct. 1931	C	57.5	28.7	13.8
14 Nov. 1935	C	56.8	43.2	-

Ladywood constituency
(the following wards [1918 boundaries] were included in Ladywood:
Ladywood, Rotton Park)

General election	Winner	Conservative %	Labour %	Liberal %
14 Dec. 1918	Co C	69.5	19.0	11.5
15 Nov. 1922	C	55.2	44.8	-
6 Dec. 1923	C	53.2	46.8	-
29 Oct. 1924	C	49.1	48.9	2.0
30 May 1929	Lab	50.0	50.0	-
27 Oct. 1931	C	71.8	28.2	-
14 Nov. 1935	C	71.7	28.3	-

Moseley constituency
(the following wards [1918 boundaries] were included in Moseley:
Acock's Green, Balsall Heath [part], King's Norton [part],
Sparkhill, Moseley [part], Sparkbrook [part])

General election	Winner	Conservative %	Labour %	Liberal %
14 Dec. 1918	Co C	69.2	16.2	14.6
15 Nov. 1922	C	-	-	-
6 Dec. 1923	C	71.3	-	28.7
29 Oct. 1924	C	77.2	22.8	-
30 May 1929	C	56.8	26.4	15.7
27 Oct. 1931	C	79.8	20.2	-
14 Nov. 1935	C	71.4	28.6	-

Parliamentary election results *(continued)*

Sparkbrook constituency
(the following wards [1918 boundaries] were included in Sparkbrook:
Balsall Heath [part], Moseley [part], Sparkbrook [part])

General election	Winner	Conservative %	Labour %	Liberal %
14 Dec. 1918	Co C	78.1	-	6.4
15 Nov. 1922	C	49.5	23.4	27.1
6 Dec. 1923	C	56.0	24.6	19.4
29 Oct. 1924	C	58.1	36.1	5.8
30 May 1929	C	46.2	37.4	16.4
27 Oct. 1931	C	73.4	26.6	-
14 Nov. 1935	C	68.5	31.5	-

West constituency
(the following wards [1918 boundaries] were included in West:
St Paul's, All Saints' [part], Lozells [part])

General election	Winner	Conservative %	Labour %	Liberal %
14 Dec. 1918	Co C	-	-	-
15 Nov. 1922	C	61.6	38.4	-
6 Dec. 1923	C	58.3	41.7	-
29 Oct. 1924	C	67.4	-	-
30 May 1929	C	50.1	49.9	-
27 Oct. 1931	C	68.1	31.9	-
14 Nov. 1935	C	64.3	35.7	-

Yardley constituency
(the following wards [1918 boundaries] were included in Yardley:
Saltley, Small Heath, Yardley)

General election	Winner	Conservative %	Labour %	Liberal %
14 Dec. 1918	Co C	56.3	38.3	5.4
15 Nov. 1922	C	58.1	41.9	-
6 Dec. 1923	C	53.5	46.5	-
29 Oct. 1924	C	53.2	46.8	-
30 May 1929	Lab	39.9	48.9	11.2
27 Oct. 1931	C	65.2	33.8	-
14 Nov. 1935	C	57.7	42.3	-

Acock's Green ward

Candidate	Party	Votes	%	Electors	Turnout	Gains
1919						
S.J. Gray	Ind	2,721	60.8	12,784	35.0	Ind from Lab
F. Atkins	Lab	1,758	39.2			
Total votes		4,479				
1920						
W.D. Hiorns	Ind	2,606	51.3	12,862	39.5	Ind from L
F. Atkins	Lab	1,459	28.7			
F.L. Hilton	T	1,011	19.9			
Total votes		5,076				
1921						
W.J. Davis	C	2,462	61.7	13,103	30.5	-
F.L. Hilton	T	1,531	38.3			
Total votes		3,993				
1922						
S.J. Grey	R	Unopp.	-		-	-
1923						
W.D.Hiorns*	Ind	Unopp.	-		-	-
1924						
W.J. Davis*	C	3,983	70.3	13,682	41.4	-
E.W. Hampton	Lab	1,679	29.7			
Total votes		5,662				
1925						
S.J. Grey*	Ind	Unopp.	-		-	-
1926						
Dr L.L. Hadley	C	4,125	66.4	15,097	41.1	C from Ind
F. Coleman	Lab	2,086	33.6			
Total votes		6,211				
1927						
W.J. Davis*	C	3,845	66.8	15,908	36.2	-
F. Coleman	Lab	1,912	33.2			
Total votes		5,757				

Acock's Green ward *(continued)*

Candidate	Party	Votes	%	Electors	Turnout	Gains
1928						
S.J. Grey*	Ind	3,570	77.0	18,288	25.3	-
P.F. Vale	I.Lab	1,065	23.0			
Total votes		4,635				
1929						
A.E.B. Cox	C	2,690	61.9	23,068	18.8	-
J.V. Sweeney	Lab	1,655	38.1			
Total votes		4,345				
1930						
J.T. Mason*	C	3,891	62.8	26,140	23.7	-
Mrs E.E. Reynolds	Lab	2,309	37.2			
Total votes		6,200				
1931						
O.F. Gloster*	C	6,376	74.9	28,113	30.3	-
Mr.E.E. Reynolds	Lab	2,136	25.1			
Total votes		8,512				
1932						
A.E.B. Cox*	C	4,550	54.2	29,205	28.7	-
T.W. Hill	Lab	3,845	45.8			
Total votes		8,395				
1933						
W.T. Brain	C	5,117	57.5	30,228	29.4	-
A.T. Doust	Lab	3,781	42.5			
Total votes		8,898				
1934						
O.F. Gloster*	C	2,774	58.6	16,620	28.5	-
A.T. Doust	Lab	1,958	41.4			
Total votes		4,732				
1935						
A.E.B. Cox*	C	3,726	62.5	16,932	35.2	-
A.T. Doust	Lab	2,238	37.5			
Total votes		5,964				

Acock's Green ward *(continued)*

Candidate	Party	Votes	%	Electors	Turnout	Gains
1936						
A.J. Harrison	C	3,120	63.4	17,282	28.5	-
H.F. Beck	Lab	1,803	36.6			
Total votes		4,923				
1937						
O.F. Gloster*	C	3,078	61.0	17,303	29.2	-
A.J. Gapper	Lab	1,966	39.0			
Total votes		5,044				
1938						
A.E.B. Cox*	C	4,157	67.1	17,303	35.8	-
A.E. Onley	Lab	2,038	32.9			
Total votes		6,195				
Overall Labour vote		**32.9%**		**Overall turnout**		**30.6%**

All Saints' ward

Candidate	Party	Votes	%	Electors	Turnout	Gains
1919						
W. Partridge	Lab	2,400	67.7	15,988	22.2	Lab from C
W. Brown*	C	1,143	32.3			
Total votes		3,543				
1920						
T.E. Smith*	C	3,981	70.9	16,034	35.0	-
H. Barrow	Lab	1,633	29.1			
Total votes		5,614				
1921						
J. Hall	Lab	4,368	58.0	16,259	46.3	Lab from C
S.T. Talbot*	C	3,166	42.0			
Total votes		7,534				
1922						
H. Barrow	Lab	4,558	55.2	16,493	50.0	-
W.H.V. Baker	C	3,692	44.8			
Total votes		8,250				
1923						
F. Stanley*	Lab	3,375	54.3	16,579	37.5	-
C.G. Lewis	C	2,841	45.7			
Total votes		6,216				
1924						
W. Blackwell	C	4,126	52.9	16,699	46.7	C from Lab
J. Hall*	Lab	3,674	47.1			
Total votes		7,800				
1925						
F.B. O'Dowd	C	3,824	52.7	16,878	43.0	C from Lab
H. Barrow*	Lab	3,430	47.3			
Total votes		7,254				
1926						
F. Stanley*	Lab	3,709	58.7	16,741	37.7	-
J.H. Wynn	C	2,609	41.3			
Total votes		6,318				

All Saints' ward *(continued)*

Candidate	Party	Votes	%	Electors	Turnout	Gains
1927						
W. Blackwell*	C	3,309	50.8	16,590	39.2	-
A.H. Bayes	Lab	3,201	49.2			
Total votes		6,510				
1928						
A. Jones	Lab	3,598	52.4	16,425	41.8	Lab from C
T.M. Sapcote	C	3,159	46.0			
H. Shepperson	Com	115	1.7			
Total votes		6,872				
1929						
F. Stanley*	Lab	3,613	58.0	17,497	35.6	-
T.C. Pepper	C	2,616	42.0			
Total votes		6,229				
1930						
W. Blackwell*	C	3,977	59.0	17,002	39.7	-
F. Griffiths	Lab	2,766	41.0			
Total votes		6,743				
1931						
D.W. Heath	C	5,316	68.9	16,794	45.9	C from Lab
E.C. Wright	Lab	2,398	31.1			
Total votes		7,714				
1932						
E.C. Wright	Lab	3,401	55.9	16,747	36.4	Lab from C
F. Stanley*	C	2,688	44.1			
Total votes		6,089				
1933						
F. Stanley	C	3,049	53.8	16,610	34.1	-
J. Davies	Lab	2,619	46.2			
Total votes		5,668				
1934						
D.W. Heath*	C	2,817	56.4	13,967	35.7	-
R.F. Aston	Lab	2,175	43.6			
Total votes		4,992				

All Saints' ward *(continued)*

Candidate	Party	Votes	%	Electors	Turnout	Gains
1935						
P.H.H. Baker	C	3,108	56.9	13,954	39.2	C from Lab
W.S. Walters	Lab	2,355	43.1			
Total votes		5,463				
1936						
F. Stanley*	C	2,605	61.9	13,835	30.4	-
W.S. Walters	Lab	1,603	38.1			
Total votes		4,208				
1937						
J. Brewin	C	2,537	61.4	13,708	30.2	-
Mrs M.A. Griffiths	Lab	1,597	38.6			
Total votes		4,134				
1938						
P.H.H. Baker*	C	3,007	64.6	13,651	34.1	-
H.J. Scott	Lab	1,649	35.4			
Total votes		4,656				

Overall Labour vote   **47.7%**   **Overall turnout**   **38.2%**

Aston ward

Candidate	Party	Votes	%	Electors	Turnout	Gains
1919						
W.E. Stevens	Lab	2,402	74.2	14,952	21.7	-
J.W. Kerr	C	836	25.8			
Total votes		3,238				
1920						
E. Moorby	Lab	2,453	54.6	15,080	29.8	Lab from C
J.M. Swingler*	C	2,036	45.4			
Total votes		4,489				
1921						
F. Smith*	C	3,902	52.2	15,302	48.8	-
H. Holland	Lab	3,569	47.8			
Total votes		7,471				
1922						
W.E. Stevens*	Lab	3,780	51.0	15,490	47.9	-
J.W. Kerr	C	3,635	49.0			
Total votes		7,415				
1923						
W.E. Smith	C	2,943	50.2	15,671	37.4	C from Lab
A. Lane	Lab	2,925	49.8			
Total votes		5,868				
1924						
J.W. Kerr*	C	4,110	51.2	15,575	51.6	-
A. Lane	Lab	3,923	48.8			
Total votes		8,033				
1925						
W.E. Stevens*	Lab	3,905	55.7	15,598	44.9	-
W. Duckett	C	3,106	44.3			
Total votes		7,011				
1926						
J.E. Corrin	Lab	4,189	62.4	15,431	43.5	Lab from C
W.E. Smith*	C	2,524	37.6			
Total votes		6,713				

Aston ward *(continued)*

Candidate	Party	Votes	%	Electors	Turnout	Gains
1927						
C.G. Spragg	Lab	3,897	53.0	15,333	48.0	Lab from C
J.W. Kerr*	C	3,462	47.0			
Total votes		7,359				
1928						
W.E. Stevens*	Lab	4,346	59.7	15,215	47.9	-
J.W. Kerr	C	2,939	40.3			
Total votes		7,285				
1929						
J.E. Corrin*	Lab	3,017	59.0	16,319	31.3	-
F.W. Moorfield	C	2,099	41.0			
Total votes		5,116				
1930						
F.W. Moorfield	C	3,466	54.8	15,887	39.8	C from Lab
C.G. Spragg*	Lab	2,861	45.2			
Total votes		6,327				
1931						
J. Mundy	C	3,980	59.9	15,596	42.6	C from Lab
W.E. Stevens*	Lab	2,669	40.1			
Total votes		6,649				
1932						
W.E. Stevens	Lab	3,230	55.8	15,615	37.1	Lab from C
Dr P. Thornton*	C	2,396	41.4			
E.J. Fletcher	ILP	103	1.8			
Mrs J. Eden	Com	57	1.0			
Total votes		5,786				
1933						
F.W. Moorfield*	C	2,904	51.1	15,605	36.4	-
F. Wetherall	Lab	2,666	46.9			
T. Roberts	Com	110	1.9			
Total votes		5,680				
1934						
J. Mundy*	C	2,687	51.8	15,546	33.4	-
F. Wetherall	Lab	2,498	48.2			
Total votes		5,185				

Aston ward *(continued)*

Candidate	Party	Votes	%	Electors	Turnout	Gains
1935						
W.E. Stevens*	Lab	2,901	52.3	15,454	35.9	-
A. Brown	C	2,647	47.7			
Total votes		5,548				
1936						
F.W. Moorfield*	C	3,141	62.7	15,207	33.0	-
F. Wetherall	Lab	1,872	37.3			
Total votes		5,013				
1937						
J. Mundy*	C	2,488	59.8	15,014	27.7	-
J. Wood	Lab	1,676	40.2			
Total votes		4,164				
1938						
D.W. Heath	C	3,024	58.7	14,790	34.8	C from Lab
F. Wetherall	Lab	2,129	41.3			
Total votes		5,153				

Overall Labour vote	**51.0%**	**Overall turnout**	**38.7%**

Balsall Heath ward

Candidate	Party	Votes	%	Electors	Turnout	Gains
1919						
E.W. Hampton	Coop	2,527	58.9	15,738	27.2	Coop from C
G.F. Heath	C	1,761	41.1			
Total votes		4,288				
1920						
W.E. Edwards	C	3,949	67.3	15,994	36.7	-
Ms H. Andrews	Lab	1,421	24.2			
J.C. Wells	L	495	8.4			
Total votes		5,865				
1921						
F.A.H. Owen-Lewis	C	4,147	60.0	16,300	42.4	-
D. Davies	Lab	2,761	40.0			
Total votes		6,908				
1922						
J.R. Menlove	C	4,604	59.2	16,259	47.8	C from Lab
E.W. Hampton*	Lab	3,167	40.8			
Total votes		7,771				
1923						
E.W. Fletcher	C	3,668	54.8	16,308	41.1	-
E.W. Hampton	Lab	3,031	45.2			
Total votes		6,699				
1924						
F.A.H. Owen-Lewis*	C	5,260	67.8	16,278	47.7	-
J.E. Corrin	Lab	2,498	32.2			
Total votes		7,758				
1925						
J. Baldwin-Webb*	C	4,055	64.2	16,100	39.2	-
J. Hammond	Lab	2,260	35.8			
Total votes		6,315				
1926						
E.W. Fletcher*	C	3,395	53.0	16,036	39.9	-
G. Craddock	Lab	3,011	47.0			
Total votes		6,406				

Balsall Heath ward *(continued)*

Candidate	Party	Votes	%	Electors	Turnout	Gains
1927						
F.A.H. Owen-Lewis*	C	4,412	59.1	15,918	46.9	-
G. Craddock	Lab	3,054	40.9			
Total votes		7,466				
1928						
J. Baldwin-Webb*	C	4,003	56.4	15,679	45.2	-
G. Craddock	Lab	3,091	43.6			
Total votes		7,094				
1929						
E.W. Fletcher*	C	2,631	53.2	16,658	29.7	-
J. Wood	Lab	2,319	46.8			
Total votes		4,950				
1930						
F.A.H. Owen-Lewis*	C	3,775	68.6	16,247	33.9	-
J. Wood	Lab	1,728	31.4			
Total votes		5,503				
1931						
J. Baldwin-Webb MP*	C	4,764	80.6	16,080	36.7	-
B.G. Marsden	Lab	1,145	19.4			
Total votes		5,909				
1932						
W.E. Fletcher*	C	2,787	58.4	16,098	29.6	-
P. Palmer	Lab	1,985	41.6			
Total votes		4,772				
1933						
Mrs E.A. Jackson*	C	2,874	61.5	16,103	29.0	-
P. Palmer	Lab	1,801	38.5			
Total votes		4,675				
1934						
J. Baldwin-Webb MP*	C	2,920	65.6	15,947	27.9	-
J.B. McGrath	Lab	1,530	34.4			
Total votes		4,450				

Balsall Heath ward *(continued)*

Candidate	Party	Votes	%	Electors	Turnout	Gains
1935						
E.W. Fletcher*	C	3,002	65.1	15,922	29.0	-
J.B. McGrath	Lab	1,610	34.9			
Total votes		4,612				
1936						
W.H. Dare*	C	2,963	68.6	15,728	27.4	-
Miss J.S. Wells	Lab	1,354	31.4			
Total votes		4,317				
1937						
J. Baldwin-Webb MP*	C	3,092	65.6	15,673	30.1	-
Miss J.S. Wells	Lab	1,618	34.4			
Total votes		4,710				
1938						
E.W. Fletcher*	C	2,930	65.2	15,567	28.8	-
Miss J.S. Wells	Lab	1,561	34.8			
Total votes		4,491				
Overall Labour vote		**35.6%**		**Overall turnout**		**35.9%**

Bromford ward
(created from the eastern parts of Erdington North and South wards, and new land brought in by the extension of the borough, in the reorganisation of 1934)

Candidate	Party	Votes	%	Electors	Turnout	Gains
1934						
C.J. Simmonds	Lab	2,197	18.5	12,066	33.8	-
Mrs A. Bradshaw	Lab	2,040	17.2			
J.R. Pessall	Lab	2,028	17.1			
J.A.C. Wright	C	1,892	15.9			
G.S. Incledon- Webber	C	1,867	15.7			
H. Ruxton	C	1,849	15.6			
Total votes		11,873				
Total voters		*4,080*				
(3 elected)						
1935						
C.V.G. Simpson	C	2,225	25.4	12,590	35.8	C from Lab
J.E. Cowdrill	C	2,206	25.2			C from Lab
Mrs F.M. Whatley	Lab	2,191	25.0			
T.W. Hawkes	Lab	2,127	24.3			
Total voters		*4,510*				
(2 elected)						
1936						
V.W. Grosvenor	C	2,304	58.4	13,088	30.1	-
T.W. Hawkes	Lab	1,639	41.6			
Total votes		3,943				
1937						
F.T. Monk	C	2,791	53.4	13,521	38.6	C from Lab
C.J. Simmons*	Lab	2,432	46.6			
Total votes		5,223				
1938						
C.V.G. Simpson*	C	2,774	55.1	13,740	36.7	-
T.W. Hawkes	Lab	2,262	44.9			
Total votes		5,036				

Overall Labour vote   **47.0%**   **Overall turnout**   **35.1%**

Duddeston and Nechells ward

Candidate	Party	Votes	%	Electors	Turnout	Gains
1919						
N.G.C. Dean	T	2,408	49.2	15,136	32.3	T from Lab
G.F. Sawyer	Lab	1,376	28.1			
J.F. White	C	1,109	22.7			
Total votes		4,893				
1920						
J.F. White	C	3,073	53.0	15,274	38.0	C from Lab
W.W. Saunders*	Lab	2,729	47.0			
Total votes		5,802				
1921						
G.F. Sawyer	Lab	3,053	55.3	16,414	33.6	-
J.W. Kerr	C	2,467	44.7			
Total votes		5,520				
1922						
N.G.C. Dean	T	Unopp.	-		-	-
1923						
J.F. White*	C	3,405	58.3	15,875	36.8	-
J. Wallis	Lab	2,431	41.7			
Total votes		5,836				
1924						
G.F. Sawyer*	Lab	4,908	58.1	15,934	53.0	-
W.E. Lovesey jun.	C	3,534	41.9			
Total votes		8,442				
1925						
C.J. Simmons*	Lab	4,510	58.9	15,992	47.9	-
D.D. James	C	3,144	41.1			
Total votes		7,654				
1926						
H. Barrow	Lab	4,824	63.4	15,845	48.0	Lab from C
Dr J. Sangster	C	2,783	36.6			
Total votes		7,607				
1927						
G.F. Sawyer*	Lab	3,874	65.8	15,831	37.2	-
F.G. Lee	C	2,017	34.2			
Total votes		5,891				

Duddeston and Nechells ward *(continued)*

Candidate	Party	Votes	%	Electors	Turnout	Gains
1928						
C.J. Simmons*	Lab	Unopp.	-		-	-
1929						
H. Barrow*	Lab	2,851	70.8	16,920	23.8	-
F. Lannon	C	1,173	29.2			
Total votes		4,024				
1930						
G.F. Sawyer*	Lab	2,764	56.8	16,356	29.8	-
F. Lannon	C	2,013	41.3			
A.E. Swain	Com	93	1.9			
Total votes		4,870				
1931						
W.R. Lewis	C	2,540	50.4	16,058	31.4	C from Lab
G.F. Godrich	Lab	2,499	49.6			
Total votes		5,039				
1932						
Mrs E.A. Wills*	Lab	3,466	75.7	15,995	28.6	-
S. Rogers	C	1,112	24.3			
Total votes		4,578				
1933						
G.F. Sawyer*	Lab	3,371	75.6	15,917	28.0	-
S. Rogers	C	1,088	24.4			
Total votes		4,459				
1934						
G.F. Godrich	Lab	2,325	67.8	15,149	22.6	Lab from C
J.F.R. Ritchie	C	1,105	32.2			
Total votes		3,430				
1935						
Mrs E.A. Wills*	Lab	2,266	66.4	15,087	22.6	-
G.M.E. Chivers	C	1,145	33.6			
Total votes		3,411				
1936						
G.F. Sawyer*	Lab	2,318	67.1	14,913	23.2	-
E. Dodd	C	1,137	32.9			
Total votes		3,455				

Duddeston and Nechells ward *(continued)*

Candidate	Party	Votes	%	Electors	Turnout	Gains
1937						
G.F. Godrich*	Lab	1,933	59.2	14,661	22.3	-
A.E.G. Hewkin	C	1,334	40.8			
Total votes		3,267				
1938						
Mrs E.A. Wills*	Lab	2,581	59.2	14,561	29.9	-
A.E.G. Hewkin	C	1,778	40.8			
Total votes		4,359				

Overall Labour vote   **58.4%**   **Overall turnout**   **32.8%**

Edgbaston ward

Candidate	Party	Votes	%	Electors	Turnout	Gains
1919						
Miss C. Martineau	C	Unopp.	-		-	-
1920						
R.H. Hume	C	4,259	80.1	14,468	36.8	-
W. Darby	Ind	1,060	19.9			
Total votes		5,319				
1921						
J.B. Burman	C	Unopp.	-		-	-
1922						
Miss C. Martineau*	C	Unopp.	-		-	-
1923						
R.H. Hume*	C	Unopp.	-		-	-
1924						
S.T. Talbot*	C	5,735	82.8	14,787	46.8	-
S.L. Treleaven	Lab	1,188	17.2			
Total votes		6,923				
1925						
Miss C. Martineau*	C	5,131	84.0	14,925	40.9	-
W.T. Chenoweth	Lab	978	16.0			
Total votes		6,109				
1926						
R.H. Hume*	C	Unopp.	-		-	-
1927						
H.E. Parkes	C	Unopp.	-		-	-
1928						
Miss C. Martineau*	C	Unopp.	-		-	-
1929						
R.H. Hume*	C	Unopp.	-		-	-
1930						
H.E. Parkes*	C	4,489	83.1	14,766	36.6	-
J. Perry	Lab	915	16.9			
Total votes		5,404				

Edgbaston ward *(continued)*

Candidate	Party	Votes	%	Electors	Turnout	Gains
1931						
Miss C. Martineau*	C	Unopp.	-		-	-
1932						
R.H. Hume*	C	Unopp.	-		-	-
1933						
R.C. Yates*	C	Unopp.	-	14,670	-	-
1934						
W.F. Higgs	C	Unopp.	-		-	-
1935						
J.C. Burman*	C	Unopp.	-	11,662	-	-
1936						
R.C. Yates*	C	Unopp.	-		-	-
1937						
E.V.Horton	C	Unopp.	-	11,939	-	-
1938						
J.C. Burman*	C	Unopp.	-		-	-

Overall Labour vote   **13.0%**   **Overall turnout**   **40.3%**

Erdington ward
(created from the western part of the old Erdington North ward in the 1934 reorganisation)

Candidate	Party	Votes	%	Electors	Turnout	Gains
1934						
Mrs G.F. Clarke	C	2,760	59.3	13,217	35.2	-
A.G. Chattaway	Lab	1,896	40.7			
Total votes		4,656				
1935						
R.W. Brosch*	C	3,268	64.2	13,392	38.0	-
A.G. Chattaway	Lab	1,821	35.8			
Total votes		5,089				
1936						
W.T. Wiggins-Davies*	C	2,822	64.8	13,517	32.2	-
A.J. Gapper	Lab	1,532	35.2			
Total votes		4,354				
1937						
Mrs G.F. Clarke*	C	2,502	58.5	13,651	31.3	-
A. Ellis	Lab	1,775	41.5			
Total votes		4,277				
1938						
R.W. Brosch*	C	3,074	61.8	13,937	35.7	-
A. Ellis	Lab	1,898	38.2			
Total votes		4,972				
Overall Labour vote		**38.2%**		**Overall turnout**		**34.5%**

Erdington North ward
(abolished in the 1934 reorganisation, the eastern part going into the new
Bromford ward and the western part into the new Erdington ward)

Candidate	Party	Votes	%	Electors	Turnout	Gains
1919						
W.B. Featherstone*	C	Unopp.	-		-	-
1920						
E.J. Houlston*	C	2,732	77.7	7,390	47.6	-
D.A.C. Harris	Lab	783	22.3			
Total votes		3,515				
1921						
S.J. Dixon	C	2,414	77.4	7,570	41.2	-
Ms A.M. Davies	Lab	705	22.6			
Total votes		3,119				
1922						
W.B. Featherstone*	C	Unopp.	-		-	-
1923						
E.W. Anderson	C	Unopp.	-		-	-
1924						
S.J. Dixon*	C	3,178	78.1	8,435	48.2	-
J. Hammond	Lab	890	21.9			
Total votes		4,068				
1925						
W.B. Featherstone*	C	Unopp.	-		-	-
1926						
J. Nicholls	C	3,217	63.1	11,509	44.3	-
J.S. Barr	Lab	1,884	36.9			
Total votes		5,101				
1927						
W.T. Wiggins-Davies	C	3,583	60.0	13,637	43.8	-
J.S. Barr	Lab	2,386	40.0			
Total votes		5,969				

Erdington North ward *(continued)*

Candidate	Party	Votes	%	Electors	Turnout	Gains
1928						
W.B. Featherstone*	C	3,104	52.4	15,034	39.4	-
J.S. Barr	Lab	2,235	37.8			
W. Sinclair	L	581	9.8			
Total votes		5,920				
1929						
R.W. Brosch	C	2,744	48.2	17,024	33.5	-
A.R. Bloxham	Lab	2,450	43.0			
W. Sinclair	L	504	8.8			
Total votes		5,698				
1930						
W.T. Wiggins-Davies*	C	3,996	55.5	19,050	37.8	-
A.R. Bloxham	Lab	3,207	44.5			
Total votes		7,203				
1931						
W.B. Featherstone*	C	5,376	69.2	19,233	40.4	-
A.R. Bloxham	Lab	2,397	30.8			
Total votes		7,773				
1932						
R.W. Brosch*	C	3,698	50.5	19,395	37.8	-
G.M. Thompson	Lab	3,629	49.5			
Total votes		7,327				
1933						
W.T. Wiggins-Davies*	C	4,271	57.1	19,821	37.7	-
A.G. Chattaway	Lab	3,205	42.9			
Total votes		7,476				
Overall Labour vote		**37.6%**			**Overall turnout**	**40.0%**

Erdington South ward
(abolished in the 1934 reorganisation, the eastern part going into the new Bromford ward and the western part into the new Graveley Hill ward)

Candidate	Party	Votes	%	Electors	Turnout	Gains
1919						
R.R. Gelling*	C	1,769	69.2	8,223	31.1	-
A.H. Spencer	Lab	789	30.8			
Total votes		2,558				
1920						
H. Bown*	C	2,533	77.2	8,340	39.4	-
H. James	Lab	749	22.8			
Total votes		3,282				
1921						
W.E. Lee*	C	2,420	78.0	8,578	36.2	-
F. Barker	Lab	682	22.0			
Total votes		3,102				
1922						
R.R. Gelling*	C	2,764	70.2	8,717	45.2	-
M.B. Shipsey	Lab	1,174	29.8			
Total votes		3,938				
1923						
F.G. Whittall	C	Unopp.	-		-	-
1924						
W.E. Lee*	C	3,001	74.6	9,428	42.7	-
M.B. Shipsey	Lab	1,021	25.4			
Total votes		4,022				
1925						
R.R. Gelling*	C	3,402	75.9	9,554	46.9	-
G. Horwill	Lab	1,078	24.1			
Total votes		4,480				
1926						
F.G. Whittall*	C	2,731	68.0	9,738	41.3	-
Mrs M.J. Simmonds	Lab	1,287	32.0			
Total votes		4,018				

Erdington South ward *(continued)*

Candidate	Party	Votes	%	Electors	Turnout	Gains
1927						
W.E. Lee*	C	2,581	67.2	9,976	38.5	-
Mrs M.J. Simmonds	Lab	1,259	32.8			
Total votes		3,840				
1928						
R.R. Gelling*	C	2,447	72.3	10,302	32.9	-
Mrs L.A.H. Burrell	Lab	939	27.7			
Total votes		3,386				
1929						
F.G. Whittall*	C	2,369	70.1	11,139	30.3	-
Mrs L.A.H. Burrell	Lab	1,009	29.9			
Total votes		3,378				
1930						
W.E. Lee*	C	2,920	68.5	12,583	33.9	-
J.G. Tottie	Lab	1,340	31.5			
Total votes		4,260				
1931						
R.R. Gelling*	C	4,000	79.4	12,858	39.2	-
J.G. Tottie	Lab	1,039	20.6			
Total votes		5,039				
1932						
F.G. Whittall*	C	3,185	60.6	12,954	40.5	-
C.J. Simmons	Lab	2,067	39.4			
Total votes		5,252				
1933						
W.E. Lee*	C	2,973	59.7	13,378	37.2	-
C.J. Simmons	Lab	2,007	40.3			
Total votes		4,980				

Overall Labour vote   **29.6%**   **Overall turnout**   **38.1%**

Gravelly Hill ward
(created from the western part of the old Erdington South ward in the 1934 reorganisation)

Candidate	Party	Votes	%	Electors	Turnout	Gains
1934						
S.J. Dixon*	C	3,216	69.7	14,222	32.4	-
Mrs H.L. Radford	Lab	1,395	30.3			
Total votes		4,611				
1935						
N. Tiptaft	C	4,022	67.8	14,657	40.5	-
A.J. Gapper	Lab	1,913	32.2			
Total votes		5,935				
1936						
J.A.C. Wright*	C	3,457	73.1	15,037	31.5	-
Mrs H.L. Radford	Lab	1,275	26.9			
Total votes		4,732				
1937						
S.J. Dixon*	C	2,965	69.5	15,173	28.1	-
Mrs H.L. Radford	Lab	1,304	30.5			
Total votes		4,269				
1938						
N. Tiptaft*	C	Unopp.	-		-	-
Overall Labour vote		**30.1%**		**Overall turnout**		**33.1%**

Hall Green ward
(created from the southern parts of Acock's Green and Sparkhill wards in the reorganisation of 1934)

Candidate	Party	Votes	%	Electors	Turnout	Gains
1934						
E.W. Dawkins	C	3,395	20.3	17,995	32.0	-
A.W. Gurden	C	3,374	20.2			
O.L. Richards	C	3,349	20.0			
H.F. Beck	Lab	2,235	13.3			
G.A. Carless	Lab	2,197	13.1			
E.H. Cox	Lab	2,194	13.1			
Total votes		16,744				
Total voters		*5,754*				
(3 elected)						
1935						
O.L. Richards*	C	3,971	61.8	19,077	33.7	-
H.F. Beck	Lab	2,455	38.2			
Total votes		6,426				
1936						
A.W. Gurden*	C	3,251	65.9	19,694	25.1	-
E.H. Cox	Lab	1,684	34.1			
Total votes		4,935				
1937						
W.H. Griggs	C	4,426	70.0	20,991	30.1	-
Mrs A.M. Durrant	Lab	1,893	30.0			
Total votes		6,319				
1938						
O.L. Richards*	C	4,371	64.1	21,976	31.0	-
W.W. Adams	Lab	2,443	35.9			
Total votes		6,814				

Overall Labour vote		**35.5%**			**Overall turnout**	**30.3%**

Handsworth ward

Candidate	Party	Votes	%	Electors	Turnout	Gains
1919						
N. Tiptaft*	Ind	4,319	70.7	11,423	53.5	-
R.H. Thornton	C	1,793	29.3			
Total votes		6,112				
1920						
B. Alderson	Ind C	3,206	61.3	11,621	45.0	-
E. Brindley	Prog	2,026	38.7			
Total votes		5,232				
1921						
D. Rose Jnr	C	Unopp.	-		-	-
1922						
N. Tiptaft*	Prog	3,830	56.8	12,018	56.1	-
Ms E. McDonald	Ind	2,915	43.2			
Total votes		6,745				
1923						
B. Alderson*	C	3,327	67.5	12,056	40.9	-
E. Hallas	Lab	1,601	32.5			
Total votes		4,928				
1924						
D. Rose*	C	Unopp.	-		-	-
1925						
T. Hampson	C	4,427	73.8	12,133	49.4	C from Ind
J. Hall	Lab	1,568	26.2			
Total votes		5,995				
1926						
B. Alderson*	C	2,996	71.6	12,146	34.4	-
W. Brown	Lab	1,186	28.4			
Total votes		4,182				
1927						
D. Rose*	C	3,688	73.6	12,350	40.6	-
A.E. Handel	Lab	1,323	26.4			
Total votes		5,011				

Handsworth ward *(continued)*

Candidate	Party	Votes	%	Electors	Turnout	Gains
1928						
W.G. Griffith*	C	3,453	67.7	12,548	40.7	-
A.C. Hodson	Lab	1,651	32.3			
Total votes		5,104				
1929						
B. Alderson*	C	Unopp.	-		-	-
1930						
J.H. Wynn	C	Unopp.	-		-	-
1931						
J.W. Kerr	C	Unopp.	-		-	-
1932						
B. Alderson*	C	Unopp.	-		-	-
1933						
W.C. Skinner	C	Unopp.	-		-	-
1934						
J.W. Kerr*	C	Unopp.	-		-	-
1935						
B. Alderson*	C	Unopp.	-	13,509	-	-
1936						
W.C. Skinner*	C	Unopp.	-		-	-
1937						
J.W. Kerr*	C	Unopp.	-	13,954	-	-
1938						
B. Alderson*	C	4,438	81.2	14,338	38.1	-
Ms H.L. Radford	Lab	1,026	18.8			
Total votes		5,464				

Overall Labour vote		**17.1%**		**Overall turnout**		**44.1%**

Harborne ward

Candidate	Party	Votes	%	Electors	Turnout	Gains
1919						
J. Oldfield	C	1,625	60.4	7,001	38.4	C from L
J.R. Turner*	L	1,065	39.6			
Total votes		2,690				
1920						
C.T. Appleby*	C	2,018	64.1	7,118	44.3	-
W.C. Wright	Sydn.	1,132	35.9			
Total votes		3,150				
1921						
W.B. Kenrick*	C	1,902	68.8	7,186	38.4	-
W.C. Wright	Ind	861	31.2			
Total votes		2,763				
1922						
W.T. Farncombe	C	2,691	71.1	7,301	51.8	-
W.C. Wright	T	1,093	28.9			
Total votes		3,784				
1923						
C.T. Appleby*	C	2,326	80.4	7,301	39.6	-
Ms F.L. Reynolds	Lab	567	19.6			
Total votes		2,893				
1924						
W.B. Kenrick*	C	2,855	79.7	7,292	49.1	-
C.E. Morgan	Lab	726	20.3			
Total votes		3,581				
1925						
W.T. Farncombe*	C	2,456	71.0	7,454	46.4	-
J. Dugmore	Lab	1,005	29.0			
Total votes		3,461				
1926						
T.B. Hooper*	C	2,088	68.0	7,488	41.0	-
J. Dugmore	Lab	982	32.0			
Total votes		3,070				

Harborne ward *(continued)*

Candidate	Party	Votes	%	Electors	Turnout	Gains
1927						
W.B. Kenrick*	C	2,308	78.2	7,719	38.2	-
P.F. Reynolds	Lab	642	21.8			
Total votes		2,950				
1928						
W.J. Loxley	C	Unopp.	-		-	-
1929						
T.B. Hooper*	C	Unopp.	-		-	-
1930						
T.F. Goode	C	Unopp.	-		-	-
1931						
W.J. Loxley*	C	3,901	85.5	10,485	43.5	-
W.M. Scarth	Lab	664	14.5			
Total votes		4,565				
1932						
T.B. Hooper*	C	Unopp.	-		-	-
1933						
T.F. Goode*	C	Unopp.	-	11,069	-	-
1934						
W.J. Loxley*	C	Unopp.	-		-	-
1935						
T.B. Hooper*	C	Unopp.	-	12,233	-	-
1936						
T.F. Goode*	C	Unopp.	-		-	-
1937						
F. Mountford*	C	Unopp.	-	15,177	-	-
1938						
J.H. Lewis*	C	Unopp.	-		-	-

| **Overall Labour vote** | | **13.9%** | | **Overall turnout** | | **43.1%** |

King's Norton ward

Candidate	Party	Votes	%	Electors	Turnout	Gains
1919						
W. Hood	Coop	2,136	63.3	8,358	40.4	Coop from
G. Yoxall*	C	1,241	36.7			C
Total votes		3,377				
1920						
J. Fryer*	L	3,882	81.1	8,647	55.4	-
W.J.J. Chamberlain	Lab	905	18.9			
Total votes		4,787				
1921						
Mrs G. Cadbury	L	Unopp.	-		-	-
1922						
W. Hood*	Lab	2,526	51.7	9,586	51.0	-
G.Yoxall	Ind	2,360	48.3			
		4,886				
1923						
J. Fryer*	L	Unopp.	-		-	-
1924						
T.B. Pritchett	C	2,807	48.3	10,038	57.8	C from L
S. Child	Lab	2,159	37.2			
R.V. Jones	L	840	14.5			
Total votes		5,806				
1925						
Miss F.E. Sant	C	2,848	53.5	10,079	52.8	-
R.W. Farrow	Lab	2,471	46.5			
Total votes		5,319				
1926						
J. Fryer*	L	4,204	65.2	10,183	63.4	-
J.V. Sweeney	C	2,248	34.8			
Total votes		6,452				
1927						
T.B. Pritchett*	C	3,037	57.2	10,261	51.8	-
J.V. Sweeney	Lab	2,276	42.8			
Total votes		5,313				

King's Norton ward *(continued)*

Candidate	Party	Votes	%	Electors	Turnout	Gains
1928						
Miss F.E. Sant*	C	2,590	50.8	10,502	48.5	-
A. Hill	Lab	2,508	49.2			
Total votes		5,098				
1929						
J. Fryer*	L	3,727	72.0	11,103	46.6	-
J. Parry	Lab	1,446	28.0			
Total votes		5,173				
1930						
T.B. Pritchett*	C	3,290	57.5	10,888	52.6	-
A. Hill	Lab	2,435	42.5			
Total votes		5,725				
1931						
Miss F.E. Sant*	C	3,571	68.5	10,836	48.1	-
R.T. Wothers	Lab	1,639	31.5			
Total votes		5,210				
1932						
J. Fryer*	L	3,889	74.0	10,943	48.0	-
R.T. Wothers	Lab	1,365	26.0			
Total votes		5,254				
1933						
T.B. Pritchett*	C	2,828	53.7	11,022	47.8	-
Mrs A.M.F. Farow	Lab	2,441	46.3			
Total votes		5,269				
1934						
Miss F.E. Sant*	C	3,441	57.1	13,841	43.6	-
Mrs A.M.F. Farrow	Lab	2,587	42.9			
Total votes		6,028				
1935						
J. Fryer*	L	5,044	74.1	14,805	46.0	-
Mrs A.M.F. Farrow	Lab	1,765	25.9			
Total votes		6,809				

King's Norton ward *(continued)*

Candidate	Party	Votes	%	Electors	Turnout	Gains
1936						
T.B. Pritchett*	C	3,564	59.0	15,875	38.1	-
Mrs A.M.F. Farrow	Lab	2,478	41.0			
Total votes		6,042				
1937						
Miss F.E. Sant*	C	3,813	59.0	16,680	38.7	-
V.J. Jackson	Lab	2,646	41.0			
Total votes		6,459				
1938						
J. Fryer*	L	Unopp.	-		-	-

Overall Labour vote   **34.0%**   **Overall turnout**   **48.0%**

Ladywood ward

Candidate	Party	Votes	%	Electors	Turnout	Gains
1919						
E.J. Parnell	Lab	1,758	56.3	11,160	28.0	Lab from C
H.E. Parkes	C	1,367	43.7			
Total votes		3,125				
1920						
R.H. Thornton	C	2,674	60.6	11,182	39.4	C from Lab
F.R. Sharkey*	Lab	1,737	39.4			
Total votes		4,411				
1921						
F.R. Sharkey	Lab	2,751	51.6	11,266	47.3	Lab from L
H.E. Parkes	C	2,577	48.4			
Total votes		5,328				
1922						
J. Bowater	C	2,960	53.2	11,468	48.6	C from Lab
F.E. Willis	Lab	2,608	46.8			
Total votes		5,568				
1923						
R.H. Thornton*	C	2,866	61.5	11,597	40.2	-
F.E. Willis	Lab	1,794	38.5			
Total votes		4,660				
1924						
E.P. Booth	C	3,139	53.5	11,557	50.7	C from Lab
A.H. Bayes	Lab	2,724	46.5			
Total votes		5,863				
1925						
J. Bowater*	C	2,441	51.5	11,667	40.6	-
C. Auger	Lab	2,296	48.5			
Total votes		4,737				
1926						
C. Auger*	Lab	2,688	57.5	11,600	40.3	-
Dr J.H.E.Trout	C	1,990	42.5			
Total votes		4,678				

Ladywood ward *(continued)*

Candidate	Party	Votes	%	Electors	Turnout	Gains
1927						
V.F. Yates	Lab	2,944	56.5	11,536	45.2	Lab from C
A.W. Gurden	C	2,271	43.5			
Total votes		5,215				
1928						
R.F. Dempster	Lab	2,682	57.6	11,373	40.9	Lab from C
H. Hopkins	C	1,974	42.4			
Total votes		4,656				
1929						
L. Glass	C	3,130	55.6	12,275	45.8	C from Lab
C. Auger*	Lab	2,497	44.4			
Total votes		5,627				
1930						
L.G.H. Alldridge	C	3,331	54.0	11,699	52.7	C from Lab
V.F. Yates*	Lab	2,838	46.0			
Total votes		6,169				
1931						
C.J. Print	C	2,823	57.6	11,393	43.0	C from Lab
R.F. Dempster*	Lab	1,306	26.6			
Mrs F. Potts	Ind	772				
Total votes		4,901				
1932						
L. Glass*	C	2,688	54.4	11,383	43.4	-
G.A. Carless	Lab	2,250	45.6			
Total votes		4,938				
1933						
L.G.H. Alldridge*	C	2,859	59.0	11,278	43.0	-
J. Webb	Lab	1,989	41.0			
Total votes		4,848				
1934						
C.J. Print*	C	2,479	58.3	13,040	32.6	-
R.F. Dempster	Lab	1,773	41.7			
Total votes		4,252				

Ladywood ward *(continued)*

Candidate	Party	Votes	%	Electors	Turnout	Gains
1935						
L. Glass*	C	3,405	68.3	12,860	38.8	-
G.A. Matthews	Lab	1,579	31.7			
Total votes		4,984				
1936						
L.G.H. Aldridge*	C	3,050	72.3	12,634	33.4	-
V.J. Jackson	Lab	1,167	27.7			
Total votes		4,217				
1937						
C.J. Print*	C	2,409	65.3	12,177	30.3	-
T. Simmonds	Lab	1,282	34.7			
Total votes		3,691				
1938						
L. Glass*	C	2,777	71.9	11,890	32.5	-
T. Simmonds	Lab	1,085	28.1			
Total votes		3,862				

Overall Labour vote		**43.6%**			**Overall turnout**	**40.7%**

Lozells ward

Candidate	Party	Votes	%	Electors	Turnout	Gains
1919						
J.C. Tillotson	L	1,991	44.9	13,513	32.8	-
G. Elliot	C	1,561	35.2			
G. Haynes	Lab	885	19.9			
Total votes		4,437				
1920						
W.C. Woodward	Ind	2,789	47.8	13,620	42.8	Ind from C
C.H. Clutterbuck*	C	2,240	38.4			
F.Moody	Lab	805	13.8			
Total votes		5,834				
1921						
W.F. Sabin*	C	3,784	55.3	13,748	49.7	-
F. Moody	Lab	3,053	44.7			
Total votes		6,837				
1922						
J.C. Tillotson*	L	4,528	67.5	13,824	48.5	-
F. Moody	Lab	2,183	32.5			
Total votes		6,711				
1923						
W.C. Woodward*	T	3,563	60.3	13,967	42.3	-
A. James	C	2,341	39.7			
Total votes		5,904				
1924						
J. Thacker	C	4,732	63.4	13,868	53.9	-
F. Griffiths	Lab	2,736	36.6			
Total votes		7,468				
1925						
A.E. Parker	C	3,008	45.1	13,920	47.9	C from L
J.C. Tillotson*	L	2,024	30.4			
T. Robinson	Lab	1,636	24.5			
Total votes		6,668				
1926						
G. Elliot	C	2,996	62.7	13,819	34.6	C from Ind
J. Webb	Lab	1,786	37.3			
Total votes		4,782				

Lozells ward *(continued)*

Candidate	Party	Votes	%	Electors	Turnout	Gains
1927						
J. Thacker*	C	3,737	67.3	13,790	40.3	-
Ms H. Andrews	Lab	1,814	32.7			
Total votes		5,551				
1928						
J.C. Tillotson*	L	2,935	61.7	13,687	34.8	-
J. Webb	Lab	1,822	38.3			
Total votes		4,757				
1929						
G. Elliott*	C	2,893	58.2	14,612	34.0	-
J. Webb	Lab	2,074	41.8			
		4,967				
1930						
J. Thacker*	C	4,252	71.4	14,235	41.8	-
J.V. Sweeney	Lab	1,702	28.6			
Total votes		5,954				
1931						
J.C. Tillotson*	L	4,298	82.6	14,316	36.3	-
F. Coleman	Lab	905	17.4			
Total votes		5,203				
1932						
A.H. Adcock	C	2,680	58.9	14,281	31.9	-
C.G. Spragg	Lab	1,872	41.1			
Total votes		4,552				
1933						
F.H. Normansell	C	3,734	68.2	14,258	38.4	-
J.L.G Kelly	Lab	1,741	31.8			
Total votes		5,475				
1934						
J.C. Tillotson*	L	2,766	71.9	14,236	27.0	-
J.L.G. Kelly	Lab	1,081	28.1			
Total votes		3,847				

Lozells ward *(continued)*

Candidate	Party	Votes	%	Electors	Turnout	Gains
1935						
A.H. Adcock*	C	3,097	71.5	14,101	30.7	-
J.L.G. Kelly	Lab	1,232	28.5			
Total votes		4,329				
1936						
F.H. Normansell*	C	3,155	75.3	14,019	29.9	-
F.L. Nicholls	Lab	1,037	24.7			
Total votes		4,192				
1937						
Dr P. Thornton	C	3,009	82.6	13,699	26.6	C from L
R.G. Crane	Com	635	17.4			
Total votes		3,644				
1938						
A.H. Adcock*	C	3,388	85.5	13,571	29.2	-
B. Williams	Com	574	14.5			
Total votes		3,962				

Overall Labour vote	**27.0%**			**Overall turnout**	**37.6%**

Market Hall ward

Candidate	Party	Votes	%	Electors	Turnout	Gains
1919						
C. Combridge*	C	940	64.9	9,904	14.6	-
C.J. Mann	Lab	508	35.1			
Total votes		1,448				
1920						
H.K. Beale	C	Unopp.	-		-	-
1921						
W.A.G. Grist*	C	1,819	51.5	9,942	35.5	-
L.G. Bradley	Lab	1,710	48.5			
Total votes		3,529				
1922						
C. Combridge*	C	2,809	68.1	10,008	41.2	-
H.A. Lacon	Lab	1,316	31.9			
Total votes		4,125				
1923						
H.K. Beale*	C	2,431	60.3	10,208	39.5	-
L.G. Bradley	Lab	1,601	39.7			
Total votes		4,032				
1924						
W.A.G. Grist*	C	2,715	73.5	10,150	36.4	-
E.H. Cox	Lab	979	26.5			
Total votes		3,694				
1925						
J.D. Lea*	C	2,419	69.4	10,127	34.4	-
E.H. Cox	Lab	1,066	30.6			
Total votes		3,485				
1926						
H.K. Beale*	C	2,133	63.8	9,981	33.5	-
J. Wood	Lab	1,208	36.2			
Total votes		3,341				

Market Hall ward (continued)

Candidate	Party	Votes	%	Electors	Turnout	Gains
1927						
W.A.G. Grist*	C	2,160	63.7	10,026	33.8	-
J. Perry	Lab	1,231	36.3			
Total votes		3,391				
1928						
J.D. Lea*	C	1,993	66.7	9,771	30.6	-
G. Bridgen	Lab	995	33.3			
Total votes		2,988				
1929						
H.K. Beale*	C	Unopp.	-		-	-
1930						
W.A.G. Grist*	C	Unopp.	-		-	-
1931						
H.A. Sale*	C	Unopp.	-		-	-
1932						
W. Martineau*	C	Unopp.	-		-	-
1933						
A.P. Morley*	C	1,805	76.9	7,817	30.0	-
B. Moore	Com	541	23.1			
Total votes		2,346				
1934						
H.A. Sale*	C	Unopp.	-		-	-
1935						
W. Martineau*	C	2,581	73.4	10,571	33.3	-
I.B.R. Cater	Lab	937	26.6			
Total votes		3,518				
1936						
A.P. Morley*	C	2,261	75.5	10,109	29.6	-
I.B.R. Cater	Lab	732	24.5			
Total votes		2,993				

Market Hall ward *(continued)*

Candidate	Party	Votes	%	Electors	Turnout	Gains
1937						
H.A. Sale*	C	2,096	72.2	9,843	29.5	-
J.H. Mills	Lab	806	27.8			
Total votes		2,902				
1938						
W. Martineau*	C	Unopp.	-		-	-

Overall Labour vote   **31.3%**   **Overall turnout**   **32.5%**

Moseley and King's Heath ward

Candidate	Party	Votes	%	Electors	Turnout	Gains
1919						
H.E. Goodby	Ind	2,664	63.8	12,877	32.4	Ind from C
F.J. Gibbs*	C	1,514	36.2			
Total votes		4,178				
1920						
S. James	C	Unopp.	-		-	-
1921						
F.D. Tippetts	C	Unopp.	-		-	-
1922						
H.E. Goodby*	C	Unopp.	-		-	-
1923						
S.A. Lamplugh	C	Unopp.	-		-	-
1924						
F.D. Tippetts*	C	Unopp.	-		-	-
1925						
H.E. Goodby*	C	Unopp.	-		-	-
1926						
S.A. Lamplugh*	C	Unopp.	-		-	-
1927						
F.D. Tippetts*	C	5,555	79.0	16,441	42.8	-
J. Hammond	Lab	1,475	21.0			
Total votes		7,030				
1928						
H.E. Goodby*	C	Unopp.	-		-	-
1929						
S.A. Lamplugh*	C	3,390	73.7	18,023	25.5	-
W.A. George	Lab	1,212	26.3			
Total votes		4,602				
1930						
F.T. Beddoes*	C	5,126	80.5	17,499	36.4	-
W.A. George	Lab	1,243	19.5			
Total votes		6,369				

Moseley and King's Heath ward *(continued)*

Candidate	Party	Votes	%	Electors	Turnout	Gains
1931						
H.E. Goodby*	C	7,863	88.7	18,837	47.0	-
A.L. Gibson	Lab	998	11.3			
Total votes		8,861				
1932						
S.A. Lamplugh*	C	4,615	74.7	18,979	32.5	-
A.L. Gibson	Lab	1,562	25.3			
Total votes		6,177				
1933						
F.T. Beddoes*	C	Unopp.	-		-	-
1934						
H.S. Goodby*	C	4,790	78.9	18,814	32.3	-
J.H. Edwards	Lab	1,280	21.1			
Total votes		6,070				
1935						
S.A. Lamplugh*	C	4,780	77.5	18,974	32.5	-
Mrs M.A. Durrant	Lab	1,387	22.5			
Total votes		6,167				
1936						
F.T. Beddoes*	C	Unopp.	-		-	-
1937						
H.S. Goodby*	C	Unopp.	-	20,096	-	-
1938						
S.A. Lamplugh*	C	5,125	75.1	20,479	33.3	-
Ms C. Braithwaite	Lab	1,698	24.9			
Total votes		6,823				

| **Overall Labour vote** | | **19.3%** | | **Overall turnout** | | **35.0%** |

Northfield ward

Candidate	Party	Votes	%	Electors	Turnout	Gains
1919						
O. Morland	Ind	1,136	71.9	3,287	48.1	Ind from C
A.J. Leeson	C	444	28.1			
Total votes		1,580				
1920						
W.W. Longford	C	1,071	65.9	3,376	48.1	-
H. Stubbs	Lab	554	34.1			
Total votes		1,625				
1921						
P.F. Jones	C	1,181	49.6	3,534	67.4	-
E.H. Cox	Lab	682	28.6			
Dame E.M.R. Shakespear	Ind	520	21.8			
Total votes		2,383				
1922						
O. Morland	L	Unopp.	-		-	-
1923						
W.W. Longford*	C	Unopp.	-		-	-
1924						
W.C. Houldey	C	1,411	62.0	4,060	56.0	-
C. Watkin	Lab	864	38.0			
Total votes		2,275				
1925						
O. Morland*	L	Unopp.	-		-	-
1926						
W.W. Longford*	C	1,765	67.9	4,365	59.5	-
G. Horwill	Lab	833	32.1			
Total votes		2,598				
1927						
A.W. Barker	C	1,313	46.2	4,689	60.6	-
P.S. Cadbury	L	801	28.2			
R.W. Farrow	Lab	729	25.6			
Total votes		2,843				

Northfield ward *(continued)*

Candidate	Party	Votes	%	Electors	Turnout	Gains
1928						
O. Morland*	Ind	1,436	64.3	4,886	45.7	-
R.W. Farrow	Lab	799	35.7			
Total votes		2,235				
1929						
W.W. Longford*	C	1,503	70.6	5,336	39.9	-
R.W. Farrow	Lab	625	29.4			
Total votes		2,128				
1930						
W.T. Hodge*	C	2,658	72.7	7,922	46.2	-
W.H. Adey	Lab	999	27.3			
Total votes		3,657				
1931						
O. Morland*	C	2,695	69.7	10,135	38.1	-
T. Paton	Lab	1,170	30.3			
Total votes		3,865				
1932						
T. Hackett	Lab	3,125	57.0	11,415	48.0	Lab from C
W.W. Longford*	C	2,355	43.0			
Total votes		5,480				
1933						
W.T. Hodge*	C	3,791	55.7	14,368	47.4	-
S.P. Dobbs	Lab	3,019	44.3			
Total votes		6,810				
1934						
O. Morland*	C	3,468	51.2	16,287	41.6	-
S.P. Dobbs	Lab	3,302	48.8			
Total votes		6,770				
1935						
T. Hackett*	Lab	4,772	55.0	17,083	50.8	-
A.C. Hodge	C	3,908	45.0			
Total votes		8,680				

Northfield ward *(continued)*

Candidate	Party	Votes	%	Electors	Turnout	Gains
1936						
W.T. Hodge*	C	4,524	53.9	18,400	45.6	-
G.H. Humphreys	Lab	3,863	46.1			
Total votes		8,387				
1937						
G.H. Humphreys	Lab	4,567	53.8	20,291	41.8	Lab from C
W. Shelley	C	3,924	46.2			
Total votes		8,491				
1938						
T. Hackett*	Lab	5,652	54.0	21,626	48.4	-
G.H. Butler	C	4,810	46.0			
Total votes		10,462				

Overall Labour vote **44.3%** **Overall turnout** **46.9%**

Perry Bar ward
(added by extension of the borough in 1929)

Candidate	Party	Votes	%	Electors	Turnout	Gains
1931
L. Holland*	C	1,773	61.9	10,104	28.3	-
W.J. Warren	Lab	1,090	38.1
Total votes		2,863
1932
(no election)
1933
W.J. Warren	Lab	2,382	30.3	13,056	31.0	-
Mrs N. Hyde	Lab	2,294	29.2
G.H. Walker	C	1,601	20.4
J.F.R. Ritchie	C	1,587	20.2
Total votes		7,864
Total voters		*4,054*
(2 elected)
1934
J. Silverman	Lab	2,312	53.4	14,015	30.9	Lab from C
L. Holland*	C	2,021	46.6
Total votes		4,333
1935
Mrs N. Hyde*	Lab	2,562	55.4	16,278	28.4	-
G.H. Walker	C	2,063	44.6
Total votes		4,625
1936
W.S. Lewis	Lab	Unopp.	-		-	-
1937
J. Silverman*	Lab	3,911	61.1	25,022	25.6	-
A.G. Tremaine	C	2,488	38.9
Total votes		6,399
1938
E.C. West	C	5,165	53.0	29,483	33.1	C from Lab
Mrs N. Hyde*	Lab	4,582	47.0
Total votes		9,747
Overall Labour vote		**52.7%**			**Overall turnout**	**29.7%**

Rotton Park ward

Candidate	Party	Votes	%	Electors	Turnout	Gains
1919						
C.F. Chance	C	2,323	50.2	15,406	30.0	C from Lab
C.J. Simmons	Lab	2,305	49.8			
Total votes		4,628				
1920						
E.J. Denton	C	4,241	61.4	15,670	44.1	C from Lab
T. Hacket*	Lab	2,662	38.6			
Total votes		6,903				
1921						
C.J. Simmons	Lab	4,228	54.7	15,700	49.2	Lab from L
E.C.R. Marks*	L	3,498	45.3			
Total votes		7,726				
1922						
J.F. Hall-Edwards*	C	4,848	59.8	15,993	50.7	-
D.H. Martin	Lab	3,253	40.2			
Total votes		8,101				
1923						
E.J. Denton*	C	4,074	56.3	16,051	45.1	-
D.H. Martin	Lab	3,157	43.7			
Total votes		7,231				
1924						
A.E.W. Hird	C	5,638	57.4	16,257	60.4	C from Lab
C.J. Simmons*	Lab	4,177	42.6			
Total votes		9,815				
1925						
J.F. Hall-Edwards*	C	4,558	58.3	16,244	48.2	-
F.T. Hawkins	Lab	3,264	41.7			
Total votes		7,822				
1926						
E.H. Cox	Lab	4,040	51.9	16,104	48.4	Lab from C
E.J. Denton*	C	3,750	48.1			
Total votes		7,790				

Rotton Park ward *(continued)*

Candidate	Party	Votes	%	Electors	Turnout	Gains
1927						
E.J. Denton	C	3,827	53.2	16,154	44.5	-
W.J.J. Chamberlain	Lab	3,363	46.8			
Total votes		7,190				
1928						
A.E.W. Hird	C	4,253	52.3	16,027	50.8	C from Lab
W.H. Milner*	Lab	3,882	47.7			
Total votes		8,135				
1929						
F.W. Daniels	Ind	4,258	53.5	17,001	46.8	Ind from Lab
E.H. Cox*	Lab	3,696	46.5			
Total votes		7,954				
1930						
E.J. Denton*	C	4,644	63.1	16,693	44.1	-
Mrs E.M. Leonard	Lab	2,715	36.9			
Total votes		7,359				
1931						
T.J.W. Allen	C	6,071	74.6	16,726	48.7	-
E.H. Cox	Lab	2,067	25.4			
Total votes		8,138				
1932						
F.W. Daniels*	C	4,611	58.7	16,564	47.4	-
F. Coleman	Lab	3,238	41.3			
Total votes		7,849				
1933						
E.J. Denton*	C	3,700	59.5	16,484	37.7	-
E.H. Cox	Lab	2,263	36.4			
C.C. Bradsworth	ILP	258	4.1			
Total votes		6,221				
1934						
T.J.W. Allen*	C	3,362	66.9	14,707	34.2	-
R.C. Hughes	Lab	1,665	33.1			
Total votes		5,027				

Rotton Park ward *(continued)*

Candidate	Party	Votes	%	Electors	Turnout	Gains
1935						
C.C. Ladds*	C	4,089	68.5	14,636	40.8	-
H.G.H. Griffin	Lab	1,878	31.5			
Total votes		5,967				
1936						
J. Williams*	C	3,557	73.0	14,435	33.8	-
H.G.H. Griffin	Lab	1,316	27.0			
Total votes		4,873				
1937						
T.J.W. Allen	C	3,540	69.0	14,371	35.7	-
A. King	Lab	1,587	31.0			
Total votes		5,127				
1938						
C.C. Ladds*	C	3,627	68.2	14,298	37.2	-
A. King	Lab	1,693	31.8			
Total votes		5,320				

Overall Labour vote   **40.6%**   **Overall turnout**   **44.1%**

St Bartholomew's ward

Candidate	Party	Votes	%	Electors	Turnout	Gains
1919						
A.V. Wright*	L	1,029	65.5	13,317	11.8	-
W.A. Jackson	C	542	34.5			
Total votes		1,571				
1920						
J.W. Danielsen	C	2,435	63.3	13,335	28.9	C from Lab
J. Adams*	Lab	1,414	36.7			
Total votes		3,849				
1921						
J.R. Stephens	L	2,296	62.3	13,356	27.6	-
F.A.C. Willis	C	1,390	37.7			
Total votes		3,686				
1922						
G. Payne	Lab	2,404	62.0	13,598	28.5	Lab from L
A.V. Wright*	L	1,472	38.0			
Total votes		3,876				
1923						
J.W. Danielsen*	C	2,567	58.2	13,823	31.9	-
E.M. Podesta	Lab	1,846	41.8			
Total votes		4,413				
1924						
J.R. Stephens*	L	2,038	56.5	13,824	26.1	-
E.M. Podesta	Lab	1,567	43.5			
Total votes		3,605				
1925						
H.A. Sale	C	2,068	51.5	13,909	28.9	C from Lab
G. Payne*	Lab	1,949	48.5			
Total votes		4,017				
1926						
Mrs A. Longdon	Lab	3,063	60.9	13,762	36.5	Lab from C
J.W. Danielsen*	C	1,966	39.1			
Total votes		5,029				

St Bartholomew's ward *(continued)*

Candidate	Party	Votes	%	Electors	Turnout	Gains
1927						
W.E. Wheeldon	Lab	2,545	60.6	13,712	30.6	Lab from L
J.R. Stephens*	L	1,656	39.4			
Total votes		4,201				
1928						
J.W. Tonks	Lab	2,598	59.9	13,777	31.5	Lab from C
H.A. Sale*	C	1,740	40.1			
Total votes		4,338				
1929						
Mrs A. Longdon*	Lab	2,318	70.8	14,764	22.2	-
F. Greenhill	C	931	28.4			
H.Shepperson	Com	27	0.8			
Total votes		3,276				
1930						
W.E. Wheeldon*	Lab	2,296	54.6	14,271	29.5	-
W.H. Walter	C	1,909	45.4			
Total votes		4,205				
1931						
H.C. Smith	C	2,741	57.8	14,032	33.8	C from Lab
J.W. Tonks*	Lab	2,001	42.2			
Total votes		4,742				
1932						
Mrs A. Longdon*	Lab	3,569	72.1	13,953	35.5	-
F. Fawcett	C	1,383	27.9			
Total votes		4,952				
1933						
W.E. Wheeldon*	Lab	2,637	64.8	13,927	29.2	-
J. Brewin	C	1,431	35.2			
Total votes		4,068				
1934						
G.M. Thompson*	Lab	2,092	63.6	13,593	24.2	-
Mrs C. Elbourne	C	1,198	36.4			
Total votes		3,290				

St Bartholomew's ward *(continued)*

Candidate	Party	Votes	%	Electors	Turnout	Gains
1935						
Mrs A. Longdon*	Lab	2,274	56.9	13,390	29.9	-
J. White	C	1,726	43.2			
Total votes		4,000				
1936						
W.E. Wheeldon*	Lab	Unopp.	-		-	-
1937						
G.M. Thompson*	Lab	2,111	52.9	12,409	32.1	-
J. Morgan	C	1,877	47.1			
Total votes		3,988				
1938						
Mrs A. Longdon*	Lab	2,457	53.2	11,777	39.2	-
R.L. Dare	C	2,165	46.8			
Total votes		4,622				

Overall Labour vote		**51.7%**		**Overall turnout**		**30.9%**

St Martin's and Deritend ward

Candidate	Party	Votes	%	Electors	Turnout	Gains
1919						
A.S. Chovil*	C	872	45.3	15,507	12.4	-
F.R. Sharkey	Lab	711	37.0			
J.C. Read	Ind	340	17.7			
Total votes		1,923				
1920						
T. Bishop	C	Unopp.	-		-	-
1921						
P.L.E. Shurmer	Lab	3,633	64.8	15,612	35.9	Lab from L
E. Price*	L	1,976	35.2			
Total votes		5,609				
1922						
J. Williams	Lab	3,652	54.5	15,832	42.3	Lab from C
A.S. Chovil*	C	3,047	45.5			
Total votes		6,699				
1923						
T. Bishop*	C	2,986	53.8	15,937	34.8	-
H.C. Vincent	Lab	2,561	46.2			
Total votes		5,547				
1924						
P.L.E. Shurmer*	Lab	5,348	58.0	15,909	57.9	-
W.J. Elwood	C	3,870	42.0			
Total votes		9,218				
1925						
A.F. Bradbeer	Lab	3,664	52.8	16,051	43.2	-
W.J. Elwood	C	3,278	47.2			
Total votes		6,942				
1926						
C.L. Watkins	Lab	3,878	56.6	15,785	43.4	Lab from C
H.T. Woodhams	C	2,978	43.4			
Total votes		6,856				
1927						
P.L.E. Shurmer*	Lab	5,029	59.5	15,832	53.3	-
D.W. Heath	C	3,417	40.5			
Total votes		8,446				

St Martin's and Deritend ward *(continued)*

Candidate	Party	Votes	%	Electors	Turnout	Gains
1928						
A.F. Bradbeer*	Lab	4,080	63.0	15,601	41.5	-
W.H. Dare	C	2,392	37.0			
Total votes		6,472				
1929						
C.L. Watkins*	Lab	2,844	61.8	16,913	27.2	-
Mrs Jackson	C	1,759	38.2			
Total votes		4,603				
1930						
P.L.E. Shurmer*	Lab	3,771	58.4	16,026	40.3	-
J. White	C	2,688	41.6			
Total votes		6,459				
1931						
J. White	C	4,053	55.5	15,759	46.4	C from Lab
A.F. Bradbeer*	Lab	3,256	44.5			
Total votes		7,309				
1932						
C.L. Watkins*	Lab	4,031	69.8	15,737	36.7	-
S. Jacobs	C	1,748	30.2			
Total votes		5,779				
1933						
P.L.E. Shurmer*	Lab	4,517	67.5	15,701	42.6	-
G.M. Martineau	C	2,173	32.5			
Total votes		6,690				
1934						
P. Palmer	Lab	2,901	60.7	15,247	31.4	Lab from C
J. White*	C	1,882				
Total votes		4,783				
1935						
C.L. Watkins*	Lab	2,652	53.6	15,169	32.6	-
J. Rigby	C	2,298	46.4			
Total votes		4,950				

St Martin's and Deritend ward *(continued)*

Candidate	Party	Votes	%	Electors	Turnout	Gains
1936						
E.C. Keey	C	2,171	53.8	14,271	28.3	C from Lab
J. Perry	Lab	1,864	46.2			
Total votes		4,035				
1937						
A.E.R. Brooks	C	2,075	52.3	13,138	30.2	C from Lab
P. Palmer*	Lab	1,895	47.7			
Total votes		3,970				
1938						
G.J. Baragwanath	C	2,614	56.2	12,628	36.8	C from Lab
C.L. Watkins*	Lab	2,038	43.8			
Total votes		4,652				
Overall Labour vote		**56.2%**		**Overall turnout**		**37.9%**

St Mary's ward

Candidate	Party	Votes	%	Electors	Turnout	Gains
1919						
Miss M.L. Wilson	Ind	1,784	63.6	11,584	24.2	Ind from C
J.B. Burman*	C	1,019	36.4			
Total votes		2,803				
1920						
T. Brown*	C	2,579	54.9	11,630	40.4	-
G.F. Godrich	Ind	2,115	45.1			
Total votes		4,694				
1921						
G.F. Godrich	Ind	2,557	56.8	11,846	38.0	Ind from C
A. James	C	1,274	28.3			
F.W .Robertson	Com	668	14.8			
Total votes		4,499				
1922						
Miss M.L. Wilson*	Ind	2,504	55.6	12,031	37.4	-
C.J. Mann	Lab	1,999	44.4			
Total votes		4,503				
1923						
W. Provost*	C	2,270	70.5	12,003	26.8	-
F.W. Robertson	Lab	949	29.5			
Total votes		3,219				

(Robertson was described as a 'Communist or Labour' candidate in the Birmingham Post)

Candidate	Party	Votes	%	Electors	Turnout	Gains
1924						
G.F. Godrich*	Ind	2,296	74.9	11,947	25.7	-
F.W. Robertson	Lab	771	25.1			
Total votes		3,067				
1925						
Miss M.L. Wilson*	Ind	Unopp.	-		-	-
1926						
C.J. Mann	Lab	1,999	54.4	11,930	30.8	Lab from C
W. Provost*	C	1,679	45.6			
Total votes		3,678				

St Mary's ward (continued)

Candidate	Party	Votes	%	Electors	Turnout	Gains
1927						
G.F. Godrich*	Lab	1,962	48.8	11,936	33.7	-
H. Milnes	C	1,765	43.9			
E. Merrell	I.Lab	293	7.3			
Total votes		4,020				
1928						
Miss M.L. Wilson*	Ind	2,509	66.0	11,714	32.4	-
Mrs N. Hyde	Lab	1,231	32.4			
A. Symes	Com	60	1.6			
Total votes		3,800				
1929						
C.J. Mann*	Lab	1,365	52.1	12,681	20.7	-
H. Milnes	C	1,232	47.0			
T. Roberts	Com	23	0.9			
Total votes		2,620				
1930						
H. Milnes	C	1,864	57.6	12,017	26.9	C from Lab
G.F. Godrich*	Lab	1,374	42.4			
Total votes		3,238				
1931						
Miss M.L. Wilson*	Ind	Unopp.	-		-	-
1932						
C.J. Mann*	Lab	1,892	60.7	11,788	26.4	-
J.F.R. Ritchie	C	1,225	39.3			
Total votes		3,117				
1933						
H. Milnes*	C	1,524	52.2	11,612	25.1	-
D.K. Walker	Lab	1,395	47.8			
Total votes		2,919				
1934						
Miss M.L. Wilson*	Ind	2,048	86.9	12,027	19.6	-
G.H. Powell	Ind	310	13.1			
Total votes		2,358				

St Mary's ward *(continued)*

Candidate	Party	Votes	%	Electors	Turnout	Gains
1935						
E.W. Apps	C	1,876	56.7	11,869	27.9	C from Lab
C.J. Mann*	Lab	1,434	43.3			
Total votes		3,310				
1936						
H. Milnes*	C	1,592	77.9	11,355	18.0	-
Ms W. Lowe	Lab	451	22.1			
Total votes		2,043				
1937						
J. Pagett	C	1,554	64.7	10,698	22.5	C from Ind
C.J. Mann	Lab	848	35.3			
Total votes		2,402				
1938						
E.W. Apps*	C	2,321	74.5	10,157	30.7	-
G.A. Matthews	Lab	793	25.5			
Total votes		3,114				

Overall Labour vote		**31.1%**		**Overall turnout**		**28.2%**

St Paul's ward

Candidate	Party	Votes	%	Electors	Turnout	Gains
1919						
J. Poole*	C	1,403	59.0	13,305	17.9	-
E.A. Peacey	Nfds	974	41.0			
Total votes		2,377				
1920						
E.A. Peacey	C	2,542	60.2	13,473	31.3	C from Lab
E.C. Taylor*	Lab	1,679	39.8			
Total votes		4,221				
1921						
C. Lucas	C	Unopp.	-		-	-
1922						
J. Poole*	C	3,175	59.7	13,612	39.1	-
A.E. Need	Lab	2,146	40.3			
Total votes		5,321				
1923						
W.J. Partridge	C	2,364	53.2	13,763	32.3	-
S.B.M. Potter	Lab	2,076	46.8			
Total votes		4,440				
1924						
C. Lucas*	C	2,629	67.2	13,768	28.4	-
A. Clynes	Lab	1,282	32.8			
Total votes		3,911				
1925						
J. Poole*	C	2,460	64.4	13,726	27.8	-
W.S. Lewis	Lab	1,359	35.6			
Total votes		3,819				
1926						
W.S. Lewis	Lab	1,849	50.9	13,525	26.9	Lab from C
W.J. Partridge*	C	1,783	49.1			
Total votes		3,632				
1927						
C. Lucas*	C	2,218	52.7	13,466	31.3	-
H.W. Whateley	Lab	1,992	47.3			
Total votes		4,210				

St Paul's ward *(continued)*

Candidate	Party	Votes	%	Electors	Turnout	Gains
1928						
J. Poole*	C	3,167	56.6	13,172	42.5	-
E. McCulloch	Lab	2,344	41.9			
J.Gardiner	Com	83	1.5			
Total votes		5,594				
1929						
W.S. Lewis*	Lab	2,345	50.7	14,049	32.9	-
S. Allen	C	2,283	49.3			
Total votes		4,628				
1930						
A.J.F. Kemp*	C	3,377	62.3	12,781	42.4	-
E. McCulloch	Lab	2,044	37.7			
Total votes		5,421				
1931						
E.R. Canning*	C	4,359	81.8	12,523	42.6	-
W.D. Harvey	Lab	970	18.2			
Total votes		5,329				
1932						
W.S. Lewis*	Lab	2,673	52.2	12,380	41.4	-
R. Grant-Ferris	C	2,452	47.8			
Total votes		5,125				
1933						
R. Grant-Ferris	C	2,860	60.6	12,168	38.8	-
Mrs E.N. Lewis	Lab	1,856	39.4			
Total votes		4,716				
1934						
E.R. Canning*	C	3,345	66.5	14,374	35.0	-
J. Adshead	Lab	1,683	33.5			
Total votes		5,028				
1935						
H.J. Riddiford	C	3,221	61.0	14,218	37.1	C from Lab
W.S. Lewis*	Lab	2,057	39.0			
Total votes		5,278				

St Paul's ward *(continued)*

Candidate	Party	Votes	%	Electors	Turnout	Gains
1936						
S. Smith	C	2,774	75.2	13,952	26.4	-
J. Adshead	Lab	915	24.8			
Total votes		3,689				
1937						
E.R. Canning*	C	3,065	78.5	13,064	29.9	-
J. Baird	Lab	840	21.5			
Total votes		3,905				
1938						
H.G. Riddiford*	C	2,707	70.7	12,778	30.0	-
J. Baird	Lab	1,124	29.3			
Total votes		3,831				
Overall Labour vote		**37.0%**		**Overall turnout**		**33.2%**

Saltley ward

Candidate	Party	Votes	%	Electors	Turnout	Gains
1919						
E. Pardoe	Lab	2,582	74.5	11,900	29.1	Lab from C
J.A. Herrick*	C	882	25.5			
Total votes		3,464				
1920						
J. Crump*	Lab	2,422	55.7	12,113	35.9	-
J.A. Herrick	C	1,731	39.8			
H. Watts	Ind	196	4.5			
Total votes		4,349				
1921						
W.W. Saunders	Lab	3,272	65.5	12,248	40.8	-
J.H. Rooke	C	1,726	34.5			
Total votes		4,998				
1922						
E. Pardoe*	Lab	3,579	50.1	12,623	56.6	-
F.W. Daniels	Ind	3,571	49.9			
Total votes		7,150				
1923						
F.W. Daniels	Ind	4,375	56.6	12,627	61.2	Ind from Lab
J. Crump*	Lab	3,349	43.4			
Total votes		7,724				
1924						
W.W. Saunders*	Lab	Unopp.	-		-	-
1925						
E. Pardoe*	Lab	Unopp.	-		-	-
1926						
F.W. Daniels*	Ind	4,285	50.0	15,035	57.0	-
Mrs C.M. Stephens	Lab	4,283	50.0			
Total votes		8,568				
1927						
J. Crump*	Lab	4,518	59.5	15,687	48.4	-
P.H. Holland	C	3,075	40.5			
Total votes		7,593				

Saltley ward *(continued)*

Candidate	Party	Votes	%	Electors	Turnout	Gains
1928						
E. Pardoe*	Lab	4,970	63.7	16,201	48.1	-
P.H. Holland	C	2,830	36.3			
Total votes		7,800				
1929						
Mrs M.J. Downing	Lab	3,910	65.6	17,619	33.8	Lab from Ind
R.F. Ash	C	2,050	34.4			
Total votes		5,960				
1930						
J. Crump*	Lab	4,162	55.8	17,465	42.7	-
R.F. Ash	C	3,300	44.2			
Total votes		7,462				
1931						
W.I. Horton	C	4,173	52.6	18,028	44.0	C from Lab
E. Pardoe*	Lab	3,767	47.4			
Total votes		7,940				
1932						
Mrs M.J. Downing*	Lab	4,192	62.3	18,566	36.3	-
G.H. Walker	C	2,539	37.7			
Total votes		6,731				
1933						
J. Crump*	Lab	4,354	58.2	18,688	40.1	-
F.K. Wynn	C	3,131	41.8			
Total votes		7,485				
1934						
E. Pardoe	Lab	2,920	57.7	13,207	38.3	Lab from C
F.K. Wynn	C	2,143	42.3			
Total votes		5,063				
1935						
Mrs M.J. Downing*	Lab	2,899	56.7	13,690	37.3	-
Mrs I.M. Barton	C	2,210	43.3			
Total votes		5,109				

Saltley ward *(continued)*

Candidate	Party	Votes	%	Electors	Turnout	Gains
1936						
J. Crump*	Lab	2,750	60.8	13,661	33.1	-
J. White	C	1,774	39.2			
Total votes		4,524				
1937						
E. Pardoe*	Lab	3,157	51.4	13,624	45.1	-
C.F. Baker	C	2,990	48.6			
Total votes		6,147				
1938						
C.F. Baker	C	3,167	51.4	13,471	45.8	C from Lab
Ms E.N. Lewis	Lab	2,996	48.6			
Total votes		6,163				

Overall Labour vote   **56.1%**   **Overall turnout**   **42.9%**

Sandwell ward

Candidate	Party	Votes	%	Electors	Turnout	Gains
1919						
G.F. McDonald	Ind	3,928	80.6	8,167	59.7	Ind from C
F.H. Pepper*	C	948	19.4			
Total votes		4,876				
1920						
S. Darlington	Ind	2,950	82.2	8,336	43.0	-
G. Cook	Lab	637	17.8			
Total votes		3,587				
1921						
C.H. Clutterbuck	Ind C	2,017	56.4	8,412	42.5	-
F. Watson	Al.	1,558	43.6			
Total votes		3,575				
1922						
G.F. McDonald*	Ind	3,105	62.3	8,624	57.8	-
A.H. Cooper	Prog	1,882	37.7			
Total votes		4,987				
1923						
A.H. Cooper	Ind	2,425	50.8	8,796	54.3	-
Mrs E. McDonald	Ind	2,352	49.2			
Total votes		4,777				
1924						
C.H. Clutterbuck*	C	3,675	73.3	9,191	54.6	-
H.G. Bartle	Lab	1,339	26.7			
Total votes		5,014				
1925						
G.F. McDonald*	Ind	Unopp.	-		-	-
1926						
A.H. Cooper*	Ind	2,018	51.7	9,271	42.1	-
Mrs A.F. Wood	C	1,887	48.3			
Total votes		3,905				
1927						
C.H. Clutterbuck*	C	3,241	66.8	9,343	51.9	-
J.W. Tonks	Lab	1,611	33.2			
Total votes		4,852				

Sandwell ward *(continued)*

Candidate	Party	Votes	%	Electors	Turnout	Gains
1928						
G.F. McDonald*	Ind	3,385	72.5	9,395	49.7	-
J. Ballinger	Lab	1,285	27.5			
Total votes		4,670				
1929						
A.H. Cooper *	Ind	Unopp.	-		-	-
1930						
H. Richardson	C	3,264	65.3	9,693	51.6	C from Lab
G. Haynes*	Lab	1,738	34.7			
Total votes		5,002				
1931						
G.F. McDonald*	Ind	Unopp.	-		-	-
1932						
A.H. Cooper*	Ind	2,350	67.1	10,299	34.0	-
J. Webb	Lab	1,152	32.9			
Total votes		3,502				
1933						
H. Richardson*	C	2,805	71.2	10,496	37.5	-
Mrs M.E. McIntosh	Lab	1,134	28.8			
Total votes		3,939				
1934						
G.F. McDonald*	Ind	2,948	74.9	10,581	37.2	-
Mrs M.McIntosh	Lab	989	25.1			
Total votes		3,937				
1935						
A.H. Cooper*	Ind	2,904	75.1	10,585	36.5	-
W.B. Talbott	Lab	962	24.9			
Total votes		3,866				
1936						
H. Richardson*	C	2,681	75.3	10,861	32.8	-
W.H. Ridler	Lab	881	24.7			
Total votes		3,562				
1937						
A.P. Smith*	C	Unopp.	-		-	-

Sandwell ward *(continued)*

Candidate	Party	Votes	%	Electors	Turnout	Gains
1938						
A.H. Cooper*	Ind	Unopp.	-		-	-
Overall Labour vote		**18.3%**		**Overall turnout**		**45.1%**

Selly Oak ward

Candidate	Party	Votes	%	Electors	Turnout	Gains
1919						
S.J. Hart	Coop	2,573	57.4	10,820	41.4	Coop from
E.E. Quinton	Ind	960	21.4			Ind
W.B. Bolland	C	946	21.1			
Total votes		4,479				
1920						
W.B. Bolland	C	2,369	50.2	11,024	42.8	C from Lab
Mɜ M.E. Cottrell*	Lab	2,350	49.8			
Total votes		4,719				
1921						
G. Cadbury Jun.	Lab	5,322	76.8	11,310	61.2	-
A.H. Close	C	1,605	23.2			
Total votes		6,927				
1922						
S.J. Hart*	Lab	Unopp.	-		-	-
1923						
Mrs T.M. Wilson	Lab	3,501	60.2	11,424	50.9	Lab from C
F. Hooper	C	2,312	39.8			
Total votes		5,813				
1924						
F.B. Darling	Lab	Unopp.	-		-	-
1925						
S.J. Hart*	Lab	3,509	55.8	11,764	53.4	-
W.T.H. Cooke	C	2,775	44.2			
Total votes		6,284				
1926						
Mrs T.M. Wilson*	Lab	3,631	61.5	11,795	50.1	-
W.T.H. Cooke	C	2,276	38.5			
Total votes		5,907				
1927						
Dr J.J. Robb	Lab	3,119	54.7	11,997	47.5	-
F. Roper	C	2,584	45.3			
Total votes		5,703				

Selly Oak ward *(continued)*

Candidate	Party	Votes	%	Electors	Turnout	Gains
1928						
S.J. Hart*	Lab	3,398	57.6	12,091	48.8	-
J.F. Smith	C	2,504	42.4			
Total votes		5,902				
1929						
Mrs T.M. Wilson*	Lab	3,351	58.2	12,870	44.7	-
J.F. Smith	C	2,405	41.8			
Total votes		5,756				
1930						
J.F. Smith	C	3,942	55.9	12,899	54.7	C from Lab
Dr J.J. Robb*	Lab	3,109	44.1			
Total votes		7,051				
1931						
J. Hand	C	3,587	50.3	13,029	54.8	C from Lab
S.J. Hart*	Lab	3,548	49.7			
Total votes		7,135				
1932						
S.J. Hart	Lab	4,358	61.2	13,281	53.6	-
S.L. Ireland	C	2,765	38.8			
Total votes		7,123				
1933						
A.F. Bradbeer	Lab	4,004	58.9	13,538	50.2	Lab from C
J.F. Smith*	C	2,796	41.1			
Total votes		6,800				
1934						
V.F. Yates	Lab	2,991	46.6	13,905	46.1	Lab from C
J. Hand*	C	2,642	41.2			
J.N. Hyde	L	779	12.1			
Total votes		6,412				
1935						
Mrs M.E. McIntosh*	Lab	3,776	51.3	14,175	51.9	-
Mrs E.C. Quinton	C	3,582	48.7			
Total votes		7,358				

Selly Oak ward *(continued)*

Candidate	Party	Votes	%	Electors	Turnout	Gains
1936						
A.F. Bradbeer*	Lab	3,956	28.0	14,726	49.5	-
S.P. Dobbs	Lab	3,543	25.1			
J. Brewin	C	3,338	23.6			
J. Scott	C	3,305	23.4			
Total votes		14,142				
Total voters		*7,290*				
(2 elected)						
1937						
N.F. Haslam	C	4,446	52.5	15,505	54.6	C from Lab
V.F. Yates*	Lab	4,016	47.5			
Total votes		8,462				
1938						
D. Wood	C	4,330	50.9	16,339	52.1	C from Lab
S.P. Dobbs*	Lab	4,179	49.1			

Overall Labour vote   **52.7%**   **Overall turnout**   **50.6%**

Small Heath ward

Candidate	Party	Votes	%	Electors	Turnout	Gains
1919						
J.J. Atkins*	Lab	2,196	63.9	12,161	28.3	-
N.B. Hodgkin	C	1,109	32.3			
J.H. Rooke	PL	132	3.8			
Total votes		3,437				
1920						
J.L. Yates*	L	2,743	61.3	12,345	36.2	-
A.E. Ager	Lab	1,730	38.7			
Total votes		4,473				
1921						
A.E. Ager	Lab	2,935	50.8	12,521	46.1	Lab from C
G. Ward*	C	2,837	49.2			
Total votes		5,772				
1922						
A.D. Wimbush	C	4,053	60.9	12,751	52.2	C from Lab
J.J. Atkins*	Lab	2,597	39.1			
Total votes		6,650				
1923						
J.L. Yates*	L	Unopp.	-		-	-
1924						
E.W. Salt	C	3,887	52.6	12,832	57.6	C from Lab
A.E. Ager*	Lab	3,502	47.4			
Total votes		7,389				
1925						
A.H. Wright	C	3,337	53.2	12,871	48.7	-
A.E. Ager	Lab	2,932	46.8			
Total votes		6,269				
1926						
A.E. Ager*	Lab	2,985	55.3	13,211	40.8	-
J.H. Allen	L	2,411	44.7			
Total votes		5,396				
1927						
E.W. Salt*	C	3,298	50.5	14,152	46.1	-
H. Johnson	Lab	3,228	49.5			
Total votes		6,526				

Small Heath ward *(continued)*

Candidate	Party	Votes	%	Electors	Turnout	Gains
1928						
H. Johnson	Lab	3,351	50.6	14,399	46.0	Lab from C
A.E. Darrall	C	3,273	49.4			
Total votes		6,624				
1929						
A.E. Ager*	Lab	3,261	57.4	15,502	36.7	-
L.G.H. Alldridge	C	2,425	42.6			
Total votes		5,686				
1930						
E.W. Salt*	C	4,101	60.9	15,348	43.8	-
S. Powell	Lab	2,629	39.1			
Total votes		6,730				
1931						
Mrs A.E. Salt	C	4,697	68.7	15,132	45.2	C from Lab
H. Johnson*	Lab	2,144	31.3			
Total votes		6,841				
1932						
A.E. Ager*	Lab	3,513	54.7	15,121	42.4	-
A.H. Wright	C	2,905	45.3			
Total votes		6,418				
1933						
W.G. Elcock	C	3,154	51.7	15,160	40.2	-
H. Johnson	Lab	2,941	48.3			
Total votes		6,095				
1934						
H. Johnson	Lab	2,737	50.3	14,442	37.7	Lab from C
Mrs A.E. Salt*	C	2,708	49.7			
Total votes		5,445				
1935						
H. Bolton	C	3,211	54.2	14,414	41.1	-
F.A. Peach	Lab	2,714	45.8			
Total votes		5,925				

Small Heath ward *(continued)*

Candidate	Party	Votes	%	Electors	Turnout	Gains
1936						
W.G. Elcock*	C	3,034	57.2	14,217	37.3	-
R.P. Belben	Lab	2,274	42.8			
Total votes		5,308				
1937						
L.G. Seymour	C	2,818	51.6	14,234	38.4	C from Lab
H. Johnson*	Lab	2,644	48.4			
Total votes		5,462				
1938						
H. Bolton*	C	3,166	54.9	14,112	40.9	-
V.F. Yates	Lab	2,601	45.1			
Total votes		5,767				

Overall Labour vote   **47.2%**   **Overall turnout**   **42.4%**

Soho ward

Candidate	Party	Votes	%	Electors	Turnout	Gains
1919						
Mrs C.M. Mitchell	Lab	1,767	58.9	11,339	26.5	Lab from C
J. White jun.*	C	1,233	41.1			
Total votes		3,000				
1920						
P. Whitehouse	C	2,808	63.5	11,568	38.2	-
H.J. Odell	Lab	1,615	36.5			
Total votes		4,423				
1921						
Miss H. Bartleet*	C	2,720	50.8	11,624	46.0	-
G. Haynes	Lab	2,631	49.2			
Total votes		5,351				
1922						
H. Roberts	C	3,593	59.1	11,767	51.7	C from Lab
Mrs C.M. Mitchell*	Lab	2,488	40.9			
Total votes		6,081				
1923						
P. Whitehouse*	C	2,846	54.2	11,902	44.1	-
G. Haynes	Lab	2,404	45.8			
Total votes		5,250				
1924						
Miss H. Bartleet*	C	4,002	65.0	11,846	52.0	-
A. Hunt	Lab	2,155	35.0			
Total votes		6,157				
1925						
H. Roberts*	C	3,408	66.2	11,863	43.4	-
C.G. Spragg	Lab	1,738	33.8			
Total votes		5,146				
1926						
P. Whitehouse*	C	2,673	58.9	11,813	38.4	-
C.G. Spragg	Lab	1,865	41.1			
Total votes		4,538				

Soho ward *(continued)*

Candidate	Party	Votes	%	Electors	Turnout	Gains
1927						
Miss H. Bartleet*	C	3,107	60.3	11,841	43.5	-
F. Moody	Lab	2,043	39.7			
Total votes		5,150				
1928						
H. Roberts*	C	2,849	63.2	11,734	38.4	-
J. Hammond	Lab	1,661	36.8			
Total votes		4,510				
1929						
P. Whitehouse*	C	2,226	60.2	12,444	29.7	-
J. Hammond	Lab	1,471	39.8			
Total votes		3,697				
1930						
Miss H. Bartleet*	C	Unopp.	-		-	-
1931						
H. Roberts*	C	Unopp.	-		-	-
1932						
P. Whitehouse*	C	Unopp.	-		-	-
1933						
Miss H. Bartleet*	C	Unopp.	-	11,919	-	-
1934						
H. Roberts*	C	Unopp.	-		-	-
1935						
F.J. Wilde	C	Unopp.	-	11,915	-	-
1936						
G.H.W. Griffith*	C	Unopp.	-		-	-
1937						
P.W. Cox*	C	Unopp.	-	11,924	-	-
1938						
F.J. Wilde*	C	Unopp.	-		-	-
Overall Labour vote		**41.0%**		**Overall turnout**		**41.1%**

Sparkbrook ward

Candidate	Party	Votes	%	Electors	Turnout	Gains
1919						
T.F. Fathers	Lab	2,160	60.5	13,946	25.6	Lab from C
A.H. Stephenson*	C	1,410	39.5			
Total votes		3,570				
1920						
H. Higgins	C	2,775	53.9	14,286	36.0	-
J. Webb	Lab	1,587	30.8			
C. Chambers	L	785	15.3			
Total votes		5,147				
1921						
J. Webb	Lab	3,050	50.7	14,547	41.4	Lab from C
Ms A.J. Lloyd*	C	2,968	49.3			
Total votes		6,018				
1922						
P.H. Carter	C	3,977	57.8	14,693	46.8	C from Lab
T.F. Fathers*	Lab	2,898	42.2			
Total votes		6,875				
1923						
H. Higgins*	C	3,163	60.1	14,700	35.8	-
C. Auger	Lab	2,100	39.9			
Total votes		5,263				
1924						
G.H. Powell	C	3,780	57.3	14,662	45.0	C from Lab
J. Webb*	Lab	2,816	42.7			
Total votes		6,596				
1925						
J.B. Field	C	2,866	45.0	14,704	43.3	-
J. Webb	Lab	2,606	40.9			
G.G. Houghton	L	900	14.1			
Total votes		6,372				
1926						
H. Higgins*	C	2,512	46.3	14,499	37.4	-
G.E. Cresswell	Lab	2,460	45.3			
G.G. Houghton	Ind L	455	8.4			
Total votes		5,427				

Sparkbrook ward *(continued)*

Candidate	Party	Votes	%	Electors	Turnout	Gains
1927						
G.H. Powell*	C	2,774	46.2	14,402	41.7	-
G.E. Cresswell	Lab	2,414	40.2			
W.H. Horton	L	547	9.1			
G.G. Houghton	Rating	265	4.4			
Total votes		6,000				
1928						
J.B. Field*	C	2,552	53.0	14,219	33.9	-
G.E. Geobey	Lab	2,263	47.0			
Total votes		4,815				
1929						
H. Higgins*	C	2,206	50.9	15,074	28.7	-
H.G. Johnson	Lab	2,124	49.1			
Total votes		4,330				
1930						
W. McMullan	C	2,805	63.0	14,786	30.1	-
Mrs D. Mellichip	Lab	1,647	37.0			
Total votes		4,452				
1931						
J.B. Field*	C	3,498	70.1	14,627	34.1	-
J. Perry	Lab	1,490	29.9			
Total votes		4,988				
1932						
J. Perry	Lab	2,434	50.9	14,629	32.7	Lab from C
H. Higgins*	C	2,348	49.1			
Total votes		4,782				
1933						
W. McMullan*	C	2,285	51.4	14,640	30.3	-
R.T. Wothers	Lab	2,157	48.6			
Total votes		4,442				
1934						
J.B. Field*	C	2,283	52.3	14,607	29.9	-
R.T. Wothers	Lab	2,084	47.7			
Total votes		4,367				

Sparkbrook ward *(continued)*

Candidate	Party	Votes	%	Electors	Turnout	Gains
1935						
D.A. Pearson	C	3,167	57.3	14,459	38.2	C from Lab
J. Perry*	Lab	2,360	42.7			
Total votes		5,527				
1936						
W. McMullan*	C	2,498	56.9	14,387	30.5	-
R.T. Wothers	Lab	1,893	43.1			
Total votes		4,391				
1937						
J.B. Field*	C	2,350	56.4	14,345	29.1	-
R.T. Wothers	Lab	1,818	43.6			
Total votes		4,168				
1938						
D.A. Pearson*	C	2,737	56.5	14,280	33.9	-
R.T. Wothers	Lab	2,104	43.5			
Total votes		4,841				

Overall Labour vote **43.4%** **Overall turnout** **35.2%**

Sparkhill ward

Candidate	Party	Votes	%	Electors	Turnout	Gains
1919						
E.J. Smith	C	1,566	52.7	10,416	28.5	-
E.H. Cox	Lab	1,406	47.3			
Total votes		2,972				
1920						
W.B. Griffin	C	2,253	50.1	10,567	42.5	-
T.W. Hill	Lab	1,266	28.2			
R. Nicklin	Ind	977	21.7			
Total votes		4,496				
1921						
Dr A.I. Esslemont	L	Unopp.	-		-	-
1922						
B.D. Elt	C	3,561	74.3	11,606	41.3	-
T.W. Hill	Lab	1,231	25.7			
Total votes		4,792				
1923						
W.B. Griffin*	C	3,009	75.6	11,932	33.4	-
W.H. Parke	Coop	971	24.4			
Total votes		3,980				
1924						
W.J. Dalton	C	4,117	75.6	12,446	43.8	C from L
J.L. Palmer	Lab	1,330	24.4			
Total votes		5,447				
1925						
B.D. Elt*	C	4,170	75.5	13,152	42.0	-
H.W. Whatley	Lab	1,352	24.5			
Total votes		5,522				
1926						
W.B. Griffin*	C	Unopp.	-		-	-
1927						
W.J. Dalton*	C	4,168	68.3	16,245	37.6	-
J. Webb	Lab	1,933	31.7			
Total votes		6,101				

Sparkhill ward *(continued)*

Candidate	Party	Votes	%	Electors	Turnout	Gains
1928						
B.D. Elt*	C	Unopp.	-		-	-
1929						
W.B. Griffin*	C	2,915	64.3	19,968	22.7	-
W. Bennett	Lab	1,619	35.7			
Total votes		4,534				
1930						
W.J. Dalton*	C	4,112	72.7	20,300	27.8	-
E.H. Cox	Lab	1,541	27.3			
Total votes		5,653				
1931						
B.D. Elt*	C	Unopp.	-		-	-
1932						
W.B. Griffin*	C	4,186	64.4	21,788	29.8	-
H.F. Beck	Lab	2,310	35.6			
Total votes		6,496				
1933						
W.J. Dalton*	C	4,133	50.2	22,155	37.1	-
H.F. Beck	Lab	2,539	30.9			
J.R. Stephens	Non-party	1,553	18.9			
Total votes		8,225				
1934						
W. Gordon*	C	Unopp.	-		-	-
1935						
W.B. Griffin*	C	3,712	70.2	16,732	31.6	-
A. Fellows	Lab	1,576	29.8			
Total votes		5,288				
1936						
W.J. Dalton*	C	Unopp.	-		-	-
1937						
Dr W. Gordon*	C	Unopp.	-	17,064	-	-

Sparkhill ward *(continued)*

Candidate	Party	Votes	%	Electors	Turnout	Gains
1938						
J. Rigby*	C	4,087	73.9	17,126	32.3	-
H.G.H. Griffin	Lab	1,443	26.1			
Total votes		5,530				

Overall Labour vote   **28.3%**   **Overall turnout**   **33.8%**

Stechford ward
(created by extension of the borough in the reorganisation of 1934)

Candidate	Party	Votes	%	Electors	Turnout	Gains
1934						
Ms F.H. Kenrick	C	2,037	16.3	11,244	41.3	-
W.R. Hunt	C	2,032	16.2			
W.W. Adams	Lab	2,005	16.0			
R.G. Tranter	Lab	1,946	15.5			
T.F. Watson	C	1,939	15.5			
Ms F.M. Whatley	Lab	1,878	15.0			
Ms L. White	L	689	5.5			
Total votes		12,526				
Total voters		*4,639*				
(3 elected)						
1935						
T.F. Watson	C	2,649	54.8	11,783	41.1	C from Lab
W.W. Adams*	Lab	2,189	45.2			
Total votes		4,838				
1936						
W.R. Hunt*	C	2,299	50.6	13,045	34.8	-
R.G. Tranter	Lab	2,245	49.4			
Total votes		4,544				
1937						
Ms F.H. Kenrick*	C	2,494	50.5	15,389	32.1	-
Ms F.M. Whatley	Lab	2,443	49.5			
Total votes		4,937				
1938						
T.F. Watson*	C	Unopp.	-		-	-

Overall Labour vote		**47.7%**			**Overall turnout**	**36.8%**

Washwood Heath ward

Candidate	Party	Votes	%	Electors	Turnout	Gains
1919						
A. Shakespeare	Lab	3,100	63.6	14,085	34.6	Lab from C
E.A.B. Cox*	C	1,773	36.4			
Total votes		4,873				
1920						
A.J. Teal	L	2,863	51.3	14,292	39.0	-
G.D. Jeffcoat	Lab	2,718	48.7			
Total votes		5,581				
1921						
Ms A.M. Howes*	Lab	3,142	53.2	14,611	40.4	-
Ms H.M. Smith	C	2,761	46.8			
Total votes		5,903				
1922						
A. Shakespeare	Lab	Unopp.	-		-	-
1923						
A.J. Teall*	L	3,657	48.8	15,104	49.6	-
W. Luckcuck	Lab	3,535	47.2			
S.L. Treleaven	Ind	303	4.0			
Total votes		7,495				
1924						
Ms A.M. Howes	Lab	Unopp.	-		-	-
1925						
A. Shakespeare*	Lab	Unopp.	-		-	-
1926						
W. Luckcuck	Lab	4,860	57.0	15,965	53.4	Lab from Ind
A.J. Teall	Const.	3,670	43.0			
Total votes		8,530				
1927						
Ms A.M. Howes*	Lab	3,865	58.0	16,268	41.0	-
W.H. Walter	C	2,797	42.0			
Total votes		6,662				
1928						
Mrs E.A. Shakespeare	Lab	Unopp.	-		-	-

Washwood Heath ward *(continued)*

Candidate	Party	Votes	%	Electors	Turnout	Gains
1929						
J.N. Spalton	Lab	2,883	59.6	17,457	27.7	-
H. Simpson	C	1,953	40.4			
Total votes		4,836				
1930						
A.E. Eyton*	Lab	2,967	50.9	17,325	33.6	-
S. Allen	C	2,862	49.1			
Total votes		5,829				
1931						
H. Simpson*	C	4,013	59.3	17,814	38.0	-
R. Moffatt	Lab	2,757	40.7			
Total votes		6,770				
1932						
J.N. Spalton*	Lab	3,936	61.4	18,656	34.4	-
J. Hosking	C	2,475	38.6			
Total votes		6,411				
1933						
R. Moffatt	Lab	3,682	57.9	18,736	33.9	-
J. Hosking	C	2,673	42.1			
Total votes		6,355				
1934						
H. James	Lab	2,475	53.0	13,798	33.9	Lab from C
H. Simpson*	C	2,197	47.0			
Total votes		4,672				
1935						
J.N. Spalton*	Lab	2,812	52.6	14,175	37.7	-
J.F.R. Ritchie	C	2,531	47.4			
Total votes		5,343				
1936						
J.F.R. Ritchie	C	2,492	51.3	14,558	33.4	C from Lab
G.A. Matthews	Lab	2,366	48.7			
Total votes		4,858				

Washwood Heath ward *(continued)*

Candidate	Party	Votes	%	Electors	Turnout	Gains
1937						
H. James*	Lab	2,896	52.2	14,964	37.1	-
P.B. Belfield	C	2,651	47.8			
Total votes		5,547				
1938						
J.N. Spalton*	Lab	3,125	50.7	15,852	38.9	-
P.B. Belfield	C	3,039	49.3			
Total votes		6,164				

Overall Labour vote   **53.3%**   **Overall turnout**   **37.8%**

Yardley ward

Candidate	Party	Votes	%	Electors	Turnout	Gains
1919						
G. Perry*	Lab	1,245	55.4	7,199	31.2	-
I.A. Kenning	R	1,002	44.6			
Total votes		2,247				
1920						
M.L. Lancaster*	Ind	2,778	88.6	7,281	43.1	-
H. Shepperson	Lab	357	11.4			
Total votes		3,135				
1921						
H. Muscott*	C	2,298	65.8	7,433	47.0	-
H. Shepperson	Com	759	21.7			
D.A. Cole	Lab	436	12.5			
Total votes		3,493				
1922						
I.A. Kenning*	Ind	2,050	69.5	7,723	38.2	-
E.H. Cox	Lab	899	30.5			
Total votes		2,949				
1923						
W.H. Painter	Ind	2,232	73.9	7,816	38.7	-
E.H. Cox	Lab	789	26.1			
Total votes		3,021				
1924						
H. Muscott*	Ind	2,403	74.3	8,154	39.7	-
G.E. Geobey	Lab	831	25.7			
Total votes		3,234				
1925						
I.A. Kenning*	Ind	Unopp.	-		-	-
1926						
W.H. Painter*	Ind	2,516	68.1	8,575	43.1	-
G. Butler	Lab	1,179	31.9			
Total votes		3,695				
1927						
H. Muscott*	Ind	2,374	58.7	10,450	38.7	-
T.C. Pearson	Lab	1,670	41.3			
Total votes		4,044				

Yardley ward *(continued)*

Candidate	Party	Votes	%	Electors	Turnout	Gains
1928						
I.A. Kenning*	C	2,848	51.9	12,606	43.4	-
T.C. Pearson	Lab	2,618	48.1			
Total votes		5,466				
1929						
W.H. Painter*	C	2,396	51.3	13,968	33.5	-
T.C. Pearson	Lab	2,279	48.7			
Total votes		4,675				
1930						
A.S. Giles	C	3,234	60.7	13,632	39.1	C from Ind
H.G. Johnson	Lab	2,090	39.3			
Total votes		5,324				
1931						
I.A. Kenning*	C	4,487	76.5	14,762	39.8	-
H.F. Beck	Lab	1,381	23.5			
Total votes		5,868				
1932						
W.H. Painter*	C	3,162	61.2	15,349	33.7	-
Mrs N. Hyde	Lab	2,003	38.8			
Total votes		5,165				
1933						
A.S. Giles*	C	3,143	61.2	15,659	32.8	-
G.A. Carless	Lab	1,993	38.8			
Total votes		5,136				
1934						
A.H. Wright*	C	2,102	59.1	12,109	29.4	-
J. Webb	Lab	1,454	40.9			
Total votes		3,556				
1935						
W.H. Painter*	C	2,636	61.0	12,503	34.6	-
J. Webb	Lab	1,684	39.0			
Total votes		4,320				

Yardley ward *(continued)*

Candidate	Party	Votes	%	Electors	Turnout	Gains
1936						
A.S. Giles	C	2,592	62.3	13,663	30.5	-
J.W. Chambers	Lab	1,571	37.7			
Total votes		4,163				
1937						
A.H. Wright*	C	2,662	60.7	14,513	30.2	-
J.W. Chambers	Lab	1,720	39.3			
Total votes		4,382				
1938						
W.H. Painter*	C	2,683	43.9	15,708	38.9	-
R.F. Dempster	Lab	1,832	30.0			
E.L.Cochrane	Ind	1,591	26.1			
Total votes		6,106				

Overall Labour vote		**35.0%**			**Overall turnout**	**36.5%**

SIX
Blackburn

BLACKBURN

Blackburn became a municipal borough in 1851. Its development was inextricably linked to the rise to global importance of Lancashire's cotton industry during the nineteenth century. The town was made by cotton spinning initially, and then more importantly by cotton weaving. Indeed for a long time the town's economy was based overwhelmingly on the single industry of weaving. In 1890 the Blackburn Chamber of Commerce warned: 'In Blackburn they had only one string to their bow ... they might some day deeply regret it'.[1] The domination of King Cotton in the local economy was to be both the making of the borough and the agent of its inter-war difficulties.

Situated by the river Blakewater, at the junction of the Calder and Darwen valleys, Blackburn developed as an important centre of cotton textiles after the Napoleonic Wars. Its initial breakthrough was in cotton spinning although weaving had been carried on since the thirteenth century. The nineteenth-century successes were erected on the base of the earlier domestic system and merchant manufacturers. Blackburn's plentiful supplies of water and later local coal aided the development of power looms and the weaving side of the industry. Excellent rail, canal and road communications ensured that the town was firmly in touch with the world market.[2] By the late Victorian age weaving was its predominant activity and the spinning side of the cotton industry had shrunk to lesser importance. Blackburn was 'the cotton weaving capital of the world. By 1914 the town was at its peak both in terms of population and output'.[3] In 1911 Blackburn had a population of over 130,000, but it had declined slightly to just over 120,000 by 1931, making it the thirty-fourth largest county borough. The town had lost 6,429 people between 1921 and 1931, and there was a further decline of 9 per cent in the years 1931 to 1939.[4]

By 1931 over 35,000 women and 11,000 men, just over 47 per cent of the labour force overall, were still engaged in the cotton textile industry. The town was thus ranked third in the top fifteen textile towns in that year and was the premier centre for weaving. Given the wage structure, P.F. Clarke's comment that here 'was a town in which a whole family would work in the mill in order to secure a decent household income' probably still held good.[5] Commerce and finance was the second largest employer in 1931, but engineering with 9.1 per cent of the male labour force, was also significant. Blackburn was thirteenth in the borough rankings in terms of the percentage of male workers in engineering. Here, even in the 1930s, the manufacture of textile machinery was important. Ironically the manufacture of the machines that underpinned Lancashire's supremacy in cotton was to help develop Britain's global competitors, especially

---

[1] Beattie, D., *Blackburn: The Development of a Lancashire Cotton Town*, (Halifax, 1992), p. 27.

[2] Freeman, T.W., *The Conurbations of Great Britain*, (Manchester, 1959), p. 237.

[3] Beattie, *Blackburn*, p. 15.

[4] Beattie, *Blackburn*, p. 149.

[5] Clarke, P.F., 'British Politics and Blackburn Politics 1900–1910', *The Historical Journal*, XII, 2 (1969), p. 303.

India and Japan. The demise of the Lancashire cotton industry in the inter-war years led eventually to the decline of the manufacture of textile machinery in Blackburn. Employment in engineering was anyway comparatively smaller in Blackburn than in other cotton towns such as Bolton, Rochdale or Oldham

Nearly a fifth of males were classified as 'managerial and own account' in 1931. This helps to account for a reasonably substantial lower-middle class of factory managers, overlookers, independent tradesmen and shopkeepers. Such social groups supported the Conservative Party in Blackburn politics. Although there was a powerful and established upper-middle class of cotton masters, brewers, and less important engineering industrialists, numerically they were few. The lack of an extensive and substantial middle class can be deduced by the fact that in 1931 the borough had only two percent of females in domestic service as a proportion of the whole population. This placed Blackburn seventy-ninth of the eighty-three county boroughs in this category. The low percentage of domestic service assumes all the more importance when it is noted that women formed over 45 per cent of the total workforce. Thus Blackburn came top of that ranking of females as a percentage of the total workforce.

The landed class, who were in any case unimportant in Blackburn, declined sooner in this locality than elsewhere. From the nineteenth century, the political elite was largely drawn from the cotton industrialists. These 'masters' had substantial paternalistic influence, even control, over their workforces. By the last third of the nineteenth century, families like the Feildens, Sudells, Cardwells, Birleys, Chippendales, Maudes, and above all the Hornbys, were stalwarts of the local establishment. Forming an upper-middle class, these industrialists at first lived in large houses on or near the Preston New Road in St Silas's and St John's wards. These were both solid Conservative wards in the inter-war years, with a Liberal presence in St John's. By the twentieth century the cotton masters, joined by brewers like the Thwaites, and some engineering entrepreneurs, had moved out of the town and purchased country estates. John Walton refers to the early Victorian millowners as 'squirearchical industrialists', a trait utilised politically for the rest of the century.[6] Aping a country gentry lifestyle, this largely Tory elite had 'far reaching effects on Blackburn's social, political, educational, and cultural development'.[7]

The Conservative Party dominated both parliamentary and municipal politics in Blackburn in the twenty years of this study, prolonging a long tradition. For Beattie the borough just after the Second Reform Act was 'the Gibraltar of Toryism' in mainly Liberal Lancashire.[8] Trodd also portrays nineteenth-century Blackburn as 'the stronghold of working class Toryism where Liberalism was in an extremely weak position'.[9] In parliamentary terms before 1918, Pelling makes the point that 'over the long term Blackburn's Conservatism, though not quite as

---

[6]   Walton, J.K., *Lancashire; A Social History, 1558-1939*, (Manchester, 1987), p. 132.
[7]   Beattie, *Blackburn*, p. 32.
[8]   Beattie, *Blackburn*, p. 38.
[9]   Trodd, G., 'Political Change and the Working Class in Blackburn and Burnley, 1880–1914', (Ph.D. thesis, Lancaster University, 1978), p. 106.

strong as Preston's was firm enough to make this normally a safe seat'.[10] The Conservative average share of the poll over the six elections between 1885 and 1910 was high (54.6 per cent).[11] Philip Snowden broke the Conservative monopoly for Labour by winning one of the two seats in 1906 and 1910, but he failed to secure re-election after his refusal to support the war, a sign of the enduring strength of patriotic working-class Toryism. Between the wars the parliamentary seats remained mainly Conservative, though one seat fell to the Liberals in both 1923 and 1924, while Labour took both seats on its flood tide of 1929.

The Conservative Party also controlled inter-war Blackburn at the municipal level with confidence and an iron grip on power. Only once, in 1935, did Labour have more members in the council chamber, but with Liberal and Independent backing Conservative control was maintained. As in many inter-war boroughs, an anti-Labour, or as it was called at the time, an 'anti-Socialist' alliance operated relatively openly at the polls. Walton notes an anti-Labour working arrangement in the council chamber as early as 1905. In that year the borough secured a peak of twelve councillors in the Labour interest. This consisted of an amalgam of Social Democratic Federation, ILP and Trades Council nominees, but the traditional parties consistently combined to outvote Labour. Earlier, in the late nineteenth century, there had been few contested elections. Conservative domination had been so great that the Liberals came to pre-election agreements to maintain at least a presence on the council.[12]

Such tacit electoral pacts were maintained between the wars. Liberals and Tories rarely stood against each other when Labour was contesting a ward. Thus though there were six three-cornered contests in 1919, these declined thereafter. In 1920 J.A. Omerod, a Liberal cotton spinning manufacturer, proposed an apolitical alliance with the Conservatives. Blackburn, he argued, should be governed on non-party lines, at least expense to the ratepayers. To achieve this the two parties should help each other as no principles divided them in municipal work.[13] The Conservatives did not stand against the Liberal Harrison in St Paul's that year. He was the recipient of, he thought, trade union votes, and 'was greatly indebted to the Conservative Party, who had fought fairly strongly on his behalf'.[14] The following year Omerod himself received help from the Conservatives in his victory in St Silas's ward.[15] Overall that year there were three contests with more than two candidates, but only one where a Conservative fought a Liberal. All the 1922 contests were straight fights between Conservative and Labour with no Liberals standing, and in 1923 Liberals and Conservatives did not stand against each other. According to G.B. Eddie, secretary of the Labour Party, speaking at the ILP Institute, Liberals and Tories were working together in

[10] Pelling, H., *Social Geography of British Elections, 1885–1910*, (Aldershot, 1994), p. 262.
[11] Pelling, *Social Geography*, p. 260.
[12] Beattie, *Blackburn*, p. 39.
[13] *Northern Daily Telegraph (NDT)*, 2 Nov., 1920.
[14] *NDT*, 2 Nov. 1920.
[15] *NDT*, 2 Nov. 1921.

the municipal elections 'though they might try to camouflage the fact'.[16] Unofficial electoral pacts seemed to operate between Conservatives and Liberals right through the twenty years of inter-war elections. Occasionally they must have broken down for in 1926 and 1931 there were some three-way contests involving the two traditional parties and Labour, but this was rare. A speech by a Mr Hurley at the ILP Institute in 1924, after Labour had lost two council seats to Conservatives expressed the Labour view of the Tory–Liberal alliance plainly:

> If anyone had said fourteen years ago in Blackburn that the Conservatives would have to depend on Liberal votes to secure their return, they would have been laughed at and told they were only fit for a lunatic asylum.[17]

Turning to the spatial distribution of political loyalties, three wards, St John's, St Mark's and St Thomas's, were rock-solid Conservative with nineteen victories for that party in each ward between the wars. The latter two were outer suburban wards to the west and east of the town centre respectively, while St John's was part of the older-established middle-class heartland noted earlier. Walton indicates that in pre-1914 years St Thomas's was already a middle-class outpost, as was the Witton district which lay partly in St Mark's.[18] Park and St Michael's were also outer suburban wards to the south and north respectively, recording sixteen Conservative victories each. By contrast, another suburban ward to the south-west, St Andrew's, and the affluent St Silas's, were the two wards where Tories and Liberals tended to share power amicably. St Stephen's was a large ward which sprawled across the east and north of the town, taking in some working-class enclaves but also extending into the suburbs, and was predominantly Tory, but with occasional lapses to Labour.

Labour's main strength lay in St Matthew's, St Luke's, St Paul's, St Peter's, and Trinity wards. All these wards were situated in or near the town centre, and their housing stock mainly consisted mainly of modest terraces. They were among the highest for the borough in terms of persons per room, reflecting their predominantly working-class nature. However, the centrally placed St Mary's ward, with the highest persons per room figure in the borough, and the main site of Irish settlement in the nineteenth century, was much more marginal. Labour won only a quarter of the twenty inter-war contests here, with Tories and Liberals maintaining a joint anti-Labour pact with considerable success. It should be noted as well that even Labour's best wards were not the absolute strongholds that it could expect to hold in other boroughs. The *Northern Daily Telegraph* claimed that St Peter's was 'traditionally a socialist stronghold', but this was plainly only by Blackburn standards.[19] In fact St Matthew's and St Luke's were Labour's safest seats, but the Conservative–Liberal vote was always respectable there, and on only three occasions was Labour given a walkover in the two wards.

---

[16] *NDT*, 2 Nov. 1923.
[17] *NDT*, 3 Nov. 1924.
[18] Walton, *Lancashire*, p. 235.
[19] *NDT*, 3 Nov. 1930.

The housing structure of Blackburn had some relevance to the politics of the borough. Between 1870 and the 1890's virtual mill colonies existed, where the cotton industrialists built and owned housing around their mills. Industrial and residential development was intermixed, but most of the mill-owned housing was sold off by the end of the century.[20] There was also a low proportion of owner-occupied housing, standing at around 8 per cent in 1906 compared to between 30 and 50 per cent in nearby Burnley.[21] Blackburn appeared to have had higher quality housing than surrounding towns and most of the old back-to-backs had been demolished by 1914.[22] Much of the borough's housing consisted of mid to late Victorian terraces, and only thirty-eight houses were designated for slum clearance under the 1930 Housing Act.[23] Population decline in the 1920s also meant that there was no shortage of housing stock in the inter-war period. There were only three small council estates built in inter-war Blackburn, amounting to 1,993 houses. Two of the estates, Brownhill and Intack, were in the aforementioned St Stephen's ward, making its political volatility more explicable. The Green Lane estate was in St Andrew's, but it was too small to affect the ward's suburban character, or its solid Tory–Liberal allegiance.

The pattern of inter-war municipal politics in Blackburn over time can be summarised briefly. As elsewhere, 1919 was a year of success for Labour in Blackburn with five gains at the expense of the Conservatives and a 43 per cent share of the poll, just below its twenty-year average. Labour nationally fared badly in most parts of the country in municipal elections in the first half of the 1920s, and this was reflected locally. Seats were lost overall, with 1922 representing Labour's nadir when four losses were sustained. Its jump up to 48 per cent of the poll in 1922 and 1923 was an illusion, caused by Labour declining to contest most of its weakest seats in those years. The years 1926 to 1929 saw the fortunes of Labour in Blackburn reflect national performance, as these were years of solid achievement locally. Council seats increased each year, culminating in the dramatic five gains of 1929, with 47 per cent of the poll. The poor performances of 1930 and 1931 again mirrored the national disaster for Labour. 1931 was especially traumatic, after Ramsay MacDonald's 'betrayal' nationally, with the loss of five seats to the Conservatives, and the Labour share of the poll falling to its lowest point between the wars at less than 34 per cent. Labour's recovery was swift though, with 43 per cent of the poll won in 1932, though it was masked by the loss of four seats that year. These losses were in wards where Labour had made windfall gains in the exceptional year of 1929, and which were only now coming up for re-election in the three-year cycle of borough politics. Labour in Blackburn continued its recovery in the following three years, reaching its high point in 1935 when it held twenty-five of the fifty-six seats on the council. This was a false dawn however, as Labour fell away for the rest of the decade. This reflected the picture in many other boroughs, and gainsays any suggestion that the 1945 Labour landslide was prefigured by the trends of the late 1930s. In

[20] Beattie, *Blackburn*, pp. 51–54.
[21] Walton, *Lancashire*, p. 307.
[22] Beattie, *Blackburn*, p. 54.
[23] Beattie, *Blackburn*, pp. 156–7.

1938 Labour held barely one-third of the seats on the council, and still seemed far away from wresting control of the borough from the firm grip of the Tories.

As the analysis so far suggests, any discussion of politics in Blackburn must account for the phenomenon of working-class Toryism, for here was a borough where the working class was numerically predominant and yet Conservatism ruled the roost. Significant changes in political attitudes had occurred by the inter-war years, and were to continue through the years of economic crisis in the town, but the survival of past traditions of thought, belief and action was still important. Tory control had its origins in the nineteenth-century industrial structure of the town, the paramountcy of cotton manufacturing, and the organisation of the mill. For many reasons, including the obvious electoral ones, but also due to wider considerations of status and control, both traditional parties maintained close social contacts with the working class. The economic and social centrality of the cotton elite and other wealthy industrialists resulted in their domination of both parliamentary and local politics.

Blackburn has been fertile ground as a case study for the historical analysis of working-class Conservatism, and a number of these studies are worth examining here. One such is the impressive thesis written by Geoffrey Trodd. Trodd has suggested that the local ties of the industrial upper-middle class to working people were 'all-important, political parties less so. And both at parliamentary and local level it was the elite of cotton owners and other industrialists who ran affairs'.[24] He goes on to make a number of points about working-class Toryism and the paternalism of the manufacturers in the town. First, the Conservatives and Liberals needed working-class support for electoral success by the twentieth century, yet both avoided obvious class ideology or stress on class differences. A paternalistic framework of politics developed which involved both hierarchical justification and popular local action. This served the requirements of the Tory elite and the Liberals were forced along the same route. This Tory paternalism however was never narrowly political, nor a case of simply crude manipulation. It rested on a broad network of both cultural and social ties, but in the last resort emanated from the mill, where munificence and control were joint bedfellows. Thus:

> Personal Benevolence by the employers built up mill loyalty, strengthened by the key positions held by long-service overseers who owed their promotion to religious or political activity on behalf of their employers. At the same time, strict hierarchy was maintained by autocratic discipline, company housing and an anti-union policy.[25]

Trodd sees this paternalism emanating from the mill to the rest of society in the town, especially through authority positions. Millowners were party chairmen and overseers controlled the local ward committees. The Tory leaders managed to identify with popular activity and yet at the same uphold societal hierarchies. Class differences and populist links with working people were thus both

[24] Trodd, 'Political Change', p. 106.
[25] Trodd, 'Political Change', p. 107.

maintained. The Church of England's incestuous ties with local Toryism also helped to uphold authority and deference. The local Tory MP W.H. Hornby personified this paternalism and appeal to the local working class before 1914. In his person working-class Toryism had an almost apolitical quality that would continue to serve the local Conservative association well in the inter-war years. The local economy was still dominated by the cotton industry and although the cotton masters were less directly involved with the council, the tradition lingered on. Even though the industry was ailing, the loyalty of many of the working people remained to the mill, which provided a livelihood, leisure activities and conviviality. Employers took this on board and made it a factor of political mobilisation.

Another analysis of deference and paternalism based in part on evidence for Blackburn emerges in Patrick Joyce's study of the culture of the factory in late Victorian England.[26] Joyce's argument is complex and at times controversial, but some of his ideas are pertinent to a consideration the nature of politics in Blackburn between the wars. For Joyce, support for the local Conservative elite by the working class could well have been a matter of calculation. The relationship of master and men was perceived as one of interdependence, no matter how hollow that quality was in reality.[27] The overlookers, with their position of authority in the mill, could reinforce both the paternalism of the mill owner and the deference of the operatives at the same time. But this was not simply a coercive relationship. The overlookers, though the bosses' men and perhaps chosen for their political bias, looked after the workers interests too, and exerted leadership and influence through running the committees of the Co-op, friendly societies and chapel.[28] The centrality of the mill for the consolidation of a sense of neighbourhood and community bolstered paternalism, deference and working-class Tory allegiance. Thus Joyce suggests:

> Dominated by the influence and authority of the employer and his
> factory regime, the operation of factory neighbourhood feeling
> would have merged any differences of cultural style and status in
> a common allegiance to the neighbourhood employer.[29]

Joyce suggests that the family, and the importance of female labour in Blackburn, might be seen as reinforcing the politics of deference and paternalism in the cotton industry. It was noted that women were rarely in the trade unions of the late nineteenth century and were allegedly less concerned than men with long term goals. Joyce does assert that women had achieved 'a real breakthrough in mentality' in the early twentieth century, but whether this heralded the end or continuation of the old order in Blackburn is an open question.[30] To a considerable degree in nineteenth-century Lancashire, with Liberalism holding to

---

[26] Joyce. P., *Work, Society and Politics: The Culture of the Factory in Later Victorian England*, (London, 1982).
[27] Joyce, *Work, Society and Politics*, p. 91.
[28] Joyce, *Work, Society and Politics*, pp. 100–103.
[29] Joyce, *Work, Society and Politics*, p. 111.
[30] Joyce, *Work, Society and Politics*, p. 115.

the cold comfort farm of *laissez-faire*, Conservatism could be portrayed as the working man's friend. Joyce points to the stirring of the Labour interest from 1885 onwards in Blackburn, and perhaps the decline of the old paternal order. Yet the hold of the past was powerful. Joyce sees Blackburn socialists of the 1890s deferring to gentlemen, and argues that 'the poorer people' were 'happy to be represented by their superiors'. As late as 1907 the Trades Council reported that though the cotton masters, brewers and lawyers who ran the town were on the run, trade unionists still 'clung loyally' to the two established parties.[31] Joyce notes the loosening hold of the employers in the mill and factory towns by the First World War. Employer-owned housing and mill-dominated neighbourhoods were, he argues, swamped by urban development and growth.[32] This may not have been as relevant to Blackburn as to other textile towns, though. In Blackburn the nineteenth-century pattern of modest terraced housing persisted, as suggested above. Suburban sprawl was at a minimum, and council-house estates were fewer than elsewhere. It is arguable that older traditions of political allegiance and belief could be sustained longer in Blackburn's relatively stable environment.

A third, more general, study of relevance here is Neville Kirk's analysis of labour and society in Britain and the USA. Kirk suggests that the proponents of popular Conservatism did their best to see that the inhumane doctrines of the Manchester School and unbridled *laissez-faire* were associated with the Liberal employers in the consciousness of working men.[33] Kirk sees a number of factors at work in the popular Conservatism of the mid-nineteenth century. He argues that:

> Conservatism, with its various emphases upon social radicalism and Tory Democracy, its links with Orangism and 'No Popery', employer paternalism, and a relaxed and expansive political style rooted in the culture of beer, bonhomie and Britannia', had by the late 1860's, established important bases in many working class communities.[34]

For Kirk, popular Conservatism among other qualities stressed a patriotic appeal to 'the people', emphasising community with toleration of the 'weaknesses' of respectable working men, while offering an alternative to the moral conceits of Liberalism:

> Conservatism thus situated itself within the culture of 'conviviality and bonhomie', of 'beer, 'bacca, billiards, and Britannia' rather than within the strait-jacketed Liberal domain of 'moral exhortation' and the 'improving tract'.[35]

---

[31] Joyce, *Work, Society and Politics*, p. 333.
[32] Joyce, *Work, Society and Politics*, p. 338.
[33] Kirk, N., *Labour and Society in Britain and the USA, Volume 2: Challenge and Accommodation, 1850–1939*, (Aldershot, 1994), p. 181 and pp. 189–190.
[34] Kirk, *Labour and Society*, p. 188–189.
[35] Kirk, *Labour and Society*, p. 195.

Blackburn then, in the second half of the nineteenth century, Kirk suggests, was a stronghold of working-class or 'clog' Toryism, dominated by cotton employers like the Hornbys. Tory hegemony prevailed   and 'revolved around social radicalism, paternalism and that mixture of "traditional" "John-Bull"-like qualities depicted above'.[36]

Another factor reinforcing popular Toryism is raised by John Walton. He points out the changing destination of the county's cotton exports over the nineteenth century, and how dependence in late Victorian and Edwardian times had shifted to the Indian market. Just before the First War, 45 per cent of Britain's cotton exports went to India and this might well have had political repercussions strengthening Conservatism in Lancashire:

> This dependence on India and on long sea routes no doubt helped to push Lancashire politics into a Palmerstonian and later imperialist mould, encouraging the rise of a flag-waving, Navy-loving, jingoistic popular Toryism in some of the late Victorian cotton towns.[37]

A militant Anglicanism too supported the Conservative grip on the local politics of Blackburn. Bishop Fisher could in 1878 write of Blackburn that 'the alliance between Conservatism and the Church – religion not having much to do with the compact – is closer than in any other Lancashire town.'[38] Neville Kirk too lays emphasis on the connections between extreme Protestantism and Conservatism in the cotton districts.[39] The Church of England was by far the strongest religious affiliation in the town and managed to keep the spread of Nonconformity, largely of immigrants from the Pennines, at bay. Nonconformity had a wide variety of sects but overall was weak in total numbers. The Anglicans had the most elementary schools by far, extending their influence over succeeding generations. Only four Board Schools were built in Blackburn by 1900, while there were twenty-five Anglican, eleven Nonconformist, and eight Catholic establishments. The situation was little changed by the inter-war years. Church and chapel dominated education and probably imparted attitudes broadly in favour of traditional ideas. No doubt this indirectly bolstered the two traditional political parties.

Even more militant expressions of religion were also evident in Blackburn. The Orange movement was quite strong with over 1,200 members in seventeen lodges at the beginning of the twentieth century.[40] Kirk argues that Orangemen and militant Protestants repeatedly linked 'virulent attacks on Roman Catholicism with support for the social and economic grievances of English workers'.[41] With over 2,500 Irish living in the Penny Street area early this century, anti-Catholicism could be utilised as another Conservative ploy. Its efficacy may perhaps be

---

[36] Kirk, *Labour and Society*, p. 196.
[37] Walton, *Lancashire*, pp. 200–201.
[38] Quoted in Clarke, 'British Politics and Blackburn Politics', p. 303.
[39] Kirk, *Labour and Society*, p. 193.
[40] Beattie, *Blackburn*, p. 41.
[41] Quoted in Kirk, *Labour and Society*, p. 191.

relevant to the fact that the predominantly working-class St Mary's ward, in which Penny Street is located, was a relatively weak area of Labour support in the inter-war era.

There are a number of criticisms that can be made of the 'working-class Toryism' thesis. Walton for instance makes a number of points concerning Joyce's insistence on working-class deference, though these would also apply to the general argument of Conservatism's grip on the working class. First, deference might well have been only skin-deep, especially where the weavers had rival cultures to the mill. Second, such a relationship with employers mainly benefited the skilled and supervisory workers. What was attractive to the overlookers may not have been to the operatives. Third, the endemic industrial conflict which existed damages the thesis.[42] Beattie also suggests that changes in the dominant cotton industry may have undermined the basis of working-class Toryism. Amalgamations and take-overs in the industry, and the concentration of production, created limited companies, shareholders and a managerial layer. This reduced the ties, and widened the divide, between the cotton industrialists and their workers. With the political hold of the old elite slipping, and with only a weak Liberal alternative on offer between the wars, some workers crossed to the left in politics.[43] These factors go some way to explaining what successes the Labour Party had in municipal politics. But the factors of international competition, discussed below, and the depression in the cotton industry, were probably as important for any weakening of working-class Toryism in the 1920s.

Nevertheless, there is strong electoral evidence that the working-class Tory tradition was still alive in inter-war Lancashire, and in particular Blackburn. There is little doubt that this tradition was no straightforward process of class manipulation in the interests of the Cotton Kings. Toryism as an ideology could appeal to some textile workers in their own perceived interests. The differentiation of the labour force, aspirations of the overseers and an atavistic belief in the independence and skill of the weavers, perhaps led to an acceptance by some of the advantages of popular Toryism over the collectivism of the new Labour Party. But the full extent and ramifications of its existence, and the potency of its hold over the people of the borough, requires deeper investigation than can be attempted here. What can be asserted is that to some degree it aided the survival of Conservative control of the council chamber in what was essentially a working-class town.

The other side of the coin was the weakness of Labour. A number of points can be made which suggest long-standing problems in working-class politics in Blackburn. Chartism had not been strong here. Later, the first Labour Representation League parliamentary candidate for the town was a wealthy local cotton master, suggesting a far from independent streak in the local labour movement. The local Trades Council was very much in the Lib-Lab tradition, even expelling a member in 1896 for espousing Socialism.[44] Blackburn's trade unions were cautious and stood against 'extreme' political views. In the early

---

[42] Walton, *Lancashire*, p. 249.
[43] Beattie, *Blackburn*, p. 47.
[44] Beattie, *Blackburn*, p. 45.

twentieth century, the Weavers Protection Society broke away from the main union and openly backed the Conservatives. There had also been established a Conservative Working Men's Vigilance Committee in 1894.[45] Even though both the Social Democratic Federation and the Blackburn Fabian Society were established before the First War, the labour movement was weak in the town and shunned radicalism, hindering the development of a vibrant opposition to the Conservative Party in Blackburn. This weakness was still evident in the inter-war period. Complaints at the lack of party organisation and the paucity of active supporters were regularly made by Labour Party leaders. After the electoral gains of 1919 one representative was quoted as follows:

> He could not congratulate the members of the ILP, or of the Labour Party, or of trade union organisations on their share in the work which had made the success possible. He could only ascribe that success to the fact that the people had read of the aims of the Labour movement in the local and national newspapers. In the wards ... he had been extremely disappointed with the measure of the assistance the candidate had received.[46]

Members of the local Labour Party were also well aware of the extent of working-class Tory support that they faced. In St Matthew's ward in 1923, for instance, the Tory candidate, who Labour claimed 'had camouflaged himself as a working-class representative', won over many potential Labour voters.[47] Even more explicitly, a Labour councillor in 1921 observed that a Conservative alderman had claimed 'as much right to speak as the representative of labour as the Labour party'. The Labour man conceded the point, saying that Tories would not have won 'if they had not received a majority of working-class votes' in some wards.[48]

The impact of the decline of the staple cotton industry, along with the repercussions of the international slump of the 1930s, were two other key factors in inter-war politics in Blackburn which need investigation. The two phenomena, which devastated both Blackburn and Lancashire, were to a degree separate, though the Depression exacerbated the earlier decline of cotton. After an initial post-war boom, by 1921 Lancashire's cotton industry was in difficulties. The Indian and Chinese markets had helped make Blackburn 'the commercial capital of the weaving district'.[49] As already noted, 45 per cent of Britain's pre-1914 cotton exports went to India. With the growth of Indian and Japanese domestic cotton production during and after the First World War, Lancashire and Blackburn's cotton industry went into terminal decline. In 1918 the town had 150 mills and 90,000 working looms, but by October 1921 just under a third of the looms had stopped production, and more than a half by early 1922. In the seventeen years after 1919, seventy-nine mills closed down, forty-four of them for good as the machinery was sold off. Those still operating were undercapitalised

---

[45] Beattie, *Blackburn*, p. 45.
[46] *NDT*, 3 Nov. 1919.
[47] *NDT*, 2 Nov. 1923.
[48] *NDT*, 2 Nov. 1921.
[49] Walton, *Lancashire*, p. 200.

and not working at anything like full capacity. The weaving side of the industry never really recovered from this decline, and the smaller sector in Blackburn, spinning, collapsed altogether.[50] The international slump from 1929 heralded the virtual eclipse of the Far Eastern export market. Walton points out that in 1929 British cotton cloth exports amounted to just over 50 per cent of their 1913 level. By 1930–31 the volume had been halved again, and by 1938–39 exports were below the level of the mid-nineteenth century. The worst hit were towns like Blackburn and Darwen exporting cheap shirts and dhotis to India and the Far East. Slump conditions in these towns lasted longer than in the Lancashire towns manufacturing higher quality fabric.[51]

Unemployment in the cotton industry depressed the whole local economy. In June 1930 unemployment in Blackburn peaked at 51.8 per cent of insured workers. It was still at 28.8 per cent in 1936, and 31.4 per cent in 1938. These figures also hide the extent of short-time working and underemployment. Wages fell, as did trade union membership and resources. For example the membership of the Blackburn Weavers Association fell 48.3 per cent between 1929 and 1938.[52] As the Manchester area had some economic bright spots, Lancashire was not included in the Special Areas Act of 1934, even though the weaving districts were as hard hit as anywhere. Thus no central government funds were forthcoming to bring in new industry until late in the day. Under the Special Areas (Amendment) Act of 1937, Blackburn was covered and loans to attract new firms to the borough became available. The council had set up an Industrial Development Sub-Committee in 1935 which offered firms sites or buildings at low rents or low purchase price. Some foreign firms were attracted, including Czech and French firms manufacturing man-made fibres and fine fabrics. This was yet further competition for the ailing King Cotton. Even more short-lived was to be a German slipper company.[53] A new industrial estate came in 1938 too late to have much effect before the war. Ironically one of the success stories of engineering was the British Northrop Loom Company established in Philips Road in St Stephen's ward by the late 1920s. Its automatic looms were exported around the world and aided the competitors to Blackburn's weaving industry.

What was the political impact of economic decline? No doubt unemployment strained the links between employers and workers, but the effect was not straightforward. For instance, it was reported:

> in a sample inquiry among cotton-weaving firms at Blackburn that over a period of six months in 1931, in which the nominal percentage of unemployment among workers at the mills concerned was 16.5 per cent, the true proportion would have been

[50] Beattie, *Blackburn*, p. 146.
[51] Walton, *Lancashire*, p. 329.
[52] Beattie, *Blackburn*, p. 149
[53] Beattie, *Blackburn*, p. 147.

26 per cent; the fall in demand had been met by reducing the number of looms operated by each weaver, not by dismissals.[54]

Vestiges of employer paternalism and worker deference were plainly still in operation here. Moreover, the political fallout of the long decline of the cotton industry was mixed. It was a perennial issue for the Blackburn Labour Party, but not always to its advantage. The disappointing results in 1920, for instance, were accounted for by two local leaders as the result of the 'depression in trade' being blamed on Labour.[55] On the other hand, Tory leaders in 1923 claimed much the same excuse for their own failures, as the ruling party suffered politically for the 'difficulties of trade and unemployment', when in fact 'the depression was world-wide'.[56] There is certainly no doubt that Labour suffered in 1930 and 1931 as result of the second Labour government's unemployment policies. In 1930 the defeated Labour candidate in St Michael's cited the unemployment factor as a reason for Labour's poor performance:

> If you carefully analyse the figures ... you will find that it is in the poorer districts of the town, where the people are suffering most unemployment, that we have gone down ... Faced with the unemployment situation, the people simply did not understand, and they would not understand until they had a few years of Tory government. They would learn sense by getting the kicks.[57]

1931 was an even greater debacle in Blackburn for Labour, following the collapse of the Labour government, but contemporary comment also suggests that working-class women voters were especially disillusioned. Labour's 1930–31 Anomalies Act, which excluded large numbers of married women from claiming benefit, was bitterly resented in a town where so many married women worked.

Given the vital place of women in the local economy, their role in borough politics might have been expected to be significant, especially with the extensions of the female franchise that took place between the wars. Women comprised 71.3 per cent of the labour force in the cotton industry in 1931, and as early as 1871, from a sample of census returns, Walton noted that four out of every ten households contained a working wife.[58] Joyce even points to millowners in the borough in the 1870s dismissing spinners who refused to bring their wives as weavers to their factories. The paternalism of the factory regime and the employer was in 'conjunction' with the paternalism of the operative's family.[59] How far the lingering traditions of Tory paternalism applied especially to women in the inter-war period is an open question. The extensive unionisation of women in the 1890's may have led to a degree of radicalisation of union politics in Blackburn, and may also have affected women's political views and aspirations. However,

---

[54] Fogarty, M.P., *Prospects of the Industrial Areas of Great Britain*, (London, 1945), p. 203.

[55] *NDT*, 2 Nov. 1920.

[56] *NDT*, 2 Nov. 1923.

[57] *NDT*, 3 Nov. 1930.

[58] Walton, *Lancashire*, p. 288.

[59] Joyce, *Work, Society and Politics*, pp. 112, 115.

unlike some other textile boroughs such as Preston for which evidence has been assembled, in Blackburn the influence of women as activists and policy-makers in local politics seems to have been slight.[60] Issues which were assumed to be of special interest to women, such as health and housing, were not a particular focus of any of the main parties in the borough, as far as the annual hustings for municipal elections were concerned at least. As far as Labour was concerned, when women were referred to at all, it was usually as a political liability. In 1919, for instance, a defeated candidate 'was certain that the cause had been beaten by the women'.[61] Nor were women well represented by any of the main parties as candidates for the council. All told eighteen women candidates stood in the inter-war period, some standing more than once. There were six Labour, five Conservative, five Communist and two Liberal candidates. These were a very small proportion of all candidates, except in the case of the Communist Party. Only three women were successful, two Conservatives (St Peter's, 1931 and Park, 1937) and one Labour (St Stephen's, 1934).

While the gender balance of the council chamber had hardly altered, the nature of its personnel changed in other ways, and this is another issue that needs to be considered. As late as 1881, cotton manufacturers had dominated the council with 79 per cent of the aldermen and 41 per cent of councillors. This situation reflected the charter of incorporation which stated: 'It is expected that men of business habits ... should be the men for municipal business'. By 1900 though, half of the council were shopkeepers and professionals, and barely one-sixth from the 'cottonocracy'.[62] By the inter-war period this trend had gone even further. In the elections of 1920, 1921 and 1923, for which complete evidence is available, out of thirty-four Conservative candidates, only four were described as cotton manufacturers or managers. Small-businessmen, professionals, builders, shopkeepers and agents made up the bulk of the Tory representation. Amongst their ranks also were an artisan, a trade union secretary and a sheet-metalworker, reflecting the strength of working-class Toryism. Of the thirty-three candidates standing for Labour in the same years, twelve were trade union officials, six small-businessmen, five cotton weavers and spinners, four public sector workers, and two professionals.[63] A political leadership based primarily on the shopocracy and skilled working class had replaced the cotton elite. This elite was to decline even further as the cotton industry collapsed, only retaining a toe-hold on power by way of the aldermanic bench, with three aldermen and only one councillor remaining at the end of the inter-war period.[64]

In a sense this was an unexceptional development, repeated with slight variation in all other boroughs. The withdrawal of elite groups from local government has been widely discussed, and complaints about the 'low calibre' of municipal representation, as John Stuart Mill put it in 1861, have been

[60] On Preston, see Savage, M., *The Dynamics of Working-Class Politics: The Labour Movement in Preston, 1880–1940*, pp. 167–187.

[61] *NDT*, 3 Nov. 1919.

[62] Beattie, *Blackburn*, p. 38.

[63] *NDT*, 2 Nov. 1920; 2 Nov. 1921; 2 Nov. 1923.

[64] Beattie, *Blackburn*, p. 153.

numerous.[65] It is also the case that retreat from the council chamber did not necessarily imply an equivalent loss of local power. As a leading authority on municipal politics has put it, 'the elite did not require council membership to influence council decisions. They had access through numerous channels, business, private and social, to make opinions known to councillors and officials, to organize mutual protection, and to challenge or modify the adoption of policies which might disturb their interests'.[66] Nevertheless, at a symbolic level the retirement of the 'cottonocracy' from Blackburn council must have had some significance. Certainly it suggests that in this arena at least, the intimate paternalistic connections between cotton masters and the wider populace, which were noted so widely in the nineteenth century, had declined.

A final question to be explored is whether the operation of the aldermanic bench was used to bolster Conservative strength on the council. Plainly this was the case in the 1920s, with Labour being allowed no aldermen at all. Only after the 1929 campaign, with Labour having a majority amongst the councillors with twenty-two to the other parties' twenty, was it able to elect seven aldermen, replacing four Tories, two Liberals and an Independent. This brought Labour up to its proportional share, but more importantly it meant that if Labour had been able to win all the resultant by-elections, it could have gained control of the council. This was not to be, however, and in 1935 its opponents took their revenge. As the local newspaper put it:

> Six years ago the Socialists used their power to turn out six
> retiring Conservative and Liberal aldermen. What will happen to
> the Socialist aldermen this time?[67]

All five Labour aldermen up for re-election were cleared out at the first council meeting after the election on 9 November. Thereafter Labour remained badly under-represented on the aldermanic bench, and this plainly made its already weak position on the council that much worse.

In conclusion, inter-war Blackburn was indelibly marked by the influence of the cotton industry, which was all-pervading in most aspects of life in the borough. The tenacious grip of Conservatism in a working-class town can be largely explained by this, through the workings of the remaining vestiges of a paternalist relationship between cotton operatives and masters. The decline of cotton between the wars certainly placed great strains on this relationship, and speeded its eventual demise, but the full political effects were not to be manifested before 1945. The Labour party by contrast was not a powerful force in the borough, despite the wider inter-war trends in its favour. Even more striking, the crisis of the local weaving industry did not result in a radicalisation of the local working class, or a permanent shift to Labour support. Indeed at times the causes of economic crisis and unemployment seemed to be laid at Labour's door by Blackburn's electors, much to the detriment of the party's advance.

---

[65] On these issues, see Waller, P.J., *Town, City and Nation: England 1850–1914*, (Oxford, 1983), pp. 288–293.
[66] Waller, *Town, City and Nation*, pp. 292–293.
[67] *NDT*, 2 Nov. 1935.

A guide to further reading

Newspapers

Blackburn Times
Manchester Guardian
Northern Daily Telegraph

Works of reference

Barrett's Directory of Blackburn and District (1935)

Secondary sources

Beattie, D., *Blackburn: The Development of a Lancashire Cotton Town*, (Halifax, 1992).
Bullen, A., *The Lancashire Weavers Union: A Commemorative History*, (Manchester, 1984).
Clarke, P.F., 'British Politics and Blackburn Politics 1900–1910', *The Historical Journal*, XII, 2 (1969).
Fogarty, M.P., *Prospects of the Industrial Areas of Great Britain*, (London, 1945).
Freeman, T.W., *The Conurbations of Great Britain*, (Manchester, 1959).
Howell, D., *British Workers and the Independent Labour Party 1888–1906*, (Manchester, 1983), ch. 3.
Joyce, P., *Work, Society and Politics: The Culture of the Factory in Later Victorian England*, (London, 1982).
Kirk, N., *Labour and Society in Britain and the USA, Volume 2: Challenge and Accommodation, 1850–1939*, (Aldershot, 1994).
Pelling, H., *Social Geography of British Elections, 1885–1910*, (Aldershot, 1994), p. 262.
Trodd, G., 'Political Change and the Working Class in Blackburn and Burnley, 1880-1914', (Ph.D. Thesis, Lancaster University, 1978).
Walton, J.K., *Lancashire: A Social History, 1558–1939*, (Manchester, 1987).

Blackburn wards 1919–1938

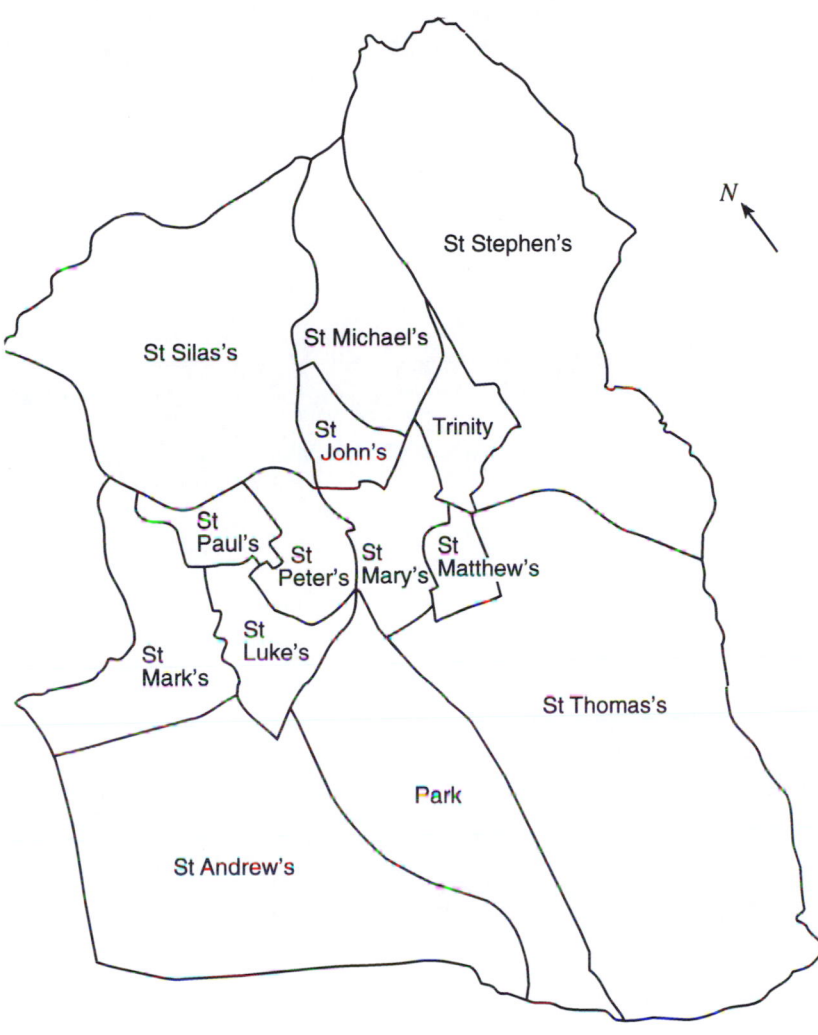

St Stephen's

St Silas's

St Michael's

St John's

Trinity

St Paul's

St Peter's

St Mary's

St Matthew's

St Luke's

St Mark's

St Thomas's

Park

St Andrew's

N

Persons aged fourteen and over classified by industry 1931

	Male	%	Female	%	Total	%
Metal and engineering	5,343	12.9	511	1.5	5,854	7.7
- *Engineering*	*3,763*	*9.1*	*431*	*1.3*	*4,194*	*5.5*
Textiles	11,723	28.4	24,804	72.1	36,527	48.3
- *Cotton*	*11,076*	*26.8*	*24,534*	*71.3*	*35,610*	*47.1*
Building	2,282	5.5	24	0.1	2,306	3.0
Transport	2,839	6.9	44	0.1	2,883	3.8
Commerce and finance	6,791	16.5	2,384	6.9	9,175	12.1
Public admin. and defence	2,818	6.8	1,063	3.1	3,881	5.1
- *Local government*	*2,309*	*5.6*	*913*	*2.7*	*3,222*	*4.3*
Personal service	1,318	3.2	2,471	7.2	3,789	5.0
Other	8,147	19.7	3,098	9.0	11,245	14.9
Total (a)	**41,261**		**34,399**		**75,660**	
Total population (b)	56,238		66,459		122,697	
(a) as % of (b)	73.4		51.8		61.7	
Total out of work (c)	10,473		14,302		24,775	
(c) as % of (a)	25.4		41.6		32.7	
Managerial and own account	5,437	17.7	1,667	8.3	7,104	14.0
Operative	25,351	82.3	18,430	91.7	43,781	86.0
Total (excluding out of work)	30,788		20,097		50,885	

Population statistics 1931

Ward	Acres	Population	Persons/acre	Persons/room
Park	651	9,052	13.9	0.85
St Andrew's	1,146	10,783	9.4	0.84
St John's	101	6,520	64.6	0.79
St Luke's	168	7,333	43.6	0.91
St Mark's	403	9,979	24.8	0.78
St Mary's	174	5,147	29.6	0.93
St Matthew's	107	8,561	80.0	0.87
St Michael's	623	8,580	13.8	0.80
St Paul's	123	8,929	72.6	0.82
St Peter's	133	6,213	46.7	0.91
St Silas's	985	9,108	9.2	0.62
St Stephen's	1,171	13,215	11.3	0.83
St Thomas's	1,718	11,255	6.6	0.82
Trinity	150	8,022	53.5	0.88
Total	**7,653**	**122,697**	**16.0**	**0.82**

Overall position on the council 1919–38

	Position				Gains				Losses			
	C	Lab	L	Ind	C	Lab	L	Ind	C	Lab	L	Ind
1919	37	10	6	3	0	5	2	0	7	0	0	0
1920	37	11	5	3	2	0	0	1	1	0	1	1
1921	35	11	6	4	2	2	1	0	3	1	0	1
1922	39	7	6	4	4	0	0	0	0	4	0	0
1923	36	10	7	3	1	2	0	0	2	1	0	0
1924	38	8	7	3	2	0	0	0	0	2	0	0
1925	41	7	6	2	3	0	0	0	0	2	1	0
1926	40	8	6	2	0	1	0	0	1	0	0	0
1927	35	12	5	4	0	4	0	1	4	0	1	0
1928[a]	29	16	6	4	0	4	0	0	4	0	0	0
1929	27	22	4	3	0	5	0	0	2	0	2	1
1930[b]	27	24	2	2	4	0	0	0	0	4	0	0
1931	35	18	1	2	6	0	0	0	0	5	1	0
1932	36	16	2	2	3	1	1	0	1	4	0	0
1933[c]	30	18	4	2	0	4	1	0	5	0	0	0
1934[d]	24	24	5	2	0	6	0	0	6	0	0	0
1935	24	25	5	2	0	1	0	0	1	0	0	0
1936	26	22	6	2	2	2	0	0	2	1	1	0
1937	29	20	5	2	2	0	0	0	0	2	0	0
1938	30	19	5	2	1	1	0	0	0	1	0	1

Aldermen 1919–38

1919 C–13, L–1
1920 C–13, L–1
1921 C–12, L–1, Ind–1
1922 C–12, L–1, Ind–1
1923 C–12, L–1, Ind–1
1924 C–12, L–1, Ind–1
1925 C–12, L–1, Ind–1
1926 C–12, L–1, Ind–1
1927 C–12, L–1, Ind–1
1928 C–11, L–2, Ind–1

1929 C–11, L–2, Ind–1
1930[b] C–5, Lab–7, Ind–1
1931 C–6, Lab–7, Ind–1
1932 C–6, Lab–7, Ind–1
1933 C–8, Lab–5, Ind–1
1934 C–8, Lab–5, Ind–1
1935 C–8, Lab–5, Ind–1
1936 C–9, Lab–1, L–2, Ind–2
1937 C–9, Lab–1, L–2, Ind–2
1938 C–9, Lab–1, L–2, Ind–2

[a] 1928 - 1 seat vacant.
[b] 1930 - 1 aldermanic seat vacant.
[c] 1933 - 2 seats vacant.
[d] 1934 - 1 scat vacant.

Municipal elections: winning party 1919–28

Ward	1919	1920	1921	1922	1923	1924	1925	1926	1927	1928
Park	C	C	C	C	**C**	C	**C**	**C**	C	C
St Andrew's	L	C	L	**L**	**C**	L	**L**	**C**	**L**	L
St John's	Lab	C	C	C	**C**	**C**	**C**	C	**C**	**C**
St Luke's	Lab	C	Lab	Lab	C	Lab	Lab	Lab	Lab	**Lab**
St Mark's	C	C	C	C	C	C	C	**C**	C	C
St Mary's	Lab	C	C	C	**L**	C	**C**	**L**	**C**	**C**
St Matthew's	Lab	Lab	C	Lab	Lab	C	Lab	Lab	Lab	**Lab**
St Michael's	Ind	C	C	**Ind**	**C**	C	C	C	Lab	Lab
St Paul's	Lab	L	Lab	C	L	C	C	L	C	Lab
St Peter's	Lab	C	C	Lab	Lab	C	**Lab**	Lab	Lab	Lab
St Silas's	L	C	L	**L**	**C**	**L**	C	**C**	Ind	**C**
St Stephen's	Lab	Ind	Lab	C	Ind	C	C	**Ind**	**C**	Lab
St Thomas's	C	C	C	**C**	**C**	C	C	C	C	C
Trinity	Ind	C	C	**Ind**	Lab	C	C	Lab	Lab	Lab

Municipal elections: party wins per year 1919–28

	1919	1920	1921	1922	1923	1924	1925	1926	1927	1928
C	3	11	9	7	8	11	10	7	7	6
Lab	7	1	3	3	3	1	3	4	5	7
L	2	1	2	2	2	2	1	2	1	1
Ind	2	1	0	2	1	0	0	1	1	0
Total	14	14	14	14	14	14	14	14	14	14
Turnout %	66.5	70.5	69.3	70.9	69.8	70.4	68.4	68.5	68.5	71.6
Labour %	43.2	38.8	39.8	47.8	47.5	41.6	38.6	48.3	44.4	45.7

Municipal elections: winning party 1929–38

Ward	1929	1930	1931	1932	1933	1934	1935	1936	1937	1938
Park	C	C	**C**	C	Lab	Lab	Lab	Lab	C	C
St Andrew's	C	**L**	C	C	L	C	L	C	C	**L**
St John's	**C**	**C**	**C**	**C**	**C**	C	C	C	**C**	C
St Luke's	Lab	**Lab**	C	Lab	-	Lab	Lab	Lab	**Lab**	Lab
St Mark's	Lab	C	C	C	C	C	C	C	C	C
St Mary's	Lab	C	**C**	L	C	Lab	L	Lab	**Lab**	L
St Matthew's	Lab	Lab	Lab	Lab	Lab	Lab	Lab	Lab	**Lab**	Lab
St Michael's	C	C	C	**C**	C	C	C	C	C	C
St Paul's	Lab	C	Lab	Lab	Lab	**Lab**	Lab	Lab	Lab	Lab
St Peter's	Lab	C	C	Lab	C	Lab	Lab	Lab	Lab	Lab
St Silas's	Ind	C	**C**	Ind	L	**C**	**Ind**	L	L	**C**
St Stephen's	Lab	C	C	C	Lab	Lab	C	C	C	C
St Thomas's	Lab	C	C	C	C	C	C	C	C	C
Trinity	Lab	C	C	Lab	Lab	Lab	Lab	Lab	Lab	Lab

Municipal elections: party wins per year 1929–38

	1929	1930	1931	1932	1933	1934	1935	1936	1937	1938
C	4	11	12	7	6	6	5	6	7	7
Lab	9	2	2	5	5	8	6	7	6	5
L	0	1	0	1	2	0	2	1	1	2
Ind	1	0	0	1	0	0	1	0	0	0
Total	14	14	14	14	13	14	14	14	14	14
Turnout %	68.8	69.0	69.0	69.8	69.2	69.8	71.8	73.3	69.7	68.4
Labour %	47.4	37.4	33.8	43.3	43.8	49.6	48.5	44.3	42.9	47.7

Municipal elections: party wins per ward 1919–28

	C	Lab	L	Ind	Total	Turnout %	Labour % of all votes
Park	16	4	0	0	20	74.5	44.9
St Andrew's	9	0	11	0	20	62.4	32.1
St John's	19	1	0	0	20	67.7	37.4
St Luke's	3	16	0	0	19	73.7	55.5
St Mark's	19	1	0	0	20	69.2	41.2
St Mary's	10	5	5	0	20	66.5	44.8
St Matthew's	2	18	0	0	20	71.3	53.4
St Michael's	16	2	0	2	20	67.6	44.9
St Paul's	5	12	3	0	20	71.7	50.5
St Peter's	6	14	0	0	20	70.8	50.7
St Silas's	9	0	7	4	20	71.3	1.9
St Stephen's	11	6	0	3	20	69.4	46.2
St Thomas's	19	1	0	0	20	70.0	41.7
Trinity	6	12	0	2	20	68.2	51.4
Total	**150**	**92**	**26**	**11**	**279**	**69.7**	**43.6**

Seats won by Labour as a percentage of all wins 1919–38 **33.0**

Parliamentary election results

Blackburn constituency *(double-member seat)*
(all wards within the borough [1918 boundaries] were included in the constituency)

General election	Winner	Conservative %	Labour %	Liberal %
14 Dec. 1918	Co L (1)	38.9	19.7	41.4
	Co C (2)	-	-	-
15 Nov. 1922	C (1)	25.5	21.7	24.4
	NL (2)	-	21.1	7.3
6 Dec. 1923	L (1)	26.6	23.8	29.1
	C (2)	-	20.5	-
29 Oct. 1924	L (1)	26.6	21.8	28.3
	C (2)	-	21.8	-
30 May 1929	Lab (1)	24.7	26.1	24.2
	Lab (2)	-	25.0	-
27 Oct. 1931	C (1)	33.3	17.0	-
	C (2)	33.1	16.6	-
14 Nov. 1935	C (1)	26.2	23.9	-
	C (2)	26.1	23.8	-

Park Ward

Candidate	Party	Votes	%	Electors	Turnout	Gains
1919						
J. Fryars*	C	1,430	57.9	3,857	64.0	-
R. Beardwood	Lab	1,039	42.1			
Total votes		2,469				
1920						
J.W. Forrest*	C	2,022	66.8	3,975	76.2	-
R. Beardwood	Lab	1,006	33.2			
Total votes		3,028				
1921						
C. Cotton*	C	1,998	66.3	4,010	75.2	-
R. Beardwood	Lab	1,017	33.7			
Total votes		3,015				
1922						
J. Fryars*	C	1,827	63.8	4,018	71.3	-
R. Beardwood	Lab	1,037	36.2			
Total votes		2,864				
1923						
R.M. Oddie*	C	Unopp.	-	4,043	-	-
1924						
J. Holden*	C	1,871	66.0	4,048	70.1	-
R. Beardwood	Lab	965	34.0			
Total votes		2,836				
1925						
J. Fryars*	C	Unopp.	-		-	-
1926						
R.M. Oddie*	C	Unopp.	-		-	-
1927						
J. Holden*	C	1,588	53.0	4,089	73.2	-
T. McNamee	Lab	1,406	47.0			
Total votes		2,994				
1928						
J. Cotton	C	1,812	53.0	4,130	82.8	-
T. McNamee	Lab	1,609	47.0			
Total votes		3,421				

Park Ward *(continued)*

Candidate	Party	Votes	%	Electors	Turnout	Gains
1929						
J. Blackshaw	C	1,869	54.5	*4,218*	81.4	-
T. McNamee	Lab	1,563	45.5			
Total votes		3,432				
1930						
J. Holden*	C	1,998	62.1	4,305	74.7	-
T. Swarbrick	Lab	1,219	37.9			
Total votes		3,217				
1931						
J. Cotton*	C	Unopp.	-		-	-
1932						
L. Holden	C	1,715	54.4	4,375	72.0	-
I. Caswell	Lab	1,437	45.6			
Total votes		3,152				
1933						
I. Caswell	Lab	1,853	51.4	5,090	70.8	Lab from C
J. Holden*	C	1,750	48.6			
Total votes		3,603				
1934						
T. Vipond	Lab	2,010	53.0	5,067	74.9	Lab from C
S. Greenwood	C	1,784	47.0			
Total votes		3,794				
1935						
F. Wilkinson	Lab	1,982	51.2	*5,047*	76.7	Lab from C
L. Holden*	C	1,887	48.8			
Total votes		3,869				
1936						
I. Caswell*	Lab	2,029	52.8	5,028	76.4	-
Mrs S. Buckley	C	1,812	47.2			
Total votes		3,841				
1937						
Mrs S. Buckley	C	1,956	50.7	5,097	75.7	C from Lab
T. Vipond*	Lab	1,902	49.3			
Total votes		3,858				

Park Ward *(continued)*

Candidate	Party	Votes	%	Electors	Turnout	Gains
1938						
D. Nightingale	C	1,991	51.8	5,121	75.0	C from Lab
F. Wilkinson*	Lab	1,850	48.2			
Total votes		3,841				

Overall Labour vote **44.9%** **Overall turnout** **74.5%**

St Andrew's ward

Candidate	Party	Votes	%	Electors	Turnout	Gains
1919						
J.W. Makin	L	1,004	35.2	4,613	61.9	L from C
W.A. Duckworth	C	937	32.8			
D.B. Lawley	Lab	914	32.0			
Total votes		2,855				
1920						
W.A. Duckworth	C	1,331	38.7	4,631	74.3	-
T. Greenwood	L	1,190	34.6			
D.B. Lawley	Lab	920	26.7			
Total votes		3,441				
1921						
E. Hamer*	L	1,783	62.9	4,661	60.8	-
D.B. Lawley	Lab	1,053	37.1			
Total votes		2,836				
1922						
J.W. Makin*	L	Unopp.	-		-	-
1923						
W.A. Duckworth*	C	Unopp.	-	4,962	-	-
1924						
E. Hamer*	L	2,331	73.8	4,970	63.6	-
T. Patterson	Lab	829	26.2			
Total votes		3,160				
1925						
J.W. Makin*	L	Unopp.	-		-	-
1926						
W.A. Duckworth*	C	Unopp.	-		-	-
1927						
E. Hamer*	L	Unopp.	-		-	-
1928						
J.W. Makin*	L	1,392	51.3	5,156	52.7	-
R. Ibbotson	C	1,323	48.7			
Total votes		2,715				

St Andrew's ward *(continued)*

Candidate	Party	Votes	%	Electors	Turnout	Gains
1929						
W.A. Duckworth*	C	1,692	55.1	*5,337*	57.5	-
J. Calvert	Lab	1,379	44.9			
Total votes		3,071				
1930						
T. Greenwood*	L	Unopp.	-	5,518	-	-
1931						
R.H.G. Horne	C	2,291	57.3	*5,544*	72.1	C from L
Miss H.M. Eccles	L	1,062	26.6			
A. Rae	Lab	642	16.1			
Total votes		3,995				
1932						
W.A. Duckworth*	C	1,823	60.3	5,570	54.2	-
J. Rae	Lab	1,198	39.7			
Total votes		3,021				
1933						
T. Greenwood*	L	1,964	64.0	5,611	54.7	-
J. Rae	Lab	1,107	36.0			
Total votes		3,071				
1934						
R.H.G. Horne*	C	2,082	62.4	5,611	59.4	-
J. Rae	Lab	1,252	37.6			
Total votes		3,334				
1935						
T. Leach*	L	2,148	62.3	*5,697*	60.5	-
Mrs R. Sugden	Lab	1,298	37.7			
Total votes		3,446				
1936						
J. Dean	C	1,772	41.9	5,784	73.1	C from L
Mrs R. Sugden	Lab	1,567	37.1			
H. Hindle*	L	887	21.0			
Total votes		4,226				

St Andrew's ward *(continued)*

Candidate	Party	Votes	%	Electors	Turnout	Gains
1937						
R.H.G. Horne*	C	2,277	57.7	5,885	67.1	-
Mrs R. Sugden	Lab	1,669	42.3			
Total votes		3,946				
1938						
T.Leach*	L	Unopp.		6,094	-	-

Overall Labour vote	**32.1%**	**Overall turnout**	**62.4%**

St John's ward

Candidate	Party	Votes	%	Electors	Turnout	Gains
1919						
A. Townsend	Lab	805	40.5	3,079	64.6	Lab from C
J. Towers	C	713	35.8			
J. Rutherford	L	472	23.7			
Total votes		1,990				
1920						
C.A. Critchley*	C	913	41.2	3,158	70.1	-
T. Hurley	Lab	771	34.8			
T. Holden	L	415	18.7			
F. Turner	Ind	116	5.2			
Total votes		2,215				
1921						
B. Holden	C	1,313	58.1	3,171	71.3	-
A. Harkin	Lab	568	25.1			
T. Holden	L	380	16.8			
Total votes		2,261				
1922						
Dr E.M. Payne	C	1,295	63.6	3,145	64.7	C from Lab
A. Townsend*	Lab	741	36.4			
Total votes		2,036				
1923						
C.A. Critchley*	C	Unopp.	-	3,157	-	-
1924						
B. Holden*	C	Unopp.	-		-	-
1925						
Dr E.M. Payne*	C	Unopp.	-		-	-
1926						
C.A. Critchley*	C	1,135	60.1	3,145	60.1	-
T. McNamee	Lab	754	39.9			
Total votes		1,889				
1927						
B. Holden*	C	Unopp.	-		-	-
1928						
Dr E.M. Payne*	C	Unopp.	-		-	-

St John's ward *(continued)*

Candidate	Party	Votes	%	Electors	Turnout	Gains
1929						
C.A. Critchley*	C	Unopp.	-		-	-
1930						
B. Holden*	C	Unopp.	-	3,281	-	-
1931						
W. Hare	C	Unopp.	-		-	-
1932						
C.A. Critchley*	C	Unopp.	-		-	-
1933						
B. Holden*	C	Unopp.	-		-	-
1934						
W. Hare*	C	1,223	58.2	3,214	65.3	-
J. Cowell	Lab	877	41.8			
Total votes		2,100				
1935						
R.F. Mottershead*	C	1,354	61.2	*3,185*	69.4	-
E.O. Mason	Lab	857	38.8			
Total votes		2,211				
1936						
J.J. Pickering	C	1,147	50.1	3,155	72.5	-
J. Fish	Lab	836	36.5			
D. Harper	L	305	13.3			
Total votes		2,288				
1937						
W. Hare*	C	Unopp.	-		-	-
1938						
R.F. Mottershead*	C	1,275	56.6	3,156	71.4	-
Mrs R. Sugden	Lab	979	43.4			
Total votes		2,254				
Overall Labour vote		**37.4%**		**Overall turnout**		**67.7%**

St Luke's ward

Candidate	Party	Votes	%	Electors	Turnout	Gains
1919						
J. Fish	Lab	1,319	64.2	3,255	63.1	Lab from C
W. Edmundson*	C	736	35.8			
Total votes		2,055				
1920						
R. Wareing*	C	1,157	50.5	3,248	70.5	-
R. Croasdale	Lab	1,134	49.5			
Total votes		2,291				
1921						
T. Hurley	Lab	1,294	54.9	3,259	72.3	Lab from C
A. Read*	C	1,061	45.1			
Total votes		2,355				
1922						
J. Fish*	Lab	1,536	60.9	3,275	77.0	-
W. Harris	C	986	39.1			
Total votes		2,522				
1923						
J. Driver	C	1,359	51.1	3,266	81.4	C from Lab
L. Pickering*	Lab	1,298	48.9			
Total votes		2,657				
1924						
T. Hurley*	Lab	1,355	52.1	3,310	78.6	-
S. Sharples	C	1,247	47.9			
Total votes		2,602				
1925						
J. Fish*	Lab	1,622	60.2	3,364	80.1	-
S. Sharples	C	1,072	39.8			
Total votes		2,694				
1926						
J. Smethurst	Lab	1,524	55.6	3,384	81.1	Lab from C
Rev J. Dimmock	C	1,219	44.4			
Total votes		2,743				

St Luke's ward *(continued)*

Candidate	Party	Votes	%	Electors	Turnout	Gains
1927						
T. Hurley*	Lab	1,497	57.7	3,428	75.7	-
W. Tempest	L	1,098	42.3			
Total votes		2,595				
1928						
J. Fish*	Lab	Unopp.	-		-	-
1929						
J. Smethurst*	Lab	1,523	63.8	*3,560*	67.1	-
H.N. Pomfret	C	865	36.2			
Total votes		2,388				
1930						
T. Hurley*	Lab	Unopp.	-	3,647	-	-
1931						
T. Marsden	C	1,419	50.7	*3,662*	76.4	C from Lab
T.H. Duxbury*	Lab	1,010	36.1			
Mrs I. Haworth	L	369	13.2			
Total votes		2,798				
1932						
T. McNamee*	Lab	1,553	55.6	3,677	76.0	-
W.E. Lang	C	1,164	41.7			
W. Marriot	Com	77	2.8			
Total votes		2,794				
1933						
(no election due to recent death of T.Hurley)						
1934						
J.W. Taylor	Lab	1,539	57.7	3,708	72.0	Lab from C
T. Marsden*	C	1,130	42.3			
Total votes		2,669				
1935						
T. McNamee*	Lab	1,608	61.5	*3,681*	71.0	-
A. Fairhurst	C	1,006	38.5			
Total votes		2,614				

St Luke's ward *(continued)*

Candidate	Party	Votes	%	Electors	Turnout	Gains
1936						
H.V. Dowdall*	Lab	1,527	58.1	3,654	71.9	-
T. Marsden	C	1,102	41.9			
Total votes		2,629				
1937						
J.W. Taylor*	Lab	Unopp.	-		-	-
1938						
T. McNamee*	Lab	1,313	55.2	3,573	66.6	-
V. Hounslow	C	1,067	44.8			
Total votes		2,380				

Overall Labour vote   **55.5%**   **Overall turnout**   **73.7%**

St Mark's ward

Candidate	Party	Votes	%	Electors	Turnout	Gains
1919						
J.W. Walsh	C	1,423	47.9	4,331	68.6	-
T. Mooney	Lab	1,216	40.9			
T. Holden	L	332	11.2			
Total votes		2,971				
1920						
T.H. Heatley*	C	1,771	57.3	4,424	69.9	-
T. Mooney	Lab	1,321	42.7			
Total votes		3,092				
1921						
G. Mayor	C	1,607	56.1	4,450	64.4	-
J.T. Alty	Lab	1,115	38.9			
J.B. Catterall	Ind	144	5.0			
Total votes		2,866				
1922						
J.H. Campbell	C	1,600	53.2	4,444	67.6	-
J.W. Taylor	Lab	1,406	46.8			
Total votes		3,006				
1923						
J. Walsh*	C	1,683	53.4	4,460	70.7	-
J.W. Taylor	Lab	1,470	46.6			
Total votes		3,153				
1924						
G. Mayor*	C	1,849	59.0	4,463	70.3	-
J.W. Taylor	Lab	1,287	41.0			
Total votes		3,136				
1925						
J.H. Campbell*	C	1,840	62.2	4,492	65.8	-
J. Calvert	Lab	1,117	37.8			
Total votes		2,957				
1926						
J. Walsh*	C	Unopp.	-		-	-

St Mark's ward *(continued)*

Candidate	Party	Votes	%	Electors	Turnout	Gains
1927						
G. Mayor*	C	1,513	53.0	4,670	61.1	-
H.V. Dowdall	Lab	1,342	47.0			
Total votes		2,855				
1928						
J.H. Campbell*	C	1,670	50.7	4,664	70.6	-
H.V. Dowdall	Lab	1,621	49.3			
Total votes		3,291				
1929						
H.V. Dowdall	Lab	1,729	50.7	*4,774*	71.4	Lab from C
J. Walsh*	C	1,681	49.3			
Total votes		3,410				
1930						
J. Grimshaw	C	2,262	65.7	4,884	70.5	-
J. Haworth	Lab	1,131	32.8			
Mrs B. Dickenson	Com	51	1.5			
Total votes		3,444				
1931						
J.H. Campbell*	C	2,340	95.0	*4,922*	50.1	-
T. Coughlin	Com	124	5.0			
Total votes		2,464				
1932						
J. Livesey	C	2,010	52.1	4,960	77.8	C from Lab
H.V. Dowdall*	Lab	1,791	46.4			
T. Coughlin	Com	60	1.6			
Total votes		3,861				
1933						
J. Grimshaw*	C	1,959	51.0	4,966	77.3	-
H.V. Dowdall	Lab	1,848	48.1			
T. Coughlin	Com	33	0.9			
Total votes		3,840				
1934						
J.H. Campbell*	C	1,910	52.0	5,037	73.0	-
S. Higham	Lab	1,765	48.0			
Total votes		3,675				

St Mark's ward *(continued)*

Candidate	Party	Votes	%	Electors	Turnout	Gains
1935						
J. Livesey*	C	2,143	57.5	*5,037*	74.0	-
A. Ford	Lab	1,583	42.5			
Total votes		3,726				
1936						
C.W. Eastwood	C	1,916	50.2	5,036	75.8	-
J. Miller	Lab	1,317	34.5			
G.F. Singleton	L	585	15.3			
Total votes		3,818				
1937						
W.T. Matthews*	C	2,144	61.6	5,097	68.3	-
J. Miller	Lab	1,338	38.4			
Total votes		3,482				
1938						
J. Livesey*	C	2,074	61.4	5,139	65.7	-
J. Reddington	Lab	1,303	38.6			
Total votes		3,377				

Overall Labour vote   **41.2%**   **Overall turnout**   **69.2%**

St Mary's ward

Candidate	Party	Votes	%	Electors	Turnout	Gains
1919						
J.M. Lomax	Lab	706	50.6	2,294	60.8	Lab from C
W.J. Turner	C	688	49.4			
Total votes		1,394				
1920						
W. Kenyon*	C	849	55.3	2,364	64.9	-
A. Harkin	Lab	685	44.7			
Total votes		1,534				
1921						
W.H. Grimshaw*	C	937	59.0	2,411	65.8	-
T. Mooney	Lab	650	41.0			
Total votes		1,587				
1922						
W.R. Hargreaves	C	832	54.1	2,445	62.9	C from Lab
J.M. Lomax*	Lab	707	45.9			
Total votes		1,539				
1923						
J. Stanworth*	L	Unopp.	-	2,443	-	-
1924						
W.H. Grimshaw*	C	999	67.1	2,430	61.3	-
J.T. Alty	Lab	490	32.9			
Total votes		1,489				
1925						
W.R. Hargreaves*	C	Unopp.	-		-	-
1926						
J. Stanworth*	L	Unopp.	-		-	-
1927						
W.H. Grimshaw*	C	Unopp.	-		-	-
1928						
W.R. Hargreaves*	C	Unopp.	-		-	-

St Mary's ward *(continued)*

Candidate	Party	Votes	%	Electors	Turnout	Gains
1929						
W. Hammond	Lab	737	51.3	*2,502*	57.4	Lab from L
W. Coupe	L	699	48.7			
Total votes		1,436				
1930						
W.H. Grimshaw*	C	1,067	60.4	2,625	67.3	-
C. Baron	Lab	699	39.6			
Total votes		1,766				
1931						
W.R. Hargreaves*	C	Unopp.	-		-	-
1932						
W.E. Woolley	L	898	51.9	2,566	67.5	L from Lab
W. Hammond*	Lab	833	48.1			
Total votes		1,731				
1933						
R.R. Fielding*	C	843	52.1	2,552	63.4	-
W. Bond	Lab	776	47.9			
Total votes		1,619				
1934						
W. Hammond	Lab	902	51.4	2,552	68.8	Lab from C
W.R. Hargreaves*	C	854	48.6			
Total votes		1,756				
1935						
W.E. Woolley*	L	981	54.3	*2,518*	71.8	-
J. Cowell	Lab	827	45.7			
Total votes		1,808				
1936						
F. Hargreaves	Lab	946	51.1	2,484	74.6	Lab from C
R.R. Fielding*	C	907	48.9			
Total votes		1,853				
1937						
W. Hammond*	Lab	Unopp.	-		-	-

St Mary's ward *(continued)*

Candidate	Party	Votes	%	Electors	Turnout	Gains
1938						
W.E. Woolley*	L	1,200	67.5	2,277	78.0	-
F. Beardsworth	Lab	577	32.5			
Total votes		1,777				

Overall Labour vote   **44.8%**   **Overall turnout**   **66.5%**

St Matthew's ward

Candidate	Party	Votes	%	Electors	Turnout	Gains
1919						
L. Bates*	Lab	1,556	61.2	3,805	66.9	-
D. Dewhurst	C	988	38.8			
Total votes		2,544				
1920						
D.E. Brierley*	Lab	1,437	51.3	3,901	71.8	-
D. Dewhurst	C	1,363	48.7			
Total votes		2,800				
1921						
D. Dewhurst	C	1,380	47.6	3,945	73.5	C from Ind
R.H. Welch	Lab	1,220	42.1			
W. Hammond*	Ind	299	10.3			
Total votes		2,899				
1922						
L. Bates*	Lab	1,552	55.1	3,979	70.8	-
D.B. Worden	C	1,267	44.9			
Total votes		2,819				
1923						
A. Heyes	Lab	1,414	52.1	4,016	67.6	-
D.B. Worden	C	1,299	47.9			
Total votes		2,713				
1924						
D. Dewhurst*	C	1,536	51.8	4,034	73.5	-
G.B. Eddie	Lab	1,429	48.2			
Total votes		2,965				
1925						
L. Bates*	Lab	1,559	56.0	4,045	68.8	-
D.B. Worden	C	1,225	44.0			
Total votes		2,784				
1926						
A. Heyes*	Lab	1,473	52.5	4,068	69.0	-
R. Culshaw	C	1,335	47.5			
Total votes		2,808				

St Matthew's ward *(continued)*

Candidate	Party	Votes	%	Electors	Turnout	Gains
1927						
R. Sugden	Lab	1,484	53.9	4,071	67.6	Lab from C
D. Dewhurst*	C	1,267	46.1			
Total votes		2,751				
1928						
L. Bates*	Lab	Unopp.	-		-	-
1929						
A. Heyes*	Lab	1,652	57.5	*4,163*	69.0	-
D. Dewhurst	C	1,221	42.5			
Total votes		2,873				
1930						
R. Sugden*	Lab	1,541	53.1	4,252	68.3	-
F. Swales	C	1,361	46.9			
Total votes		2,902				
1931						
J. Shorrock*	Lab	1,564	51.4	*4,211*	72.2	-
A. Dinham	C	1,421	46.7			
Mrs M. Nelson	Com	57	1.9			
Total votes		3,042				
1932						
C. Cross*	Lab	1,390	48.1	4,170	69.2	-
D. Dewhurst	C	1,366	47.3			
G.C. Jane	Com	131	4.5			
Total votes		2,887				
1933						
R. Sugden*	Lab	1,574	50.1	4,185	75.1	-
E. Woolley	L	1,527	48.6			
G.C. Jane	Nuwm	41	1.3			
Total votes		3,142				
1934						
J. Shorrock*	Lab	2,068	62.8	4,164	79.0	-
E. Woolley	L	1,223	37.2			
Total votes		3,291				

St Matthew's ward *(continued)*

Candidate	Party	Votes	%	Electors	Turnout	Gains
1935						
J. Whitehead	Lab	1,673	51.9	*4,142*	77.8	-
E. Woolley	L	1,551	48.1			
Total votes		3,224				
1936						
R. Sugden*	Lab	1,716	57.9	4,119	71.9	-
T.H. Counsell	C	1,246	42.1			
Total votes		2,962				
1937						
J. Shorrock*	Lab	Unopp.	-		-	-
1938						
J. Whitehead*	Lab	1,618	56.0	4,080	70.8	-
S. Sharples	C	1,269	44.0			
Total votes		2,887				

Overall Labour vote   **53.4%**   **Overall turnout**   **71.3%**

St Michael's ward

Candidate	Party	Votes	%	Electors	Turnout	Gains
1919						
J.W.M. Jamieson*	Ind	1,698	65.4	3,800	68.4	-
J. Ward	Lab	900	34.6			
Total votes		2,598				
1920						
G. Hargreaves	C	1,487	53.1	3,831	73.1	C from Ind
C. Cross	Lab	1,315	46.9			
Total votes		2,802				
1921						
Dr A.A.P. Moffatt	C	1,580	59.7	3,885	68.1	-
J. Ward	Lab	1,067	40.3			
Total votes		2,647				
1922						
J.W.M. Jamieson*	Ind	Unopp.	-		-	-
1923						
J. Riley*	C	Unopp.	-	3,922	-	-
1924						
Dr A.A.P. Moffat*	C	1,491	56.6	3,905	67.5	-
G.H. Kirby	Lab	1,145	43.4			
Total votes		2,636				
1925						
J. Ashton	C	1,483	55.7	4,004	66.5	C from Lab
G.B. Eddie	Lab	1,178	44.3			
Total votes		2,661				
1926						
J. Riley*	C	1,420	53.8	4,044	65.3	-
G.B. Eddie	Lab	1,219	46.2			
Total votes		2,639				
1927						
G.B. Eddie	Lab	1,376	50.7	4,102	66.2	Lab from C
Dr A.A.P. Moffat*	C	1,339	49.3			
Total votes		2,715				

St Michael's ward *(continued)*

Candidate	Party	Votes	%	Electors	Turnout	Gains
1928						
G.H. Kirby	Lab	1,523	51.8	4,198	70.1	Lab from C
J. Ashton*	C	1,418	48.2			
Total votes		2,941				
1929						
J. Riley*	C	1,536	51.4	*4,354*	68.7	-
C. Cross	Lab	1,454	48.6			
Total votes		2,990				
1930						
T.G. Markland	C	1,764	55.7	4,510	70.2	C from Lab
G.B. Eddie*	Lab	1,402	44.3			
Total votes		3,166				
1931						
A. Hodgkinson	C	2,154	70.7	*4,596*	66.3	C from Lab
C.Baron	Lab	894	29.3			
Total votes		3,048				
1932						
J. Riley*	C	Unopp.	-	-	-	-
1933						
T.G. Markland*	C	1,525	52.1	4,767	61.4	-
P. Lord	Lab	1,403	47.9			
Total votes		2,928				
1934						
A. Hodgkinson*	C	1,605	53.8	4,803	62.1	-
J.R. Grocott	Lab	1,380	46.2			
Total votes		2,985				
1935						
J. Riley*	C	1,898	56.3	*4,871*	69.3	-
J.R. Grocott	Lab	1,476	43.7			
Total votes		3,374				
1936						
J.W. Baker	C	1,817	53.6	4,940	68.7	-
J.R. Grocott	Lab	1,576	46.4			
Total votes		3,393				

St Michael's ward *(continued)*

Candidate	Party	Votes	%	Electors	Turnout	Gains
1937						
W.A. Henshall	C	1,824	51.9	5,065	69.4	-
J.R. Grocott	Lab	1,693	48.1			
Total votes		3,517				
1938						
G. Proctor	C	1,841	52.0	5,129	69.0	-
J.R. Grocott	Lab	1,699	48.0			
Total votes		3,540				

Overall Labour vote   **44.9%**   **Overall turnout**   **67.6%**

St Paul's ward

Candidate	Party	Votes	%	Electors	Turnout	Gains
1919						
J.W. Ellison	Lab	1,276	43.4	3,949	74.5	Lab from C
W.H. Ainsworth	C	886	30.1			
F. Harrison	L	779	26.5			
Total votes		2,941				
1920						
F. Harrison	L	1,616	53.7	4,054	74.2	-
J. Smethurst	Lab	1,392	46.3			
Total votes		3,008				
1921						
J. Smethurst	Lab	1,547	51.8	4,100	72.8	Lab from C
W.H. Ainsworth	C	1,438	48.2			
Total votes		2,985				
1920						
W.H. Ainsworth	C	1,651	54.5	4,141	73.2	C from Lab
J.W. Ellison*	Lab	1,379	45.5			
Total votes		3,030				
1923						
F. Harrison*	L	1,500	53.0	4,167	67.9	-
J. Calvert	Lab	1,328	47.0			
Total votes		2,828				
1924						
J.H. Chadburn	C	1,656	52.9	4,131	75.8	C from Lab
J. Smethurst*	Lab	1,475	47.1			
Total votes		3,131				
1925						
W.H. Ainsworth*	C	1,589	53.9	4,181	70.6	-
G.H. Kirby	Lab	1,361	46.1			
Total votes		2,950				
1926						
W.F. Dean	L	1,601	55.4	4,223	68.5	-
G.H. Kirby	Lab	1,290	44.6			
Total votes		2,891				

St Paul's ward *(continued)*

Candidate	Party	Votes	%	Electors	Turnout	Gains
1927						
J.H. Chadburn*	C	1,496	51.4	4,268	68.2	-
J. Beardsworth	Lab	1,414	48.6			
Total votes		2,910				
1928						
J. Beardsworth	Lab	1,678	54.9	4,253	71.9	Lab from C
W.H. Ainsworth*	C	1,378	45.1			
Total votes		3,056				
1929						
H. Beardwood	Lab	1,592	52.4	*4,351*	69.9	Lab from L
W.F. Dean*	L	1,447	47.6			
Total votes		3,039				
1930						
A. McLeod	C	1,751	57.3	4,448	68.8	-
J.W. Taylor	Lab	1,160	37.9			
T.B. Pace	Ind	147	4.8			
Total votes		3,058				
1931						
J. Beardsworth*	Lab	1,884	54.9	*4,480*	76.5	-
G. Davies	C	1,545	45.1			
Total votes		3,429				
1932						
H. Johnson	Lab	1,645	51.2	4,512	71.3	-
S. Greenwood	C	1,485	46.2			
Mrs M. Nelson	Com	86	2.7			
Total votes		3,216				
1933						
G.B. Eddie	Lab	1,719	50.8	4,463	75.8	Lab from C
S. Greenwood	C	1,100	32.5			
H. Hindle	L	563	16.6			
Total votes		3,382				
1934						
J. Beardsworth*	Lab	Unopp.	-		-	-

St Paul's ward *(continued)*

Candidate	Party	Votes	%	Electors	Turnout	Gains
1935						
H. Johnson*	Lab	1,862	56.1	*4,439*	74.7	-
C.W. Eastwood	C	1,455	43.9			
Total votes		3,317				
1936						
G.B. Eddie*	Lab	1,872	57.4	4,426	73.7	-
S. Greenwood	C	1,389	42.6			
Total votes		3,261				
1937						
J. Beardsworth*	Lab	1,960	64.2	4,393	69.5	-
F. Campbell	C	1,094	35.8			
Total votes		3,054				
1938						
H. Johnson*	Lab	1,609	56.8	4,325	65.5	-
S. Dean	C	1,223	43.2			
Total votes		2,832				

Overall Labour vote		**50.5%**		**Overall turnout**		**71.7%**

St Peter's ward

Candidate	Party	Votes	%	Electors	Turnout	Gains
1919						
E. Porter*	Lab	1,100	65.7	2,428	69.0	-
J. Walsh	C	575	34.3			
Total votes		1,675				
1920						
T. Dugdale	C	1,090	57.9	2,552	73.7	-
A. McHugh	Lab	792	42.1			
Total votes		1,882				
1921						
Dr C.M. Bradley	C	1,061	53.9	2,611	75.4	C from Lab
J. Miller*	Lab	907	46.1			
Total votes		1,968				
1922						
E. Porter*	Lab	1,084	54.9	2,618	75.4	-
A.T. Heatley	C	891	45.1			
Total votes		1,975				
1923						
J. Charnley	Lab	902	52.7	2,611	65.5	Lab from C
M. Brierley	C	809	47.3			
Total votes		1,711				
1924						
Dr C.M. Bradley*	C	1,035	56.3	2,638	69.7	-
T. McNamee	Lab	804	43.7			
Total votes		1,839				
1925						
E. Porter*	Lab	Unopp.			-	-
1926						
J. Charnley*	Lab	964	53.9	2,683	66.7	-
W.R. Rowe	C	825	46.1			
Total votes		1,789				
1927						
J. Frankland	Lab	986	53.6	2,733	67.3	Lab from C
Dr C.M. Bradley*	C	852	46.4			
Total votes		1,838				

St Peter's ward *(continued)*

Candidate	Party	Votes	%	Electors	Turnout	Gains
1928						
E. Porter*	Lab	1,117	55.7	2,727	73.6	-
D. Dewhurst	C	858	42.8			
Ms B. Dickinson	Com	32				
Total votes		2,007				
1929						
J. Charnley*	Lab	1,140	57.3	2,831	70.3	-
J. Ainsworth	C	828	41.6			
J. Abbot	Nuwm	22	1.1			
Total votes		1,990				
1930						
J. Ainsworth	C	1,221	59.9	2,934	69.5	C from Lab
E. Atherton	Lab	741	36.3			
J. Wilkinson	Chtr	77	3.8			
Total votes		2,039				
1931						
Mrs M. Bradley	C	1,275	61.9	2,904	70.9	C from Lab
J. Calvert*	Lab	754	36.6			
Mrs B. Jane	Com	31	1.5			
Total votes		2,060				
1932						
J. Charnley*	Lab	1,052	52.9	2,875	69.2	-
J.E. Webster	C	937	47.1			
Total votes		1,989				
1933						
J. Ainsworth*	C	1,074	51.5	2,867	72.8	-
A. Townsend	Lab	1,013	48.5			
Total votes		2,087				
1934						
A. Townsend	Lab	1,052	52.0	2,823	71.7	Lab from C
Mrs M. Bradley*	C	971	48.0			
Total votes		2,023				
1935						
J. Charnley*	Lab	1,198	58.7	2,745	74.4	-
J. Middleton	C	843	41.3			
Total votes		2,041				

St Peter's ward *(continued)*

Candidate	Party	Votes	%	Electors	Turnout	Gains
1936						
E. Porter	Lab	1,036	51.6	2,667	75.2	Lab from C
J. Ainsworth*	C	970	48.4			
Total votes		2,006				
1937						
A. Townsend*	Lab	916	54.1	2,540	66.6	-
S. Greenwood	C	776	45.9			
Total votes		1,692				
1938						
J. Charnley*	Lab	884	51.1	2,509	69.0	-
Mrs M. Bradley	C	846	48.9			
Total votes		1,730				

Overall Labour vote		**50.7%**		**Overall turnout**		**70.8%**

St Silas's ward

Candidate	Party	Votes	%	Electors	Turnout	Gains
1919						
J.W. Carmichael	L	1,444	46.5	4,158	74.7	L from C
T. Sharples*	C	1,295	41.7			
J. Frankland	Lab	366	11.8			
Total votes		3,105				
1920						
T. Sharples	C	2,232	87.8	4,182	60.8	C from L
C. Murfitt	Lab	309	12.2			
Total votes		2,541				
1921						
J.A. Omerod	L	1,530	51.1	4,221	71.0	L from C
J. Leigh*	C	1,467	48.9			
Total votes		2,997				
1922						
J.W. Carmichael*	L	Unopp.	-		-	-
1923						
T. Sharples*	C	Unopp.	-	4,241	-	-
1924						
J.A. Ormerod*	L	Unopp.	-		-	-
1925						
E. Coward	C	1,835	56.2	4,351	75.1	C from L
W. Coupe	L	1,432	43.8			
Total votes		3,267				
1926						
T. Sharples*	C	Unopp.	-		-	-
1927						
C.W. Eastwood	Ind	2,017	60.4	4,456	74.9	Ind from L
J.A. Ormerod*	L	1,321	39.6			
Total votes		3,338				
1928						
J. Taylor	C	Unopp.	-		-	-

St Silas's ward *(continued)*

Candidate	Party	Votes	%	Electors	Turnout	Gains
1929						
R. Culshaw*	Ind	1,651	46.8	*4,650*	75.8	-
W. Carmichael	L	1,191	33.8			
A. McLeod	C	684	19.4			
Total votes		3,526				
1930						
C.W. Eastwood*	C	1,709	58.2	4,747	61.8	-
R.H.G. Horne	R	1,226	41.8			
Total votes		2,935				
1931						
J. Taylor*	C	Unopp.	-		-	-
1932						
R. Culshaw*	Ind	2,150	60.8	4,818	73.4	-
C.A. Milford	C	1,387	39.2			
Total votes		3,537				
1933						
W. Carmichael	L	1,478	43.6	4,847	69.9	L from C
C.W. Eastwood*	C	958	28.3			
H. Ashworth	Ind	954	28.1			
Total votes		3,390				
1934						
J. Taylor*	C	Unopp.	-		-	-
1935						
R. Culshaw*	Ind	Unopp.	-		-	-
1936						
W. Carmichael*	L	1,814	50.1	4,851	74.6	-
E. Holden	C	1,804	49.9			
Total votes		3,618				
1937						
E. Woolley*	L	1,913	54.0	4,910	72.1	-
H. Yates	C	1,629	46.0			
Total votes		3,542				

St Silas's ward *(continued)*

Candidate	Party	Votes	%	Electors	Turnout	Gains
1938						
C.R. Davies*	C	Unopp.	-	4,979	-	-

Overall Labour vote   **1.9%**   **Overall turnout**   **71.3%**

St Stephen's ward

Candidate	Party	Votes	%	Electors	Turnout	Gains
1919						
A. Heyes	Lab	1,506	50.5	4,530	65.9	Lab from C
F. Hargreaves	C	1,063	35.6			
E. Rudd	L	415	13.9			
Total votes		2,984				
1920						
J. Eddleston	Ind	2,266	66.5	4,590	74.3	Ind from C
E. Atherton	Lab	1,144	33.5			
Total votes		3,410				
1921						
J. Johnson*	Lab	1,743	58.1	4,629	64.9	-
G.M. Dean	C	1,259	41.9			
Total votes		3,002				
1922						
D.C. Cayley	C	1,775	52.0	4,683	72.9	C from Lab
A. Heyes*	Lab	1,639	48.0			
Total votes		3,414				
1923						
J. Eddleston*	Ind	2,096	63.2	4,754	69.8	-
W. Scott	Lab	1,223	36.8			
Total votes		3,319				
1924						
J. Atkinson	C	2,002	56.8	4,794	73.6	C from Lab
J. Johnson*	Lab	1,525	43.2			
Total votes		3,527				
1925						
D.C. Cayley*	C	2,035	57.1	4,919	72.5	-
J. Johnson	Lab	1,532	42.9			
Total votes		3,567				
1926						
J. Eddleston*	Ind	Unopp.	-	-		-
1927						
J. Atkinson*	C	Unopp.	-	-		-

St Stephen's ward *(continued)*

Candidate	Party	Votes	%	Electors	Turnout	Gains
1928						
H. Johnson	Lab	2,116	52.2	5,747	70.6	Lab from C
D.C. Cayley*	C	1,939	47.8			
Total votes		4,055				
1929						
T. Vipond	Lab	2,058	51.6	*6,197*	64.3	Lab from Ind
P. Hargreaves	C	1,928	48.4			
Total votes		3,986				
1930						
J. Atkinson	C	2,564	58.7	6,647	65.7	-
H. Smith	Lab	1,801	41.3			
Total votes		4,365				
1931						
G. Haworth	C	2,944	61.8	*6,949*	68.6	C from Lab
H. Johnson*	Lab	1,820	38.2			
Total votes		4,764				
1932						
J.T. Taylor	C	2,449	51.9	7,252	65.0	C from Lab
T. Vipond*	Lab	2,268	48.1			
Total votes		4,717				
1933						
H. Earnshaw	Lab	2,392	46.8	7,265	70.4	Lab from C
J. Atkinson*	C	2,192	42.9			
T. Holden	L	529	10.3			
Total votes		5,113				
1934						
Mrs Smethhurst	Lab	2,390	46.0	7,321	71.0	Lab from C
G. Haworth*	C	2,302	44.3			
T. Holden	L	509	9.8			
Total votes		5,201				
1935						
G. Haworth	C	2,732	52.4	*7,404*	70.4	-
F. Beardsworth	Lab	2,479	47.6			
Total votes		5,211				

St Stephen's ward *(continued)*

Candidate	Party	Votes	%	Electors	Turnout	Gains
1936						
J. Atkinson	C	2,763	50.1	7,488	73.6	C from Lab
H. Earnshaw*	Lab	2,749	49.9			
Total votes		5,512				
1937						
B.S. White	C	2,620	50.7	7,499	68.9	C from Lab
F. Beardsworth*	Lab	2,545	49.3			
Total votes		5,165				
1938						
G. Haworth*	C	2,782	53.2	7,605	68.8	-
H. Earnshaw	Lab	2,452	46.8			
Total votes		5,234				

Overall Labour vote   **46.2%**   **Overall turnout**   **69.4%**

St Thomas' ward

Candidate	Party	Votes	%	Electors	Turnout	Gains
1919						
G. Burke*	C	1,719	52.1	4,618	71.5	-
N. Cronshaw	Lab	1,583	47.9			
Total votes		3,302				
1920						
J.W. Keighley*	C	1,892	60.0	4,849	65.0	-
N. Cronshaw	Lab	1,259	40.0			
Total votes		3,151				
1921						
W. Jenkins*	C	1,779	53.2	4,698	71.1	-
N. Cronshaw	Lab	1,562	46.8			
Total votes		3,341				
1922						
G. Burke*	C	Unopp.	-		-	-
1923						
T.W. Hitchen*	C	Unopp.	-	4,697	-	-
1924						
W. Jenkins*	C	1,957	60.6	4,703	68.6	-
L. Pickering	Lab	1,271	39.4			
Total votes		3,228				
1925						
G. Burke*	C	2,109	84.8	4,761	52.3	-
A. Leacy	Lab	379	15.2			
Total votes		2,488				
1926						
R.H. Barnes	C	1,557	47.1	4,811	68.7	-
N. Cronshaw	Lab	1,381	41.8			
J.T. Duckworth	L	368	11.1			
Total votes		3,306				
1927						
W. Jenkins*	C	1,730	53.8	4,852	66.2	-
N. Cronshaw	Lab	1,484	46.2			
Total votes		3,214				

St Thomas' ward *(continued)*

Candidate	Party	Votes	%	Electors	Turnout	Gains
1928						
G. Burke*	C	2,214	54.5	4,883	83.2	-
R. Weir	Lab	1,847	45.5			
Total votes		4,061				
1929						
R. Weir	Lab	1,885	50.5	*4,980*	75.0	Lab from C
S. Jenner	C	1,850	49.5			
Total votes		3,735				
1930						
W. Tempest	C	2,346	61.8	5,076	74.8	C from Lab
A. Rigby	Lab	1,450	38.2			
Total votes		3,796				
1931						
D.B. Worden*	C	2,483	69.7	*5,104*	69.7	-
A. Rigby	Lab	1,077	30.3			
Total votes		3,560				
1932						
H. Stuart	C	2,121	55.5	5,132	74.5	C from Lab
R. Weir*	Lab	1,653	43.2			
T.M. Fay	Com	50	1.3			
Total votes		3,824				
1933						
W. Tempest*	C	1,966	54.6	5,159	69.8	-
F. Wilkinson	Lab	1,636	45.4			
Total votes		3,602				
1934						
D.B. Worden*	C	2,096	56.2	5,199	71.8	-
F. Wilkinson	Lab	1,635	43.8			
Total votes		3,731				
1935						
J.T. Taylor	C	2,143	54.9	*5,282*	73.9	-
M. Rourke	Lab	1,763	45.1			
Total votes		3,906				

St Thomas' ward *(continued)*

Candidate	Party	Votes	%	Electors	Turnout	Gains
1936						
W. Tempest*	C	2,144	55.6	5,365	71.9	-
M. Rourke	Lab	1,712	44.4			
Total votes		3,856				
1937						
D.B. Worden*	C	2,280	62.1	5,455	67.3	-
F. Green	Lab	1,393	37.9			
Total votes		3,673				
1938						
J.T. Taylor*	C	2,124	59.5	5,502	64.8	-
W. Poulton	Lab	1,443	40.5			
Total votes		3,567				

Overall Labour vote   **41.7%**   **Overall turnout**   **70.0%**

Trinity ward

Candidate	Party	Votes	%	Electors	Turnout	Gains
1919						
Dr F.J. Greeves*	Ind	1,149	60.9	3,559	53.0	-
J.T. Alty	Lab	738	39.1			
Total votes		1,887				
1920						
P. Prebble	C	1,307	54.2	3,592	67.1	-
J.T. Alty	Lab	1,104	45.8			
Total votes		2,411				
1921						
H.R. Hornby*	C	1,377	56.2	3,646	67.2	-
I. Flint	Lab	1,072	43.8			
Total votes		2,449				
1922						
Dr F.J. Greeves*	Ind	Unopp.	-		-	-
1923						
A. Townsend	Lab	1,315	53.8	3,712	65.9	Lab from C
P. Prebble*	C	1,131	46.2			
Total votes		2,446				
1924						
T. Lucas*	C	1,365	52.8	3,669	70.4	-
Mrs L. Flint	Lab	1,218	47.2			
Total votes		2,583				
1925						
H. Bolton	C	1,271	50.3	3,738	67.5	C from Lab
J.M. Lomax*	Lab	1,254	49.7			
Total votes		2,525				
1926						
A. Townsend*	Lab	1,362	53.0	3,775	68.1	-
Rev G.S. Perry	C	1,207	47.0			
Total votes		2,569				
1927						
J.M. Lomax	Lab	1,301	52.0	3,792	65.9	Lab from C
T. Lucas*	C	1,199	48.0			
Total votes		2,500				

Trinity ward *(continued)*

Candidate	Party	Votes	%	Electors	Turnout	Gains
1928						
R. Beardwood	Lab	1,429	51.6	3,804	72.8	Lab from C
H. Bolton*	C	1,341	48.4			
Total votes		2,770				
1929						
A. Townsend*	Lab	1,468	58.5	*3,894*	64.5	-
J.C. Hindle	C	1,018	40.5			
H. Dickenson	Com	25				
Total votes		2,511				
1930						
E. Leaver	C	1,379	50.6	3,984	68.4	C from Lab
J.M. Lomax*	Lab	1,345	49.4			
Total votes		2,724				
1931						
F. Smith	C	1,626	58.2	*3,931*	71.1	C from Lab
H. Smith	Lab	1,167	41.8			
Total votes		2,793				
1932						
H. Smith	Lab	1,448	51.3	3,877	72.7	Lab from C
F. Hargreaves*	C	1,303	46.2			
Mrs B. Jane	Com	69	2.4			
Total votes		2,820				
1933						
R. Weir	Lab	1,559	56.5	3,885	71.0	Lab from C
E. Leaver*	C	1,031	37.4			
E.O. Mason	L	169	6.1			
Total votes		2,759				
1934						
W. Bond	Lab	1,614	59.4	3,876	70.1	Lab from C
C.W. Eastwood	C	1,104	40.6			
Total votes		2,718				
1935						
J. Rogerson	Lab	1,559	55.7	*3,831*	73.0	-
A. Gleeson	C	1,239	44.3			
Total votes		2,798				

Trinity ward *(continued)*

Candidate	Party	Votes	%	Electors	Turnout	Gains
1936						
R. Weir*	Lab	1,534	55.0	3,786	73.6	-
A. Gleeson	C	1,253	45.0			
Total votes		2,787				
1937						
W. Bond*	Lab	1,427	52.7	3,770	71.8	-
Dr A.H. Gregson	C	1,281	47.3			
Total votes		2,708				
1938						
J. Fish	Lab	1,288	56.6	3,747	60.7	Lab from Ind
J. Rogerson*	Ind	986	43.4			
Total votes		2,274				

Overall Labour vote		**51.4%**		**Overall turnout**		**68.2%**

SEVEN
Blackpool

BLACKPOOL

Blackpool's confident adaptation to change in the half century before the First World War was neatly encapsulated in the town's motto, 'Progress'. In the two decades between the wars, however, this premier holiday resort of Britain's working class faced far more uncertain economic circumstances which were to tax the confidence and skill of the municipal government. But before the problems of Blackpool's local politics in this period can be analysed, its historical development needs to be explained.

Until the mid-nineteenth century, Southport, and even Lytham, were larger and more important tourist resorts than the few fishermen's cottages and hotels of Blackpool. When the railway reached Blackpool in 1846, however, the town began to grow rapidly. In terms of population growth and the development of its staple industries, leisure and tourism, Blackpool's foundations were laid between 1851 and 1871. Its establishment as incomparably Britain's largest resort occurred in the last quarter of the nineteenth century. Its growth was encouraged by an accidental advantage that lasted from 1879 until after the First World War. A civil servant's mistake which became part of a parliamentary Act allowed the council to levy a twopenny rate to advertise the town or provide a band.[1] This gave Blackpool an enormous advantage over its seaside rivals. The corporation's first advertising manager, Charles Noden, became known as 'Mr Blackpool' with the motto 'We cater for quantity and we give them quality'. The industrial working class of Lancashire based on King Cotton and coal were to provide the basis for this growth and prosperity. As one analysis has pointed out:

> The spread of prosperity down the social scale in the urban populations of the coalfield together with the institution of the annual holiday of the 'wakes week' gave Blackpool an immense stimulus in the closing decades of the nineteenth century.[2]

The most prominent historian of the borough, John Walton, has shown that late nineteenth-century Blackpool had become 'the world's first specialised working-class seaside resort.'[3] A number of factors explained this development. First, there was no dominant landlord intent on creating a high-class resort. Second, with private enterprise lacking, it was the town's municipal authorities which intervened to augment the natural attractions and ensure entertainment provision. This was to lead to ever-increasing municipal involvement in the local economy on a relatively large scale for that period. Third, the municipal authorities fostered an ambience of 'homeliness', and Blackpool's lack of 'pretensions and petty restrictions' soon made the borough attractive to working-class visitors.[4]

[1] Walton, J.K., *The Blackpool Landlady: A Social History*, (Manchester, 1978), p. 55.
[2] Freeman, T.W., Rodgers, H.R. and Kinvig, R.H., *Lancashire, Cheshire and the Isle of Man*, (London, 1966), p. 241.
[3] Walton, J.K., *Lancashire: A Social History 1558–1939*, (Manchester, 1987), p. 295.
[4] Walton, J.K., 'Municipal government and the holiday industry in Blackpool, 1876–1914' in Walton, J.K. and Walvin, J., (eds), *Leisure in Britain 1780–1939*, (Manchester, 1983), pp 162–165.

By 1904, then, Blackpool had grown so large as to became a county borough. By the time of the 1931 census it had a population of around 100,000, and was the forty-second largest of the county boroughs. In terms of the social indicators used in these volumes, Blackpool was ranked respectively first and third among the county boroughs with regard to the self-employed and personal service sectors. Tourism and the connected leisure industries were at the heart of Blackpool's inter-war economy. These service industries were all-pervasive in the social fabric. The wealthy leisure-company owners and managers, building developers, and hotel owners at one end of the spectrum, the precariously comfortably-off shopkeepers, publicans, and lodging-house keepers in the middle, and the poor seasonal labourers at the other end, were all fundamentally affected by tourism. The lodging-house keepers, publicans, shopkeepers, and other small-businessmen and women, who were in business on their own account, or as managers, accounted for nearly 29 per cent of the male and just over 30 per cent of the female workforce classified by industry in 1931. Most of these were connected directly or indirectly to tourism. Commerce and finance accounted for just over a quarter of the working population in the same year. A high percentage of these, together with the 6.1 per cent in entertainment and sport were also reliant on the ubiquitous leisure and tourist industries. Furthermore nearly 13 per cent of the male and over 59 per cent of the female labour force worked in the personal services category with many workers servicing the lodging houses and small hotels. Given this economic structure, it is no surprise that women made up a relatively high proportion of 38 per cent of the total workforce in 1931, the town ranking twelfth of the county boroughs in this regard. Lastly the builders, a prominent interest in the council chamber, employed 14 per cent of the male labour force.

The central importance of municipal government to the development of Blackpool needs to be stressed. Across the country, the involvement of municipal authorities in the provision of 'gas and water' amenities in mid-Victorian Britain was followed by deeper involvement in the local economy. The development of tramways and electrical supply was later added to by broader involvement of councils in areas of welfare such as housing and education. In this respect Blackpool was no different from other municipal authorities, and like them became an important employer of labour. If self-improvement and philanthropy can be seen at work in cities such as Manchester and Birmingham, though, Blackpool spent its rates for commercial return. Walton argues that commercial justification for rate expenditure was all-pervasive. This was especially so with the heavy investment in promenades and parks constructed to attract working-class visitors.[5] Such expenditure in support of leisure-connected industries made Blackpool, more than most comparable authorities, an interventionist advocate of big local government.

With some justification, Walton sees the pre-1914 council run the town like a limited company, with little alternative put forward to 'the businessman's idea of municipal government'.[6] Rising rateable values and profitable utilities meant that

[5] Walton, 'Municipal government', p. 163.
[6] Walton, 'Municipal government', p. 171.

municipal enterprise and improvements to the infrastructure of Blackpool occurred without substantial rate rises. D.L. Harbottle, the town clerk, when surveying Blackpool in 1936, itemised the council's municipal enterprise from the vital ownership of the promenades and foreshore, to the transport, gas, electrical and water utilities. Even in the recession-hit 1930s most of these enterprises remained profitable.[7] Although post-1918 private capital was scarce, the municipal authorities continued to spend on the development of the town. In the mid-1920s, Blackpool's capital investment was around £80,000 per year compared to £70,000 in 1910.[8] In 1923, for example, the council was rebuilding the North Promenade, constructing a new boating pool and open-air baths, completely re-laying all the tram-tracks in the town, and laying out Stanley Park.

The directors and managers of the leisure companies, together with the builders and others with business interests, played the most important role in running Blackpool's corporation during the inter-war period. These interests dominated local politics and were often referred to by their opponents as the 'ring', 'gang' or 'clique'. The obvious implication was that such interest groups ran the town to their own economic advantage. They worked largely within the Conservative and Liberal parties in the town. Given the weakness of Labour, there being no industrial working class before aircraft production in the Second World War, municipal politics had a tenor of muted competition between the two established parties. Walton's judgement of pre-First World War local politics, namely that ruling groups recruited from the Liberals as well as from the Tories, holds good for the inter-war years.[9] National party labels were probably more relevant after 1918, but apart from sniping in the pre-November electoral meetings, Conservatives, Liberals and Independents ruled Blackpool and were drawn for the same class and from similar occupational groups.

Like many other councils in this period Blackpool was dominated by businessmen, both employers and self-employed. Very unusually the borough had no working-class councillors before 1919. Between 1876 and 1914 Walton estimated that 36 per cent of councillors had directorships in the leisure and holiday enterprises or sea-front hotels. More than half of councillors were known to be shareholders in local entertainment firms. Again more than half of all councillors were engaged in land speculation and property development. The building trades usually composed one sixth of the council, the shopkeepers and 'lower reaches' of the hotel trade another sixth, while the drink trade's representation was almost as powerful as the builders'.[10] Again this analysis still applied to inter-war municipal politics. There were constant complaints from the Labour Party and sometimes Independents of 'rings' and 'cliques' at work. Matthew Burns, a candidate representing the National Federation of Discharged and Demobilised Sailors and Soldiers (NFDDSS) in Talbot ward in 1919, elaborated upon these shady interest groups in his election address:

---

[7]   Curnow, W.I., 'The growth of Blackpool as a health and holiday resort', in Grime, A., (ed.), *A Scientific Study of Blackpool and District*, (London, 1936), pp. 79–80.
[8]   Turner, B. and Palmer, S., *The Blackpool Story*, (Blackpool, 1994), p. 119.
[9]   Walton, 'Municipal government', p. 170.
[10]   Walton, 'Municipal government', p. 167.

The Sectional Groups in the Town are Three in number, namely: (1) Building Trades, (2) Amusement Caterers, and (3) Food Purveyors and Caterers. They may be classified as follows: 12 Building Trades (embracing Builders and Contractors, Land and Property Speculators), 10 Amusement Caterers; 13 Food Purveyors and Caterers: a total of 35 out of the 52 members of the Council. The remaining number consist of 2 tradesmen, 5 Professional men, 1 Company-House Keepers representative, and 9 of miscellaneous occupations. The three Dominating Groups embracing 35 have interests which unite them.'[11]

The influence of the directors and managers of the leisure companies, sitting as councillors, cannot be underestimated. The best example of this powerful vested interest was W.G. Bean, whose family still run one of the largest leisure enterprises in the town. Bean, who was managing director of Blackpool Pleasure Beach Ltd, was the Conservative councillor for Waterloo for many years before becoming an alderman in 1926. The power of his company, together with the Tower Company and the Winter Gardens, should not be understated. In the inter-war period, the Tower Company employed more than 1,500 people in the season.[12] Indeed, by 1928 the Tower Company controlled its greatest competitor, the Winter Gardens. There was usually a harmony of interests between the private enterprise of the leisure companies and the public expenditure plans and enterprise of the council. In return for the granting of some land for the new South Promenade extension in 1926, for instance, the Pleasure Beach received free advertising on the trams with the terminus destination always to show 'Pleasure Beach' instead of the old 'South Pier'.[13]

Spending the rates on leisure-related projects made Blackpool attractive and made sound economic sense to the politicians representing the holiday trades. Large capital expenditure was rarely directly in the interests of the locals unless they were in business, or an employee in a holiday trade. Projects such as parks and libraries could be rejected as the holiday industry was not involved, and in these cases municipal parsimony gained the upper hand. Demands for economy and the abolition of waste were made by some. Thus Councillor J. Potter (Layton ward) supporting a fellow Conservative in Talbot ward in 1920 urged a curb on waste.[14] This was a consistent theme, but more typical of the small shopkeepers and company house keepers of inter-war Blackpool. This echoes the pattern of other towns. When times were harsh, the economically insecure small-businessman or woman usually called for municipal economy. Conversely large-scale capital projects were consistently supported when advantage could be discerned for the leisure and holiday interests. A whole range of middling to large council-sponsored projects were undertaken in the 1920s: the Poor Children's Holiday Camp and the North Shore Open Air Bath in 1923, a new promenade at

[11] *Gazette–News for Blackpool, Fleetwood, Lytham, St Annes and Fylde District*, 31 Oct. 1919.
[12] Curnow, 'The growth of Blackpool', pp. 82–83.
[13] Turner and Palmer, *The Blackpool Story*, p. 103.
[14] *Blackpool Gazette & Herald*, 25 Oct. 1920.

South Shore in 1926, and a new school at Tyldesley and the opening of the new municipal aerodrome in 1929.

The 1930s saw even greater municipal investment with further road building to add to the new roads and extensions of the 1920s. The year 1930 saw extensive works on the North Shore cliffs, the Olympia building opened, the construction of three new schools, a new gas main and a new refuse disposal works. A new hospital, the Victoria, in 1933, and the foundation of a new technical college followed. Right up to the £2 million redevelopment scheme of 1938, approved by parliament but abandoned because of the war, the borough was plainly prepared to spend ratepayers' money. Few of these projects aroused much contention, yet public works specifically for the relief of unemployment, and municipal housing, invariably did. Most schemes that were carried forward, with the possible exceptions of the hospital and technical college, were beneficial to the staple industries. councillors with business largely connected to the holiday trade could see both the direct and indirect returns on rate expenditure.

By contrast with the 'insider' cliques that dominated the council, the Company-House Keepers' Association (CHKA) was an important 'outsider' group in inter-war Blackpool representing the lodging-house interest. This active and aggressive association had begun in a period of economic uncertainty for the trade in the 1890s. The numerous and predominantly female lodging-house keepers had previously been little represented on the council. Only five out of 150 councillors elected between 1876 and 1914 described themselves as lodging-house keepers.[15] Membership of the CHKA was composed mainly of the landladies who ran small company-houses or took in paying guests in quite small and humble terraced housing. This was an important area of female economic activity and also independence, and the CHKA was an important political pressure group which amounted almost to a political party in inter-war Blackpool. The Blackpool landlady, of course, was and is viewed as the epitome of the seaside landlady and has entered the popular consciousness of Britain through the Donald McGill postcard.

The CHKA put forward its claims strongly in the years immediately after the First World War. The association's successful candidate for Brunswick ward in 1919, G.R. Johnson, claimed that the company-house business was 'the staple of Blackpool' and that the ward had 'the highest number of people who take in visitors and may be considered the business centre'.[16] A year later another CHKA councillor, J. Hitchen, said company-house keeping was the 'bread and butter of Blackpool. Take the company-house keepers away and there would be little of Blackpool left. The company-house keepers were therefore entitled to greatly increased representation in the Town Council.'[17] In another meeting in 1920, Councillor Hitchen also claimed that the company-house keepers were 'collectively the largest ratepayers of the town'.[18]

[15]   Walton, *The Blackpool Landlady*, p. 161.
[16]   *Gazette–News*, 31 Oct. 1919.
[17]   *Blackpool Gazette & Herald*, 30 Oct. 1920.
[18]   *Blackpool Gazette & Herald*, 28 Oct. 1920.

The objectives of the association emerged quite clearly. One was to protect its members from unfair competition among themselves, and thereby prevent self-exploitation. Another was to help maintain the company-house keepers' income. The need to increase charges to visitors in line with increases in the cost of living was a pressing issue throughout the period. W.H. Hudson, the CHKA candidate in Brunswick ward in 1920, was quoted in the local press as follows:

> The company-house business was the foundation on which the prosperity of Blackpool rested. Speaking of the work of the Company-House Keepers' Association, Mr Hudson said that the 2/- a night in pre-war days was not sufficient and the present 4/- a night was insufficient when they came to consider the cost of living. They were the worst paid community in England.[19]

Other themes emerged at another meeting at Warley Road congregational school on 29 October 1920. Some of the positions taken were to become typical of the company-house keepers' stance. Councillor J.W. Bellarby argued for the abolition of the rates.

> He noticed that on the previous day the Manchester corporation ... decided to include in their new Parliamentary Bill a clause empowering Manchester to levy a charge of five per cent on the value of all the land in the city, whether developed or undeveloped, as a means of reducing the rates ... if this land tax came to be levied it would result in reducing the rates in Manchester from the present 16s. to 6s. 8d. in the £. If a similar plan were followed in Blackpool our rates would be nothing at all. (Laughter). He did not see why vested interests in land should not be taxed for the benefit of the community.'[20]

This desire for parsimony was plainly on behalf of the hard-pressed small-businessman and woman. At the same time, the CHKA attempted to win over working-class voters by claiming that they also would benefit from such a policy, but with little success. For at the same meeting, instead of sympathising with a questioner concerned at the poor quality of the new municipal houses being built, Councillor Bellarby put the blame on the standards demanded by the Ministry of Health. He then ominously referred to municipal housing as a 'white elephant', hardly words likely to attract working-class support.[21]

It is no wonder given the above that the CHKA was often accused of only 'bringing out' Liberal candidates. The association's response was predictable. It claimed to know no politics and that all parties were represented on its executive committee. Municipal economy and efficiency was its stated aims again and again. By 1920, the membership of the association had risen to 1,800, and it had become the mouthpiece for one-third of the Blackpool lodging-house business. By 1923, the Blackpool branch of the company-house keepers dominated the national

[19] *Blackpool Gazette & Herald*, 28 Oct. 1920.
[20] *Blackpool Gazette & Herald*, 30 Oct. 1920.
[21] *Blackpool Gazette & Herald*, 30 Oct. 1920.

federation of the association. But in the highly individualistic world of the landlady, the CHKA was on difficult ground. As a trade organisation its weaknesses were its failure in the long run to recruit the majority of Blackpool landladies, and its conspicuous lack of success at election time. Walton argues that it increasingly sounded more like a skilled trade union than a trade association of the self-employed.[22]

Throughout the period of this study, the CHKA never had more than three councillors at any one time. The association did well in its expansionist period just after the First World War but then fell away. Thus it made gains in Brunswick and Claremont wards in 1919, both wards being predominately Liberal and Progressive in the period. Both seats were lost subsequently when they came up for re-election in 1922. The only other intermittent successes for the CHKA were made in the wards where Labour had its only two victories, Foxhall and Tyldesley. Over the twenty-year period then the association was an unsuccessful vehicle in council elections. It failed to shift the grip of the dominant Conservative and Liberal parties in local politics, and thus the more established interests, namely the leisure companies, builders and the drinks trade.

Turning now to inter-war politics, in terms of parliamentary representation, Blackpool, together with the adjoining urban district of Lytham St Anne's and a small part of the rural district of Fylde, formed a single member constituency. Apart from a Liberal victory in 1923, reversed the following year, Blackpool remained a safe seat for the Conservatives at Westminster. 'Traces of Liberal strength' were noted by Pelling in his study of pre-First World War parliamentary elections.[23] Before the 1918 parliamentary boundary changes, the Blackpool seat had included a large agricultural hinterland where Liberalism and Nonconformity were weak. The new seat was more urban, and what Liberal strength there was became more significant therefore. This partly explains the 1923 parliamentary victory and the presence of Liberalism in municipal politics. Though a safe Conservative seat, the Liberal Party's percentage of the poll did not fall below 36 per cent until the 1931 election.

The strong performance of the two traditional parties was reflected in municipal politics. Conservative and Liberal councillors dominated the borough, and the Conservative party controlled the council throughout the twenty years of this study. The strongest Conservative wards were Warbreck and Waterloo, located in the peripheral north and south locations. Both wards were noted for their upmarket residential housing, together with private hotels and smarter sea-front terraces. Here lived the resident local businessmen, professionals and those who had retired from other Lancashire towns after successful business or professional careers. Talbot ward too can be viewed in this category where the Conservatives suffered only one defeat. Bank Hey, known as 'the businessman's ward', was relatively evenly split between the Conservative and Liberal parties. Claremont, towards the North Shore was largely controlled by the Liberals, as was Brunswick. Liberal Claremont was referred to by Councillor J.W. Bellarby as

---

[22] Walton, *The Blackpool Landlady*, p. 173.
[23] Pelling, H., *Social Geography of British Elections, 1885–1910*, (Aldershot, 1994), p. 278.

the 'aristocratic ward'. Beyond the North Shore Bispham ward can be viewed as a relatively safe suburban ward for the Conservatives. The other inland suburban wards of Layton and Marton the Conservatives shared with the Liberals.

The non-partisan and somewhat apolitical stance of the Conservatives and Liberals has already been referred to. Both parties largely represented the same economic interests connected to leisure, tourism, drink and the building trades. The ruling groups, as Walton commented on the pre-war situation, recruited from Liberals as well as Conservatives with national party labels largely irrelevant.[24] Councillors would have worked on the boards of the various leisure companies and no doubt socialised together too. Both the Wainwright Conservative Club rooms and the Liberal Club were situated in Victoria Street. They were close neighbours in both the sense of proximity of space and politics. Interlocking networks no doubt played their part in council decision-making. Occasionally the Conservatives could get hot under the collar concerning the charge of vested interests. Councillor Thickett, speaking in support of the Conservative candidate in Warbreck ward in 1930, could say 'that there had been a lot of talk about interests on the Town Council and that they should not be there. I have heard more blather talked about that than on any other subject'. 'I know', he added, 'you all have your interests'.[25] Sometimes, too, there were Liberal complaints about overwhelming Tory domination. Thus Councillor Kershaw, the Liberal candidate in Victoria ward in 1926 could say 'they needed a better balanced Council, as it was not good that one Party should be in such a large majority as was the case on Blackpool Council'.[26]

Only on the issue of the liquor trade and the influence of the publicans, brewers and small licensees did the two main parties differ. Here Nonconformity was important. John Walton has noted a relaxed and uniquely pioneering attitude to Sunday observance in the borough. Sunday trading and entertainment were allowed thus catering both for the needs of working-class visitors and the profits of the town's businessmen.[27] Nonetheless some tensions emerged in the arena of inter-war municipal politics. There seems little doubt that the Anglicanism of the Conservatives and the minority status of Nonconformity at times exercised the minds of Liberal councillors. In their election-night victory celebrations at the Liberal Club in 1919, J. Booth, the secretary of Bank Hey ward, proclaimed: 'too long had the town been ruled by the brewing interest.' He claimed five victories for temperance that night. Of these five, however, only one was a Liberal (Dean of Bank Hey), while the others were two CHKA candidates, an Independent and a Labour councillor.[28] Indeed temperance was as much an issue for Labour or the CHKA. At a pre-election meeting at Layton ward, the Labour candidate, E. Stevenson, agreed that, with seven out of eight members on the Watch Committee, the liquor trade was over-represented on the council.[29] The usual

24   Walton, 'Municipal government', p. 170.
25   *Blackpool Gazette & Herald*, 1 Nov. 1930.
26   *Blackpool Gazette & Herald*, 30 Oct. 1926.
27   Walton, 'Municipal government', p. 180.
28   *Gazette–News*, 4 Nov. 1919.
29   *Gazette–News*, 31 Oct. 1919.

pairing of the brewing interest with Conservatism created tension, but apart from this little of real import divided the two major parties.

Independents had some strength in the 1920s mainly in Bispham and Foxhall, while in the next decade they had three successes in the new ward of Stanley. They also had a presence in Layton, Tyldesley and Victoria. W.S. Ashton, the Independent candidate for Brunswick in 1920, stated the usual case for such candidates when he said that 'he thought the town could be better managed if it was entirely free from party politics'. He claimed the freedom to exercise his own judgement in municipal affairs and 'so be free of political leaders '. Opting for a pro-imperial position, 'he also made it clear he was a Liberal'.[30] The Independents however were the only ones who persistently raised the issue of corruption on the council. The Rev. H. Boydell Smith, a supporter of William Grundy (Independent) in Alexandra ward in 1919,

> declared that in a municipality like Blackpool there was always the danger that municipal affairs would be carried on in the interests of cliques. What was required was that there should be watch dogs, as it were, exercising watching control and supervision over what took place. Men who had been on the Council for a very long time had been men who had become among the richest of the inhabitants of the town.[31]

Smith was aware of the recently made post of elective auditor, but hinted at him being the elective nominee of the parties. and called for a genuinely independent auditor.

The Labour Party in Blackpool was probably the weakest in all the county boroughs. On only two occasions between the wars were Labour councillors ever elected, in Foxhall ward in 1919 and Tyldesley in 1936, and Labour's overall share of votes cast was extraordinarily low. Even by comparison with other boroughs in this volume such as Bath and Bournemouth, which were by no means Labour strongholds, Blackpool Labour lagged far behind. This unique lack of political success requires explanation. The lack of an industrial working class was obviously significant, but also the preponderance of people engaged in tourism and the leisure industries. Those such as the house keepers were often small-property owners who believed in competition and individual effort. The Labour Party would have had few attractions for this important group, whose petit bourgeois mentality was similar to that of the shopkeepers and small traders who survived economically through the holiday industry. Those in the entertainment industry also would not have found a home in the Labour movement, especially the middle class who owned and ran the entertainment industries, and also their intermediate middle-class managerial cadres. Lower down the scale, the thousands of small entertainers, traders, barkers and hustlers who existed on the margins of the local economy were typically extreme individualists. Finally, transitory and migrant workers were significant in Blackpool, especially during the season from April to late autumn. Such poorly-paid workers, even if they had

[30] *Blackpool Gazette & Herald*, 28 Oct. 1920.
[31] *Gazette–News*, 4 Nov. 1919.

had Labour sympathies, would seldom have had the municipal franchise. They would rarely have been ratepayers, and many would also have been disqualified by the permanent residence qualification. In the Depression years of the early 1930s especially, up to 10,000 seasonal workers wintered in Blackpool and were unemployed. Few of these would have met the requirements of the local government franchise.

It is also the case that Labour's weakness was accentuated by the aggressive tactics of its opponents. When Labour narrowly won its seat in Foxhall in 1919, in a ward that contained a concentration of gas, tramway and railway workers, the consternation among the established parties was palpable. When a more radical Labour candidate, Ernest Machin, contested the same ward at a by-election in September 1920, Liberals and Tories combined against him to support an 'Independent' opponent. Machin was denounced as a 'Bolshevik' and a 'revolutionary' in a campaign of unusual bitterness for Blackpool, and harshly treated in the local press. He was soundly defeated, a forewarning of Labour's disappointments in the annual elections two months later. As Walton comments, it was as if the threat of Labour and industrial unrest was especially frightening in Blackpool: 'if seaside resorts were not "safe" from this contagion, then nowhere was'. As a Lancashire businessmen put it, 'Blackpool stands between us and revolution. May it long continue as the protector of social order'.[32]

The national trends in favour of the rise of the Labour Party were only very faintly reflected in Blackpool. The gain of 1919 did coincide with the substantial gains by Labour nationally in that year, although the low turnout that prevailed elsewhere was not evident. The upsurge of Labour support in 1926 was barely visible in Blackpool, though, nor was the arrival of a Labour government in 1929 reflected in the local results. Encouraged more by the national success the Blackpool Labour Party put up candidates for all thirteen wards in the following year, the only occasion it was to do so between the wars. The results were predictably disastrous, given the nationwide slump in Labour support in 1930. All thirteen candidates lost heavily, a heavy blow in terms of morale and spent resources, and Labour's subsequent interventions were highly selective. Labour's lack of organisation on the ground was also a problem. Labour's best performance in 1930 was surprisingly in the predominantly suburban ward of Layton, but organisational weakness there meant that it was never contested again by the party before the war.

Women did not make much headway in the municipal politics of Blackpool between the wars, despite the fact that they constituted a large majority of the electoral roll.[33] The combination of plentiful female employment in the hotel and leisure trade, and in domestic service for the extensive middle class, plus large numbers of retired couples of whom the wives tended to outlive the husbands, ensured this female majority. The first woman councillor, Mrs Quayle, was elected in Alexandra ward in 1932 and returned for the Conservatives in walkovers in 1935 and 1938. She was to be the only woman to serve on the council in the inter-war years. Her husband was another Conservative councillor

---

[32] Walton, J.K., *Blackpool*, (Edinburgh, 1998), ch. 5.
[33] *Blackpool Gazette & Herald*, 28 Oct. 1920.

for the same ward. It was the Labour Party and the CHKA who put up most female candidates. In 1920 Mrs M. Harrison, the CHKA candidate in Tyldesley ward pointed out that the greater part of the membership of her organisation were women. Women, she argued at a pre-election meeting, 'should have one of their sex to speak for them'. Her mission was 'to elevate the women workers and to minimise their slavery'.[34] This kind of talk was rare, however, and it failed to win over sufficient voters in this case, Mrs Harrison losing to a Liberal by some distance.

In other boroughs the aldermanic elections were often a bone of contention sometimes involving chicanery by the controlling party. In Blackpool, however, the relative aldermanic strengths of Conservatives and Liberals reflected an even-handedness which came partly from Conservative security and partly from the interrelationship of the two parties' vested interests. The lack of manipulation of aldermanic elections was part and parcel of an apolitical consensus of the dominant business interests. The Liberals' six aldermen in the 1920s and five in the late 1930s represented a benevolent tolerance on the part of the Conservatives. Alternatively it might be argued it just did not matter, for both parties were effectively the same in occupational background and broad ideological outlook. Equally, gerrymandering of ward boundaries in Blackpool was of no significance.

The provision of municipal housing was a significant political issue in Blackpool. The town clerk noted in 1936 that the borough had ten council housing estates, and nearly 1400 dwellings had been provided.[35] Compared to boroughs of comparable size this was a low figure, although he could point out that building development by private enterprise 'has been phenomenal in Blackpool during the last few years'.[36] In the years from 1925 to 1935, an average of 1,250 dwelling houses had been built by private enterprise. There had been a greater commitment to council housing for a brief period in the immediate post-war years, with over 600 houses being constructed under the Addison Act by 1923. This was in part a response to the perceived threat posed by Labour in these years, which was to fade as the years went on.[37] Certainly the Labour Party raised the question of housing in the first post-war election. E. Stevenson, the Labour candidate in Layton, saw the housing problem as one of the main issues. His speech though was very general, deploring the unhealthy conditions of working-class accommodation and demanding good housing along with recreation grounds and better education to create 'an A1 population'. Unusually an Independent Conservative councillor, H. Bateson, in a Bank Hey ward meeting on the same day, saw housing as an issue of importance too. He pointed a finger of accusation at the builders on the council. Bateson said that the 'housing question was the one serious problem before the people and many were in a fix. They were up against the interests of the builders of Blackpool of whom there were eleven on the

---

[34] *Blackpool Gazette & Herald*, 16 Oct. 1920.
[35] D.L. Harbottle, 'Municipal life in Blackpool', in Grime, *A Scientific Study of Blackpool*, p. 91.
[36] Harbottle, 'Municipal life in Blackpool', p. 93.
[37] Walton, *Blackpool*, ch. 5.

council. The interests of the ordinary ratepayer was not the interest of the builders'.[38]

In 1920, W.S. Ashton, an Independent candidate for Brunswick, argued that the builders should be encouraged to build houses to rent and not just to sell.[39] Councillor Bellarby, of the CHKA, who saw municipal housing as a 'white elephant', also raised the issue of empty private-sector housing and homelessness. He claimed that over 400 empty houses existed, some of them not in the rate books and hence undetectable. He implied that this was because the builders kept them empty and hoped to sell them. He quoted, with apparent approval, a suggestion raised in the council chamber: 'If the soldiers of the town would only create a little bit of unrest, I would lead them, and I would do the same as the Manchester Councillors did. I would install them and their families in the empty houses until they were all filled up'.[40] Later J. Parkinson, an official Conservative candidate in Talbot ward in 1926, pushed the issue of council housing too. Saying that the borough had long waiting lists and a serious shortage, he promised 'to urge the corporation to make provision for more municipal houses at fair and reasonable rents'.[41] Parkinson, who secured the ward for the Conservatives, was a solicitor by profession not a builder. Councillor Rice, defending Claremont for the Liberals, argued the case for better housing for the working class in the same year. Houses were required to let and not just for sale. Houses should be built at a reasonable price as working people could not afford more than ten shillings a week. Rice went on: 'If the housing Committee set about it as businessmen this could be done. I consider that a programme of 500 houses in five years is totally inadequate.'[42] Rice was not a builder either. Housing, or the lack of it, was most often an issue for the Labour Party, however, and it remained so throughout the inter-war period. Given the weakness of the party, however, it was seldom placed on the agenda of the council chamber, and anyway the ruling Conservatives and Liberals had more pressing interests to service through public expenditure. With the Depression in 1931, government subsidies were abolished, which slowed down even more what little council building there was.

Lastly, the issue of unemployment was a social ill that afflicted Blackpool as elsewhere in the inter-war period. The percentage of workers unemployed, expressed as a monthly average, was 12.7 per cent (1929); 23.7 per cent (1931); 21.6 per cent (1932); and 18.0 per cent (1937).[43] Thus in 1932, Blackpool was ranked forty-fourth in the unemployed league table of the eighty-three county boroughs. Seasonal unemployment exacerbated Blackpool's problems. The 1936 survey of Blackpool noted that there had been a rapid growth of the borough's population since the Depression.[44] A high percentage of this influx of seasonal workers did not return to the industrial areas at the end of the season. With the

---

[38] *Gazette–News*, 31 Oct. 1919.

[39] *Blackpool Gazette & Herald*, 26 Oct. 1920.

[40] *Blackpool Gazette & Herald*, 16 Oct. 1920.

[41] *Blackpool Gazette & Herald*, 28 Oct. 1926.

[42] *Blackpool Gazette & Herald*, 30 Oct. 1926.

[43] Fogarty, M.P., *Prospects of the Industrial Areas of Great Britain*, (London, 1945), p. 32.

[44] Curnow, 'Growth of Blackpool', p. 84.

Depression there was no industry to return to, so most remained unemployed until the next season as permanent residents of Blackpool. The fluctuation was greater than in the southern resorts such as Brighton and Bournemouth which attracted a winter clientele. The borough tried to extend the winter season and promote itself as 'Congress City', but these projects, although having some success, did not eradicate mass seasonal unemployment. Most of the working people who were unemployed would not have achieved the local franchise, which perhaps muted the issue in municipal politics. There is no doubt though that the Anomalies Act of 1930–31, passed by the Labour government, adversely affected seasonal and casual workers, along with married women. This may have been a factor in the disastrous Labour results in Blackpool in 1930.

The 1930s saw some industrial development with a confectionery firm, two large biscuit factories and some light engineering, including motor coach building, being established. The real breakthrough in industrial employment, in the form of aircraft construction, did not come until the Second World War, however. Nevertheless Blackpool appears to have adapted its facilities and survived the Depression better than some. In most years comfortable seasons were recorded for the holiday and leisure industries. The continually buoyant rate revenues allowed the borough to spend hundreds of thousands of pounds on development schemes that lowered the unemployment statistics. In 1920, ex-servicemen were used on sea defences for the North Shore cliffs. In November of the same year the unemployed were set to work on Devonshire New Road.[45] Various other promenade and shoreworks provided temporary relief for the unemployed and did not appear politically contentious. This culminated in 1928 with winter relief schemes put into place by the council. This did not stop unemployment demonstrations in Talbot Square on 16 November 1932, and the National Unemployed Workers' Movement (NUWM) claimed a local membership of 1,500 in the early 1930s. But the fate of the unemployed rarely affected electioneering for the council. In 1938, however, Spencer Hudson, the Communist candidate for Foxhall ward did raise the issue of unemployment amongst seasonal workers. He highlighted the question in a meeting at the Manor Hall, Singleton Street, as well as emphasising the dangers of the international situation and the rise of fascism.[46] He won 32.6 per cent of the poll, which was a surprisingly high figure for a communist in most boroughs, let alone in a socialist backwater like Blackpool. On the whole, though, to the self-satisfied ratepayers of Blackpool, in what was still the foremost working-class resort in the 1930s, the issue of unemployment was never really to be on the agenda. Despite the Depression and mass unemployment, the holiday industry had remained largely resilient. Relative to the times the corporation too, did more than most in terms of public works relief.

In conclusion, the political domination of the borough by the Tory and Liberal parties, underpinned by their shared economic interest in the leisure industry,

---

[45] Eyre, K., *Seven Golden Miles: The Fantastic Story of Blackpool*, (Clapham, N. Yorks., 1975), p. 116.

[46] *West Lancs. Evening Gazette & Herald*, 26 Oct. 1938; the claim of 1,500 NUWM members in the early 1930s was also made in this speech.

stands out in Blackpool. As a consequence, Liberalism appeared to survive here better than it did nationally between the wars, although it is doubtful if Blackpool Liberalism was very easy to distinguish from Toryism. At the same time, the lack of manufacturing industry and working-class organisation, the exclusion from the municipal franchise of seasonal workers, and the predominance of a petit bourgeois property-owning ideology, all contributed to the overwhelming weakness of the Labour Party in Blackpool. In the political discourse of the borough there were no high ideals, no parallel of Birmingham's 'civic gospel', but instead in John Walton's phrase a 'philistine pragmatism' in which the borough 'owed its municipal success to the adoption of a business ethic in the Council chamber'. Success lay in serving its working-class holiday-makers and the council's role was to aid the entertainment industry by providing the services and infrastructure without unduly bothering the ratepayers.[47] In the case of Bournemouth, included later in this volume, ratepayers' money was spent mainly in the interests of incomers as retired residents, and in the promotion of a higher-class holiday and leisure industry. On the other hand, Blackpool remained the premier working-class resort in our period by using ratepayers' money to support the provision of working-class tastes and pleasures. In the main, the council was run to that end, controlled by the traditional parties to the advantage of the borough's most important economic interest groups. In its own terms the approach seems to have worked, for there is little doubt that Blackpool corporation played its part in providing for the holiday dreams of those who toiled in the factories and mills of industrial Britain.

[47] Walton, 'Municipal government', pp. 180, 171.

A guide to further reading

Newspapers

Blackpool Gazette & Herald
Blackpool Times
Manchester Guardian
West Lancs. Evening Gazette & Herald

Works of reference

Barrett's Directory for Blackpool and the Fylde

Other secondary sources

Clarke, A., *The Story of Blackpool*, (London, 1923).
Cross, G., *Worktowners at Blackpool*, (London, 1990).
Eyre, K., *Seven Golden Miles: The Fantastic Story of Blackpool*, (Clapham, N. Yorks., 1975).
Fogarty, M.P., *Prospects of the Industrial Areas of Great Britain*, (London, 1945).
Freeman, T.W., *The Conurbations of Great Britain*, (Manchester, 1959).
Freeman, T.W., Rodgers, H.R. and Kinvig, R.H., *Lancashire, Cheshire and the Isle of Man*, (London, 1966).
Grime, A., (ed.), *A Scientific Study of Blackpool and District*, (London, 1936).
Municipal Journal and Public Works Engineer, 'Municipal enterprise in seaside towns', Vol. 43, (6 Apr. 1934), p. 481.
Pelling, H., *Social Geography of British Elections*, 1885–1910, (Aldershot, 1994), p. 278.
Turner, B. and Palmer, S., *The Story of Blackpool*, (Blackpool, 1994).
Walton, J.K., *The Blackpool Landlady: A Social History*, (Manchester, 1978).
Walton, J.K., *Lancashire: A Social History, 1558–1939*, (Manchester, 1987).
Walton, J.K., 'Municipal government and the holiday industry in Blackpool, 1876–1914' in Walton, J.K. and Walvin, J., (eds), *Leisure in Britain 1780–1939*, (Manchester, 1983).
Walton, J.K., 'Leisure towns in wartime: the impact of the First World War in Blackpool and San Sebastian', *Journal of Contemporary History*, 31, (1996).
Walton, J.K., 'The seaside resorts of England and Wales, 1900–1950', in Shaw, G. and Williams, A., (eds), *The Rise and Fall of British Coastal Resorts*, (London, 1997).
Walton, J.K., *Blackpool*, (Edinburgh, 1998).

Blackpool wards 1919–1938

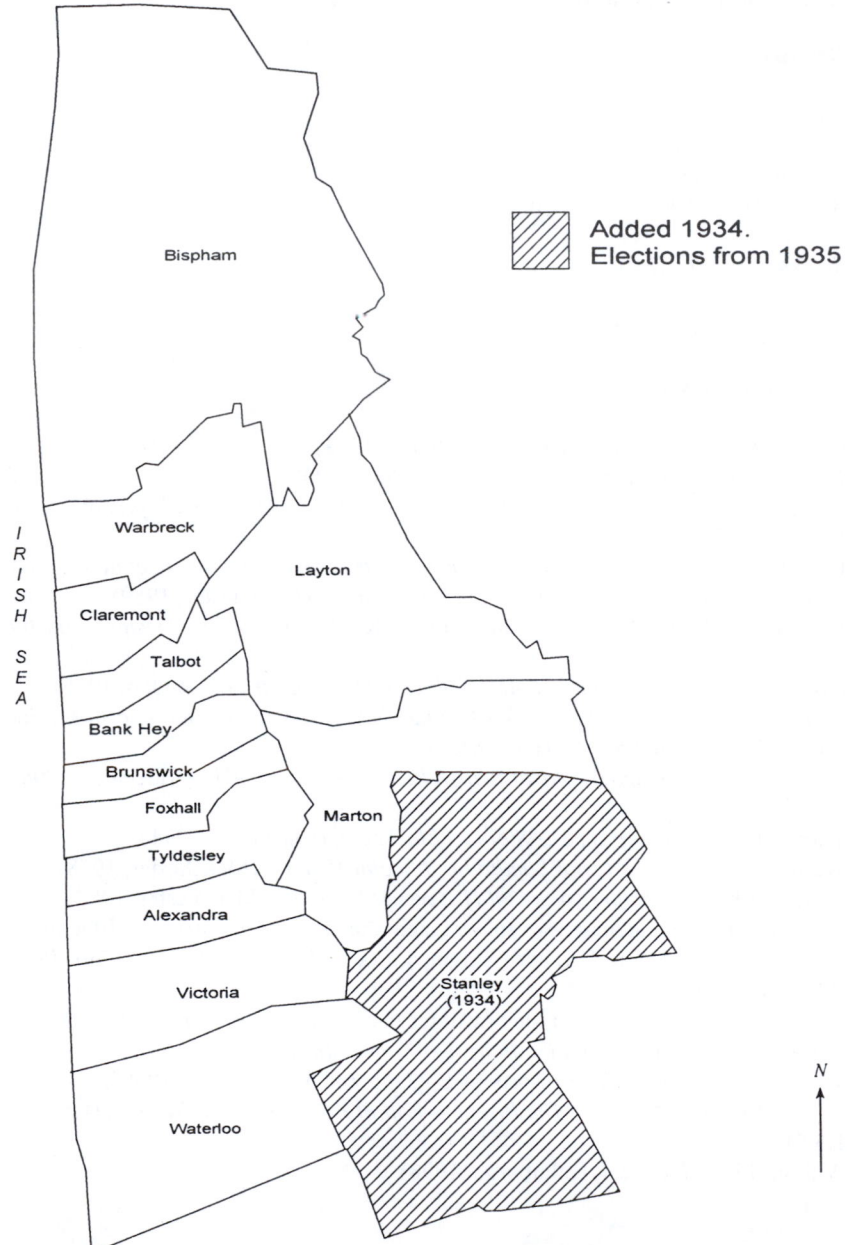

Added 1934.
Elections from 1935

I R I S H   S E A

Bispham

Warbreck

Layton

Claremont

Talbot

Bank Hey

Brunswick

Foxhall

Marton

Tyldesley

Alexandra

Victoria

Stanley
(1934)

Waterloo

N

Persons aged fourteen and over classified by industry 1931

	Male	%	Female	%	Total	%
Metal and engineering	1,601	6.1	90	0.5	1,691	4.0
Building	3,664	14.0	46	0.3	3,710	8.7
Transport	3,033	11.6	100	0.6	3,133	7.3
- Road	*1,976*	*7.6*	*67*	*0.4*	*2,040*	*4.8*
- Tram	*781*	*3.0*	*14*	*0.1*	*795*	*1.9*
Commerce and finance	7,364	28.2	3,725	22.4	11,089	26.0
Public admin. and defence	2,786	10.7	606	3.7	3,392	7.9
- Local government	*2,198*	*8.4*	*450*	*2.7*	*2,648*	*6.2*
Entertainment and sport	1,896	7.3	698	4.2	2,594	6.1
Personal service	3,375	12.9	9,820	59.2	13,195	30.9
Other	2,378	9.1	1,508	9.1	3,886	9.1
Total (a)	26,097		16,593		42,690	
Total population (b)	**43,870**		**57,683**		**101,553**	
(a) as % of (b)	59.5		28.8		42.0	
Total out of work (c)	4,909		2,441		7,350	
(c) as % of (a)	18.8		14.7		17.2	
Managerial and own account	7,513	28.8	5,031	30.3	12,544	29.4
Operative	18,584	71.2	11,562	69.7	30,146	70.6
Total (excluding out of work)	26,097		16,593		42,690	

Population statistics 1931

Ward	Acres	Population	Persons/acre	Persons/room
Alexandra	168	6,739	40.1	0.67
Bank Hey	98	4,600	46.9	0.70
Bispham	1,586	8,137	5.1	0.57
Brunswick	137	6,307	46.0	0.60
Claremont	139	6,471	46.6	0.66
Foxhall	141	8,121	57.6	0.71
Layton	738	11,014	14.9	0.75
Marton	457	9,948	21.8	0.71
Talbot	135	7,212	53.4	0.76
Tyldesley	232	8,818	38.0	0.71
Victoria	348	9,942	28.6	0.72
Warbreck	388	5,265	13.6	0.56
Waterloo	622	8,979	14.4	0.62
Total	**5,189**	**101,553**	**19.6**	**0.67**

Overall position on the council 1919–38

	Position				Gains				Losses			
	C	Lab	L	Other	C	Lab	L	Other	C	Lab	L	Other
1919	31	1	15	5	0	1	1	3	5	0	0	0
1920	30	1	14	7	1	0	0	2	2	0	1	0
1921	31	1	13	7	1	0	0	0	0	0	1	0
1922	32	0	13	7	1	0	0	3	0	1	0	3
1923	29	0	15	8	0	0	2	1	3	0	0	0
1924	28	0	15	9	2	0	2	0	2	0	1	1
1925	34	0	11	7	0	0	0	1	0	0	1	0
1926	34	0	11	7	0	0	0	1	1	0	0	0
1927	36	0	13	3	1	0	1	0	0	0	1	1
1928	34	0	14	4	0	0	0	0	0	0	0	0
1929	34	0	15	3	0	0	1	0	0	0	0	1
1930[a]	32	0	17	1	1	0	1	0	1	0	1	0
1931	34	0	17	1	1	0	0	0	0	0	1	0
1932	34	0	15	3	1	0	0	1	1	0	1	0
1933	32	0	15	5	0	0	1	2	3	0	0	0
1934	33	0	14	9	0	0	0	0	0	0	0	0
1935	33	0	15	8	1	0	1	0	1	0	1	0
1936	33	1	14	8	2	1	0	0	1	0	0	2
1937	32	1	14	9	0	0	1	0	1	0	0	0
1938	32	1	15	8	1	0	2	0	2	0	1	0

Aldermen 1919–38

1919 C–5, L–6, Other–2
1920 C–5, L–6, Other–2
1921 C–5, L–6, Other–2
1922 C–5, L–6, Other–2
1923 C–5, L–6, Other–2
1924 C–5, L–6, Other–2
1925 C–5, L–6, Other–2
1926 C–5, L–6, Other–2
1927 C–5, L–6, Other–2
1928 C–5, L–6, Other–2

1929 C–5, L–6, Other–2
1930 C–7, L–6
1931 C–7, L–6
1932 C–7, L–6
1933 C–7, L–6
1934 C–8, L–6
1935 C–8, L–6
1936 C–8, L–6
1937 C–8, L–5, Other–1
1938 C–8, L–5, Other–1

[a] 1930 - 2 seats vacant.

Municipal elections: winning party 1919–28

Ward	1919	1920	1921	1922	1923	1924	1925	1926	1927	1928
Alexandra	Ind	C	**C**	C	L	L	C	L	**L**	**C**
Bank Hey	L	**C**	C	C	R	C	**C**	C	C	C
Bispham	C	C	**Ind**	C	C	Ind	**C**	C	**Ind**	C
Brunswick	Chka	C	L	Prog	**C**	Prog	L	Prog	Prog	L
Claremont	Chka	Ind	**L**	Prog	L	**L**	Prog	L	L	L
Foxhall	Lab	C	Ind	Ind	**C**	**Ind**	C	C	L	C
Layton	C	C	C	**C**	L	C	C	**L**	C	**C**
Marton	C	**C**	**C**	**C**	**C**	C	**C**	C	C	**C**
Stanley	-	-	-	-	-	-	-	-	-	-
Talbot	C	C	C	C	C	L	C	C	C	**C**
Tyldesley	**L**	L	**Chka**	**L**	L	C	Chka	L	C	**Chka**
Victoria	**C**	**C**	**L**	**C**	**C**	C	C	C	**C**	**C**
Warbreck	C	C	**C**	**C**	**C**	**C**	C	C	**C**	**C**
Waterloo	C	**C**	**C**	**C**	**C**	**C**	**C**	**C**	**C**	C

Municipal elections: party wins per year 1919–28

	1919	1920	1921	1922	1923	1924	1925	1926	1927	1928
C	7	11	7	9	8	7	10	8	8	10
Lab	1	0	0	0	0	0	0	0	0	0
L	2	1	3	1	4	3	1	4	3	2
Other	3	1	3	3	1	3	2	1	2	1
Total	13	13	13	13	13	13	13	13	13	13
Turnout %	**63.0**	**62.5**	**54.8**	**62.4**	**68.5**	**69.2**	**71.0**	**58.9**	**50.3**	**55.1**
Labour %	**13.2**	**14.0**	**13.7**	**7.7**	**5.2**	**-**	**-**	**5.1**	**10.5**	**-**

Municipal elections: winning party 1929–38

Ward	1929	1930	1931	1932	1933	1934	1935	1936	1937	1938
Alexandra	L	L	C	C	L	C	C	L	C	C
Bank Hey	L	L	C	L	L	C	L	L	C	L
Bispham	C	C	C	C	C	C	C	C	C	C
Brunswick	L	L	L	L	L	L	L	L	L	L
Claremont	L	C	L	L	C	L	L	C	L	L
Foxhall	C	L	C	Chka	L	C	Ind	L	C	C
Layton	L	C	C	L	Ind	C	C	C	L	L
Marton	C	C	C	C	L	L	L	L	L	C
Stanley	-	-	-	-	-	-	Ind	C	Ind	Ind
Talbot	C	C	C	C	C	C	C	C	C	C
Tyldesley	L	C	Chka	L	C	Ind	C	Lab	Ind	C
Victoria	C	C	C	C	Ind	C	C	Ind	C	L
Warbreck	C	C	C	C	C	C	C	C	C	C
Waterloo	C	C	C	C	C	C	C	C	C	C

Municipal elections: party wins per year 1929–38

	1929	1930	1931	1932	1933	1934	1935	1936	1937	1938
C	7	9	10	7	6	9	8	7	8	8
Lab	0	0	0	0	0	0	0	1	0	0
L	6	4	2	5	5	3	4	5	4	5
Other	0	0	1	1	2	1	2	1	2	1
Total	13	13	13	13	13	13	14	14	14	14
Turnout %	**47.4**	**53.7**	**61.4**	**52.4**	**54.7**	**50.2**	**51.8**	**51.5**	**48.9**	**43.3**
Lab %	**15.3**	**16.2**	**3.5**	**–**	**5.0**	**3.8**	**–**	**8.8**	**10.9**	**3.9**

Municipal elections: party wins per ward 1919–38

	C	Lab	L	Other	Total	Turnout %	Labour % of all votes
Alexandra	11	0	8	1	20	67.4	2.7
Bank Hey	11	0	8	1	20	62.2	0.8
Bispham	17	0	0	3	20	61.6	1.2
Brunswick	2	0	13	5	20	63.8	0.5
Claremont	3	0	13	4	20	65.9	2.8
Foxhall	10	1	4	5	20	56.5	19.3
Layton	13	0	6	1	20	49.9	5.6
Marton	15	0	5	0	20	45.4	9.7
Stanley	1	0	0	3	4	44.4	-
Talbot	19	0	1	0	20	54.9	17.1
Tyldesley	6	1	7	6	20	58.4	13.4
Victoria	16	0	2	2	20	54.4	2.6
Warbreck	20	0	0	0	20	59.4	1.0
Waterloo	20	0	0	0	20	56.9	1.9
Total	164	2	67	31	264	55.5	6.9

Seats won by Labour as a percentage of all wins 1919–38   **0.8**

Parliamentary election results

Blackpool constituency
*(all wards within the borough [1918 boundaries] were included in the
constituency, along with the urban district of Lytham and St Anne's-on-the-Sea,
and part of the rural district of Fylde)*

General election	Winner	Conservative %	Labour %	Liberal %
14 Dec. 1918	C	55.9	9.2	-
15 Nov. 1922	C	50.2	-	49.8
6 Dec. 1923	L	46.3	-	53.7
29 Oct. 1924	C	58.0	-	42.0
30 May 1929	C	46.8	17.1	36.1
27 Oct. 1931	C	73.1	-	26.9
14 Nov. 1935	C	65.2	18.3	16.5

Alexandra ward

Candidate	Party	Votes	%	Electors	Turnout	Gains
1919						
W. Grundy	Ind	930	60.7	2,162	70.9	Ind from C
T.W. Boden*	C	602	39.3			
Total votes		1,532				
1920						
T.W. Boden	C	716	46.9	2,248	67.9	C from L
I.S. Beaumont	L	687	45.0			
J. Wallace	Lab	124				
Total votes		1,527				
1921						
W.R. Duckworth*	C	Unopp.	-	2,360	-	-
1922						
J. Quayle*	C	871	53.1	2,362	69.4	-
H. Renwick	L	739	45.1			
S. Smith	Ind	30				
Total votes		1,640				
1923						
H. Renwick	L	1,005	57.0	2,446	72.0	L from C
T.W. Boden*	C	757	43.0			
Total votes		1,762				
1924						
D.J. Bailey	L	1,007	51.9	2,441	79.5	L from C
W.R. Duckworth*	C	933	48.1			
Total votes		1,940				
1925						
J.R. Quayle*	C	1,090	54.7	2,694	73.9	-
I.E. Beaumont	L	782	39.3			
A. Wallis	Prog	120				
Total votes		1,992				
1926						
H. Renwick*	L	953	52.1	2,694	67.9	-
W. Ward	C	876	47.9			
Total votes		1,829				
1927						
D.J. Bailey*	L	Unopp.	-		-	-

Alexandra ward *(continued)*

Candidate	Party	Votes	%	Electors	Turnout	Gains
1928						
J.R. Quayle*	C	Unopp.	-	2,791	-	-
1929						
H. Renwick*	L	Unopp.	-		-	-
1930						
D.J. Bailey*	L	1,424	82.5	3,322	52.0	-
W. Giles	Lab	302	17.5			
Total votes		1,726				
1931						
J.R. Quayle*	C	Unopp.	-		-	-
1932						
Mrs M. Quayle	C	1,087	51.5	3,459	61.0	C from L
H. Renwick*	L	1,023	48.5			
Total votes		2,110				
1933						
D.J. Bailey*	L	Unopp.	-		-	-
1934						
J.R. Quayle*	C	Unopp.	-		-	-
1935						
Mrs M. Quayle*	C	Unopp.	-	3,476	-	-
1936						
D.J. Bailey*	L	Unopp.	-		-	-
1937						
F.R. Boydell	C	Unopp.	-		-	-
1938						
Mrs M. Quayle*	C	Unopp.	-		-	-

Overall Labour vote   **2.7%**   **Overall turnout**   **67.4%**

Bank Hey ward

Candidate	Party	Votes	%	Electors	Turnout	Gains
1919						
T. Dixon	L	510	36.0	2,148	65.9	L from C
H. Bateson	Ind C	465	32.9			
J. Monk	C	440	31.1			
Total votes		1,415				

(Bateson stood as an Ex-services and Conservative candidate)

1920						
T. Masheter*	C	Unopp.	-	2,473	-	-
1921						
W. Taylor*	C	753	51.2	2,528	58.1	-
H. Wilde	L	717	48.8			
Total votes		1,470				
1922						
H. Bateson	C	979	62.4	2,553	61.5	C from L
H. Eastwood	Ind	591	37.6			
Total votes		1,570				
1923						
J.W. Roberts	R	959	56.4	2,527	67.3	R from C
J.R. Huddlestone	C	741	43.6			
Total votes		1,700				
1924						
C.S. Westwell	C	898	51.2	2,489	70.5	-
H. Wilde	R	856	48.8			
Total votes		1,754				
1925						
H. Bateson*	C	Unopp.			-	-
1926						
J.W. Roberts*	C	756	52.2	2,549	56.8	-
E. Holt	L	691	47.8			
Total votes		1,447				
1927						
C.S. Westwell	C	963	66.5	2,500	57.9	-
S.H. Thomas	L	485	33.5			
Total votes		1,448				

Bank Hey ward *(continued)*

Candidate	Party	Votes	%	Electors	Turnout	Gains
1928						
F.I. Nickson	C	701	51.5	2,671	51.0	-
C.E. Lindley	Ind	660	48.5			
Total votes		1,361				
1929						
E. Holt*	L	Unopp.	-		-	-
1930						
J.R. Furness	L	639	45.3	2,228	63.3	L from C
C.S. Westwell*	C	620	43.9			
E. Stevenson	Lab	152				
Total votes		1,411				
1931						
F.I. Nickson*	C	Unopp.	-		-	-
1932						
E. Holt*	L	942	63.3	2,326	64.0	-
E.G. Packer	C	547	36.7			
Total votes		1,489				
1933						
J.R. Furness*	L	823	51.5	2,327	68.6	-
C.S. Westwell	C	774	48.5			
Total votes		1,597				
1934						
F.I. Nickson*	C	Unopp.	-		-	-
1935						
E. Holt*	L	Unopp.	-	2,216	-	-
1936						
J.R. Furness*	L	770	57.4	2,116	63.4	-
E.W. Garsden	C	572	42.6			
Total votes		1,342				
1937						
F.I. Nickson*	C	Unopp.	-		-	-
1938						
E. Holt*	L	Unopp.	-		-	-

Overall Labour vote		**0.8%**		**Overall turnout**		**62.2%**

Bispham ward

Candidate	Party	Votes	%	Electors	Turnout	Gains
1919						
W. Harris	C	486	49.5	1,371	71.6	-
S. Barnes	Ind	331	33.7			
S.H. Wilson	Ind	164	16.7			
Total votes		981				
1920						
S. Coop	C	634	65.0	1,413	69.0	
S. Barnes	Ind	341	35.0			-
Total votes		975				
1921						
T.G. Lumb*	Ind	Unopp.	-	1,477	-	-
1922						
H.A. Thickett	C	635	56.8	1,601	69.8	-
A.E. Elliott	Ind	483	43.2			
Total votes		1,118				
1923						
R.H. Lord	C	688	51.7	1,702	78.3	-
E.A. Elliott	R	644	48.3			
Total votes		1,332				
1924						
T.G. Lumb*	Ind	1,019	69.4	1,886	77.9	-
A.E. Elliott	Ind	450	30.6			
Total votes		1,469				
1925						
H.A. Thickett*	C	Unopp.	-		-	-
1926						
S.H. Coop	C	1,146	67.5	2,486	68.3	-
J. Whalley	L	551	32.5			
Total votes		1,697				
1927						
T.G. Lumb*	Ind	Unopp.	-	2,760	-	-

Bispham ward *(continued)*

Candidate	Party	Votes	%	Electors	Turnout	Gains
1928						
H.A. Thickett*	C	1,214	65.6	3,079	60.1	-
J. Whalley	L	638	34.4			
Total votes		1,852				
1929						
A.E. Elliott	C	1,159	55.5	3,599	58.0	-
J.R. Handy	R	928	44.5			
Total votes		2,087				
1930						
J.R.F. Hill*	C	1,399	89.9	4,074	38.2	-
W. Entwhistle	Lab	158	10.1			
Total votes		1,557				
1931						
H.A. Thickett*	C	Unopp.	-		-	-
1932						
A.E. Elliott*	C	Unopp.	-		-	-
1933						
J.R.F. Hill*	C	Unopp.	-		-	-
1934						
H.A. Thickett*	C	Unopp.	-		-	-
1935						
A.E. Elliott*	C	Unopp.	-	6,940	-	-
1936						
J.R.F. Hill*	C	Unopp.	-		-	-
1937						
H.A. Thickett*	C	Unopp.	-		-	-
1938						
C. Dunn*	C	Unopp.	-		-	-

Overall Labour vote		**1.2%**		**Overall turnout**		**61.6%**

Brunswick ward

Candidate	Party	Votes	%	Electors	Turnout	Gains
1919						
G.R. Johnson	Chka	747	53.2	2,253	62.4	Chka from C
W.C. Standerwick*	C	658	46.8			
Total votes		1,405				
1920						
J. Monk	C	686	40.3	2,397	71.1	-
W.H. Hudson	Chka	517	30.3			
W.F. Ashton	Ind	501				
Total votes		1,704				
1921						
W.F. Ashton	L	910	58.7	2,516	61.6	-
G. Bonny	C	641	41.3			
Total votes		1,551				
1922						
G. Burton	Prog	978	61.0	2,507	63.9	Prog from
W. Stairzakar	Chka	624	39.0			CHKA
Total votes		1,602				
1923						
J. Monk*	C	Unopp.	-	2,529	-	-
1924						
W.S. Ashton*	Prog	1,149	65.6	2,678	65.4	-
J.W. Bellarby	C	603	34.4			
Total votes		1,752				
1925						
P. Rounds	L	960	50.6	2,766	68.6	L from Prog.
J. Gaunt	C	937	49.4			
Total votes		1,897				
1926						
F. Taylor	Prog	978	50.3	2,783	69.9	Prog from C
J.P. Bamber	C	968	49.7			
Total votes		1,946				
1927						
W.S. Ashton*	Prog	1,088	57.6	2,848	66.4	-
E.W. Hough	C	802	42.4			
Total votes		1,890				

Brunswick ward *(continued)*

Candidate	Party	Votes	%	Electors	Turnout	Gains
1928						
P. Round*	L	1,131	57.4	2,867	68.7	-
J.B. Singleton	C	839	42.6			
Total votes		1,970				
1929						
G.F. Burton	L	1,138	66.1	3,125	55.1	L from Prog
W.H. Orry	C	584	33.9			
Total votes		1,722				
1930						
W.S. Ashton*	L	1,257	68.7	2,931	62.4	-
W.T. Russell	C	459	25.1			
J.H. Carter	Lab	114	6.2			
Total votes		1,830				
1931						
P. Round*	L	Unopp.	-		-	-
1932						
G.F. Burton*	L	948	51.5	2,924	63.0	-
J. Parr	C	894	48.5			
Total votes		1,842				
1933						
W.S. Ashton*	L	1,143	66.1	2,960	58.4	-
Miss E.A. Hudson	C	586	33.9			
Total votes		1,729				
1934						
P. Round*	L	Unopp.	-		-	-
1935						
G.F. Burton*	L	Unopp.	-	2,808	-	-
1936						
H. Smith	L	Unopp.	-		-	-
1937						
P. Round*	L	Unopp.	-		-	-

Brunswick ward *(continued)*

Candidate	Party	Votes	%	Electors	Turnout	Gains
1938						
G.F. Burton*	L	801	50.1	2,750	58.1	-
S.Jenkinson	C	798	49.9			
Total votes		1,599				

Overall Labour vote   **0.5%**   **Overall turnout**   **63.8%**

Claremont ward

Candidate	Party	Votes	%	Electors	Turnout	Gains
1919						
J.W. Bellarby	Chka	809	55.7	2,458	59.1	Chka from C
T.H. Sergenson*	C	644	44.3			
Total votes		1,453				
1920						
F. Rice	Ind	796	45.5	2,569	68.2	Ind from C
Ms L. Dewhurst	C	487	27.8			
A. Turner	Chka	468	26.7			
Total votes		1,751				
1921						
T.P. Fletcher*	L	Unopp.	-	2,618	-	-
1922						
J. Leavesley	Prog	855	53.2	2,593	61.9	Prog from
J.W. Bellarby*	Ind	626	39.0			Chka
W. Hulme	C	125	7.8			
Total votes		1,606				
1923						
F.H. Rice*	L	1,114	59.9	2,643	70.3	-
E. Law	C	745	40.1			
Total votes		1,859				
1924						
T.P. Fletcher*	L	Unopp.	-	2,759	-	-
1925						
J. Leavesley*	Prog	1,165	54.5	2,850	74.9	-
R. Saxon	C	971	45.5			
Total votes		2,136				
1926						
F.H. Rice*	L	1,089	54.7	2,869	69.4	-
F.W. Halton	C	901	45.3			
Total votes		1,990				
1927						
H. Wilde*	L	1,086	80.7	2,917	46.1	-
G.E. Human	Lab	260	19.3			
Total votes		1,346				

Claremont ward *(continued)*

Candidate	Party	Votes	%	Electors	Turnout	Gains
1928						
J.M. Masterson	L	1,130	53.4	2,951	71.7	-
J. Smith	C	987	46.6			
Total votes		2,117				
1929						
F.H. Rice*	L	Unopp.	-		-	-
1930						
W. Salisbury	C	1,297	55.3	3,346	70.1	C from L
H. Wilde*	L	851	36.3			
S.W. Wakefield	Lab	198	8.4			
Total votes		2,346				
1931						
J. Anderson jun.	L	Unopp.	-		-	-
1932						
J. Anderson sen.*	L	Unopp.	-		-	-
1933						
A. Salisbury*	C	Unopp.	-		-	-
1934						
J. Anderson jun.*	L	Unopp.	-		-	-
1935						
J. Anderson jun.*	L	Unopp.	-	2,901	-	-
1936						
A. Salisbury*	C	Unopp.	-		-	-
1937						
J. Anderson jun.*	L	Unopp.	-		-	-
1938						
J. Anderson jun.*	L	Unopp.	-		-	-

| **Overall Labour vote** | | **2.8%** | | **Overall turnout** | | **65.9%** |

Foxhall ward

Candidate	Party	Votes	%	Electors	Turnout	Gains
1919						
J.W. Mitchell	Lab	1,040	52.7	3,114	63.4	Lab from C
F. Seed*	C	935	47.3			
Total votes		1,975				
1920						
P.J. Tomlinson	C	1,277	66.3	3,128	61.6	-
B.H. Rushworth	Lab	649	33.7			
Total votes		1,926				
1921						
F. Boothroyd*	Ind	1,104	67.7	3,329	49.0	-
B.H. Rushworth	Lab	526	32.3			
Total votes		1,630				
1922						
E. Stevenson	Ind	1,145	57.3	3,394	58.9	Ind from Lab
J.W. Mitchell*	Lab	853	42.7			
Total votes		1,998				
1923						
P.J. Tomlinson*	C	Unopp.	-	3,445		-
1924						
F. Boothroyd*	Ind	Unopp.	-	3,478		-
1925						
E. Stevenson*	C	1,360	53.6	3,614	70.1	-
D. Dickinson	Prog	1,175	46.4			
Total votes		2,535				
1926						
P.J. Tomlinson*	C	1,218	52.1	3,626	64.4	-
J.D. Ryan	Lab	690	29.5			
Mrs M.F. Rainford	Ind	428	18.3			
Total votes		2,336				
1927						
J.A. Ward	L	1,087	48.3	3,689	61.0	L from Ind
T. Pye	C	740	32.9			
J.D. Ryan	Lab	424	18.8			
Total votes		2,251				

Foxhall ward *(continued)*

Candidate	Party	Votes	%	Electors	Turnout	Gains
1928						
E. Stevenson*	C	1,193	55.2	3,696	58.5	-
A. Oldfield	Chka	969	44.8			
Total votes		2,162				
1929						
P.J. Tomlinson*	C	Unopp.	-		-	-
1930						
J.A. Ward*	L	1,485	77.8	3,882	49.1	-
L. Tattersall	Lab	423	22.2			
Total votes		1,908				
1931						
E. Stevenson*	C	1,275	51.3	3,882	64.0	-
A. Talbot	L	1,210	48.7			
Total votes		2,485				
1932						
A. Talbot	Chka	Unopp.	-		-	Chka from C
1933						
J.A. Ward*	L	Unopp.	-		-	-
1934						
E. Stevenson*	C	1,312	71.4	3,921	46.9	-
G.E. Human	Lab	526	28.6			
Total votes		1,838				
1935						
A. Talbot*	Ind	1,159	55.5	3,966	52.6	-
C.P. Dewhirst	C	928	44.5			
Total votes		2,087				
1936						
J.A. Ward*	L	Unopp.	-		-	-
1937						
E. Stevenson*	C	Unopp.	-		-	-

Foxhall ward *(continued)*

Candidate	Party	Votes	%	Electors	Turnout	Gains
1938						
A. Talbot*	C	997	67.4	3,879	38.1	-
S. Hudson	Com	482	32.6			
Total votes		1,479				

Overall Labour vote   **19.3%**   **Overall turnout**   **56.5%**

Layton ward

Candidate	Party	Votes	%	Electors	Turnout	Gains
1919						
R. Swarbrick*	C	750	44.3	2,636	64.2	-
J. Bond	L	567	33.5			
E. Stevenson	Lab	375				
Total votes		1,692				
1920						
C.W. Callis	C	973	75.4	2,746	47.0	-
E. Stevenson	Lab	317	24.6			
Total votes		1,290				
1921						
J. Potter*	C	1,119	81.5	2,850	48.2	-
J.S. Bradshaw	A–W	254	18.5			
Total votes		1,373				
1922						
R. Swarbrick*	C	Unopp.	-	3,140	-	-
1923						
W. Smith	L	1,492	61.8	3,344	72.2	L from C
T.M. Watson	C	922	38.2			
Total votes		2,414				
1924						
J. Potter*	C	1,457	61.8	3,411	69.1	-
A.J. Hollings	L	900	38.2			
Total votes		2,357				
1925						
R. Swarbrick*	C	1,674	61.8	3,644	74.3	-
A.J. Hollings	L	1,033	38.2			
Total votes		2,707				
1926						
W. Smith*	L	Unopp.	-	-	-	-
1927						
J. Whittaker*	C	1,230	62.5	4,109	47.9	
T.H. McGlynn	L	739	37.5			
Total votes		1,969				

Layton ward *(continued)*

Candidate	Party	Votes	%	Electors	Turnout	Gains
1928						
R. Swarbrick*	C	Unopp.	-	4,524	-	-
1929						
W. Smith*	L	1,127	59.8	5,070	37.2	-
M. Crossley	Lab	699	37.1			
S. Smith	Ind	60	3.2			
Total votes		1,886				
1930						
J. Whittaker*	C	1,455	63.5	5,276	43.4	-
M. Crossley	Lab	837	36.5			
Total votes		2,292				
1931						
R. Swarbrick*	C	Unopp.	-		-	-
1932						
J.C. Bond	L	1,373	54.7	5,578	45.0	-
H. Rawcliffe	C	1,137	45.3			
Total votes		2,510				
1933						
A.N. Hartley	Ind	1,212	51.6	5,487	42.8	Ind from C
J. Whittaker*	C	1,135	48.4			
Total votes		2,347				
1934						
J.E. Horsman*	C	1,733	63.3	6,359	43.0	-
J. Leavesley	L	1,003	36.7			
Total votes		2,736				
1935						
J. Whittaker	C	1,517	50.0	6,747	44.9	C from L
J.C. Bond*	L	1,515	50.0			
Total votes		3,032				
1936						
J.W. Whittaker	C	1,563	50.9	7,010	43.8	C from Ind
A.N. Hartley*	Ind	1,508	49.1			
Total votes		3,071				

Layton ward *(continued)*

Candidate	Party	Votes	%	Electors	Turnout	Gains
1937						
J.C. Bond	L	1,978	55.0	*7,401*	48.6	L from C
T. Brierley	C	1,617	45.0			
Total votes		3,595				
1938						
H. Grimbledeston	L	3,189	72.4	7,792	56.5	L from C
C. Bagot	C	1,216	27.6			
Total votes		4,405				
Overall Labour vote		**5.6%**		**Overall turnout**		**49.9%**

Marton ward

Candidate	Party	Votes	%	Electors	Turnout	Gains
1919						
C.E. Tatham	C	684	56.4	2,244	54.0	-
J. Spencer	Ind	528	43.6			
Total votes		1,212				
1920						
R. Cardwell*	C	Unopp.	-	2,335	-	-
1921						
R. Eaves	C	Unopp.	-	2,443	-	-
1922						
C.E. Tatham*	C	Unopp.	-	2,516	-	-
1923						
R. Cardwell*	C	Unopp.	-	2,679	-	-
1924						
C. Bagot*	C	1,023	57.9	2,807	62.9	-
N. Naylor	R	743	42.1			
Total votes		1,766				
1925						
C.E. Tatham*	C	Unopp.	-		-	-
1926						
J. Cardwell*	C	810	77.4	3,761	27.8	-
S. Smith	Ind	237	22.6			
Total votes		1,047				
1927						
C. Bagot*	C	634	85.0	4,152	18.0	-
S. Smith	Ind	112	15.0			
Total votes		746				
1928						
C.E. Tatham*	C	563	81.8	4,443	15.5	-
S. Smith	Ind	125	18.2			
Total votes		688				

Marton ward (*continued*)

Candidate	Party	Votes	%	Electors	Turnout	Gains
1929						
J. Cardwell*	C	1,206	58.3	4,988	41.4	-
W.P.B. Hammersley	Lab	861	41.7			
Total votes		2,067				
1930						
C. Bagot*	C	1,642	73.2	5,088	44.1	-
W.P.B. Hammersley	Lab	601	26.8			
Total votes		2,243				
1931						
C.E. Tatham*	C	Unopp.	-		-	-
1932						
T. Pye*	C	1,257	49.0	5,462	47.0	-
H.C. Peckett	L	1,253	48.8			
S. Smith	Ind	57	2.2			
Total votes		2,567				
1933						
H.C. Peckett	L	2,225	61.7	5,274	68.4	L from C
C. Bagot*	C	1,380	38.3			
Total votes		3,605				
1934						
C. Wilkinson*	L	2,228	61.9	6,000	60.0	-
F. Ayre	C	1,372	38.1			
Total votes		3,600				
1935						
W. Cowels	L	Unopp.	-	6,201	-	L from C
1936						
H.C. Peckett*	L	1,798	54.5	6,420	51.4	-
E. Pendlebury	C	1,503	45.5			
Total votes		3,301				
1937						
C. Wilkinson*	L	2,029	74.7	*6,503*	41.8	-
W. Dalby	Lab	687	25.3			
Total votes		2,716				

Marton ward *(continued)*

Candidate	Party	Votes	%	Electors	Turnout	Gains
1938						
J.E. Dugdale	C	1,661	49.6	6,586	50.8	C from L
W. Cowels*	L	1,032	30.8			
Mrs Fairclough	Lab	655	19.6			
Total votes		3,348				

Overall Labour vote	**9.7%**		**Overall turnout**	**45.4%**

Stanley ward
(created by extension of the borough in 1934)

Candidate	Party	Votes	%	Electors	Turnout	Gains
1935						
W.H. Winstanley*	Ind	2,138	62.0	5,558	62.0	-
C. Bagot	C	1,310	38.0			
Total votes		3,448				
1936						
J. Moore	C	1,723	52.5	6,342	51.7	C from Ind
A. Webster*	Ind	1,486	45.3			
S. Smith	Ind	70				
Total votes		3,279				
1937						
W. Dugdale*	Ind	2,535	69.6	6,862	53.1	-
J. Chambers	C	1,109	30.4			
Total votes		3,644				
1938						
W.H. Winstanley*	Ind	1,147	92.7	7,383	16.8	-
S. Smith	Ind	90	7.3			
Total votes		1,237				

Overall Labour vote — **Overall turnout** **44.4%**

Talbot ward

Candidate	Party	Votes	%	Electors	Turnout	Gains
1919						
G. Whittaker	C	647	42.0	2,463	62.5	-
M. Shea	Lab	542	35.2			
M. Burns	Nfds	350	22.7			
Total votes		1,539				
1920						
R. Fenton	C	892	55.4	2,701	59.6	-
M. Shea	Lab	718	44.6			
Total votes		1,610				
1921						
J. Gaunt	C	634	38.4	2,769	59.6	C from L
M. Shea	Lab	523	31.7			
J. Kay*	L	493	29.9			
Total votes		1,650				
1922						
C. Whittaker*	C	1,014	65.3	2,760	56.3	-
J. Kay	L	540	34.7			
Total votes		1,554				
1923						
R. Fenton*	C	945	59.0	2,803	57.2	-
M. Shea	Lab	658	41.0			
Total votes		1,603				
1924						
J. Masterson	L	917	53.5	2,824	60.7	L from C
J. Gaunt*	C	796	46.5			
Total votes		1,713				
1925						
G. Whittaker*	C	1,334	72.6	2,893	63.5	-
T.H. McGlynn	L	504	27.4			
Total votes		1,838				
1926						
J. Parkinson	C	813	48.6	2,977	56.2	-
S.A. Thomas	L	558	33.4			
G. Human	Lab	302	18.1			
Total votes		1,673				

Talbot ward *(continued)*

Candidate	Party	Votes	%	Electors	Turnout	Gains
1927						
W. Coop	C	726	42.4	3,093	55.4	C from L
J.M. Masterson*	L	686	40.0			
M. Shea	Lab	301	17.6			
Total votes		1,713				
1928						
G. Whittaker*	C	Unopp.	-	3,084	-	-
1929						
J. Parkinson*	C	862	60.9	3,346	42.3	-
Mrs L.A. Chew	Lab	553	39.1			
Total votes		1,415				
1930						
J.B. Singleton	C	792	47.3	3,080	54.3	-
F. Waterhouse	L	636	38.0			
Mrs L.A. Chew	Lab	245	14.6			
Total votes		1,673				
1931						
G. Whittaker*	C	Unopp.	-		-	-
1932						
J. Parkinson*	C	781	54.2	3,135	46.0	-
J. Haworth	Chka	661	45.8			
Total votes		1,442				
1933						
J.B. Singleton*	C	860	58.5	3,073	47.8	-
J. Haworth	Chka	609	41.5			
Total votes		1,469				
1934						
A. Whiteside*	C	886	56.1	2,996	52.7	-
E.W. Garsden	Ind C	694	43.9			
Total votes		1,580				
1935						
J. Parkinson*	C	Unopp.	-	3,022	-	-
1936						
J.B. Singleton*	C	Unopp.	-		-	-

Talbot ward *(continued)*

Candidate	Party	Votes	%	Electors	Turnout	Gains
1937						
A. Whiteside*	C	Unopp.	-		-	-
1938						
J. Parkinson*	C	Unopp.	-		-	-
Overall Labour vote		**17.1%**			**Overall turnout**	**54.9%**

Tyldesley ward

Candidate	Party	Votes	%	Electors	Turnout	Gains
1919						
E.H. Howe	L	Unopp.	-		-	-
1920						
L. Newsome	L	781	62.9	2,165	57.3	-
Mrs M. Harrison	Chka	460	37.1			
Total votes		1,241				
1921						
J. Hitchen*	Chka	Unopp.	-	2,263	-	-
1922						
E.H. Howe*	L	Unopp.	-	2,498	-	-
1923						
L. Newsome*	L	988	52.4	2,862	65.8	-
J.E. Dugdale	C	896	47.6			
Total votes		1,884				
1924						
J.E. Dugdale	C	1,145	52.6	3,064	71.1	C from Chka
H.E. Evans	Chka	1,033	47.4			
Total votes		2,178				
1925						
H.E. Evans	Chka	1,430	55.9	3,421	74.7	Chka from L
J. Parkinson	C	1,127	44.1			
Total votes		2,557				
1926						
L. Newsome*	L	1,259	60.4	3,546	58.8	-
G. Morrison	C	825	39.6			
Total votes		2,084				
1927						
J.E. Dugdale*	C	1,189	51.4	3,886	59.5	-
F. Robinson	L	668	28.9			
E. Spencer	Lab	455	19.7			
Total votes		2,312				
1928						
H.E. Evans*	Chka	Unopp.	-	4,009	-	-

Tyldesley ward *(continued)*

Candidate	Party	Votes	%	Electors	Turnout	Gains
1929						
L. Newsome*	L	1,164	54.1	4,294	50.1	-
A. Talbot	Chka	989	45.9			
Total votes		2,153				
1930						
J.E. Dugdale*	C	1,121	42.4	4,357	60.7	-
A. Talbot	Chka	986	37.3			
J.D. Ryan	Lab	539				
Total votes		2,646				
1931						
H.E. Evans*	Chka	1,677	59.5	4,440	63.4	-
E. Smith	C	1,140	40.5			
Total votes		2,817				
1932						
L. Newsome*	L	Unopp.	-		-	-
1933						
J.E. Dugdale*	C	1,123	59.1	4,440	42.8	-
G.E. Human	Lab	776	40.9			
Total votes		1,899				
1934						
H.E. Evans*	Ind	Unopp.	-		-	-
1935						
E. Smith*	C	1,383	54.0	4,735	54.0	
S. Morris	Ind	1,176	46.0			
Total votes		2,559				
1936						
E. Machin	Lab	1,502	56.3	4,626	57.7	Lab from C
J.E. Dugdale*	C	1,166	43.7			
Total votes		2,668				
1937						
S. Morris*	Ind	1,746	72.4	*4,517*	53.4	-
C. Rushfirth	Lab	666	27.6			
Total votes		2,412				

Tyldesley ward *(continued)*

Candidate	Party	Votes	%	Electors	Turnout	Gains
1938						
E.Smith*	C	Unopp.	-		-	-

Overall Labour vote   **13.4%**   **Overall turnout**   **58.4%**

Victoria ward

Candidate	Party	Votes	%	Electors	Turnout	Gains
1919						
G.W. Gath	C	Unopp.	-		-	-
1920						
W.D. Halstead*	C	Unopp.	-	1,623	-	-
1921						
D. Dickinson*	L	Unopp.	-	1,751	-	-
1922						
G.W. Gath*	C	Unopp.	-	1,888	-	-
1923						
W.D. Halstead*	C	Unopp.	-	2,232	-	-
1924						
F.W. Corns	C	1,086	60.0	2,591	69.8	C from L
D. Dickinson*	L	723	40.0			
Total votes		1,809				
1925						
G.W. Gath*	C	1,268	62.4	3,099	65.6	-
R. Foster	R	637	31.3			
P. Pye	Ind	127	6.3			
Total votes		2,032				
1926						
W.D. Halstead*	C	1,146	58.4	3,470	56.5	-
S. Kershaw	L	815	41.6			
Total votes		1,961				
1927						
F.W. Corns*	C	Unopp.	-		-	-
1928						
G.W. Gath*	C	Unopp.	-	4,182	-	-
1929						
E.H. Altman	C	1,361	54.4	4,762	52.6	-
F. Robinson	L	1,142	45.6			
Total votes		2,503				

Victoria ward *(continued)*

Candidate	Party	Votes	%	Electors	Turnout	Gains
1930						
F.W. Corns*	C	1,206	42.9	4,590	61.2	-
F. Robinson	L	1,150	40.9			
G.S. Worthington	Lab	432	15.4			
S. Smith	Ind	23	0.8			
Total votes		2,811				
1931						
R.W. Marshall	C	1,275	45.3	4,895	57.5	C from L
F. Robinson*	L	1,255	44.6			
L. Tattersall	Lab	283	10.1			
Total votes		2,813				
1932						
E.H. Altman*	C	1,576	57.1	5,204	53.0	-
J. Hill	L	1,182	42.9			
Total votes		2,758				
1933						
J. Hill	Ind	1,532	52.4	4,895	59.7	Ind from C
J. Fenton	C	1,390	47.6			
Total votes		2,922				
1934						
R.W. Marshall*	C	1,636	59.8	5,395	50.8	-
F. Robinson	L	1,102	40.2			
Total votes		2,738				
1935						
E.H. Altman*	C	1,568	59.8	5,526	47.5	-
F. Robinson	Ind L	1,055	40.2			
Total votes		2,623				
1936						
J. Hill*	Ind	Unopp.	-		-	-
1937						
R.W. Marshall*	C	Unopp.	-		-	-
1938						
J. Parker	L	1,488	59.5	6,031	41.5	L from C
E.H. Altman*	C	1,012	40.5			
Total votes		2,500				

Overall Labour vote		**2.6%**		**Overall turnout**		**54.4%**

Warbreck ward

Candidate	Party	Votes	%	Electors	Turnout	Gains
1919						
M.G. Wilde	C	528	80.1	1,301	50.7	-
Rev. F. Hibbert	L	131	19.9			
Total votes		659				
1920						
H. Brook	C	496	56.3	1,285	68.6	-
H. Wilde	L	385	43.7			
Total votes		881				
1921						
T. Fielding*	C	Unopp.	-	1,305	-	-
1922						
W. Newman*	C	Unopp.	-	1,437	-	-
1923						
H. Brooks*	C	Unopp.	-	1,553	-	-
1924						
T. Fielding*	C	Unopp.	-	1,680	-	-
1925						
W. Newman*	C	830	58.5	1,923	73.8	-
J.W. Docking	L	589	41.5			
Total votes		1,419				
1926						
R. Saxon*	C	870	64.6	2,095	64.3	-
O.W. Scott	L	477	35.4			
Total votes		1,347				
1927						
T. Fielding*	C	Unopp.	-		-	-
1928						
W. Newman*	C	Unopp.	-	2,391	-	-
1929						
R. Saxon*	C	Unopp.	-		-	-

Warbreck ward *(continued)*

Candidate	Party	Votes	%	Electors	Turnout	Gains
1930						
F.W. Halton	C	1,024	55.2	2,565	72.3	-
J. Anderson jun.	L	731	39.4			
A. Weaver	Lab	99				
Total votes		1,854				
1931						
P. Fairhurst*	C	Unopp.	-		-	-
1932						
R. Saxon*	C	Unopp.	-		-	-
1933						
F.W. Halton*	C	Unopp.	-		-	-
1934						
P. Fairhurst*	C	1,256	86.7	3,085	46.9	-
J.H. Sheard	Ind	192	13.3			
Total votes		1,448				
1935						
J. Smith	C	Unopp.	-	3,385	-	-
1936						
F.W. Halton*	C	Unopp.	-		-	-
1937						
P. Fairhurst*	C	Unopp.	-		-	-
1938						
J. Smith*	C	1,333	63.6	4,085	51.3	-
J.E. Perry	L	763	36.4			
Total votes		2,096				

| **Overall Labour vote** | | **1.0%** | | | **Overall turnout** | **59.4%** |

Waterloo ward

Candidate	Party	Votes	%	Electors	Turnout	Gains
1919						
W. Hardman*	C	615	62.6	1,430	68.7	-
E. Lawson	Nfds	367	37.4			
Total votes		982				
1920						
W.G. Bean*	C	Unopp.	-	1,441	-	-
1921						
T. Fenton*	C	Unopp.	-	1,546	-	-
1922						
F.W. Millington*	C	Unopp.	-	1,660	-	-
1923						
W.G. Bean*	C	Unopp.	-	1,772	-	-
1924						
T. Fenton*	C	Unopp.	-	2,067	-	-
1925						
F.W. Millington*	C	Unopp.	-		-	-
1926						
W.R. Duckworth*	C	Unopp.	-		-	-
1927						
T. Fenton*	C	Unopp.	-	3,544	-	-
1928						
F.W. Millington*	C	1,499	53.8	3,777	73.8	-
A. Brooks	Ind	1,287	46.2			
Total votes		2,786				
1929						
W.R. Duckworth*	C	Unopp.	-		-	-
1930						
T. Fenton*	C	1,985	91.8	4,569	47.3	-
D. Holland	Lab	177	8.2			
Total votes		2,162				

Waterloo ward *(continued)*

Candidate	Party	Votes	%	Electors	Turnout	Gains
1931						
F.W. Millington*	C	Unopp.	-		-	-
1932						
W.R. Duckworth*	C	Unopp.	-		-	-
1933						
J.W. Roberts*	C	Unopp.	-		-	-
1934						
F.W. Millington*	C	Unopp.	-		-	-
1935						
W.R. Duckworth*	C	Unopp.	-	6451	-	-
1936						
J.W. Roberts*	C	2,103	61.1	6,698	51.4	-
T. Whiteside	Ind	1,340	38.9			
Total votes		3,443				
1937						
W. Ogden	C	Unopp.	-		-	-
1938						
H. Henson*	C	Unopp.	-		-	-
Overall Labour vote		**1.9%**		**Overall turnout**		**56.9%**

EIGHT
Bolton

BOLTON

Bolton was ranked twentieth in size of the eighty-three inter-war county boroughs in 1931, with a population of almost 180,000. Given the epithet of the 'Geneva of the North' in the seventeenth century, Nonconformity continued to be prominent in the town into the next century.[1] By the twentieth century this influence seems to have been insignificant in local politics, although Anglicanism was to play its part in Conservative domination of the borough. Bolton's population growth from just over 17,000 in 1801 was largely based on the activity of cotton manufacture and related industries. Although weaving survived in Bolton, the town developed in the eighteenth and nineteenth centuries mainly as a centre of fine spinning.[2] By the Napoleonic Wars the canal to Manchester flourished, and the first goods railway to Liverpool was opened in 1828, two years before that port's connection to Manchester. In 1889, Bolton became a county borough. In 1898 its population was over 160,000.[3] Like many other big municipalities in the late Victorian age, the responsibilities of local government were extended. The borough acquired its own gas company, electric generation, and by 1900 was running the electric trams.

By 1900, 50 per cent of employed males in Bolton were engaged in cotton textiles. Spinning produced the fine cloths and yarns which ensured that Bolton's pre-1914 prosperity was based on exports. The cotton industry continued to expand in Bolton until just before the Depression, with the last large mill, of Sir John Holden and Sons, being constructed at Astley Bridge in 1920. The number of equivalent spindles in Bolton increased from 4,853,000 in 1910 to 5,617,000 in 1938.[4] Most of the raw cotton came from Egypt and the Sudan, the remaining 20 per cent coming from the Americas. Also of importance alongside cotton were the connected industries of engineering, especially of textile machinery, and coal mining. As John Walton has pointed out, 'cotton Lancashire' was also 'engineering Lancashire'.[5] Pelling points out that engineering had become increasingly independent of the cotton industry, gaining ground while cotton remained static or declined.[6] Textile engineering initially aided Lancashire's capture of world markets, but, as has been noted for Blackburn, also helped to dig the grave of the inter-war cotton industry. Bolton's textile machines were by the 1920s to build up the indigenous cotton industries of Lancashire's rivals. Apart from the production of cotton spinning machinery, general engineering was also important in Bolton. Although the borough was not in the first division in iron and steel founding, it was still an important industry in the town. The Dobson and Barlow foundry at Bradley Fold, though situated just outside the borough boundaries, employed around 3,000 workers from the town. The main production

[1] Saxelby, C.H., (ed.), *Bolton Survey*, (Wakefield, 1971), p. 48.
[2] Walton, J.K., *Lancashire: a Social History, 1558–1939*, (Manchester, 1987), pp. 200–203.
[3] Saxelby, *Bolton*, p. 79.
[4] Saxelby, *Bolton*, pp. 93–4.
[5] Walton, *Lancashire*, p. 208.
[6] Pelling, H., *Social Geography of British Elections 1885–1910*, (Aldershot, 1994), p. 248.

of iron and steel was to help maintain plant in the local mills. Also of importance was locomotive manufacture (the Horwich works in Red Moss) and further iron and engineering works in the neighbourhood of Trinity Street and the Rose Hill Sidings. Also of some significance was structural engineering, the chemical industry, brass and lead foundries, lubricating oils, paper manufacture, timber and brewing. Finally in 1938, the Montagu Burton clothing firm opened in Bolton.[7]

By the time of this study, Bolton could with some justification claim to be 'the fine cotton spinning centre of the world'. The *Chamber of Commerce Yearbook* for 1919 noted that there were 'about 112 firms engaged in the cotton trade ... representing capital at over £12,000,000'. These were spinning firms. In addition there were 'some seventy firms engaged in the manufacture of cotton fabrics'. Around 50,000 skilled operatives were employed in the cotton mills, approximately another 12,000 in engineering and machine making, 10,000 in coal mining, 8,000 in bleaching and dyeing and lastly 5,000 in the building trade.[8] In 1923, the *Bolton and District Yearbook* noted that in the top ten industries spinning was the most important, followed by weaving, engineering, bleaching and dying, tanning, coal mining and corn milling.[9]

Yet by the early 1920s the borough was in severe economic difficulties. The First World War had seen the decline in the production of yarn and cloth as industrial production was diverted to the war effort. India and the Far East were cut off from their source of supply and dependency was broken. The indigenous cotton industries of India and Japan were further developed and in the 1920s the greatest decrease in demand for Lancashire cotton came from India. But as the Far Eastern trade was mainly in coarser and medium yarns, Bolton was to an extent less hard hit than the rest of Lancashire in the first decade after the war. Bolton's finer yarns had substantial European markets, especially in Germany, Switzerland and the Netherlands.[10] Nonetheless the Depression hit Bolton hard and there was a European challenge for its medium yarns which damaged that part of local production. By 1939 Lancashire's cotton goods no longer commanded the world market.[11] The economic consequences of renewed international competition from Far Eastern cotton manufacture and the ravages of the 1930s slump, laid Bolton low. The traditional staples of cotton and engineering were virtually wrecked, at least as important industries. The national reorganisation of the industrial structure had its parallel in Bolton. Textile machinery manufacture and coal mining suffered too along with King Cotton. The ravaging of Bolton's local economy resulted in mass unemployment, poverty and severe deprivation. The health, prosperity and happiness of the town's working class was fundamentally affected in the period of this study.

---

[7] Saxelby, *Bolton*, pp. 98–9.
[8] Harris, P.A., 'Social Attitudes and Social Leadership in Bolton 1919–1939', (Ph.D. thesis, University of Lancaster, 1973), p. 1.
[9] Quoted in Harris, 'Social Attitudes', p. 2.
[10] Massey, D., 'The Cotton Industry in Bolton', (B.A. Dissertation, University of Liverpool, 1948), pp. 10–13 and 53–54.
[11] Massey, 'The Cotton Industry', p. 14.

The 1931 census confirms the still largely Victorian structure of Bolton's industrial base. Cotton textiles employed over a quarter of the male labour force and 58 per cent of the female, that sector employing as a whole over 36,000 workers. Textiles as a category, including dyeing and printing, employed over 30 per cent of the males and nearly 64 per cent of the females of the borough. Thus Bolton was ranked fifth in the league table of county boroughs in terms of the percentage of male and female workers engaged in the textile industry. Commerce and finance came second as an employer of labour in 1931 with nearly 12,000 so employed, just over 12 per cent of the labour force. Metal and engineering was an important category of male labour employing nearly 16 per cent overall with 10 per cent in engineering alone. Thus Bolton was ranked eleventh in our league table of county boroughs for that category. The sector of those in managerial roles or business on their own account, with nearly 14 per cent of the male labour force and just over 7 per cent of the female, ensured that Bolton was ranked low at fifty-third in our county borough league table of the self-employed. This picture of a largely working-class Bolton is reinforced with personal service taking just over 10 per cent of the female labour force in 1931. Indeed the absence of a substantial middle class is further established with the town ranked at a lowly seventy-fifth in the league table for females in personal service. With only 2.1 per cent as a proportion of the whole population of the town employed in domestic service and hotel work, this is a strong indicator of the social class of the town. The absence of a numerically strong middle-class and petit bourgeois cadre again points to the electoral importance of working-class voters in Conservatism's control of municipal politics. Lastly, the importance of female labour should be noted. With women comprising over 37 per cent of the total workforce, Bolton was sixteenth in the league table of county boroughs in 1931. With a measure of financial independence, the female vote was to become more important from the 1928 election onwards.

Turning to the politics of the borough, by 1919 the Conservative Party had run Bolton's politics for half a century, and it continued to do so for the whole of inter-war period. The first decade of electoral politics after the First War saw far more contests than previously and thus keen competition between the parties. Calling themselves 'The True Progressive Party' in 1919, the Conservatives developed tactics that served them in subsequent elections. The central theme was to present themselves as the party that could preserve the ratepayers' money by keeping the rates low and championing municipal economy. From Bath to Southend this will be seen in other borough studies to be a tried and trusted Tory tactic in local elections. The changing Conservative slogans over time were variations on the same theme: 'Economy with Efficiency', 'Wise Spending', 'No Extravagance'. Conversely, as in other county boroughs, the Labour party were portrayed as 'the spendthrift Socialists'. The Tories' appeal was:

> to the ratepayer who was seen as the eternal prey of a host of parasitic money-grabbers. This was coupled with an appeal to the people as 'your trustees', as the natural and most experienced

rulers of Bolton. It was up to the opposition to prove that they could do better at less cost.[12]

These tactics were on the whole to prove highly successful. The Conservative Party had an overall majority on the council from 1919 to 1932, and again from 1937. Only in the years between 1933 and 1936 did the Conservatives require Liberal backing to keep Labour out of power, although they still remained the largest single party in the council chamber.

Deep-rooted historical traditions need to be examined, though, to fully explain the survival of Tory strength in Bolton, despite the travails of unemployment and poverty in the 1930s. As in the case of Blackburn, dealt with earlier in this volume, the traditional conservatism of the mass electorate in Bolton needs to be emphasised. In Bolton too the paternalism of the industrialists and the survival of a working-class Toryism were living traditions from its Victorian heyday. Part of this stemmed from the continued importance of the cotton spinning industry. Conservative control was maintained by the strength of the local elite, even after it had undergone considerable change. This political tradition continued to act both as an ideology and as a basis for political mobilisation in Bolton. It is intended here to give only a brief account of this political phenomenon which was important in many of Lancashire's cotton towns as well as Bolton.

Disraeli's Crystal Palace speech in 1872 laid one of the planks of working-class Toryism, and has been viewed 'as one of the most important speeches ever made by a Conservative leader'.[13] For Disraeli the three main purposes of the Conservative Party were 'to maintain the institutions of the country ..., to uphold the empire of England ..., [and] to elevate the condition of the people'.[14] Conservatives argued that the Liberals, and later Labour, should not be trusted to uphold the defence of the country or imperial interests. Those parties, it was alleged, had no concern for the greatness of the country. The parties of the left should not be trusted for:

> in their domestic policies, by their attacks on British institutions – the monarchy, the House of Lords, religion, and the established economic order, including all the institutions of property – and by their attempts to foment jealousy between classes, [they] represent a fatal threat to the unity and well being of the national community.[15]

Further Conservative propaganda insinuated that even the claims of the Labour party and Liberals to look after the underprivileged was a sham. Unencumbered by the albatross of *laissez-faire*, the Tories claimed in a paternalistic fashion to protect the working class by welfare legislation and support for collective bargaining. Even the issue of tariff reform was portrayed as sustaining employment for working people. Claiming to be the only party competent to

[12] Harris, 'Social Attitudes', p. 408.
[13] McKenzie, R. and Silver, A., *Angels in Marble: Working Class Conservatives in Urban England,* (London, 1968), p. 49.
[14] McKenzie and Silver, *Angels,* pp. 49–50.
[15] McKenzie and Silver, *Angels,* p. 72.

manage the economy, Conservatism sought to appeal to all classes including the workers. Condemning selfish class interests, 'One Nation' Toryism claimed to stand above class and serve all of society. Thus Tory self-representation to be the true friend of the working man was established and bore rich dividends way beyond the 'Villa Toryism' previously noted by Lord Derby.

Conservative municipal control in Bolton however had its origins even before that speech. It was located in the nineteenth-century industrial structure of the town, the central importance of cotton manufacturing and the organisation of the mill. The cotton and manufacturing elite, to effect status and control, preserved close social contacts with the working class. The economic and social centrality of the cotton elite and other wealthy industrialists resulted in their command of both parliamentary and local politics. The economic and social ties of the cotton elite to their workers aided the processes of political leadership, and ensured that the cottonocracy and associated manufacturers were the MPs for the borough, as well as the preponderant influence in municipal affairs. Paternalistic policies in the mill, local philanthropy, control of mill housing, the avoidance of a censorious attitude to working-class leisure and sporting activities, all contributed to the cotton masters maintaining close relations with their workforce. The result was the legitimising of their leadership functions and political influence with the working-class constituency. As diverse writers on the locality such as Trodd, Joyce and Kirk have shown, this was a subtle process involving close relationships of legitimation and no simplistic matter of crude social control.[16]

Bolton Conservatism, which later so hamstrung the Labour party in the town, also emphasised popular nationalism and imperialism, and stressed Disraeli's heritage of 'One Nation' Toryism. It avoided class ideology or stress on class differences, while Anglicanism's close ties with local Toryism also helped uphold authority and deference. For Neville Kirk, popular Conservatism among other qualities also stressed a patriotic appeal to 'the people', emphasising community, with toleration of the 'weaknesses' of respectable working men, while offering an alternative to the high moral tones of Liberalism. From the early years of the Industrial Revolution, Liberalism's identification with the cold comfort of unfettered *laissez-faire* had given paternalistic Toryism an advantage which it seized. The Conservative alternative was more attractive because it tolerated the simple pleasures that improving Liberalism deplored. Lancashire's 'clog' Toryism of the working class, dominated by the big local employers, 'revolved around social radicalism, paternalism and that mixture of "traditional" "John-Bull"-like qualities'.[17] John Walton too has emphasised the jingoistic popular Toryism of late Victorian cotton towns such as Bolton.[18] Finally, as Patrick Joyce has argued, working-class support for the local elite was a matter of calculation, perceived

---

[16] Joyce, P., *Work, Society and Politics: The Culture of the Factory in Later Victorian England*, (London, 1982); Kirk, N., *Labour and Society in Britain and the USA, Volume 2: Challenge and Accommodation, 1850–1939*, (Aldershot, 1994); Trodd, G., 'Political Change and the Working Class in Blackburn and Burnley, 1880–1914', (Ph.D. thesis, University of Lancaster, 1978).

[17] Kirk, *Labour and Society*, p. 196.

[18] Walton, *Lancashire*, pp. 200–201.

interdependence, and a sense of neighbourhood and community, all of which underlay deferential attitudes.[19]

Even though the new century had seen the success of Labour in other urban industrial centres, and the first stirrings of Labour in Bolton itself, the paternalistic framework of politics developed in the nineteenth century was sustained into the period of this study. It was still based upon a broad network of both cultural and social ties, and in the last resort emanated from the mill, where open-handedness and control were joint bedfellows. Conservative leaders still managed to a degree to identify with popular activity while upholding societal hierarchies. Class differences and populist links with working people were thus both upheld. Working-class Toryism continued to serve the local Conservative association well in inter-war municipal elections mainly because the local economy was still dominated by the cotton industry. By the late twenties the cotton masters were less directly involved with the council, but even when King Cotton was failing, so great a proportion of workers were still employed in this staple industry that the millowners still exerted the preponderant political influence in the borough. The loyalty of many working people remained to the mill which provided a livelihood, and leisure and recreational activities.

It is important to note here that there are criticisms of the notion of working-class Toryism, which have been elaborated upon in the earlier chapter on Blackburn. It is also the case that Tory dominance in Bolton did fluctuate over the inter-war period, and was threatened especially in the mid-1930s, as shown below. The Labour presence did grow significantly after 1918, challenging the influence of the old elite, and the identification of that elite with Conservatism also began to wane. It should be stressed especially that the paternalistic activities of the cotton elite were never able to entirely eliminate class tensions from the industry or locality. Whatever the ideological power of Tory ideas, the divergent interests of employers and workers could not always be disguised, especially in times of economic downturn. The existence of cotton trade-unionism, however moderate and deferential, and of sporadic industrial disputes, are testament to that fact.[20] Nevertheless, the strength of working-class conservatism was to a degree reflected in important working-class institutions, including crucially the trade unions. By the twentieth century, the spinning and weaving unions had developed a sophisticated process of collective bargaining, minimising and localising industrial conflict. Walton argues that to a considerable degree these unions had 'accepted and internalised the political economy of their employers'.[21] The sense of obligation the workers had to their employers is brought out by the socialist journalist Allen Clarke, writing in 1899:

> They have no idea of life. They believe they are born to work;
> they do not see that work is but a means to life ... They think that

[19] Joyce, *Work, Society and Politics*, p. 91.

[20] On cotton trade unionism, see White, J., *The Limits of Trade Union Militancy: The Lancashire Textile Workers, 1910–1914*, (Westport, 1978); Fowler, A. and Wyke, T., (eds), *The Barefoot Aristocrats: A History of the Amalgamated Association of Operative Cotton Spinners*, (Littleborough, 1987).

[21] Walton, *Lancashire*, pp. 268–269.

the masters build factories and workshops not to make a living for themselves by trading but in order to find the people employment. They honestly believe that if there were no mills and workshops the poor people would all perish.[22]

Later developments are instructive as to working-class attitudes. John Walton points to the Bolton Spinners Union whose general and superannuation funds had invested 58 per cent of their reserves in mill investments by 1925. Spinners investing as individuals in their own mills were quite common too.[23] This leaching of funds into the ailing industry ensured that the unions were less able to aid their members during the Depression. This highlights the continuing conservatism of the spinners, the largest single sector of Bolton's workforce.

The electoral evidence presented here does suggest that the working-class Tory tradition was still alive in inter-war Lancashire, and in particular Bolton. This makes some qualification necessary to P.F. Clarke's well-known argument that working-class Conservatism was weakened by the rise of the New Liberalism in Lancashire.[24] Clarke suggests that the Labour party was performing badly, and that New Liberal ideas were penetrating the working class in the years leading up to the First War. The Liberals, putting a greater emphasis upon social reform, and stressing the acceptance of class politics, advocated 'social justice, state intervention and alliance with Labour' after 1906.[25] In doing so, Clarke argues, they adapted, survived, and indeed revived, before 1914. For the post-1918 years, Clarke's thesis at the very least seems muted in operation in Bolton.

This leads to consideration of the fortunes of Liberalism in inter-war Bolton. The Liberal party was the second largest party on Bolton council until 1924, and had been the traditional rival to Tory control before the First War. Harris's study points to the influence of the old cottonocracy and industrialists beginning to wane in the power centres of local Conservatism during this period, while holding on in a much reduced Liberal Party.[26] In parliamentary elections Bolton was a double-member constituency, and the Liberals did not perform strongly at this level between the wars. Apart from Labour's bonanza year of 1929, the seats were largely won by the Conservatives or their ersatz brethren the National Liberals. Only in 1918 was one Liberal returned unopposed, and he was in fact a Coalition Liberal. In municipal elections, though, Liberalism maintained a foothold. The high tide of success for Liberalism in inter-war Bolton came in 1920 when the party had twenty-four seats. Then the Liberals sank to a low of a dozen seats in 1926 and 1927, but later from 1935 onwards made somewhat of a recovery, to finish with nineteen seats in 1938, only two fewer than Labour.

The relatively strong inter-war performance of the Liberals does require further investigation. On the face of it, the Liberals here were not swamped by Labour as the radical party, nor entirely subsumed under the Conservatives as part of a middle class *ralliement* against the left, as they were in some other boroughs.

---

[22] Quoted in Joyce, *Work, Society and Politics*, p. 90.
[23] Walton, *Lancashire*, p. 352.
[24] Clarke, P.F., *Lancashire and the New Liberalism*, (Cambridge, 1971).
[25] Clarke, *Lancashire and the New Liberalism*, pp. 397–8.
[26] Harris, 'Social Attitudes', p. 47.

Their support came mainly from a well-defined section of the town's electorate, most Liberal councillors being elected in outer middle-class suburbs. One explanation for their survival might be that the social leadership of the Liberals had become little different to the Conservatives by this time. If this was the case, then the social and political processes of paternalism and deference could to a degree have operated as a force for Liberalism as well as Toryism. It may also be the case that the ideological differences between local Tories and Liberals had become insignificant.

Harris indicates that the social origins of Liberal leadership were slightly more mixed than the Conservatives. Provision merchants from the Warburton (Astley Bridge and North wards) and Steele (Exchange) families, leading lights in the party, were of a lower social standing than generally found amongst the dominant figures of the Tories. Nonetheless he points out that the leader of the party and caucus was first J.P. Taylor (Halliwell), and later A. Pilling (Heaton), both 'capitalists of the old social leadership', while the 'cotton capitalists' remained 'a potent force' in the local Liberal leadership. He also notes a plethora of local big employers representing the Liberal Party on, or aspiring to, the council. A.E. Holt (West), J.W. Lomax, W.A. Greenhalgh, and also the Edge and Hollas families were all present in local Liberalism. Four prominent Liberals, J.W. Lomax, T. Jackson, A. Hollas (Heaton), and J.C. Holdsworth were to later become Conservatives.

The distinction between Tories and Liberals does seem to have become blurred, therefore, and this in turn appears to be supported by the fact that many Liberal councillors, especially in the 1930s, were elected as a result of intermittent electoral pacts with the Tories, sometimes openly acknowledged as anti-socialist and at other times tacit. In double-member wards, such as Halliwell or Exchange, one Tory and one Liberal would be nominated, while in single-member seats such as Rumworth or Heaton, Liberals would be given a free run in some years and then defer to Tories in other years. So the revival of Liberalism in Bolton may well have been more apparent than real, reflecting a merging of interests with the dominant Toryism. This may also be linked with more general shifts in the social leadership of the borough.

Harris's account of Bolton's social leadership begins by posing the question as to whether or not there was a single cohesive elite in Bolton dominating most aspects of society, economy and politics, or a competing plurality of groups controlling separate facets of the system. He comes down on the side of a socially integrated leadership in Bolton, with ties of marriage, social membership in the local authority and voluntary societies, and above all what he calls an economic 'kinterlock'. The social leaders came mainly from cotton, an elite made all the more cohesive with the amalgamations and rationalisations in the industry before the First War. The cottonocracy was made up of sixteen key families, augmented by the owners of the secondary industries of engineering, coal, tanning and corn milling.[27] As a counterpoint to writers such as Joyce, who paints a rather rosy view of class relations in cotton towns, Harris points to a huge divide between Bolton's elite and the working class. Workers were 'cowed under', and viewed

---

[27] Harris, 'Social Attitudes', p. 3.

the town council and those of power and status as a 'class above'.[28] The poor feared the officials, police, and authorities generally.

In the immediate post-war years the old industrialists were still important in the borough's economic and social leadership functions. They remained dominant on the council, mainly through the Conservative Party, but also to an extent in the Liberal opposition. There was however, a gradual dilution of local control after the cotton boom. The cotton elite was replaced in the council chamber by 'the shopkeeping stratum', and 'thus trade had replaced industry in local politics'.[29] The cotton boom led many of the cotton elite to cash in and sell up, leaving for the Home Counties and the south of France. Further amalgamations and rationalisations accelerated this southward migration. This left Bolton bereft of its traditional elite in leadership positions on the council, in charitable organisations, on the Board of Guardians, and by the 1930s, on the Public Assistance Committee as well. Although some of the old industrial leaders remained on the boards of the local firms, there were far less of them serving the municipality. Thus for instance the leader of the Conservative Party caucus for most of the period, and chair of the Finance Committee from 1922 to 1939 and the Public Assistance Committee from 1931 to 1933, was Alderman Edmund Aspinall, a wealthy retired pork butcher. He was succeeded to the chair of the Public Assistance Committee by Alderman A. Lawson, a solicitor. The vice-chairmen of the council's Finance Committee, J. W. Lomax (1933–35) and A. Pilling (1935–39), were by contrast from the old Bolton elite of cotton and industry.[30] But in the main the personnel of the old elite retreated from public and municipal life over the period. John Walton also refers to a new 'more complex and less cohesive elite'. Many of the cotton masters who remained had diversified into advertising and entertainment.[31] This change did not necessarily equate with a complete surrender of real power and influence. The withdrawal of elites from local government had taken place elsewhere, often much earlier than in Bolton, but without the loss of control from behind the scenes.[32] As Harris states, 'the Conservative section of old leadership certainly did not relinquish its ties with political power, although it left council affairs to the control of Aspinall and his fellow small traders and capitalists'.[33]

This did result in some changes in the attitudes of the council leadership, however, and the citizens of Bolton were very much to suffer from these changes. Paternalism and pride in the borough had made the old elite more expansive and more committed to local investment than the new leadership. The new leaders had a more parsimonious desire to keep the rates low. As indicated earlier, this could be a vote-winner amongst the ratepayers, but it also prevented much-needed social expenditure, and was to prove politically unpopular for some of the inter-war years. The changing structure of Bolton's elite and new social attitudes were

[28] Harris, 'Social Attitudes', p. 103.
[29] Harris, 'Social Attitudes', p. 46.
[30] Harris, 'Social Attitudes', p. 46.
[31] Walton, *Lancashire*, pp. 347–8.
[32] See Waller, P.J., *Town, City and Nation: England 1850–1914*, (Oxford, 1983), pp. 288–293.
[33] Harris, 'Social Attitudes', pp. 47–48.

especially evident after the economic slump of 1929, with measures of economy and reduced local government spending being introduced locally. This paralleled wage cuts in the mills and a reduction of public assistance costs, and hit the poor and unemployed hard. However, like other boroughs at the time, the degree of manoeuvre of the council was reduced by the state's greater control in the rudimentary welfare and unemployment benefits.[34] Harris also portrays Bolton's upper class as both elitist and anti-democratic, viewing the poor of the working class as lacking ability or initiative, unable to help themselves. The poor required discipline, the Conservatives believed, and both local and state expenditure would never make up for the deficiencies of the working class itself. Thus the responsibility for poverty and unemployment was shifted onto the working class themselves, and restrictions in municipal spending were justified accordingly. On this the new leadership was generally in accord, and distinctions between Tories and Liberals were confined to incidental issues. It is in this light that the Liberal survival in Bolton should be viewed.

The Labour party was the main challenger to the two established parties in Bolton, as would be expected. In terms of the performance of the local Labour party when compared to national fortunes of the party, strong performances were achieved in both 1919 and 1920 with five gains in each year. This was similar at least with the national performance in 1919 but locally in 1920 Labour went against the trend by performing so strongly in the borough. Nationally Labour did not do well between 1921 and 1925, the party's performance nearing collapse in 1920–21. Locally however Labour again to some extent did rather better than the national trend, with the party's percentage of the poll rising from 28 per cent in 1921 to 40 per cent in 1925. Labour increased its position on the council from thirteen in 1920 to nineteen in 1925, making thirteen gains against six losses in the five-year period. By 1925 it had become the second party to the Conservatives, which it was to remain until 1938. Labour was in its strongest position on the council in the years from 1927 to 1936 inclusive, never holding fewer than 30 council seats in the ten-year period. The years 1926 to 1929 saw Labour perform strongly both locally and nationally. In those four years Labour made fifteen gains to three losses. Seven Labour gains were made in 1926 when Labour recorded a 40 per cent share of the poll. Surprisingly in 1929, its peak nationally, Labour lost a seat and made no gains. This was for the most part an anomaly produced by the vagaries of the three-year cycle of elections, so that very few seats that Labour was likely to gain from opponents came up that year. Labour's percentage share of the poll in that year however, at 41.4 per cent, was its second highest of the period.

Nationally the years 1930–31 were disaster years for Labour, seeing a widespread and deep collapse of electoral support. Labour in Bolton, however, was spared the worst effects by two strokes of good fortune. First, in 1930 Labour was unopposed in a number of seats which it might otherwise have lost. In both of the double-member wards of Bradford and West, incumbent Labour councillors received a walkover, in return for which the sitting Tory and Liberal respectively was unopposed by Labour. In Derby ward two Labour candidates were opposed

---

[34]   Harris, 'Social Attitudes', p. vi.

by a single Tory. The Tory took one seat off Labour by topping the poll comfortably, but Labour was still left with one seat. In all three of these cases Labour would very probably have lost a seat if it had faced full opposition. As it was Labour's overall share of the vote fell to a disastrous 21.3 per cent, its worst performance between the wars, and it still lost three seats in 1930, including both incumbents in East ward, showing how much it might have lost if it had been fully challenged in its double-member strongholds. Through electoral understandings with its opponents, based on shared expectations of how the elections would have gone in a 'normal' year, Labour was cushioned from the full effects of the 1930 collapse in support.

Labour was even luckier in 1931. With the National Government's advent to power in 1931 came the lead from the centre for economy in all aspects of administration. This was to lead to electoral pacts being arranged across the country, to varying degrees according to the borough, in order to cut costs. The three major parties in Bolton came to a comprehensive pact, and only the intervention of NUWM or Communist candidates forced contests in four wards. There is evidence that Labour locally entered into this pact because it was short of cash.[35] It also made good tactical sense for Labour, given the political climate after the collapse of the Labour government. It was a defensive strategy of 'what we have we hold'. Whether by good luck or good judgement, Labour avoided any losses in 1931, and its opponents missed a major opportunity. This also produced a freak result in terms of Labour's share of the overall vote, which at 45.7 per cent was on paper its best performance between the wars. This was caused, though, by the fact that Labour won abnormally large majorities over its NUWM or Communist opponents, and was not a true reflection of Labour's popularity.

Locally, as nationally, the years 1932–35 were years of recovery for Labour, with the party peaking at its inter-war high of thirty-five seats in 1934 and 1935. There were no gains in Bolton in 1932, partly due to the fact that vestiges of the previous year's pact were maintained, but also partly due again to the vagaries of the three-year cycle. However, Labour secured a massive seven gains in 1933, including all three that had been lost in 1930, and further gains in 1934 and 1935 consolidated its position. Labour clearly benefited in these years from Tory unpopularity over the administration of unemployment relief, as mentioned above. Conservative policy on municipal expenditure was always characterised by a parsimonious attitude, but it was perceived as especially mean-spirited by those who suffered at the hands of the Poor Law Guardians and their successors the Public Assistance Committee. In 1926, for instance, Tory-controlled committees had cut off all relief from families of striking miners. By 1932, Walton informs us, Labour had withdrawn from the administration of the Means Test, having previously only fought symbolic battles such as over the provision of butter rather than margarine for children in council homes.[36] Refusal of benefit ran at 43 per cent in Bolton during 1931–35 compared to 33 per cent for Lancashire as a whole. Labour's trump card in the 1933 election campaign was the refusal to administer the Means Test, and in both 1929 and 1934 the dominant issue was

---

[35] Harris, 'Social Attitudes', p. 411.
[36] Walton, *Lancashire*, p. 347.

unemployment. Labour instead put forward municipal works schemes as a measure to reduce unemployment locally, and advocated the employment of direct labour to build council houses for the poor in the thirties. Other Labour policies, such as free secondary education put forward in 1926, and free nursery schools in 1934, began to attract a more receptive audience in these years.[37]

The trend towards Labour was very much reversed, though, between 1936 and 1938, with the party's percentage share of the poll falling back. Labour suffered a net loss of thirteen seats in these three years, and its seats on the council fell quite dramatically from the high of thirty-five in 1935 to twenty-one in 1938, the lowest total since 1925. Remarkably, the Liberals had only two fewer seats than Labour in 1938. No pointers can be detected here then for Labour's overwhelming success in the general election of 1945, as its fortunes were plainly in decline before the Second War. There is a deeper trend that needs to be considered here. Notwithstanding the general strength of working-class Conservatism in Bolton, the later 1930s appears to a period of growing malaise, not only in terms of working-class support for Labour electorally, but also in terms of commitment to, and involvement with, politics at all. One measure of this is the decline in voter turnout at municipal elections. Overall turnout in the 1920s fluctuated in the mid-60s range, but after the freak years of 1931 and 1932 when the electoral pact and the NUWM intervention caused abnormally low turnout, the low 50s range was more the norm. More impressionistic evidence conveys the same message. Passivity and deference have been noted as features of the borough's working class by some commentators. One has written of the 1930s, 'The majority of the Lancashire working class remained stolidly politically apathetic and conservative in all senses of the word, which made them as impervious to the forces of the radical right as to those of the left'.[38]

There were other factors too that may have contributed to Labour's ultimate failure in inter-war Bolton. Harris makes the point that increasingly in the 1930s Labour bowed to the pressure of working-class conservatism by moving to more moderate and cautious policies. This was particularly the case in the early 1930s when Communist and NUWM candidates, infused with the anti-reformist rhetoric of the 'third-period' Comintern, raised radical and ambitious demands on behalf of the unemployed. Labour sought to distance itself from such radicalism, and in the short term, given Tory unpopularity over the Means Test, its caution yielded political dividends. As the 1930s wore on, however, the rightward drift of the party contributed to its decline, and to the increasing disillusionment and apathy of late 1930s municipal politics. To an extent Labour lost some of its distinctive appeal, and all three major parties in Bolton were aiming for an increasingly crowded middle ground. This was not purely a local phenomenon of course. Nationally there was a shift towards more cautious policies by Labour in the 1930s. In Bolton, though, Harris argues it may well have contributed to Labour's faltering performance. He makes one other point that is relevant, and that is the financial weakness of the Labour party in Bolton. In county boroughs up and down the land, local Labour parties bemoaned the fact that they lost votes because

---

[37] Harris, 'Social Attitudes', p. 410.
[38] Quoted in Walton, *Lancashire*, p. 351.

they lacked the motor transport to convey voters to the poll that other parties possessed. This was equally the case in Bolton, but Labour's relative lack of funds was even more important when it came to affording advertisements in the local press. In this regard, the Tories and Liberals were clear winners in the battle of propaganda.[39]

Harris also makes the claim that Labour suffered politically in the 1930s by the movement of population from terraced slums in traditionally stronger Labour inner-city wards to suburban Conservative and Liberal strongholds. Mostly working-class voters were transferred to scattered and relatively small council-housing estates, where their votes were swamped by suburban middle-class voters.[40] 6,385 council houses were erected in Bolton between the wars, and by 1939 one-ninth of the total housing stock was corporation owned.[41] Nearly all of these were built in the suburbs. These included in the 1920s the Platt Hill estate (Deane ward), Green Lane (Great Lever), Firwood, Castleton Street and Hall i' th' Wood (all Tonge), Castle Hill and the first phase of Cameron Street (Astley Bridge) and lastly Snow Hill (Darcy Lever). None of these were large estates, the biggest being Firwood (279 houses) and Green Lane (237). The years between 1930 and 38 saw both the extension of earlier sites and the building of new developments further out in the suburbs, including Johnson Fold (Smithills), the Crescent Road flats (Great Lever), Higher Swan Lane (mainly Great Lever), Cameron Street (Astley Bridge), Top o' th' Brow (Darcy Lever), the Long Lane estate in the Breightmet development (Darcy Lever), Entwistle Street and the Moorfield estate (Tonge).

Plainly the council-housing developments were scattered across the suburbs of Bolton, but this was not a feature unique to the borough. Council houses naturally tended to be developed on greenfield suburban sites, where land was cheaper and more plentiful, although in some boroughs they were concentrated into larger estates, as in the case of Birmingham for instance. Certainly it was the case that none of the estates in Bolton were big enough to significantly alter the political complexion of the wards they were situated in. This was not just a case of numbers, though. Council-house rents were relatively high, and the new council-house tenants tended to be better-off members of the working class, and even white-collar workers. Many of them were upwardly mobile, and some at least tended to reject the old close-knit ties of working-class community, identifying more with their social superiors in the suburbs.[42] They were by no means automatically Labour voters, and may very well have comprised a high proportion of the working-class Conservatives of the borough. By contrast it was predominantly the unemployed and disadvantaged who tended to be left in the crumbling back-to-backs of the early phase of industrialisation.[43]

---

[39] Harris, 'Social Attitudes', p. 411.
[40] Harris, 'Social Attitudes', p. 403.
[41] Harris, 'Social Attitudes', p. 414; Sale, S., 'Some Aspects of Industry and Population in the County Borough of Bolton', (B.A. dissertation, University of Liverpool, 1965), unpaginated.
[42] Harris, 'Social Attitudes', p. 403.
[43] Walton, *Lancashire*, p. 346.

Conversely, argues Harris, the loss of working-class voters in the inner city could transform previously strong Labour wards into more marginal territory. This was particularly the case if wards near the city centre contained retail and shopping districts, which would have had large numbers of generally anti-Labour plural business voters. Exchange ward's electorate, for instance, was almost halved between 1929 and 1938, and East ward's fell by roughly 20 per cent in the same period. The *Bolton Evening News* attributed Labour's loss of four seats in these wards in 1936 to slum clearance.[44] In total seven seats were lost by Labour in these two wards between 1936 and 1938. It is impossible to be sure of the overall political impact of these population shifts, and Harris's claim that 'the middle class areas were made safe for the Conservatives and Liberals, the working class wards not so for Labour', cannot be fully substantiated.[45] It may, however, have had at least some marginal effect contributing to Labour's retreat in the late 1930s.

This leads on to the consideration of the spatial distribution of political support in Bolton. A fairly clear-cut pattern emerges. Labour's main support was concentrated in six city-centre wards, namely Bradford, Derby, East, Exchange, North and West, all with the exception of North being double-member seats. Apart from their central location, these wards shared one other obvious common characteristic, the working-class nature of their population. They were comprised largely of Victorian terraced housing interspersed with mills and other industrial premises. If the examples of Bradford and Exchange wards are taken, the pattern of mill, factory and working-class housing can be put into clear relief. Thus Weston Street on the southern ward boundary of Bradford had five mills alone situated along it, including Ainsworth's, Winder and McKean's, Charles Heaton's and Knowles's.[46] Further north were situated Marsden's No.3 and No.4 mills, Chatwood's Safe Works, and the old cattle market, all set in the midst of tiny single houses (one room up, one room down) and the back-to-backs around John Taylor Street, Foundry Street, Coe Street, York Street and Sidney Street.[47] In Exchange ward, the iron and steel firms of Hick and Hargreaves', the Atlas Forge, and Bessemer's Forge were also all situated in the middle of working-class housing. Bessemer's was at the Moor Lane–New Street junction on the ward boundary of Exchange and Derby.[48] This site was cleared in 1930 and became Moor Lane Bus Station. There were also iron and engineering works near Trinity Street on the ward boundary of Exchange and Bradford. Additionally the Dobson and Barlow textile machinery firm operated in Blackhorse Street in Exchange from 1850 until as late as 1970.[49] These Labour heartlands were described in the 1890s by Allen Clarke, a socialist writer of working-class background, as follows:

---

[44] Quoted in Harris, 'Social Attitudes', p. 404.
[45] Harris, 'Social Attitudes', p. 404.
[46] Horrocks, B., *Reminiscences of Bolton*, (Manchester, 1984), p. 21.
[47] Horrocks, *Reminiscences*, p. 5.
[48] Horrocks, *Reminiscences*, p. 11.
[49] Readyhough, G., *Bolton Town Centre: A Modern History*, (Manchester, undated), pp. 3–4.

a terrible heap of houses and buildings, with blackened church spires standing here and there, and hundreds of high chimneys belching forth, like huge fiery dragons, till the whole place looks like a city sunk in a sea of smoke. Amidst that sickening jerry-jumble of cheap bricks and cheaper British industry, over a hundred thousand men, women and children toil and exist, sweating in the vast, hot stuffy mills and sweltering forges ... growing up stunted, breeding thoughtlessly. Dying prematurely. Knowing not, nor dreaming ... of aught better than this shrieking, steamy sphere of slime and sorrow.[50]

Clarke's description would have been recognisable to Boltonians thirty years on, as even during the inter-war period much of Bolton's inter-war housing stock was at best of mid and late Victorian vintage. The nature of these wards is also confirmed by the persons per room data. Varying between 0.87 persons per room in West and 1.09 in Exchange, these wards had the most crowded housing in the borough. It should be noted that Labour also won the occasional seat in two other wards just outside the central area, Halliwell and Rumworth, adjoining West and Derby wards respectively. These both had some concentration of terraced working-class housing, such as the Daubhill area in Rumworth,

By contrast, Conservative and Liberal strength was found mainly in residential and suburban wards, surrounding the central Labour wards. Heaton, for instance, was an exclusive suburb, a fashionable area to live with grand houses where the wealthiest families lived. Smithills had some of the 'upper class' with many middle-class residential areas, while Hulton too was dominated largely by middle-class housing.[51] Labour never won a single seat in any of these wards between the wars. Astley Bridge, Darcy Lever, Deane, Great Lever, and Tonge wards also fitted this category. The person per room figures for these wards were low, ranging from 0.60 in Heaton to 0.86 in Tonge. Almost the only clear exception to the pattern established so far was Church ward, the only central ward that was also a Tory stronghold. Here, though, were the smartest parts of the town centre, and also a concentration of business voters, revealed again by the very low person per room figure of 0.74. One can conclude from this clear-cut spatial pattern of political allegiance one clear point. Despite the significance of working-class Conservatism in Bolton, which put a limitation on the strength of the Labour party, class was still highly relevant to voters' preferences. Labour's strength, however limited, was in working-class districts, while Tory and Liberal support was strongest in middle-class areas.

In conclusion a number of points emerge concerning inter-war municipal politics in the county borough of Bolton. Conservative control of an industrial borough with a substantial working class was maintained for the entire period. The role of King Cotton, with the domination of the spinning mill and related engineering in the local economy, together with the politics of economic decline, created the conditions for the operation of a specific ideology that mobilised

---

[50] Quoted in Walton, *Lancashire,* p. 316.
[51] Harris, 'Social Attitudes', p. 99.

significant numbers of working men and women towards the right in municipal politics. In the context of a tradition of employer paternalism and working-class Toryism, sufficient numbers of working-class voters stayed faithful to their old loyalties to stave off the muted Labour challenge. Commanding a pyramid of power, wealth and status, a 'ruling class', which changed in its composition in significant ways during the period, nevertheless continued to provide the political and social leadership of the borough. Bolton remained an elitist society dominated by Conservative rule.[52] The Liberals did survive in Bolton, but the Liberal elite was drawn from much the same social group as the Conservatives. The Liberals helped to sustain Conservative control of the town in the middle thirties, and the two parties moved inexorably closer to each other, with electoral pacts between themselves sustaining the Liberal presence, and ideological differences between them becoming increasingly insignificant.

Labour did increase its strength over the whole period from 1919 to 1935, and was fortunate that local electoral pacts in the 1930–31 period allowed it to escape the effects of the collapse in Labour support of those years. This good fortune made Labour's progress seem more effective than it actually was, as was shown in the late 1930s when Labour support fell away substantially. Labour ended the decade almost as far away from power in Bolton as it had been in 1919, and apathy and disillusionment had to a large degree replaced the confident hopes of twenty years earlier. This makes the political transformation of 1945 seem all the more remarkable in contrast. That a majority of working-class people did not put in power the 'working-class' party in an age of class politics shows the limitations of straightforward explanations of voting behaviour. Arguments that Labour's increasing association with trade unionism from 1910 to 1924 ensured working-class support for the party also have to be qualified in the case of Bolton.[53] Instead paternalism and the ideology of working-class Toryism must be linked to the conservatism of the trade unions in the cotton industry. In this context, the onset of the Depression forced the local Labour party towards the middle, taking on board some of the shibboleths of Conservatism and a moderate stance in local affairs.

[52]   Harris, 'Social Attitudes', p. 68.
[53]   McKibbin, R., *The Evolution of the Labour Party 1910–1924*, (Oxford, 1974).

A guide to further reading

Newspapers

Bolton Evening News
Manchester Guardian

Works of reference

Tillotson's Bolton Directory (various years)

Other secondary sources

Clarke, P.F., *Lancashire and the New Liberalism*, (Cambridge, 1971).

Fowler, A. and Wyke, T., (eds), *The Barefoot Aristocrats: A History of the Amalgamated Association of Operative Cotton Spinners*, (Littleborough, 1987).

Harris, P.A., 'Social Attitudes and Social Leadership in Bolton 1919–1939', (Ph.D. thesis, University of Lancaster, 1973).

Horrocks, B., *Reminiscences of Bolton*, (Manchester, 1984).

Joyce, P., *Work, Society and Politics: The Culture of the Factory in later Victorian England*, (London, 1982).

Howell, D., *British Workers and the Independent Labour Party 1888–1906*, (Manchester, 1983), ch. 3.

Kirk, N., *Labour and Society in Britain and the USA, Volume 2: Challenge and Accommodation, 1850–1939*, (Aldershot, 1994).

McKibbin, R., *The Evolution of the Labour Party 1910–1924*, (Oxford, 1974).

Massey, D., 'The Cotton Industry in Bolton', (B.A. dissertation, University of Liverpool, 1948).

Municipal Journal and Public Works Engineer, 'Municipal progress in Bolton', vol. 40, (13 Mar. 1931), pp. 385–6; 'Bolton's clearance method', vol. 43, (1 Jun. 1934), p. 752.

Pelling, H., *Social Geography of British Elections 1885–1910*, (Aldershot, 1994), pp. 252–260.

Readyhough, G., *Bolton Town Centre: A Modern History*, (Manchester, undated).

Sale, S., 'Some Aspects of Industry and Population in the County Borough of Bolton', (B.A. dissertation, University of Liverpool, 1965).

Saxelby, C.H., (ed.), *Bolton Survey*, (Wakefield, 1971).

Trodd, G., 'Political Change and the Working Class in Blackburn and Burnley, 1880–1914', (Ph.D. thesis, University of Lancaster, 1978).

Walton, J.K., *Lancashire: a Social History, 1558–1939*, (Manchester, 1987).

White, J., *The Limits of Trade Union Militancy: The Lancashire Textile Workers, 1910–1914*, (Westport, 1978)

Bolton wards 1919–1938

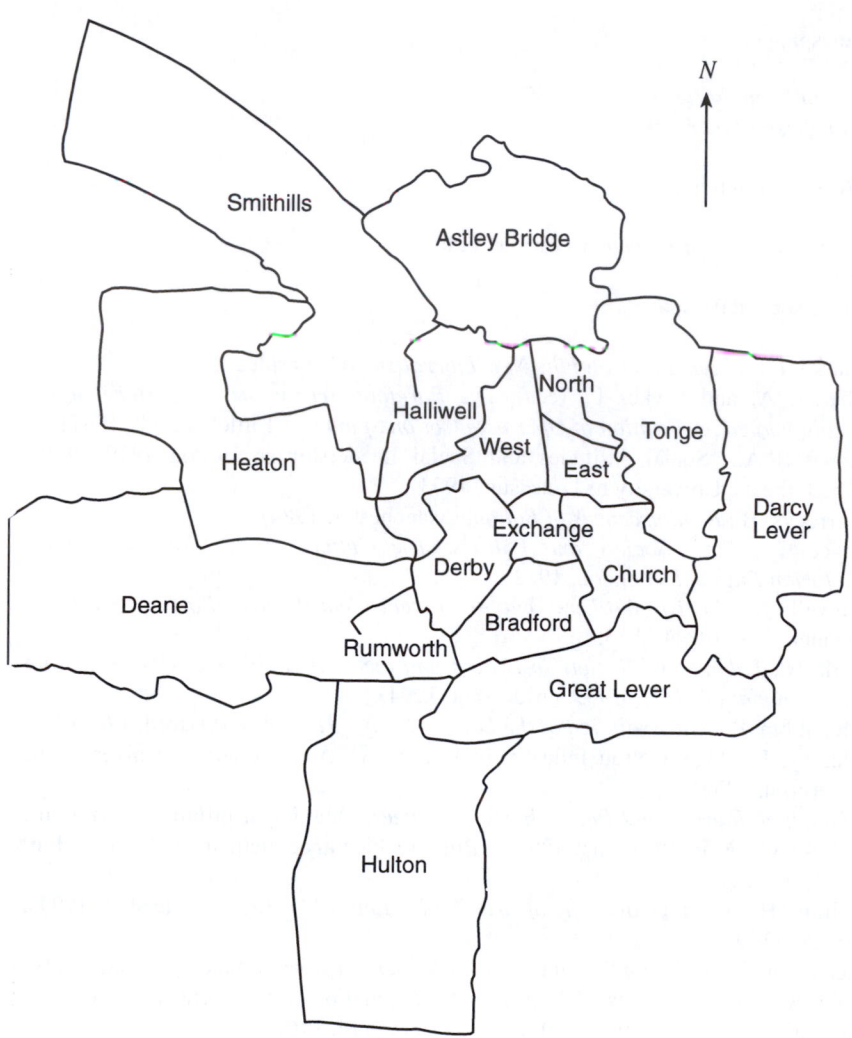

N

Persons aged fourteen and over classified by industry 1931

	Male	%	Female	%	Total	%
Metal and engineering	9,495	15.7	531	1.5	10,026	10.4
- Engineering	*6,048*	*10.0*	*373*	*1.0*	*6,421*	*6.6*
Textiles	18,551	30.6	22,976	63.9	41,527	43.0
- Cotton	*15,188*	*25.1*	*20,849*	*58.0*	*36,037*	*37.3*
- Dyeing, printing, etc.	*2,923*	*4.8*	*941*	*2.6*	*3,864*	*4.0*
Building	4,174	6.9	48	0.1	4,222	4.4
Transport	3,564	5.9	86	0.2	3,650	3.8
Commerce and finance	8,224	13.6	3,551	9.9	11,775	12.2
Public admin. and defence	3,097	5.1	1,280	3.6	4,377	4.5
- Local government	*2,493*	*4.1*	*1,090*	*3.0*	*3,583*	*3.7*
Personal service	1,687	2.8	3,658	10.2	5,345	5.5
Other	11,798	19.5	3,846	10.7	15,644	16.2
Total (a)	**60,590**		**35,976**		**96,566**	
Total population (b)	82,997		94,253		177,250	
(a) as % of (b)	73.0		38.2		54.5	
Total out of work (c)	10,097		4,458		14,555	
(c) as % of (a)	16.7		12.4		15.1	
Managerial and own account	6,917	13.7	2,230	7.1	9,147	11.2
Operative	43,576	86.3	29,288	92.9	72,864	88.8
Total (excluding out of work)	50,493		31,518		82,011	

Population statistics 1931

Ward	Acres	Population	Persons/acre	Persons/room
Astley Bridge	1,776	8,525	4.8	0.79
Bradford	282	15,711	55.7	0.96
Church	391	7,226	18.5	0.74
Darcy Lever	1,374	5,297	3.9	0.85
Deane	2,604	5,873	2.3	0.80
Derby	312	16,618	53.3	0.91
East	158	8,080	51.1	1.04
Exchange	109	2,629	24.1	1.09
Great Lever	867	13,712	15.8	0.79
Halliwell	358	19,464	54.4	0.84
Heaton	1,746	4,420	2.5	0.60
Hulton	1,615	6,456	4.0	0.82
North	157	6,241	39.8	0.90
Rumworth	163	9,236	56.7	0.89
Smithills	2,127	10,181	4.8	0.74
Tonge	829	13,502	16.3	0.86
West	412	24,079	58.4	0.87
Total	**15,280**	**177,250**	**11.6**	**0.85**

Overall position on the council 1919–38

	Position				Gains				Losses			
	C	Lab	L[a]	Other	C	Lab	L[a]	Other	C	Lab	L[a]	Other
1919	65	9	22	0	2	5	0	0	5	0	2	0
1920	59	13	24	0	4	5	1	0	5	1	4	0
1921	63	15	17	1	5	2	0	1	0	0	8	0
1922	67	13	15	1	5	2	1	0	2	3	3	0
1923	64	14	17	1	2	2	1	0	3	1	1	0
1924	62	14	19	1	0	2	2	0	2	2	0	0
1925	59	19	17	1	2	5	1	0	5	0	3	0
1926	55	25	15	1	2	7	2	0	6	1	4	0
1927	54	30	12	0	3	6	1	0	4	1	4	1
1928	51	33	12	0	0	2	1	0	2	0	1	0
1929[b]	49	33	13	0	1	0	1	0	0	1	1	0
1930[c]	50	30	14	0	5	0	1	0	1	3	2	0
1931	52	30	14	0	0	0	0	0	0	0	0	0
1932	51	31	14	0	0	0	0	0	0	0	0	0
1933	47	34	15	0	0	7	2	0	7	1	1	0
1934	46	35	15	0	2	2	1	0	3	1	1	0
1935[b]	43	35	17	0	1	1	3	0	3	1	1	0
1936[b]	45	31	17	2	4	0	2	2	2	5	1	0
1937	52	24	17	3	6	0	0	1	0	6	0	1
1938	53	21	19	3	2	1	3	0	3	3	0	0

Aldermen 1919–38

1919 C–21, L–3	1929[b] C–17, L–3, Lab–4
1920 C–21, L–3	1930[c] C–11, L–3, Lab–9
1921 C–22, L–2	1931 C–11, L–3, Lab–10
1922 C–20, L–3, Lab–1	1932 C–11, L–3, Lab–10
1923 C–18, L–5, Lab–1	1933 C–13, L–4, Lab–7
1924 C–18, L–5, Lab–1	1934 C–13, L–4, Lab–7
1925 C–19, L–3, Lab–2	1935[b] C–13, L–4, Lab–7
1926 C–19, L–3, Lab–2	1936[b] C–11, L–5, Lab–8
1927 C–19, L–3, Lab–2	1937 C–11, L–5, Lab–8
1928 C–19, L–3, Lab–2	1938 C–13, L–5, Lab–7

[a] Sir T. Flitcroft, intermittently labelled L or Ind L, counted as L in this table.
[b] 1929, 1935, 1936 - 1 seat vacant.
[c] 1930 - 2 seats vacant, including 1 aldermanic seat.

Municipal elections: winning party 1919–28

Ward	1919	1920	1921	1922	1923	1924	1925	1926	1927	1928
Astley Bridge	C	C	C	**C**	**C**	C	**C**	C	C	**C**
Bradford (1)	Lab	Lab	Lab	C	C	Lab	Lab	Lab	Lab	Lab
Bradford (2)	Lab	Lab	C	Lab	Lab	Lab	Lab	Lab	C	Lab
Church (1)	C	C	L	C	C	**L**	**C**	C	C	C
Church(2)	C	C	C	C	C	**C**	**C**	C	C	C
Darcy Lever	**C**	C	**C**	**C**	**C**	**C**	**C**	C	C	C
Deane	C	C	**C**	C	**C**	**C**	**C**	**C**	**C**	C
Derby (1)	Lab	C	C	Lab	C	C	Lab	Lab	Lab	Lab
Derby (2)	L	C	C	C	L	Lab	Lab	C	Lab	Lab
East (1)	Lab	Lab	C	Lab	Lab	C	Lab	Lab	Lab	Lab
East (2)	C	C	C	C	C	C	Lab	Lab	Lab	Lab
Exchange (1)	**L**	C	C	Lab	C	C	Lab	**C**	Lab	Lab
Exchange (2)	**L**	Lab	Lab	L	Lab	L	C	**Lab**	C	C
Great Lever	L	C	C	**C**	**C**	**C**	C	L	C	L
Halliwell (1)	L	C	C	L	C	L	L	Lab	L	L
Halliwell (2)	Lab	L	L	C	L	C	C	C	C	Lab
Heaton	C	C	C	L	L	**C**	**L**	C	**C**	L
Hulton	C	C	C	L	C	C	C	C	L	C
North	**L**	Lab	C	L	Lab	C	Lab	Lab	C	Lab
Rumworth	C	C	Lab	C	C	L	C	Lab	L	C
Smithills	L	L	WCA	C	C	**WCA**	L	L	C	L
Tonge	Lab	C	C	C	Lab	C	C	C	C	C
West (1)	Lab	C	L	C	C	L	L	Lab	Lab	Lab
West (2)	L	L	L	L	L	L	Lab	Lab	Lab	Lab

Municipal elections: party wins per year 1919–28

	1919	1920	1921	1922	1923	1924	1925	1926	1927	1928
C	9	16	16	14	15	14	11	11	13	9
Lab	7	5	3	4	5	3	9	11	8	11
L[a]	8	3	4	6	4	6	4	2	3	4
Other	0	0	1	0	0	1	0	0	0	0
Total	24	24	24	24	24	24	24	24	24	24
Turnout %	60.2	66.1	68.9	67.3	65.2	61.2	63.5	63.1	61.0	68.5
Labour %	26.6	21.6	26.8	32.1	29.7	37.4	38.6	39.9	37.1	40.7

[a] Sir T. Flitcroft, intermittently labelled L or Ind L, counted as L in this table.

Municipal elections: winning party 1929–38

Ward	1929	1930	1931	1932	1933	1934	1935	1936	1937	1938
Astley Bridge	C	L	C	C	L	C	C	C	C	L
Bradford (1)	Lab	Lab	Lab	C	Lab	Lab	Lab	Lab	C	C
Bradford (2)	Lab	C	Lab	Lab	Lab	Lab	Lab	Lab	Lab	Lab
Church (1)	C	C	C	C	C	C	C	C	C	C
Church(2)	C	C	C	C	C	C	C	C	C	C
Darcy Lever	C	C	C	C	C	C	C	C	C	C
Deane	C	C	C	C	C	C	C	C	C	C
Derby (1)	C	C	Lab	C	Lab	Lab	C	C	C	C
Derby (2)	Lab	Lab	Lab	Lab	Lab	Lab	Lab	Lab	Lab	Lab
East (1)	Lab	C	Lab	Lab	Lab	Lab	Lab	C	C	Lab
East (2)	Lab	C	Lab	Lab	Lab	Lab	Lab	C	C	C
Exchange (1)	Lab	Lab	Lab	Lab	Lab	Lab	Lab	Ind	C	L
Exchange (2)	C	C	C	C	C	C	C	Ind	Ind	C
Great Lever	L	C	L	L	C	C	C	L	C	C
Halliwell (1)	Lab	L	L	C	L	C	L	L	C	L
Halliwell (2)	C	C	Lab	C	Lab	L	C	Lab	L	C
Heaton	C	L	L	C	L	L	L	L	C	L
Hulton	C	C	C	C	L	L	C	L	L	L
North	Lab	L	Lab	Lab	Lab	Lab	Lab	Lab	C	Lab
Rumworth	Lab	C	C	Lab	Lab	C	L	Lab	C	L
Smithills	C	C	L	C	C	L	C	L	C	L
Tonge	C	C	C	C	C	C	C	C	C	Lab
West (1)	L	Lab	C	L	L	Lab	L	L	C	C
West (2)	Lab	L	Lab	Lab	L	Lab	Lab	C	Lab	L

Municipal elections: party wins per year 1929–38

	1929	1930	1931	1932	1933	1934	1935	1936	1937	1938
C	12	15	10	14	8	10	12	10	18	11
Lab	10	4	10	8	10	10	8	6	3	5
L[a]	2	5	4	2	6	4	4	6	2	8
Other	0	0	0	0	0	0	0	2	1	0
Total	24	24	24	24	24	24	24	24	24	24
Turnout %	56.1	58.5	30.4	30.0	47.4	51.0	55.6	50.9	53.5	53.8
Labour %	41.4	21.3	45.7	34.9	39.6	42.1	36.9	34.5	37.8	37.6

[a] Sir T. Flitcroft, intermittently labelled L or Ind L, counted as L in this table.

Municipal elections: party wins per ward 1919–38

	C	Lab	L[a]	Other	Total	Turnout %	Labour % of all votes
Astley Bridge	17	0	3	0	20	62.2	23.3
Bradford	8	32	0	0	40	53.1	63.5
Church	38	0	2	0	40	57.4	3.1
Darcy Lever	20	0	0	0	20	60.0	31.9
Deane	20	0	0	0	20	63.1	9.4
Derby	15	23	2	0	40	52.2	49.0
East	15	25	0	0	40	58.3	49.2
Exchange	17	15	5	3	40	60.3	34.4
Great Lever	13	0	7	0	20	52.0	13.1
Halliwell	16	7	17	0	40	58.3	31.0
Heaton	9	0	11	0	20	74.9	0.3
Hulton	13	0	7	0	20	72.5	14.8
North	4	13	3	0	20	64.8	52.0
Rumworth	10	6	4	0	20	68.3	39.7
Smithills	9	0	9	2	20	66.3	4.4
Tonge	17	3	0	0	20	60.0	43.7
West	7	16	17	0	40	49.4	40.4
Total	**248**	**140**	**87**	**5**	**480**	**58.0**	**34.7**

Seats won by Labour as a percentage of all wins 1919–38   **29.2**

[a] Sir T. Flitcroft, intermittently labelled L or Ind L, counted as L in this table.

Parliamentary election results

Bolton constituency *(double-member seat)*
(all wards within the borough [1918 boundaries] were included in the constituency)

General election	Winner	Conservative %	Labour %	Liberal %
14 Dec. 1918	**Co L** (1)	-	-	-
	Lab (2)	-	-	-
15 Nov. 1922	C (1)	29.3	16.1	24.3
	NL (2)	-	15.8	14.5
6 Dec. 1923	Lab (1)	16.9	18.6	16.5
	C (2)	16.8	15.6	15.6
29 Oct. 1924	C (1)	23.7	20.9	6.9
	C (2)	22.8	19.8	5.9
30 May 1929	Lab (1)	20.3	24.0	15.0
	Lab (2)	19.8	20.9	-
27 Oct. 1931	C (1)	33.9	17.3	-
	C (2)	32.4	16.4	-
14 Nov. 1935	C (1)	29.0	21.4	-
	C (2)	28.2	21.4	-

Astley Bridge ward

Candidate	Party	Votes	%	Electors	Turnout	Gains
1919						
J. Hesketh	C	978	42.1	3,456	67.2	C from L
J. Redford	Lab	709	30.5			
W. Roscroft	L	634	27.3			
Total votes		2,321				
1920						
F. Robinson	C	1,618	66.5	3,533	68.8	-
J. Redford	Lab	814	33.5			
Total votes		2,432				
1921						
A. Dawson	C	1,194	47.4	3,544	71.0	-
S.R. Walsh	L	853	33.9			
J. Redford	Lab	471	18.7			
Total votes		2,518				
1922						
J. Hesketh*	C	Unopp.	-	3,557	-	-
1923						
F. Robinson*	C	Unopp.	-	3,542	-	-
1924						
A. Dawson*	C	1,483	69.8	3,589	59.2	-
R. Mather	Lab	641	30.2			
Total votes		2,124				
1925						
E.G.R. Lloyd*	C	Unopp.	-	3,658	-	-
1926						
J. Simms*	C	1,477	67.2	3,668	59.9	-
J. Leach	Lab	721	32.8			
Total votes		2,198				
1927						
A. Dawson*	C	1,302	55.5	3,766	62.3	-
T. Bolton	L	1,043	44.5			
Total votes		2,345				
1928						
E.G.R. Lloyd*	C	Unopp.	-	3,841	-	-

Astley Bridge ward *(continued)*

Candidate	Party	Votes	%	Electors	Turnout	Gains
1929						
Mrs E. Lawson	C	1,163	42.6	4,058	67.3	-
T. Higham	L	919	33.6			
W.M. Farrington	Lab	651	23.8			
Total votes		2,733				
1930						
G. Warburton*	L	1,469	50.0	4,106	71.5	-
C.R. Shaw	C	1,468	50.0			
Total votes		2,937				
1931						
C.R. Shaw	C	Unopp.	-	4,295	-	-
1932						
S. Wadsworth	C	Unopp.	-	4,302	-	-
1933						
E. Huck	L	Unopp.	-	4,789	-	-
1934						
C.R. Shaw*	C	Unopp.	-	4,978	-	-
1935						
S. Wadsworth*	C	1,963	73.9	5,145	51.6	-
A. Hall	Lab	694	26.1			
Total votes		2,657				
1936						
E. Huck*	C	Unopp.	-	5,286	-	-
1937						
C.R. Shaw*	C	1,676	59.4	5,464	51.6	-
S. Bentley	Lab	1,145	40.6			
Total votes		2,821				
1938						
A.W. Talbot	L	Unopp.	-	5,547	-	-

Overall Labour vote		**23.3%**		**Overall turnout**		**62.2%**

Bradford ward
(2 councillors elected each year)

Candidate	Party	Votes	%	Electors	Turnout	Gains
1919						
R.B. Heywood	Lab	2,247	32.8	6,895	51.9	Lab from C
G.F. Vickers	Lab	2,194	32.0			Lab from C
W. Hill	C	1,239	18.1			
J.A. Smethurst	C	1,174	17.1			
Total votes		6,854				
Total voters		3,576				
1920						
T. Halstead	Lab	2,061	27.5	6,916	56.2	Lab from C
J. Pearson	Lab	1,986	26.5			Lab from C
T. Gibbs	C	1,725	23.1			
J. Coppell	C	1,711	22.9			
Total votes		7,483				
Total voters		3,888				
1921						
F. Cheadle*	Lab	1,965	29.8	6,928	62.5	-
T. Gibbs	C	1,865	28.3			
H.H. Bell	Lab	1,792	27.2			
J. Hilton	L	963	14.6			
Total votes		6,585				
Total voters		4,327				
1922						
J.W. McDougall	C	2,350	38.7	7,009	59.4	C from Lab
H.H. Bell	Lab	1,899	31.2			
R. Heywood	Lab*	1,830	30.1			
Total votes		6,079				
Total voters		4,166				
1923						
J.A. Drinkwater	C	2,095	38.9	7,040	53.0	C from Lab
T. Halstead*	Lab	1,719	32.0			
J. Pearson*	Lab	1,566	29.1			
Total votes		5,380				
Total voters		3,728				

Bradford ward *(continued)*

Candidate	Party	Votes	%	Electors	Turnout	Gains
1924						
R. Heywood*	Lab	1,947	36.2	6,959	54.3	
J. Pearson	Lab	1,743	32.4			Lab from C
T. Gibbs*	C	1,682	31.3			
Total votes		5,372				
Total voters		3,782				
1925						
B. Robinson	Lab	2,305	28.6	6,994	59.2	
G. Thompson	Lab	2,211	27.4			Lab from C
J.W. McDougall*	C	1,823	22.6			
J.A. Lindley	C	1,728	21.4			
Total votes		8,067				
Total voters		4,141				
1926						
T. Halstead*	Lab	2,464	38.1	6,974	57.6	
Mrs E. Hailwood	Lab	2,427	37.5			Lab from C
J.A. Lindley*	C	1,583	24.5			
Total votes		6,474				
Total voters		4,017				
1927						
R. Heywood*	Lab	2,278	34.9	6,959	61.5	
W.E .Walker	C	2,156	33.0			C from Lab
J. Pearson*	Lab	2,091	32.0			
Total votes		6,525				
Total voters		4,279				
1928						
B. Robinson*	Lab	2,419	35.1	6,908	64.3	-
G. Thompson*	Lab	2,351	34.1			
J.W. McCann	C	2,124	30.8			
Total votes		6,894				
Total voters		4,442				
1929						
T. Halstead*	Lab	2,015	35.7	7,291	50.0	-
Mrs E. Hailwood*	Lab	1,945	34.4			
J.W. McCann	C	1,688	29.9			
Total votes		5,648				
Total voters		3,647				

Bradford ward *(continued)*

Candidate	Party	Votes	%	Electors	Turnout	Gains
1930						
A.B. Grealey*	Lab	Unopp.	-	7,100	-	-
A.W. Ainsworth*	C	Unopp.	-			
1931						
G. Thompson*	Lab	Unopp.	-	7,100	-	-
W.J. Knight	Lab	Unopp.	-			
1932						
J.W. McCann*	C	1,147	53.6	7,164	26.9	-
J. Pearson*	Lab	804	37.6			
J.W. Smith	Com	188				
Total votes		2,139				
Total voters		1,928				
1933						
A.B. Grealey*	Lab	1,871	29.0	7,266	46.0	
E.D. Jones	Lab	1,735	26.9			Lab from C
H. Harding*	C	1,431	22.2			
G. Unsworth	C	1,405	21.8			
Total votes		6,442				
Total voters		3,345				
1934						
P. Lowe	Lab	1,757	35.8	7,163	43.6	
J.W. Banks	Lab	1,757	35.8			Lab from C
W.J. Knight*	C	1,391	28.4			
Total votes		4,905				
Total voters		3,126				
1935						
H. Jones	Lab	2,012	36.1	7,120	50.2	
E. Clarke	Lab	1,985	35.6			Lab from C
J.W. McCann*	C	1,575	28.3			
Total votes		5,572				
Total voters		3,576				
1936						
F. Cheadle	Lab	Unopp.	-	7,079	-	-
A.B. Grealey*	Lab	Unopp.	-			

492

Bradford ward *(continued)*

Candidate	Party	Votes	%	Electors	Turnout	Gains
1937						
Dr H.N. Savage	C	2,131	36.9	6,988	55.5	C from Lab
P. Lowe*	Lab	1,846	32.0			
J.W. Banks*	Lab	1,794	31.1			
Total votes		5,771				
Total voters		3,875				
1938						
Mrs E. Savage	C	1,935	36.3	6,830	52.0	C from Lab
E. Clarke*	Lab	1,701	31.9			
H. Jones*	Lab	1,688	31.7			
Total votes		5,324				
Total voters		3,553				

Overall Labour vote   **63.5%**   **Overall turnout**   **53.1%**

Church ward
(2 councillors elected each year)

Candidate	Party	Votes	%	Electors	Turnout	Gains
1919						
R.E. Roberts*	C	1,007	29.3	3,172	56.0	-
W. Russell	C	960	27.9			
R. Kirk	L	769	22.4			
J.W. Sefton	L	701	20.4			
Total votes		3,437				
Total voters		1,775				
1920						
A. Hamer*	C	1,145	35.7	3,234	63.6	-
R. Kenyon*	C	1,115	34.8			
R. Kirk	L	945	29.5			
Total votes		3,205				
Total voters		2,058				
1921						
R. Kirk*	L	1,196	27.4	3,270	70.2	-
R. Morris	C	1,128	25.9			
W. Sykes	C	1,073	24.6			
T. Bolton	L	963	22.1			
Total votes		4,360				
Total voters		2,296				
1922						
W.Russell*	C	1,211	37.0	3,287	62.2	-
R.E. Roberts*	C	1,181	36.1			
T. Bolton	L	882	26.9			
Total votes		3,274				
Total voters		2,043				
1923						
F.R. Mallett*	C	1,320	39.1	3,331	62.6	-
R. Kenyon*	C	1,152	34.1			
T. Bolton	L	907	26.8			
Total votes		3,379				
Total voters		2,086				
1924						
R. Kirk*	L	Unopp.	-	3,292	-	-
R. Morris*	C	Unopp.	-			

Church ward *(continued)*

Candidate	Party	Votes	%	Electors	Turnout	Gains
1925						
R.E. Roberts*	C	Unopp.	-	3,339	-	-
W. Russell*	C	Unopp.	-			
1926						
F.R. Mallett*	C	1,197	38.7	3,333	57.9	-
R. Kenyon*	C	1,094	35.3			
T.Bolton	L	806	26.0			
Total votes		3,097				
Total voters		1,931				
1927						
J.S. Lomax	C	1,117	35.1	3,387	59.8	C from L
R. Morris*	C	1,108	34.9			
R. Kirk*	L	953	30.0			
Total votes		3,178				
Total voters		2,024				
1928						
R.E. Roberts*	C	1,179	37.9	3,330	63.3	-
W. Russell*	C	1,178	37.8			
W. Howard	L	757	24.3			
Total votes		3,114				
Total voters		2,109				
1929						
F.R. Mallett*	C	Unopp.	-	3,513	-	-
J.R. Massey*	C	Unopp.	-			
1930						
J.S. Lomax*	C	Unopp.	-	3,362	-	-
R. Morris*	C	Unopp.	-			
1931						
J. Shuttleworth	C	Unopp.	-	3,377	-	-
R.E. Roberts*	C	Unopp.	-			
1932						
J.R. Massey*	C	Unopp.	-	3,356	-	-
F.R. Mallett*	C	Unopp.	-			

Church ward *(continued)*

Candidate	Party	Votes	%	Electors	Turnout	Gains
1933						
J.S. Lomax*	C	Unopp.	-	3,366	-	-
R. Morris*	C	Unopp.	-			
1934						
J. Shuttleworth*	C	1,022	42.3	3,375	41.7	-
F. Berry*	C	1,018	42.1			
J. Paulden	Lab	378	15.6			
Total votes		2,418				
Total voters		1,408				
1935						
D. Hewitson	C	1,442	42.7	3,351	54.2	-
A. Crossley*	C	1,311	38.8			
F. Haslam	Lab	367	10.9			
J. Paulden	Lab	256	7.6			
Total votes		3,376				
Total voters		1,815				
1936						
J.S. Lomax*	C	1,156	47.3	3,298	39.9	-
T.E. Marsden*	C	1,136	46.5			
J. Paulden	Lab	153	6.3			
Total votes		2,445				
Total voters		1,317				
1937						
F. Berry*	C	Unopp.	-	3,342	-	-
J. Shuttleworth*	C	Unopp.	-			
1938						
A. Crossley*	C	Unopp.	-	3,331	-	-
D.G. Hewitson*	C	Unopp.	-			

Overall Labour vote		**3.1%**			**Overall turnout**	**57.4%**

Darcy Lever-cum-Breightmet ward

Candidate	Party	Votes	%	Electors	Turnout	Gains
1919						
H. Twisse	C	Unopp.	-	1,617	-	-
1920						
G. Glaister*	C	959	70.4	1,660	82.0	-
T.T. Ramsden	Lab	403	29.6			
Total votes		1,362				
1921						
J. Lund	C	Unopp.	-	1,691	-	-
1922						
N.B. Stringfellow	C	Unopp.	-	1,713	-	-
1923						
T. Glaister*	C	Unopp.	-	1,724	-	-
1924						
J.H. Lund*	C	Unopp.	-	1,766	-	-
1925						
H. Twisse*	C	Unopp.	-	1,847	-	-
1926						
T. Glaister*	C	941	65.8	1,974	72.5	-
Ms G.F. Cain	Lab	490	34.2			
Total votes		1,431				
1927						
H.D. Scowcroft	C	950	63.2	2,219	67.7	-
J. Taylor	Lab	553	36.8			
Total votes		1,503				
1928						
H. Twisse*	C	1,039	63.5	2,366	69.1	-
T. Connor	Lab	596	36.5			
Total votes		1,635				
1929						
T. Glaister*	C	1,041	63.5	2,585	63.4	-
T. Connor	Lab	598	36.5			
Total votes		1,639				

Darcy Lever-cum-Breightmet ward *(continued)*

Candidate	Party	Votes	%	Electors	Turnout	Gains
1930						
H.D. Scowcroft*	C	Unopp.	-	2,577	-	-
1931						
J.J. Haslam	C	Unopp.	-	2,670	-	-
1932						
J.C. Cort	C	Unopp.	-	2,670	-	-
1933						
H.D. Scowcroft*	C	Unopp.	-	2,702	-	-
1934						
J.J. Haslam*	C	Unopp.	-	2,986	-	-
1935						
J.C. Cort*	C	1,303	69.0	3,480	54.3	
J. Williams	Lab	586	31.0			
Total votes		1,889				
1936						
H.D. Scowcroft*	C	Unopp.	-	3,672	-	-
1937						
J.J. Haslam*	C	1,129	83.3	3,739	36.3	
Mrs M.E. Dawson	Lab	227	16.7			
Total votes		1,356				
1938						
W. Collinson*	C	Unopp.	-	3,801	-	-
Overall Labour vote		**31.9%**			**Overall turnout**	**60.0%**

Deane-cum-Lostock ward

Candidate	Party	Votes	%	Electors	Turnout	Gains
1919						
G. Dootson*	C	561	53.7	1,634	64.0	-
J.H. Beardmore	Lab	264	25.3			
W. Holden	L	220	21.1			
Total votes		1,045				
1920						
J.R Horrocks*	C	798	72.3	1,646	67.0	-
J. Ford	Lab	305	27.7			
Total votes		1,103				
1921						
J.H. Taylor	C	Unopp.	-	1,673	-	-
1922						
R. Platt	C	952	72.2	1,816	72.6	-
W. Holden	L	366	27.8			
Total votes		1,318				
1923						
J.R. Horrocks*	C	Unopp.	-	2,000	-	-
1924						
J.H. Taylor*	C	Unopp.	-	2,035	-	-
1925						
R. Platt*	C	Unopp.	-	2,067	-	-
1926						
W.W. Tong	C	Unopp.	-	2,114	-	-
1927						
J. Bleakley*	C	Unopp.	-	2,081	-	-
1928						
R. Platt*	C	1,088	67.9	2,167	74.0	-
Mrs M. Reid	L	515	32.1			
Total votes		1,603				
1929						
W.W. Tong*	C	1,063	75.2	2,284	61.9	-
Mrs M. Reid	L	351	24.8			
Total votes		1,414				

Deane-cum-Lostock ward *(continued)*

Candidate	Party	Votes	%	Electors	Turnout	Gains
1930						
J. Bleakley*	C	Unopp.	-	2,268	-	-
1931						
R Platt*	C	Unopp.	-	2,728	-	-
1932						
W. Tong*	C	Unopp.	-	2,742	-	-
1933						
J. Bleakley*	C	Unopp.	-	2,756	-	-
1934						
R. Platt*	C	1,125	68.5	2,783	59.0	-
L.L.W. Litting	Lab	518	31.5			
Total votes		1,643				
1935						
W.W. Tong*	C	Unopp.	-	2,892	-	-
1936						
J. Bleakley*	C	Unopp.	-	2,891	-	-
1937						
R. Platt*	C	1,054	65.1	2,865	56.5	-
Mrs M. Reid	L	564	34.9			
Total votes		1,618				
1938						
W.W. Tong*	C	1,198	67.7	3,048	58.1	-
Mrs M. Reid	L	572	32.3			
Total votes		1,770				

Overall Labour vote		**9.4%**		**Overall turnout**	**63.1%**

Derby ward
(2 councillors elected each year)

Candidate	Party	Votes	%	Electors	Turnout	Gains
1919						
J.H. Hampson	Lab	1,285	30.5	6,758	49.0	Lab from C
A.T. Peters*	L	1,024	24.3			
J. Kearsley*	C	1,007	23.9			
Mrs J. Taylor	WCA	502	11.9			
Mrs M. Higgins	Coop	400	9.5			
Total votes		4,218				
Total voters		3,309				
1920						
J.F. Wright	C	2,140	31.4	6,770	63.2	
J. Kearsley	C	1,888	27.7			C from Lab
E. Bates	Lab	1,652	24.3			
J. Wilcocks	L	1,127	16.6			
Total votes		6,807				
Total voters		4,277				
1921						
J. Jackson*	C	1,900	24.3	6,866	64.4	
J.A. Taylor	C	1,813	23.2			C from L
E. Bates	Lab	1,675	21.4			
H.A. Duncan	Lab	1,470	18.8			
J. Wilcox	L	969	12.4			
Total votes		7,827				
Total voters		4,425				
1922						
E. Bates	Lab	1,843	23.6	6,795	67.1	
Mrs J. Taylor	C	1,594	20.4			C from L
J.H. Hampson*	Lab	1,484	19.0			
W. Heap	C	1,471	18.9			
A.T. Peters*	L	1,408	18.1			
Total votes		7,800				
Total voters		4,559				
1923						
J.W. Makant*	C	1,959	28.2	6,802	66.0	
A.T. Peters	L	1,789	25.7			L from C
J. Kearsley*	C	1,703	24.5			
G. Rickman	Lab	1,499	21.6			
Total votes		6,950				
Total voters		4,492				

Derby ward *(continued)*

Candidate	Party	Votes	%	Electors	Turnout	Gains
1924						
J. Jackson*	C	1,893	28.4	6,808	64.5	
R. Demaine	Lab	1,882	28.2			Lab from C
W. Heap	C	1,714	25.7			
C. Brady	L	1,184	17.7			
Total votes		6,673				
Total voters		4,392				
1925						
S. Davies	Lab	2,188	28.5	6,820	57.6	
H. Eastwood	Lab	2,177	28.4			Lab from C
W. Openshaw	C	1,706	22.3			
A. Lambourn	C	1,594	20.8			
Total votes		7,665				
Total voters		3,926				
1926						
J.W .Allanson	Lab	2,173	37.4	6,757	64.3	Lab from L
J.W. Makant*	C	1,621	27.9			
A.T. Peters*	L	1,328	22.9			
Ms A.F. Mawson	WCA	683	11.8			
Total votes		5,805				
Total voters		4,342				
1927						
R. Demaine*	Lab	2,247	37.2	6,824	57.4	
J.H. Hampson	Lab	1,986	32.9			Lab from C
J. Jackson*	C	1,805	29.9			
Total votes		6,038				
Total voters		3,918				
1928						
H. Eastwood*	Lab	2,552	35.3	6,866	67.6	-
S. Davies*	Lab	2,543	35.2			
E.T. Vizard	C	2,126	29.4			
Total votes		7,221				
Total voters		4,641				

Derby ward *(continued)*

Candidate	Party	Votes	%	Electors	Turnout	Gains
1929						
J.W. Makant*	C	2,142	36.5	7,257	54.3	-
J.W. Allanson*	Lab	1,942	33.1			
T.H. Lee	Lab	1,781	30.4			
Total votes		5,865				
Total voters		3,942				
1930						
T.P. Dunning	C	1,867	37.5	7,439	46.2	C from Lab
J.H. Hampson*	Lab	1,617	32.4			
T. Lee	Lab	1,501	30.1			
Total votes		4,985				
Total voters		3,438				
1931						
H. Eastwood*	Lab	1,440	46.4	7,330	21.6	-
S. Davies*	Lab	1,411	45.5			
R. Ramsden	Nuwm	134	4.3			
R. Anderson	Nuwm	118	3.8			
Total votes		3,103				
Total voters		1,583				
1932						
J. Jackson*	C	1,413	39.3	7,271	36.3	-
T.H. Lee*	Lab	1,178	32.8			
C. Brady	Ind	607	16.9			
C. Walsh	Com	207	5.8			
J. Derbyshire	Com	187	5.2			
Total votes		3,592				
Total voters		2,641				
1933						
J.H. Hampson*	Lab	1,484	37.4	7,239	35.0	
A.J. Penston	Lab	1,405	35.4			Lab from C
T.P. Dunning*	C	1,076	27.1			
Total votes		3,965				
Total voters		2,534				
1934						
H. Eastwood*	Lab	Unopp.		7,318	-	-
S. Davies*	Lab	Unopp.				

Derby ward *(continued)*

Candidate	Party	Votes	%	Electors	Turnout	Gains
1935						
Dr H.W. Taylor	C	1,863	35.1	7,323	49.7	
T.H. Lee*	Lab	1,729	32.5			
R. Tankard	Lab	1,722	32.4			
Total votes		5,314				
Total voters		3,643				
1936						
H. Ratcliffe	C	1,614	36.4	7,097	42.2	C from Lab
R. Tankard*	Lab	1,460	32.9			
A.J. Penston*	Lab	1,358	30.6			
Total votes		4,432				
Total voters		2,992				
1937						
A. Brownlow	C	1,339	27.3	7,100	44.1	C from Lab
H. Eastwood*	Lab	1,289	26.2			
J. Hitchen	Lab	1,170	23.8			
J. Rushton	L	1,114	22.7			
Total votes		4,912				
Total voters		3,130				
1938						
Dr H.W. Taylor*	C	1,787	32.3	7,242	48.3	-
J. Gradwell	Lab	1,383	25.0			
T.H. Lee*	Lab	1,238	22.4			
J. Rushton	L	1,124	20.3			
Total votes		5,532				
Total voters		3,496				

Overall Labour vote	**49.0%**		**Overall turnout**	**52.2%**

East ward
(2 councillors elected each year)

Candidate	Party	Votes	%	Electors	Turnout	Gains
1919						
A. Potts	Lab	1,084	35.3	2,966	67.2	-
J. Entwhistle	C	658	21.4			
Mrs S.M. Mothersole	WCA	439	14.3			
T.H. Dawson	C	438	14.2			
R. Westwood	L	243	7.9			
J. Seed	Coop	212	6.9			
Total votes		3,074				
Total voters		1,993				
1920						
W.H. Grime	Lab	860	28.4	3,002	61.7	Lab from C
D. Heap	C	732	24.2			
J.H. Bromilow	C	630	20.8			
Mrs S.M. Mothersole	WCA	420	13.9			
W.J. Greenhalgh	L	389	12.8			
Total votes		3,031				
Total voters		1,851				
1921						
Dr H.C.D. Cross	C	1,548	42.1	3,035	68.1	C from L
T. Caless*	C	1,287	35.0			
J. Murphy	Lab	553	15.0			
P. Meagher	Lab	292	7.9			
Total votes		3,680				
Total voters		2,067				
1922						
H.A. Johnson	Lab	995	35.0	3,021	63.6	Lab from C
J. Entwhistle*	C	978	34.4			
J.H. Bromilow*	C	866	30.5			
Total votes		2,839				
Total voters		1,922				
1923						
J. Clayton	Lab	879	34.7	3,022	55.7	Lab from C
D. Heap*	C	856	33.8			
W.H. Grime*	C	801	31.6			
Total votes		2,536				
Total voters		1,684				

East ward *(continued)*

Candidate	Party	Votes	%	Electors	Turnout	Gains
1924						
Dr H.C.D. Cross*	C	1,065	33.9	2,999	67.3	-
T. Caless*	C	1,041	33.2			
T. Little	Lab	1,031	32.9			
Total votes		3,137				
Total voters		2,017				
1925						
T. Little	Lab	1,237	31.2	3,034	67.8	Lab from C
H.A. Duncan*	Lab	1,154	29.1			
J. Entwhistle*	C	810	20.4			
W.H. Grime	C	761	19.2			
Total votes		3,962				
Total voters		2,058				
1926						
J. Clayton*	Lab	1,162	36.4	3,058	66.5	
A. Haines	Lab	1,121	35.1			Lab from C
D. Heap*	C	909	28.5			
Total votes		3,192				
Total voters		2,034				
1927						
R. Birchby	Lab	1,005	26.7	3,112	62.9	Lab from C
F.V. Gilliver	Lab	941	25.0			Lab from C
Dr H.C.D. Cross*	C	926	24.6			
T. Caless*	C	896	23.8			
Total votes		3,768				
Total voters		1,959				
1928						
T. Little*	Lab	1,264	29.8	3,095	69.8	-
Mrs F.C. Cain	Lab	1,198	28.3			
D. Heap	C	898	21.2			
T. Caless	C	875	20.7			
Total votes		4,235				
Total voters		2,160				

East ward *(continued)*

Candidate	Party	Votes	%	Electors	Turnout	Gains
1929						
J. Clayton*	Lab	1,107	26.9	3,357	62.3	-
W. Geere*	Lab	1,074	26.1			
W.T. Settle	C	969	23.5			
F. Sharples	C	969	23.5			
Total votes		4,119				
Total voters		2,092				
1930						
D. Heap	C	1,011	27.4	3,261	58.1	C from Lab
T.P. Longworth	C	993	26.9			C from Lab
R. Birchby*	Lab	846	22.9			
F.V. Gilliver*	Lab	845	22.9			
Total votes		3,695				
Total voters		1,896				
1931						
W.M. Farrington*	Lab	756	46.6	3,190	27.2	-
J. Kilcommins*	Lab	746	46.0			
Mrs A.E. Rose	Com	121	7.5			
Total votes		1,623				
Total voters		867				
1932						
W. Geere*	Lab	705	40.9	3,118	28.1	-
T. Connor*	Lab	688	39.9			
Mrs A.E. Rose	Com	175	10.2			
T. Lomax	Com	155	9.0			
Total votes		1,723				
Total voters		877				
1933						
E. Faulkner	Lab	784	25.7	3,047	51.8	Lab from C
T. McCall	Lab	778	25.5			Lab from C
T.P. Longworth*	C	702	23.0			
D. Heap*	C	674	22.1			
P.N. Harker	Com	113	3.7			
Total votes		3,051				
Total voters		1,579				

East ward *(continued)*

Candidate	Party	Votes	%	Electors	Turnout	Gains
1934						
J. Kilcommins*	Lab	915	36.5	2,998	52.4	-
W.M. Farrington*	Lab	908	36.2			
T.C. Longworth	C	682	27.2			
Total votes		2,505				
Total voters		1,571				
1935						
Mrs E.A. Ashmore	Lab	926	28.1	2,936	58.2	-
T. Connor*	Lab	909	27.6			
D. Heap	C	744	22.6			
J. Grimshaw	C	720	21.8			
Total votes		3,299				
Total voters		1,708				
1936						
P. Norris	C	803	27.3	2,829	53.1	C from Lab
J.T. Harfield	C	738	25.1			C from Lab
E. Faulkner*	Lab	714	24.2			
T. McCall*	Lab	690	23.4			
Total votes		2,945				
Total voters		1,503				
1937						
J.L. Howard	C	981	28.8	2,752	63.4	C from Lab
J. Grimshaw	C	872	25.6			C from Lab
J. Kilcommins*	Lab	789	23.2			
W.M. Farrington*	Lab	763	22.4			
Total votes		3,405				
Total voters		1,744				
1938						
Mrs E.A. Ashmore*	Lab	885	27.5	2,637	62.6	
J.S. Walmsley	C	782	24.3			C from Lab
T. Connor*	Lab	778	24.1			
F. Sharples	C	778	24.1			
Total votes		3,223				
Total voters		1,650				
Overall Labour vote		**49.2%**			**Overall turnout**	**58.3%**

Exchange ward
(2 councillors elected each year)

Candidate	Party	Votes	%	Electors	Turnout	Gains
1919						
J.E. Sheppard	L	Unopp.		1,588	-	-
M. Lundy	L	Unopp.				
1920						
R.J. Berry	C	444	33.3	1,642	60.0	C from L
G. O'Neil	Lab	323	24.2			Lab from L
J. Sherry*	L	322	24.1			
W.R. Lythgoe*	L	246	18.4			
Total votes		1,335				
Total voters		985				
1921						
T.E. Norbury	C	544	37.5	1,637	60.5	C from L
T. White	Lab	257	17.7			Lab from L
J. Ford	Lab	242	16.7			
W. Nicholson	L	240	16.6			
W. Kearns*	L	166				
Total votes		1,449				
Total voters		990				
1922						
H. Rushton	Lab	365	26.4	1,623	59.3	Lab from L
H. Steele	L	363	26.3			
P. Walsh	C	353	25.6			
J. Parkinson	C	299	21.7			
Total votes		1,380				
Total voters		963				
1923						
R.J. Berry*	C	453	38.1	1,631	59.4	-
G. O'Neil*	Lab	382	32.1			
F. Bentley	L	354	29.8			
Total votes		1,189				
Total voters		968				
1924						
T.E. Norbury*	C	468	39.6	1,599	56.9	
F. Bentley	L	374	31.6			L from Lab
T. White*	Lab	340	28.8			
Total votes		1,182				
Total voters		910				

Exchange ward *(continued)*

Candidate	Party	Votes	%	Electors	Turnout	Gains
1925						
H. Rushton*	Lab	460	35.9	1,600	61.0	
J.A. Smethurst	C	449	35.0			C from L
H. Steele*	L	373	29.1			
Total votes		1,282				
Total voters		976				
1926						
R.J. Berry	C	Unopp.		1,624	-	-
G. O'Neil	Lab	Unopp.				
1927						
T. White	Lab	433	35.4	1,633	58.4	Lab from L
J.E. Norbury*	C	423	34.6			
F. Bentley*	L	367	30.0			
Total votes		1,223				
Total voters		953				
1928						
H. Rushton*	Lab	506	39.7	1,624	65.6	-
J. Kearsley	C	449	35.2			
H. Mason	L	320	25.1			
Total votes		1,275				
Total voters		1,066				
1929						
G. O'Neil*	Lab	421	47.3	1,659	46.5	-
R.J. Berry*	C	334	37.5			
H. Steel	L	135	15.2			
Total votes		890				
Total voters		772				
1930						
T. White*	Lab	Unopp.		1,320	-	-
T.E. Norbury*	C	Unopp.				
1931						
J. Murphy	Lab	Unopp.		1,294	-	-
J. Kearsley*	C	Unopp.				
1932						
O. Keenan	Lab	Unopp.		1,281	-	-
R.J. Berry*	C	Unopp.				

Exchange ward *(continued)*

Candidate	Party	Votes	%	Electors	Turnout	Gains
1933						
J. Stobbs*	Lab	370	36.1	1,211	64.9	-
G.F. Duggan*	C	366	35.7			
G. Brown	L	289	28.2			
Total votes		1,025				
Total voters		786				
1934						
J. Murphy*	Lab	Unopp.		1,204	-	-
J. Kearsley*	C	Unopp.				
1935						
O. Keenan*	Lab	310	39.0	1,127	68.9	-
R.J. Berry*	C	266	33.5			
W.J. Maine	L	218	27.5			
Total votes		794				
Total voters		776				
1936						
J. Parkes	Ind	432	30.3	1,130	65.6	Ind from Lab
E. Walkden	Ind	380	26.7			Ind from Lab
M. Lundy*	Lab	319	22.4			
J.S. Stobbs*	Lab	293	20.6			
Total votes		1,424				
Total voters		741				
1937						
W. Bleakley	C	310	37.9	1,041	60.1	
H. Barker	Ind	256	31.3			Ind from Lab
J. Murphy*	Lab	253	30.9			
Total votes		819				
Total voters		626				
1938						
F. Hartley	L	292	37.4	869	65.4	L from Lab
R. Aspinall*	C	252	32.3			
O. Keenan*	Lab	237	30.3			
Total votes		781				
Total voters		568				

Overall Labour vote		**34.4%**		**Overall turnout**		**60.3%**

Great Lever ward

Candidate	Party	Votes	%	Electors	Turnout	Gains
1919						
A. Wilson*	L	1,057	37.9	4,950	56.3	-
T.R. Boardman	C	876	31.4			
Mrs M.E. Farrington	Coop	853	30.6			
Total votes		2,786				
1920						
N. Crowther	C	1,815	60.1	4,946	61.1	-
Mrs M.E. Farrington	Coop	1,207	39.9			
Total votes		3,022				
1921						
R. Greenhalgh	C	1,588	49.3	5,024	64.1	-
H.G. Cooper	Lab	966	30.0			
D. Winkley	L	667	20.7			
Total votes		3,221				
1922						
R. Carter	C	Unopp.		5,208	-	-
1923						
J. Coppell	C	Unopp.		5,380	-	-
1924						
R. Greenhalgh*	C	Unopp.		5,378	-	-
1925						
R. Carter*	C	1,496	54.2	5,523	50.0	-
D. Winkley	L	1,263	45.8			
Total votes		2,759				
1926						
D. Winkley	L	1,396	51.9	5,619	47.9	L from C
A.W.G. Holland	C	1,293	48.1			
Total votes		2,689				
1927						
R. Greenhalgh*	C	1,782	60.0	5,751	51.7	-
B.F. Davies	Lab	1,190	40.0			
Total votes		2,972				

Great Lever ward *(continued)*

Candidate	Party	Votes	%	Electors	Turnout	Gains
1928						
W.A. Hindley	L	1,834	52.1	6,061	58.1	L from C
R. Carter*	C	1,685	47.9			
Total votes		3,519				
1929						
D. Winkley*	L	1,613	50.4	6,433	49.8	-
G.B. Slater	C	1,588	49.6			
Total votes		3,201				
1930						
R. Greenhalgh*	C	1,694	56.4	6,629	45.3	-
J. West	L	1,310	43.6			
Total votes		3,004				
1931						
W.A. Hindley*	L	Unopp.		6,683	-	-
1932						
D. Winkley*	L	Unopp.		6,625	-	-
1933						
R. Greenhalgh*	C	Unopp.		6,688	-	-
1934						
H. Harding	C	1,631	46.6	6,883	50.9	C from L
W. Hadley	Lab	946	27.0			
W.A. Hindley*	L	924	26.4			
Total votes		3,501				
1935						
S. Howarth	C	1,476	39.9	7,047	52.5	C from L
D. Winkley*	L	1,337	36.1			
J.E. Hassett	Lab	890	24.0			
Total votes		3,703				
1936						
D. Winkley	L	1,720	52.4	7,144	45.9	L from C
F. Young	C	1,562	47.6			
Total votes		3,282				

Great Lever ward *(continued)*

Candidate	Party	Votes	%	Electors	Turnout	Gains
1937						
H. Harding*	C	2,177	61.0	7,234	49.3	-
W. Hadley	Lab	1,389	39.0			
Total votes		3,566				
1938						
S. Howarth*	C	Unopp.		7,413	-	-

Overall Labour vote	**13.1%**	**Overall turnout**	**52.0%**

Halliwell ward
(2 councillors elected each year)

Candidate	Party	Votes	%	Electors	Turnout	Gains
1919						
J.P. Taylor*	L	2,018	28.2	8,715	63.2	
B. Kirkman	Lab	1,830	25.6			Lab from C
G. Sykes	C	1,790	25.0			
Mrs B.L. Agnew	WCA	1,144	16.0			
T. Greenlees	Coop	379	5.3			
Total votes		7,161				
Total voters		5,512				
1920						
G. Sykes	C	2,364	25.9	8,852	65.9	-
T.Y. Ritson*	L	2,028	22.2			
E. Wardle	C	1,744	19.1			
Mrs B.L. Agnew	WCA	1,561	17.1			
J. Edge	Lab	1,429	15.7			
Total votes		9,126				
Total voters		5,833				
1921						
E. Wardle	C	2,797	31.3	8,973	71.2	C from L
T.E Flitcroft	L	2,702	30.2			
W. Bowcock*	L	1,918	21.4			
J. Orr	Lab	1,529	17.1			
Total votes		8,946				
Total voters		6,391				
1922						
J.P. Taylor*	L	2,263	32.8	8,987	65.7	
G.B. Row	C	2,413	34.9			C from Lab
B. Kirkman*	Lab	2,233	32.3			
Total votes		6,909				
Total voters		5,907				
1923						
G. Sykes*	C	2,524	38.8	8,968	63.5	-
W. Bowcock	L	2,051	31.5			
J.H. Hampson	Lab	1,928	29.6			
Total votes		6,503				
Total voters		5,691				

Halliwell ward *(continued)*

Candidate	Party	Votes	%	Electors	Turnout	Gains
1924						
T.E. Flitcroft*	Ind L	2,663	41.2	8,997	61.4	-
J.T. Greenhalgh	C	2,126	32.9			
J.H. Hampson	Lab	1,668	25.8			
Total votes		6,457				
Total voters		5,527				
1925						
J.P. Taylor*	L	2,124	33.8	8,980	61.2	-
G.B. Row*	C	2,094	33.4			
J.H. Hampson	Lab	2,058	32.8			
Total votes		6,276				
Total voters		5,500				
1926						
B. Kirkman	Lab	2,451	39.4	8,946	59.4	Lab from L
G. Sykes*	C	1,990	32.0			
H. Steele*	L	1,772	28.5			
Total votes		6,213				
Total voters		5,315				
1927						
Sir T.E. Flitcroft*	L	2,538	39.1	8,958	60.1	-
J.T. Greenhalgh*	C	1,983	30.6			
J.R. Holland	Lab	1,962	30.3			
Total votes		6,483				
Total voters		5,388				
1928						
J.P. Taylor*	L	2,407	26.7	8,915	68.0	
J.R. Holland	Lab	2,339	25.9			Lab from C
G.B. Row*	C	2,229	24.7			
J. Isherwood	Lab	2,052	22.7			
Total votes		9,027				
Total voters		6,059				
1929						
B. Kirkman*	Lab	2,227	28.3	9,543	56.0	-
G. Sykes*	C	2,082	26.5			
J. Isherwood	Lab	1,922	24.4			
F. Bentley	L	1,636	20.8			
Total votes		7,867				
Total voters		5,348				

Halliwell ward *(continued)*

Candidate	Party	Votes	%	Electors	Turnout	Gains
1930						
Sir T.E. Flitcroft*	Ind L	2,248	39.3	9,609	51.5	-
J.T. Greenhalgh*	C	2,016	35.2			
W.M. Farrington	Lab	1,460	25.5			
Total votes		5,724				
Total voters		4,948				
1931						
F. Bentley	L	Unopp.		9,585	-	-
J.R. Holland*	Lab	Unopp.				
1932						
G. Sykes*	C	2,044	46.4	9,573	24.8	-
G.W. Hudson*	C	1,761	40.0			
C. Bentley	Com	310	7.0			
J.E. Holland	Com	291	6.6			
Total votes		4,406				
Total voters		2,374				
1933						
K. Edge*	L	2,611	42.0	9,522	54.5	
J. Vickers	Lab	2,044	32.9			Lab from C
J.T. Greenhalgh*	C	1,561	25.1			
Total votes		6,216				
Total voters		5,188				
1934						
H. Crossley	C	2,366	29.6	9,524	56.6	C from Lab
F. Bentley*	L	2,021	25.3			
E. Clarke*	Lab	1,841	23.0			
Mrs C. Leece	Lab	1,770	22.1			
Total votes		7,998				
Total voters		5,392				
1935						
T.S Barlow	L	2,753	40.3	9,548	58.9	L from C
T.P. Longworth	C	2,096	30.7			
Mrs C. Leece	Lab	1,985	29.0			
Total votes		6,834				
Total voters		5,626				

Halliwell ward *(continued)*

Candidate	Party	Votes	%	Electors	Turnout	Gains
1936						
K. Edge*	L	2,845	39.4	9,517	58.7	-
J. Vickers*	Lab	2,436	33.8			
D. Heap	C	1,932	26.8			
Total votes		7,213				
Total voters		5,586				
1937						
H. Crossley*	C	2,499	38.0	9,500	57.0	-
F. Bentley*	L	2,186	33.2			
Mrs C. Leece	Lab	1,898	28.8			
Total votes		6,583				
Total voters		5,414				
1938						
T.S. Barlow*	L	2,509	39.1	9,492	52.9	-
T.P Longworth*	C	2,137	33.3			
Mrs C. Leece	Lab	1,772	27.6			
Total votes		6,418				
Total voters		5,021				

Overall Labour vote   **31.0%**   **Overall turnout**   **58.3%**

Heaton ward

Candidate	Party	Votes	%	Electors	Turnout	Gains
1919						
P. Higson*	C	513	52.4	1,330	73.6	-
C.H. Beswick	L	466	47.6			
Total votes		979				
1920						
J.W. Thompson*	C	556	53.1	1,339	78.2	-
C.H. Beswick	L	491	46.9			
Total votes		1,047				
1921						
S. Bellis	C	539	50.3	1,319	81.3	C from L
Ms E. Taylor	L	533	49.7			
Total votes		1,072				
1922						
C.H. Beswick*	L	561	50.6	1,342	82.6	-
E.A. Walker	C	548	49.4			
Total votes		1,109				
1923						
Ms E. Taylor*	L	579	50.3	1,412	81.4	-
F.S. Hampson	C	571	49.7			
Total votes		1,150				
1924						
S. Bellis*	C	Unopp.		1,489	-	-
1925						
C.H. Beswick*	L	Unopp.		1,568	-	-
1926						
J.W. Lomax	C	701	54.5	1,644	78.2	C from L
Ms E. Taylor*	L	585	45.5			
Total votes		1,286				
1927						
S. Bellis*	C	Unopp.		1,853	-	-
1928						
C. H.Beswick*	L	835	52.6	1,927	82.4	-
J. Lomax	C	752	47.4			
Total votes		1,587				

Heaton ward *(continued)*

Candidate	Party	Votes	%	Electors	Turnout	Gains
1929						
J.W. Lomax*	C	785	54.5	2,084	69.1	-
Mrs E. Hodkinson	L	655	45.5			
Total votes		1,440				
1930						
A. Pilling	L	776	50.9	2,204	69.2	L from C
E. Moss	C	749	49.1			
Total votes		1,525				
1931						
C.H. Beswick*	L	Unopp.		2,160	-	-
1932						
J.W. Lomax*	C	Unopp.		2,208	-	-
1933						
A. Pilling*	L	873	57.0	2,265	67.6	-
E. Moss	C	658	43.0			
Total votes		1,531				
1934						
C.H. Beswick*	L	Unopp.		2,373	-	-
1935						
A. Hollas	L	859	48.8	2,470	71.3	L from C
J.W. Lomax*	C	858	48.7			
T. Bentley	Lab	45	2.6			
Total votes		1,762				
1936						
A. Pilling*	L	Unopp.		2,582	-	-
1937						
J.W. Lomax*	C	Unopp.		2,640	-	-
1938						
A. Hollas*	L	Unopp.		2,713	-	-
Overall Labour vote		**0.3%**		**Overall turnout**		**74.9%**

Hulton ward

Candidate	Party	Votes	%	Electors	Turnout	Gains
1919						
T. Entwhistle	C	1,243	62.2	2,703	73.9	-
E. Bates	Lab	754	37.8			
Total votes		1,997				
1920						
A. Crook	C	1,053	52.4	2,712	74.0	-
F. Battle	L	955	47.6			
Total votes		2,008				
1921						
R.C. Smith	C	1,132	48.5	2,727	85.7	-
F. Battle	L	728	31.2			
W. Geere	Lab	476	20.4			
Total votes		2,336				
1922						
F. Battle	L	1,153	52.3	2,663	82.7	L from C
W. Dickinson	C	1,050	47.7			
Total votes		2,203				
1923						
A. Crook*	C	1,185	57.1	2,730	76.0	-
J. Walker	L	890	42.9			
Total votes		2,075				
1924						
A. Burns	C	1,179	58.6	2,804	71.8	-
J.T. Geere	Lab	833	41.4			
Total votes		2,012				
1925						
C. Lindley	C	1,203	52.6	2,936	77.9	C from L
F. Battle*	L	1,084	47.4			
Total votes		2,287				
1926						
A. Crook*	C	1,266	55.7	2,976	76.4	-
J.T. Geere	Lab	1,007	44.3			
Total votes		2,273				

Hulton ward *(continued)*

Candidate	Party	Votes	%	Electors	Turnout	Gains
1927						
F. Battle	L	1,153	50.5	2,998	76.2	L from C
A. Burns*	C	1,131	49.5			
Total votes		2,284				
1928						
C. Lindley*	C	1,326	55.6	3,019	79.0	-
W. Geere	Lab	1,059	44.4			
Total votes		2,385				
1929						
A. Crook*	C	1,318	61.2	3,208	67.1	-
A. Corkhill	Lab	836	38.8			
Total votes		2,154				
1930						
W. Dickinson	C	1,215	51.2	3,256	72.82	C from L
F. Battle*	L	1,156	48.8			
Total votes		2,371				
1931						
Mrs E. Crook	C	Unopp.		3,266	-	-
1932						
A. Crook*	C	Unopp.		3,265	-	-
1933						
H. Crompton	L	1,203	57.9	3,277	63.4	L from C
W. Dickinson*	C	875	42.1			
Total votes		2,078				
1934						
F. Battle	L	1,328	60.1	3,420	64.6	L from C
H. Ashurst	C	881	39.9			
Total votes		2,209				
1935						
A. Crook*	C	1,252	52.8	3,537	67.0	-
W.C. Thomasson	L	1,118	47.2			
Total votes		2,370				
1936						
H. Crompton*	L	Unopp.		3,699	-	-

Hulton ward *(continued)*

Candidate	Party	Votes	%	Electors	Turnout	Gains
1937						
F. Battle*	L	1,516	64.8	3,752	62.4	-
M. Smith	C	825	35.2			
Total votes		2,341				
1938						
W.C. Thomasson	L	1,101	40.3	3,868	70.7	L from C
C.L. Hurst	C	969	35.4			
J.B. O'Hara	Lab	664	24.3			
Total votes		2,734				

Overall Labour vote   **14.8%**   **Overall turnout**   **72.5%**

North ward

Candidate	Party	Votes	%	Electors	Turnout	Gains
1919						
H. Warburton	L	Unopp.		2,771	-	-
1920						
E. Collinge	Lab	942	43.9	2,834	75.7	Lab from C
F.W. Morris	C	620	28.9			
G. Warburton	L	582	27.1			
Total votes		2,144				
1921						
P. Knott*	C	1,161	57.3	2,842	71.3	-
W. Houson	Lab	866	42.7			
Total votes		2,027				
1922						
H. Warburton*	L	1,009	55.1	2,869	63.8	-
Mrs A.E. Dowling	Lab	822	44.9			
Total votes		1,831				
1923						
E. Collinge*	Lab	1,171	58.0	2,852	70.8	-
J. Jackson	C	847	42.0			
Total votes		2,018				
1924						
P. Knott*	C	1,068	53.2	2,846	70.5	-
Mrs A.E. Dowling	Lab	939	46.8			
Total votes		2,007				
1925						
Mrs A.E. Dowling	Lab	1,046	52.4	2,867	69.6	Lab from L
A. Hamer*	L	950	47.6			
Total votes		1,996				
1926						
E. Collinge*	Lab	1,275	63.5	2,853	70.4	-
R. Booth	C	733	36.5			
Total votes		2,008				
1927						
P. Knott*	C	1,056	50.9	2,920	71.0	-
J. Leach	Lab	1,017	49.1			
Total votes		2,073				

North ward *(continued)*

Candidate	Party	Votes	%	Electors	Turnout	Gains
1928						
Mrs A.E. Dowling*	Lab	1,055	47.3	2,895	77.0	-
S. Crossley	C	628	28.2			
A. Hamer	L	546	24.5			
Total votes		2,229				
1929						
R.H. Patterson*	Lab	976	60.9	3,033	52.9	-
E. Eccleshare	L	627	39.1			
Total votes		1,603				
1930						
E. Eccleshare*	L	1,057	56.2	3,043	61.8	-
A. Dearden	Lab	824	43.8			
Total votes		1,881				
1931						
Mrs A.E. Dowling*	Lab	Unopp.		2,998	-	-
1932						
R.H. Patterson*	Lab	825	90.6	2,976	30.6	-
W.H. Wainwright	Com	86	9.4			
Total votes		911				
1933						
A. Booth	Lab	873	53.4	2,982	54.8	Lab from L
E. Eccleshare*	L	762	46.6			
Total votes		1,635				
1934						
Mrs A.E. Dowling*	Lab	943	57.7	2,951	55.3	-
F.H. York	L	690	42.3			
Total votes		1,633				
1935						
R.H. Patterson*	Lab	918	51.2	2,966	60.4	-
J.W. Chadwick	C	874	48.8			
Total votes		1,792				
1936						
A. Booth*	Lab	1,091	54.6	2,924	68.4	-
Mrs S.J. Chadwick	C	908	45.4			
Total votes		1,999				

North ward *(continued)*

Candidate	Party	Votes	%	Electors	Turnout	Gains
1937						
J.W. Chadwick*	C	1,174	53.3	2,924	75.3	-
B. Vickers	Lab	1,028	46.7			
Total votes		2,202				
1938						
B. Vickers	Lab	1,081	53.1	2,936	69.3	-
Mrs S.J. Chadwick	C	955	46.9			
Total votes		2,036				
Overall Labour vote		**52.0%**			**Overall turnout**	**64.8%**

Rumworth ward

Candidate	Party	Votes	%	Electors	Turnout	Gains
1919						
W. Grundy	C	1,089	39.9	3,749	72.7	C from L
J. Booth	L	943	34.6			
C.P. Unsworth	Ind	559	20.5			
Mrs C. Darby	Coop	136	5.0			
Total votes		2,727				
1920						
J.W. Keighley*	C	1,059	35.3	3,886	77.2	-
C.P. Unsworth	Lab	997	33.2			
J. Booth	L	945	31.5			
Total votes		3,001				
1921						
C.P. Unsworth	Lab	1,296	41.3	3,933	79.8	Lab from L
E. Hirst	C	1,209	38.5			
P. Sutcliffe	L	635	20.2			
Total votes		3,140				
1922						
J.E. Parkinson	C	1,123	38.0	3,930	75.3	-
G. Thompson	Lab	1,035	35.0			
W. Dore	L	801	27.1			
Total votes		2,959				
1923						
J.W. Keighley*	C	1,284	41.7	3,901	79.0	-
G. Thompson	Lab	1,236	40.1			
W. Dore	L	560	18.2			
Total votes		3,080				
1924						
J. Booth	L	1,643	55.3	3,917	75.8	L from Lab
C.P. Unsworth*	Lab	1,326	44.7			
Total votes		2,969				
1925						
J.E. Parkinson*	C	1,481	52.0	3,948	72.1	-
C.P. Unsworth	Lab	1,366	48.0			
Total votes		2,847				

Rumworth ward *(continued)*

Candidate	Party	Votes	%	Electors	Turnout	Gains
1926						
C.P. Unsworth	Lab	1,539	53.9	3,929	72.7	Lab from C
J. Johnson	C	1,317	46.1			
Total votes		2,856				
1927						
J. Booth*	L	1,339	50.1	3,975	67.3	-
W. Geere	Lab	1,336	49.9			
Total votes		2,675				
1928						
J. Parkinson*	C	1,714	51.3	4,044	82.7	-
E. Bates	Lab	1,630	48.7			
Total votes		3,344				
1929						
E. Bates	Lab	1,434	54.3	4,319	61.2	-
W. Heap	C	1,208	45.7			
Total votes		2,642				
1930						
H. Ashurst	C	1,088	35.7	4,321	70.4	C from L
E.Y. Kitchen	Lab	1,055	34.7			
J. Booth*	L	901	29.6			
Total votes		3,044				
1931						
J. Parkinson*	C	2,191	94.4	4,349	53.3	-
C. Walsh	Com	129	5.6			
Total votes		2,320				
1932						
E. Bates*	Lab	Unopp.		4,339	-	-
1933						
P. Flanagan	Lab	1,278	51.7	4,306	57.4	Lab from C
H. Ashurst*	C	1,192	48.3			
Total votes		2,470				

Rumworth ward *(continued)*

Candidate	Party	Votes	%	Electors	Turnout	Gains
1934						
J. Parkinson*	C	1,693	49.7	4,315	79.0	-
J.R. Pryce	Lab	963	28.3			
Dr Jean Marshall	L	752	22.1			
Total votes		3,408				
1935						
Dr Jean Marshall	L	1,384	53.5	4,353	59.4	L from Lab
E. Bates*	Lab	1,201	46.5			
Total votes		2,585				
1936						
P. Flanagan*	Lab	1,215	51.1	4,403	54.1	-
J. Booth	L	1,165	48.9			
Total votes		2,380				
1937						
T.P. Dunning*	C	1,551	55.6	4,482	62.3	-
J. Hale	Lab	1,241	44.4			
Total votes		2,792				
1938						
Dr Jean Marshall*	L	1,293	52.0	4,585	54.2	-
J.W. Banks	Lab	1,194	48.0			
Total votes		2,487				

Overall Labour vote **39.7%**   **Overall turnout** **68.3%**

Smithills ward

Candidate	Party	Votes	%	Electors	Turnout	Gains
1919						
J.H. Edge	L	1,493	67.6	3,422	64.6	-
F.S. Hampson	C	717	32.4			
Total votes		2,210				
1920						
J. Lonsdale	L	1,445	53.9	3,430	78.1	L from C
P. Edge	C	1,234	46.1			
Total votes		2,679				
1921						
Mrs B.L. Agnew	WCA	1,269	53.9	3,439	68.5	WCA from L
R. Fairhurst*	L	1,086	46.1			
Total votes		2,355				
1922						
P. Edge	C	1,466	55.3	3,426	77.4	C from L
F. Bentley	L	1,187	44.7			
Total votes		2,653				
1923						
G. Bullock	C	1,341	52.3	3,429	74.7	C from L
W. Bentley*	L	1,221	47.7			
Total votes		2,562				
1924						
Mrs B.L. Agnew*	WCA	Unopp.		3,508	-	-
1925						
R. Fairhust	L	1,458	52.5	3,745	74.2	L from C
Ms E. Lomax	C	1,320	47.5			
Total votes		2,778				
1926						
J. Brown	L	1,479	52.5	4,110	68.5	L from C
G. Fell	C	1,336	47.5			
Total votes		2,815				
1927						
T. Profit	C	1,591	52.4	4,477	67.9	C from WCA
Mrs B.L. Agnew*	WCA	1,447	47.6			
Total votes		3,038				

Smithills ward *(continued)*

Candidate	Party	Votes	%	Electors	Turnout	Gains
1928						
R. Fairhurst*	L	2,073	56.3	4,673	78.9	-
J. Morris	C	1,612	43.7			
Total votes		3,685				
1929						
B.A.P. Dobson	C	1,767	50.8	5,142	67.7	C from L
J.E. Hayes	L	1,712	49.2			
Total votes		3,479				
1930						
T. Profit*	C	2,069	54.3	5,421	70.3	-
J.E. Hayes	L	1,744	45.7			
Total votes		3,813				
1931						
R. Fairhurst*	L	Unopp.		5,431	-	-
1932						
B.A.P. Dobson*	C	Unopp.		5,635	-	-
1933						
T. Profit*	C	Unopp.		5,922	-	-
1934						
R. Fairhurst*	L	Unopp.		6,743	-	-
1935						
A. Lawson	C	1,846	40.8	6,888	65.7	-
R. Kirk	L	1,747	38.6			
R. Daulby	Lab	930	20.6			
Total votes		4,523				
1936						
R. Kirk	L	2,050	49.7	7,037	58.7	L from C
G.L. Barnes	C	1,539	37.3			
Mrs M.E. Dawson	Lab	539	13.1			
Total votes		4,128				

Smithills ward *(continued)*

Candidate	Party	Votes	%	Electors	Turnout	Gains
1937						
A. Farnworth	C	1,881	45.6	7,156	57.7	C from L
J. Brown*	L	1,582	38.3			
W. Gleave	Lab	663	16.1			
Total votes		4,126				
1938						
T. Bent	L	1,927	52.5	7,393	49.7	L from C
A. Lawson*	C	1,746	47.5			
Total votes		3,673				

Overall Labour vote   **4.4%**   **Overall turnout**   **66.3%**

Tonge ward

Candidate	Party	Votes	%	Electors	Turnout	Gains
1919						
L. Shaw	Lab	1,474	50.3	4,200	69.8	Lab from C
W.R. Rostron*	C	1,132	38.6			
N. Ramsden	L	327	11.1			
Total votes		2,933				
1920						
J.J. Haslam	C	1,573	49.5	4,224	75.3	C from L
W.T. Holt*	L	965	30.3			
T.V. Gilliver	Lab	642	20.2			
Total votes		3,180				
1921						
W. Bradley	C	1,673	51.2	4,235	77.2	-
C Wells	L	822	25.1			
W. Whiteside	Lab	775	23.7			
Total votes		3,270				
1922						
C. Smith	C	1,663	50.7	4,311	76.1	C from Lab
L. Shaw*	Lab	1,618	49.3			
Total votes		3,281				
1923						
L. Shaw	Lab	1,931	53.3	4,662	77.7	Lab from C
J.J. Haslam*	C	1,691	46.7			
Total votes		3,622				
1924						
W. Bradley*	C	1,921	59.9	4,715	68.1	-
A. Haines	Lab	1,288	40.1			
Total votes		3,209				
1925						
C. Smith*	C	1,806	54.0	4,812	69.5	-
A. Haines	Lab	1,538	46.0			
Total votes		3,344				
1926						
J. Entwhistle	C	1,602	49.2	4,919	66.2	C from Lab
F. Hart	Lab	1,189	36.5			
W.P. Crankshaw	L	464	14.3			
Total votes		3,255				

Tonge ward *(continued)*

Candidate	Party	Votes	%	Electors	Turnout	Gains
1927						
W. Bradley*	C	1,666	48.8	5,145	66.3	-
G.W. Jones	Lab	1,261	37.0			
W.P. Crankshaw	L	484	14.2			
Total votes		3,411				
1928						
C. Smith*	C	1,876	51.4	5,670	64.4	-
G.W. Jones	Lab	1,776	48.6			
Total votes		3,652				
1929						
J. Entwhistle*	C	1,955	54.7	6,207	57.6	-
W. Whiteside	Lab	1,618	45.3			
Total votes		3,573				
1930						
W. Bradley*	C	Unopp.		6,533	-	-
1931						
C. Smith*	C	Unopp.		6,676	-	-
1932						
T. Bailey	C	Unopp.		7,552	-	-
1933						
W. Bradley*	C	1,846	52.8	7,604	46.0	-
W. Robertson	Lab	1,651	47.2			
Total votes		3,497				
1934						
C. Smith*	C	1,886	51.4	7,664	47.8	-
W. Robertson	Lab	1,781	48.6			
Total votes		3,667				
1935						
Dr E.P. Johnson	C	2,494	57.1	7,730	56.5	-
W. Whiteside	Lab	1,875	42.9			
Total votes		4,369				

Tonge ward *(continued)*

Candidate	Party	Votes	%	Electors	Turnout	Gains
1936						
W. Bradley*	C	2,179	54.3	7,927	50.6	-
W. Whiteside	Lab	1,831	45.7			
Total votes		4,010				
1937						
C. Smith*	C	1,926	51.1	8,124	46.4	-
S. Lomax	Lab	1,842	48.9			
Total votes		3,768				
1938						
A. Ainscow	Lab	2,207	52.8	8,192	51.0	Lab from C
E. Taylor	C	1,969	47.2			
Total votes		4,176				

Overall Labour vote   **43.7%**   **Overall turnout**   **60.0%**

West ward
(2 councillors elected each year)

Candidate	Party	Votes	%	Electors	Turnout	Gains
1919						
S. Lomax*	Lab	2,050	30.2	9,683	52.9	-
J. Taylor*	L	1,856	27.3			
G.B. Row	C	1,537	22.6			
Mrs S.E. Jones	WCA	1,349	19.9			
Total votes		6,792				
Total voters		5,122				
1920						
G. Crowther	C	2,383	30.7	9,655	58.1	C from L
H. Bommer*	L	2,029	26.1			
J.F. Steele*	L	1,780	22.9			
Mrs Rose	Lab	1,580	20.3			
Total votes		7,772				
Total voters		5,605				
1921						
J.F. Steele	L	2,626	23.4	9,821	62.6	-
A.E. Holt*	L	2,091	18.6			
T. Jones	C	1,976	17.6			
Mrs F. Knott	C	1,799	16.0			
J.T. Agnew	Lab	1,367				
J. Whittam	Lab	1,359				
Total votes		11,218				
Total voters		6,150				
1922						
W. Whitehead	Co C	2,206	22.4	9,928	61.8	C from Lab
J.A. Swainson	Co L	2,141	21.8			
S. Lomax*	Lab	2,049	20.8			
J. Clayton	Lab	1,726	17.6			
Miss M.E. Taylor	L	1,707	17.4			
R.E. Fogg	L	1,549	15.8			
Total votes		9,829				
Total voters		6,134				

West ward *(continued)*

Candidate	Party	Votes	%	Electors	Turnout	Gains
1923						
G. Crowther*	C	2,282	26.8	9,930	58.3	-
H. Bommer*	L	2,225	26.2			
S. Lomax	Lab	2,076	24.4			
Miss M.E. Taylor	L	1,921	22.6			
Total votes		8,504				
Total voters		5,791				
1924						
J.F. Steele*	L	2,759	37.3	9,936	48.5	-
A.E. Holt*	L	2,450	33.2			
G.J. Briggs	Lab	2,181	29.5			
Total votes		7,390				
Total voters		4,815				
1925						
Dr R.D. Mothersole	L	2,694	25.9	10,000	62.8	
S. Lomax	Lab	2,660	25.6			Lab from C
W. Whitehead*	C	2,522	24.3			
A.B. Grealey	Lab	2,512	24.2			
Total votes		10,388				
Total voters		6,279				
1926						
A.B. Grealey	Lab	2,817	27.5	10,027	61.7	Lab from C
P. Gleaves	Lab	2,801	27.4			Lab from L
W. Whitehead*	C	2,520	24.6			
H. Bommer*	L	2,099	20.5			
Total votes		10,237				
Total voters		6,191				
1927						
G.J. Briggs	Lab	2,494	24.2	10,103	52.1	Lab from L
J.M. Ashworth	Lab	2,230	21.6			Lab from L
Mrs S.J. Chadwick	C	2,056	19.9			
A. Worthington	C	2,051	19.9			
T. Whittle	L	1,490	14.4			
Total votes		10,321				
Total voters		5,263				

West ward *(continued)*

Candidate	Party	Votes	%	Electors	Turnout	Gains
1928						
S. Lomax*	Lab	2,843	28.3	10,020	63.0	
L. Shaw	Lab	2,603	25.9			Lab from L
Dr R.D. Mothersole*	L	2,229	22.2			
J. Whittle	C	2,212	22.0			
H. Shaw	Com	149	1.5			
Total votes		10,036				
Total voters		6,310				
1929						
Dr R.D. Mothersole	L	2,655	38.6	10,682	44.3	L from Lab
P. Gleaves*	Lab	2,133	31.0			
A.B. Grealey*	Lab	2,092	30.4			
Total votes		6,880				
Total voters		4,729				
1930						
J.N. Ashworth*	Lab	Unopp.	-	10,518	-	-
D. Gray*	L	Unopp.	-			
1931						
G.L. Barnes*	C	2,328	50.4	10,621	28.0	-
Mrs H. Wright*	Lab	1,996	43.2			
H. Shaw	Com	293	6.3			
Total votes		4,617				
Total voters		2,973				
1932						
Dr R.D. Mothersole*	L	2,532	51.9	10,613	32.7	-
P. Gleaves*	Lab	1,603	32.8			
H. Shaw	Com	427	8.7			
A.T. Rostron	Com	321	6.6			
Total votes		4,883				
Total voters		3,466				
1933						
D. Grey*	L	2,177	38.1	10,577	32.5	
W. Simpson	L	1,745	30.5			L from Lab
Mrs B. Jones*	Lab	1,352	23.7			
H. Shaw	Com	271	4.7			
J.W. Warbrick	Com	171	3.0			
Total votes		5,716				
Total voters		3,435				

West ward *(continued)*

Candidate	Party	Votes	%	Electors	Turnout	Gains
1934						
Mrs H. Wright*	Lab	2,057	27.5	10,466	36.8	
W.J. Allen	Lab	1,898	25.4			Lab from C
G.L. Barnes*	C	1,677	22.4			
F. Wright	C	1,665	22.2			
Mrs C. Bentley	Ind	190	2.5			
Total votes		7,487				
Total voters		3,854				
1935						
Dr R.D. Mothersole*	L	2,153	27.9	10,543	45.3	-
P. Gleaves*	Lab	1,936	25.1			
J.H. Shaw	C	1,771	22.9			
J.M. Fagan	Lab	1,754	22.7			
M. Cunningham	Ind	104	1.3			
Total votes		7,718				
Total voters		4,780				
1936						
D. Grey*	L	2,099	26.8	10,468	43.0	C from L
J.H. Shaw	C	1,727	22.0			
J.M. Fagan	Lab	1,430	18.2			
R. Daulby	Lab	1,390	17.7			
W. Simpson*	L	1,192	15.2			
Total votes		7,838				
Total voters		4,502				
1937						
T. Holt	C	2,421	28.5	10,355	51.3	C from Lab
Mrs H. Wright*	Lab	2,282	26.9			
W.J. Allen*	Lab	2,159	25.5			
S. Porter	L	1,618	19.1			
Total votes		8,480				
Total voters		5,315				

West ward *(continued)*

Candidate	Party	Votes	%	Electors	Turnout	Gains
1938						
W. Crumblehume*	C	2,709	33.5	10,383	49.3	-
Dr R.D. Mothersole*	L	1,968	24.3			
J. Kilcommins	Lab	1,731	21.4			
W.J. Allen	Lab	1,684	20.8			
Total votes		8,092				
Total voters		5,117				

Overall Labour vote		**40.4%**		**Overall turnout**		**49.4%**

NINE
Bootle

BOOTLE

Bootle was situated on the banks of the River Mersey to the north of its much larger neighbour Liverpool. It had developed as a separate county borough from 1868, but in economic and social terms it had become an extension of the larger city well before the inter-war years. One study described Bootle as 'an industrial offshoot of Liverpool at all times indistinguishable from it to the ordinary traveller'. Another investigation found that it had 'no clear line of division from Liverpool', and that as a borough it was hard for Bootle to 'maintain its own life and identity'.[1] Along its waterfront were situated the Brocklebank, Langton, Alexandra, Hornby and Gladstone docks, which then formed the northernmost outposts of the port of Liverpool. 'The northern wall of the Gladstone dock is the northern boundary of the Bootle foreshore.'[2] Adjacent to the docks lived a community that was very similar in its occupational structure, religion and culture to the docklands community of the north end of Liverpool. There was some nineteenth-century deprecation of Bootle by its Liverpool neighbours. The borough was characterised as 'Brutal Bootle' – 'where the bugs wear clogs', but in reality the differences between north Liverpool and Bootle were insignificant.[3] Despite being administratively separate, therefore, Bootle had more of the characteristics of a suburb than of a distinct and complete conurbation in its own right. Like a suburb, it had a concentration of economic function that skewed its occupational structure unusually.

Bootle had a population of just over 75,000 in 1931, being the fifty-ninth largest county borough. The economic functions of the borough were dominated by the docks and associated industries and services. Almost 30 per cent of its male workforce was employed in the water and dock transport categories of the 1931 industry tables, a higher proportion than in any other county borough, and almost double the proportion in Liverpool. Liverpool was no less a maritime city, of course, but it had a wider variety of occupations overall, as befitted a large, regionally significant centre of population. The higher concentration of dock-related workers in Bootle reflected its subordinate role within the Liverpool conurbation as a whole, then. Apart from work on the docks and on board ships, there were few other sources of large-scale employment for men. Processing of goods coming in through the port, especially foodstuffs, was the only significant factory-based work, and road and rail transport away from the dockside provided some jobs. There was some employment in the metal and engineering sector, mostly concentrated in small-scale shipbuilding and repairing and marine engineering. There was also a substantial commerce and finance sector, much being accounted for by clerical work connected with dock and shipping companies. In a maritime economy like this, women's employment opportunities were restricted. The food and commerce sectors were significant areas of female

[1]   Freeman, T.W., *The Conurbations of Great Britain*, (Manchester, 1959), p.108; Caradog Jones, D., *Social Survey of Merseyside*, (Liverpool, 1934), vol. 1, p. 37.
[2]   Caradog Jones, *Social Survey of Merseyside*, vol. 1, p.56.
[3]   Quoted in Waller, P.J., *Democracy and Sectarianism: A Political and Social History of Liverpool 1868–1939,* (Liverpool, 1981), p. 94.

work, but by far the most important was domestic service. The total female workforce as recorded in the 1931 industrial tables amounted to only a quarter of the total female population of the borough. Finally, it should be obvious that Bootle was a strongly working-class borough, as borne out by the fact that its proportion of managerial and self-employed workers was the fifth lowest of all the county boroughs. It is significant that West Ham on the eastern edge of London also ranked low in this regard, another borough that formed part of a much larger conurbation, and with a similarly distorted occupational structure.

The spatial distribution of Bootle's population and its political effects can be summarised briefly. As might be expected, the three wards along the river, Mersey, Knowsley and Linacre, were the most proletarian, reflected in their relatively high persons per room figures. Over the whole period these were also the strongest Labour wards, although not in the early and mid-1920s, for reasons which will become clear below. By contrast, the two inland wards of Derby and, especially, Stanley were relatively more white-collar and petit bourgeois in nature, with a sprinkling of skilled working-class inhabitants particularly evident in Derby. These were clearly the main anti-Labour wards in the borough. Orrell ward was harder to categorise, in part because it was the ward where most change and population growth took place in this period. Snaking out along the boundary with Liverpool, it was the only suburban ward in the borough, but it was also the site of most of the council-house developments in this period. In total 2,647 council houses were constructed between 1919 and 1938. A small proportion were situated in the Marsh Lane area straddling Linacre and Knowsley wards, but the majority of them were in the southern end of Orrell ward in the vicinity of the cemetery. Interestingly, over 600 council houses were built for sale, and these along with 1,160 privately-constructed houses were mostly in Orrell.[4] Orrell was also the only ward to be significantly affected by the boundary changes that took place in 1928, being extended outwards to include land and housing on the outskirts of the borough, and also taking in a predominantly working-class corner of the north of Derby ward. The net effect of all these changes was to make Orrell a predominantly anti-Labour ward, but to a varying degree over the inter-war period.

The other striking feature of Bootle's population was its ethnic and religious origin. The north end docks of Liverpool were an enclave of Catholic employment, as opposed to the southern docks which were predominantly Protestant. The boundary between the two boroughs was of no significance here in that Bootle's docklands were simply a continuation of the Catholic north end. Bootle's Catholic working class, mostly originating from Irish migration in the nineteenth century, was if anything of greater preponderance than that of Liverpool. There was a Protestant working class situated some distance inland from the docks mainly in Derby ward, composed mainly of such occupational groups as carters, railway workers and engineers, as was the case in north

---

[4]   Social Science Department, University of Liverpool, *Handbook of Social Statistics Relating to Merseyside*, (Liverpool, 1938), p. 29; County Borough of Bootle, *Municipal Government Centenary, County Borough of Bootle: Merseyside Celebrations, February 17 to February 24*, (Bootle, 1935), pp. 14–16.

Liverpool. But without the counterbalance of the south end docks, Bootle was even more Catholic than Liverpool. Proving this by way of the census reports is difficult, as religious affiliation was not covered in the census forms. The proportion of the population which was born in Ireland can be identified, but this is by no means a perfect indicator of Catholicism. Some Irish-born would not have been Catholic, and some Catholics would not have been born in Ireland. Second and succeeding generations of Irish migrants would have been especially significant in the latter category. Moreover, Bootle was only covered as a separate borough for the first time in the census of 1901. Nevertheless, the comparative figures for that year are revealing. Irish-born made up 10 per cent of the total population of Bootle, compared with 6.7 per cent in Liverpool, and 4.8 per cent in Birkenhead just across the river Mersey. Even more significant, of the 5,857 Irish-born in Bootle, 3,372, or 58 per cent, were men. This gender imbalance was not found amongst the Irish-born of Liverpool or Birkenhead, nor amongst the general population. What this suggests is that there were many young, male recent migrants in Bootle, in turn indicative of close social and cultural ties with Ireland still being maintained.

As has been well documented, the Catholic–Protestant divide in the Liverpool working class had a profound impact on local politics.[5] It was no less significant in Bootle. A description of events as a mixed crowd of Labour and Conservative supporters gathered to await the results of the 1921 elections gives some idea of the tenor of municipal politics in the borough at the time:

> Liveliness was caused by the approach of a drum and fife band, accompanied by boys waving Union Jacks. The tune was one that was played with zest by a procession on the Twelfth of July, and though the singing accompaniment was omitted the emphatic beat of the drums more than made up for it. Soon after, a section of the crowd outside the Town Hall started to sing the 'Soldiers' Song', for which they were applauded. They then broke into the dirge-like 'Wrap the green flag round me, boys', which gained even louder applause. Thus encouraged they became a little more cheerful – and defiant – with 'All round my hat I wear the tri-colour ribbon', ending up with 'God save Ireland'. They seemed to find special pleasure in treating the police force to this serenade.[6]

In the early 1920s in particular, with the backdrop of war and partition taking place across the Irish Sea, religious sectarianism seemed to dominate Bootle politics. The Conservative party, especially in its guise of the Conservative Working Men's Association (CWMA), represented Protestantism, as was made

---

[5]   See for example, Davies, S., *Liverpool Labour: Social and Political Influences on the Development of the Labour Party in Liverpool, 1900–1939*, (Keele, 1996); Smith, J., 'Labour tradition in Liverpool and Glasgow', *History Workshop*, 17, (Spring 1984); Smith, J., 'Class, skill and sectarianism in Glasgow and Liverpool', in Morris, R.J., (ed.), *Class, Power and Social Structure in British Nineteenth-Century Towns*, (Leicester, 1986).
[6]   *Bootle Times*, 4 Nov. 1921.

abundantly clear on numerous occasions. When Conservatives met in the Constitutional Club after their losses in the 1919 elections, an alderman exhorted the audience to 'defend the honour of our country and our borough', only for a lady to interject: 'And our religion'. A defeated Conservative candidate later appealed: 'Protestants would have to pull themselves together and work'. The following year after an improved showing in the elections they met in the Masonic Hall, where it was agreed that 'the splendid meeting held ... on the previous Friday evening by the Orange Lodges had also been of very great assistance. (Hear, Hear)'. One of the Conservative candidates avowed: 'He had not introduced religion into the fight, although, as most of them knew, he was a Protestant, and a man who put religion first, and politics second'. At a Conservative election meeting before the poll, the Anglican vicar of St Leonard's had advised his parishioners to vote for the Conservative candidate as he was a 'churchman'. The following year in 1921, after good results for the Conservatives again, a councillor asserted that as long as the voters of Bootle continued to support them, 'the keys of the Town Hall would remain safely wrapped in the Union Jack'.[7] Conversely, the Labour party was presented by some as the natural home of the Catholic working class of Bootle. After the 1920 poll the Labour meeting was addressed by a Catholic priest who 'was received with vociferous cheering', and who congratulated the electors of the predominantly Catholic dockside Mersey ward for returning two Labour councillors. Another speaker said 'they wanted religious teaching in all schools of the borough', and the meeting closed with a 'rousing chorus' of 'God save Ireland'. A year later a councillor found it hard to understand how the voters of Mersey ward could have turned against Labour. He was mystified not only 'socially, and politically', but also 'spiritually'. A Tory opponent expressed the view that 'whenever they fought Mersey ward, they had to reckon on fighting religion, and not politics'.[8]

However, the apparently straightforward correlation between religion and party that characterised these years needs some qualification. Before 1914 the association of Toryism with Protestantism had been plain. The MP for Bootle between 1885 and 1911 for instance, Thomas Sandys, was a prominent Orangeman. But Catholic sympathies before 1914 lay with Liberalism, and not the Labour party. Unlike Liverpool with its lofty patrician Liberalism, there had been no necessity to put forward Irish Nationalist candidates as Bootle Liberalism was deep-rooted enough to represent Catholic interests. The transport strike of 1911 and widespread unionisation of the dock labour force first placed strains on this relationship, and the events in Ireland between the Easter Rising of 1916 and Partition in 1922 further undermined it. So Labour in the early 1920s began to be the new repository of the hopes of some of Bootle's Catholic working class, partly for industrial and partly for nationalistic reasons. Yet this was an inherently unstable position.

At the parliamentary level Liberalism still remained strong, with Liberal victories in the 1922 and 1923 general elections. In municipal politics, Mersey ward, which had been triumphantly captured by Labour in 1919 and 1920, was

---

[7] *Bootle Times*, 7 Nov. 1919, 29 Oct. 1920, 5 Nov. 1920, 4 Nov. 1921.
[8] *Bootle Times*, 5 Nov. 1920, 4 Nov. 1921.

lost without a fight in 1922 to Independents of a decidedly Catholic nature. Others who had switched to Labour returned to Liberalism. The two successful Labour candidates in Mersey ward in 1920 reappeared as Liberals in 1923, and heavily defeated their new Labour rivals. This was partly a reflection of growing contradictions between the Catholic church and the Labour party. The secular and socialistic aims of Labour nationally sat uneasily with the views of the church hierarchy, and at a local level this had become increasingly problematic by 1923. The Catholic Archbishop of Liverpool in that year declared:

> We hope that the Catholic vote in the November elections will be cast for Catholic candidates wherever they are nominated, in all parts of the Archdiocese ... no political party can be trusted to safeguard Catholic interests so loyally as we can safeguard our own.[9]

His message was taken up in Liverpool with the development of a Catholic party, but his flock in Bootle also responded. In 1924, while Liberals again defeated Labour in Mersey ward, candidates for the Irish Democratic League contested the other two dockside wards of Knowsley and Linacre. They came a poor third behind the Tories and Labour in both cases, and one of the Labour candidates claimed that this demonstrated that 'two parties are not required to represent the working class', and that 'the Irish people had shown that the Labour party represented the interests of the workers irrespective of nationalities'. His hope that the election had 'cleared the air on that issue' was unfounded though as hostilities continued, and a Liberal councillor hit the nail on the head when he bemoaned the fact that 'the anti-Tory elements in the town are divided'.[10] A year later a Catholic priest stood in Mersey ward and topped the poll, while the Labour candidates came bottom. By contrast, in Knowsley ward the sitting Labour councillor had been deselected by the party for his pro-Catholic views. He stood instead as 'Independent Labour', but was soundly beaten by the official Labour nominee, who proclaimed that 'they had not watered down their policy, but had fought the issue on a full Socialist programme'.[11]

It was only from 1926 that Labour began to command the allegiance of the majority of the Catholic working class in Bootle. Labour gained two seats in the dockside wards in 1926, all six contested in 1927, and five more in 1928, and by then held all eighteen seats in these wards. This was in some measure a mirror of national trends, but it was to a greater degree the culmination of the process of struggle between the Bootle Labour party and its politico-religious rivals. It was also very similar to a corresponding series of events taking place in Liverpool over the same period.[12] In both cases, it should be stressed that the association between Labour and its Catholic supporters was by no means automatic, and was

---

[9] *The Liverpool Catholic Parishioner*, vol. VI, no. 11, Nov. 1923.

[10] *Bootle Times*, 7 Nov. 1924.

[11] *Bootle Times*, 6 Nov. 1925.

[12] On this, see Davies, S., ' "A stormy political career": P.J. Kelly and Irish Nationalist and Labour politics in Liverpool, 1891–1936', *Transactions of the Historic Society of Lancashire and Cheshire*, no. 148, (1999, forthcoming).

only achieved by winning voters away from a more overtly sectarian politics. In Liverpool, this resulted in a Catholic caucus within the Labour party vying for control with other important wings of the party. In Bootle, Catholic influence on the party was much more dominant, simply because the Catholic element within the working class was more significant. The effects were to be long-lasting. By 1934 the council Labour group was led by a prominent Catholic, Simon Mahon. One of his sons, Simon jun., was to be Labour MP for Bootle for many years after 1955. Another son, Peter, was Labour MP for Preston South between 1964 and 1970, and stood as a Labour and Anti-Abortion candidate in a 1971 by-election for the Liverpool Scotland constituency. He lost to the official Labour nominee, and was expelled from the party, completing a long political exodus by joining the Liberals in 1973.

Control of Bootle council very much reflected the inter-war shifts in political support that have been outlined here. Despite Labour's gains in 1919 and 1920, the large pre-war Tory majority was still retained. Labour had held only two seats compared to the Tories' twenty-five and the Liberals' fifteen after the last contested elections before the war in 1913.[13] Conservative control was also strengthened when for municipal purposes a Tory–Liberal 'Constitutional' alliance was formed in 1920 and 1921. When Liberal independence was reasserted in 1922, Labour emerged as the second party in the council. However, the subsequent politico-religious conflict saw the Labour party dip to its lowest point in 1924. Only when Labour had secured the support of the Catholic working-class wards from 1926 did it begin to improve its position on the council markedly. After the sweeping gains of 1928, the Labour celebrations were enlivened by a soloist singing 'My day shall come to rule this world', but his optimism was premature.[14] Labour had a majority of the councillors by this point, but it was severely under-represented on the aldermanic bench. Labour offered an agreement with the other parties that aldermen should be elected in future on the basis of proportionality, but this was rejected by the Conservatives.[15] By 1929 Labour had drawn level with the Tories overall, but Conservative control was maintained by the support of the remaining handful of Liberals and Independents. Labour's chance to seize power was expected to come in 1930 when a number of aldermen were due for re-election, but the national trend was reflected locally in four Labour losses, and the opportunity was missed.

The importance of the aldermanic system had by this time been fully recognised by all sides in Bootle, and it remained a crucial factor throughout the 1930s. Labour made a rapid recovery in 1932 and 1933, and with the support of one Co-operative party member had a majority of the councillors when six aldermen came up for re-election after the 1933 elections.[16] Labour replaced all six with their own aldermen, and took control of Bootle council for the first time. Three years later Labour lost four seats, so Labour had eighteen councillors to the Conservatives' seventeen. Six aldermen were due for re-election, and the sole

---

[13] *Liverpool Daily Post*, 3 Nov. 1913.
[14] *Bootle Times*, 2 Nov. 1928.
[15] *Bootle Times*, 1 Nov. 1929.
[16] *Manchester Guardian*, 2 Nov. 1933.

Liberal councillor, James Burnie (MP for Bootle from 1922 to 1924), who was also the newly-elected Lord Mayor, held the balance. With his casting vote he could have reinstated Tory rule in the borough, but he chose to abstain as he did not want to appear partisan ten minutes after he had been elected mayor. Labour proceeded to take the opportunity to make a clean sweep of the aldermanic bench, thereby consolidating their control. The Conservative councillors were so disgusted with this series of events that they walked out of the chamber in protest, and there were rumours, later denied, that they intended to boycott all local government business for a month. Mayor Burnie's 'fairmindedness' was commended by all sides, but twelve months later the electors of Stanley ward repaid him for his actions by voting him off the council.[17] Despite the Labour party losing seats in 1936, 1937 and 1938, therefore, it remained in power by virtue of its stranglehold on the aldermanic system. The Conservative leader on the council made his party's position clear in 1938:

> Next year, if we retain what we have got ... we will have to elect six aldermen. Needless to say, the six aldermen will be Conservatives (applause).[18]

Only the intervention of war stopped this prediction being fulfilled.

Plainly the politics of the council chamber in Bootle were tough and uncompromising, but this was matched at the hustings and in the streets of the borough. The overt religious sectarianism of the early 1920s was one obvious source of discord that has already been mentioned, but other political divisions were also expressed intemperately. In 1920 one of the 'Constitutional' candidates was happy to be described as the 'anti-Bolshevist' candidate, another accused his 'Socialist and Bolshevist' opponents of 'trying to overthrow the constitution of the country', and a third thought his victory was a rejection of 'revolution, Bolshevism, or a Soviet government'. Ten years later a Tory victor hoped the election results in Bootle signalled 'a nation-wide revulsion against the satellites of Moscow'. In 1935 and 1936, in the 'most scurrilous campaign ... in the history of Bootle' according to Labour, Tories accused their opponents again of being soft on Communism and seeking to affiliate the Communist party to Labour. The reality of the Catholic-influenced Bootle Labour party bore little resemblance to these lurid claims, but there was nevertheless a bitter edge to local campaigning.

The effects of poverty and unemployment were an important and contentious issue in the politics of Bootle, and account for some of the bitterness in local municipal affairs. Casual employment at the docks meant irregular earnings and insecurity for many of the families living in the borough. The impact of the inter-war Depression only worsened the customary poverty and deprivation. The slump in world trade hit all British ports, but Liverpool, as the main export port, was hit especially hard by the disproportionate collapse of export trade. In 1931 the total volume of goods through the port was only 42 per cent of the 1924 figure.[19] Bootle did have the advantage of being the site of the only major expansion of the

---

[17] *Bootle Times*, 6 Nov. and 13 Nov. 1936, 5 Nov. 1937.

[18] *Bootle Times*, 4 Nov. 1938.

[19] Caradog Jones, *Social Survey of Merseyside*, vol. II, p. 63.

dock system in the inter-war period, with the Gladstone dock, designed to take the largest new ships in operation at the time, opening in 1927.[20] Other industrial expansion in the borough was minimal, though. The unemployment rate in Bootle and Liverpool in 1932 was identical at just under 30 per cent.

Unsurprisingly, one of the strongest and most active branches of the National Unemployed Workers' Movement (NUWM) in the Merseyside area was established in Bootle throughout the inter-war years.[21] In electoral terms its direct influence was minimal, but indirectly it played an important role in keeping the issue of unemployment to the forefront. Only one NUWM candidate ever stood in Bootle, in Mersey ward in 1922. He gained a respectable 460 votes in a total poll of 2,500, but this was when Labour–NUWM co-operation was still possible. The NUWM candidate, William Keenan, became the leader of the Labour council only a few years later. Subsequent relations between the Communist-dominated NUWM and the Labour party were for the most part inharmonious, and even worse after Labour took control of the borough. In 1935 for instance the NUWM mounted a vigorous campaign for increases in the rates of relief paid by the Labour-controlled Public Assistance Committee, and was condemned by the then Labour leader, Simon Mahon sen., for its 'irresponsible' actions.[22] However, before Labour took power it had made much of the unemployment issue in its election strategy. In 1932 in particular, following the riots by the unemployed in Birkenhead and Liverpool, Labour attacked Tory administration of public assistance, and claimed to have won many votes as a result.[23] Conversely, in 1930 rising unemployment under a Labour government was seen as a vote loser. One of Labour's defeated candidates even complained that his support had been cut because on a polling day of heavy and wintry showers,

> In the lower wards some of the people had been so poverty stricken that they were unable to go to the polls because they had not got decent boots.[24]

There were other indications of the hardship and hard feeling that affected the polls. After the Conservative successes in 1921, one report described

> a small boy with bare feet, a brown jersey, and a face so dirty one could hardly tell where jersey ended and face began. Round each eye there was a patch of white that had evidently been irrigated with tears. He was starting to 'pitch in' to another little boy [a Tory supporter] ... the brown-eyed one remarked, 'I'm not afraid, yer know. I've 'ad four fights today with kids like 'im'.[25]

---

[20] Freeman, *The Conurbations of Great Britain*, pp. 105–107.
[21] See Lane, T., 'Some Merseyside militants of the 1930s', in Hikins, H., (ed.), *Building the Union: Studies on the Growth of the Workers' Movement: Merseyside 1756–1967*, (Liverpool, 1973), pp. 159–177; Davies, S. *et al., Genuinely Seeking Work: Mass Unemployment on Merseyside in the 1930s*, (Liverpool, 1992), pp. 177–200.
[22] *Liverpool Daily Post*, 24 Jan. 1935.
[23] *Bootle Times*, 4 Nov. 1932.
[24] *Bootle Times*, 7 Nov. 1930.
[25] *Bootle Times*, 4 Nov. 1921.

On another occasion a woman was fined ten shillings for being drunk and disorderly in Kirk Street at 10.25 on the night of the 1924 Labour disappointments. She was 'shouting and bawling, and wanted to fight', after being taunted by another woman celebrating the Tory wins. 'I was not the only one who should have been locked up – other people were shouting', she claimed, and added, 'I don't know why she ... should tell me who had got in at the elections'. After the 1927 results were declared, a near-riotous celebration was held at the Bootle Labour Club, where many youths described as 'bootless and in many cases stockingless' cheered raucously at every Labour win. The evening of the 1928 poll was described as 'a typical election night, with its public-house politics and vociferous children parading the streets singing "Vote, vote, vote!" '. Allegations of hooliganism were levelled against Labour supporters. Two young boys delivering Liberal leaflets near the docks in Linacre ward had been attacked and their leaflets torn up, and other similar attacks had followed. One of the Tory candidates in Mersey ward also alleged that cars and workers of his party had been pelted with stones on several occasions on Derby Road near the docks.[26]

One final point of interest is the apparent importance of women to campaigning in Bootle. In the early 1920s in particular the Conservatives were perceived to have a distinct advantage due to their superior organisation of women. In 1922 for instance two successful Tory candidates attributed their victories to female support, while a Labour loser bemoaned his party's lack of women workers. Similar sentiments were expressed by both sides in 1924. A Labour leader stated that 'the greatest tribute that could be paid to the women's organisation of the Conservatives was that the elections were won by them', and went on to urge the formation of women's sections in his own party. There was certainly no shortage of female interest in Labour's fortunes. It was reported that the audience for Labour's 1921 and 1925 post-election meetings was composed mostly of women.[27]

There is evidence as well that Labour eventually succeeded in organising its female support. In 1927 Miss Lily Thorpe was elected in Linacre ward, at twenty-two years old the youngest woman councillor in the country according to the local press, and the only woman on the council. Her win was hailed by Labour as a 'blow at Conservatism on behalf of the "Flappers" as they were called (applause and laughter)'. By the following year it was Labour, rather than the Conservative party, which was attributing its victories to the great work of women supporters.[28] It was significant that between 1925 and 1930 Labour put forward five women candidates in total, whereas before that it had never put up a woman. Yet the position seemed to change again in the 1930s, and after 1930 Labour nominated only four women in the eight years up to the war. This pattern of increased women's activity and influence in the Labour party during the second half of the 1920s, and retreat for women in the more defensively-minded 1930s, has been

---

[26] *Bootle Times*, 7 Nov. 1924, 4 Nov. 1927, 2 Nov. 1928.
[27] *Bootle Times*, 4 Nov. 1921, 3 Nov. 1922, 7 Nov. 1924, 6 Nov. 1925.
[28] *Bootle Times*, 4 Nov. 1927, 2 Nov. 1928.

reflected in other local studies.[29] By 1938 in Bootle it was the Tories again who were hailing the work of the Women's Conservative Association, while Labour's female organisation had atrophied.[30] It would be interesting to explore further the reasons for this change, and its deeper implications. Michael Savage's work on Preston suggests a shift in working-class politics away from 'economistic' concerns during the time when women became more influential in the Labour party. Whether such a shift can be identified in Bootle as well remains to be uncovered by more extensive research than can be attempted here.

In conclusion, it could be argued that a number of distinctive features of the county borough of Bootle had an important influence on its municipal politics between the wars. Its status as an administratively separate neighbour, but socio-economic part, of the city of Liverpool, gave it a distorted and incomplete social structure. As a result, its economic functions were concentrated in dock-related activities. In turn, this meant that Bootle was a strongly working-class borough, and one where a predominantly unskilled and casually-employed proletariat was the key to winning political control. It was also skewed in that there was a unusually high proportion of Catholics amongst that working class, in an area where religious sectarianism was an historically important force. Politico-religious questions were therefore of great significance in Bootle, and municipal politics was an arena of bitter conflict. Political divisions were made even more stark by the prevailing poverty and unemployment of the borough. Once the Labour party had been established as the main political vehicle of working-class Catholic voters, Labour strength in the key dockside wards, and therefore the borough, was assured. Finally, though, the vagaries of the municipal electoral system could be used to frustrate the popular political will, and control of the aldermanic bench became a crucial factor in Bootle. While across the border in Liverpool in the same period Labour's opponents blatantly fixed the system, in Bootle it was Labour politicians who learned to be the cynical manipulators.

[29] See Davies, *Liverpool Labour*, pp. 167–185; Savage, M., *The Dynamics of Working-Class Politics: The Labour Movement in Preston, 1880–1940*, pp. 167–187; for a different pattern in London, see Thane, P., 'The women of the British Labour Party and feminism, 1906–1945', in Smith, H., (ed.), *British Feminism in the Twentieth Century*, (Aldershot, 1990).
[30] *Bootle Times*, 4 Nov. 1938.

A guide to further reading

Newspapers

Bootle Times
Liverpool Daily Post
Manchester Guardian

Works of reference

Kelly's Directory of Liverpool, (annual).
Liverpool Official Red Book, (annual).

Other secondary sources

Caradog Jones, D., *Social Survey of Merseyside*, (Liverpool, 1934), 3 Vols.
County Borough of Bootle, *Municipal Government Centenary, County Borough of Bootle: Merseyside Celebrations, February 17 to February 24*, (Bootle, 1935).
Davies, S., *et al., Genuinely Seeking Work: Mass Unemployment on Merseyside in the 1930s*, (Liverpool, 1992).
Davies, S., *Liverpool Labour: Social and Political Influences on the Development of the Labour Party in Liverpool, 1900–1939*, (Keele, 1996).
Davies, S., ' "A stormy political career": P.J. Kelly and Irish Nationalist and Labour politics in Liverpool, 1891–1936', *Transactions of the Historic Society of Lancashire and Cheshire*, no. 148, (1999, forthcoming).
Lane, T., 'Some Merseyside militants of the 1930s', in Hikins, H., (ed.), *Building the Union: Studies on the Growth of the Workers' Movement: Merseyside 1756–1967*, (Liverpool, 1973).
Lane, T., *Liverpool: City of the Sea*, (Liverpool, 1997).
McManus, P., 'Industrial Bootle: A Study of its Present Distribution and its Past Evolution', (B.A. dissertation, University of Liverpool, 1965).
Smith, J., 'Labour tradition in Liverpool and Glasgow', *History Workshop*, 17, (Spring, 1984).
Smith, J., 'Class, skill and sectarianism in Glasgow and Liverpool', in Morris, R.J., (ed.), *Class, Power and Social Structure in British Nineteenth-Century Towns*, (Leicester, 1986).
Social Science Department, University of Liverpool, *Handbook of Social Statistics Relating to Merseyside*, (Liverpool, 1938).
Waller, P.J., *Democracy and Sectarianism: A Political and Social History of Liverpool 1868–1939,* (Liverpool, 1981).

Bootle wards 1919–1938

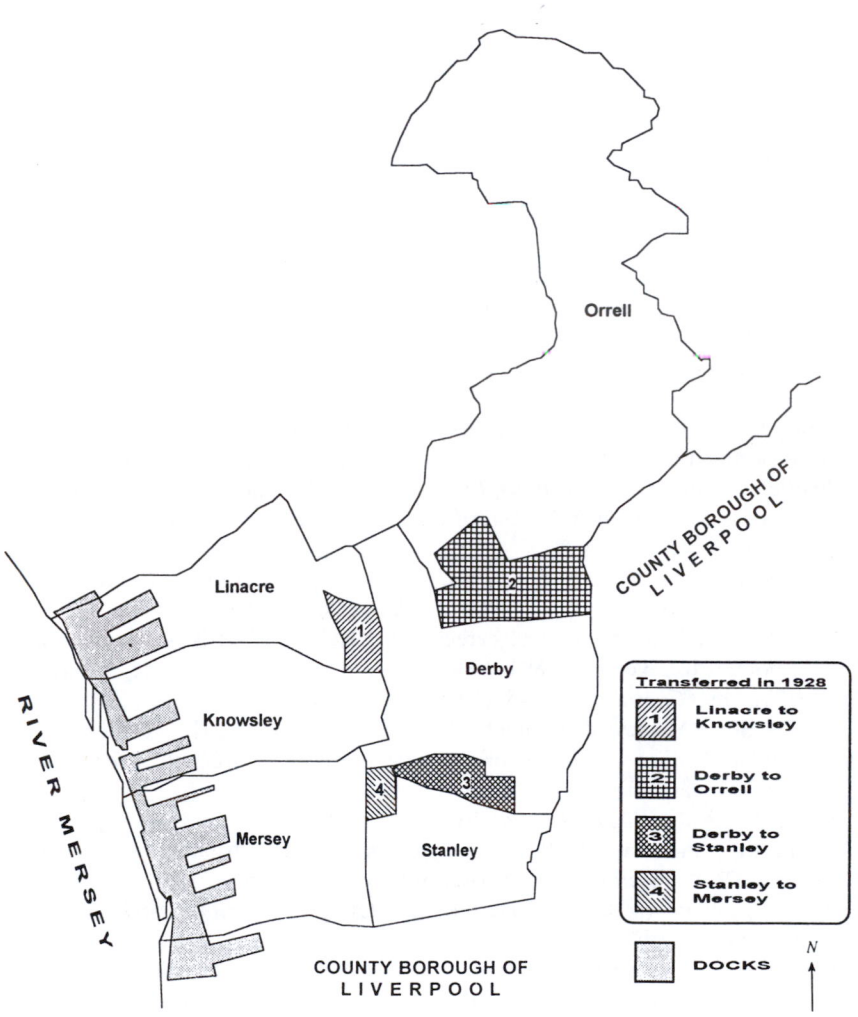

Persons aged fourteen and over classified by industry 1931

	Male	%	Female	%	Total	%
Metal and engineering	3,095	12.6	592	5.8	3,687	10.6
Textiles	172	0.7	577	5.6	749	12.6
Building	1,219	5.0	19	0.2	1,238	3.6
Food, drink and tobacco	1,100	4.5	1,290	12.6	2,390	40.3
Transport	9,037	36.7	256	2.5	9,293	26.7
- Rail	*664*	*2.7*	*18*	*0.2*	*682*	*2.0*
- Road	*1,026*	*4.2*	*36*	*0.4*	*1,062*	*3.0*
- Water	*4,729*	*19.2*	*172*	*1.7*	*4,901*	*6.4*
- Docks	*2,334*	*9.5*	*21*	*0.2*	*2,355*	*3.1*
Commerce and finance	3,922	15.9	2,127	20.7	6,049	17.3
Public admin. and defence	1,555	6.3	582	5.7	2,137	6.1
- Local government	*1,303*	*5.3*	*473*	*4.6*	*1,776*	*5.1*
Personal service	747	3.0	2,645	25.8	3,392	9.7
Other	3,768	15.3	2,167	21.1	5,935	17.0
Total (a)	**24,615**		**10,255**		**34,870**	
Total population (b)	36,838		39,932		76,487	
(a) as % of (b)	66.8		25.7		45.6	
Total out of work (c)	5,975		1,460		7,435	
(c) as % of (a)	24.3		14.2		21.3	
Managerial and own account	1,660	8.9	690	7.8	2,350	8.5
Operative	17,040	91.1	8,105	92.2	25,145	91.5
Total (excluding out of work)	18,700		8,795		27,495	

Population statistics 1931

Ward	Acres	Population	Persons/acre	Persons/room
Derby	330	12,352	37.4	0.88
Knowsley	335	13,573	40.5	1.09
Linacre	253	14,478	57.2	0.98
Mersey	336	11,992	35.7	1.03
Orrell	483	13,178	27.3	1.04
Stanley	210	11,197	53.3	0.74
Total	**1,947**	**76,770**	**39.4**	**0.95**

Overall position on the council 1919–38

	Position				Gains				Losses			
	C	Lab	L	Other	C	Lab	L	Other	C	Lab	L	Other
1919	20	10	10	4	0	5	0	1	6	0	0	0
1920[a]	28	13	-	3	1	2	0	0	1	0	1	1
1921[b]	30	13	-	1	1	1	0	0	0	1	0	1
1922[c]	27	8	4	5	3	0	0	2	0	4	0	1
1923[c]	29	4	5	6	0	0	2	0	0	2	0	0
1924	31	3	5	5	2	0	1	0	0	1	1	1
1925	30	5	5	4	0	2	0	1	1	0	0	2
1926	30	7	5	2	0	2	0	0	1	0	1	0
1927	25	13	4	2	0	6	0	0	5	0	1	0
1928[d]	23	19	4	1	0	5	0	0	3	0	1	1
1929	22	22	3	1	0	1	0	0	1	0	0	0
1930[d]	27	17	2	1	4	0	0	0	0	4	0	0
1931[d]	32	12	2	1	2	0	0	0	0	2	0	0
1932[d]	32	12	2	1	1	1	0	0	1	1	0	0
1933	26	18	2	2	0	5	0	1	6	0	0	0
1934	18	27	1	2	0	3	0	0	3	0	0	0
1935	17	29	1	1	0	0	0	0	0	0	0	0
1936[d]	20	25	1	1	4	0	0	0	0	4	0	0
1937	21	27	0	0	4	0	0	0	0	3	1	0
1938	23	25	0	0	1	0	0	0	0	1	0	0

Aldermen 1919–38

1919 C–6, L–4, Other–1	1929 C–8, L–2, Lab–2
1920 C–11	1930[d] C–7, L–1, Lab–3
1921 C–11	1931[d] C–9, L–1, Other–1
1922 C–7, L–4	1932[d] C–9, L–1, Other–1
1923 C–9, L–2	1933 C–10, L–1, Other–1
1924 C–9, L–2	1934 C–4, Other–1, Lab–7
1925 C–9, L–2	1935 C–4, Other–1, Lab–7
1926 C–9, L–2	1936[d] C–3, Other–1, Lab–7
1927 C–8, L–3	1937 Lab–12
1928[d] C–8, L–3	1938 Lab–12

[a] 1920 - C–Co L coalition.
[b] 1921 - C–L–Ind coalition.
[c] 1922 and 1923 - C = Constitutionalists.
[d] 1928, 1930, 1931, 1932, 1936 - 1 aldermanic vacancy.

Municipal elections: winning party 1919–28

Ward	1919	1920	1921	1922	1923	1924	1925	1926	1927	1928
Derby (1)	C	C	C	C	C	C	C	C	C	C
Derby (2)	Coop	C	C	C	C	C	C	C	C	C
Knowsley (1)	Lab	**Lab**	C	C	Lab	C	Lab	Lab	Lab	Lab
Knowsley (2)	Lab	**Lab**	C	Lab	Lab	C	C	Lab	Lab	Lab
Linacre (1)	Lab	**Lab**	C	C	C	C	C	Lab	Lab	Lab
Linacre (2)	Lab	**C**	C	Lab	I Lab	C	C	Lab	Lab	Lab
Linacre (3)	-	-	-	-	-	-	-	-	-	-
Mersey (1)	Lab	Lab	C	Ind	L	C	Ind	L	Lab	Lab
Mersey (2)	Lab	Lab	Lab	Ind	L	L	L	Lab	Lab	Lab
Orrell (1)	Lab	Ind	Ind	Ind	Ind	C	Lab	Ind	C	C
Orrell (2)	-	-	-	-	-	-	-	-	-	Lab
Orrell (3)	-	-	-	-	-	-	-	-	-	C
Orrell (4)	-	-	-	-	-	-	-	-	-	C
Stanley (1)	L	C	C	C	C	C	C	C	C	L
Stanley (2)	C	C	C	C	C	C	C	C	C	C

Municipal elections: party wins per year 1919–28

	1919	1920	1921	1922	1923	1924	1925	1926	1927	1928
C	2	5	9	6	5	10	7	4	5	6
Lab	7	5	1	2	2	0	2	5	6	7
L	1	0	0	0	2	1	1	1	0	1
Other	1	1	1	3	2	0	1	1	0	0
Total	11	11	11	11	11	11	11	11	11	14
Turnout %	56.2	64.2	60.7	49.5	55.7	51.5	53.4	43.4	53.0	55.8
Labour %	41.3	32.6	32.3	24.7	19.7	21.5	26.1	44.6	40.8	38.5

Municipal elections: winning party 1929–38

Ward	1929	1930	1931	1932	1933	1934	1935	1936	1937	1938
Derby (1)	C	C	C	C	C	C	C	C	C	C
Derby (2)	C	C	C	C	Coop	C	C	C	C	C
Knowsley (1)	Lab	C	Lab	Lab	Lab	Lab	Lab	Lab	Lab	Lab
Knowsley (2)	Lab	C	Lab	Lab	Lab	Lab	Lab	Lab	Lab	Lab
Linacre (1)	Lab	C	C	Lab	Lab	Lab	Lab	C	C	C
Linacre (2)	Lab	C	C	Lab	Lab	Lab	Lab	Lab	C	C
Linacre (3)	-	-	-	-	-	-	-	-	Lab	-
Mersey (1)	Lab	Lab	Lab	**Lab**	Lab	Lab	Lab	Lab	Lab	Lab
Mersey (2)	Lab	Lab	Lab	**Lab**	Lab	Lab	Lab	Lab	Lab	Lab
Orrell (1)	Lab	C	C	C	Lab	C	C	C	C	C
Orrell (2)	Ind	C	C	C	Lab	Lab	C	C	C	C
Orrell (3)	-	-	-	-	-	-	-	-	-	-
Orrell (4)	-	-	-	-	-	-	-	-	-	-
Stanley (1)	C	C	**L**	C	C	L	C	C	C	C
Stanley (2)	C	C	**C**	C	C	C	C	C	C	C

Municipal elections: party wins per year 1929–38

	1929	1930	1931	1932	1933	1934	1935	1936	1937	1938
C	4	10	7	6	3	4	6	7	8	8
Lab	7	2	4	6	8	7	6	5	5	4
L	0	0	1	0	0	1	0	0	0	0
Other	1	0	0	0	1	0	0	0	0	0
Total	12	12	12	12	12	12	12	12	13	12
Turnout %	48.2	46.8	54.5	45.9	49.0	43.6	50.5	55.4	58.2	52.8
Labour %	50.4	35.1	47.7	49.2	53.3	48.3	41.3	43.0	39.3	41.4

Municipal elections: party wins per ward 1919–38

	C	Lab	L	Other	Total	Turnout %	Labour % of all votes
Derby	38	0	0	2	40	50.0	19.0
Knowsley	8	32	0	0	40	52.5	62.6
Linacre	18	22	0	1	41	50.5	48.6
Mersey	2	30	5	3	40	57.9	49.0
Orrell	20	7	0	6	33	54.3	41.6
Stanley	36	0	4	0	40	48.3	10.2
Total	**122**	**91**	**9**	**12**	**234**	**52.0**	**38.8**

Seats won by Labour as a percentage of all wins 1919–38   **38.9**

Parliamentary election results

Bootle constituency
(all wards within the borough [1918 boundaries] were included in the constituency)

General election	Winner	Conservative %	Labour %	Liberal %
14 Dec. 1918	Co C	63.0	-	-
15 Nov. 1922	L	41.9	-	56.3
6 Dec. 1923	L	42.1	13.8	44.1
29 Oct. 1924	C	45.5	34.7	19.8
30 May 1929	Lab	40.7	43.6	15.7
27 Oct. 1931	C	61.9	38.1	-
14 Nov. 1935	C	48.6	38.8	12.6

Derby ward
(2 councillors elected each year)

Candidate	Party	Votes	%	Electors	Turnout	Gains
1919						
W.E. Hughes*	C	1,522	34.8	5,374	50.2	
Mrs E.H. Smith	Coop	1,465	33.5			Coop from C
T.A. Patrick	C	1,386	31.7			
Total votes		4,373				
Total voters		2,697				
1920						
F.W. Baucher*	C	2,304	36.0	5,452	60.5	
T.A. Patrick	C	2,215	34.6			C from Co L
W. Gowling	Lab	970	15.2			
J. Kinley	Lab	907	14.2			
Total votes		6,396				
Total voters		3,299				
1921						
J. Spence*	C	2,328	42.9	5,498	60.9	-
B. Wolfenden*	C	2,303	42.5			
T. Garnett	Lab	790	14.6			
Total votes		5,421				
Total voters		*3,346*				
1922						
D.S. Eaton	C	2,006	34.1	5,703	54.8	C from Coop
W.E. Hughes*	C	1,834	31.2			
J.M. Smith	Ind	1,058	18.0			
Mrs E.H. Smith*	Coop	982	16.7			
Total votes		5,880				
Total voters		3,126				
1923						
T.A. Patrick*	C	1,733	29.4	5,879	55.7	-
F.W. Baucher*	C	1,525	25.9			
Mrs E.H. Smith	Coop	929	15.8			
T. Lawrenson	L	648	11.0			
J.M. Smith	Ind C	613	10.4			
T.A. Pritchard	L	442	7.5			
Total votes		5,890				
Total voters		3,274				

Derby ward *(continued)*

Candidate	Party	Votes	%	Electors	Turnout	Gains
1924						
B. Wolfenden*	C	2,134	36.9	5,995	53.7	-
W.A. Hanlon	C	2,121	36.7			
Mrs E.H. Smith	Coop	976	16.9			
J. Jackson	Lab	550	9.5			
Total votes		5,781				
Total voters		3,221				
1925						
D.S. Eaton*	C	1,663	25.7	6,108	57.8	-
W.E. Hughes*	C	1,549	23.9			
J. Burnie	L	1,432	22.1			
W.H. Rose	L	947	14.6			
Mrs B. Wait	Lab	883	13.6			
Total votes		6,474				
Total voters		3,533				
1926						
F.W. Baucher*	C	1,096	24.4	6,133	41.8	-
T.A. Patrick*	C	1,055	23.5			
J. Burnie	L	1,038	23.1			
A. McLeod	Lab	656	14.6			
W.H. Rose	L	644	14.3			
Total votes		4,489				
Total voters		2,563				
1927						
W.A. Hanlon*	C	1,589	28.5	6,121	52.3	-
A.B. Spencer*	C	1,400	25.1			
J. Burnie	L	1,269	22.7			
B.R. Otter	Lab	755	13.5			
H. Parry	Lab	569	10.2			
Total votes		5,582				
Total voters		3,199				
1928						
D.S. Eaton*	C	1,378	28.7	5,407	44.4	-
W.E. Hughes*	C	1,336	27.8			
G. Thorpe	Lab	772	16.1			
T. Lawrenson	L	677	14.1			
J.B. Grafton	L	636	13.3			
Total votes		4,799				
Total voters		2,666				

Derby ward *(continued)*

Candidate	Party	Votes	%	Electors	Turnout	Gains
1929						
F.W. Baucher*	C	1,471	28.5	5,626	48.7	-
T.A. Patrick*	C	1,423	27.6			
Mrs E.H. Smith	Coop	1,226	23.7			
W.A. Hounslea	Lab	1,045	20.2			
Total votes		5,165				
Total voters		2,740				
1930						
J. Spence*	C	1,873	39.2	5,746	43.1	-
A.B. Spencer*	C	1,813	37.9			
W.A. Hounslea	Lab	549	11.5			
A. Cleary	Lab	545	11.4			
Total votes		4,780				
Total voters		2,474				
1931						
D.S. Eaton*	C	2,129	43.5	5,712	46.2	-
J.T. Hackett*	C	1,948	39.8			
W. McNiffe	Lab	475	9.7			
T.A. Gilligan	Lab	339	6.9			
Total votes		4,891				
Total voters		2,640				
1932						
F. Hughes	C	1,534	31.6	6,200	40.4	-
R.A. Black*	C	1,522	31.4			
J.G. Corlett	Lab	899	18.5			
W. Atherton	Lab	892	18.4			
Total votes		4,847				
Total voters		2,505				
1933						
J. Spence*	C	1,504	26.9	6,259	46.2	
Mrs E.H. Smith	Coop	1,421	25.4			Coop from C
A.B. Spencer*	C	1,408	25.2			
W. Atherton	Lab	1,252	22.4			
Total votes		5,585				
Total voters		2,892				

Derby ward *(continued)*

Candidate	Party	Votes	%	Electors	Turnout	Gains
1934						
D.B. Black*	C	1,413	28.4	6,385	39.9	-
J.T. Hackett*	C	1,392	28.0			
Mrs M.C. Hevey	Coop	1,063	21.4			
S. Williams	Lab	1,105	22.2			
Total votes		4,973				
Total voters		2,546				
1935						
R.A. Black*	C	2,078	35.4	6,607	45.4	-
F. Hughes*	C	2,060	35.1			
W. Tewkesbury	Lab	870	14.8			
C. Williams	Lab	861	14.7			
Total votes		5,869				
Total voters		3,001				
1936						
J. Spence*	C	2,370	34.0	6,839	52.8	C from Lab
W.E. Hughes	C	2,322	33.3			
Mrs E.H. Smith*	Lab	1,219	17.5			
M. Connolley	Lab	1,053	15.1			
Total votes		6,964				
Total voters		3,608				
1937						
D.B. Black*	C	2,637	37.0	6,863	53.0	-
J.T. Hackett*	C	2,595	36.4			
J.C. Hevey	Lab	963	13.5			
Mrs M.C. Hevey	Lab	928	13.0			
Total votes		7,123				
Total voters		3,636				
1938						
R.A. Black*	C	2,424	37.0	6,822	49.2	-
T.A. Patrick*	C	2,367	36.1			
J.C. Hevey	Lab	895	13.7			
Mrs M.C. Hevey	Lab	868	13.2			
Total votes		6,554				
Total voters		3,359				

Overall Labour vote **19.0%**   **Overall turnout** **50.0%**

Knowsley ward
(2 councillors elected each year)

Candidate	Party	Votes	%	Electors	Turnout	Gains
1919						
P. Quigley	Lab	1,812	35.1	4,295	62.0	Lab from C
E. Connolly	Lab	1,678	32.5			Lab from C
H. Pennington*	C	931	18.0			
H. Kay	C	746	14.4			
Total votes		5,167				
Total voters		2,665				
1920						
S. Mahon sen.*	Lab	Unopp.	-		-	-
P. Marmion*	Lab	Unopp.	-			
1921						
A. Malins	C	1,324	25.7	4,228	62.8	C from Lab
R.A. Black	C	1,291	25.0			
J. Murphy	Lab	1,279	24.8			
W.A. Ainsworth	Lab	1,261	24.5			
Total votes		5,155				
Total voters		*2,657*				
1922						
J. Benson	C	1,220	34.7	4,432	49.0	C from Lab
C. Flynne	Lab	1,177	33.5			
A. Hankey*	Lab	1,120	31.8			
Total votes		3,517				
Total voters		2,173				
					2171.0	
1923						
S. Mahon sen.*	Lab	1,570	38.3	4,806	52.6	-
A. Hankey	Lab	1,380	33.7			
W.B. Thompson	C	1,150	28.0			
Total votes		4,100				
Total voters		2,529				

Knowsley ward *(continued)*

Candidate	Party	Votes	%	Electors	Turnout	Gains
1924						
J.A. Stewart	C	1,033	24.7	4,970	46.6	-
R.A. Black*	C	1,003	23.9			
W. Keenan	Lab	855	20.4			
M. Connolly	Lab	849	20.3			
P. Marmion	IDL	379	9.0			
J.Farrell	IDL	71	1.7			
Total votes		4,190				
Total voters		2,317				
1925						
W. Keenan	Lab	1,073	27.2	4,924	52.6	Lab from
G.A. Rogers	C	974	24.7			I Lab
A. Campbell	Lab	929	23.6			
C. Flynne*	I.Lab	718	18.2			
J.M. Smith	Ind	250				
Total votes		3,944				
Total voters		2,591				
1926						
S. Mahon sen.*	Lab	1,525	41.2	4,937	46.3	-
A. Hankey*	Lab	1,415	38.3			
J. Benson	C	757	20.5			
Total votes		3,697				
Total voters		2,287				
1927						
J.W. Clark	Lab	1,732	34.4	5,044	51.8	Lab from C
T.A. Jones	Lab	1,672	33.2			Lab from C
R.A. Black*	C	817	16.2			
J.A. Stewart*	C	812	16.1			
Total votes		5,033				
Total voters		2,611				
1928						
W. Keenan*	Lab	1,865	29.4	5,468	59.9	
J. Kinley	Lab	1,849	29.1			Lab from C
A. Holden	C	1,336	21.0			
R.A. Black	C	1,304	20.5			
Total votes		6,354				
Total voters		*3,275*				

Knowsley ward *(continued)*

Candidate	Party	Votes	%	Electors	Turnout	Gains
1929						
J.S. Kelly*	Lab	1,745	40.2	5,913	45.9	-
R.O. Jones	Lab	1,656	38.1			
A. Holden	C	942	21.7			
Total votes		4,343				
Total voters		2,714				
1930						
L.S. Lawton	C	1,549	27.3	5,800	50.4	C from Lab
I. Timon	C	1,500	26.5			C from Lab
J.W. Clark*	Lab	1,334	23.5			
T.A. Jones*	Lab	1,288	22.7			
Total votes		5,671				
Total voters		2,922				
1931						
J. Kinley*	Lab	1,991	29.4	5,702	61.0	-
W. Keenan*	Lab	1,915	28.3			
J. Bradley	C	1,450	21.4			
W.G. Timon	C	1,418	20.9			
Total votes		6,774				
Total voters		3,479				
1932						
J.S. Kelly*	Lab	1,596	30.5	5,606	48.8	-
R.O. Jones*	Lab	1,525	29.2			
D.B. Black	C	953	18.2			
H. Wardle	C	935	17.9			
J. Byrne	Com	217	4.2			
Total votes		5,226				
Total voters		2,738				
1933						
J.W. Clark	Lab	1,774	38.8	5,709	48.9	Lab from C
E. Smith*	Lab	1,767	38.7			
L.S. Lawton*	C	1,029	22.5			
Total votes		4,570				
Total voters		2,794				

Knowsley ward *(continued)*

Candidate	Party	Votes	%	Electors	Turnout	Gains
1934						
J. Kinley*	Lab	1,598	39.1	5,619	44.8	-
T.A. Caine	Lab	1,593	39.0			
J. Ingham	C	893	21.9			
Total votes		4,084				
Total voters		2,520				
1935						
J.S. Kelly*	Lab	1,763	30.8	5,607	51.9	-
R.O. Jones*	Lab	1,754	30.7			
H. Knight	C	1,128	19.7			
P. Love	C	1,075	18.8			
Total votes		5,720				
Total voters		2,908				
1936						
T. Connolly*	Lab	1,752	30.6	5,412	54.3	-
A.F. Campbell*	Lab	1,733	30.3			
Mrs L .Riley	C	1,122	19.6			
P. Grainger	C	1,111	19.4			
Total votes		5,718				
Total voters		2,940				
1937						
T.A. Cain*	Lab	1,964	32.9	5,264	58.1	-
J.R. Dunn*	Lab	1,915	32.0			
R.J. Craft	C	1,053	17.6			
C. Smith	C	1,044	17.5			
Total votes		5,976				
Total voters		3,058				
1938						
A. Cleary*	Lab	1,574	29.9	5,060	52.6	-
A. Small*	Lab	1,485	28.2			
J. Black	C	1,127	21.4			
R.J. Craft	C	1,074	20.4			
Total votes		5,260				
Total voters		2,662				

Overall Labour vote   **62.6%**   **Overall turnout**   **52.5%**

Linacre ward
(2 councillors elected each year)

Candidate	Party	Votes	%	Electors	Turnout	Gains
1919						
A.M. McLeod	Lab	1,805	28.2	5,934	55.6	Lab from C
W. Hayward	Lab	1,719	26.8			Lab from C
W.S. Scott	C	1,520	23.7			
E. Gardiner	C	1,366	21.3			
Total votes		6,410				
Total voters		3,302				
1920						
J. Rafter*	Lab	Unopp.	-		-	-
W.C. Scott*	C	Unopp.	-			
1921						
D. Mitchell*	C	1,976	31.5	5,832	55.5	
P. Grainger	C	1,927	30.7			
J. Kinley	Lab	1,195	19.0			
C. Flynne	Lab	1,181	18.8			
Total votes		6,279				
Total voters		*3,237*				
1922						
H.L. Scholefield	C	1,690	43.5	6,368	37.7	C from Lab
W. Hayward*	Lab	1,106	28.4			
A.M. McLeod*	Lab	1,092	28.1			
Total votes		3,888				
Total voters		2,398				
1923						
W.C. Scott*	C	1,802	38.6	6,532	47.0	-
J. Rafter*	I Lab	1,180	25.3			
A.M. McLeod	I Lab	899	19.3			
J. Kinley	Lab	416	8.9			
A. Cleary	Lab	368	7.9			
Total votes		4,665				
Total voters		3,071				

Linacre ward *(continued)*

Candidate	Party	Votes	%	Electors	Turnout	Gains
1924						
P. Grainger*	C	1,515	30.6	6,546	43.3	C from L
J.T. Hackett	C	1,500	30.3			
D. Phillips	Lab	701	14.2			
T. McElroy	Lab	699	14.1			
C. O'Connor	IDL	533	10.8			
Total votes		4,948				
Total voters		2,836				
1925						
H.L. Scholefield*	C	1,416	26.4	6,689	42.0	-
H.D. Bailey	C	1,407	26.2			
H. Jones	Lab	1,282	23.9			
J. Haworth	Lab	1,262	23.5			
Total votes		5,367				
Total voters		2,810				
1926						
E. Smith*	Lab	1,427	32.3	6,703	41.0	
J. Haworth	Lab	1,422	32.2			Lab from C
W.C. Scott*	C	1,062	24.0			
T.A. Pritchard	L	507	11.5			
Total votes		4,418				
Total voters		2,746				
1927						
J. Tunney	Lab	1,433	22.0	6,684	51.2	Lab from C
Miss L. Thorpe	Lab	1,374	21.1			Lab from C
P. Grainger*	C	1,068	16.4			
J.T. Hackett*	C	1,026	15.7			
Dr T.M. Jones	L	984	15.1			
T.G. Anderson	L	639	9.8			
Total votes		6,524				
Total voters		3,423				

Linacre ward *(continued)*

Candidate	Party	Votes	%	Electors	Turnout	Gains
1928						
S. Reeves	Lab	1,571	24.9	6,110	54.4	Lab from C
T.A. Gilligan	Lab	1,546	24.5			Lab from C
H.L. Scholefield*	C	1,211	19.2			
H.D. Bailey*	C	1,051	16.7			
D. Mitchell	L	487	7.7			
W. Adamson	L	446	7.1			
Total votes		6,312				
Total voters		*3,322*				
1929						
E. Smith*	Lab	1,592	28.6	6,547	44.5	-
J. Haworth*	Lab	1,589	28.5			
W.C. Scott	C	1,254	22.5			
J. Spence	C	1,141	20.5			
Total votes		5,576				
Total voters		2,913				
1930						
W.C. Scott	C	1,743	29.9	6,409	47.6	C from Lab
A. Redding	C	1,659	28.4			C from Lab
J. Tunney*	Lab	1,237	21.2			
Miss L. Thorpe*	Lab	1,194	20.5			
Total votes		5,833				
Total voters		3,049				
1931						
F.W. Baucher	C	1,707	28.1	6,323	49.0	C from Lab
J.B. Stewart*	C	1,606	26.5			
E. Smith	Lab	1,440	23.7			
J. Tunney	Lab	1,316	21.7			
Total votes		6,069				
Total voters		3,099				
1932						
Dr D. Harris	Lab	2,096	34.7	6,275	50.3	Lab from C
J. Haworth*	Lab	1,736	28.8			
P. Grainger*	C	1,131	18.7			
Mrs B. Mulhern	C	986	16.3			
T.A. Jones	ILP	84	1.4			
W.G. McNiffe	ILP	64	1.1			
Total votes		6,033				
Total voters		3,155				

Linacre ward *(continued)*

Candidate	Party	Votes	%	Electors	Turnout	Gains
1933						
J. Olswang	Lab	1,992	30.5	6,232	54.0	Lab from C
W.C. Harrison	Lab	1,887	28.9			Lab from C
A. Redding*	C	1,328	20.4			
D. Brown	C	1,317	20.2			
Total votes		6,524				
Total voters		3,367				
1934						
W. Atherton	Lab	1,569	29.6	6,166	45.0	Lab from C
P. Monks	Lab	1,569	29.6			Lab from C
W.H. Skilling	C	1,115	21.0			
J.B. Stewart*	C	1,046	19.7			
Total votes		5,299				
Total voters		2,774				
1935						
Dr.D. Harris*	Lab	1,856	27.1	6,158	57.4	-
T.P. McNeill	Lab	1,722	25.1			
W.H. Skilling	C	1,683	24.5			
R.W. Evans	C	1,600	23.3			
Total votes		6,861				
Total voters		3,534				
1936						
W.H. Skilling	C	1,807	26.1	5,953	60.1	C from Lab
W.C. Harrison*	Lab	1,711	24.7			
R.W. Evans	C	1,705	24.6			
J. Olswang*	Lab	1,704	24.6			
Total votes		6,927				
Total voters		3,578				
1937						
A. Redding	C	2,060	17.2	5,928	69.5	C from Lab
R.W. Evans	C	2,029	16.9			C from Lab
S. Mahon sen.	Lab	2,008	16.7			
T. Harris	C	1,991	16.6			
W. Atherton*	Lab	1,957	16.3			
P. Monks*	Lab	1,949	16.2			
Total votes		11,994				
Total voters		4,119				

(3 elected)

(Mahon was a sitting alderman at the time)

Linacre ward *(continued)*

Candidate	Party	Votes	%	Electors	Turnout	Gains
1938						
T. Harris	C	1,804	25.8	5,984	59.1	C from Lab
P. Grainger	C	1,785	25.6			
S. Williams	Lab	1,730	24.8			
T.J. Griffiths	Lab	1,664	23.8			
Total votes		6,983				
Total voters		3,539				

Overall Labour vote   **48.6%**   **Overall turnout**   **50.5%**

Mersey ward
(2 councillors elected each year)

Candidate	Party	Votes	%	Electors	Turnout	Gains
1919						
J.J. King*	Lab	1,594	33.9	3,857	62.9	Lab from C
A. Hankey	Lab	1,532	32.6			
T. Mansergh*	C	795	16.9			
H. Coleman	C	779	16.6			
Total votes		4,700				
Total voters		2,425				
1920						
H.J. Sankey	Lab	1,451	30.6	3,868	65.1	Lab from C
E. Smith	Lab	1,261	26.6			Lab from Ind
R.A. Black	Const Lab	1,087	22.9			
J.G. Blackledge*	Ind	938	19.8			
Total votes		4,737				
Total voters		2,518				
1921						
W.E. Marsh	C	1,515	41.3	3,735	60.7	
R. Carroll	Lab	1,096	29.9			Lab from Ind
J. Maguire	Lab	1,060	28.9			
Total votes		3,671				
Total voters		2,266				
1922						
P.L. Regan	Ind	1,295	26.6	4,214	61.5	Ind from Lab
J. Garvey	Ind	1,102	22.6			Ind from Lab
J.T. Hackett	C	1,046	21.5			
D. Cantor	C	967	19.9			
W. Keenan	Nuwm	460	9.4			
Total votes		4,870				
Total voters		2,592				
1923						
H.J. Sankey*	L	1,969	39.1	4,407	75.2	L from Lab
J.J. King	L	1,217	24.1			L from Lab
H. Jones	C	1,105	21.9			
E. Smith*	Lab	394	7.8			
G. Bookless	Lab	231	4.6			
B. Turner	Ind	126	2.5			
Total votes		5,042				
Total voters		3,315				

Mersey ward *(continued)*

Candidate	Party	Votes	%	Electors	Turnout	Gains
1924						
H. Jones	C	1,317	30.8	4,529	62.1	
J.A. Mulhern	L	1,092	25.5			L from Lab
T. Lawrenson	L	1,033	24.2			
A. Cleary	Lab	449	10.5			
T. Newton	Lab	383	9.0			
Total votes		4,274				
Total voters		2,812				
1925						
Rev. F. Blanchard	Ind	1,474	31.4	4,551	65.2	Ind from C
T. Lawrenson*	L	1,425	30.4			
W.H. McConnell	C	1,084	23.1			
J. Cullen	Lab	353	7.5			
Miss M. Maguire	Lab	351	7.5			
Total votes		4,687				
Total voters		2,969				
1926						
F.W. King*	L	1,030	26.2	4,555	45.8	
M. Connolly	Lab	1,025	26.1			Lab from L
J. Cullen	Lab	967	24.6			
W. Begely	L	906	23.1			
Total votes		3,928				
Total voters		2,086				
1927						
J. O'Neill	Lab	1,253	28.9	4,617	61.3	Lab from C
N. Cullen	Lab	1,201	27.7			Lab from L
H. Jones*	C	1,139	26.2			
J. Mulhern*	L	748	17.2			
Total votes		4,341				
Total voters		2,832				
1928						
D. Kelly	Lab	1,331	26.5	4,657	53.9	Lab from Ind
N. Kennedy	Lab	1,317	26.2			Lab from L
W. Halpin	C	1,193	23.8			
J.H. Woolam	C	1,181	23.5			
Total votes		5,022				
Total voters		*2,589*				

Mersey ward *(continued)*

Candidate	Party	Votes	%	Electors	Turnout	Gains
1929						
J. McNamara	Lab	1,430	34.4	5,070	50.4	-
Mrs A.F. Coupe*	Lab	1,427	34.3			
J.B. Stewart	C	856	20.6			
T. Lawrenson	L	449	10.8			
Total votes		4,162				
Total voters		2,553				
1930						
N. Cullen*	Lab	1,100	25.1	4,988	45.7	-
J. O'Neill*	Lab	1,083	24.7			
W.R. Ellison	C	1,076	24.6			
R.A. Black	C	1,071	24.5			
W. Johnson	Ind	49	1.1			
Total votes		4,379				
Total voters		2,280				
1931						
S. Mahon sen.	Lab	1,794	36.7	5,047	60.9	-
D. Kelly*	Lab	1,672	34.2			
Miss M.L. Halpin	C	1,422	29.1			
Total votes		4,888				
Total voters		3,073				
1932						
A. Hankey*	Lab	Unopp.	-		-	-
J. Maguire*	Lab	Unopp.	-			
1933						
C.D. McMullan	Lab	1,488	38.6	4,947	48.6	-
J. O'Neill*	Lab	1,484	38.5			
Mrs M.A. Upton	C	881	22.9			
Total votes		3,853				
Total voters		2,403				
1934						
P. Mahon*	Lab	1,607	33.0	4,864	51.1	-
D. Kelly*	Lab	1,561	32.1			
R. Raw	C	860	17.7			
A.O. Hughes	C	839	17.2			
Total votes		4,867				
Total voters		2,484				

Mersey ward *(continued)*

Candidate	Party	Votes	%	Electors	Turnout	Gains
1935						
J. Maguire*	Lab	1,423	29.4	4,572	54.0	-
S. Williams*	Lab	1,395	28.8			
G. Hodgson	C Ch	1,014	20.9			
J. Hodgins	C Ch	1,013	20.9			
Total votes		4,845				
Total voters		2,468				
1936						
J. O'Neill*	Lab	1,398	27.5	4,401	59.6	-
M. Kennedy	Lab	1,390	27.4			
H.E. Scholefield	C	1,153	22.7			
R.J. Rogerson	C	1,139	22.4			
Total votes		5,080				
Total voters		2,621				
1937						
P. Mahon*	Lab	1,554	30.3	4,215	61.9	-
M. Connolley*	Lab	1,516	29.5			
A. Williams	C	1,042	20.3			
G. Hodgson	C	1,019	19.9			
Total votes		5,131				
Total voters		2,610				
1938						
R.J. Rainford*	Lab	1,403	28.6	4,196	59.5	-
E. Westhoff	Lab	1,379	28.1			
A. Williams	C	1,068	21.7			
G. Hodgson	C	1,063	21.6			
Total votes		4,913				
Total voters		2,495				

Overall Labour vote **49.0%** **Overall turnout** **57.9%**

Orrell ward
(expanded in 1928 by extension of the borough; 1 councillor elected each year before 1928, 2 each year thereafter)

Candidate	Party	Votes	%	Electors	Turnout	Gains
1919						
J.H. Johnson*	Lab	660	62.0	1,799	59.2	-
J. Whitehall	Ind	405	38.0			
Total votes		1,065				
1920						
T. Harris*	Ind	742	62.5	1,841	64.5	-
T. Garnett	Lab	445	37.5			
Total votes		1,187				
1921						
T. Ashton	Ind	717	66.3	1,908	56.7	-
J. Corlett	Lab	365	33.7			
Total votes		1,082				
1922						
A. Roberts*	Ind	804	58.6	2,311	59.4	-
T. Garnett	Lab	569	41.4			
Total votes		1,373				
1923						
T. Harris*	Ind	772	53.5	2,775	52.0	-
H.E. Summers	Lab	422	29.2			
J.A. Mulhern	L	250	17.3			
Total votes		1,444				
1924						
J. Fairlie	C	532	40.8	2,529	51.6	C from Ind
T. Ashton*	Ind	426	32.7			
H.E. Summers	Lab	346	26.5			
Total votes		1,304				
1925						
J. Kinley	Lab	545	35.1	2,612	59.5	Lab from Ind
J.H. Woolam	C	544	35.0			
A. Roberts*	Ind	464	29.9			
Total votes		1,553				

Orrell ward *(continued)*

Candidate	Party	Votes	%	Electors	Turnout	Gains
1926						
T. Harris*	Ind	517	51.6	2,749	36.4	-
R.J. Rainford	Lab	485	48.4			
Total votes		1,002				
1927						
J.A. Fairlie*	C	760	46.5	2,904	56.3	-
R.J. Rainford	Lab	662	40.5			
C.A. Cooke	L	213	13.0			
Total votes		1,635				
1928						
Mrs M. Ballantyne	C	1,177	13.2	3,465	66.5	-
R.J. Rainford	Lab	1,177	13.2			
J.H. Abbott	C	1,173	13.1			
J. Williams	C	1,137	12.7			
G.A. Rogers*	C	1,131	12.6			
H.E. Summers	Lab	1,066	11.9			
K. Hughes	Lab	1,059	11.8			
C. Read	Lab	1,027	11.5			
Total votes		8,947				
Total voters		*2,306*				
(4 elected)						
1929						
H. Summers	Lab	1,153	26.0	4,145	59.0	Lab from C
T. Harris*	Ind	1,112	25.1			
K. Hughes	Lab	1,097	24.7			
J. Scott	C	1,074	24.2			
Total votes		4,436				
Total voters		2,444				
1930						
J.A. Fairlie*	C	1,651	29.9	5,009	56.6	-
J.H. Abbott*	C	1,641	29.8			
K.M. Hughes	Lab	1,163	21.1			
J. Corlett	Lab	1,059	19.2			
Total votes		5,514				
Total voters		2,837				

Orrell ward *(continued)*

Candidate	Party	Votes	%	Electors	Turnout	Gains
1931						
A. Roberts	C	1,850	29.6	5,637	56.9	C from Lab
Mrs M. Ballantyne*	C	1,757	28.1			
R.J. Rainford*	Lab	1,448	23.1			
W.J. Wormald	Lab	1,200	19.2			
Total votes		6,255				
Total voters		3,206				
1932						
H.O. Cullen*	C	1,609	28.3	5,744	51.0	
A.E. Abbott	C	1,471	25.8			C from Lab
T.A. Gilligan	Lab	1,311	23.0			
A. Cleary	Lab	1,303	22.9			
Total votes		5,694				
Total voters		2,932				
1933						
R.J. Rainford	Lab	1,666	27.6	5,992	51.5	Lab from C
A. Cleary	Lab	1,499	24.8			Lab from C
J.H. Abbott*	C	1,444	23.9			
J.A. Fairlie*	C	1,427	23.6			
Total votes		6,036				
Total voters		3,083				
1934						
C.G. Anderson	C	1,493	25.5	6,214	47.8	
P. McLaren	Lab	1,471	25.1			Lab from C
J.R. Dunn	Lab	1,450	24.8			
A. Jones	C	1,435	24.5			
Total votes		5,849				
Total voters		2,968				
1935						
H.O. Cullen*	C	2,160	31.3	6,652	52.5	-
A.E. Abbott*	C	2,123	30.7			
T. Gutcher	Lab	1,318	19.1			
J.M. Butler	Lab	1,307	18.9			
Total votes		6,908				
Total voters		3,489				

Orrell ward *(continued)*

Candidate	Party	Votes	%	Electors	Turnout	Gains
1936						
D. Brown	C	2,687	32.4	7,232	58.6	C from Lab
N. Robinson	C	2,520	30.4			C from Lab
R.J. Rainford*	Lab	1,575	19.0			
A. Cleary*	Lab	1,503	18.1			
Total votes		8,285				
Total voters		4,239				
1937						
C.G. Anderson*	C	2,468	32.5	7,363	52.6	C from Lab
J. Craig	C	2,423	31.9			
M. Brown	Lab	1,354	17.8			
P. McLaren*	Lab	1,345	17.7			
Total votes		7,590				
Total voters		3,872				
1938						
H.O. Cullen*	C	2,355	32.2	7,277	51.6	-
A.E. Abbott*	C	2,297	31.5			
H.E. Summers	Lab	1,394	19.1			
P. McLaren	Lab	1,257	17.2			
Total votes		7,303				
Total voters		3,752				

Overall Labour vote   **41.6%**   **Overall turnout**   **54.3%**

Stanley ward
(2 councillors elected each year)

Candidate	Party	Votes	%	Electors	Turnout	Gains
1919						
J.R. Barbour*	Co L	1,346	33.0	4,110	51.1	-
J. Scott	C	1,322	32.4			
J. Kinley	Nfds	710	17.4			
J. Hudson	Nfds	702	17.2			
Total votes		4,080				
Total voters		2,101				
1920						
E. Gardiner	C	2,047	44.4	4,174	68.3	-
C.H. Warburton	C	1,994	43.2			
W. Mills	Lab	572	12.4			
Total votes		4,613				
Total voters		2,850				
1921						
R. Turner*	C	2,146	47.2	4,163	67.4	-
W. Vaux*	C	1,983	43.6			
W. Mills	Lab	416	9.2			
Total votes		4,545				
Total voters		2,806				
1922						
H. Pennington*	C	1,443	48.1	4,298	43.0	-
J. Scott*	C	1,335	44.5			
A.J.V. Reeves	Ind	223	7.4			
Total votes		3,001				
Total voters		1,850				
1923						
E. Gardiner*	C	1,409	29.3	4,509	55.0	-
C.H. Warburton*	C	1,405	29.2			
F.W. King	L	1,032	21.5			
G. Sutherland	L	959	20.0			
Total votes		4,805				
Total voters		2,479				

Stanley ward *(continued)*

Candidate	Party	Votes	%	Electors	Turnout	Gains
1924
M.S. Webster	C	1,497	35.9	4,609	54.7	-
W. Vaux*	C	1,462	35.0			
L. Roberts	L	754	18.1			
W. Mills	Lab	459	11.0			
Total votes		4,172				
Total voters		2,523				
1925
H. Pennington*	C	1,258	27.8	4,683	50.1	-
J. Scott*	C	1,275	28.2			
P. Rogerson	L	1,013	22.4			
W. Adamson	L	979	21.6			
Total votes		4,525				
Total voters		2,346				
1926
E. Gardiner*	C	1,072	26.9	4,649	47.6	-
J.S. Riley	C	1,003	25.2			
P. Rogerson	L	760	19.1			
W. Adamson	L	713	17.9			
B.R. Otter	Lab	438	11.0			
Total votes		3,986				
Total voters		2,213				
1927
M.S Webster*	C	1,073	26.3	4,703	47.8	-
W. Vaux*	C	1,053	25.9			
P. Rogerson	L	778	19.1			
W. Adamson	L	730	17.9			
T.J. Harrison	Lab	439	10.8			
Total votes		4,073				
Total voters		2,246				
1928
J. Burnie	L	1,378	27.1	4,967	52.7	L from C
W.E. Marsh*	C	1,313	25.9			
J. Scott*	C	1,259	24.8			
P. Rogerson	L	1,129	22.2			
Total votes		5,079				
Total voters		*2,618*				

Stanley ward *(continued)*

Candidate	Party	Votes	%	Electors	Turnout	Gains
1929						
E. Gardiner*	C	1,364	31.5	5,378	44.3	-
J.S. Riley*	C	1,241	28.6			
P. Rogerson	L	620	14.3			
R. Halstead	Lab	576	13.3			
F.J. Maunder	Lab	531	12.3			
Total votes		4,332				
Total voters		2,382				
1930						
M.S. Webster*	C	1,305	32.3	5,369	37.8	-
W. Vaux*	C	1,250	31.0			
P. Rogerson	L	751	18.6			
T. Lawrenson	L	730	18.1			
Total votes		4,036				
Total voters		2,031				
1931						
J. Burnie*	L	Unopp.	-	5,369	-	-
W.E. Marsh*	C	Unopp.				
1932						
J.S. Riley*	C	1,347	34.1	5,367	38.5	-
G.A. Rogers*	C	1,299	32.9			
A. Sebborn	Lab	667	16.9			
J.R. Dunne	Lab	641	16.2			
Total votes		3,954				
Total voters		2,064				
1933						
A. Holden*	C	1,191	29.7	5,305	44.0	-
M.S. Webster*	C	1,006	25.1			
P. Mahon	Lab	614	15.3			
P. Rogerson	L	603	15.0			
J.R. Dunn	Lab	594	14.8			
Total votes		4,008				
Total voters		2,333				

Stanley ward *(continued)*

Candidate	Party	Votes	%	Electors	Turnout	Gains
1934						
J. Burnie*	L	1,007	29.2	5,281	33.6	-
W.E. Marsh*	C	900	26.1			
J.H. Hort	C	788	22.9			
P. Rogerson	L	750	21.8			
Total votes		3,445				
Total voters		1,773				
1935						
J.S. Riley*	C	1,645	37.6	5,324	41.9	-
G.A. Rogers*	C	1,628	37.2			
E. Gowling	Coop	549	12.5			
M.J. Murray	Coop	555	12.7			
Total votes		4,377				
Total voters		2,230				
1936						
M.S. Webster*	C	1,739	38.3	5,158	46.8	-
A. Holden*	C	1,679	37.0			
T.J. Griffiths	Lab	567	12.5			
Mrs M.J. Murray	Lab	556	12.2			
Total votes		4,541				
Total voters		2,416				
1937						
J.D. Crighton	C	1,746	31.6	5,025	57.2	C from L
E. Gardner	C	1,702	30.8			
J. Burnie*	L	1,191	21.6			
N. Landau	L	881	16.0			
Total votes		5,520				
Total voters		2,872				
1938						
J.S. Riley*	C	1,760	37.6	5,135	46.5	-
G.A. Rogers*	C	1,758	37.6			
A.F. Riley	Lab	603	12.9			
G. Cresswell	Lab	558	11.9			
Total votes		4,679				
Total voters		2,387				
Overall Labour vote		**10.2%**			**Overall turnout**	**48.3%**

TEN
Bournemouth

BOURNEMOUTH

Bournemouth in the late Victorian age was one of the three large towns of the distinct region of Wessex, the others being Southampton and Portsmouth.[1] In 1901 the recently established county borough had a population of almost 60,000, and by 1931 had almost doubled again to 116,000. Yet Bournemouth district in the mid-nineteenth century had had a population of just 695. The phenomenal growth of Bournemouth started between 1871 and the formation of the borough in 1891. The economic development that explained this rapid rise requires examination. The railway did not come directly to Bournemouth until 1870. Before that, from 1862 passenger trains had run only to Christchurch. There were grumbles by Bournemouth hoteliers in the 1870s that there was an uncomfortable six-hour journey from London on wooden seats for an exorbitant fare of twenty-eight shillings. This, it was alleged, caused a shortage of summer visitors. Nonetheless the town developed economically in the last three decades of the century.

Taking advantage of its location on the south coast, good beaches, a healthy climate with mild winters and long hours of sunshine, Bournemouth's late Victorian developers encouraged it to grow first as a health and later as a pleasure resort. The climate and location brought an influx of the wealthier middle class, who built up residential Bournemouth with its expensive properties, flats and nursing accommodation. The retired, and especially well-to-do widows, were to have an important impact on the town. Bournemouth also became a pleasure resort, and mass summer tourism was to have a significant effect. By 1900 Bournemouth had established itself as a high-quality resort, and a predominantly middle-class borough.[2] It was as a residential centre for large numbers of the retired wealthy classes that the service sector of Bournemouth developed. The hotels and lodging houses, together with the entertainment industry, also grew as tourism became more important.

The occupational structure requires some comment. There was very little employment in manufacturing industry in Bournemouth in the inter-war years. The metal and engineering sectors were of some significance, but still only 5 per cent of men and less than 1 per cent of women were employed in these categories in the industry tables of the 1931 census. The commercial and financial sectors were far more developed with a total labour force of 11,790, being over 25 per cent of the males and 17 per cent of the females classified by industry. The predominance of residential property and the tourist and leisure industries meant that 21 per cent of the workforce were in the managerial and self-employed categories, the fourth-highest proportion amongst all the county boroughs. This latter sector was to provide most of the councillors for the allegedly apolitical independents, eager to keep the rates down and public expenditure on a parsimonious string. As noted in other resorts, hotel owners and villa residents were predominantly conservative.[3] Again, personal service, accounting for 3,836

---

[1] Pelling, H. *Social Geography of British Elections*, (Aldershot, 1967), p. 125.
[2] Pelling, *Social Geography*, p. 131.
[3] Pelling, *Social Geography*, p. 170.

men (12.3 per cent) and 13,400 women (59.8 per cent), was politically significant. The proportion of domestic servants was still very high. However, many of these working-class people were denied the local government franchise at this time, putting a limit on the effect they could have on municipal elections.[4] Lastly, growing central government and defence industries accounted for 3,052 males (just under 10 per cent) and 814 females (3.6 per cent) in the 1931 census. The traditional conservatism with a small 'c' of this sector was reinforced by organised Conservative strength at parliamentary elections. Conservative central government was also more closely associated with greater defence expenditure and the latter had some importance in Bournemouth. This factor will be examined in greater depth in the analysis of Portsmouth and Plymouth, where it was of much greater significance, in Volume Seven of this series. It should be noted finally that to some degree the various factors which latterly had encouraged Conservatism in Bournemouth were offset by an older tradition of Nonconformity and Liberalism in the city.

Before 1918, the electors of Bournemouth voted in the single-member constituency of Christchurch. Conservative MPs were elected seven times between 1885 and 1910, but the Liberals had won in 1906 and generally performed strongly. Christchurch then, was in Pelling's estimation a very marginal Tory area. He notes a number of factors that made for some Liberal strength in Bournemouth, namely Nonconformity and the prevalence of leasehold property.[5] The former, with the collapse of the Liberal vote in the new single-member constituency of Bournemouth after 1918, was probably translated into support for Labour in at least two of the borough's wards. The second factor, leasehold property enfranchisement, was supported by the Liberals before the Great War, but the issue was certainly extinct in the inter-war municipal elections. In the new Bournemouth constituency after 1918 the vestiges of Liberal support were in rapid decline, Conservatives being returned in all Westminster elections between the wars.

Turning to municipal politics, Bournemouth became a municipal borough in 1890, elevation to county borough status following in 1900. In 1931 the Bournemouth Corporation Act saw further extension with the parishes of Holdenhurst and Kinson being incorporated. Holdenhurst was divided up and absorbed into the existing wards of Boscombe East, Malmesbury Park, Moordown, Southbourne and Springbourne. Kinson was annexed from residential Poole and became a distinct new ward. Conservative strength in Bournemouth was reflected in municipal politics, but in a faintly-disguised fashion. The Labour Party was weak overall, with only a few small pockets of support, but it was also alone in proclaiming its existence as an organised party in council politics. Its opponents, who had complete control over the city council, eschewed party labels, assuming an apolitical but in reality anti-Labour orientation. In all but name, the ruling councillors were overwhelmingly Conservatives, but they articulated a politics of 'small government' and local 'economy', aiming to keep the rates as low as was politically possible. There is no doubt that the nature of the inter-war

[4]   On the inter-war franchise, see the notes in this volume, pp. 671.
[5]   Pelling, *Social Geography*, p. 131.

municipal electorate, consisting essentially of ratepayers, made an emphasis on 'economy' more likely. This was especially so in an upmarket retirement and health resort like Bournemouth. Conversely, as noted above, the large percentage of domestic servants and low-paid hotel and lodging-house workers, who might have had rather different attitudes towards the level of rates and local government spending priorities, were mainly excluded from the franchise.

The occupations of candidates for the council also tell us something about the nature of the political conflict in Bournemouth. Although the available evidence is only for occasional years, the class orientation of the Labour and 'anti-Labour' forces can be clearly seen. Thus in 1920, the following occupations for independent candidates were recorded: two 'gentlemen', a retired agent, a dyer's supervisor, a retired leather merchant, a florist, an Admiralty accountant, an insurance agent, a proprietor of a lodging house, a hotel proprietress, a jeweller and a wholesale tobacconist. By contrast, standing for Labour were an insurance agent, a general labourer, a locomotive engineer, a trade-union organiser, and an agent.[6] Again in 1935, the *Echo* gave the employment of candidates for the elections as follows: for Labour, a railway employee, a medical practitioner, a general engraver, and a works foreman; for the independents, a company director, a hotel proprietor, a retired doctor of medicine, two building contractors, a retired coal merchant and a widow.[7] The broad class differences between the two sides of the political divide on the council were quite plain to see. Nor were those differences glossed over at the hustings. In opposing a Labour candidate in Moordown in 1927, the independent appealed to the electorate with the following placard: 'Don't stop to read this. Hurry to the poll and vote for Barnes; Do you want a sound man, do you want a businessman ...'[8]

Considering the inter-war social composition and character of the wards, three broad categories can be identified in Bournemouth. First there existed a coastal belt of wards along the channel from Westbourne, through West Cliff, Central, East Cliff, and Boscombe West and East, to Southbourne. These all included expensive accommodation, with a good proportion of detached housing and hotels, and with broad streets and formal parks. In this group Westbourne, for example, had an exceptionally low figure of only 0.47 persons per room in 1931, the lowest in the borough. All the other wards here had low persons per room figures, with Boscombe West the highest at 0.63, reflecting a great deal of affluence. The wards in this category were rock solid for the independents and returned councillors who wished to keep council projects at a minimum and the rates low. Only in East Cliff was there some slight variation, in that this ward contained some enclaves of poorer housing. G.W. Spicer, commenting on his defeat for Labour in 1934, indicated this with perhaps a degree of overstatement when he said:

> I think we may congratulate ourselves on our figures to within
> 200 this time ... I shall continue to fight for East Cliff because I

[6] *Bournemouth Daily Echo*, 26 Oct. 1920.
[7] *Bournemouth Daily Echo*, 31 Oct. 1935.
[8] *Bournemouth Daily Echo*, 1 Nov. 1927.

think a working-class ward should have working-class representatives.[9]

A second category which can be identified was comprised of the central wards, or more accurately a 'coastal hinterland' group, north of the coastal belt. With their terraced housing, narrower streets and newer housing developments, some of them council built, these wards mainly returned Labour councillors in this period. The poorer-quality housing and lower social class can be discerned in the persons per room data. Labour's stronghold of Moordown had 0.83 persons per room, the highest in the borough, while Springbourne, the other solid Labour ward was also relatively high with 0.73 persons per room. Springbourne, with fourteen Labour councillors returned between 1919 and 1932, was Labour's bastion. It had the main line of the London–South-West Railway running through a district of largely crowded terrace housing. It also had a brickworks, cemetery and the Sanitary Hospital within its boundaries. In the late Victorian age Springbourne was viewed 'as a small and somewhat self-contained workman's hamlet', with a mission church and a Wesleyan Chapel.[10] There was a hint of radicalism in that its streets were named not after 'Royals' but US presidents. With some boundary modifications, King's Park was Springbourne's successor ward in the 1933 reorganisation. The ward, however, remained solid for Labour returning a clean sweep of councillors up to the end of the period. Moordown was Labour's other fortress. In 1853, it was described as 'a tract of heath-land on which many poor families are settled'.[11] The tram sheds were built at Moordown in 1906. Although consisting mainly of poorer terraced housing, in the 1920's some council-house building took place in this ward. The *Bournemouth Daily Echo* referred to the class nature of Moordown in the 1927 election. Reporting apathy on the day of the poll despite excellent weather, the *Echo* commented 'that it is expected that there will be a real rush after six o'clock, it being pointed out that as Moordown is a working class ward people cannot vote in large numbers until the evening'.[12] Similarly in 1931 Springbourne was described as 'a ward largely populated by the working-classes'.[13]

A third group was made up of the outer suburban wards, largely green belt and farmland at the start of the period. New private housing development occurred here after the First War. Malmesbury Park (Queens Park from the 1933 reorganisation) with Winton and Kinson (from 1931) fell into this category. Winton had substantial detached houses especially in Talbot village, although some new developments pushed it up to 0.62 person per room by 1931. These wards were again barren territory for Labour, except that after the 1933 reorganisation the new ward of Redhill Park became an area of some Labour strength, primarily due to the spread of council housing. The onset of the Depression saw council-house building slow to a virtual halt in the 1930s, especially in the light of the political complexion of the borough. However, much

---

9 *Bournemouth Daily Echo*, 2 Nov. 1934.
10 Young, D.S., *The Story of Bournemouth* , (London, 1970), p. 88.
11 Popham, D. and R., *The Book of Bournemouth*, (Buckingham, 1985), p. 17.
12 *Bournemouth Daily Echo*, 1 Nov. 1927.
13 *Bournemouth Daily Echo*, 2 Nov. 1931.

of the council housing stock that had already been built was incorporated into Redhill Park, taken from the northern part of Winton and the south-east of Kinson.

Given the dominance of the independents and the lack of contests, 'municipal apathy' was to be a recurring headline in the local press in early November each year. In 1919, the *Echo* noted that municipal government was now more important than before, given the growth of local government bodies together with the problems of post-war reconstruction. But with a prescience based on pre-war local politics, the *Echo* noted:

> Interest in local affairs has reached a very low ebb, so much so ...
> as to bring the system of representation into serious disrepute. But
> there is evidence on all hands of a new life in local politics. There
> certainly never was a time when a condemnation of apathy and
> inertia was more necessary.[14]

The year 1919 saw greater opportunity for women in local politics and increased the electoral roll from 13,431 to 28,827, of whom almost 50 per cent voted. Although 1919 was a good year for the Labour Party nationally, this was not quite the case in Bournemouth. Labour had eight candidates defeated, including two women. There was only one Labour success in which George Tiller retained Moordown with 52 per cent of the poll. The following year saw a Labour gain with E.J. Stocker winning Moordown. The main interest in 1921 was a public works project to help in the relief of the unemployed, an issue especially significant in Southbourne. Here the retiring councillor was defeated because of his support for the Pavilion scheme in any works undertaken for the relief of the unemployed. This did not meet the approval of the voters of the more affluent eastern end of the ward, or of the Middle Classes' Union.[15] Again the Pavilion scheme was the main local interest in 1922, with the *Echo* believing the town was now favourable towards the project, as shown by the fact that all of the retiring councillors were returned.[16]

Largely the 1920s were poor years for Labour with the party never holding more than half-a-dozen council seats. In 1921, Labour lost Moordown for the only time before reorganisation, but at the same time gained a seat in Springbourne. Housing was made a Labour issue in 1923, but Mrs Tiller was defeated in Winton where the issue was aired. By winning two contests in 1925, Labour at least had all six council seats in Moordown and Springbourne. On the local scale this could be seen as a reflection of Labour's growth in the mid and late 1920s nationally. However, apathy ruled in 1926 with only one contest in which Labour held Moordown, and despite a clash of two middle-class independents in Winton in 1927, the third Labour candidate contrived to come bottom of the poll. 1929 did not see any great success for Labour as a reflection of the party's achievements at Westminster. The *Echo* commented that it was difficult to realise that an election

---

[14] *Bournemouth Daily Echo*, 31 Nov. 1919.
[15] *Bournemouth Daily Echo*, 2 Nov. 1921.
[16] *Bournemouth Daily Echo*, 2 Nov. 1922.

was in progress, with only three contests taking place.[17] It is worth noting that two of the candidates were Guardians who had been rendered redundant by the recent reform of the old Poor Law system. Their desire for council seats was in order to continue their work in this field through the newly-created Public Assistance Committee of the council.

There were no contests whatsoever in 1930, followed by only one contest in 1931 in which Labour held Springbourne, despite the incorporation of the more affluent Holdenhurst area in the ward because of the borough extension. In the 1932 election Labour made housing an issue. The *Echo* reported a Labour Party meeting in which Bournemouth was compared unfavourably with nearby Eastleigh, where Hampshire county council had built 1,000 council houses. Two Labour candidates, Dr R.A. Lyster and Miss M.M. Whitehead, held a joint public meeting in which Lyster suggested that the high rents pertaining in the borough were due to a housing ring which was operating in the town. Pleading for fair medical and health treatment for the poor, he hammered home what he saw as the difference between Labour and the rest of the council: 'Economy, with ruling authorities, too often meant economy at the expense of the poorest. (hear, hear)'.[18] In another part of his speech Lyster made further allusions to the ruling bloc of non-party councillors, making the following accusation that went down very well with his audience:

> During his 35 years experience of public administration, he said,
> he had noted that candidates labelling themselves 'independent'
> could generally be depended upon to 'vote reactionary'.

Miss Whitehead too raised an issue dear to Labour and received an enthusiastic reception:

> Among the planks of her programme was more and better council
> houses, built by direct labour; wider roads in the county borough,
> as needed by present day traffic; justice not charity, for the
> unemployed.

At another meeting at the Labour Hall on the eve of the poll, once more the issues of rents and council-house building were raised. This was one of the rare occasions when a clear reference to the activities of the Conservative Party in the municipal politics of Bournemouth was reported in the *Echo*. Usually their presence was cloaked in their independent disguise, but at this meeting Councillor Wilkinson declared that the whole forces of Tory organisation were being mobilised against Dr Lyster. Dr Lyster had apparently been referred to elsewhere as the most hated member of the Bournemouth council, which the meeting saw approvingly as a sign of his progressive stance. Miss Whitehead and Lyster were portrayed as 'the only progressive candidates, the only employment candidates,' standing 'for everything worth living'. When Dr Lyster addressed the meeting, he made great play of the housing issue. He once again referred to the high rents in the town and the existence of a housing ring, saying:

[17] *Bournemouth Daily Echo.*, 1 Nov. 1929.
[18] *Bournemouth Daily Echo*, 28 Oct. 1932.

the only way to break that ring is to build a large number of houses and those landlords in Bournemouth will come to heel ... We stand for public interest before private interest.[19]

Lastly there was an interesting allusion to class-based politics by Councillor Tom Peaty:

When the working class representatives are denounced by the other side, in the main they are on the right track.

With reorganisation, the elections of 1933 were hectic and saw a dozen contests. Labour fought the two Moordown wards where four seats were available in total, Redhill Park where three seats were up for election, and the one seat in King's Park. Public transport was a major issue in the election. At a crowded meeting in the Co-operative Hall in Winton, both J.H. Collingbourne and another Labour man, W.H. Duell, argued that the motor and trolley bus system should remain under the control of the town council and not be handed over to private enterprise as the council leaders were considering. Duell further said that publicly-owned transport benefited ratepayers, while the benefits of a system run by private enterprise 'would go into shareholders' pockets'.[20] M.J. Dando, who came top of the poll for Labour in Moordown South, spoke at the same meeting. Dando was not a typical resident of Bournemouth. He claimed he had been connected to the trade-union movement for over twenty years, having started work as a miner at the age of thirteen. Part of his platform for election was the building of council houses to keep private rents low. Public works, he said, could be effected in Wimborne Road between Winton Library and Brassey Road, 'putting the unemployed to useful work'. Later Miss Whitehead, who was one of the two Labour successes in Moordown North, addressed the meeting. She wanted a large number of council houses built by direct labour. She also condemned any move to hand over the transport system to private enterprise, seeing the system as one of the town's greatest assets. Advocating a decrease in fares, Miss Whitehead 'said that during the summer season many people living in the northern wards could not afford to take their families down to the beach continuously'.

1933 was a good year for the Labour party, with its representation on the augmented council increasing by three councillors. Notably for Labour, two women councillors, Mrs Tiller and Miss Whitehead, joined the independent Mrs Laney on the council. Another woman, Mrs Boyce in Southbourne ward, was also added to the independent ranks. The party's strength after the November elections of 1933 stood at an all time high of ten, which included two aldermen. Labour was to retain this strength of nearly a fifth of the council until the World War. Labour's local success reflected its national performance in the municipal elections of 1933. The national resurgence appeared all the more impressive because Labour made many gains by recouping the numerous losses of three years previously in the disastrous campaign of 1930. In Bournemouth this factor did not apply, making Labour's successes all the more notable locally.

---

[19] *Bournemouth Daily Echo*, 1 Nov. 1932.
[20] *Bournemouth Daily Echo*, 28 Oct. 1933.

However, Labour made no further headway in Bournemouth for the rest of the 1930s. 1934 was uneventful, with only one change in six contests, with one independent replacing another. The headline for the *Echo* in 1935 was 'Labour's "No Change" ' in Bournemouth, but in effect it was a poor year for the party, with Dr Lyster being the only candidate to retain his seat. Labour lost out in East Cliff, Queens Park, Kinson and more surprisingly failed in Moordown North by eighty-five votes. The following year saw 'No Change in Bournemouth' as the headline yet again, although Labour this time held Moordown North in a straight fight with an independent. The year 1937 saw little activity with only two contests. In West Cliff, a declared 'Independent' unseated an unlabelled independent councillor, a rare rebellion on behalf of the hoteliers' interest against the ruling clique. The rebel in his acceptance speech said that he had no party backing and 'wanted to see hoteliers as one in the town',[21] although he himself was actually a jeweller. The last election before the war saw six contests in the town. Few issues arose and only one Labour candidate faced opposition. He was defeated by ninety-five votes on a 40 per cent turnout in Moordown North, a clear indication of Labour's faltering performance in the second half of the 1930s.

The question of ward boundaries and their revision was an issue of some significance in inter-war Bournemouth politics. While ward size had been relatively equal in 1919, by the early 1930s inequities had developed. Labour's strongest ward, Moordown, had tripled in size to over 7,000 voters, reflecting lower-cost housing developments there, some of them council financed. By contrast the affluent West Cliff ward, and Central ward which contained a high proportion of plural voters, had barely 2,000 voters each. Local Labour politicians believed that they had a number of grievances which they aired to the commissioner appointed to prepare the new scheme of redistribution of ward boundaries in October 1932. Mr W.H. Duell was reported as follows:

> Speaking of the present representation, Mr. Duell said that the electorate of the Central, West Cliff and Westbourne wards totalled 6,970 as compared with 7,098 in Moordown alone – a thing that could not be tolerated. The first three wards had 12 representatives including aldermen, as compared with four in Moordown.
>
> He quoted figures in the proposed scheme, viz. Southbourne, 2,725 electorate, Central, 2,040, Southbourne East, 3,259, ... and said the revision still left great inequalities.
>
> Developments in nearly all cases were going on in the outside wards, Southbourne, Moordown, Winton, Malmesbury Park, and Springbourne. During the year ended April 1st 1932, 849 houses were erected in the borough, the greater number in the outside wards, 286 being in the added area. The development in the Central, West Cliff and Westbourne wards was practically nil, a great deal of development in rateable value, but a decrease in the electorate. These wards showed a far greater proportion of non-

---

[21] *Bournemouth Daily Echo*, 2 Nov. 1937.

residents than the other wards, which decreased their claim from the electorate point of view.[22]

To the same committee of enquiry Councillor J.H. Collingbourne (Labour) highlighted the same unfairness to Moordown. The 1933 reorganisation went a good way to satisfy the demands of the Labour Party. Moordown was split into the North and South wards. These two wards, with 4,107 and 3,813 voters respectively, were still the first and fourth largest wards, but the differentials were much smaller, and the overall allocation was considerably fairer. Even so, the coastal and suburban wards dominated by the independents remained marginally smaller. Thus Central, Kinson, Queens Park and West Southbourne had an average of 500 voters less when compared to the three strongest Labour wards, the Moordowns and Kings Park.

Turning to the aldermanic system, as Bournemouth was so overwhelmingly controlled by the small-businessmen and hoteliers backed electorally by the well-off, unsurprisingly the aldermen were selected solely from amongst their number from 1919 to 1930. This unabashed use of power on behalf of the ruling group gave way to a sense of 'fair play' soon after, with Labour's first success in the aldermanic elections coming with the elevation of J.J. Empson, who was joined later in 1933 by George Tiller, the Moordown Labour councillor. Given the overwhelming majority held by the ruling group, it was no great risk to concede some ground to Labour in the interest of damping down bad feeling in the council chamber. In relation to councillor strength, Labour was still marginally under-represented at the aldermanic level. Between 1920 and 1926 Labour should have had one alderman in proportion to their number of councillors, two between 1927 and 1933, and three by 1935.

The issue of gender was of some significance in Bournemouth. Given the important residential and retirement role of Bournemouth, and the greater longevity of women, women far outnumbered men on the local government electoral registers throughout the inter-war years. However, as table 10.1 at the end of this chapter shows, the ratio of females to males on an individual ward basis reveals that Moordown, probably Labour's strongest ward, had by far the lowest differential, and Springbourne, its other main stronghold, had a less than average differential. There was plainly a class dimension to the gender imbalance of the borough. Working-class women were alleged to been more interested than men in housing, health and education as affected by council policies, all issues which appear to have been given much priority by Labour in Bournemouth. This was made explicit in 1923, when Mrs Tiller, the defeated Labour candidate in Winton, used housing as an issue. She declared that housing conditions were 'absolutely terrible', saying the housing problem should be 'solved for the sake of the women and children'.[23] Perhaps the gender imbalance of the borough helped to push Labour's policies in this direction.[24]

[22] *Bournemouth Daily Echo*, 28 October, 1932.
[23] *Bournemouth Daily Echo*, 2 Nov. 1923.
[24] On women and municipal services in other boroughs, see Davies, S,. *Liverpool Labour: Social and Political Influences on the Development of the Labour Party in Liverpool, 1900–1939*, (Keele, 1996), pp. 167–195.

However, the numerical advantage of women on the local electoral roll was more important in the wealthier wards of the coastal and central belt. Here mainly retired and wealthy women from the higher social classes living in the residential wards almost certainly favoured the independents. The politics of parsimonious small government at the local level would have been attractive to middle- and high-income residents. This was especially so as many lived on fixed incomes from annuities and pensions, or the proceeds of sold businesses. The *Bournemouth Daily Echo* certainly saw gender as a political factor in local politics. On the eve of the 1919 municipal elections, it noted that women outnumbered men in all wards of the town. It considered whether women would use their power as many of the chief problems of the town were 'those in which woman are closely concerned'.[25] However great the preponderance of women in the borough, this was plainly not reflected in their representation on the council. In a speech to the returning officer for Boscombe East in 1929, Miss Mott, the defeated candidate, was reported to have 'created some amusement when she said Bournemouth was a place with more women voters than men and yet women could only send one of their number to the council. "I think", she added "that there should be more than one woman among forty-two men." '[26] As indicated earlier, it was only Labour's two women victors in 1933 that helped to change this picture significantly.

In conclusion, what can be said about inter-war municipal elections in Bournemouth? First, the electoral importance of well-to-do retired people together with the residential character of the town ensured the overwhelming dominance of independents who assumed an apolitical guise. The economic structure of Bournemouth, with tourism to the fore and little manufacturing industry, reinforced the political presence of hoteliers and other small-businessmen in the council chamber. This control resulted in a dominant political ethos of 'small government', with the objective of keeping public services on a tight rein, and the rates as low as was feasible. Thus capital improvement projects for tourism could be contemplated, while council-house construction, rudimentary social expenditure and improvements to public transport were a low priority.

Second, the Labour Party was weak in Bournemouth. This reinforced the low-key nature of political conflict and the virtual absence of formal party politics on the council. Labour's lack of success was due to the smallness of the working class of the borough, which was primarily a product of the service nature of the town's economy. Labour's support was also very much concentrated in two wards in the 1920s, and three wards in the 1930s. This limited any possibility of it making gains elsewhere in the borough, but on the other hand it also guaranteed it a permanent minority bloc of councillors in this period. Labour also suffered some political disadvantage from the operation of the aldermanic system, and from the inequity of ward boundaries, but these were only marginal factors in its overall weakness.

Third, the decline of Liberalism, noted as a force in Bournemouth before the First War, was significant. In safe Conservative seats at the parliamentary level,

---

[25] *Bournemouth Daily Echo*, 31 Oct. 1919.
[26] *Bournemouth Daily Echo*, 2 Nov. 1929.

and where independents or other such non-party groupings ruled the roost locally, it seems apparent that organised Liberalism was subsumed in a broad anti-Labour alliance. Bournemouth was a good example of this, but similar developments applied in a number of other boroughs, as will become apparent in this and later volumes. Where such an anti-Labour alliance held, the ideological distinction between the political traditions of Liberalism and Conservatism became blurred. Many voters supported the grouping they thought best able to fend off Labour, while some others of a more radical bent might have gone over to Labour. In the process the identity of local Liberalism was seriously undermined.

Fourth, the numerical strength of women on the local electoral register differentiated Bournemouth from many other county boroughs. The political significance of this was varied. Most numerous in the affluent middle-class wards of the borough, women voters here probably reinforced the independents' control of the council and the avoidance of political labels. On the other hand, the preponderance of women may have influenced Labour to stress issues that were assumed to be of greater interest to them, such as housing and social policy. In terms of political representation, though, women made only small gains on the council, despite their majority in the local electorate.

Last, geography and climate were twin influences on the economy of the town. Bournemouth was made by the importance of its residential nature and by twentieth-century tourism. This in turn shaped the politics of low social expenditure and the control of independent councillors. The Labour councillor Dr Lyster expressed the belief that such politicians would always 'vote reactionary' in policy-making, and there is some evidence here to support that view, but only a much deeper investigation of local politics could fully substantiate it.

Table 10.1 Women voters as a percentage of total municipal electorate in
Bournemouth 1919–38

Ward	1919	1930	Ward	1938
Boscombe East	56.9	58.1	Boscombe East	60.7
Boscombe West	61.4	61.1	Boscombe West	60.9
Central	60.5	59.1	Central	59.1
East Cliff	57.8	57.2	East Cliff	57.9
Malmesbury Park	57.8	58.2	King's Park	55.6
Moordown	52.2	53.7	Kinson	52.0
Southbourne	60	59.6	Moordown North	53.3
Springbourne	53.8	55.5	Moordown South	54.6
Westbourne	63.6	63.6	Queen's Park	58.4
West Cliff	60.2	61.2	Redhill Park	55.2
Winton	56.3	57.3	Southbourne	57.2
Total	**57.6**	**57.9**	Westbourne	62.9
			West Southbourne	60.0
			West Cliff	61.5
			Winton	56.1
			Total	**57.4**

Source: Sidney J. Mate's Bournemouth and Poole Directory and Year Book

A guide to further reading

Newspapers

Bournemouth Daily Echo
Bournemouth Times and Directory
Bournemouth Graphic

Works of reference

Sidney J. Mate's Bournemouth and Poole Directory and Year Book, various
    volumes.
Kelly's Directory of Bournemouth, Boscombe etc., various volumes.

Other secondary sources

Mate, C.H. and Riddle, C., *Bournemouth*, (1910).
Municipal Journal and Public Works Engineer, 'Beautiful Bournemouth', vol. 40, (4 Dec. 1931), pp. 1793–1794.
Pelling, H., *Social Geography of British Elections*, (Aldershot, 1967).
Popham, D. and R., *The Book of Bournemouth*, (Buckingham, 1985).
Roberts, R.W., 'The Development of the Economic Functions of Local Government in England and Wales, 1880–1914, with Special Reference to Bournemouth', (Ph.D. thesis, University of Cambridge, 1981).
Roberts, R., 'Leasehold estates and municipal enterprise: landowners, local government and the development of Bournemouth, c.1850–1914', in Cannadine, D., (ed.), *Patricians, Power and Politics in Nineteenth-Century Towns*, (Leicester, 1982).
Soane, J., 'The Significance of the Development of Bournemouth, 1840–1940', (Ph.D. thesis, University of Surrey, 1977).
Young, D.S., *The Story of Bournemouth* , (London, 1970).

Bournemouth wards 1919–1932

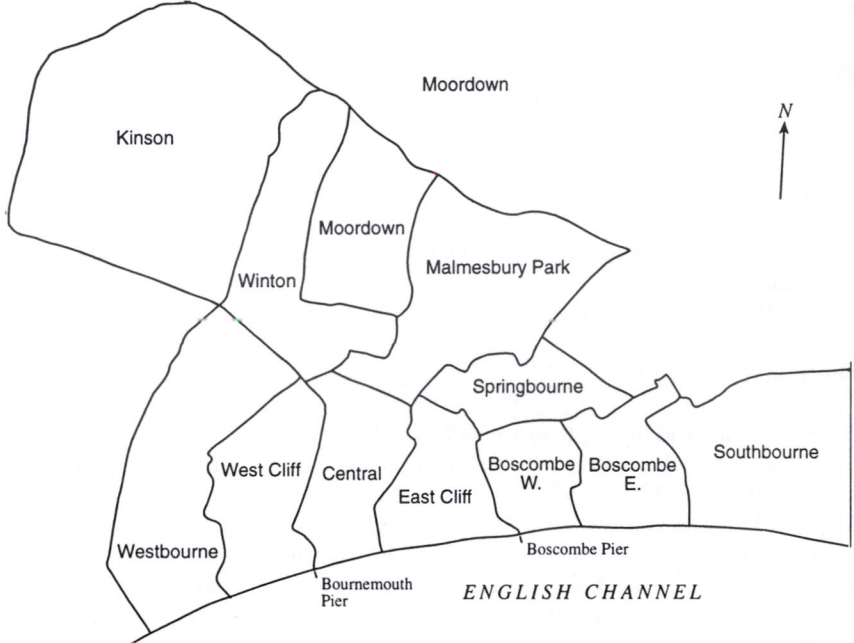

Bournemouth wards 1933–1938

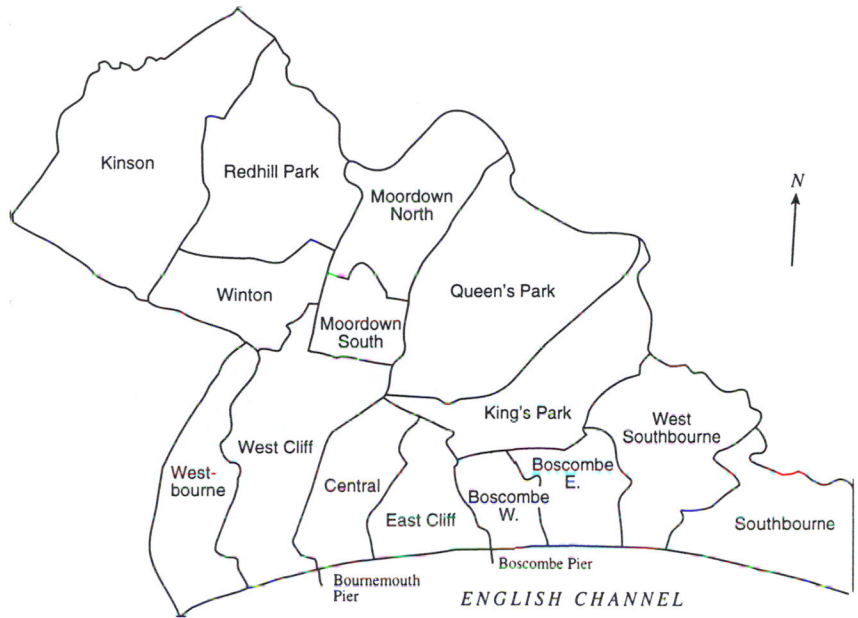

Persons aged fourteen and over classified by industry 1931

	Male	%	Female	%	Total	%
Metal and engineering	1,568	5.0	103	0.5	1,671	3.1
- Vehicle construction and repair	*613*	*2.0*	*36*	*0.2*	*649*	*1.2*
Building	4,614	14.8	44	0.2	4,658	8.7
Transport	2,689	8.6	118	0.5	2,807	5.2
- Road	*1,862*	*6.0*	*99*	*0.4*	*1,961*	*3.7*
Commerce and finance	7,957	25.6	3,833	17.1	11,790	22.0
Public admin. and defence	3,052	9.8	814	3.6	3,866	7.2
- Local government	*2,065*	*6.6*	*525*	*2.3*	*2,590*	*4.8*
Professions	1,515	4.9	2,130	9.5	3,645	6.8
Personal service	3,836	12.3	13,400	59.8	17,236	32.2
Others	5,884	18.9	1,955	8.7	7,839	14.6
Total (a)	**31,115**		**22,397**		**53,512**	
Total population (b)	47,060		69,737		116,797	
(a) as % of (b)	66.1		32.1		45.8	
Total out of work (c)	2,085		908		2,993	
(c) as % of (a)	6.7		4.1		5.6	
Managerial and own account	7,295	25.1	3,320	15.4	10,615	21.0
Operative	21,735	74.9	18,169	84.6	39,904	79.0
Total (excluding out of work)	29,030		21,489		50,519	

Population statistics 1931

Ward	Acres	Population	Persons/acre	Persons/room
Boscombe East	641	9,352	14.6	0.62
Boscombe West	278	8,720	31.4	0.63
Central	447	6,656	14.9	0.51
East Cliff	377	8,611	22.8	0.65
Kinson	2,769	8,496	3.1	0.81
Malmesbury Park	1,456	8,104	5.6	0.59
Moordown	1,012	15,541	15.4	0.83
Southbourne	1,485	15,465	10.4	0.60
Springbourne	804	7,637	9.5	0.73
Westbourne	865	6,484	7.5	0.47
West Cliff	490	8,913	18.2	0.57
Winton	589	12,818	21.8	0.62
Total	**11,213**	**116,797**	**10.4**	**0.64**

Overall position on the council 1919–38

	Position		Gains		Losses	
	Other	Lab	Other	Lab	Other	Lab
1919	42	2	0	0	0	0
1920	41	3	0	1	1	0
1921	39	5	0	1	1	0
1922	39	5	0	0	0	0
1923	39	5	0	0	0	0
1924	39	5	0	0	0	0
1925	39	5	0	0	0	0
1926	39	5	0	0	0	0
1927	38	6	0	1	1	0
1928	38	6	0	0	0	0
1929	38	6	0	0	0	0
1930	37	7	0	0	0	0
1931[a]	41	7	0	0	0	0
1932	41	7	0	0	0	0
1933[b]	50	10	0	0	0	0
1934	50	10	0	0	0	0
1935	50	10	0	0	0	0
1936	50	10	0	0	0	0
1937	50	10	0	0	0	0
1938	50	10	0	0	0	0

Aldermen 1919–38

1919	Other–11	1929	Other–11
1920	Other–11	1930	Other–11
1921	Other–11	1931[a]	Other–11, Lab–1
1922	Other–11	1932	Other–11, Lab–1
1923	Other–11	1933[b]	Other–14, Lab–1
1924	Other–11	1934	Other–13, Lab–2
1925	Other–11	1935	Other–13, Lab–2
1926	Other–11	1936	Other–13, Lab–2
1927	Other–11	1937	Other–13, Lab–2
1928	Other–11	1938	Other–13, Lab–2

[a] 3 councillors and 1 alderman added in 1931.
[b] 9 councillors and 3 aldermen added in 1933.

Municipal elections: winning party 1919–28

Ward	1919	1920	1921	1922	1923	1924	1925	1926	1927	1928
Boscombe East	O	O	O	O	O	O	**O**	**O**	**O**	**O**
Boscombe West	O	**O**	**O**	O	**O**	**O**	O	**O**	**O**	**O**
Central	O	**O**	**O**	**O**	**O**	**O**	**O**	**O**	O	**O**
East Cliff	O	**O**	O	O	O	**O**	**O**	**O**	**O**	**O**
King's Park	-	-	-	-	-	-	-	-	-	-
Kinson	-	-	-	-	-	-	-	-	-	-
Malmesbury Park	O	O	O	O	**O**	**O**	**O**	**O**	**O**	O
Moordown	Lab	Lab	O	**Lab**	**Lab**	O	Lab	Lab	Lab	Lab
Moordown N. (1)	-	-	-	-	-	-	-	-	-	-
Moordown N. (2)	-	-	-	-	-	-	-	-	-	-
Moordown N. (3)	-	-	-	-	-	-	-	-	-	-
Moordown South	-	-	-	-	-	-	-	-	-	-
Queen's Park	-	-	-	-	-	-	-	-	-	-
Redhill Park	-	-	-	-	-	-	-	-	-	-
Redhill Park (2)	-	-	-	-	-	-	-	-	-	-
Redhill Park (3)	-	-	-	-	-	-	-	-	-	-
Southbourne	O	O	O	**O**	O	**O**	**O**	**O**	O	O
Southbourne (2)	-	-	-	-	-	-	-	-	-	-
Southbourne (3)	-	-	-	-	-	-	-	-	-	-
Springbourne	O	Lab	Lab	Lab	**Lab**	**Lab**	Lab	**Lab**	**Lab**	**Lab**
Westbourne	O	**O**	**O**	**O**	**O**	**O**	**O**	**O**	**O**	**O**
West Cliff	O	O	O	O	**O**	**O**	O	**O**	**O**	**O**
West Southbourne	-	-	-	-	-	-	-	-	-	-
Winton	O	O	**O**	**O**	O	O	**O**	**O**	O	O

Municipal elections: party wins per year 1919–28

	1919	1920	1921	1922	1923	1924	1925	1926	1927	1928
Lab	1	2	1	2	2	1	2	2	2	2
Others	10	9	10	9	9	10	9	9	9	9
Total	11	11	11	11	11	11	11	11	11	11
Turnout %	49.7	45.2	50.9	57.7	44.1	49.2	59.6	48.6	54.4	48.4
Labour %	26.0	33.0	19.2	24.2	27.0	27.1	34.8	54.9	25.4	18.2

Municipal elections: winning party 1929–38

Ward	1929	1930	1931	1932	1933	1934	1935	1936	1937	1938
Boscombe East	O	O	O	O	O	O	O	O	O	O
Boscombe West	O	O	O	O	O	O	O	O	O	O
Central	O	O	O	O	O	O	O	O	O	O
East Cliff	O	O	O	O	O	O	O	O	O	O
King's Park	-	-	-	-	Lab	Lab	Lab	Lab	Lab	Lab
Kinson	-	-	O	O	O	O	O	O	O	O
Malmesbury Park	O	O	O	O	-	-	-	-	-	-
Moordown	Lab	Lab	Lab	Lab	-	-	-	-	-	-
Moordown N. (1)	-	-	-	-	Lab	Lab	O	Lab	Lab	O
Moordown N. (2)	-	-	-	-	O	-	-	-	-	-
Moordown N. (3)	-	-	-	-	Lab	-	-	-	-	-
Moordown South	-	-	-	-	Lab	O	Lab	Lab	O	Lab
Queen's Park	-	-	-	-	O	O	O	O	O	O
Redhill Park	-	-	-	-	O	Lab	O	O	Lab	O
Redhill Park (2)	-	-	-	-	O	-	-	-	-	-
Redhill Park (3)	-	-	-	-	Lab	-	-	-	-	-
Southbourne	O	O	O	O	O	O	O	O	O	O
Southbourne (2)	-	-	-	-	O	-	-	-	-	-
Southbourne (3)	-	-	-	-	O	-	-	-	-	-
Springbourne	Lab	Lab	Lab	Lab	-	-	-	-	-	-
Westbourne	O	O	O	O	O	O	O	O	O	O
West Cliff	O	O	O	O	O	O	O	O	O	O
West Southbourne	-	-	-	-	O	O	O	O	O	O
Winton	O	O	O	O	O	O	O	O	O	O

Municipal elections: party wins per year 1929–38

	1929	1930	1931	1932	1933	1934	1935	1936	1937	1938
Lab	2	2	2	2	5	3	2	3	3	2
Others	9	9	10	10	16	12	13	12	12	13
Total	11	11	12	12	21	15	15	15	15	15
Turnout %	43.8	-	58.2	45.4	47.6	45.9	44.5	34.4	35.2	44.5
Labour %	-	-	69.8	24.7	29.8	32.1	33.1	55.9	22.9	14.7

Municipal elections: party wins per ward 1919–38

	Lab	Other	Total	Turnout %	Labour % of all votes
Boscombe East	0	20	20	43.2	17.0
Boscombe West	0	20	20	49.7	5.4
Central	0	20	20	55.6	-
East Cliff	0	20	20	49.6	31.8
King's Park	6	0	6	48.5	61.2
Kinson	0	8	8	42.8	31.9
Malmesbury Park	0	14	14	49.2	12.8
Moordown	12	2	14	51.1	50.3
Moordown North	5	3	8	36.9	52.4
Moordown South	4	2	6	47.4	44.1
Queen's Park	0	6	6	46.8	6.2
Redhill Park	3	5	8	42.3	37.3
Southbourne	0	22	22	44.2	8.1
Springbourne	13	1	14	59.5	55.5
Westbourne	0	20	20	47.4	8.2
West Cliff	0	20	20	52.9	2.0
West Southbourne	0	6	6	61.2	-
Winton	0	20	20	47.1	14.2
Total	**43**	**209**	**252**	**48.1**	**26.6**

Seats won by Labour as a percentage of all wins 1919–38   **17.1**

Parliamentary election results

Bournemouth constituency
(all wards within the borough [1918 boundaries] were included in the constituency)

General election	Winner	Conservative %	Labour %	Liberal %
14 Dec. 1918	NP	-	25.0	8.7
15 Nov. 1922	C	52.3	-	33.9
6 Dec. 1923	C	50.4	19.5	30.1
29 Oct. 1924	C	72.7	27.3	-
30 May 1929	C	52.2	15.9	31.9
27 Oct. 1931	C	80.0	20.0	-
14 Nov. 1935	C	71.1	28.9	-

Boscombe East ward

Candidate	Party	Votes	%	Electors	Turnout	Gains
1919						
J.R. Edgecombe		790	42.9	2,860	64.3	-
W.J. McCabe*		634	34.5			
E.J. Stocker	Lab	416				
Total votes		1,840				
1920						
G. Newman*		450	73.8	3,034	20.1	-
J.A. Neppiras	Lab	160	26.2			
Total votes		610				
1921						
F.B. Summerbee*		908	70.2	3,168	40.8	-
F. Mills		386	29.8			
Total votes		1,294				
1922						
J.R. Edgecombe*		967	65.2	3,220	46.1	-
E.G. Stay	Lab	517	34.8			
Total votes		1,484				
1923						
G. Newman*		534	43.2	3,314	37.3	-
J.R. Goodchild	Lab	527	42.7			
G.A. Parker		174	14.1			
Total votes		1,235				
1924						
F.B. Summerbee*		1,308	79.7	3,438	47.8	-
E.G. Stay	Lab	334	20.3			
Total votes		1,642				
1925						
J.R. Edgecombe*		Unopp.	-	3,632	-	-
1926						
A.H. Abbott		Unopp.	-	3,709	-	-
1927						
F.B. Summerbee*		Unopp.	-	3,806	-	-
1928						
J.R. Edgecombe*		Unopp.	-	3,850	-	-

Boscombe East ward *(continued)*

Candidate	Party	Votes	%	Electors	Turnout	Gains
1929						
H.A. Abbot*		1,099	55.6	4,114	48.0	-
W.J. Arnold		518	26.2			
Miss A. Mott		358	18.1			
Total votes		1,975				
1930						
A.H. Little*		Unopp.	-	4,131	-	-
1931						
J.R. Edgecombe*		Unopp.	-	4,508	-	-
1932						
H.A. Abbott*		Unopp.	-	4,576	-	-
1933						
A.H. Little*		Unopp.	-	3,484	-	-
1934						
A.C. Meader*		Unopp.	-	3,451	-	-
1935						
L.V. Barney		Unopp.	-	3,461	-	-
1936						
A.H. Little*		Unopp.	-	3,472	-	-
1937						
A.C. Meader*		Unopp.	-	3,389	-	-
1938						
L.V. Barney*		906	64.4	3,422	41.1	-
H.C. King		500	35.6			
Total votes		1,406				

Overall Labour vote	**17.0%**			**Overall turnout**		**43.2%**

Boscombe West ward

Candidate	Party	Votes	%	Electors	Turnout	Gains
1919						
J. Wilson*		248	42.8	2,575	22.5	-
Mrs E.S. Hull	Lab	332	57.2			
Total votes		580				
1920						
Mrs F.E. Laney*		Unopp.	-	2,730	-	-
1921						
W. Jones		Unopp.	-	2,885	-	-
1922						
W.J. McCabe		1,283	75.6	2,927	58.0	-
H. Hook		414	24.4			
Total votes		1,697				
1923						
Mrs F.E. Laney*		Unopp.	-	2,985	-	-
1924						
W. Jones*		Unopp.	-	3,060	-	-
1925						
W.J. McCabe*		937	51.6	3,113	58.3	-
W.F. Street		878	48.4			
Total votes		1,815				
1926						
Mrs F.E. Laney*		Unopp.	-	3,087	-	-
1927						
W. Jones*		Unopp.	-	3,633	-	-
1928						
A.J. Playdon		Unopp.	-	3,195	-	-
1929						
Mrs F.E .Laney*		Unopp.	-		-	-
1930						
W. Jones*		Unopp.	-	3,194	-	-

Boscombe West ward *(continued)*

Candidate	Party	Votes	%	Electors	Turnout	Gains
1931						
A.J. Playdon*		Unopp.	-	3,211	-	-
1932						
Mrs F.E. Laney*		Unopp.	-	3,208	-	-
1933						
W. Jones*		Unopp.	-	3,808	-	-
1934						
A.J. Playdon*		1,469	71.9	3,732	54.7	-
W.J. Pharo		573	28.1			
Total votes		2,042				
1935						
W.F. Street		Unopp.	-	3,871	-	-
1936						
E.L.A. Hockey*		Unopp.	-	3,864	-	-
1937						
A.J. Playdon*		Unopp.	-	3,824	-	-
1938						
W.F. Street*		Unopp.	-	3,788	-	-

Overall Labour vote	**5.4%**			**Overall turnout**	**49.7%**

Central ward

Candidate	Party	Votes	%	Electors	Turnout	Gains
1919						
J.D. Mann		435	57.8	1,613	46.6	-
R. Hodges*		317	42.2			
Total votes		752				
1920						
C.H. Cartwright*		Unopp.	-	1,723	-	-
1921						
F.J. Webb*		Unopp.	-	1,820	-	-
1922						
H.J. Thwaites*		Unopp.	-	1,869	-	-
1923						
H.E.G. Beale*		Unopp.	-	1,947	-	-
1924						
F.J. Webb*		Unopp.	-	1,996	-	-
1925						
H.J. Thwaites*		Unopp.	-	2,061	-	-
1926						
H.E.G. Beale*		Unopp.	-	2,008	-	-
1927						
T.V. Rebbeck		713	56.5	2,012	62.7	-
F.J. Webb*		549	43.5			
Total votes		1,262				
1928						
E.J. Mapp*		Unopp.	-	2,010	-	-
1929						
H.E.G. Beale*		Unopp.	-		-	-
1930						
T.V. Rebbeck*		Unopp.	-	2,040	-	-
1931						
E.J. Mapp*		Unopp.	-	2,052	-	-

Central ward *(continued)*

Candidate	Party	Votes	%	Electors	Turnout	Gains
1932						
H.E. George*		Unopp.	-	2,004	-	-
1933						
T.V. Rebbeck*		Unopp.	-	3,435	-	-
1934						
R.H. Old*		Unopp.	-	3,442	-	-
1935						
J.B.C. Beale		Unopp.	-	3,466	-	-
1936						
T.V. Rebbeck*		Unopp.	-	3,379	-	-
1937						
R.C.H. Old*		Unopp.	-	3,455	-	-
1938						
J.B.C. Beale*		Unopp.	-	3,519	-	-

Overall Labour vote   -   **Overall turnout**   **55.6%**

East Cliff ward

Candidate	Party	Votes	%	Electors	Turnout	Gains
1919						
W.E. Crowther		643	46.4	2,529	54.8	-
H.J. Thwaites*		463	33.4			
C.E. Richards	Lab	279				
Total votes		1,385				
1920						
C.A. George*		Unopp.	-	2,622	-	-
1921						
J.J. Brazier*		877	63.3	2,700	51.3	-
Mrs R. Gubby		509	36.7			
Total votes		1,386				
1922						
J. Fox		752	40.7	2,889	63.9	-
J.H. Collingbourne	Lab	606	32.8			
W. Hale		489	26.5			
Total votes		1,847				
1923						
C.A.D. George*		873	63.4	2,993	46.0	-
F.D. Roberts	Lab	504	36.6			
Total votes		1,377				
1924						
J.J. Brazier*		Unopp.	-	3,024	-	-
1925						
J. Fox*		Unopp.	-	3,014	-	-
1926						
P.M. Bright*		Unopp.	-	2,920	-	-
1927						
J.J. Brazier*		Unopp.	-	2,971	-	-
1928						
J. Fox*		Unopp.	-	2,946	-	-
1929						
P.M. Bright*		Unopp.	-		-	-

East Cliff ward *(continued)*

Candidate	Party	Votes	%	Electors	Turnout	Gains
1930						
L.F. King*		Unopp.	-	3,100	-	-
1931						
J. Fox*		Unopp.	-	3,099	-	-
1932						
A.J. Marsh*		Unopp.	-	3,087	-	-
1933						
L.F. King*		Unopp.	-	3,703	-	-
1934						
H.E. Harding*		912	56.5	3,697	43.7	-
G.W. Spicer	Lab	702	43.5			
Total votes		1,614				
1935						
A.J. Marsh*		1,194	58.8	3,761	54.0	-
G.W. Spicer	Lab	838	41.2			
Total votes		2,032				
1936						
L.F. King*		Unopp.	-	3,855	-	-
1937						
H.E. Harding*		Unopp.	-	3,765	-	-
1938						
H.C. Brown*		843	58.6	3,788	38.0	-
E.T. Eames	Lab	596	41.4			
Total votes		1,439				

Overall Labour vote   **31.8%**   **Overall turnout**   **49.6%**

King's Park ward
(created out of Springbourne ward with minor alterations in the 1933 reorganisation)

Candidate	Party	Votes	%	Electors	Turnout	Gains
1933						
W. Wilkinson*	Lab	1,304	58.7	3,850	57.7	-
J.N. Hardy		918	41.3			
Total votes		2,222				
1934						
T. Peaty*	Lab	Unopp.	-	4,077	-	-
1935						
Dr R.A. Lyster*	Lab	1,103	64.4	4,262	40.2	-
S.H. Snell		611	35.6			
Total votes		1,714				
1936						
W. Wilkinson*	Lab	Unopp.	-	4,435	-	-
1937						
T. Peaty*	Lab	Unopp.	-	4,574	-	-
1938						
Dr R.A. Lyster*	Lab	Unopp.	-	4,792	-	-

Overall Labour vote **61.2%** **Overall turnout** **48.5%**

Kinson ward
(created by extension of the borough in 1931; part transferred to Redhill Park ward in the 1933 reorganisation)

Candidate	Party	Votes	%	Electors	Turnout	Gains
1931						
J. Burt*		Unopp.	-	4,524	-	-
1932						
F.F. Hawkins*		Unopp.	-	4,924	-	-
1933						
H.A. Benwell*		Unopp.	-	3,339	-	-
1934						
A.A. Cull*		Unopp.	-	3,675	-	-
1935						
F.F. Hawkins*		1,172	68.1	4,027	42.8	-
S. Dyer	Lab	550	31.9			
Total votes		1,722				
1936						
H.A. Benwell*		Unopp.	-	4,386	-	-
1937						
A.A. Cull*		Unopp.	-	4,853	-	-
1938						
F.F. Hawkins*		Unopp.	-	5,286	-	-
Overall Labour vote		**31.9%**		**Overall turnout**		**42.8%**

Malmesbury Park ward
(becomes Queen's Park ward with minor alterations in the 1933 reorganisation)

Candidate	Party	Votes	%	Electors	Turnout	Gains
1919						
T. Pratten*		584	38.2	2,863	53.4	-
W.H. Willoughby		493	32.3			
C. Cox	Lab	451	29.5			
Total votes		1,528				
1920						
W.H. Ridout*		1,258	80.0	3,041	51.7	-
C. Cox	Lab	314	20.0			
Total votes		1,572				
1921						
F. Court*		1,036	71.1	3,035	48.0	-
H.C. James		421	28.9			
Total votes		1,457				
1922						
T. Pratten*		782	54.2	3,064	47.1	-
W. Taylor		661	45.8			
Total votes		1,443				
1923						
W.H. Ridout*		Unopp.	-	3,191	-	-
1924						
F. Court*		Unopp.	-	3,327	-	-
1925						
T. Pratten*		Unopp.	-	3,444	-	-
1926						
P.W.T. Hayward*		Unopp.	-	3,450	-	-
1927						
F. Court*		Unopp.	-	3,522	-	-
1928						
C.D. Newton		989	58.7	3,574	47.2	-
F. Corbin		697	41.3			
Total votes		1,686				

Malmesbury Park ward *(continued)*

Candidate	Party	Votes	%	Electors	Turnout	Gains
1929						
P.W.T. Hayward*		Unopp.	-		-	-
1930						
H. Salt		Unopp.	-	3,855	-	-
1931						
C.D. Newton*		Unopp.	-	4,036	-	-
1932						
P.W.T. Hayward*		1,560	76.4	4,205	48.6	-
Miss M.M. Whitehead	Lab	483	23.6			
Total votes		2,043				

Overall Labour vote	**12.8%**		**Overall turnout**	**49.2%**

Moordown ward
(divided into Moordown North and Moordown South wards in the 1933 reorganisation)

Candidate	Party	Votes	%	Electors	Turnout	Gains
1919						
G. Tiller*	Lab	807	52.0	2,477	62.6	-
J. Martin	Nfds	666	42.9			
N.H. Arter		78	5.0			
Total votes		1,551				
1920						
E.J. Stocker	Lab	1,051	58.9	3,715	48.0	Lab from O
G. Evans*		733	41.1			
Total votes		1,784				
1921						
T. Cole*		1,081	55.0	3,861	50.9	-
F. Perriman	Lab	884	45.0			
Total votes		1,965				
1922						
G. Tiller*	Lab	Unopp.	-	4,140	-	-
1923						
E.J. Stocker*	Lab	Unopp.	-	4,415	-	-
1924						
A.J. Seal		1,254	58.0	4,852	44.6	-
J.H. Collingbourne	Lab	909	42.0			
Total votes		2,163				
1925						
G. Tiller*	Lab	1,407	51.7	5,238	51.9	-
H.C. Barnes		1,312	48.3			
Total votes		2,719				
1926						
J.H. Collingbourne*	Lab	1,495	54.9	5,595	48.6	-
H.C. Barnes		1,226	45.1			
Total votes		2,721				

Moordown ward *(continued)*

Candidate	Party	Votes	%	Electors	Turnout	Gains
1927						
W.C. Street	Lab	1,342	44.0	5,991	50.9	Lab from O
H.C. Barnes		1,224	40.1			
T.J. Rowley		484	15.9			
Total votes		3,050				
1928						
G. Tiller*	Lab	1,862	53.8	6,241	55.4	-
H.C. Barnes		1,597	46.2			
Total votes		3,459				
1929						
J.H. Collingbourne*	Lab	Unopp.	-		-	-
1930						
W.C. Street*	Lab	Unopp.	-	7,098	-	-
1931						
G. Tiller*	Lab	Unopp.	-	7,556	-	-
1932						
J.H. Collingbourne*	Lab	Unopp.	-	7,755	-	-

Overall Labour vote   **50.3%**   **Overall turnout**   **51.1%**

Moordown North ward
(created out of part of Moordown ward in the 1933 reorganisation)

Candidate	Party	Votes	%	Electors	Turnout	Gains
1933						
W.C. Street*	Lab	927	23.1	3,813	36.8	-
S.H.C. Lorie		909	21.7			
Miss M.M. Whitehead	Lab	727	17.4			
A.S. Ritchie	Lab	680	16.2			
W.H. Thomas		666	15.9			
G.W. Miller		236	5.6			
Total votes		4,145				
Total voters		1,405				
(3 elected)						
1934						
Miss M.M. Whitehead*	Lab	866	52.0	3,859	43.1	-
W. Taylor		798	48.0			
Total votes		1,664				
1935						
W. Taylor		868	52.6	3,984	41.4	-
A.S. Ritchie	Lab	783	47.4			
Total votes		1,651				
1936						
W.C. Street*	Lab	824	55.9	4,280	34.4	-
S. Lawrance		649	44.1			
Total votes		1,473				
1937						
Miss M.M. Whitehead*	Lab	700	59.2	4,552	26.0	-
R.C. Kellaway		482	40.8			
Total votes		1,182				
1938						
W. Taylor*		1,042	52.4	4,905	40.6	-
F.W. Purdy	Lab	947	47.6			
Total votes		1,989				
Overall Labour vote		**52.4%**		**Overall turnout**		**36.9%**

Moordown South ward
(created out of part of Moordown ward in the 1933 reorganisation)

Candidate	Party	Votes	%	Electors	Turnout	Gains
1933						
M.J. Dando	Lab	782	41.8	4,107	45.5	-
H.C. Barnes		728	39.0			
Mrs E. Bizby		359	19.2			
Total votes		1,869				
1934						
H.C. Barnes*		1,081	53.9	4,072	49.3	-
G.M. Troke	Lab	926	46.1			
Total votes		2,007				
1935						
J.H. Collingbourne	Lab	Unopp.	-	4,072	-	-
1936						
M.J. Dando*	Lab	Unopp.	-	4,056	-	-
1937						
H.C. Barnes*		Unopp.	-	3,981	-	-
1938						
J.H. Collingbourne*	Lab	Unopp.	-	3,949	-	-
Overall Labour vote		**44.1%**		**Overall turnout**		**47.4%**

Queen's Park ward
(created out of Malmesbury Park ward with minor alterations in the 1933 reorganisation)

Candidate	Party	Votes	%	Electors	Turnout	Gains
1933						
H. Salt*		Unopp.	-	3,396	-	-
1934						
C.D. Newton*		Unopp.	-	3,549	-	-
1935						
P.W.T. Hayward*		1,252	85.3	3,577	41.0	-
Mrs K. Burbidge	Lab	215	14.7			
Total votes		1,467				
1936						
H. Salt*		Unopp.	-	3,558	-	-
1937						
C.D. Newton*		Unopp.	-	3,669	-	-
1938						
D.E. Richards		1,400	70.5	3,808	52.2	-
A.W. Thresher*		586	29.5			
Total votes		1,986				

Overall Labour vote   **6.2%**   **Overall turnout**   **46.8%**

Redhill Park ward
(Created from parts of Kinson and Winton wards in the 1933 reorganisation)

Candidate	Party	Votes	%	Electors	Turnout	Gains
1933						
R.J. Raggett		1,412	28.9	3,508	46.6	-
J.E. Bevis		1,140	23.3			
Mrs A. Tiller	Lab	875	17.9			
G.F. Rider		515	10.5			
W.J. Clapcott		476	9.7			
T.C. George		466	9.5			
Total votes		4,884				
Total voters		1,634				
(3 elected)						
1934						
Mrs A. Tiller*	Lab	835	60.1	3,643	38.2	-
F. Jarvis		555	39.9			
Total votes		1,390				
1935						
J.E. Bevis		Unopp.	-	3,831	-	-
1936						
R.J. Raggett*		Unopp.	-	4,011	-	-
1937						
Mrs A. Tiller*	Lab	Unopp.	-	4,242	-	-
1938						
J.E. Bevis*		Unopp.	-	4,331	-	-

Overall Labour vote   **37.3%**   **Overall turnout**   **42.3%**

Southbourne ward
(part transferred to West Southbourne ward in 1933 reorganisation)

Candidate	Party	Votes	%	Electors	Turnout	Gains
1919						
C. Hussey		998	75.0	2,928	45.5	-
J.A. Neppiras	Lab	333	25.0			
Total votes		1,331				
1920						
W.G. Roff		889	72.4	3,130	39.2	-
T. Slade		339	27.6			
Total votes		1,228				
1921						
H. Sparkes		1,223	83.3	3,364	43.6	-
H. Hook*		245	16.7			
Total votes		1,468				
1922						
A. Sutton*		Unopp.	-	3,569	-	-
1923						
W.G. Roff*		702	44.0	3,768	42.4	-
A.W. Phillips		610	38.2			
H. Hook		284	17.8			
Total votes		1,596				
1924						
H.M. Sparkes*		Unopp.	-	4,148	-	-
1925						
A. Sutton*		Unopp.	-	4,533	-	-
1926						
R.G. Ash-Moody		Unopp.	-	4,883	-	-
1927						
H.M.P. Sparkes*		1,942	74.7	5,253	49.5	-
E.G. Stay	Lab	656	25.3			
Total votes		2,598				
1928						
J. Richards		1,429	56.5	5,462	46.3	-
A. Sutton*		1,099	43.5			
Total votes		2,528				

Southbourne ward *(continued)*

Candidate	Party	Votes	%	Electors	Turnout	Gains
1929						
R.G. Ash-Moody*	Unopp.	-			-	-
1930						
W. Taylor*	Unopp.	-		6,438	-	-
1931						
J. Richards*	Unopp.	-		7,392	-	-
1932						
A. Langton*	Unopp.	-		7,858	-	-
1933						
J.H. Turner		1,303	86.3	3,829	39.4	-
G. Haigh		1,262	83.6			
Mrs F.E. Boyce		1,145				
J.H. Sugden		685				
Total Votes		4,395				
Total poll		*1,510*				
(3 elected)						
1934						
Mrs F.E. Boyce	Unopp.	-		4,194	-	-
1935						
G. Haigh*	Unopp.	-		4,516	-	-
1936						
J.H. Turner*	Unopp.	-		4,764	-	-
1937						
Mrs F.E. Boyce*	Unopp.	-		4,963	-	-
1938						
G. Haigh*	Unopp.	-		5,091	-	-
Overall Labour vote		**8.1%**		**Overall turnout**		**44.2%**

Springbourne ward
(becomes King's Park ward with minor alterations in the 1933 reorganisation)

Candidate	Party	Votes	%	Electors	Turnout	Gains
1919						
T. Peaty	Nfds	784	56.0	2,870	48.8	Nfds from O
R. Chamberlain*		499	35.6			
W. Notton		118	8.4			
Total votes		1,401				
1920						
J.J. Empson*	Lab	986	70.2	3,079	45.6	-
Mrs R. Gubby		419	29.8			
Total votes		1,405				
1921						
W. Wilkinson	Lab	1,189	59.0	3,132	64.3	Lab from O
W. Taylor*		825	41.0			
Total votes		2,014				
1922						
T. Peaty*	Lab	1,294	54.3	3,227	73.9	-
P.W.T. Hayward		1,090	45.7			
Total votes		2,384				
1923						
J.J. Empson*	Lab	Unopp.	-	3,212	-	-
1924						
W. Wilkinson*	Lab	Unopp.	-	3,245	-	-
1925						
T. Peaty*	Lab	1,459	64.0	3,323	68.6	-
Dr W. Asten		821	36.0			
Total votes		2,280				
1926						
J.J. Empson*	Lab	Unopp.	-	3,317	-	-
1927						
W. Wilkinson*	Lab	Unopp.	-	3,334	-	-
1928						
T. Peaty*	Lab	Unopp.	-	3,364	-	-

Springbourne ward *(continued)*

Candidate	Party	Votes	%	Electors	Turnout	Gains
1929						
J.J. Empson*	Lab	Unopp.	-		-	-
1930						
W. Wilkinson*	Lab	Unopp.	-	3,629	-	-
1931						
T. Peaty*	Lab	1,513	69.8	3,727	58.2	-
Dr S.H. Snell		656	30.2			
Total votes		2,169				
1932						
Dr R.A. Lyster*	Lab	1,190	56.9	3,728	56.1	-
F.G.R. Heather		902	43.1			
Total votes		2,092				
Overall Labour vote		**55.5%**		**Overall turnout**		**59.5%**

Westbourne ward

Candidate	Party	Votes	%	Electors	Turnout	Gains
1919						
W.J.L. Beaton*		534	72.9	1,692	43.3	-
Dr A.B. Scott	Lab	199	27.1			
Total votes		733				
1920						
A. Youngman*		Unopp.	-	1,791	-	-
1921						
W.E. Odlum*		Unopp.	-	1,872	-	-
1922						
J. Frost*		Unopp.	-	1,904	-	-
1923						
A. Youngman*		Unopp.	-	1,976	-	-
1924						
H.B. Norton		Unopp.	-	2,079	-	-
1925						
J. Frost*		Unopp.	-	2,120	-	-
1926						
C. Fox*		Unopp.	-	2,165	-	-
1927						
D.E. Hillier*		Unopp.	-	2,206	-	-
1928						
J. Frost*		Unopp.	-	2,322	-	-
1929						
C. Fox*		Unopp.			-	-
1930						
D.E. Hillier*		Unopp.	-	2,420	-	-
1931						
J. Frost*		Unopp.	-	2,505	-	-
1932						
W.G. Hale*		Unopp.	-	2,472	-	-

Westbourne ward *(continued)*

Candidate	Party	Votes	%	Electors	Turnout	Gains
1933						
D.E. Hillier*	Unopp.	-		3,063	-	-
1934						
R.F. Seward*	Unopp.	-		3,160	-	-
1935						
W.G. Hale*	Unopp.	-		3,245	-	-
1936						
J.W. Moore*	Unopp.	-		3,336	-	-
1937						
S.A. Thomson*	Unopp.	-		3,398	-	-
1938						
Mrs C.I. Hilyer		919	53.9	3,454	49.4	-
W.G. Hale*		787	46.1			
Total votes		1,706				

Overall Labour vote   **8.2%**   **Overall turnout**   **47.4%**

West Cliff ward

Candidate	Party	Votes	%	Electors	Turnout	Gains
1919						
T. Mattocks*		691	73.4	1,765	53.4	-
W.H. Duell	Lab	251	26.6			
Total votes		942				
1920						
C. Fox*		546	52.4	1,810	57.6	-
H.G. Harris		496	47.6			
Total votes		1,042				
1921						
H.G. Harris		606	50.8	1,918	62.1	-
Dr R.N. Hart*		586	49.2			
Total votes		1,192				
1922						
T. Mattocks*		573	51.3	1,965	56.8	-
Miss G.M. Saye		543	48.7			
Total votes		1,116				
1923						
Dr T.B. Scott*		Unopp.	-	2,045	-	-
1924						
H.G. Harris		Unopp.	-	2,107	-	-
1925						
T. Mattocks*		636	44.9	2,123	66.7	-
I.W. Dickinson		549	38.8			
A.R. Baker		230				
Total votes		1,415				
1926						
E.R. Whitfield*		Unopp.	-	2,098	-	-
1927						
H.G. Harris*		Unopp.	-	2,115	-	-
1928						
I.W. Dickinson*		Unopp.	-	2,071	-	-

West Cliff ward *(continued)*

Candidate	Party	Votes	%	Electors	Turnout	Gains
1929						
Dr A. Lee		940	72.0	2,207	59.1	-
O.C. Porter		365	28.0			
Total votes		1,305				
1930						
H.G. Harris*		Unopp.	-	2,150	-	-
1931						
I.W. Dickinson*		Unopp.	-	2,147	-	-
1932						
Dr A. Lee*		Unopp.	-	2,140	-	-
1933						
S.J.J. Wise*		Unopp.	-	3,869	-	-
1934						
I.W. Dickinson*		Unopp.	-	3,962	-	-
1935						
W.J. Clapcott		1,050	54.1	4,042	48.0	-
F.J. McInnes		892	45.9			
Total votes		1,942				
1936						
F.J. McInnes		Unopp.	-	4,007	-	-
1937						
G.W. Pascall		997	53.1	4,134	45.4	-
H. Brown		879	46.9			
Total votes		1,876				
1938						
W.J. Clapcott*		1,146	58.1	4,227	46.6	-
R.F. Seward		825	41.9			
Total votes		1,971				

Overall Labour vote		**2.0%**		**Overall turnout**		**52.9%**

West Southbourne ward
(created out of part of Southbourne ward in the 1933 reorganisation)

Candidate	Party	Votes	%	Electors	Turnout	Gains
1933						
F. Curtis		906	45.4	3,263	61.2	-
W. Taylor*		678	34.0			
S.E. Hayes		413	20.7			
Total votes		1,997				
1934						
J. Richards*		Unopp.	-	3,544	-	-
1935						
A. Langton		Unopp.	-	3,573	-	-
1936						
R.W. Scott		Unopp.	-	3,722	-	-
1937						
J. Richards*		Unopp.	-	3,757	-	-
1938						
A. Langton*		Unopp.	-	3,781	-	-

Overall Labour vote   -   **Overall turnout**   **61.2%**

Winton ward
(part transferred to Redhill Park ward in the 1933 reorganisation)

Candidate	Party	Votes	%	Electors	Turnout	Gains
1919						
G.J. Luckham*		823	46.5	3,646	48.5	-
Mrs A. Tiller	Lab	522	29.5			
J. Mason		424	24.0			
Total votes		1,769				
1920						
R. Chamberlain*		1,414	66.5	3,776	56.3	-
F. Jeans	Lab	711	33.5			
Total votes		2,125				
1921						
J.A. Nethercoate		Unopp.	-	3,900	-	-
1922						
G.J. Luckham*		Unopp.	-	4,039	-	-
1923						
R. Chamberlain*		1,393	67.9	4,129	49.7	-
Mrs A. Tiller	Lab	660	32.1			
Total votes		2,053				
1924						
C. Long*		1,166	48.5	4,338	55.4	-
T.M. Morgan		796	33.1			
H.W. Schofield	Lab	443	18.4			
Total votes		2,405				
1925						
T.M. Morgan*		Unopp.	-	4,718	-	-
1926						
R. Chamberlain*		Unopp.	-	5,135	-	-
1927						
Dr W. Asten		1,568	47.0	5,566	59.9	-
W.G. Hale		1,159	34.8			
Dr A.A. Hill	Lab	608				
Total votes		3,335				

Winton ward *(continued)*

Candidate	Party	Votes	%	Electors	Turnout	Gains
1928						
T.M. Morgan*		1,428	56.3	5,797	43.7	-
T.J. Rowley		1,107	43.7			
Total votes		2,535				
1929						
R. Chamberlain*		1,210	53.3	6,346	35.8	-
T.J. Rowley		1,062	46.7			
Total votes		2,272				
1930						
Dr W. Asten*		Unopp.	-	6,584	-	-
1931						
T.M. Morgan*		Unopp.	-	6,785	-	-
1932						
R. Chamberlain*		1,392	53.0	6,977	37.7	-
W.J. Clapcott		1,235	47.0			
Total votes		2,627				
1933						
Dr W. Asten*		Unopp.	-	3,565	-	-
1934						
G.F. Rider		634	38.4	3,569	46.3	-
H.P.E. Mears		609	36.9			
T.M. Morgan*		408	24.7			
Total votes		1,651				
1935						
S.C. Hoddinott		Unopp.	-	3,610	-	-
1936						
Dr W. Asten*		Unopp.	-	3,744	-	-
1937						
G.F. Rider*		Unopp.	-	3,779	-	-
1938						
S.C. Hoddinott*		Unopp.	-	3,795	-	-
Overall Labour vote		**14.2%**		**Overall turnout**		**47.1%**

CONCLUSION
The aggregate and comparative analysis

Conclusion – the aggregate and comparative analysis

It is intended that as each volume of this publication is completed, the electoral data for the individual boroughs will be themselves consolidated to give an aggregate analysis of electoral trends over the inter-war period. As the series develops, therefore, a more and more representative picture of the overall trends will emerge. At the same time, the boroughs will also be compared to one another statistically in terms of turnout and various measures of Labour party support. As further boroughs are covered in later volumes, it will also be possible to categorise them in various ways and analyse them comparatively. Thus regional trends, or trends in larger cities, or in textile towns, for instance, will be revealed. It is also intended that more qualitative comparative analysis of the different boroughs will be undertaken, taking up various contentious and important issues relating to inter-war politics such as the rise of Labour, the decline of Liberalism, the consolidation of Toryism, gender and politics, and so on. In this way these volumes should throw light on many aspects of the politics of the period.

However, these intentions can only be partially fulfilled in this first volume. Only ten of the eighty-three county boroughs have been analysed so far, and it would be wrong to assume that these ten constitute a representative sample of the whole. It is the case that by covering the boroughs alphabetically, a suitably random selection has been made in each volume, but the aggregate data could only be considered representative in statistical terms when two or perhaps three volumes have been completed. Only a brief consideration of the list of ten boroughs in this volume makes this point obvious. The regional spread is limited, notable omissions being the North-East and Wales, and the Midlands is represented only by Birmingham, and Yorkshire by Barnsley. Birmingham, the largest county borough, by its sheer size is also likely to have a disproportionate impact on the aggregate figures so far. This may distort the overall trends, especially given both the very low turnout and low Labour support found in England's second city. For the same reasons, it would also be premature to present any definitive comparative analysis of the boroughs, whether of a quantitative or qualitative nature, at this stage. These tasks must await the completion of future volumes. For now, only tentative suggestions can be made.

The aggregate analysis

Consolidated figures for the ten Volume One boroughs, consisting of various measures of voter support and involvement in municipal elections, are presented below. These provide at least some provisional view of the overall inter-war trends in the county boroughs, but in addition to the proviso about the representative nature of the ten boroughs, it is also important to be aware of other limitations to the data collected in the series as a whole. First, these figures relate to county boroughs in England and Wales only, excluding Scotland and Ireland (pre- and post-partition). Second, the county boroughs themselves mainly comprised the larger urban centres, all but three of them having a population over 50,000 in 1931. However, there were a number of other local authorities, mostly fast-growing urban district councils in the south-east such as Willesden, Tottenham and Dagenham, and one or two others such as Rhondda and Stretford, which also had populations of over 50,000. As already stated in the introduction to this volume, these authorities held their elections in the spring, and therefore cannot be directly compared with the county boroughs. The biggest urban centre of all, London, was largely represented in its own metropolitan boroughs, with only three county boroughs in the London area, West and East Ham and Croydon, persisting in their own right after the 1899 legislation. Elections were held every three years in the London boroughs, with all councillors coming up for election at the same time. Additionally, there was only one alderman to every six councillors in these authorities, and for both these reasons the metropolitan boroughs were also not directly comparable to the county boroughs. Third, a significant proportion of the parliamentary electorate (varying somewhere between 10 and 20 per cent over the whole inter-war period) was excluded from municipal elections due to differences in the franchise.[1]

In sum then, the county borough elections reflected the voters' preferences of the municipal electorate of most of the larger provincial urban centres of England and Wales. They cannot be taken to be fully representative of the whole voting-age population of Great Britain. In terms of political allegiance, relatively strong Labour-supporting areas at this time such as London, south-west Scotland, and most of the semi-rural coal-mining districts such as South Wales and the North-East, are not included. On the other hand, the predominantly Conservative agrarian rural areas are also missing. It may also be the case that the franchise exclusions favoured Labour's opponents in municipal elections, although this is by no means certain.[2]

One further qualification needs to be considered. In parliamentary elections between the wars most constituencies were usually contested. Only the 1918 and 1931 general elections were exceptions to this rule, for contingent reasons. The effect of unopposed coalition candidates and Sinn Fein candidates in Ireland in 1918 resulted in 107 out of the total of 707 seats being uncontested. The national coalition of 1931 resulted in sixty-seven no-contests out of 615 seats. Fewer than 10 per cent of constituencies were uncontested in all other cases, and in 1929 only three seats in the whole of England, Wales and Scotland were not contested.[3] By contrast, far more elections tended to be uncontested at the municipal level. This was especially the case in the smaller, or more rural, authorities, and also in the London boroughs. At the municipal level, the county boroughs on the whole had

---

[1] On the franchise and aldermanic systems, see the notes at the end of this volume, pp. 670–671.
[2] Evidence for Liverpool may support this possibility. See Davies, S., *Liverpool Labour: Social and Political Influences on the development of the Labour Party in Liverpool, 1900–1939*, (Keele, 1996), pp. 119–126.
[3] See Craig, F.W.S., *British Electoral Facts 1832–1987*, (Dartmouth, 5th edn, 1989), pp. 21–33.

the lowest level of no-contests. Even so, as the evidence for Bath or Bournemouth in this volume plainly shows, many seats could still be uncontested. The majority of no-contests in this period took place in seats where Labour had little chance of success, and therefore did not put up candidates against its opponents. This tended to make Labour's performance seem better than it really was. Many non-Labour votes, that would have been cast in great numbers in these seats if contests had taken place, were excluded. The decision in these volumes to calculate the Labour vote as a percentage of all votes cast, rather than as a percentage of votes cast only in the seats Labour contested, partially compensates for this. The greater the number of wards Labour conceded without a contest, then the less its total vote tended to be as a proportion of all votes. This was because non-Labour votes would build up in those seats where parties other than Labour confronted each other. This measure thus gives a more realistic impression of Labour's support. Nevertheless, no-contests still produce a distorting effect on the electoral data that cannot be precisely quantified. Summary figures for uncontested seats in the ten Volume One boroughs are shown below at the end of this chapter in Table 11.3.[4]

Taking all these factors together, one other point needs to be made. However imperfect or unrepresentative the aggregate figures of county borough elections may be, the data will still constitute a valuable indicator of trends over time. The distortions can be regarded for the most part as constant factors, affecting the data more or less equally from year to year. The eighty-three county boroughs can be seen in themselves as a large and constant sample, providing a unique view of changes in political support over the twenty-year period. Keeping all these qualifications in mind, therefore, the aggregate figures for the ten boroughs of this volume are summarised at the end of this chapter in Tables 11.1, 11.2 and 11.3. It should be noted that the decision to measure party support only in terms of the Labour Party has been taken on entirely pragmatic grounds. Labour was the only party that consistently stood under its proper name throughout the country in municipal politics at this time. In some boroughs the other main parties were sometimes in alliance, and also adopted different names at times. Only Labour, therefore, can be clearly identified for these purposes.

Analysing the trends shown in the three tables, Labour started in the November 1919 municipal elections by winning just over one-third of the votes cast in these ten boroughs. This was a dramatic increase from its pre-war position, and a far better performance than it had managed in the 'coupon' general election of December 1918. The heightened social tension and industrial conflict that came in 1919 may have been an underlying factor in Labour's rise this year. Labour may also have been helped by its new constitution, including the famous Clause IV commitment to greater public ownership, and its new and more effective organisational structure. Labour's good performance was also reflected in the fact that it won one-third of all seats decided that year. Labour success was achieved on a low turnout of only 42.7 per cent, a feature that was to be repeated on a number of occasions between the wars. This contrasts very much with the

---

[4]   The figures for no-contests in this volume tend to conflict with the view put elsewhere that there were 'relatively few uncontested elections' in the 1920s; see Cook, C., *The Age of Alignment: Electoral Politics in Britain, 1922–1929*, (London, 1975), pp. 49, 66.

post-1945 conventional political wisdom, which has maintained that low turnout has usually hurt Labour most. It should also be noted that Labour did not contest almost one-third of all the seats available, but less than 10 per cent of all seats were actually no-contests. This meant that Labour's share of the overall vote would have been lowered, as many non-Labour votes were cast in contests where they had no candidate. As a result of the 1919 net gains, thirty-one in total, Labour held 16.8 per cent of all the seats on the ten councils after the elections. This total included aldermanic seats as well, of which Labour held very few.

After this good start, Labour fell back sharply in 1920 on a much higher turnout of 50 per cent. Its share of the vote fell to its lowest point between the wars, although the fall from the previous year did not appear so dramatic. This was to some extent due to the contrast being with the artificially-lowered 1919 figure described above. This time far fewer seats where Labour did not stand were contested by other parties, so large numbers of non-Labour votes were not piled up in them. In terms of seats won, the decline was much clearer, Labour winning only one in five of the seats available, and making only six net gains. The early 1920s down to 1925 remained disappointing for Labour. Its vote share recovered, but this was in part an artificial boost caused by the increased number of uncontested seats where Labour put up no candidate. This was a result mainly of decreasing Liberal candidatures, and Liberal and Tory pacts or mergers in municipal politics. Labour's share of seats won revealed the real picture, fluctuating in the 15 to 20 per cent range. Overall in the ten boroughs between 1920 and 1924, there were nine net Labour losses. In 1922, defending the big gains of three years previously, Labour suffered net losses of twenty-three seats in these boroughs. In 1924, the county borough elections took place three days after the general election in which the 'Zinoviev letter' had played its part. Labour's losses in parliament and the downfall of the first Labour government were faithfully reflected at the municipal level. Labour won only 15 per cent of all the seats contested in the ten boroughs, its worst performance between the wars. Turnout remained fairly constant through this period at 50 to 55 per cent.

Labour support showed a marked shift upwards from 1926, peaking in 1929. The great industrial defeat experienced by the labour movement in the General Strike of May 1926 was accompanied by a swing to the Labour Party at the municipal elections six months later. Further success in 1927 and 1928 presaged the election of the second Labour government in the general election of May 1929. The party's vote share in the ten boroughs climbed to the 40 per cent range in this period, hitting 45.4 per cent in 1929, and it made substantial net gains of eighty-one seats between 1925 and 1929. In 1929 Labour won 42.3 per cent of all seats available, its best inter-war performance, and by that year it held roughly one-third of all the seats on the ten councils, a reflection also of increases in its share of aldermen. In three of the boroughs in this volume, Barnsley, Barrow and Birkenhead, Labour won control of the council for the first time between 1926 and 1928. The negative correlation between Labour's performance and turnout was also manifested in this period, turnout declining back to its 1919 level to near 40 per cent in 1929.

The electoral trends in these ten boroughs were reversed sharply by the impact of the second Labour government. Its increasing problems, especially over unemployment policy, led to its disastrous collapse in 1931 and the formation of Ramsay MacDonald's 'national' coalition. These developments took place in the context of the onset of the Depression from 1929. Labour candidates at municipal elections were the recipients of a severe backlash by the voters as a result of these developments. This was manifested quite plainly in November 1930, significantly before the political crisis developed in mid-1931, reflecting general dissatisfaction by the voters with government policies. Unsurprisingly the strong trend against Labour was continued in the 1931 elections, which were held only five days after Labour had suffered calamitous defeat in the general election. Turnout increased in these two years, almost reaching 50 per cent again in 1931. In 1930 and 1931 Labour's vote share fell by roughly a quarter, its share of all wins was more than halved, and a net loss of forty-nine seats was recorded over these two miserable years for the party. For the first time since 1924 Labour's share of seats held on the ten councils began to decline again. Labour lost control of the council in Barnsley and Birkenhead in 1930 and 1931 respectively, and by 1932 had lost its overall majority in Barrow. It ought to be stressed that Labour's slump was disguised to an extent by the all-party electoral pacts that were instituted on grounds of economy in many boroughs between 1930 and 1932. Thus 43.8 per cent of all seats were uncontested in 1931. In boroughs such as Bolton and Bath, Labour was spared even greater losses by this stroke of good fortune.

The rest of the 1930s saw a general trend towards lower turnout, the mid to low 40 per cent range becoming the norm. This may well have been the beginning of a much longer-term decline for municipal elections that has continued in the post-1945 period.[5] Two distinct periods in Labour performance from 1932 to 1938 can be distinguished. First, in the years from 1932 to 1934, Labour made a rapid recovery from the 1930–31 disasters. Its strong performance in 1932 was all the more remarkable given that only twelve months previously it had been so demoralised by its heavy parliamentary and municipal defeats. Labour's share of the vote increased by over ten points in 1932 to 45.4 per cent, taking it back to the high point of 1929. The party won 38 per cent of all seats up for election in 1932 as well. However, Labour made only three net gains in the year, precisely because it was defending seats won in the bonanza of three years previously. For the same reason, and also because of aldermanic losses that had followed its 1930–31 decline, its share of seats held actually fell marginally between 1931 and 1932. Labour's strong recovery persisted into 1933 and 1934 however, fifty-three net gains being made in the ten boroughs in the two years. The party won 36 per cent and 38 per cent of all seats up for election in these two years respectively, and its consistent performance in this period reinstated it as a serious challenger to Conservative dominance. This was reflected as well in the fact that by 1934 Labour held 33.7 per cent of all seats on the ten councils, the highest proportion between the wars. Four of the ten councils were held by Labour in that year. Control was restored in Barnsley and Birkenhead, an overall majority for Labour was secured again in Barrow, and in 1934 Bootle was won for the first time.

---

[5]   For an interesting early attempt to evaluate trends in turnout, see Rhodes, E.C., 'Voting at municipal elections', *Political Quarterly*, vol. 9, pt. 2, (1938), pp. 271–280.

The period from 1935 to 1938 saw a further reversal of the trend, though. The downturn for Labour in the municipal elections in 1935 was a harbinger of what was to happen in the general election held less than two weeks later. Labour was expected to do far better in the parliamentary poll than it actually did, an expectation based on its by-election successes in previous months, and its good showing in the 1933 and 1934 municipal elections. Labour's rise had peaked in those years though, and the party's support was declining by the November elections. Nine net losses were recorded in the ten boroughs in 1935, and Labour won only 32.3 per cent of all the seats up for election. Labour's fall continued in the years leading up to the Second World War, with the party suffering a net loss of fifty-three seats between 1935 and 1938. By 1938 it held only 27.7 per cent of all seats in the ten councils, fewer than it had held in 1927. Labour lost control of Birkenhead, and its hold on Bootle was only sustained by taking a disproportionate share of aldermanic seats.

The reasons for Labour's decline in this period are hard to pinpoint. The downward trend in turnout suggests that a generalised apathy towards municipal politics may have been developing amongst voters. The buffeting of the British economy by global factors had perhaps by this time been seen by some voters as demonstrating the limited effect local government could have on the resulting mass unemployment and poverty. Conversely, in those areas where the economy was relatively healthy, a degree of complacency amongst voters may have set in, as already suggested in the case of Birmingham. The mounting international crisis which was to lead to war may perhaps have diverted attention from seemingly trivial local affairs. There was also a general tendency, noted in a number of the boroughs covered in this volume, for Labour to present a more moderate and cautious face in the 1930s. A certain blandness crept in to its municipal policies by contrast with its peak years of dynamism and radical intent from 1926 to 1929. Arguably some of its distinctive electoral appeal was lost in this period. It may also be the case that improvements in Conservative organisation and propaganda at a local level swung support. As recent research has emphasised, the Tory party, described by some as 'the most successful political organization in the modern world', had to remake itself in the inter-war years. Faced with democracy, the rise of Labour, and a more secular and class-conscious society, Tory electoral hegemony was by no means assured. 'Conservatives were actively engaged throughout this period in trying to understand the nature of their new audience and reconstructing the social alliances from which their electoral strength derived'.[6] Perhaps they had best achieved this by the late 1930s, when the base of their electoral support seemed as secure and as stable as at any point between the wars. The intervention of war was to disturb this stability though. Whatever the causes of Labour's late 1930s decline, the point that has been made in respect of a number of the boroughs in this volume needs to be repeated here. There was no sign in the years leading up to the war of the massive increases that Labour would

---

[6]   Jarvis, D., 'The shaping of Conservative electoral hegemony, 1918–39', in Lawrence, J. and Taylor, M., *Party, State and Society: Electoral Behaviour in Britain since 1820*, (Aldershot, 1997), p. 146.

make in 1945. On the contrary, Labour's future prospects looked bleak before war halted the electoral process.

The comparative analysis

The comparative data on turnout and Labour performance for the ten boroughs covered in this volume are shown below in Tables 11.4 and 11.5. Some brief comments can be made. First, the turnout figures suggest that interest in municipal elections was considerably higher over these years than it has been in the post-1945 period. With the significant exception of Birmingham, turnout in the other nine boroughs averaged near or over 50 per cent in all cases over the whole inter-war period. Turnout was especially high in Barnsley, Barrow and Blackburn at almost 70 per cent.[7] It is possible that variations in turnout may have been a regional phenomenon, or alternatively they may have been influenced by differences in size of place, but at this stage there are not enough cases here to test such hypotheses. Nor is it possible yet to establish whether there was any connection between turnout and Labour performance, although the evidence here so far is interesting, if inconclusive. Labour was strongest in Barrow and Barnsley with high turnout, and very weak in Birmingham with low turnout. On the other hand, Labour was relatively successful in Birkenhead and Bootle with fairly low turnout. Further data in future volumes will make it possible to establish whether any consistent patterns existed.[8]

Turning to the comparison of Labour's performance in the ten boroughs, the problem of uncontested seats alluded to above clouds the issue somewhat, but nevertheless a reasonably clear picture can be discerned. Labour's success has been evaluated in three ways in Tables 11.4 and 11.5: in terms of its share of all votes, of its share of all contests won, and of its share of seats held on the councils near the beginning (1919), middle (1929) and end (1938) of the period. By all three criteria, Barnsley and Barrow emerge as Labour's strongest boroughs, with around half of all votes and all contests being won there, and a majority of all seats being held in 1929 and 1938. A second group can be identified, comprised of Birkenhead and Bootle, where Labour won roughly 40 per cent of all votes and contests, and attained a majority of seats in at least one of the years 1929 and 1938. Blackburn and Bolton made up a third category, where Labour picked up 30–40 per cent of all votes, won around 30 per cent of all contests, but held only 20–30 per cent of all seats. Birmingham was unique, with Labour gaining 40 per cent of all votes, but less than a quarter of all wins, and holding less than 30 per cent of all seats even at the high point of 1929. Finally, Bath, Blackpool and Bournemouth were plainly Labour's weakest boroughs by all three criteria, the party having 30 per cent or less of all votes, less than 20 per cent of all wins, and holding 20 per cent or less of all the seats on the council at all three specified dates. Within that category, though, Blackpool can be identified as exceptionally

---

[7] The exceptionally low turnout in Birmingham has been commented on already on pp. 229–230 in this volume.
[8] On variations in turnout, see Rhodes, 'Voting in municipal elections'.

barren territory for the party, with well under 10 per cent of votes, wins and seats being gained by Labour.

Various reasons for these widespread differences in Labour's performance have been advanced in the chapters on each borough in this volume, and readers are referred to the individual essays for the full details. Some brief comments are appropriate here. The varying socio-economic character of the boroughs was clearly an important influence. Labour's strongest boroughs of Barnsley and Barrow were both overwhelmingly industrial, and in both cases dominated by one industry (mining and shipbuilding respectively). Well-organised, cohesive, and predominantly male workforces in these boroughs produced solid labour movements and relatively strong Labour parties. Conversely, the lack of industry in Bath, Blackpool and Bournemouth produced predominantly middle-class boroughs, and thus the domination of middle-class political organisations. Somewhere between these extremes, Birkenhead had a significant working class, (although not confined to one dominant industry) but it also had a substantial middle class. Municipal politics in the borough to some degree reflected the interests of both these groups, with Labour beginning to threaten the dominant position of Tory and Liberal parties in the inter-war years.

However, this rather deterministic type of analysis can only be taken so far, and is easiest to sustain for the extreme cases. On the evidence for the ten boroughs analysed so far, in most cases there was a far more complex interaction between socio-economic structures and other factors which underlay political practice. For instance, the significance of cultural and political traditions has been stressed to different degrees in this volume. In Bootle religious sectarianism was an important influence, weakening Labour's position in the early 1920s, but then later providing a mainly Catholic base of support on which it could build a real challenge to Conservatism. In Bath, on the other hand, Nonconformist traditions of a popular and radical nature ensured a slightly stronger Labour presence than might have been expected in such a borough. Again, the Nonconformist roots of Birmingham's 'civic gospel' was clearly important in explaining the powerful tradition of Liberal Unionism in the city. Most complex of all was the experience of the two cotton-textile towns dealt with in this volume, Blackburn and Bolton. A tradition of working-class Toryism was plainly still of importance here, and held back the rise of the Labour party in what were predominantly industrial and working-class boroughs. This tradition was based on a number of social, cultural and ideological components, including employer-worker relations (at work and elsewhere) and employer paternalism, gender relations in the cotton industry, economic self-interest, religious beliefs, cultural attitudes to questions such as temperance, and nationalistic and jingoistic sentiments.

It is also the case that more contingent and short-term factors could be of importance in municipal politics. Each borough's particular experience of the 1930s Depression was significant, for instance. It is arguable that Birmingham's relatively healthy economy and low unemployment had something to do with the growing strength of the ruling Unionist party there in the 1930s. Blackpool's survival as a major tourist resort through the inter-war period may have encouraged the self-satisfaction of its voters, and thus their solid support for its traditional ruling groups. Conversely, unemployment in Barnsley in particular appears to have been a political issue which Labour used very effectively to its own advantage. Another contingent issue was the impact of the General Strike in 1926. While a noticeable surge in Labour support in the ten boroughs overall was seen in the November 1926 elections, it was especially obvious in Birkenhead and Bootle, and unsurprisingly most of all in Barnsley, where a massive turnout of 80 per cent reflected the heightened political interest of that year. A third example of the importance of short-term contingencies was the effect of the second Labour government of 1929–31 and its disastrous collapse. There was a general slump in Labour support in all ten boroughs as a whole in the elections of 1930 and 1931. In Bolton, however, the existence of electoral pacts in both years saved Labour from experiencing the dramatic loss of seats that it otherwise could have expected. This significantly boosted Labour's strength on the council in Bolton in the 1930s, while in other boroughs Labour took three years up to 1934 just to recoup the losses of 1930–31. A similar pattern of abstentions benefitted Labour in Bath over the same period.

In addition, there were elements of the system of municipal politics itself which influenced Labour's political performance in the different boroughs. The limitations of the municipal franchise at this time, excluding some residents while giving plural votes to others, may have been a factor working against Labour in all boroughs. When more boroughs have been covered in these volumes a more systematic analysis can be applied to give a definitive answer to that question. There were certainly differential effects as well. The case of Blackpool is one obvious example in this volume. Large numbers of temporary workers in the holiday trade were excluded from the municipal franchise there, either because they did not meet the six-month (later three-month) residency test, or because they lived in furnished lodgings and therefore did not pay rates. Labour almost certainly suffered politically for this, perhaps helping to explain its extremely poor performance in the borough. Similar comments can be made about the vagaries of the system of ward boundaries in municipal politics at this time. In this volume, Birkenhead is a good example of where gerrymandering the boundaries could be used to political advantage. There is little doubt that Labour was disadvantaged by the ward reorganisation that took place in 1934 in this borough.

Most plain of all is the significance of the aldermanic system. A quarter of all the seats in the various boroughs were decided by the elected councillors, rather than by the voters. The evidence from this volume shows that the aldermanic seats could be crucial in determining political power. A clear pattern can be identified in the ten boroughs covered here. In all cases, Labour was initially under-represented on the aldermanic bench. Where Labour remained very weak, the dominant parties eventually conceded one or two aldermanic vacancies to it (in Bath from 1925–6 and in Bournemouth from 1930–1, for instance), as this posed no threat to overall political control. In other Boroughs where Labour won a greater degree of support, but still did not endanger the traditional ruling party, rough parity of representation on the aldermanic bench might eventually be conceded (by the mid 1920s in Birmingham, by 1929–30 in Blackburn and Bolton). However, where Labour grew strong enough to gain a majority of the elected councillors, and therefore fill aldermanic vacancies to its own advantage, then the aldermanic system became a major and permanent political issue. This was the case in Barnsley (from as early as 1921–2), Barrow (from 1928–9), Birkenhead (from 1926–7) and Bootle (from 1933–4). In these boroughs, control of the council by the late 1930s was largely determined by the coincidence of the timing of the three-year cycle of aldermanic elections in relation to the annual round of council elections. In Barnsley, Barrow and Bootle, Labour control was secured by taking all or most of the aldermanic vacancies while its position on the council enabled it to do so in the late 1930s. Conversely, Labour's opponents in Birkenhead seized the opportunity after the 1931 council elections to oust half its aldermen. Labour recouped some of these losses in the mid 1930s, but not enough to put itself back into power on a secure footing.

One final point of a general nature needs to be made. It is striking that in all the boroughs considered so far, the political struggle at the municipal level resolved itself quite rapidly after 1918 into more or less a straight fight between Labour and anti-Labour forces. This was equally true for boroughs where Labour's opponents retained their distinctive party labels for municipal purposes (as in Bath, Birkenhead, Birmingham, Blackburn, Blackpool, Bolton and Bootle), adopted a common label such as Citizen or Independent (as in Barnsley and Barrow), or eschewed political labels altogether and presented themselves in a supposedly apolitical guise (as in Bournemouth). This was also the case despite the fact that at the level of parliamentary politics, Liberals and Tories usually retained their separate identities and continued to fight each other politically at least up to 1929.

There are two important implications that flow from this. One is related to the decline of Liberalism between the wars. In one of the few studies to consider this decline at the municipal level, Chris Cook has seen the fall in the number of Liberal candidates and the shift to municipal alliances primarily as a symptom of the weakness of Liberalism.[9] Arguably it could also be seen as a contributory cause of the decline of the Liberal party. The apparently widespread and early tendency for Liberals to sink their differences with Tories and present an anti-Labour front as far as municipal elections were concerned must have weakened their distinctive political identity in the minds of voters. Cause and effect may be hard to disentangle here, but the evidence of this volume tends to support the view that these anti-labour fronts 'forced the radical working-class Liberal vote into the Labour camp'.[10] The only clear variant to this may be found in Birkenhead, where it seems possible that one group of local voters at least, namely shipbuilders, transferred their allegiance to Labour in municipal elections, but for pragmatic reasons still retained their loyalty to Liberalism in general elections.

The other implication of this tendency is related to the rise of Labour. There has been a long and contentious argument amongst historians as to whether or not the growth of the Labour party before 1918 can be attributed primarily to

---

[9]   Cook, *The Age of Alignment*, pp. 49–70.
[10]   Cook, *The Age of Alignment*, p. 56.

increasing class consciousness.[11] For the years after 1918 covered in these volumes, the significance of class in municipal politics stands out. The anti-Labour alliances were only the formal manifestation of the often fiercely-expressed language of class that dominated the discourse of municipal politics in these boroughs. This applies as much to boroughs where Labour was relatively strong, such as Barnsley or Birkenhead, as it does where Labour was at its weakest, in Blackpool. Another apposite case is Bootle, where the language of sectarian politics was dominant at first, but was quite soon subsumed into a Labour–anti-Labour discourse, even if sectarian undertones remained. It should also be stressed that the anti-socialist sentiments of candidates were usually reflected in the local press, which tended to be stridently partisan in its coverage and continually stress the 'dangers of socialism'. On the starkly different political terrain of Blackpool and Bootle, Labour was denounced in strikingly similar language as a 'Bolshevist' threat.[12]

Concluding comments on the comparative method

The remarks made in this conclusion of a comparative nature are only brief and selective, and more detailed and rigorous analysis will be applied at later stages of the production of these volumes. One of the problems of attempting comparative analysis is that at the beginning of the process there is little to compare the initial evidence with. A leading exponent of the method has commented, 'comparison which begins by regarding one particular case as the norm against which comparisons are made with other cases is flawed from the outset', and again, 'the first requirement of a proper comparative history is to be equally interested in all the cases under consideration'. Until an extensive amount of what he calls 'comparative descriptive work' has been carried out, it is hard to make comparative conclusions.[13] These recommendations must be borne in mind both by the authors and the readers of this first volume in an eight-volume series. It remains to be seen how much the evidence of future volumes in this series will modify both the aggregate patterns and the comparative suggestions that have been put forward here. Their implications will also need to be considered carefully, both within the series and elsewhere, and not only by the authors of these volumes alone. To repeat the warning made in the introduction to Volume One, election results need to be fully contextualised and analysed for their full significance to be realised. On their own, they have clear limitations, and no straightforward conclusions can be derived from them. Much detailed and subtle work will be required to put the flesh on the bare bones of an analysis that has been given here. It is hoped, though, that a start has been made in these pages.

[11] See, for example, arguing for the significance of class consciousness, McKibbin, R., *The Evolution of the Labour Party 1910–1924*, (Oxford, 1974); and against, Tanner, D., *Political Change and the Labour Party 1900–1918*, (Cambridge, 1990).
[12] See pp. 414 and 549 in this volume.
[13] Breuilly, J., *Labour and Liberalism in Nineteenth-Century Europe: Essays in Comparative History*, (Manchester, 1992), pp. 1–2, 14.

Table 11.1   Overall turnout, Labour % of votes, Labour % of wins, and
Labour % of council seats held, in all ten Volume One
county boroughs, 1919–38

	Turnout %	Labour % of all votes	Labour % of all wins	Labour % of seats held
1919	42.7	33.7	34.5	16.8
1920	50.2	31.2	20.0	19.3
1921	52.6	36.7	21.2	21.2
1922	54.7	36.5	17.6	17.3
1923	50.2	35.9	22.3	17.3
1924	55.4	35.9	15.5	16.9
1925	54.0	36.8	25.0	18.3
1926	50.9	43.4	38.5	23.0
1927	49.8	42.2	33.8	28.1
1928	51.4	41.8	37.7	31.7
1929	41.7	45.4	42.3	33.6
1930	45.9	36.4	19.3	31.6
1931	48.5	34.4	18.3	25.5
1932	44.4	45.4	38.0	25.0
1933	45.1	44.8	36.0	28.2
1934	42.1	42.9	38.0	33.7
1935	46.0	40.7	32.3	33.5
1936	44.1	39.4	26.4	30.9
1937	43.4	40.6	25.0	29.0
1938	45.0	38.6	25.6	27.7
1919-38	**47.5**	**39.2**	**28.4**	**25.6**

Table 11.2   Labour net gains or losses in all ten Volume One county boroughs,
1919–38

1919	31	1929	5
1920	6	1930	-22
1921	5	1931	-27
1922	-23	1932	3
1923	4	1933	25
1924	-1	1934	28
1925	10	1935	-9
1926	23	1936	-17
1927	23	1937	-18
1928	20	1938	-9
1919-28	**98**	**1929–38**	**-41**
1919-38	**57**		

Table 11.3   Uncontested seats in all ten Volume One county boroughs
1919–1938

	Labour un-contested wins	Other un-contested wins	All seats	% of all seats un-contested	Contested seats with no Labour candidate	% of all seats with no Labour candidate
1919	0	13	145	9.0	35	33.1
1920	9	17	145	17.9	20	25.5
1921	3	29	156	20.5	28	36.5
1922	4	37	148	27.7	25	41.9
1923	6	45	148	34.5	21	44.6
1924	5	35	148	27.0	11	31.1
1925	3	40	148	29.1	20	40.5
1926	2	31	148	22.3	19	33.8
1927	2	31	148	22.3	11	28.4
1928	8	33	151	27.2	20	35.1
1929	7	27	149	22.8	12	26.2
1930	8	38	150	30.7	8	30.7
1931	9	58	153	43.8	5	41.2
1932	10	43	150	35.3	11	36.0
1933	1	44	161	28.0	15	36.6
1934	10	36	166	27.7	19	33.1
1935	8	34	161	26.1	9	26.7
1936	8	43	163	31.3	12	33.7
1937	9	44	160	33.1	12	35.0
1938	7	42	160	30.6	14	35.0
1919–38	**119**	**720**	**3058**	**27.4**	**327**	**34.2**

Table 11.4 Overall turnout, Labour % of all votes and Labour % of all wins in each of the ten Volume One county boroughs 1919–38
(rankings in brackets)

Borough	Turnout %	Labour % of all votes	Labour % of all wins
Barnsley	*(2)* 69.6	*(2)* 49.1	*(2)* 49.5
Barrow	*(3)* 69.2	*(1)* 49.9	*(1)* 55.0
Bath	*(6)* 53.2	*(8)* 31.5	*(8)* 18.2
Birkenhead	*(8)* 50.3	*(4)* 41.6	*(3)* 42.2
Birmingham	*(10)* 37.9	*(5)* 40.8	*(7)* 23.3
Blackburn	*(1)* 69.7	*(3)* 43.6	*(5)* 33.0
Blackpool	*(5)* 55.5	*(10)* 6.9	*(10)* 0.8
Bolton	*(4)* 58.0	*(7)* 34.7	*(6)* 29.2
Bootle	*(7)* 52.0	*(6)* 38.8	*(4)* 38.9
Bournemouth	*(9)* 48.1	*(9)* 26.6	*(9)* 17.1
All	**47.5**	**39.2**	**28.4**

Table 11.5 Labour % of all council seats held in each of the ten Volume One county boroughs in 1919, 1929 and 1938
(rankings in brackets)

Borough	Labour % of all council seats held 1919	Labour % of all council seats held 1929	Labour % of all council seats held 1938
Barnsley	*(1)* 37.5	*(3)* 52.8	*(1)* 65.0
Barrow	*(2)* 31.3	*(1)* 68.8	*(2)* 62.5
Bath	*(7)* 12.5	*(8)* 14.3	*(9)* 14.3
Birkenhead	*(3)* 26.8	*(2)* 55.9	*(4)* 41.9
Birmingham	*(5)* 20.2	*(7)* 29.8	*(8)* 16.2
Blackburn	*(6)* 17.9	*(5)* 39.3	*(5)* 33.9
Blackpool	*(10)* 1.9	*(10)* 0.0	*(10)* 1.8
Bolton	*(8)* 9.4	*(6)* 34.7	*(6)* 21.9
Bootle	*(4)* 22.7	*(4)* 45.8	*(3)* 52.1
Bournemouth	*(9)* 4.5	*(9)* 13.6	*(7)* 16.7
All	**16.8**	**33.6**	**27.7**

NOTES

NOTES

Notes on maps, tables and appendices

MAPS

Ward boundary maps

Ward boundaries have been identified from various sources. The contemporary 2½ inch Ordnance Survey maps showed ward boundaries, but their large scale makes them difficult to use, especially in the case of large towns. Other locally-produced maps were sometimes located in local record offices, and newspapers sometimes showed, or listed, changes in boundaries. Where no maps showing boundaries could be found, as a last resort, all streets listed in contemporary electoral registers by ward were identified on maps in order to establish boundaries. All maps were first hand-drawn by the authors, and then converted to digital form by Phil Cubbin, of the Human Geography section of Liverpool John Moores University, to give working copies. The final versions used in this volume were drawn by Ian Wileman.

TABLES

Persons aged 14 and over classified by industry 1931

These tables have been constructed from the industrial tables of the 1931 census reports. It should be noted that the numbers included separately for each category as 'out of work' in the census tables have been aggregated with the employed in the tables included here. All industrial categories that amounted to 5 per cent or more of the total (working and 'out of work') population enumerated, for either men or women, have been included in these tables. Very exceptionally, where the numbers classified in a locally notable industry (which other sources have highlighted) did not quite amount to 5 per cent, these categories may also be included.

Population statistics 1931

These tables have been constructed from the county tables of the 1931 census reports.

Overall position on the council; and aldermen

In these tables, the position on the council and on the aldermanic bench is that which pertained in the immediate aftermath of the elections held on the first day in November. The position could often change very soon after the elections, especially when the aldermanic elections took place at the first council meeting after the election, and also sometimes because councillors changed parties in the light of the results. It is impossible to reflect these changes in a consistent fashion for all boroughs. The first council meeting after the election took place after intervals varying from one borough to another. Vacancies created by the election of new aldermen then had to be filled in by-elections, which were again held after varying intervals, and in which new gains or losses might be made to further confuse the situation. The position immediately after the election is therefore the only acceptable one, as it at least has the merit of being directly comparable across the board.

It should also be noted that the position on the council, and the balance of aldermen, were not always recorded accurately, or even at all, in press reports and directories. The figures given in these volumes have been constructed in many cases from a detailed analysis of the effects of the election results on each individual councillor and alderman.

Gains and losses for parties are only those which took place as a direct result of the elections themselves. Changes which had taken place in between the three-year cycle of elections, due to retirements, deaths, elections to the aldermanic bench, or councillors changing parties, were sometimes recorded in the press as gains, but this was often very misleading as the change might have occurred months or even years before. The gains recorded here reflect the real changes in party strength at the annual elections.

Municipal elections: winning party

In these summary tables of results, no-contests are marked in bold and underlined.

Municipal elections: party wins per year; and per ward

In these tables, it has only been possible to assess Labour Party performance, as Labour was the only party to consistently appear under its own name across the country. Tory and Liberal alliances, and the use of indeterminate labels such as 'Independent' or 'Citizens', make it impossible to assess the other two major parties' support on a comparable basis across the country.

The 'Labour per cent' figure is calculated from the total number of votes won by Labour candidates (in any one year, or ward), as a proportion of all votes cast (in any one year, or ward). This calculation gives a more realistic picture of actual Labour support than if all votes cast only in wards contested by Labour are counted. If this latter method were employed, then in boroughs where Labour was very weak and thus contested very few seats, it could misleadingly appear to do quite well.

In the case of double-member seats, in each individual contest all votes won by Labour candidates have been calculated as a proportion of all votes cast, and then scaled down as a proportion of all electors voting. This ensures that where only one candidate is put up by Labour, this 'weaker' position than if it had fielded two candidates is reflected, on the same principle as applied for single-member seats. The scaling down to take account of all electors voting, as opposed to all votes cast, also ensures that voters' preferences are not double-counted in the aggregated figures for all boroughs.

Parliamentary election results

These tables have been constructed from the full lists of results contained in Craig, F.W.S., *British Parliamentary Election Results, 1918–1949*, (2nd edn, Aldershot, 1989). The details of the wards which were contained within constituencies have been taken from Craig, F.W.S., *Boundaries of Parliamentary Constituencies 1885–1971*, (Chichester, 1972).

Municipal elections (full ward-by-ward results)

Candidates

All female candidates are given the title used in press reports or directories (Miss or Mrs). In some cases women candidates were denoted by the use of their Christian names, with no titles given. For reasons of space, this practice cannot be employed in these tables, and these women have been denoted by the title of Ms, of modern usage. Other titles, especially military titles, have had to be omitted, again for reasons of space. Sitting candidates are indicated by an asterix after their name.

Party

Party labels have been recorded as far as possible as they appeared in the press etc., except where local usage may be misleading. In Birmingham, for instance, Unionist, rather than Conservative, was customarily used for 'Conservative and Unionist' candidates, for good historical reasons. For consistency across these volumes they have been recorded in these tables as Conservatives. Note, though, that the local usage is employed in the text of the essay on Birmingham. Again, some of the more virulently anti-Labour newspapers, such as the *Yorkshire Post*, would only record Labour candidates as Socialists, but the correct party label of Labour has been employed in these tables.

Co-operative Party candidates in some boroughs were treated by the press as if they were Labour candidates. However, in all cases, including the **overall position on the council** tables, they have been treated in these volumes as follows: where candidates were simply labelled Co-operative, they have been treated as Co-operative candidates, separate from Labour (most of these cases occurred in 1919 and the early 1920s, when they were still separate parties); where candidates were labelled 'Labour and Co-operative' or 'Co-operative and Labour', they have been treated as Labour candidates (whether or not formal merger had occurred, these clearly must have had the official endorsement of the local Labour Party).

Votes

The figures for votes given in the tables of results have been derived from a number of sources, including press reports from both regional and local newspapers, or directories of various kinds. As a general rule, where occasionally conflicting figures were given in different sources, directories have usually been preferred to the press, on the assumption that the speed required for newspaper reports was likely to cause more errors or misprints. Similarly, results printed in the newspaper of the particular borough concerned have usually been preferred to those given in national or regional press coverage. This was on the assumption that locally-based reporters picking up the results at the counts were likely to get the right figures. National and regional papers would have got the results for most of the smaller boroughs through agency reports, and transcription errors must have occurred at times. However, these decisions were also dependent on a judgement of the overall quality and reliability of particular newspapers.

In single-member seats, the 'total votes' figure is simply the sum of all votes cast. In double-member seats, an additional figure of 'total voters' has been given. This is the number of voters who actually voted in the poll, which in most cases was given in the press. In a small number of cases where it was not given, estimated figures have been calculated, which have been denoted by printing in italics. These 'total voters' figures have been used in the calculation of the turnout figures (see below), as they reflect the actual turnout of voters. 'Total voter' estimates could be calculated by simply halving the 'total votes', assuming that each individual voter used both his or her available votes. This, however, would result in a significant underestimate of turnout in cases where major parties do not put up two candidates, and where therefore large numbers of voters may not have used both their votes. The estimates in these volumes have been constructed on a different basis to try and take account of this problem, as follows.

A sample of 100 cases in Birkenhead, Bolton and Bootle where 'total voters' figures were given in the press were collated, and then classified into various categories according to the number of candidates put up by parties (e.g. 2 Labour, 2 Tory; 2 Labour, 1 Tory; 2 Labour, 2 Tory, 1 Liberal; etc.) For each category, the number of actual voters was compared with the halved 'total votes' figure, and consistent patterns emerged. Five main categories emerged, in each of which the degree of underestimation of 'total voters' produced by the halving of 'total votes' varied very little, as shown here:

Group A *(10 cases)*
2 C, 2 L, 2 Lab
Highest underestimation - 6.1 %
Lowest underestimation - 3.2 %
Mean underestimation (rounded) - 5 %

Group B *(12 cases)*
2 Lab, 1 C; 2 C, 1 Lab, etc.
Highest underestimation - 21.5 %
Lowest underestimation - 17.2 %
Mean underestimation - 19 %

Group C *(44 cases)*
2 C, 2 Lab; 2 C, 2 L, etc.
Highest underestimation - 7.3 %
Lowest underestimation - 1.0 %
Mean underestimation - 3 %

Group D *(10 cases)*
2 C, 1 Lab, 1 L; 2 Lab, 1 C, 1 L, etc.
Highest underestimation - 23.4 %
Lowest underestimation - 17.3 %
Mean underestimation - 20 %

Group E *(24 cases)*
2 C, 2 Lab, 1 L; 2 C, 2 L, 1 Lab, etc.
Highest underestimation - 14.1 %
Lowest underestimation - 4.6 %
Mean underestimation - 10 %

In each group, the mean underestimation was taken to be representative. In all cases where no 'total voters' figures were available, therefore, the 'total votes' figures were first halved, and then raised by the proportion appropriate for each group. There were too few cases where other minor parties intervened for any patterns to be gauged, so these have been treated as if they were one of the major parties.

The resultant estimates cannot be taken as being entirely accurate, of course, but they will produce turnout figures which will reflect the real situation better than any other alternative.

Per cent

The per cent figures for candidates are the votes cast for each candidate as a proportion of the total votes cast. This applies to both single- and double-member seats.

Electors

As in the case of the figures for votes noted above, the figures for electors in these tables have been derived from a variety of sources, and the same principles of selection have been applied where discrepancies between different sources have been identified. In some cases, turnout figures were provided, from which it was possible to calculate electorate figures once the total number of votes cast was known.

Where it has been impossible to locate electorates, then estimates have been made based on the trend between the last and the next figures known. Thus if one year is missing, and the difference between the previous and the following year is an increase of 100 voters, then it has been assumed that the electorate for the missing year had increased by fifty votes. For missing 1919 or 1938 figures, the succeeding or preceding trends have been used. So if the electorate increased by fifty voters between 1936 and 1937, then it has been assumed that the missing 1938 figure had seen another fifty-voter increase. In all cases, such estimates are shown in italics in the tables of results.

In cases where seats were uncontested, if figures for electors are available, they have been quoted. If no figures are available, no estimates have been made, as they cannot be used for any useful purpose such as calculating turnout. Blanks appear on the tables in these latter cases.

Turnout

The turnout figures have been calculated as the total votes cast as a proportion of the total electorate in single-member seats. In double-member seats they are the 'total voters' figures as a proportion of the electorate, as explained above under *Votes*.

Gains

As explained under **overall position of the council**, gains are only those that took place as a direct result of the November elections. Any earlier changes within the three-year cycle of elections which resulted in gains to parties are discounted.

APPENDICES

Appendix 1

Population of all eighty-three county boroughs 1931

This appendix has been constructed from table XXII of the general report for the 1931 census, which lists all towns with populations over 50,000. The figures quoted here were estimates taking account of seasonal movements, rather than the enumerated populations. It should be noted therefore that these figures vary very slightly from the population figures quoted in the tables for the individual boroughs, which are based on enumerated population. They are used in this appendix because they are more likely to accurately reflect the real size of the boroughs. The enumerated figures have had to be used for the individual boroughs, however, as the individual ward figures were based on the enumerated population. As will be seen, the variations are small, and do not affect the overall ranking of boroughs.

Appendix 2

Persons per room in all eighty-three county boroughs 1931

This appendix has been constructed from the data given in the county tables of the 1931 census for the various county boroughs. To an extent this table can be taken as a general indicator of social class: the more working-class the borough, the higher the person per room figure tended to be. However, differences in types of housing, by borough and by region, obviously complicates this apparently simple relationship.

Appendix 3

Female domestic servants as a percentage of total population in all eighty-three county boroughs 1931

This appendix has been constructed from the data given in the industrial tables of the 1931 census for the various county boroughs. Domestic servants (or 'personal service' in the original tables, and including 'hotels and catering') have been expressed as a percentage of the total population, rather than of the female workforce. The proportion of the female population which was officially defined as working varied greatly from one borough to another, so the proportionate weight of domestic servants could be distorted accordingly. The figures shown here best indicate the significance of domestic service in the boroughs as a whole. As such, they are another indicator of social class: the more middle-class a borough, the higher the proportion of domestic servants tended to be. Again, though, other factors enter into the situation which complicate the picture, a proviso that needs to be made in all these appendixes.

Appendix 4

Percentage of workforce in own account and managerial categories in all eighty-three county boroughs 1931

This appendix has been constructed from the data given in the industrial tables of the 1931 census for the various county boroughs. The total workforce that was recorded as working at the time of the census was divided into three categories: 'working on own account' (taken to mean 'self-employed' in modern parlance), 'managerial' and 'operative'. Those who were recorded as 'out of work' were excluded from these categories. The percentage of the working population defined as 'managerial' and 'working on own account' expressed in this appendix can again be taken as an indicator of social class; the higher the proportion, the more middle-class the borough tended to be. However, special care needs to be taken in interpreting these figures, as varying rates of unemployment may have had a distorting effect. Where unemployment was high, it may have been that a higher proportion of 'operatives' were affected (although there is no absolute proof of this). If so, then these figures would tend to overestimate the 'middle-class' nature of those boroughs where unemployment was especially high.

Appendix 5

Percentage of workforce in professional category in all eighty-three county boroughs 1931

This appendix has been constructed from the data given in the industrial tables of the 1931 census for the various county boroughs. It may again be taken as a general indicator of social class: the higher the proportion of professionals, the more middle-class a borough tended to be. However, the size of a borough was another factor that cut across this possible relationship. In general, larger boroughs tended to have a greater concentration of professionals.

Appendix 6

Percentage of workforce recorded as out of work in 1931 industry tables in all eighty-three county boroughs

This appendix has been constructed from the data given in the industrial tables of the 1931 census for the various county boroughs. All those who stated they were out of work to the enumerator were put in this category. They were all placed in industrial categories as well, on the basis of what job they had previously or usually held, as an addition to those recorded as working.

These figures may have been in one sense a more accurate record of unemployment, as they reflect the attitudes of people themselves as to whether they were 'out of work' or not. The official unemployment figures, of course, recorded only those insured workers who were entitled to benefit. In the case of women particularly, and especially after the Anomalies Act of 1930–31 which excluded many married women and part-time women workers from claiming benefit, many may have been cut out of the official statistics, despite regarding themselves as unemployed.

Appendixes 7 and 8

Percentage of workforce (male and female) in textiles category, top fifteen county boroughs 1931

Percentage of female workforce in textiles category, top fifteen county boroughs 1931

These appendices have been constructed from the data given in the industrial tables of the 1931 census for the various county boroughs. Workers in all types of textiles have been included. The figures have been expressed both in terms of all workers, and women workers only. Both say something about the industrial structure of a borough. The former shows the overall significance of textile production and employment in the local economy. The latter emphasises how significant employment in the textile industries was for women in certain boroughs and regions.

Appendix 9

Percentage of male workforce in mining category, top fifteen county boroughs 1931

This appendix has been constructed from the data given in the industrial tables of the 1931 census for the various county boroughs. All men have been included from the category 'mining and quarrying, and treatment of non-metalliferous mine and quarry products'. The figures have been expressed in terms of male workers only, as in all cases there were so few women in this category that they made no difference to the overall ranking of boroughs.

Appendix 10

Percentage of male workforce in docks and water transport categories, top fifteen county boroughs 1931

This appendix has been constructed from the data given in the industrial tables of the 1931 census for the various county boroughs. All men from the two subcategories of 'water transport' and 'docks, lighthouses, canals, etc.' were included. Again, women were so few in this category that they would make no difference to the overall standings.

Appendix 11

Percentage of male workforce in rail category, top fifteen county boroughs 1931

This appendix has been constructed from the data given in the industrial tables of the 1931 census for the various county boroughs. All men in the 'railways' sub-category have been included. Again, there were very few women in this category.

Appendix 12

Percentage of workforce (male and female) in metalworking categories, top fourteen county boroughs 1931

This appendix has been constructed from the data given in the industrial tables of the 1931 census for the various county boroughs. These figures include all workers (male and female) in the following six subcategories (as numbered in the census): 1. smelting, converting, refining and rolling of iron and steel; 2. extracting and refining of other metals and alloys; 3. founding and other secondary processes in metal working; 8. cutlery, and small tools (not machine tools); 9. other metal industries (not precious metals, jewellery or plate); 10. precious metals, jewellery, plate.

Appendix 13

Percentage of male workforce in shipbuilding categories, top ten county boroughs 1931

This appendix has been constructed from the data given in the industrial tables of the 1931 census for the various county boroughs. These figures include all male workers in the subcategory 'ship building and repairing and marine engineering'. Women workers were again very rare in this category.

Appendix 14

Percentage of male workforce in engineering category, top sixteen county boroughs 1931

This appendix has been constructed from the data given in the industrial tables of the 1931 census for the various county boroughs. These figures include all male workers in the subcategory 'engineering (not marine or electrical)'. Women workers were again very rare in this category.

Appendix 15

Percentage of workforce (male and female) in vehicle construction category, top six county boroughs 1931

This appendix has been constructed from the data given in the industrial tables of the 1931 census for the various county boroughs. These figures include all workers (male and female) in the subcategory 'construction and repair of vehicles'. These vehicles included motor transport, rail transport and aeroplanes, and also horse-drawn vehicles etc.

Appendix 16

Houses constructed by county boroughs to 31 Mar. 1939

This appendix has been constructed from data given in *The Municipal Yearbook*, (1939), pp. 250–278; (1938), pp. 325–340; (1937), pp. 287–308; (1936), pp. 946–965. Superficially these figures show the generosity of boroughs in providing council housing, but factors entered into this which complicated the picture. Varying levels of provision of housing by employers were especially significant. As an example, the very low level of provision in Barrow was clearly related to the fact that the dominant local employer, Vickers, provided large numbers of houses for its workers (see above, p. 64).

General notes

Aldermen

In the county boroughs, there were most commonly three councillors for each ward, and one alderman to every three councillors on the council. Where there were double-member wards, for every six councillors per ward there were two aldermen. Overall then aldermen made up a quarter of the total membership of the council. In exceptional circumstances these rules were broken if a ward with a very small electorate was added to a county borough, in which case the new ward might only be allocated one or two councillors, and no alderman would be added to the council.

Aldermen sat for a term of office of six years. In most cases they were elected on a three-year cycle, with half the aldermanic seats coming up for election three years after the other half. They were usually elected from the ranks of the elected councillors, although of course retiring aldermen could also be re-nominated. It was also possible to nominate people from outside the council, but this was very rarely done. Only councillors, and not the sitting aldermen, were entitled to vote on aldermanic vacancies. If aldermen were voted out of office they left the council immediately. The councillors who succeeded them took their place on the aldermanic bench, and their council seats became vacant and had to be filled in by-elections.

When aldermen retired after their six years of service, the elections to replace them took place at the first full council meeting after the annual council elections on 1 November. This was usually at the end of the following week. When an alderman died in office, or retired prematurely, then the vacancy created could be filled at the next meeting of the council, and a by-election would again ensue.

There were no rules as to whether the numbers of aldermen should be proportional to the number of seats a party held on the council, and each borough decided its own conventions. In some, aldermanic vacancies were filled on the basis of seniority of service on the council, regardless of party, and retiring aldermen were often re-elected without opposition. In others, the principle of proportionality prevailed. In most cases where the balance of power on the council changed hands or was seriously challenged during the inter-war period, party advantage became the determinant of the outcome of aldermanic elections. The party holding the largest number of council seats took all or most of the aldermanic vacancies, thus bolstering its control or enabling it to take control.[1]

---

[1]   For further discussion of the aldermanic system in the inter-war period, see Davies, S., *Liverpool Labour: Social and Political Influences on the Development of the Labour Party in Liverpool, 1900–1939*, (Keele, 1996), pp. 110–119, 156–163.

Municipal franchise

The municipal franchise differed significantly from the parliamentary franchise in the inter-war years. The essential principle of the municipal franchise was that only those who paid rates, and their spouses, were entitled to vote. Ratepayers were those who owned property, or occupied unfurnished property. In addition, they had to prove that they had been resident in the property for the six months previous to registration (this period was reduced to three months in 1926). Registration took place twice a year, with the autumn register being the one in force at the annual November elections. Female spouses of ratepayers aged thirty or over gained the municipal vote in the 1918 Representation of the People Act, and this age threshold was reduced to twenty-one in the 1928 Act.

This meant that significant numbers were excluded from the municipal franchise, most notably those who had moved within six months (later three months), non-spouse family members of voting age living in the house of ratepayers (most commonly sons and daughters, and aged relatives), and occupiers of lodging houses and other furnished premises. These exclusions were of significant proportions. At all levels of local government in England and Wales in 1938, there were 21.4 million municipal voters, compared with 28.2 million parliamentary voters, an exclusion rate of 24 per cent.[2]

It should also be noted that the owners or occupiers of business premises were entitled to a vote in the ward where those premises were situated. There were 360,000 of these plural voters in the whole of England and Wales in 1938, amounting to 1.7 per cent of the municipal electorate. However, the business vote could be much more significant in city centre wards, where most business premises were usually situated. No figures are available for municipal wards, but in some parliamentary constituencies the figures were very high. For instance, plural voters in Manchester Exchange amounted to 34 per cent of the parliamentary electorate, 26 per cent in Liverpool Exchange, 18 per cent in Sheffield Central, and an extraordinary 84 per cent in City of London. Obviously city-centre wards, being much smaller, would have had even higher proportions of business voters than these constituency-level figures.[3]

---

[2] For these and other figures quoted on the franchise, see *Registrar General's Statistical Review of England and Wales, (1938)*, pt. II, Civil Tables, pp. 61–93.

[3] For further discussion of the inter-war municipal franchise, see Davies, *Liverpool Labour*, pp. 119–129, 156–163.

Housing and inter-war housing Acts

This note serves as a background to the various Acts that impacted on the housing policies of the county boroughs in the inter-war years. Various Victorian Acts had established the principle of state intervention and local authority responsibility in eradicating slums. The 1890 Housing of the Working Class Act gave local authorities further powers to demolish insanitary houses and construct council houses using the local rates. The First World War saw the enactment of rent controls as an emergency measure. In July 1919, the Housing and Town Planning Act (the 'Addison' Act, after the Coalition-Liberal Dr Christopher Addison, the Minister of Health) was the first of a series of Acts to encourage large-scale state intervention, in conjunction with the local authorities, to increase the supply of working-class housing. The local authorities, already responsible for slum clearance, 'could be given the job of providing the working-class houses which were urgently needed, for it was assumed that temporarily private enterprise would be neither willing nor able to do so'.[4] The first Addison Act gave open-ended subsidies to local authorities to cover the cost of municipal housing schemes. The county boroughs were obligated to survey the housing needs within their boundaries and produce housing development plans. A second Act provided a subsidy of £260 per house for houses to be built for sale or rent by private enterprise. In 1922, because of central government economy measures, grants from the centre under Addison stopped. By then the Addison scheme had aided the construction of over 200,000 houses.[5] The Housing Act of 1923 (the 'Chamberlain' Act, after Neville Chamberlain, then Tory Health Minister) replaced Addison. The 1923 Act offered a £6 subsidy for twenty years, the houses to be built by the local authorities or private enterprise. Around 500,000 houses were built, largely by private enterprise. By 1929 the subsidy was withdrawn and the Act 'was regarded as a failure in terms of council-house building'.[6] The 1924 Housing Act (or 'Wheatley' Act, after John Wheatley, the first Labour Minister of Health) increased the state subsidy to £9 a year for forty years on houses built to let at a controlled rent. Under this scheme over 500,000 council houses were built before the Act was terminated in 1932. Following Wheatley, the 1930 Housing Act, (or 'Greenwood' Act, after Arthur Greenwood, Minister of Health in the second Labour government) aided further slum clearance with graduated subsidies. The level of subsidy was based on the number of families rehoused and the cost to the authority of the housing clearance. The county boroughs were required to develop five-year plans for slum clearance. The financial crisis of 1931 largely suspended the Act. Next, the 1933 Housing Act aimed at clearing 266,000 insanitary houses and constructing 285,000 new houses, with the target of rehousing 1.25 million people.[7] Finally the 1935 Housing Act (or 'Hilton Young' Act, after E. Hilton Young, Minister of Health), endeavoured to ensure

---

[4] Bowley, M., *Housing and the State 1919–1944*, (London, 1947), p. 15.
[5] Cook, C. and Stevenson, J., *The Longman Handbook of Modern British History, 1714–1980*, (London, 1985), p. 113.
[6] Cook and Stevenson, *Handbook*, p. 114.
[7] Cook and Stevenson, *Handbook*, p. 114.

that local authorities made plans to deal with overcrowding. Marian Bowley calculated that the cost of the schemes between 1923 and 1933, were in 1935–6 a 'modest' £1.9 million to the ratepayer. This was equivalent to 0.9% of the total rate expenditure.[8]

It is worth emphasising that individual county boroughs could react differently to the Acts. This was so whether or not these authorities acted in the spirit of the legislation, let alone in terms of their legal obligations. The differential rate of house construction by the county boroughs could also be the result of history, the existence of differing types and quality of housing stock and particular social needs. Relative economic decline, or otherwise, in the locality, could also be a factor in the extent of local council house building. There was obviously also the question of political will to act on central government's legislation. Obviously this was informed by the political complexion and resources of the council itself. Also the Acts themselves could work unfairly against some districts. Thus Bowley makes the point that under the 1923 Housing Act, 'better-off districts would tend to benefit from the subsidy more than the poorer districts'.[9]

The local press

The local press in the county boroughs has been examined in the writing of each chapter. It is perhaps the major source of the data and comment included in these volumes. The local press served as an instrument of record of the local election results. It also served as a major source for the debates concerning the major issues and social problems which came within the remit of the power of the local council. The press, of course, was more often than not owned by propertied and conservative interests that supported the status quo. Such local newspapers directly or indirectly favoured one or other of the established pre-1918 political parties. In some county boroughs the local press could assume a lofty position of neutrality and even-handedness, openly approving the non-politicisation of municipal affairs. In some boroughs this led to an ostensibly apolitical stance where the allegedly non-partisan 'independents' would be backed by the proprietors of the publication. Rarely were local newspapers supportive of the local Labour party or their policies. Indeed the local press was in the main antipathetic to Labour. This often emerged in open hostility to its aspiring councillors and policies, but sometimes in the more subtle use of pejorative language when discussing Labour in electoral coverage. Thus the local press has had to be used with extreme care as a source of political comment and analysis. As a journal of straightforward record of the bare results, however, the local press could, more often than not, be relied upon to be accurate.

The press reported throughout the year on various events in the political life of the borough. It has been impossible in a publication of this scale to analyse this year-round coverage for every county borough. In most cases the reports around the period of electioneering in October and November of each year have been the

---

[8]   Bowley, *Housing*, p. 47.
[9]   Bowley, *Housing*, p. 39.

main sources. Three types of report which tend to appear in all boroughs on a regular basis were especially useful. First there were reports of nomination day, when the deadline for nominating candidates was reached. These provided valuable information on candidates, including sometimes their occupations. Speeches made by the candidates were also recorded in many cases, giving their stance on the issues and major problems facing the borough. Second, reports on the declaration of the results, which often took place at the local Town Hall or some other important municipal building. Speeches were made by most of the candidates, successful and unsuccessful, to their waiting supporters, and very often the main election issues were aired at these points. Further meetings were often held later the same night by the individual parties, and these were often reported in some detail. Third, the advertisements placed by aspiring candidates in the local press prior to the November elections were an important source. Here the candidates often outlined their policies, the issues they supported or opposed, their past record of local service and sometimes their political affiliation where the official labelling was unclear.

The issues raised in these three types of reports largely reflected the political debate which had exercised both the council and electorate over the major part of the year. Only where important issues were alluded to (such as boundary changes, for instance) which had been debated at length at other times of the year, were press reports followed up outside the election period. Obviously important events and issues raised in secondary sources were also traced where appropriate.

APPENDICES

(On sources and other details, see **notes***, pp. 665–669)*

Appendix 1   Population of all eighty-three county boroughs 1931

1	Birmingham	1,004,300	43	Burnley	98,280
2	Liverpool	856,020	44	Reading	97,970
3	Manchester	766,800	45	Halifax	97,960
4	Sheffield	512,600	46	Wallasey	97,650
5	Leeds	482,900	47	Northampton	92,390
6	Bristol	399,400	48	Grimsby	91,520
7	Hull	314,100	49	Rochdale	90,770
8	Bradford	298,200	50	Newport	89,750
9	West Ham	294,200	51	Ipswich	88,000
10	Newcastle	283,900	52	York	85,600
11	Stoke	276,500	53	Wigan	85,520
12	Nottingham	269,400	54	Smethwick	84,620
13	Portsmouth	249,300	55	West Bromwich	81,230
14	Leicester	240,000	56	Oxford	80,870
15	Croydon	233,900	57	Warrington	79,510
16	Salford	223,300	58	Southport	78,260
17	Cardiff	223,200	59	Bootle	76,810
18	Plymouth	208,200	60	Darlington	72,680
19	Sunderland	186,800	61	Barnsley	71,600
20	Bolton	177,800	62	Merthyr	71,420
21	Southampton	175,600	63	Rotherham	69,600
22	Coventry	167,140	64	Bath	68,760
23	Swansea	164,800	65	West Hartlepool	68,680
24	Birkenhead	148,300	66	Barrow	66,180
25	Brighton	145,300	67	Lincoln	66,050
26	Derby	142,400	68	Exeter	65,940
27	East Ham	142,400	69	Tynemouth	64,880
28	Oldham	140,300	70	Doncaster	63,590
29	Middlesbrough	138,830	71	Hastings	63,130
30	Wolverhampton	133,000	72	Dudley	59,430
31	Norwich	126,500	73	Wakefield	58,990
32	Stockport	125,700	74	Carlisle	57,270
33	Gateshead	123,000	75	Great Yarmouth	57,170
34	Blackburn	122,700	76	Eastbourne	56,730
35	Preston	119,000	77	Bury	56,280
36	Southend	119,000	78	Dewsbury	53,960
37	South Shields	114,400	79	Gloucester	53,280
38	Huddersfield	113,600	80	Worcester	50,720
39	Bournemouth	111,190	81	Burton	49,590
40	St Helens	107,100	82	Chester	41,650
41	Walsall	103,300	83	Canterbury	24,660
42	Blackpool	99,590		**All**	**13,312,920**

Appendix 2   Persons per room in all eighty-three county boroughs 1931

1	Gateshead	1.23	43	Burnley	0.85
2	Sunderland	1.22	44	Chester	0.85
3	South Shields	1.18	45	Coventry	0.85
4	West Ham	1.14	46	Preston	0.85
5	Newcastle	1.13	47	Rochdale	0.85
6	St Helens	1.13	48	Bury	0.84
7	Tynemouth	1.08	49	York	0.84
8	Stoke	1.04	50	Birmingham	0.83
9	Middlesbrough	1.03	51	Blackburn	0.82
10	Dewsbury	1.02	52	Smethwick	0.82
11	West Bromwich	1.01	53	Stockport	0.82
12	Dudley	1.00	54	Bristol	0.81
13	West Hartlepool	1.00	55	Grimsby	0.81
14	Wigan	1.00	56	Southampton	0.80
15	Warrington	0.98	57	Brighton	0.79
16	Barnsley	0.97	58	Nottingham	0.78
17	Plymouth	0.96	59	Worcester	0.77
18	Bootle	0.95	60	Burton	0.76
19	Carlisle	0.95	61	Portsmouth	0.76
20	Salford	0.94	62	Croydon	0.75
21	East Ham	0.93	63	Derby	0.75
22	Liverpool	0.93	64	Doncaster	0.75
23	Darlington	0.91	65	Gloucester	0.75
24	Huddersfield	0.91	66	Reading	0.75
25	Rotherham	0.91	67	Lincoln	0.74
26	Wakefield	0.91	68	Exeter	0.73
27	Walsall	0.91	69	Canterbury	0.72
28	Halifax	0.90	70	Oxford	0.72
29	Swansea	0.90	71	Southend	0.72
30	Barrow	0.89	72	Norwich	0.71
31	Birkenhead	0.89	73	Wallasey	0.71
32	Hull	0.89	74	Hastings	0.70
33	Oldham	0.89	75	Northampton	0.70
34	Bradford	0.88	76	Bath	0.69
35	Merthyr	0.88	77	Eastbourne	0.69
36	Leeds	0.87	78	Ipswich	0.69
37	Manchester	0.87	79	Leicester	0.69
38	Newport	0.87	80	Southport	0.68
39	Sheffield	0.87	81	Blackpool	0.67
40	Wolverhampton	0.87	82	Great Yarmouth	0.65
41	Cardiff	0.86	83	Bournemouth	0.64
42	Bolton	0.85		**All**	**0.86**

Appendix 3 Female domestic servants as a percentage of total population in all eighty-three county boroughs 1931

1	Eastbourne	12.3	43	Barrow	3.3
2	Bournemouth	12.1	44	Sheffield	3.3
3	Blackpool	9.9	45	Wolverhampton	3.3
4	Hastings	9.8	46	Middlesbrough	3.3
5	Southport	9.3	47	South Shields	3.2
6	Brighton	8.6	48	Leeds	3.1
7	Bath	8.3	49	Manchester	3.1
8	Oxford	7.1	50	Nottingham	3.1
9	Southend	6.9	51	Huddersfield	3.1
10	Canterbury	6.3	52	Rotherham	3.0
11	Chester	6.1	53	Dewsbury	3.0
12	Exeter	5.7	54	Stockport	3.0
13	Wallasey	5.3	55	Northampton	2.9
14	Croydon	5.2	56	Salford	2.9
15	Great Yarmouth	5.0	57	Birmingham	2.9
16	Birkenhead	4.7	58	Wakefield	2.9
17	Cardiff	4.4	59	Gateshead	2.9
18	Worcester	4.3	60	Derby	2.7
19	Darlington	4.3	61	Barnsley	2.7
20	Lincoln	4.3	62	Halifax	2.6
21	Ipswich	4.2	63	East Ham	2.6
22	Southampton	4.2	64	Leicester	2.5
23	Portsmouth	4.2	65	Bradford	2.5
24	Reading	4.2	66	West Ham	2.4
25	York	4.2	67	Preston	2.4
26	Newport	4.2	68	Walsall	2.4
27	Gloucester	4.1	69	Coventry	2.2
28	Newcastle	4.1	70	Wigan	2.2
29	Grimsby	4.1	71	Smethwick	2.1
30	Bristol	4.0	72	St Helens	2.1
31	Tynemouth	3.9	73	Merthyr	2.1
32	Plymouth	3.8	74	Bury	2.1
33	Doncaster	3.8	75	Bolton	2.1
34	Sunderland	3.7	76	Dudley	2.0
35	West Hartlepool	3.7	77	Burnley	2.0
36	Hull	3.6	78	Rochdale	2.0
37	Liverpool	3.5	79	Blackburn	2.0
38	Swansea	3.5	80	Oldham	1.8
39	Norwich	3.5	81	Warrington	1.8
40	Bootle	3.4	82	Stoke	1.8
41	Carlisle	3.4	83	West Bromwich	1.8
42	Burton	3.3		**All**	**3.6**

Appendix 4   Percentage of workforce in own account and managerial
categories in all eighty-three county boroughs 1931
(excluding 'out of work')

1 Blackpool	29.4	43 Hull	11.6
2 Southport	23.3	44 Merthyr	11.6
3 Southend	21.4	45 Sheffield	11.6
4 Bournemouth	21.0	46 Preston	11.6
5 Hastings	20.9	47 Sunderland	11.5
6 Eastbourne	18.5	48 Wolverhampton	11.5
7 Great Yarmouth	18.1	49 Darlington	11.4
8 Brighton	17.8	50 Walsall	11.3
9 Wallasey	17.5	51 Burnley	11.3
10 Bath	16.8	52 Wigan	11.2
11 Canterbury	16.6	53 Bolton	11.2
12 Exeter	14.4	54 Dewsbury	11.1
13 Blackburn	14.0	55 Newcastle	11.1
14 Croydon	13.9	56 Liverpool	11.1
15 Chester	13.8	57 Leicester	11.0
16 Swansea	13.7	58 Bury	11.0
17 Grimsby	13.6	59 Birmingham	10.9
18 Cardiff	13.5	60 Plymouth	10.8
19 Gloucester	13.3	61 York	10.7
20 Tynemouth	13.2	62 Carlisle	10.7
21 Ipswich	12.9	63 Dudley	10.5
22 Stockport	12.8	64 Middlesbrough	10.5
23 Worcester	12.8	65 Rochdale	10.5
24 Birkenhead	12.7	66 Wakefield	10.3
25 Halifax	12.6	67 Burton	10.2
26 Newport	12.4	68 Barrow	9.8
27 Oxford	12.3	69 Oldham	9.7
28 Bristol	12.3	70 Coventry	9.7
29 Bradford	12.3	71 Salford	9.6
30 Norwich	12.2	72 Barnsley	9.6
31 Leeds	12.2	73 Rotherham	9.4
32 Southampton	12.1	74 Derby	9.2
33 Lincoln	12.1	75 Gateshead	9.1
34 Reading	12.0	76 Smethwick	9.0
35 West Hartlepool	12.0	77 West Bromwich	8.7
36 Northampton	12.0	78 Stoke	8.4
37 Doncaster	11.9	79 Bootle	8.3
38 Huddersfield	11.9	80 East Ham	8.3
39 Portsmouth	11.8	81 Warrington	7.9
40 Nottingham	11.8	82 St Helens	7.8
41 South Shields	11.8	83 West Ham	7.2
42 Manchester	11.7	**All**	**11.9**

Appendix 5   Percentage of workforce in professional category in all eighty-three county boroughs 1931

	M	F	All			M	F	All
1 Oxford	10.8	13.8	11.8	43 Nottingham		1.8	3.2	2.3
2 Hastings	4.8	13.1	8.1	44 Sheffield		1.6	4.0	2.3
3 Eastbourne	5.1	11.4	7.8	45 Wakefield		1.6	4.0	2.2
4 Bournemouth	4.9	9.5	6.8	46 Derby		1.4	4.3	2.2
5 Bath	4.4	10.1	6.5	47 Hull		1.5	4.2	2.2
6 Exeter	4.4	9.9	6.1	48 Preston		2.0	2.6	2.2
7 Southport	4.5	7.2	5.5	49 Leicester		1.9	2.6	2.2
8 Southend	4.3	7.4	5.3	50 Stockport		2.0	2.4	2.2
9 Canterbury	3.8	8.6	5.2	51 Halifax		1.9	2.6	2.2
10 Croydon	4.1	7.3	5.1	52 Burton		1.4	4.0	2.0
11 Brighton	3.8	7.1	4.9	53 West Ham		1.4	3.6	2.0
12 Chester	3.4	7.8	4.7	54 Huddersfield		2.0	2.1	2.0
13 Reading	3.1	7.7	4.5	55 Bradford		1.7	2.4	2.0
14 Wallasey	3.2	6.8	4.3	56 Barnsley		1.5	3.7	2.0
15 Cardiff	2.7	6.5	3.7	57 W. Hartlepool		1.3	4.3	2.0
16 Bristol	2.5	6.2	3.7	58 Tynemouth		1.4	3.5	1.9
17 Blackpool	3.3	3.8	3.5	59 Bury		2.0	1.8	1.9
18 Gloucester	2.4	5.9	3.4	60 Middlesbro'		1.1	4.7	1.9
19 York	2.5	5.6	3.4	61 Rotherham		1.1	5.3	1.9
20 Newcastle	2.3	5.8	3.3	62 Gateshead		1.4	3.1	1.9
21 Norwich	2.3	5.1	3.3	63 Salford		1.5	2.5	1.9
22 Lincoln	2.2	6.4	3.3	64 Wigan		1.4	2.6	1.8
23 Southampton	2.0	6.9	3.3	65 Bolton		1.8	1.9	1.8
24 Ipswich	2.0	6.2	3.2	66 South Shields		1.2	3.7	1.8
25 Northampton	2.4	4.9	3.2	67 Grimsby		1.3	3.3	1.8
26 Birkenhead	2.0	5.7	3.1	68 Blackburn		2.0	1.4	1.7
27 Swansea	2.1	6.6	3.1	69 Bootle		1.2	2.8	1.7
28 Newport	2.1	6.3	3.0	70 Merthyr		1.1	5.3	1.7
29 Gt. Yarmouth	2.2	4.5	3.0	71 St Helens		0.9	4.7	1.7
30 Worcester	2.2	4.2	2.9	72 Dudley		1.2	2.8	1.7
31 Plymouth	1.7	6.6	2.9	73 Barrow		0.9	4.7	1.7
32 Carlisle	2.2	4.1	2.9	74 Coventry		1.0	3.2	1.6
33 Liverpool	2.0	4.7	2.8	75 Dewsbury		1.4	2.0	1.6
34 Portsmouth	1.7	5.6	2.7	76 Walsall		1.1	2.5	1.5
35 Darlington	1.6	5.9	2.7	77 Burnley		1.6	1.2	1.4
36 Manchester	2.1	3.4	2.6	78 Oldham		1.4	1.4	1.4
37 Leeds	2.2	3.1	2.5	79 Smethwick		1.1	1.9	1.3
38 Sunderland	1.6	4.9	2.4	80 Stoke		1.1	1.7	1.3
39 Doncaster	1.6	5.0	2.4	81 Rochdale		1.2	1.0	1.1
40 East Ham	2.0	3.3	2.4	82 W. Bromwich		0.7	2.2	1.1
41 Wolverh'ton	1.5	4.6	2.4	83 Warrington		0.8	1.3	0.9
42 Birmingham	1.8	3.5	2.4	**All**		**2.0**	**4.2**	**2.7**

Appendix 6   Percentage of workforce recorded as out of work in 1931
industry tables in all eighty-threee county boroughs

1	Blackburn	32.7	43	Stockport	13.1
2	Merthyr	32.4	44	Warrington	12.9
3	South Shields	30.6	45	Derby	12.7
4	Sunderland	30.3	46	Coventry	12.6
5	West Hartlepool	29.0	47	West Ham	12.6
6	Middlesbrough	24.2	48	Leeds	12.6
7	Burnley	24.1	49	Smethwick	12.3
8	Tynemouth	23.7	50	Birmingham	12.2
9	Gateshead	23.6	51	Southampton	12.1
10	Oldham	22.8	52	Burton	12.1
11	Newcastle	22.4	53	Grimsby	11.4
12	Bootle	21.3	54	Wallasey	11.3
13	Birkenhead	21.1	55	Carlisle	11.0
14	Swansea	20.8	56	Halifax	11.0
15	Liverpool	19.6	57	Nottingham	10.9
16	Wigan	18.9	58	Bristol	10.9
17	Preston	18.6	59	Ipswich	10.8
18	Barnsley	17.9	60	Worcester	10.4
19	Sheffield	17.3	61	York	10.4
20	Walsall	17.3	62	Chester	10.3
21	Cardiff	17.1	63	Plymouth	10.3
22	Bury	16.9	64	Norwich	9.9
23	Rochdale	16.6	65	Wakefield	9.8
24	Barrow	16.6	66	Doncaster	9.7
25	Dudley	16.5	67	Huddersfield	9.2
26	Newport	16.4	68	Leicester	8.8
27	Wolverhampton	16.4	69	Southport	8.6
28	St Helens	16.1	70	East Ham	8.6
29	Stoke	16.1	71	Portsmouth	8.5
30	Darlington	15.9	72	Brighton	8.1
31	Lincoln	15.8	73	Bath	8.1
32	Salford	15.3	74	Northampton	8.1
33	Dewsbury	15.3	75	Reading	7.1
34	Manchester	15.1	76	Hastings	7.1
35	Bolton	15.1	77	Southend	7.0
36	Rotherham	14.8	78	Canterbury	7.0
37	Great Yarmouth	14.7	79	Exeter	6.9
38	Blackpool	14.7	80	Croydon	6.2
39	West Bromwich	13.9	81	Eastbourne	5.8
40	Hull	13.6	82	Bournemouth	5.6
41	Gloucester	13.4	83	Oxford	4.7
42	Bradford	13.1		**All**	**14.7**

Appendix 7   Percentage of workforce (male and female) in textiles category,
top fifteen county boroughs 1931

1 Burnley	50.4	9 Preston	32.5
2 Rochdale	49.0	10 Halifax	32.4
3 Blackburn	48.3	11 Stockport	24.8
4 Oldham	46.7	12 Leicester	24.4
5 Bolton	43.0	13 Nottingham	19.5
6 Bradford	38.8	14 Salford	12.0
7 Bury	36.7	15 Manchester	9.3
8 Huddersfield	33.0		

Appendix 8   Percentage of female workforce in textiles category, top fifteen
county boroughs 1931

1 Burnley	73.4	9 Halifax	51.7
2 Blackburn	72.1	10 Huddersfield	48.5
3 Rochdale	67.9	11 Leicester	43.3
4 Oldham	67.8	12 Stockport	38.6
5 Bolton	63.9	13 Nottingham	34.2
6 Preston	57.1	14 Salford	18.2
7 Bradford	55.0	15 Manchester	14.6
8 Bury	54.0		

Appendix 9   Percentage of male workforce in mining category, top fifteen county boroughs 1931

1 Merthyr	53.7	9 Dewsbury	14.3
2 Barnsley	44.1	10 Gateshead	12.0
3 Wigan	37.9	11 Sunderland	11.6
4 St Helens	28.5	12 Doncaster	11.3
5 Stoke	23.5	13 Nottingham	9.0
6 Rotherham	19.7	14 Walsall	8.6
7 South Shields	18.6	15 Swansea	7.5
8 Wakefield	17.5		

Appendix 10   Percentage of male workforce in docks and water transport categories, top fifteen county boroughs 1931

1 Bootle	28.7	9 Cardiff	12.1
2 Southampton	19.2	10 West Ham	10.9
3 Liverpool	16.6	11 East Ham	10.5
4 South Shields	16.5	12 Grimsby	10.1
5 Birkenhead	14.8	13 Middlesbrough	8.7
6 Hull	13.8	14 Swansea	8.0
7 Newport	12.5	15 West Hartlepool	7.3
8 Tynemouth	12.2		

Appendix 11   Percentage of male workforce in rail category, top fifteen county boroughs 1931

1 Carlisle	15.9	9 Chester	8.1
2 York	12.4	10 Burton	8.0
3 Doncaster	11.3	11 Cardiff	7.9
4 Gloucester	10.0	12 Wakefield	7.5
5 Derby	9.2	13 Gateshead	7.4
6 Newport	9.2	14 Darlington	7.3
7 Worcester	8.6	15 Hull	6.3
8 Exeter	8.5		

Appendix 12   Percentage of workforce (male and female) in metalworking categories, top fourteen county boroughs 1931

	M	F	All		M	F	All
1 W. Bromwich	40.6	31.4	38.0	8 Walsall	29.6	17.8	26.0
2 Sheffield	40.2	25.5	36.2	9 Birmingham	21.4	21.0	21.2
3 Middlesbro'	39.6	2.5	31.7	10 Wolverh'ton	21.5	17.2	20.2
4 Rotherham	36.9	7.6	31.4	11 Swansea	24.1	5.3	20.1
5 Smethwick	32.0	27.5	30.6	12 Newport	19.5	1.3	15.3
6 Warrington	37.8	10.2	29.9	13 Merthyr	13.9	1.6	12.2
7 Dudley	32.2	21.1	29.0	14 Darlington	15.5	1.0	11.8

Appendix 13   Percentage of male workforce in shipbuilding categories, top ten county boroughs 1931

1 Barrow	50.9	6 Plymouth	16.7
2 Sunderland	26.9	7 Portsmouth	16.2
3 Tynemouth	20.0	8 Birkenhead	15.7
4 West Hartlepool	18.1	9 Newcastle	13.4
5 South Shields	18.0	10 Southampton	12.6

Appendix 14   Percentage of male workforce in engineering category, top sixteen county boroughs 1931

1 Lincoln	27.9	9 Newcastle	10.5
2 Darlington	22.4	10 Coventry	10.2
3 Oldham	19.4	11 Bolton	10.0
4 Ipswich	16.3	12 Halifax	9.6
5 Derby	13.5	13 Blackburn	9.1
6 Gateshead	12.5	14 Bury	8.8
7 Rochdale	12.4	15 Leicester	8.0
8 Doncaster	11.8	16 Leeds	7.9

Appendix 15   Percentage of workforce (male and female) in vehicle construction category, top six county boroughs 1931

	M	F	All		M	F	All
1 Coventry	38.5	15.2	32.1	4 Wolverh'ton	15.2	4.5	12.0
2 Oxford	18.8	3.4	13.7	5 Birmingham	12.6	7.9	11.0
3 Smethwick	13.7	8.9	12.2	6 Derby	14.0	2.4	10.7

Appendix 16   Houses constructed by county boroughs to 31 Mar. 1939[a]

Borough	Houses	Pop./house	Borough	Houses	Pop./house
1 Carlisle	4,473	12.80	41 Birkenhead	4,365	33.97
2 Dudley	4,598	12.93	42 Middlesbro'	4,047	34.30
3 Wakefield	4,523	13.04	43 Swansea	4,798	34.35
4 Walsall	7,321	14.11	44 Bradford	8,644	34.50
5 Rotherham	4,711	14.77	45 Cardiff	6,204	35.98
6 W. Bromwich	5,485	14.81	46 Sunderland	5,184	36.03
7 Nottingham	17,265	15.60	47 Oxford[d]	2,195	36.84
8 Wolverh'ton	8,113	16.39	48 Southampton	4,719	37.21
9 Norwich	7,019	18.02	49 Brighton	3,884	37.41
10 York	4,744	18.04	50 Wigan	2,261	37.82
11 Smethwick	4,463	18.96	51 South Shields[c]	3,013	37.97
12 Doncaster	3,271	19.44	52 Gateshead	3,034	40.54
13 Manchester	37,668	20.36	53 Halifax	2,402	40.78
14 Birmingham	49,167	20.43	54 Preston	2,755	43.19
15 Barnsley	3,473	20.62	55 Gt.Yarmouth	1,307	43.74
16 Derby	6,786	20.98	56 Burnley	2,140	45.93
17 Sheffield	24,147	21.23	57 Burton	1,060	46.78
18 Northampton	4,301	21.48	58 Plymouth	4,431	46.99
19 Bury	2,456	22.92	59 Bath	1,298	52.97
20 Warrington	3,391	23.45	60 Eastbourne[b]	1,019	55.67
21 Worcester	2,138	23.72	61 Stockport	2,250	55.87
22 Tynemouth	2,703	24.00	62 W.Hartlepool	1,201	57.19
23 Newcastle[b]	11,815	24.03	63 Oldham	2,345	59.83
24 Rochdale	3,660	24.80	64 Blackburn	1,953	62.83
25 Liverpool	34,495	24.82	65 Croydon[b]	3,585	65.24
26 Leeds	18,602	25.96	66 Blackpool	1,448	68.78
27 Chester	1,543	26.99	67 Newport	1,294	69.36
28 Leicester	8,878	27.03	68 Wallasey	1,397	69.90
29 Lincoln	2,408	27.43	69 Darlington	907	80.13
30 Dewsbury	1,958	27.56	70 Southport	924	84.70
31 Bristol	13,677	29.20	71 Salford	2,615	85.39
32 Bootle	2,628	29.23	72 Hastings	730	86.48
33 Exeter	2,178	30.28	73 Portsmouth	2,736	91.12
34 Hull	10,367	30.30	74 Barrow	724	91.41
35 St Helens	3,496	30.64	75 Southend	920	129.35
36 Canterbury	786	31.37	76 Grimsby[b]	664	137.83
37 Huddersfield[b]	3,589	31.65	77 Bournemouth	732	151.90
38 Coventry	5,238	31.91	78 West Ham[d]	1,792	164.17
39 Reading	3,068	31.93	79 East Ham	690	206.38
40 Bolton	5,369	33.12	80 Gloucester	154	345.97
			All	**443,792**	**29.02**

[a] excluding 6 months to 30 Sep. 1938, in all cases; [b] excluding 1937–38 figures;
[c] excluding 1936–38 figures; [d] excluding 1935–38 figures.
No figures given for Ipswich, Merthyr Tydfil or Stoke.

The eighty-three county boroughs of England and Wales, 1931

SCOTLAND

Newcastle-on-Tyne • Tynemouth
South Shields
Gateshead • Sunderland
Carlisle
• W. Hartlepool
Darlington • Middlesbrough

Barrow-in Furness

• York

Kingston upon Hull

Blackpool • Preston Burnley Bradford
• Halifax • Leeds
Blackburn • Dewsbury
Southport Wigan Bolton Huddersfield
Rochdale • Wakefield
Bootle Bury Oldham Barnsley • Doncaster Grimsby
Liverpool Salford • Manchester
Wallasey St. Helens • Stockport • Rotherham
Warrington Sheffield
Birkenhead
• Lincoln
• Chester

Stoke on Trent Derby • Nottingham

• Burton upon Trent

Great
Yarmouth

Wolverhampton • Leicester Norwich
Dudley • Walsall
W. Bromwich • Birmingham
WALES Smethwick • Coventry

• Northampton Ipswich •
Worcester •

• Gloucester

Merthyr Tydfil • Oxford
Swansea E. Ham
Newport W. Ham • • Southend-on-Sea
Cardiff
• Bristol Reading • • Croydon
• Bath Canterbury

Brighton
Southampton Hastings
Portsmouth Eastbourne
Exeter Bournemouth

Plymouth

Index